GOVERNMENT CONTRACT GUIDEBOOK

By
Donald P. Arnavas
Counsel
Sonnenschein Nath & Rosenthal
and
Judge William J. Ruberry
Vice Chairman (retired)
Armed Services Board of Contract Appeals

Second Edition

FEDERAL PUBLICATIONS
A WEST GROUP COMPANY

1120 TWENTIETH STREET, N.W. ■ WASHINGTON, D.C. 20036

★

GOVERNMENT CONTRACT GUIDEBOOK

Second Edition

Copyright © 1994 Federal Publications—A West Group Company

Library of Congress Catalog Number 93-73024

★

This publication is designed to provide accurate and authoritative information in regard to the subject matter covered. It is sold with the understanding that the publisher is not engaged in rendering legal, accounting, or other professional service. If legal advice or other expert assistance is required, the services of a competent professional person should be sought. From a Declaration of Principles jointly adopted by a Committee of the American Bar Association and a Committee of Publishers and Associations.

7/96

Donald Arnavas

William Ruberry

The Authors

Donald P. Arnavas practices and teaches law, specializing in all aspects of Government contracting on both the domestic and international level.

Prior to entering private practice, Mr. Arnavas served as an administrative judge with the Armed Services Board of Contract Appeals and was on the legal staff of a major defense contractor.

Mr. Arnavas is an Adjunct Professor of Law at the Dickinson School of Law and a frequent lecturer on Government contract issues. He has authored or co-authored numerous articles on a wide range of Government contract topics and is a regular contributor to Federal Publications' BRIEFING PAPERS series. Mr. Arnavas has served on the Council of the American Bar Association's Section of Public Contract Law and as Senior Editor of the Section's *Public Contract Law Journal*.

Mr. Arnavas received a Bachelor of Arts degree from Iona College and a Juris Doctor degree from Georgetown University. He is a member of the Bars of the State of Virginia and the District of Columbia.

* * *

William J. Ruberry has been involved in Government procurement for over 40 years as an attorney for a number of federal procurement agencies and as an administrative judge. He was a member of the Armed Services Board of Contract Appeals beginning in 1970, and a Vice Chairman of that Board from 1979 until his retirement in May 1994.

For many years Judge Ruberry prepared the annual Procurement and Construction *Bibliographies* for the BRIEFING PAPERS and CONSTRUCTION BRIEFINGS series of Federal Publications Inc. and was Associate Editor of Federal Publications' annual YEARBOOK OF PROCUREMENT ARTICLES.

Judge Ruberry received his Juris Doctor degree from Loyola University in Chicago, where he received the Judge John B. McCormack award. He is a member of the Bar of the State of Illinois.

Attribution

Opinions and analyses contained in this book are strictly those of the authors and not represented to be those of any agency of the United States Government or any other governmental entity.

Acknowledgments

We are indebted to the authors of the other books in the GOVERNMENT CONTRACT TEXTS series and to the many authorities who have contributed to Federal Publications' BRIEFING PAPERS periodical and seminar manuals. Without the wealth of information and insights contained in the writings of these procurement professionals, this book could not have been produced. Finally, we would like to thank David Levendusky, Barbara Bares, and the staff of the Publications Division of Federal Publications for their efforts in editing and producing this Second Edition.

CONTENTS

FOREWORD / i

PART I   INTRODUCTION

chapter 1   About This Book

 A. Organization / **1-2**
 B. Guide To Use / **1-3**
  1. References / **1-4**
  2. Figures & Appendix / **1-4**
  3. Glossary / **1-5**
  4. Table Of Contents & Index / **1-5**
  5. Supplementation & Revision / **1-5**

chapter 2   The Setting

 A. Institutional Framework / **2-2**
  1. Legislative Branch / **2-2**
   a. Congress / **2-2**
   b. General Accounting Office / **2-4**
  2. Executive Branch / **2-5**
   a. President / **2-5**
   b. Executive Departments & Agencies / **2-5**
   c. Rulemaking Organizations / **2-6**
  3. Judicial Branch / **2-7**
 B. Regulations / **2-8**
  1. Federal Acquisition Regulation / **2-8**
  2. Agency Acquisition Regulations / **2-9**
  3. Deviations / **2-12**
 C. Purchasing Offices / **2-12**
  1. Department Of Defense / **2-13**
  2. Civilian Agencies / **2-14**

3. Obtaining Information / **2-14**
D. Basic Procurement Process / **2-15**
   1. Government "Requirement" / **2-15**
   2. Procurement Methods / **2-16**
      a. Competitive Contracts / **2-16**
      b. Noncompetitive Contracts / **2-17**
      c. Special Procedures For Small Purchases / **2-19**
   3. Contract Types / **2-19**
   4. Soliciting Sources / **2-21**
   5. Government Procurement Team / **2-21**
   6. Activities Of Government Representatives / **2-23**
   7. Dealing With Government Representatives / **2-24**

PART II CONTRACT BASICS

chapter 3 Sealed Bidding

A. Invitation For Bids / **3-2**
   1. Standard Forms / **3-3**
   2. Specifications / **3-3**
   3. Correction Of IFB Deficiencies / **3-11**
B. Soliciting Bids / **3-13**
C. Preparing The Bid / **3-16**
   1. Complete Bid Package / **3-17**
   2. Instructions To Bidders / **3-17**
   3. Other Aids / **3-18**
   4. Formulation Of Price Quotations / **3-19**
   5. Acknowledgment Of Amendments / **3-20**
D. Bid Opening / **3-21**
   1. Initial Handling / **3-21**
   2. Procedures / **3-22**
   3. Early Or Late Openings / **3-22**
   4. Late Bids / **3-23**

       5. Telegraphic Bids & Modifications / **3-24**
       6. Facsimile Bids & Modifications / **3-25**
       7. FACNET Bids & Modifications / **3-25**
E. Eligibility For Award / **3-25**
       1. Responsiveness Of Bids / **3-26**
          a. Minor Informalities / **3-26**
          b. Bid Acceptance Period / **3-26**
          c. Binding Legal Obligation / **3-27**
          d. Firm Price / **3-28**
          e. Completeness / **3-28**
          f. Ambiguities / **3-28**
       2. Responsibility Of Bidders / **3-29**
          a. Responsibility Determinations / **3-29**
          b. Buy-Ins / **3-30**
          c. Special Requirements / **3-30**
          d. Preaward Survey / **3-31**
F. Mistakes In Bids / **3-31**
       1. Preaward Mistakes / **3-31**
          a. Apparent Clerical Errors / **3-31**
          b. Other Preaward Mistakes / **3-32**
          c. Bid Verification / **3-32**
       2. Postaward Mistakes / **3-33**
G. Protests / **3-34**
       1. Contracting Agency / **3-35**
          a. Procedures / **3-35**
          b. Remedies / **3-36**
       2. Comptroller General / **3-36**
          a. Procedures / **3-37**
          b. Remedies / **3-38**
       3. Federal Courts / **3-38**
       4. GSBCA / **3-42**
H. Contract Award / **3-42**
       1. Award Procedures / **3-42**
       2. Rejection Of All Bids / **3-44**
I. Two-Step Sealed Bidding / **3-45**
       1. Step One: Request For Technical Proposals / **3-45**
       2. Step Two: Invitation For Bids / **3-46**

chapter 4 Competitive Negotiation

A. Conditions Permitting Use / 4-3
B. Requests For Proposals Or Quotations / 4-3
  1. RFP vs. RFQ / 4-3
  2. Standard Forms / 4-4
  3. Soliciting Offers / 4-4
  4. Amendments / 4-5
  5. Preproposal Conferences / 4-5
  6. Evaluation Factors / 4-6
  7. Cancellation / 4-8
C. Proposal Preparation & Submission / 4-8
  1. Proposal Preparation / 4-8
  2. Best Response / 4-9
  3. Timeliness / 4-9
D. Discussions / 4-10
  1. Award Without Discussions / 4-10
  2. Competitive Range Concept / 4-11
    a. Determining The Range / 4-12
    b. Responsiveness-Responsibility Relationship / 4-13
  3. Scope Of Discussions / 4-13
E. Best & Final Offers / 4-15
F. Contract Types / 4-16
  1. Fixed-Price Contracts / 4-17
    a. Firm-Fixed-Price / 4-17
    b. Fixed-Price With Economic Price Adjustment / 4-17
    c. Fixed-Price Incentive / 4-18
    d. Fixed-Price Redeterminable / 4-18
  2. Cost-Reimbursement Contracts / 4-18
    a. Cost / 4-19
    b. Cost-Sharing / 4-19
    c. Cost-Plus-Incentive-Fee / 4-19
    d. Cost-Plus-Award-Fee / 4-20
    e. Cost-Plus-Fixed-Fee / 4-21
  3. Other Contract Types / 4-21

G. Postaward Notice & Debriefing / **4-22**
H. Protests / **4-25**

chapter 5 Costs

A. Cost Principles / **5-2**
1. Applicability / **5-3**
2. Allowability / **5-5**
3. Reasonableness / **5-5**
4. Allocability / **5-7**
5. Selected Costs / **5-8**

B. Cost Accounting Standards / **5-20**
1. Applicability / **5-21**
   a. Exemptions & Waiver / **5-21**
   b. Types Of Coverage / **5-21**
2. Contractor Obligations / **5-22**
3. Disclosure Statements / **5-23**
   a. Requirements / **5-23**
   b. Time Of Submission / **5-24**
   c. Form Of Submission / **5-24**
4. Individual Standards / **5-25**

C. Truth In Negotiations Act / **5-28**
1. Applicability / **5-28**
2. Exemptions & Waiver / **5-29**
   a. Adequate Price Competition / **5-29**
   b. Established Catalog Or Market Price / **5-30**
   c. Price Set By Law Or Regulation / **5-30**
   d. Commercial Item Procurements / **5-30**
   e. Waiver / **5-30**
3. "Cost Or Pricing Data" Defined / **5-31**
4. Submission Of Data / **5-32**
   a. Form / **5-32**
   b. When Submitted / **5-32**
   c. Subcontractor Data / **5-34**
   d. Failure To Submit Data / **5-34**
5. Certification Of Data / **5-34**
6. Liability For Defective Data / **5-36**

D. Government Audit Rights / **5-36**

1. Procuring Agencies / **5-37**
   a. Price Proposal Audits / **5-37**
   b. Contract Settlement Audits / **5-37**
   c. Cost Or Pricing Data Audits / **5-38**
2. General Accounting Office / **5-39**
3. Inspectors General / **5-40**

chapter 6 Socioeconomic Considerations

A. Small Business Preferences / **6-2**
   1. Qualification / **6-3**
   2. Contract Set-Asides / **6-3**
      a. Total Set-Asides / **6-4**
      b. Partial Set-Asides / **6-4**
   3. Certificates Of Competency / **6-4**
   4. Subcontracting / **6-5**
      a. By Private Firms / **6-5**
      b. By The SBA / **6-6**
   5. Equal Access To Justice Act / **6-7**
      a. History / **6-7**
      b. Eligibility / **6-8**
      c. "Prevailing Party" / **6-8**
      d. Government Position Not "Substantially Justified" / **6-8**
      e. Amount Of Recovery / **6-9**
B. Women-Owned Small Business Preferences / **6-9**
C. Labor Surplus Area Preferences / **6-10**
   1. Qualification / **6-10**
   2. Contract Set-Asides / **6-10**
   3. Subcontracting / **6-11**
D. Nondiscrimination Requirements / **6-11**
   1. Equal Employment Opportunity / **6-11**
      a. "Equal Opportunity" Clause / **6-11**
      b. Affirmative Action Plans / **6-12**
   2. Miscellaneous Requirements / **6-12**
   3. Administration & Enforcement / **6-13**
E. Labor Standards Requirements / **6-14**
   1. Walsh-Healey Act / **6-14**

        a. Coverage / **6-14**
        b. Administration & Enforcement / **6-15**
    2. Service Contract Act / **6-16**
        a. Coverage / **6-16**
        b. Administration & Enforcement / **6-16**
F. Buy American Act Requirements / **6-17**
G. Environmental Protection Requirements / **6-19**
H. Drug-Free Workplace Requirements / **6-19**

chapter 7   Fraud And Ethical Considerations

A. Fraud / **7-2**
    1. Civil False Claims Act / **7-3**
        a. Key Definitions / **7-3**
        b. Burden Of Proof / **7-3**
        c. Penalties / **7-4**
    2. "Qui Tam" Provisions / **7-4**
        a. Relators / **7-5**
        b. Limitations / **7-5**
        c. Procedures / **7-6**
        d. Recovery / **7-6**
    3. Criminal False Claims Act / **7-7**
        a. "Claim" / **7-7**
        b. Knowledge & Intent / **7-8**
        c. Presentation Against Government / **7-8**
        d. Penalties / **7-8**
    4. False Statements Act / **7-9**
        a. Included Offenses / **7-9**
        b. Elements / **7-9**
        c. Penalties / **7-10**
    5. Mail & Wire Fraud / **7-10**
    6. Program Fraud Civil Remedies Act / **7-10**
    7. Major Fraud Act / **7-11**
B. Corruption / **7-12**
    1. Anti-Kickback Enforcement Act Of 1986 / **7-12**
        a. Prohibited Conduct / **7-13**
        b. Penalties / **7-14**
    2. Bribery & Illegal Gratuities Statutes / **7-14**

        a. Bribery Statute / **7-14**
        b. Illegal Gratuities Statute / **7-14**
    3. Procurement Integrity Act / **7-15**
        a. Prohibitions / **7-15**
        b. Penalties / **7-16**
    4. Byrd Amendment / **7-16**
        a. Prohibitions / **7-17**
        b. Penalties / **7-17**
C. Enforcement / **7-18**
    1. Inspectors General / **7-18**
    2. Department Of Justice / **7-19**
    3. Suspension & Debarment / **7-19**
        a. Suspension / **7-19**
        b. Debarment / **7-20**

PART III   PERFORMANCE

chapter 8   Specifications

A. Design vs. Performance Specifications / **8-2**
    1. Design Specifications / **8-3**
    2. Performance Specifications / **8-3**
B. Government's "Minimum Needs" / **8-3**
C. Specifications, Standards & Purchase Descriptions / **8-5**
    1. Specifications / **8-5**
        a. Federal Specifications / **8-5**
        b. Military Specifications / **8-5**
        c. Industry Specifications / **8-6**
    2. Standards / **8-6**
    3. Purchase Descriptions / **8-7**
        a. Definition / **8-7**
        b. Brand Name Or Equal / **8-7**
        c. Foreign Purchase Descriptions / **8-8**
    4. Deviations & Waivers / **8-8**
D. Qualified Products / **8-9**
E. Government Warranty Of Specifications / **8-10**
    1. The "Implied Warranty" / **8-10**

2. Government Disclaimers / **8-11**
F. Contractor Compliance With Specifications / **8-12**
  1. Strict Compliance / **8-12**
  2. Minimum Compliance / **8-12**
G. Substantial Performance / **8-13**
  1. Construction Contracts / **8-13**
  2. Supply Contracts / **8-14**
  3. Service Contracts / **8-14**
H. Defective Specifications / **8-15**
  1. Impossibility Of Performance / **8-16**
    a. Types Of Impossibility / **8-16**
    b. Allocation Of Risk / **8-17**
  2. Notice / **8-17**
  3. Right To Stop Work / **8-18**

chapter 9 Government Property

A. Overview / **9-2**
  1. Definitions / **9-2**
    a. Government Property / **9-2**
    b. Government-Furnished Property / **9-2**
  2. Neutralizing The Competitive Advantage / **9-3**
    a. Sealed Bid Procurements / **9-4**
    b. Negotiated Procurements / **9-5**
    c. Other Costs & Savings / **9-5**
  3. Standard Contract Clauses / **9-5**
  4. Title / **9-6**
B. Government Obligations / **9-11**
  1. Furnishing Property / **9-11**
  2. Timely Delivery / **9-11**
  3. Suitability Of Property / **9-12**
  4. Suitability Of Data & Information / **9-14**
C. Contractor Obligations / **9-14**
  1. Mitigation Of Damages / **9-14**
  2. Notice To Government / **9-15**
  3. Maintenance & Repair / **9-16**
D. Contractor Remedies / **9-16**
  1. Recovery Of Extra Costs / **9-16**

2. Performance Time Extension / **9-17**
　E. Risk Of Loss / **9-17**
　　　1. Competitive, Fixed-Price Contracts / **9-17**
　　　2. Other Contracts / **9-18**

chapter 10　Intellectual Property Rights

　A. Patents / **10-2**
　　　1. Title vs. License / **10-2**
　　　2. Current Government Policy / **10-3**
　　　3. FAR Coverage / **10-4**
　　　　a. Contractor Title / **10-4**
　　　　b. Government License / **10-5**
　　　4. Patent Infringement / **10-5**
　　　5. Contractor Indemnification Of Government / **10-7**
　　　6. Contractor Notice & Assistance / **10-7**
　B. Technical Data / **10-8**
　　　1. The Regulations / **10-8**
　　　2. Types Of Government Rights / **10-9**
　　　3. Government Policy / **10-9**
　　　4. DOD Policy & Procedures / **10-10**
　　　　a. Policy / **10-10**
　　　　b. Procedures / **10-10**
　　　5. Enforcing Data Rights / **10-12**
　C. Copyright / **10-12**

chapter 11　Changes

　A. Standard "Changes" Clauses / **11-2**
　　　1. Fixed-Price Contracts / **11-2**
　　　2. Cost-Reimbursement Contracts / **11-4**
　B. Changes Authority / **11-7**
　　　1. Non-Contracting Officers / **11-7**
　　　2. Changes Outside Contract's "Scope" / **11-9**
　C. Contractor's Duty To Proceed / **11-10**
　　　1. Scope Of Duty / **11-10**
　　　2. Effect Of Failure To Proceed / **11-11**
　D. Value Engineering / **11-12**

        1. Value Engineering Change Proposals / **11-12**
        2. Administration / **11-13**
   E. Formal Change Orders / **11-14**
        1. Origination / **11-14**
            a. Contractor-Proposed Changes / **11-14**
            b. Government-Originated Changes / **11-14**
        2. Procedures / **11-16**
            a. Bilateral Change Orders / **11-16**
            b. Unilateral Change Orders / **11-16**
            c. Timing / **11-16**
   F. Constructive Changes / **11-17**
        1. Development Of The Doctrine / **11-17**
        2. Types Of Constructive Changes / **11-18**
            a. Contract Interpretation / **11-18**
            b. Interference & Failure To Cooperate / **11-19**
            c. Defective Specifications / **11-20**
            d. Nondisclosure Of Vital Information / **11-20**
            e. Acceleration / **11-21**

chapter 12   Delays

   A. Compensable Delays / **12-2**
        1. Standard Contract Clauses / **12-2**
        2. Recovery For Constructive Suspensions / **12-4**
        3. Types Of Constructive Delays / **12-4**
            a. Delays Involving Changes / **12-5**
            b. Delays Involving Faulty Specifications / **12-5**
            c. Delays In Furnishing Property / **12-5**
            d. Delays In Approval Or Inspection Of Work / **12-5**
   B. Excusable Delays / **12-6**
        1. Standard Clause / **12-6**
        2. Elements & Proof / **12-7**
        3. Enumerated Causes Of Excusable Delay / **12-7**
            a. Government Sovereign Acts / **12-8**
            b. Government Contractual Acts / **12-8**

          c. Weather / **12-9**
          d. Subcontractor Delays / **12-9**
      4. Unenumerated Causes Of Excusable Delay / **12-10**

chapter 13   Equitable Adjustment Claims

    A. Basic Rules Of Computation / **13-2**
      1. Added Work / **13-3**
      2. Deleted Work / **13-4**
      3. Overhead & Profit / **13-5**
          a. Overhead / **13-5**
          b. Profit / **13-5**
    B. Proving The Equitable Adjustment Amount / **13-6**
      1. Actual Cost Data / **13-11**
      2. "Total Cost" Method / **13-12**
      3. "Jury Verdict" Method / **13-13**
    C. Claim Preparation Costs / **13-14**
    D. Interest / **13-16**
      1. Interest On Claims / **13-16**
      2. Interest On Borrowings / **13-17**
    E. Notice Of Claims / **13-17**

chapter 14   Inspection And Warranty

    A. Government Inspection Rights / **14-2**
      1. Regulations / **14-2**
      2. Standard Contract Clauses / **14-2**
    B. Inspection Procedures / **14-6**
      1. Contractor Inspection / **14-6**
      2. Time Of Inspection / **14-7**
      3. Place Of Inspection / **14-8**
      4. Costs Of Inspection / **14-8**
      5. Manner Of Inspection / **14-9**
    C. Rejection & Correction / **14-9**
      1. Rejection Notice / **14-9**
          a. Timing / **14-9**
          b. Form / **14-10**

        2. Contractor Correction / **14-10**
    D. Acceptance / **14-11**
        1. Effect / **14-11**
        2. Method Of Acceptance / **14-12**
        3. Government's Postacceptance Rights / **14-13**
            a. Latent Defects / **14-13**
            b. Fraud & Gross Mistakes / **14-14**
            c. Other Contract Terms / **14-14**
    E. Warranties / **14-15**
        1. Express Warranties / **14-15**
            a. Regulations / **14-15**
            b. Standard Contract Clauses / **14-16**
            c. Government's Remedies / **14-16**
        2. Implied Warranties / **14-20**

chapter 15   Payment

    A. Contract Payments / **15-2**
        1. Standard Contract Clauses / **15-2**
        2. Partial Payments / **15-3**
        3. Prompt Payment Act Requirements / **15-6**
            a. Interest Penalties / **15-7**
            b. "Proper" Invoices / **15-7**
            c. Applicability Of The Act / **15-7**
    B. Contract Financing / **15-8**
        1. Progress Payments / **15-8**
            a. Standard Contract Clause / **15-9**
            b. Amount / **15-15**
            c. Title To Property / **15-16**
            d. Suspension Or Reduction Of Payments / **15-16**
        2. Advance Payments / **15-17**
        3. Other Financing Methods / **15-18**
            a. Loan Guarantees / **15-18**
            b. Private Financing / **15-18**
    C. Government Withholding / **15-19**
    D. Government Debt Collection Through Offset / **15-19**
        1. Applicability Of Debt Collection Act / **15-19**
        2. Regulations / **15-20**

PART IV   TERMINATIONS

chapter 16   Termination For Default

    A. Standard "Default" Clauses / 16-2
    B. Bases For Termination / 16-6
        1. Failure To Deliver Or Perform / 16-6
            a. Timely Delivery / 16-7
            b. Compliance With Specifications / 16-8
        2. Failure To Make Progress / 16-8
        3. Failure To Perform Other Contract Provisions / 16-10
        4. Anticipatory Breach Of Contract / 16-10
    C. The Termination Decision / 16-11
        1. Contracting Officer Discretion / 16-12
        2. Improper Motive Or Grounds / 16-12
        3. Notices / 16-13
    D. Contractor Defenses / 16-14
        1. Excusable Delay / 16-14
        2. Waiver Of Due Date / 16-15
            a. Forbearance vs. Waiver / 16-16
            b. Termination After Waiver / 16-17
    E. Government Remedies / 16-17
        1. Excess Costs Of Reprocurement / 16-18
            a. Measure Of Excess Costs / 16-18
            b. Similarity Of Repurchase / 16-19
            c. Government Duty To Mitigate / 16-20
            d. Government Completion Of Work / 16-21
        2. Other Remedies / 16-21
        3. Liquidated Damages / 16-22
    F. Contesting Default Terminations / 16-23
        1. Procedures / 16-23
        2. Contractor Remedies / 16-24

chapter 17   Termination For Convenience

    A. Government's Convenience Termination Right / 17-2
        1. Standard "Termination For Convenience" Clause / 17-3

2. Scope Of Right / **17-7**
B. Termination Procedures / **17-8**
   1. Government's Obligations / **17-9**
      a. Written Notice / **17-9**
      b. Post-Termination Duties / **17-9**
   2. Contractor's Obligations / **17-10**
C. Constructive Termination / **17-11**
   1. Conversion Of Improper Default Termination / **17-11**
   2. Cancellation Of Contract, Award, Or Work / **17-11**
D. Contractor Recovery / **17-13**
   1. Settlement Proposals / **17-13**
      a. Form & Content / **17-13**
      b. Settlement Basis / **17-13**
      c. No-Cost Settlement / **17-14**
   2. Settlement Principles & Limitations / **17-14**
      a. "Fair Compensation" / **17-14**
      b. General Limitations / **17-15**
   3. Special Termination Costs / **17-16**
      a. Precontract Costs / **17-17**
      b. Initial Costs / **17-17**
      c. Termination Inventory Costs / **17-17**
      d. Post-Termination Costs / **17-18**
   4. Settlement Expenses / **17-19**
   5. Subcontractor Claims / **17-21**
   6. Profit / **17-22**
   7. Loss Adjustments / **17-22**
E. Partial Terminations / **17-23**
   1. Partial Termination vs. Deductive Change / **17-23**
   2. Contractor Recovery / **17-24**

PART V   DISPUTES AND REMEDIES

chapter 18   The Disputes Process

A. Contract Disputes Act Overview / **18-2**
   1. History / **18-2**

2. Coverage / **18-3**
     a. Excluded Contracts / **18-4**
     b. Excluded Claims / **18-4**
  B. Standard "Disputes" Clause/ **18-5**
  C. The Disputes Path / **18-7**
     1. Contracting Officer / **18-8**
     2. Board Of Contract Appeals / **18-8**
     3. Court Of Federal Claims / **18-9**
     4. Appellate Review / **18-9**
  D. Other Remedies / **18-9**
     1. Alternative Dispute Resolution / **18-11**
     2. Extraordinary Contractual Relief / **18-11**
        a. Agency Implementation / **18-12**
        b. Types Of Relief / **18-13**
        c. Procedures / **18-15**

chapter 19 The Claim And Contracting Officer Decision

  A. Contractor Claims vs. Government Claims / **19-2**
  B. Asserting A "Claim" / **19-3**
     1. Early Notice To Contracting Officer / **19-3**
     2. Definition Of "Claim" / **19-4**
     3. Need For Preexisting Dispute / **19-5**
     4. Sum Certain / **19-5**
     5. Claim Certification / **19-6**
        a. Who Signs The Certification / **19-6**
        b. Content Of Certification / **19-6**
  C. Contracting Officer's Decision / **19-8**
     1. Content / **19-8**
     2. Timing / **19-10**
     3. Contractor's Duty To Proceed / **19-11**
  D. Contractor's Decision To Appeal Or Bring Suit / **19-11**
     1. Practical Considerations / **19-11**
     2. Binding Election Of Forum / **19-12**

chapter 20   Appeal To Board Of Contract Appeals

A. Initial Steps / 20-2
  1. Notice Of Appeal / 20-2
     a. Content / 20-2
     b. Timing / 20-2
  2. Docketing / 20-3
  3. Representation / 20-3
  4. Complaint / 20-4
  5. Answer / 20-4
  6. Rule 4 File / 20-5
B. Discovery / 20-6
C. Subpoenas / 20-8
D. Motions / 20-8
E. Abbreviated Proceedings / 20-9
  1. Submission Without Hearing / 20-9
  2. Small Claims Procedures / 20-9
     a. Expedited Appeals / 20-10
     b. Accelerated Appeals / 20-10
     c. Advantages & Disadvantages / 20-10
F. Hearings / 20-11
  1. Prehearing Conference / 20-11
  2. Location & Date / 20-12
  3. Conduct / 20-13
  4. Posthearing Briefs / 20-14
G. Decision / 20-14
  1. Reconsideration / 20-15
  2. Judicial Review / 20-15

chapter 21   Federal Court Proceedings

A. History / 21-2
B. Court of Federal Claims / 21-3
  1. Complaint / 21-3
  2. Answer / 21-4
  3. Pretrial Orders & Conferences / 21-4
  4. Discovery / 21-5
  5. Motions / 21-5

        6. Trial / **21-6**
        7. Post-Trial Briefs / **21-6**
        8. Decision / **21-6**
    C. Court Of Appeals For The Federal Circuit / **21-7**
        1. Review Of Board Decisions / **21-7**
            a. Law vs. Fact Distinction / **21-7**
            b. Substantial Evidence Test / **21-8**
        2. Review Of Court Of Federal Claims Decisions / **21-9**
        3. Procedures / **21-9**
            a. Filings & Record / **21-9**
            b. Decision / **21-10**
            c. Rehearing / **21-11**

PART VI   SUBCONTRACTING

chapter 22   Subcontract Basics

    A. Nature Of Subcontracts / **22-2**
    B. Subcontractor Disputes & Remedies / **22-2**
        1. Privity Rule / **22-2**
        2. Subcontractors vs. The Government / **22-3**
        3. Subcontractors vs. Prime Contractors / **22-5**
    C. Government Control / **22-5**
        1. Contractor Purchasing System Review / **22-6**
        2. Consent To Subcontracts / **22-6**
        3. Flow-Down Clauses / **22-8**
        4. Policies Favoring Special Groups / **22-9**
        5. Payment / **22-10**

chapter 23   Subcontract Terms And Conditions

    A. Background / **23-2**
        1. Uniform Commercial Code / **23-2**
        2. Standard Government Contract Clauses / **23-3**
    B. Flow-Down Clauses / **23-4**
    C. ABA Model Terms & Conditions / **23-11**

PART VII   CONSTRUCTION CONTRACTING

chapter 24   Construction Contract Basics

    A. Overview / **24-2**
    B. Construction Contracts vs. Supply Contracts / **24-4**
        1. Similarities / **24-4**
        2. Differences / **24-4**
            a. Government Control / **24-5**
            b. Work Site / **24-5**
            c. Contract Clauses / **24-5**
            d. Bonds / **24-6**
            e. Labor Standards / **24-6**
            f. Contract Changes / **24-7**
            g. Default Termination/ **24-7**

chapter 25   Differing Site Conditions

    A. Standard "Differing Site Conditions" Clause / **25-2**
    B. Notice To Government / **25-3**
    C. Types Of Differing Site Conditions / **25-4**
        1. Type I Conditions / **25-5**
        2. Type II Conditions / **25-6**
        3. Conditions Occurring After Award / **25-7**
        4. Excluded Conditions / **25-8**
    D. Contractor's Duty To Investigate Site / **25-9**
        1. Standard "Site Investigation" Clause / **25-9**
        2. Limitations / **25-9**
        3. Failure To Investigate Or Inquire / **25-10**
        4. Government's Duty To Disclose / **25-11**
    E. Government Disclaimers / **25-11**

chapter 26   Construction Delays And Liquidated Damages

    A. Government Suspensions Of Work / **26-2**
        1. Ordered Suspensions / **26-2**
        2. Constructive Suspensions / **26-4**

    a. Government Fault / 26-4
    b. Unreasonable Delay / 26-5
   3. Recoverable Costs / 26-6
   4. Limitations On Recovery / 26-7
    a. Notice & Claim Requirements / 26-7
    b. Concurrent Delays / 26-8
  B. Excusable Delays / 26-9
   1. Weather Delays / 26-9
   2. Labor Delays / 26-11
    a. Strikes / 26-11
    b. Labor Shortages / 26-11
   3. Subcontractor Delays / 26-11
   4. Acts Of Another Contractor / 26-12
  C. Liquidated Damages / 26-12
   1. Standard Clause / 26-12
    a. Measuring The Damages Period / 26-13
    b. Per Diem Rate / 26-14
   2. Enforceability / 26-14
    a. Reasonableness Of The Forecast / 26-15
    b. Difficulty In Estimating Loss / 26-15
   3. Relief From Liquidated Damages / 26-16
    a. Substantial Completion / 26-16
    b. Excusable & Concurrent Delays / 26-16
    c. Remission By Comptroller General / 26-17

chapter 27 Construction Labor Standards

  A. Davis-Bacon Act / 27-2
   1. Coverage / 27-2
   2. Determination Of "Prevailing" Wage Rate / 27-3
   3. Contractor Obligations / 27-3
    a. Wage Schedule / 27-3
    b. Wage Payments / 27-4
    c. Fringe Benefits / 27-4
   4. Administration & Enforcement / 27-5
  B. Work Hours Act / 27-6
   1. Coverage / 27-6
   2. Contractor Obligations / 27-7

            a. Maximum Hours & Overtime Pay / **27-7**
            b. Health & Safety Standards / **27-7**
        3. Administration & Enforcement / **27-7**
            a. Maximum Hours & Overtime Pay / **27-7**
            b. Health & Safety Standards / **27-8**
    C. Construction In Foreign Countries/ **27-8**

APPENDIX
    Appendix: FAR Structure To The Subpart Level / **APP-1**

GLOSSARY / GL-1

SUBJECT INDEX / SI-1

List of Figures

Each Figure has two numbers: the first indicates the chapter in which the Figure is located; the second is the Figure's sequence within that chapter. For example, Figure 3-4 is the fourth Figure in Chapter 3.

No.		Page
2-1	Federal Acquisition Regulation Structure	2-10
3-1	Standard Form 33, "Solicitation, Offer, and Award"	3-4
3-2	Standard Form 30, "Amendment of Solicitation/Modification of Contract"	3-5
3-3	Optional Form 347, "Order for Supplies or Services"	3-7
3-4	Standard Form 1442, "Solicitation, Offer, and Award (Construction, Alteration, or Repair)"	3-9
3-5	Standard Form 129, "Solicitation Mailing List Application"	3-14
3-6	GAO Protest Time Chart	3-39
4-1	Contract Types (chart)	4-23
5-1	Standard Form 1411, "Contract Pricing Proposal Cover Sheet"	5-33
5-2	Certificate of Current Cost or Pricing Data	5-35
9-1	"Government Property (Fixed-Price Contracts)" Clause	9-7
10-1	"Authorization and Consent" Clause	10-6

No.		Page
11-1	"Changes–Fixed Price" Clause	11-3
11-2	"Changes–Cost-Reimbursement" Clause	11-6
11-3	"Engineering Change Proposals" Clause	11-15
12-1	"Government Delay of Work" Clause	12-3
13-1	Equitable Adjustment Calculations	13-7
14-1	"Inspection of Supplies–Fixed-Price" Clause	14-3
14-2	"Warranty of Supplies of a Noncomplex Nature" Clause	14-17
15-1	"Payments" Clause	15-3
15-2	"Payments Under Fixed-Price Construction Contracts" Clause	15-4
15-3	"Progress Payments" Clause	15-9
16-1	"Default (Fixed-Price Supply and Service)" Clause	16-3
16-2	"Default (Fixed-Price Construction)" Clause	16-5
17-1	"Termination for Convenience of the Government (Fixed-Price)" Clause	17-3
18-1	"Disputes" Clause	18-6
18-2	Government Contract Disputes Routes	18-10
23-1	ABA Model Fixed-Price Supply Subcontract Terms and Conditions	23-12

No.		Page
25-1	"Differing Site Conditions" Clause	25-3
25-2	"Site Investigation and Conditions Affecting the Work" Clause	25-10
26-1	"Suspension of Work" Clause	26-3
26-2	"Liquidated Damages–Construction" Clause	26-13

Foreword

It has been nine years since we published the First Edition of the GOVERNMENT CONTRACT GUIDEBOOK. Judging by the response to the First Edition, it was one of our most popular volumes on the subject of Government contracting. Providing a comprehensive, yet manageable, overview of the entire field, the GUIDEBOOK's First Edition was received by procurement professionals as an authoritative work and welcomed by novices needing direction in a complicated area.

We are now happy to present this completely revised, updated, and expanded Second Edition. Written by the same authors—Donald P. Arnavas, formerly a judge of the Armed Services Board of Contract Appeals and now a practicing Government contracts lawyer, and William J. Ruberry, retired Vice Chairman of the Armed Services Board—the GUIDEBOOK sets forth the essentials of Government contracting, from the basic principles of the contracting process to the peculiarities of subcontracts and construction contracts. Drawing on their collective Government contracts experience of over half a century, these authors have made the complex simple and the obscure accessible. Most importantly, they have done so in a book that is neither so large that it intimidates nor so small that it misses the mark.

Read and use this text both as a valuable reference tool and as a shepherd through the field of federal procurement. We have no doubt that it will serve you well.

Federal Publications Inc.

October 1994

Part I

INTRODUCTION

chapters

1 | About This Book
2 | The Setting

ABOUT THIS BOOK

1

A. Organization

B. Guide To Use
    1. References
    2. Figures & Appendix
    3. Glossary
    4. Table Of Contents & Index
    5. Supplementation & Revision

Contracting with the Federal Government can be an attractive undertaking. The United States spends billions of dollars every year on the procurement of supplies, services, and construction. But Government contracting also has unique problems and pitfalls. So, while many companies have become successful by concentrating most of their efforts on doing business with the Government, others have not fared as well.

In recent years, much has been written about Government contracting. But most of these books and studies focus on the various *particulars* of the contracts field. Little has been said about contracting as a *whole*. Moreover, there has not been a comprehensive exploration—within a single book—of the *essential* information someone considering entry into this complex area of business should know. This book fills that vacuum.

As its title indicates, this is a "Guidebook." Government contracting is a field filled with laws and regulations and countless significant legal decisions (because it is rife with disputes and litigation). It is also a field in a constant state of flux. This GOVERNMENT CONTRACT GUIDEBOOK is intended to highlight the essential elements and principles of Government contracting and provide the reader with a foundation for understanding how Government procurement works. Hopefully, this will enable business executives, contract administrators, lawyers, accountants, and students to become familiar with the fundamentals of Government contracting in a relatively short time.

Although the book's primary audience is the relative newcomer to Government procurement, those with some contracting experience should also find it of value. For them, the book will serve as a guide to specific areas with which they may be unfamiliar, and as a useful reference in those areas where they are already knowledgeable.

A. ORGANIZATION

The book covers all major areas of Government contracting. It is, of course, an overview. To cover all aspects of the subject in detail would require several books. Whole books can be—and have been—written on subjects treated in a single chapter of this book.

The book is organized in "parts," which are subdivided into 27 chapters. There are seven parts:

- Part I: Introduction
- Part II: Contract Basics
- Part III: Performance
- Part IV: Terminations
- Part V: Disputes And Remedies
- Part VI: Subcontracting
- Part VII: Construction Contracting

The text has been organized to parallel the events that someone would likely experience as a Government contractor. Thus, after Part I, which contains introductory material, the discussion turns, in Part II, to the basics of how—and from whom—the Government buys what it needs. The various aspects of contract performance are then reviewed in Part III, followed by Part IV's treatment of the Government's right to terminate a contract. Thereafter, in Part V, the focus is on the procedures for resolving disputes, claims, and lawsuits that may occur if all does not go as the parties hoped when the contract was awarded. Finally, the special areas of subcontracts and construction contracts—and their peculiarities—are discussed in Parts VI and VII.

Under the book's organizational plan, the reader who wants to review the entire scope of Government contracts can start at the beginning and proceed to the end of the book in logical sequence. On the other hand, if a specific aspect of procurement is of interest, the reader can go directly to that portion of the book in which it is discussed.

B. GUIDE TO USE

To make this book as readable as possible, certain special features have been included, and tailored techniques of presentation have been devised. They are explained below.

1. References

References (footnotes) have been included at the end of each chapter so that the reader may extend his or her understanding of the matters discussed and learn the source for the statements made in the text. Except in unusual instances, the references contain no textual information. There is no need to skip back and forth between text and references, therefore, when reading the book; refer to the references only to trace the authority for the statements in the text.

Many references in this book consist of citations to federal laws relating to Government procurement, as found in the United States Code (USC), as well as citations to Government regulations dealing with procurement, such as the Federal Acquisition Regulation (FAR) and the Department of Defense FAR Supplement (DFARS). It should be noted that the laws and rules that govern Government contracts are constantly changing. The citations that appear in this book reflect the status of these sources on the date of publication.

The references also include numerous citations to legal decisions by federal courts, agency boards of contract appeals, and the U.S. Comptroller General. References of this type will be of particular interest to the attorney-user. Especially noteworthy are those references which, in addition to citing the source in which the full text of a decision is reported, contain citations bearing the abbreviation "GC." These references indicate that a decision has been discussed in THE GOVERNMENT CONTRACTOR, Federal Publications' weekly periodical which has been analyzing decisions bearing on Government contract law for over 35 years.

Certain standard abbreviations are used in the citations to the legal decisions, statutes, regulations, and other authorities that appear in the References sections of the chapters. The common abbreviations used in citing most legal authorities may generally be found in *A Uniform System of Citation* published by the Harvard Law Review Association. Other abbreviations may be found in the Glossary at the back of this volume.

2. Figures & Appendix

Figures have been included when it appears that they will be helpful in furthering the reader's understanding of the subject being discussed. One major use of figures in this book is to provide examples of standard Government forms and contract clauses that are used as part of the procurement process.

For ease of location, each figure has two numbers—the first indicates the chapter in which the figure is located, the second is the figure's sequence within that chapter (for example, Figure 11-2 is the second figure in Chapter 11). A List of Figures appears immediately following the Table of Contents.

In addition, the book contains an appendix (following the last chapter) setting forth the structure of the FAR.

3. Glossary

As a rule, an abbreviation or acronym is never used in the text of a chapter unless it has first been identified in that chapter. (An exception is the use of "FAR" to refer to the Federal Acquisition Regulation since it appears so frequently throughout the book.) In a field as specialized as Government procurement, however, certain terms (and abbreviations) inevitably become common to the veterans—sort of a recognized shorthand—and those who wish to practice in the field should thus be aware of them. It seemed, therefore, appropriate to use some of those specialized terms throughout this volume. To aid the reader who may be unfamiliar with them, a Glossary has been included at the back of the book.

4. Table Of Contents & Index

A detailed Table of Contents listing all the chapter heads and subheads appears at the front of the book—and itself serves as a form of index. In addition, for ease of reference, each chapter opens with its own individual list of contents. Finally, a quick-reference Subject Index (alphabetically arranged by topic and subtopic) appears at the end of the book.

5. Supplementation & Revision

The hardcover version of this book has been designed as a "looseleaf"—individual pages may be easily removed from the permanent binder in which they are housed. This design, and the binder's capacity to expand, will allow for periodic supplementation and revision of the book. In addition, softcover versions of this book—with any current revisions and supplementation bound-in—will appear periodically.

EDITOR'S NOTE

Just prior to publication of this second edition of the GOVERNMENT CONTRACT GUIDEBOOK, the Federal Acquisition Streamlining Act of 1994, Public Law 103-355 (108 Stat. 3243), was signed into law by the President. The Act, intended by Congress to simplify and streamline the way the Government buys goods and services, amends many of the federal acquisition laws discussed and cited in this book. Although some of the statutory amendments were effective as of the Act's enactment date (October 13, 1994), most will become applicable in accordance with final implementing regulations or on October 1, 1995, whichever is earlier. Changes to the regulations—especially the Federal Acquisition Regulation—that will implement and trigger the applicability of many of the Act's provisions are currently underway and are expected to be completed before the statutory deadline of October 1, 1995.

To ensure the currency of the information contained in this GUIDEBOOK, the text and references reflect, where relevant, the statutory changes made by Congress in the Streamlining Act. Regulatory changes will be covered in the first Supplement to this text.

THE SETTING

2

A. Institutional Framework
1. Legislative Branch
2. Executive Branch
3. Judicial Branch

B. Regulations
1. Federal Acquisition Regulation
2. Agency Acquisition Regulations
3. Deviations

C. Purchasing Offices
1. Department Of Defense
2. Civilian Agencies
3. Obtaining Information

D. Basic Procurement Process
1. Government "Requirement"
2. Procurement Methods
3. Contract Types
4. Soliciting Sources
5. Government Procurement Team
6. Activities Of Government Representatives
7. Dealing With Government Representatives

In some ways, the study of United States Government procurement is a complex undertaking. Procurement is accomplished—and contracts are awarded, administered, and enforced—not by a single Government department but by a variety of military and civilian agencies subject to a multitude of rules and regulations. Moreover, each of the branches of Government—legislative, executive, and judicial—has a role to play in the procurement process, sometimes with divergent objectives and results.

This chapter provides an overview of the important basic aspects of Government procurement. It reviews the laws and regulations that are most important to the process and identifies the major procuring agencies and the means they use to accomplish their duties.

A. INSTITUTIONAL FRAMEWORK

Because the powers and functions (originating from the U.S. Constitution) of the three branches of the Federal Government often overlap, a discussion of them individually in terms of their roles in the procurement process is necessary.

1. Legislative Branch

Not surprisingly, the Congress, composed of the Senate and the House of Representatives, profoundly affects Government contracting both as overseer of the federal "purse strings" and as the only federal legislative body. In addition, an "agent" of Congress—the General Accounting Office (GAO)—is materially involved in the procurement process.

a. Congress. Under Article I of the U.S. Constitution, the Congress is the ultimate source of funds for Federal Government contracts. Its role in procurement is therefore a fundamental one.

Authorization for Government projects proposed by agencies commences in the various Committees of Congress. Representatives of particular Government agencies or departments (for example, the National Aeronautics and Space Administration or the Department of Defense (DOD)) request funds to carry on their functions by submitting detailed estimates (budgets) of the monies they will require for the next fiscal year. Hearings are held on many of these requests, negotiations ensue, concessions are made, and—when a budget is finally approved by the Committee charged with overseeing that particular agency's activities—it is referred to the House of Representatives and the Senate as a proposed authorization bill. The final bill does not provide the funds requested by the procuring agency but merely specifies a ceiling on its spending.

All authorization bills are eventually introduced into the House of Representatives and Senate Appropriations Committees. The Appropriations Committees have an opportunity to review the legislation and then determine whether the authorization will be matched by an appropriation. An Appropriations Committee can allot any sum for an authorized project, provided it does not exceed the authorized ceiling. Appropriation bills, after passage by both houses of Congress, are then sent to the President, who may either sign or veto them.

In addition to controlling federal expenditures, Congress enacts the laws that directly govern federal procurement. Indeed, the overall scheme of the procurement process is dictated by enactments of Congress—principally the Federal Property and Administrative Services Act of 1949[1] and the Armed Services Procurement Act.[2] Other statutes directly affect, among other things, contractors' cost accounting practices, cost controls in negotiated procurements, and disputes resolution procedures. There is no dearth of legislation directly dealing with Government contracts, and Congress is continually rethinking some of the basic principles of the contracting process.

Moreover, Congress has used Government contracts as devices for achieving social, economic, and foreign policy goals through the enactment of statutes that attach conditions to the expenditure of federal funds. An example of such a statute is the Defense Authorization Act of 1976.[3] Section 814 of this law directed DOD to initiate procedures for the acquisition of equipment that is standardized or interchangeable with equipment purchased by member countries of the North Atlantic Treaty

Organization. Thus, in this instance, Congress sought to promote a foreign policy objective in the context of a statute directed at the procurement process.

b. General Accounting Office. Congress engages in a continuing review of Executive Branch procurement policies and practices by relying heavily on the assistance of the GAO. The GAO was created by an act of Congress in 1921 as part of the Legislative Branch of the Government. It functions under the control and direction of the Comptroller General of the United States and is charged with, among other things, (a) auditing the Government's accounts, (b) settling and adjusting all claims and demands by and against the United States, and (c) deciding the merits of protests regarding contract awards or proposed awards. GAO's activities are supplemented by the Government Operations Committees of the House of Representatives and the Senate. These Committees have responsibility for (1) reviewing GAO reports and making recommendations to Congress and (2) conducting their own studies of Government procurement projects.

GAO's role in federal contracting is somewhat unusual and, at times, controversial. Although GAO does virtually no contracting for itself, its influence is far-reaching because of its audit reports on the efficiency and effectiveness of Government operations and its decisions regarding the merits of specific Government procurement actions. Specifically, among its activities, it:

(1) *Reviews* (upon the request of either a procurement agency or unsuccessful bidder) the propriety of contract awards (see Chapter 3, Section G.2).

(2) *Audits* the books and records of both the procuring agencies and Government contractors (see Chapter 5, Section D.2).

(3) *Evaluates* and *reviews*, in connection with its audit functions, Executive Branch management and programs.

(4) *Prescribes* and *reviews* the Government's accounting practices and standards as the chief accountant for the Government.

(5) *Advises* Congress not only on specific program policies, but also on specific legislation for improving federal procurement.

2. Executive Branch

The President and the heads of the various executive departments and agencies (such as DOD or the Department of Energy) exert great influence over the procurement process. For example, Department Secretaries and agency heads (through their delegates) collectively direct the procuring activities that award and administer contracts. In addition, they prescribe regulations, decide contract disputes (through boards of contract appeals), and implement social and economic policies through contracts.

a. President. Congress has directly delegated many contractual powers to the President. The most significant delegation was made under the Defense Production Act of 1950,[4] which grants the President far-reaching powers over the defense industry as well as the ability to obtain necessary supplies or services during times of national emergency. Although the direct exercise of this power is seldom undertaken, the possibility of its invocation has been used by the Executive Branch to prod resolution of disputes in critical procurements.

Presidential authority is also used to achieve desired economic and social policy goals. This is usually accomplished by means of "Executive Orders" which set forth policies or rules relating to numerous areas. Executive Orders are often incorporated into procurement regulations and contract provisions.

b. Executive Departments & Agencies. The Secretaries and heads of the various military and civilian departments and agencies—through congressional delegation—have authority over major procurement decisions affecting their departments and agencies. The Armed Services Procurement Act[5] grants the Secretaries of the various armed services the authority to make procurement decisions and outlines general guidelines under which such decisions are to be made. Similar provisions—with regard to the heads of the nonmilitary departments and agencies—are found in the Federal Property and Administrative Services Act.[6]

In addition to performing actual procurement and contract management functions, the various military and civilian agencies in the Executive Branch have boards of contract appeals that decide a wide variety of contract disputes. As discussed in Chapter 20, most Government contracts litigation is conducted before these boards. They are composed of experienced procurement attorneys (designated as "administrative judges") who are authorized to decide contract disputes on behalf of the heads of their respective agencies. In the case of most DOD appeals, the Armed Services Board of Contract Appeals (ASBCA) acts on behalf of the Secretary of Defense and the Secretaries of the various military services. In all other cases, each agency with significant procurement activities has its own board, while those with only minor contract activities have their cases assigned to one of the major boards.

At present there are 11 boards—all located in the Washington, D.C. area. The ASBCA, with nearly 40 judges, is by far the largest and busiest board. In Fiscal Year 1993, it disposed of 1,722 contract appeals, with 2,027 cases pending at the end of the fiscal year.[7] The second most active board is the General Services Administration (GSA) Board of Contract Appeals (GSBCA). The GSBCA's docket, as well as its impact on the procurement process, has grown dramatically in recent years because of its jurisdiction over protests involving the Government's procurement of automatic data processing equipment and software.[8] The bid protest decisions of the GSBCA are published in Federal Publications' BOARD OF CONTRACT APPEALS BID PROTEST DECISIONS reporter.

c. Rulemaking Organizations. The procurement process is governed by a vast array of regulations and rules. Three principal rulemaking groups, established pursuant to congressional authority, are connected to the Executive Branch. These are (a) the Office of Federal Procurement Policy (OFPP) within the Office of Management and Budget, (b) the Defense Acquisition Regulations (DAR) Council, and (c) the Civilian Agency Acquisition (CAA) Council.

Congress established OFPP in 1974 and charged it with promoting economic efficiency and effectiveness in procurement by and for the Executive Branch of the Federal Government.[9] Congress specifically envisioned that OFPP would meet the following four areas of need in the procurement process: (1) provide a central authority in charge of procurement functions, (2) act as a "court of last resort" in arbitrating agency differences, (3) serve as an information-gathering body to analyze agency procurement practices and policies, and (4) direct, develop, and evaluate uniform procurement policies.

The DAR Council and the CAA Council are jointly responsible for preparing and issuing revisions to the basic set of regulations that governs Government contracts—the Federal Acquisition Regulation, or FAR, discussed below in Section B. The DAR Council is a group composed of a representative of the Secretary of Defense and representatives from each of the military departments, the Defense Logistics Agency, and the National Aeronautics and Space Administration. Its principal function is to submit recommendations on revisions or additions to the FAR and the Defense FAR Supplement (DFARS). The CAA Council serves a function roughly comparable to the DAR Council for civilian agencies. It is chaired by a representative of the Administrator of General Services. Representatives from the civilian agencies (the Departments of Agriculture, Commerce, Energy, and Treasury, for example) make up its membership.

3. Judicial Branch

Procurement policies are also influenced by the Federal Government's Judicial Branch—principally by the U.S. Court of Appeals for the Federal Circuit, the U.S. Court of Federal Claims,[10] and, to a lesser extent, by the U.S. Supreme Court. Full reproductions of all current Government contract decisions issued by these three federal courts are available in FEDERAL COURT PROCUREMENT DECISIONS, published monthly by Federal Publications Inc.

The Court of Federal Claims can—if a contractor wishes—serve as the trial court for deciding whether a Government Contracting Officer's decision was proper. (Alternatively, the contractor may choose to appeal to an agency board of contract appeals.) The Court of Appeals for the Federal Circuit functions as the appellate reviewer of decisions of the boards of contract appeals and the Court of Federal Claims (see Chapter 21).

The U.S. District Courts and other U.S. Courts of Appeals have traditionally been the least influential of the Judicial Branch involved in the federal contracts process. This lack of influence can be attributed to their limited participation in considering contract disputes. However, these courts can have a significant indirect impact on the Government contracts practice, since they—along with state courts—decide all cases between prime contractors and subcontractors under federal contracts. Because the substantive rights and obligations between subcontractors and prime contractors can frequently turn on the construction of Government regulations and clauses, decisions of the federal courts can directly affect the interpretation and application of these rules and clauses. In addition, specific statutes or Executive Orders affecting the Government contracts process—if challenged by a contractor or other interested party—may be construed by federal courts.

The Supreme Court only infrequently agrees to review Government contract cases, and does so primarily only when important questions—usually with far-ranging implications—are involved. The effect of this relatively small number of decisions can be profound, however, and many of these cases will be discussed in this book.

B. REGULATIONS

Government procurement is procurement by regulation. The informality that often accompanies the solicitation and award of a purely commercial contract is obviously inappropriate where public funds are being expended for public purposes. Because of this, regulations play a key role in Government contracts.

1. Federal Acquisition Regulation

The basic set of regulations relating to federal procurement is the Federal Acquisition Regulation—the FAR. This set of regulations, which went into effect on April 1, 1984,[11] is the primary set of regulations for *all* federal executive agencies. It is prepared, issued, and maintained by the Secretary of Defense, the Administrator of General Services, and the Administrator of the National Aeronautics and Space Administration.[12]

Prior to the FAR, two sets of regulations governed Government contracts. One was the Defense Acquisition Regulation—the DAR as it was commonly called. The DAR (which was at one time called the Armed Services Procurement Regulation—the ASPR) governed procurements by military agencies. The other pre-FAR set of regulations was called the Federal Procurement Regulations—the FPR—governing procurements by civilian agencies.

The FAR is a massive document. At its most basic level of organization, as found in Chapter 1 of Title 48 in the *Code of Federal Regulations*, it consists of eight "subchapters," which in turn are composed of 53 "parts." Figure 2-1 on the following page lists the parts of the FAR, showing how they are arranged under each of the subchapters. In addition, Appendix A to this volume shows the structure of the FAR to the "subpart" level.

The FAR establishes uniform policies and procedures for procurement of supplies and services (including construction). It applies to all such purchases made within or outside the United States for procurements that obligate appropriated funds.[13]

The FAR is by no means a static document. As already mentioned, it is subject to frequent revision through the coordinated action of the DAR Council and the CAA Council.[14] Revision is accomplished through the issuance of Federal Acquisition Circulars (FACs).

2. Agency Acquisition Regulations

Agency acquisition regulations are limited to (a) those necessary to implement FAR policies and procedures within the agency and (b) additional policies, procedures, solicitation provisions, or contract clauses that supplement the FAR to satisfy the specific needs of the agency.[15]

Figure 2-1

FEDERAL ACQUISITION REGULATION STRUCTURE

Subchapter A: General

Part 1—Federal Acquisition Regulations System
Part 2—Definitions of Words and Terms
Part 3—Improper Business Practices and Personal Conflicts of Interest
Part 4—Administrative Matters

Subchapter B: Acquisition Planning

Part 5—Publicizing Contract Actions
Part 6—Competition Requirements
Part 7—Acquisition Planning
Part 8—Required Sources of Supplies and Services
Part 9—Contractor Qualifications
Part 10—Specifications, Standards, and Other Purchase Descriptions
Part 11—Acquisition and Distribution of Commercial Products
Part 12—Contract Delivery or Performance

Subchapter C: Contracting Methods and Contract Types

Part 13—Small Purchase and Other Simplified Purchase Procedures
Part 14—Sealed Bidding
Part 15—Contracting by Negotiation
Part 16—Types of Contracts
Part 17—Special Contracting Methods
Part 18—[Reserved]

Subchapter D: Socioeconomic Programs

Part 19—Small Business and Small Disadvantaged Business Concerns
Part 20—Labor Surplus Area Concerns
Part 21—[Reserved]
Part 22—Application of Labor Laws to Government Acquisitions
Part 23—Environment, Conservation, Occupational Safety, and Drug-Free Workplace
Part 24—Protection of Privacy and Freedom of Information
Part 25—Foreign Acquisition
Part 26—Other Socioeconomic Programs

continued

Fig. 2-1 / continued

Subchapter E: General Contracting Requirements

Part 27—Patents, Data, and Copyrights
Part 28—Bonds and Insurance
Part 29—Taxes
Part 30—Cost Accounting Standards
Part 31—Contract Cost Principles and Procedures
Part 32—Contract Financing
Part 33—Protests, Disputes, and Appeals

Subchapter F: Special Categories of Contracting

Part 34—Major System Acquisition
Part 35—Research and Development Contracting
Part 36—Construction and Architect-Engineer Contracts
Part 37—Service Contracting
Part 38—Federal Supply Schedule Contracting
Part 39—Acquisition of Information Resources
Part 40—[Reserved]
Part 41—[Reserved]

Subchapter G: Contract Management

Part 42—Contract Administration
Part 43—Contract Modifications
Part 44—Subcontracting Policies and Procedures
Part 45—Government Property
Part 46—Quality Assurance
Part 47—Transportation
Part 48—Value Engineering
Part 49—Termination of Contracts
Part 50—Extraordinary Contractual Actions
Part 51—Use of Government Sources by Contractors

Subchapter H: Clauses and Forms

Part 52—Solicitation Provisions and Contract Clauses
Part 53—Forms

Although the various civilian agencies have each issued their own sets of regulations implementing the FAR, the most comprehensive set is the DFARS (the Defense FAR Supplement), which applies to all of the military and DOD agencies. It is organized to correspond to the 53 parts of the FAR and incorporates several appendices and supplements. DOD completely rewrote the DFARS in 1991 to (1) eliminate text and clauses that were unnecessary, (2) eliminate or modify thresholds, certifications, and other regulatory burdens on Contracting Officers and contractors, and (3) rephrase all remaining text and clauses in plain English.[16]

Like the FAR, the DFARS is codified in the *Code of Federal Regulations* (designated as Chapter 2 of Title 48). The civilian agency regulations implementing the FAR are also codified in Title 48.

The DFARS is supplemented from time to time by the issuance of Defense Acquisition Circulars (DACs) or Departmental Letters.[17] A DAC may include—in addition to DFARS revisions—policies, directives, and informational items. These Circulars can be of significance to contractors. Unless otherwise stated in the DAC, any new provisions, policies, or directives are effective as of the effective date stated in the DAC.

Because the FAR is the key set of procurement regulations, most of the citations in this book will be to the FAR. Occasionally, the DFARS will also be cited.

3. Deviations

Deviations from the FAR are allowed only if they are (a) authorized and (b) approved by a designated official.[18] The same holds true for deviations from the DFARS.[19] Generally, deviations from the FAR consist of use of a contract clause containing language differing from the standard FAR language, use of forms other than prescribed forms, alteration of prescribed forms, or omission of a mandatory contract clause.

C. PURCHASING OFFICES

Actual purchasing activities and procurement management functions are accomplished by the military or civilian agencies within the Executive Branch.

1. Department Of Defense

Despite recent decreases in its budget, DOD is the biggest buying business in the world. For example, DOD figures released annually from 1986 through 1994 reveal that after reaching a high of $150.6 billion in Fiscal Year 1985, DOD's total contracting volume fell to $145.7 billion in Fiscal Year 1986, $142.5 billion in 1987, $137 billion in 1988, and $129 billion in 1989. However, DOD's total contracting volume during Fiscal Year 1990 rose to $130.8 billion and then increased every year to $138.3 billion in Fiscal Year 1993.[20] More than 80,000 contractors regularly do business with DOD.

DOD includes the Office of the Secretary of Defense, the organization of the Joint Chiefs of Staff, the military departments, the unified commands, and other agencies that the Secretary of Defense establishes to meet specific requirements—such as the Defense Contract Audit Agency (DCAA) and the Defense Logistics Agency (DLA).

Organization of the military departments is, in part, prescribed by statute. As with the Office of the Secretary of Defense, the functional area of procurement is managed at the secretarial level by an Under Secretary (Acquisition & Technology), who is a statutory appointee. Procurement operational responsibility is generally decentralized in the military services.

Organization for procurement is influenced by the manner in which procurement authority is delegated. Research and development (R&D) policies are overseen by the Assistant Secretaries for R&D. Responsibility for research, development, and acquisition of hardware and for other logistics aspects is generally delegated to major commands. Below the command level, there are hundreds of field organizations. Normally, these have a dollar limitation on their purchasing authority.

Within each DOD department, certain major commanders are designated as "Head of the Agency." The number of agency heads is small. Generally, each delegates his authority, except for certain critical functions, to contracting activities. This authority is usually further apportioned and redelegated to Contracting Officers.

Each of the three military departments buys supplies and services to support its respective functions. Other DOD component organizations, however, have a significant role in the procurement process.

The DLA, for example, provides consumable supply items and logistics services common to the military departments. Separate DLA supply centers exist for the handling of items associated with construction, electronics, fuels, general supplies, personnel support supplies, and industrial supplies. DLA provides contract administration services through its branch, the Defense Contract Management Command (formerly the Defense Contract Administration Service) with area offices located throughout the country.

The DCAA—initiated in 1965—performs contract audit functions and provides accounting and financial advisory services for all DOD components, as well as for most other Government agencies. DCAA provides services in connection with the negotiation, administration, and settlement of contracts and subcontracts, as well defective pricing and fraud situations.

2. Civilian Agencies

The Executive Office of the President, civilian agencies, boards and commissions, and other independent non-DOD establishments each year procure a wide variety of supplies, services, and construction. Yearly procurements by them now are about half of the amount for DOD procurements. For example, the GSA (the civilian equivalent of the DLA) performs a critical role in the acquisition and management of property (including construction and operation of federal buildings), procurement and distribution of supplies, utilization and disposal of property, transportation, traffic and communications management, and management of the Government-wide automatic data processing program.

3. Obtaining Information

Virtually every procuring agency has information regarding its purchasing activities and how it conducts business, which can be obtained upon request by contacting the specific agency. More general publications are also readily available. For instance, one publication, *Doing Business With the Federal Government*, can be obtained by contacting the General Services Administration, Federal Supply Service, Washington, DC 20405. It contains an overall guide to federal purchasing—both civilian and DOD. Interested contractors can also purchase the *U.S. Government Purchasing and Sales Directory* from the Superintendent of Documents, U.S. Government Printing Office, Washington, DC 20402. This booklet contains extensive address listings as well as sources of U.S. Government specifications.

D. BASIC PROCUREMENT PROCESS

Purchasing methods are not uniform throughout the Government. They vary from agency to agency. Moreover, within an individual agency, the procedures can vary from case to case according to the agency mission, dollar value, type of contract, and end-product involved.

1. Government "Requirement"

The first step in the procurement process involves approval or authority to process a Government "requirement." A requirement may be defined as a determination within an agency that a need exists that must be satisfied. The need may be real or apparent, existing or potential, and externally- or self-generated.

Once a requirement has been approved, the necessary funds must be committed. A "commitment" in this sense differs from an "obligation." Funds are obligated when a contract is awarded. Only then is there a legal obligation to make a payment. Funds may only be obligated after they are authorized and appropriated by Congress, and then pursuant only to the express limitations that may be set forth in the applicable appropriation act. A commitment, on the other hand, is the internal "earmarking" of funds by which an agency identifies both the types and amounts of dollars that are committed to certain requirements. Once committed, the funds are no longer available for other purposes.

The document setting forth the requirement (and citing the appropriated funds) is generally called a "purchase request" or "purchase requisition" (PR). However named, it contains the following minimum information: (1) a description of the desired supplies or services, including a specification, (2) a desired contract award date and delivery date, (3) recommended sources, if known, (4) shipping, marking, and packaging information, and (5) to the extent appropriate, any other pertinent information such as special terms and conditions desired or required by the contract. The degree of information and detail is usually a reflection of the dollar value of the procurement and the nature—particularly the complexity—of the contemplated effort.

This document is formally transmitted to the procurement organization. It is immaterial whether procurement is centralized or decentralized within the agency; contracting personnel are generally organizationally structured and physically located so that they are separate from technical and logistics personnel (i.e., those who generate requirements and prepare and approve PRs).

2. Procurement Methods

As the next step in the process, the Contracting Officer (the key Government person in any Government procurement, discussed below in Section D.5) determines "how" to conduct the procurement. The procurement may be either competitive or noncompetitive. In addition, there are special procedures for small purchases.

a. Competitive Contracts. Ever since enactment of the Competition in Contracting Act of 1984 (CICA),[21] "full and open competition" has become the byword of all Government procurement—a goal to be sought and achieved primarily through the use of sealed bidding and competitive proposals, the two basic methods of procurement. For this reason, noncompetitive contracts, discussed in the next section, are permitted to be used only in exceptional circumstances.

Prior to enactment of CICA, the two basic methods of procurement were (a) formal advertising and (b) negotiation. One significant effect of CICA has been its elimination of the bias under the old system in favor of formal advertising (now called sealed bidding) and its establishment of negotiation, instead, as the primary procurement method. Although CICA introduced new terminology for the basic methods of procurement, many procedures were carried over from the old system. Most of the procedures that were used for formally advertised procurements apply to "sealed bidding" (discussed in Chapter 3),[22] and the Act recodified existing practice with respect to negotiation—now referred to in terms of "competitive negotiation" (discussed in Chapter 4).

b. Noncompetitive Contracts. As mentioned above, noncompetitive contracts may be used only in exceptional circumstances because of the requirement for "full and open competition." Under the FAR, the requirement for full and open competition may be *waived* if any of these seven situations is present:[23]

(1) The property or service is available from only a single source. Also, a follow-on contract may be awarded to the incumbent contractor if using competition would be likely to cause unacceptable delays or substantial cost duplication.

(2) The agency's needs are so urgent that the Government's interest will be seriously injured unless a limit on sources is permitted.

(3) Award to a particular contractor is necessary to maintain that source in case of national emergency.

(4) The terms of an agreement or treaty between the United States and a foreign government or organization have the effect of requiring the use of noncompetitive procedures.

(5) The law expressly authorizes or requires that the procurement be made from a specified source, or the agency's need is for a brand-name commercial item for authorized resale.

(6) National security would be compromised.

(7) The agency (a) determines that noncompetitive procedures are "necessary in the public interest" and (b) provides Congress with written notice of its determination at least 30 days prior to contract award.

There are procedural requirements connected with the use of noncompetitive contracts. Under the FAR, a Contracting Officer is not permitted to (a) commence negotiations for a sole-source contract or for a contract resulting from an unsolicited proposal or (b) award any other contract without providing for full and open competition, unless he (1) justifies the use of such action in writing, (2) certifies the accuracy and completeness of the justification, and (3) obtains necessary approvals (for example, for contracts over $10 million, approval by the agency's senior procurement executive).[24]

Each justification must contain sufficient facts and rationale to justify use of the specific exception cited.[25] At a minimum, each justification must include the following information:[26]

(a) Identification of the agency and the contracting activity and specific identification of the document as a "justification for other than full and open competition."

(b) The nature and/or description of the action being approved.

(c) A description of the supplies or services required to meet the agency's needs.

(d) An identification of the statutory authority permitting other than full and open competition.

(e) A demonstration that the proposed contractor's unique qualifications or the nature of the acquisition requires use of the authority cited.

(f) A description of efforts made to ensure that offers are solicited from as many potential sources as is practicable.

(g) A determination by the Contracting Officer that the anticipated cost to the Government will be fair and reasonable.

(h) A description of the market survey conducted and the results, or a statement of the reasons a market survey was not conducted.

(i) Any other facts supporting the use of other than full and open competition.

In addition, justifications must include evidence that any supporting data that form a basis for the recommendation for other than full and open competition have been certified as complete and accurate by the technical or requirements personnel responsible for that data, and the justifications—as well as any related information—must be made available to the public consistent with the provisions of the Freedom of Information Act.[27] The FAR expressly prohibits contracting without full and open competition because of (1) a lack of advance planning or (2) concerns related to the amount of funds available to the agency for the acquisition of supplies or services.[28]

c. Special Procedures For Small Purchases. In 1994, Congress exempted two types of small purchases from the detailed "full and open competition" procedures and other contractor recordkeeping and certification requirements established by statute. One, the "simplified acquisition threshold," which can be used by agencies that have established electronic commerce capabilities, applies to procurements not exceeding $100,000 (an increase from the $25,000 small purchase threshold established in 1983). The other, the "micro-purchase threshold," applies to procurements of $2,500 or less. The streamlined procedures that apply to these types of purchases will be set forth in the FAR. Although an agency making a "simplified acquisition" must "promote competition to the maximum extent practicable," "micro-purchases" may be made without obtaining competitive quotations if the price is reasonable.[29]

3. Contract Types

Once the method of procurement has been determined as described above, the contract type must be chosen. There are a variety of contract types. Basically, they fall into two categories—fixed-price and cost-reimbursement.

At one end of the spectrum of contract types, the Government uses a *fixed-price* contract, generally what is called a "firm-fixed-price" (FFP) contract. In this type of contract, the Government and the contractor agree on a fixed price (or a lump sum, as it is sometimes called) for timely delivery of an end-item or defined service in accordance with the specification. The contractor must deliver the contract end-item within the fixed price; the profit (or loss) that the contractor experiences in doing so is of no consequence to the Government.

There are certain advantages and disadvantages to FFP contracts (most of these are summarized on the chart contained in Figure 4-1 set forth in Chapter 4). Among the advantages, FFP contracts offer the contractor the highest possibility for substantial profits. In addition, title to work-in-process, tooling, and equipment acquired in the performance of the fixed-price contract (that is not deliverable as an end-item) may be retained by the contractor. Also, Government administration and audit controls are relaxed; that is, there is a certain degree of "disengagement" by the Government, and the contractor is more fully permitted to manage its own work.

On the other hand, there are distinct disadvantages to FFP contracts. In particular, the risk of financial difficulty is greatest under these contracts. The contractor will normally be obligated to perform regardless of its actual cost experience.

At the other end of the spectrum (when financial risk is considered) is the *cost-reimbursement* contract. As discussed in Chapter 4, Section F.2, this type of contract guarantees that the contractor will be reimbursed for all "allowable" and properly "allocable" costs incurred in performance of the contract. A "Limitation of Cost" clause[30] is included in such contracts, however, to limit the Government's obligation to pay costs over a prescribed limit unless certain procedures are followed.

In the most frequently used variant of cost-reimbursement contracts, the Government also pays the contractor a fee (which remains fixed regardless of the costs the contractor incurs). This is called a "cost-plus-fixed-fee" (CPFF) contract. The so-called "cost-plus-percentage-of-cost" contract is not permitted in Government contracting because it could invite contractors to increase costs—because higher costs would lead to higher percentage-based profits.

Between the FFP contract and the CPFF contract, there are a variety of contract variations. In particular, various forms of incentive contracts have become popular in the Government. In these contracts, the Government seeks to devise ways of encouraging the contractor to keep costs down by agreeing to share savings achieved through efficient performance by paying more profits. While these modified contracts can be quite complicated, the basic point is that most Government contracts are fundamentally fixed-price or cost-reimbursement, or variations of either type.

4. Soliciting Sources

Most procurements must be advertised—in digest form—in a Government publication known as the *Commerce Business Daily* (CBD). Except for acquisitions under $100,000 in which the solicitation is made available through electronic commerce procedures, no solicitation may be issued earlier than 15 days after publication of the CBD notice, and no deadline for submission of bids can be shorter than 30 days after the date the solicitation is issued.[31] The CBD is published every business day by the Department of Commerce. It can be purchased, through subscription, by writing to the Superintendent of Documents, U.S. Government Printing Office, Washington, DC 20402, and is also available electronically.

In addition to the CBD notice, the Government solicits contractors who are listed on bidders lists (discussed in Chapter 3, Section B) for procurements in which they have an interest. Potential sources are also located by Government procurement officials in industry directories and even—in some cases—in the "yellow pages" telephone directory. Obviously, another key source of potential contractors comes from those who have previously produced the items or services that are now being sought by the Government. In general then, the Government—aided by the CBD—pursues the same types of leads that a commercial buyer would in seeking interested sellers.

5. Government Procurement Team

Every contract has, at a minimum, a seller and a buyer. In the case of Government contracts—whether from administrative expediency or out of necessity—the key Government official is known as the Contracting Officer. It is important to remember that only a duly appointed Contracting Officer has the authority to obligate the Government.[32] Many people may assist the Contracting Officer by performing contract-related tasks. However, it is his signature alone which authorizes new contracts or changes to existing contracts. Note, too, that for sensitive end-products or those exceeding certain dollar amounts, new contracts or changes to existing contracts may also require the approval of the head of the contracting activity after the contract document is signed by the Contracting Officer.

The term "Contracting Officer" may include an individual such as a Quality Assurance Representative (QAR), to the extent that he acts within the limits of the authority delegated. There may be specialized Contracting Officers also. Within DOD, for example, a Contracting Officer at a contract administration office is called an Administrative Contracting Officer, and a Contracting Officer who handles settlement of terminated contracts is a Termination Contracting Officer. On construction projects, the Contracting Officer is frequently represented by the Resident Officer in Charge of Construction or his assistant. Other individuals (variously titled buyers, contract negotiators, or contract specialists) handle bid solicitation and evaluation, negotiation, and award recommendations. These supporting members of the contracting team may also monitor contracts to ensure satisfactory and timely performance.

On major systems acquisitions, the systems acquisition manager, program manager, project manager, or system manager coordinates program development with the Contracting Officer. The roles of these managers can be compared to the role of a general manager in a private firm. They are responsible for coordinating research, development, and production to meet performance or design specifications. They are also responsible for schedule control, meeting cost objectives, and whatever is necessary to ensure the satisfactory progress of various elements in achieving the system's objective. Other acquisition and contracting team members may be required to perform the functions indicated by their titles (for example, price analyst, production specialist, industrial property specialist) and to provide support to the Contracting Officer in the awarding and administration of a contract.

THE SETTING 2-23

There are, of course, variations on the make-up of the procurement "team." Particularly in smaller civilian agencies, it is not unusual for one individual to perform virtually all of the functions that are delegated to a number of individuals in a major DOD procurement.

6. Activities Of Government Representatives

During the *presolicitation phase* of a procurement, Government activity focuses primarily on the establishment of requirements, the identification of funds, procurement planning, required internal approval, and specification preparation. In most instances, contractors deal with the "using activity"—the Government group charged with responsibility for the logistics of the procurement (what will be required, when, and in what quantities). At this point in the procurement process, there is no clearly defined Government team. The office having the requirement may be the most informed regarding the service or project that it needs. In the case of major systems acquisitions or other selected major acquisitions, there may be a nucleus in the form of a program office. Procurement personnel may or may not yet be involved. Generally, efforts on the part of contractors to communicate with procurement personnel will be resisted to avoid giving any contractor a competitive advantage.

At the *solicitation phase*, the Government team may be small. In a simple DOD procurement, it may consist of only the Contracting Officer, assisted by a contract administrator, an Administrative Contracting Officer, an attorney, an industrial specialist, and possibly an engineer. In more complex procurements, however, the Government team may consist of literally hundreds of highly specialized personnel involved with proposal evaluations, source selection, and contract awards. During the solicitation phase, all of those involved are admonished not to discuss the procurement with any contractor representatives. All such inquiries and contracts are referred to the team spokesman: the Contracting Officer.

After award of a contract, the composition of the Government team is revised, although it continues to be led by the Contracting Officer. In a DOD procurement, the Contracting Officer, in turn, generally delegates certain administration authority to the Administrative Contracting Officer or to the cognizant department's plant representative, and relies heavily upon assistance from auditors and project engineers. The contractor will have continuous contact with such personnel, as well as direct contact with the users, the program office personnel, and, in all instances, with the paying activity. In the case of disagreement or dispute, the range of contacts may be expanded to encompass superiors of the Contracting Officer.

7. Dealing With Government Representatives

The name of the buyer or Contracting Officer appears on every solicitation and contract. Normally, both the mailing address and telephone number of the Contracting Officer are also provided. In this manner, the Government attempts to make its contracting representatives accessible to the contractor.

Contractors should, at all times, be aware of the fact that the *authority* of the various Government personnel with whom they deal is very carefully delineated.[33] Thus—as has already been noted—Contracting Officers, QARs, project engineers, inspectors, and the like all have specific *limitations* on what they can and cannot do. For example, a particular Contracting Officer may have authority to sign contracts not exceeding $1 million. If he exceeds this limitation—whether willfully or inadvertently—there is a serious question regarding whether the Government is bound by his actions, and the likelihood is that it is not. As the Supreme Court has succinctly put it:[34]

> Whatever the form in which the Government functions, anyone entering into an arrangement with the Government takes the risk of having accurately ascertained that he who purports to act for the Government stays within the bounds of his authority.... And this is so even though...the agent himself may have been unaware of the limitations upon his authority.

Thus, contractors should be wary of following instructions from any and all Government personnel that present themselves during the preaward phase or during the course of contract performance. Care must be taken to ensure that the individual giving the directive has the actual authority to do so. For example, in one case, a settlement agreement entered into between counsel for a contractor and counsel for the Corps of Engineers was set aside because the Government counsel had not sought the prior approval of the Contracting Officer as he was required to do by a Corps of Engineers regulation. The Contracting Officer disclaimed any knowledge of the settlement negotiations and stated that had he been consulted he never would have approved the settlement that was reached.[35] This decision underscores the importance of determining the *actual* authority of Government personnel.[36]

A somewhat related aspect of Government/contractor communications concerns their *form*. Obviously, communications may be verbal or written. It is important, however, that any significant understandings, arrangements, or agreements between the parties be expressed in *writing*. Such writings can take the form of an amendment to the solicitation, an amendment to the contract, or a separate document incorporated by reference or that refers to the solicitation or contract. This is consistent with good commercial practice, although, in the private sector, long-established relations between the parties frequently permit reliance on oral commitments to expedite business transactions. While not completely absent in Government contracting, relying on oral commitments is perilous and usually done at the risk of the contractor.

Obviously, the need for written documentation is not caused by the fact that Government procurement personnel may be lacking in integrity or principle. The procurement regulations recognize that the sheer numbers of procurement actions in any agency make reliance on isolated or collective memory impracticable. Moreover, litigation of disputes or review by higher authority is not possible without written documentation. Reliance by the Government on written rather than oral commitments or recollections is calculated as much to protect the interest of the contractor as it is to serve the purposes of the Government.

In certain circumstances, Contracting Officers may *ratify* the acts or statements of unauthorized Government employees. The FAR sets forth detailed limitations on the use of this ratification authority, however. This authority may be exercised only when (1) the Government has obtained a benefit from the unauthorized commitment (for example, supplies or services have been provided to the Government and it has accepted them), (2) the ratifying official had the authority to enter into the contract commitment at the time it was made and still has the authority to do so, (3) the resulting contract would otherwise have been proper if it had been made by an appropriate Contracting Officer, (4) the reviewing Contracting Officer determines that the price is fair and reasonable and recommends payment, (5) legal counsel concurs in that recommendation (unless agency procedures expressly do not require such concurrence), (6) funds to make payment are available and were available at the time the unauthorized commitment was made, and (7) the ratification complies with any other agency-prescribed limitations.[37]

REFERENCES

1. P.L. 152, 63 Stat. 378, as amended.

2. 10 USC § 2301 et seq.

3. P.L. 94-106, 89 Stat. 531.

4. P.L. 774, 64 Stat. 798, as amended.

5. Note 2, supra.

6. Note 1, supra.

7. ASBCA 1993 Annual Report (Feb. 25, 1994). See 36 GC ¶ 128.

8. See, e.g., GSBCA, Report of Proceedings for First Quarter Fiscal Year 1994 (Jan. 31, 1994) (122 cases were docketed of which 40 were appeals and 55 were protests).

9. P.L. 93-400, 88 Stat. 796.

10. See P.L. 97-164, 96 Stat. 25. See also Federal Courts Administration Act of 1992, P.L. 102-572, tit. IX, § 902.

11. 48 CFR ch. 1, subchs. A–H.

12. FAR 1.102(b).

13. FAR 1.103.

14. FAR 1.201-1.

15. FAR 1.302.

THE SETTING 2-27

16. 56 Fed. Reg. 36280 (July 31, 1991, effective Dec. 31, 1991).

17. DFARS 201.304(6).

18. FAR subpt. 1.4.

19. DFARS 201.402.

20. See 28 GC ¶ 69; 29 GC ¶ 93; 30 GC ¶ 79; 31 GC ¶ 108; 32 GC ¶ 94; 33 GC ¶ 97; 34 GC ¶ 143; 35 GC ¶ 169; 36 GC ¶ 272.

21. Deficit Reduction Act of 1984, tit. VII of "Div. B," P.L. 98-369, 98 Stat. 494. See Smith, "The Procurement Reforms of 1984," Briefing Papers No. 85-6 (June 1985), 7 BPC 99.

22. See Shnitzer, Government Contract Bidding (Federal Publications Inc., 3d ed. 1987 & Supp.).

23. FAR 6.302–6.302-7.

24. FAR 6.303-1.

25. FAR 6.303-2.

26. FAR 6.303-2(a).

27. FAR 6.303-2(b), 6.305. See 5 USC § 552.

28. FAR 6.301(c).

29. Federal Acquisition Streamlining Act of 1994, P.L. 103-355, §§ 4001—4404, 108 Stat. 3243 (Oct. 13, 1994).

30. FAR 52.232-20.

31. See FAR pt. 5. See also note 29, supra (after Government-wide implementation of electronic commerce procedures, 15-day CBD notice requirement applies only to purchases over $250,000).

32. FAR 1.602-1.

33. See generally Reifel & Bastianelli, "Contracting Officer Authority," Briefing Papers No. 86-4 (Mar. 1986), 7 BPC 257; Hannah, Bond & Virden, "Who Is the Contracting Officer," Briefing Papers No. 67-2 (Apr. 1967), 1 BPC 229.

34. Federal Crop Ins. Corp. v. Merrill, 332 U.S. 380 (1947). See also VecTor, Inc., ASBCA 25807, 84-1 BCA ¶ 17145, 26 GC ¶ 154 (Note); Norman B. Henderson, ASBCA 27612, 85-1 BCA ¶ 17881, 27 GC ¶ 87.

35. J.H. Strain & Sons, Inc., ASBCA 34432, 88-3 BCA ¶ 20909.

36. See also LaCoste Builders, Inc., ASBCA 29884, 88-1 BCA ¶ 20360 (ASBCA rejected contractor's argument that Contracting Officer had waived

2-28 GOVERNMENT CONTRACT GUIDEBOOK

Buy American Act's requirements because he did not have actual authority to waive Act), 30 GC ¶ 136 (Note); Murino Const. Co., VABCA 2752, 90-1 BCA ¶ 22553; Burge & Alvin White, PSBCA 2431, 89-3 BCA ¶ 21910.

37. FAR 1.602-3.

Part II

CONTRACT BASICS

chapters

3 | Sealed Bidding
4 | Competitive Negotiation
5 | Costs
6 | Socioeconomic Considerations
7 | Fraud And Ethical Considerations

SEALED BIDDING

3

A. Invitation For Bids
 1. Standard Forms
 2. Specifications
 3. Correction Of IFB Deficiencies

B. Soliciting Bids

C. Preparing The Bid
 1. Complete Bid Package
 2. Instructions To Bidders
 3. Other Aids
 4. Formulation Of Price Quotations
 5. Acknowledgment Of Amendments

D. Bid Opening
 1. Initial Handling
 2. Procedures
 3. Early Or Late Openings
 4. Late Bids
 5. Telegraphic Bids & Modifications
 6. Facsimile Bids & Modifications
 7. FACNET Bids & Modifications

E. Eligibility For Award
 1. Responsiveness Of Bids
 2. Responsibility Of Bidders

F. Mistakes In Bids
 1. Preaward Mistakes
 2. Postaward Mistakes

G. Protests
 1. Contracting Agency
 2. Comptroller General
 3. Federal Courts
 4. GSBCA

H. Contract Award
 1. Award Procedures
 2. Rejection Of All Bids

I. Two-Step Sealed Bidding
 1. Step One: Request For Technical Proposals
 2. Step Two: Invitation For Bids

This chapter, the first in Part II of the book where the focus is on the making of a Government contract, deals with one of the two basic methods of procurement that were briefly referred to in the previous chapter (see Chapter 2, Section D.2)—*sealed bidding*. As mentioned in that chapter, this method of procurement was so designated by the Competition in Contracting Act (CICA).[1] Previously, it was called "formal advertising."

Under CICA, procuring agencies are required to procure "competitively." This means that they must solicit sealed bids if (a) time permits, (b) the award will be made on the basis of price and other price-related factors, (c) it is not necessary to conduct discussions with the responding sources about their bids, and (d) there is a reasonable expectation of receiving more than one sealed bid.[2] If sealed bids are not appropriate under these criteria, then the agency must use competitive negotiation (discussed in Chapter 4) as the procurement method.

The key to purchasing through the use of sealed bids is its *formality*—it is a closely regulated system governed by the rather rigid requirements of the FAR. Its basic objective is to give *all* interested parties an opportunity to deal with the Government on an equal basis—with the Government (theoretically at least) reaping the benefits of full and open competition. Therefore, there is little room for considering the intangible merits of a potential contractor or of its particular goods or services—award of the contract *must* be made (if at all) to the *responsible* bidder who submits the *lowest responsive* bid.

This chapter discusses sealed bidding in terms of (1) the invitation for bids and how deficiencies in it may be corrected, (2) methods for soliciting bids, (3) the preparation of a bid, (4) bid opening procedures, (5) eligibility for award, (6) bid problems (mistakes and protests), (7) the ultimate selection of a bid for award of a contract, and (8) a hybrid type of sealed bidding called two-step sealed bidding. Readers desiring an additional discussion of this subject should consult Shnitzer, GOVERNMENT CONTRACT BIDDING (Federal Publications Inc., 3d ed. 1987 & Supp.).

A. INVITATION FOR BIDS

A sealed bid procurement is initiated by an Invitation for Bids, commonly referred to as an IFB. The IFB should contain all the information required by a bidder to submit a responsive bid. Typically, as discussed below, it contains standard forms and a number of common, nonstandard, and special provisions relating to a wide variety of subjects, the most notable being specifications.

1. Standard Forms

An IFB is a collection of standard forms that includes instructions for bidders to follow, certifications to be signed, prices to be filled in, the technical requirements or specifications of the procurement, and both standard and special terms and conditions. This mass of forms is often referred to as a "bid package" and can be more or less complex, depending on the size and nature of the procurement.

For *supply* and *service* contracts, IFBs will normally include Standard Form 33, "Solicitation, Offer and Award" as the first page (a reduced reproduction appears as Figure 3-1). If the solicitation is amended, Standard Form 30, "Amendment of Solicitation/Modification of Contract" will be issued (a reduced reproduction appears as Figure 3-2). For small purchases using simplified procurement procedures, the agency may use an Optional Form 347, "Order for Supplies or Services" (see Figure 3-3), or its own form. (The figures appear on the following pages.)

For *construction* contracts, there is a far greater variety and number of forms.[3] The precise forms to be used will depend on the *estimated* price for the particular contract. Most higher-priced contracts for such work will be sought under Standard Form 1442, "Solicitation, Offer, and Award (Construction, Alteration, or Repair)" (see Figure 3-4).

2. Specifications

Specifications, which are discussed in detail in Chapter 8, provide bidders with a *description* of the work required to be performed and establish a *starting point* for determining the rights and obligations of the parties.

If the specifications are ambiguous or contain other defects (for example, an erroneous dimension or an impossible requirement),

3-4 GOVERNMENT CONTRACT GUIDEBOOK

Figure 3-1

STANDARD FORM 33, "SOLICITATION, OFFER, AND AWARD"

SEALED BIDDING 3-5

Figure 3-2

STANDARD FORM 30, "AMENDMENT OF SOLICITATION/ MODIFICATION OF CONTRACT"

continued

Fig. 3-2 / continued

INSTRUCTIONS

Instructions for items other than those that are self-explanatory, are as follows:

(a) Item 1 (Contract ID Code). Insert the contract type identification code that appears in the title block of the contract being modified.

(b) Item 3 (Effective date).

  (1) For a solicitation amendment, change order, or administrative change, the effective date shall be the issue date of the amendment, change order, or administrative change.

  (2) For a supplemental agreement, the effective date shall be the date agreed to by the contracting parties.

  (3) For a modification issued as an initial or confirming notice of termination for the convenience of the Government, the effective date and the modification number of the confirming notice shall be the same as the effective date and modification number of the initial notice.

  (4) For a modification converting a termination for default to a termination for the convenience of the Government, the effective date shall be the same as the effective date of the termination for default.

  (5) For a modification confirming the contracting officer's determination of the amount due in settlement of a contract termination, the effective date shall be the same as the effective date of the initial decision.

(c) Item 6 (Issued By). Insert the name and address of the issuing office. If applicable, insert the appropriate issuing office code in the code block.

(d) Item 8 (Name and Address of Contractor). For modifications to a contract or order, enter the contractor's name, address, and code as shown in the original contract or order, unless changed by this or a previous modification.

(e) Items 9, (Amendment of Solicitation No.–Dated), and 10, (Modification of Contract/Order No.–Dated). Check the appropriate box and in the corresponding blanks insert the number and date of the original solicitation, contract, or order.

(f) Item 12 (Accounting and Appropriation Data). When appropriate, indicate the impact of the modification on each affected accounting classification by inserting one of the following entries:

  (1) Accounting classification
      Net increase $ ....

  (2) Accounting classification
      Net decrease $ ....

  NOTE: If there are changes to multiple accounting classifications that cannot be placed in block 12, insert an asterisk and the words "See continuation sheet".

(g) Item 13. Check the appropriate box to indicate the type of modification. Insert in the corresponding blank the authority under which the modification is issued. Check whether or not contractor must sign this document. (See FAR 43.103.)

(h) Item 14 (Description of Amendment/Modification).

  (1) Organize amendments or modifications under the appropriate Uniform Contract Format (UCF) section headings from the applicable solicitation or contract. The UCF table of contents, however, shall not be set forth in this document.

  (2) Indicate the impact of the modification on the overall total contract price by inserting one of the following entries:

    (i) Total contract price increased by $ ....

    (ii) Total contract price decreased by $ ....

    (iii) Total contract price unchanged.

  (3) State reason for modification.

  (4) When removing, reinstating, or adding funds, identify the contract items and accounting classifications.

  (5) When the SF 30 is used to reflect a determination by the contracting officer of the amount due in settlement of a contract terminated for the convenience of the Government, the entry in Item 14 of the modification may be limited to –

    (i) A reference to the letter determination; and

    (ii) A statement of the net amount determined to be due in settlement of the contract.

  (6) Include subject matter or short title of solicitation/contract where feasible.

(i) Item 16B. The contracting officer's signature is not required on solicitation amendments. The contracting officer's signature is normally affixed last on supplemental agreements.

STANDARD FORM 30 BACK (REV. 10-83)

Figure 3-3

OPTIONAL FORM 347, "ORDER FOR SUPPLIES OR SERVICES"

ORDER FOR SUPPLIES OR SERVICES

PAGE 1 OF PAGES

IMPORTANT: Mark all packages and papers with contract and/or order numbers.

1. DATE OF ORDER	2. CONTRACT NO. *(If any)*	3. ORDER NO.	4. REQUISITION/REFERENCE NO.

5. ISSUING OFFICE *(Address correspondence to)*

6. SHIP TO: *(Consignee and address, ZIP Code)*

SHIP VIA:

7. TO: CONTRACTOR *(Name, address and ZIP Code)*

8. TYPE OF ORDER

☐ A. PURCHASE — Reference your ______

Please furnish the following on the terms and conditions specified on both sides of this order and on the attached sheets, if any, including delivery as indicated. This purchase is negotiated under authority of

☐ B. DELIVERY — Except for billing instructions on the reverse, this delivery order is subject to instructions contained on this side only of this form and is issued subject to the terms and conditions of the above-numbered contract.

9. ACCOUNTING AND APPROPRIATION DATA

10. REQUISITIONING OFFICE

11. BUSINESS CLASSIFICATION *(Check appropriate box(es))*

☐ SMALL ☐ OTHER THAN SMALL ☐ DISADVANTAGED ☐ WOMEN-OWNED

12. F.O.B. POINT

13. PLACE OF INSPECTION AND ACCEPTANCE

14. GOVERNMENT B/L NO.

15. DELIVER TO F.O.B. POINT ON OR BEFORE *(Date)*

16. DISCOUNT TERMS

17. SCHEDULE *(See reverse for Rejections)*

ITEM NO. (A)	SUPPLIES OR SERVICES (B)	QUANTITY ORDERED (C)	UNIT (D)	UNIT PRICE (E)	AMOUNT (F)	QUANTITY ACCEPTED (G)

SEE BILLING INSTRUCTIONS ON REVERSE

18. SHIPPING POINT

19. GROSS SHIPPING WEIGHT

20. INVOICE NO.

17(H). TOT. *(Cont. pages)*

21. MAIL INVOICE TO: *(Include ZIP Code)*

17(I). GRAND TOTAL

22. UNITED STATES OF AMERICA BY *(Signature)*

23. NAME *(Typed)*

TITLE: CONTRACTING/ORDERING OFFICER

NSN 7540-01-152-8083 50347-101

OPTIONAL FORM 347 (10-83)
Prescribed by GSA
FAR (48 CFR) 53.213(e)

continued

Fig. 3-3 / continued

PURCHASE ORDER TERMS AND CONDITIONS

52.252-2. CLAUSES INCORPORATED BY REFERENCE (Apr 84).—This contract incorporates the following clauses by reference with the same force and effect as if they were given in full text. Upon request the Contracting Officer will make their full text available:

FEDERAL ACQUISITION REGULATION (48 CFR CHAPTER 1) CLAUSES

52.203-1	Officials Not to Benefit (Apr 84)
52.203-3	Gratuities (Apr 84)
52.203-4	Covenant Against Contingent Fees (Apr 84)
52.212-9	Variation in Quantity (Apr 84) (In the preceding clause, the permissible variations are stated in the schedule)
52.222-3	Convict Labor (Apr 84)
52.222-4	Contract Work Hours and Safety Standards Act—Overtime Compensation—General (Apr 84)
52.222-26	Equal Opportunity (Apr 84)
52.222-36	Affirmative Action for Handicapped Workers (Apr 84)
52.222-40	Service Contract Act of 1965—Contracts of $2500 or Less (Apr 84)
52.222-41	Service Contract Act of 1965 (Apr 84)
52.225-3	Buy American Act—Supplies (Apr 84)
52.232-1	Payments (Apr 84)
52.232-8	Discounts for Prompt Payment (Apr 84) (With Alternate 1)
52.233-1	Disputes (Apr 84)
52.243-1	Changes — Fixed Price (Apr 84)
52.249-1	Termination for Convenience of the Government (Fixed Price) (Short Form) (Apr 84)

NOTE.—If desired, this order (or a copy thereof) may be used by the Contractor as the Contractor's invoice, instead of a separate invoice, provided the following statement, (signed and dated) is on (or attached to) the order: "Payment is requested in the amount of $ _____ . No other invoice will be submitted." However, if the Contractor wishes to submit an invoice, the following information must be provided: contract number (if any), order number, item number(s), description of supplies or services, sizes, quantities, unit prices, and extended totals. Prepaid shipping costs will be indicated as a separate item on the invoice. Where shipping costs exceed $10 (except for parcel post), the billing must be supported by a bill of lading or receipt. When several orders are invoiced to an ordering activity during the same billing period, consolidated periodic billings are encouraged.

RECEIVING REPORT

Quantity in the "Quantity Accepted" column on the face of this order has been: ☐ inspected, ☐ accepted, ☐ received by me and conforms to contract. Items listed below have been rejected for the reasons indicated.

SHIPMENT NUMBER	PARTIAL / FINAL	DATE RECEIVED	SIGNATURE OF AUTHORIZED U.S. GOV'T. REP.	DATE
TOTAL CONTAINERS	GROSS WEIGHT	RECEIVED AT	TITLE	

REPORT OF REJECTIONS

ITEM NO.	SUPPLIES OR SERVICES	UNIT	QUANTITY REJECTED	REASON FOR REJECTION

☆ U.S. GOVERNMENT PRINTING OFFICE : 1983 O - 413-930   OPTIONAL FORM 347 BACK (10-83)

SEALED BIDDING   3-9

Figure 3-4

STANDARD FORM 1442, "SOLICITATION, OFFER, AND AWARD (CONSTRUCTION, ALTERATION, OR REPAIR)"

continued

3-10 GOVERNMENT CONTRACT GUIDEBOOK

Fig. 3-4 / continued

and if the defects are discovered before bid opening, the Contracting Officer has a responsibility to (a) correct the deficiency by issuing an amendment to the IFB or a revised specification, or (b) cancel the procurement (see Section A.3 below).

When necessary for evaluation purposes, an IFB may require bidders to submit *samples* or *descriptive literature* along with their bids. The FAR, however, limits their use to situations where a particular product has certain characteristics that cannot be adequately described in the specifications or purchase descriptions.[4]

Also, the IFB may sometimes describe the product to be furnished by a *brand name* and state that bids must specify use of that brand name or its "equal" in order to be responsive. In addition, the IFB must set out the most significant physical, functional, or other characteristics (known as the "salient" characteristics) of the product that are essential to the Government. To ensure as much competition as possible under the circumstances, all known commercial items that will serve the Government's purposes should be listed as acceptable "brand names." "Brand name or equal" specifications are not particularly encouraged since they can cause misunderstanding, confusion, and protest. As a result, they should be used only when no other specification is available.[5]

Delivery dates may be a part of the specifications, but more often are in the IFB schedule. Normally, they are expressed as maximums. However, under some circumstances, the IFB may specify a *desired* delivery date and a *required* date that is somewhat later. Only the required date is significant since a bidder gains no evaluation advantage in offering to meet a desired delivery date or any other date earlier than that required. In some solicitations, the delivery date is stated in "days after award" or "days after date of contract." Generally, the date of award or date of contract is set forth, in a supply or service contract, on the first page (for example, Block 28 of Standard Form 33 set forth in Figure 3-1). This date starts the performance period.

3. Correction Of IFB Deficiencies

If the IFB is found—either by the Contracting Officer or a bidder—to be defective (i.e., it fails to meet minimum standards of clarity and precision), it is deficient. Deficiencies can arise because the IFB (1) reflects other than the reasonable needs of the Government, (2) unduly restricts competition, (3) omits required information (or fails to ask for necessary information), (4) contains erroneous information, or (5) contains some ambiguity.[6]

If the discovery of the deficiency is made *before bid opening,* and if the Contracting Officer is put on notice of the deficiency, the solution is relatively simple: the IFB can be modified by amendment to correct the defect and the time for submission of bids can be extended if necessary.[7] It is most important that a bidder *notify* the Contracting Officer immediately should the bidder discover a deficiency because a bidder may be barred from protesting an ambiguity (or other defect) after opening if it is shown that the bidder was aware of it prior to submitting its bid.[8]

If the deficiency is not noted until *after bid opening,* the problem is considerably more difficult to remedy since it is no longer possible simply to amend the IFB and proceed with the competition. Instead, a decision must be made whether to award a contract despite the deficiency or to cancel the IFB and resolicit.[9] Note that not every defect or deficiency is serious enough to warrant cancellation of the solicitation. An IFB will be canceled only for *compelling reasons,*[10] such as when the IFB, taken as a whole, can reasonably be interpreted to call for something other than what was intended by the Contracting Officer, or some bidder was misled to give the wrong response, or a competitor was discouraged from submitting a bid (because of an unintended interpretation).

For example, an IFB may be canceled after bid opening if it fails to provide for acquisition of unlimited rights in technical data where such an acquisition could result in substantial savings to the Government. On the other hand, if through inadvertence a potential supplier is not solicited (even though its name appears on the procuring agency's bidders list), this alone would not constitute a compelling reason for canceling the procurement—particularly upon a showing of adequate competition, reasonable prices, and no deliberate or conscious attempt to preclude the potential supplier from competing.[11]

B. SOLICITING BIDS

As indicated earlier, a major reason for using sealed bid procedures is to secure the benefit of wide competition. It follows, therefore, that the Government will seek to publicize its procurement efforts extensively. Thus, a principal requirement of sealed bid procedures is the distribution of the IFB to a sufficient number of prospective bidders to ensure adequate competition. Normally, this is accomplished in four ways:

(a) Display of the IFB (if unclassified) in a public place.

(b) Announcement in newspapers or trade journals.

(c) Publication in synopsis form in the *Commerce Business Daily* or public notice through electronic commerce procedures (see Chapter 2, Section D.4).

(d) A mailing to the bidders list maintained by most procuring agencies.

Until the establishment of a federal acquisition computer network, use of the *bidders list method* is probably the most efficient procedure for publicizing a solicitation. Bidders' names are placed on these lists in two ways. First, if a procuring activity through its prior contracting experience—or after conducting a search of appropriate trade publications, directories, and the like—believes that a prospective bidder is capable of meeting its procurement requirements, it may include the bidder on the list without any prior request. Second, the bidder may submit an application to be placed on the list.

Any interested bidder can apply for inclusion on a particular procuring agency bidders list by completing and filing a Standard Form 129, "Solicitation Mailing List Application" (Figure 3-5 on the following page). When a new prospective supplier is placed on a bidders mailing list, the procuring agency will notify it (the issuance of an IFB to the bidder within a reasonable time may be considered appropriate notification). Those who do not meet the criteria for placement on a list will also receive notification.[12]

The bidders list application must be signed by the supplier (or manufacturer or dealer), as distinguished from the agent of

Figure 3-5

STANDARD FORM 129, "SOLICITATION MAILING LIST APPLICATION"

SOLICITATION MAILING LIST APPLICATION	1. TYPE OF APPLICATION ☐ INITIAL ☐ REVISION	2. DATE	FORM APPROVED OMB. NO. 9000–0002

NOTE: Please complete all items on this form. Insert N/A in items not applicable. See reverse for instructions.

Public reporting burden for this collection of information is estimated to average .58 hours per response, including the time for reviewing instructions, searching existing data sources, gathering and maintaining the data needed, and completing and reviewing the collection of information, including suggestions for reducing this burden, to the FAR Secretariat (VRS), Office of Federal Acquisition Policy, GSA, Washington, DC 20405; and to the Office of Management and Budget, Paperwork Reduction Project (9000-0002), Washington, DC 20503.

3. NAME AND ADDRESS OF FEDERAL AGENCY TO WHICH FORM IS SUBMITTED (Include ZIP code)	4. NAME AND ADDRESS OF APPLICANT (Include county and ZIP code)
5. TYPE OF ORGANIZATION (Check one) ☐ INDIVIDUAL ☐ NON-PROFIT ORGANIZATION ☐ PARTNERSHIP ☐ CORPORATION, INCORPORATED UNDER THE LAWS OF THE STATE OF:	6. ADDRESS TO WHICH SOLICITATIONS ARE TO BE MAILED (If different than item 4)

7. NAMES OF OFFICERS, OWNERS, OR PARTNERS

A. PRESIDENT	B. VICE PRESIDENT	C. SECRETARY
D. TREASURER	E. OWNERS OR PARTNERS	

8. AFFILIATES OF APPLICANT (Names, locations and nature of affiliation. See definition on reverse.)

9. PERSONS AUTHORIZED TO SIGN OFFERS AND CONTRACTS IN YOUR NAME (Indicate if agent)

NAME	OFFICIAL CAPACITY	TELE. NO. (Include area code)

10. IDENTIFY EQUIPMENT, SUPPLIES, AND/OR SERVICES ON WHICH YOU DESIRE TO MAKE AN OFFER (See attached Federal Agency's supplemental listing and instructions, if any)

11A. SIZE OF BUSINESS (See definitions on reverse) ☐ SMALL BUSINESS (If checked, complete items 11B and 11C) ☐ OTHER THAN SMALL BUSINESS	11B. AVERAGE NUMBER OF EMPLOYEES (Including affiliates) FOR FOUR PRECEDING CALENDAR QUARTERS	11C. AVERAGE ANNUAL SALES OR RECEIPTS FOR PRECEDING THREE FISCAL YEARS $
12. TYPE OF OWNERSHIP (See definitions on reverse) (Not applicable for other than small businesses) ☐ DISADVANTAGED BUSINESS ☐ WOMAN-OWNED BUSINESS	13. TYPE OF BUSINESS (See definitions on reverse) ☐ MANUFACTURER OR PRODUCER ☐ REGULAR DEALER (Type 1) ☐ CONSTRUCTION CONCERN ☐ SURPLUS DEALER ☐ SERVICE ESTABLISHMENT ☐ REGULAR DEALER (Type 2) ☐ RESEARCH AND DEVELOPMENT	

14. DUNS NO. (If available)	15. HOW LONG IN PRESENT BUSINESS?

16. FLOOR SPACE (Square feet)		17. NET WORTH	
A. MANUFACTURING	B. WAREHOUSE	A. DATE	B. AMOUNT $

18. SECURITY CLEARANCE (If applicable, check highest clearance authorized)

FOR	TOP SECRET	SECRET	CONFIDENTIAL	C. NAMES OF AGENCIES WHICH GRANTED SECURITY CLEARANCES (Include dates)
A. KEY PERSONNEL				
B. PLANT ONLY				

CERTIFICATION – I certify that information supplied herein (including all pages attached) is correct and that neither the applicant nor any person (or concern) in any connection with the applicant as a principal or officer, so far as is known, is now debarred or otherwise declared ineligible by any agency of the Federal Government from making offers for furnishing materials, supplies, or services to the Government or any agency thereof.

19. NAME AND TITLE OF PERSON AUTHORIZED TO SIGN (Type or print)	20. SIGNATURE	21. DATE SIGNED

NSN 7540-01-152-8086 Previous edition usable   EXPIRATION DATE: 9-30-91   129-107   STANDARD FORM 129 (REV. 6-90) Prescribed by GSA – FAR (48 CFR) 53.214(

continued

SEALED BIDDING   3-15

Fig. 3-5 / continued

INSTRUCTIONS

Persons or concerns wishing to be added to a particular agency's bidder's mailing list for supplies or services shall file this properly completed and certified Solicitation Mailing List Application, together with such other lists as may be attached to this application form, with each procurement office of the Federal agency with which they desire to do business. If a Federal agency has attached a Supplemental Commodity list with instructions, complete the application as instructed. Otherwise, identify in item 10 the equipment, supplies, and/or services on which you desire to bid. (Provide Federal Supply Class or Standard Industrial Classification codes, if available.) The application shall be submitted and signed by the principal as distinguished from an agent, however constituted.

After placement on the bidder's mailing list of an agency, your failure to respond (submission of bid, or notice in writing, that you are unable to bid on that particular transaction but wish to remain on the active bidder's mailing list for that particular item) to solicitations will be understood by the agency to indicate lack of interest and concurrence in the removal of your name from the purchasing activity's solicitation mailing for items concerned.

SIZE OF BUSINESS DEFINITIONS
(See Item 11A.)

a. Small business concern - A small business concern for the purpose of Government procurement is a concern, including its affiliates, which is independently owned and operated, is not dominant in the field of operation in which it is competing for Government contracts, and can further qualify under the criteria concerning number of employees, average annual receipts, or the other criteria, as prescribed by the Small Business Administration. (See Code of Federal Regulations, Title 13, Part 121, as amended, which contains detailed industry definitions and related procedures.)

b. Affiliates - Business concerns are affiliates of each other when either directly or indirectly (i) one concern controls or has the power to control the other, or (ii) a third party controls or has the power to control both. In determining whether concerns are independently owned and operated and whether or not affiliation exists, consideration is given to all appropriate factors including common ownership, common management, and contractual relationship. (See Items 8 and 11A.)

c. Number of employees - (Item 11B) In connection with the determination of small business status, "number of employees" means the average employment of any concern, including the employees of its domestic and foreign affiliates, based on the number of persons employed on a full-time, part-time, temporary or other basis during each of the pay periods of the preceding 12 months. If a concern has not been in existence for 12 months, "number of employees" means the average employment of such concern and its affiliates during the period that such concern has been in existence based on the number of persons employed during each of the pay periods of the period that such concern has been in business.

TYPE OF OWNERSHIP DEFINITIONS
(See Item 12.)

a. "Disadvantaged business concern" - means any business concern (1) which is at least 51 percent owned by one or more socially and economically disadvantaged individuals; or, in the case of any publicly owned business, at least 51 percent of the stock of which is owned by one or more socially and economically disadvantaged individuals; and (2) whose management and daily business operations are controlled by one or more of such individuals.

b. "Women-owned business" - means a business that is at least 51 percent owned by a woman or women who are U.S. citizens and who also control and operate the business.

TYPE OF BUSINESS DEFINITIONS
(See Item 13.)

a. Manufacturer or producer - means a person (or concern) owning, operating, or maintaining a store, warehouse, or other establishment that produces, on the premises, the materials, supplies, articles or equipment of the general character of those listed in Item 10, or in the Federal Agency's Supplemental Commodity List, if attached.

b. Service establishment - means a concern (or person) which owns, operates, or maintains any type of business which is principally engaged in the furnishing of nonpersonal services, such as (but not limited to) repairing, cleaning, redecorating, or rental of personal property, including the furnishing of necessary repair parts or other supplies as a part of the services performed.

c. Regular dealer (Type 1) - means a person (or concern) who owns, operates, or maintains a store, warehouse, or other establishment in which the materials, supplies, articles, or equipment of the general character listed in Item 10, or in the Federal Agency's Supplemental Commodity List, if attached, are bought, kept in stock, and sold to the public in the usual course of business.

d. Regular dealer (Type 2) - In the case of supplies of particular kinds (at present, petroleum, lumber and timber products, machine tools, raw cotton, green coffee, hay, grain, feed, or straw, agricultural liming materials, tea, raw or unmanufactured cotton linters and used ADPE), Regular dealer means a person (or concern) satisfying the requirements of the regulations (Code of Federal Regulations, Title 41, 50-201.101(a) (2)) as amended from time to time, prescribed by the Secretary of Labor under the Walsh-Healey Public Contracts Act (Title 41, U.S. Code 35-45). For coal dealers see Code of Federal Regulations, Title 41, 50-201.604(a).

- COMMERCE BUSINESS DAILY - The Commerce Business Daily, published by the Department of Commerce, contains information concerning proposed procurements, sales, and contract awards. For further information concerning this publication, contact your local Commerce Field Office.

STANDARD FORM 129 (REV. 6-80) BACK

the supplier. However, suppliers are not precluded from designating their agents to receive solicitations.[13]

Where the bidders mailing list is excessively long, making mailing an IFB to every business on the list very costly, any reasonable portion of the list may be used as long as bid packages are also made available to other bidders who request them. A procuring activity may rotate the names on its mailing lists. When the rotation method is used, the successful bidder for the last procurement of the same (or similar) items, as well as those suppliers who have been added to the list since the last procurement, must be solicited.[14]

To save the expense of mailing a complete bid package to every bidder on the list, procuring agencies frequently send out digested pre-IFB notices and follow up with complete solicitations only to those who specifically request them. Names of those who have not responded to two consecutive IFBs or have been debarred, suspended, or otherwise disqualified from entering into Government contracts will normally be removed from the bidders list. It is important, therefore, to respond to each solicitation, even if the response is a simple "no bid" or a request to be retained on the list.

Whatever method of publicizing the solicitation the agency uses, it must be accomplished in sufficient time to permit bidders to prepare and submit their bids. Except for procurements under $100,000 or procurements where the Government's requirements are urgent, a bidding time (the time between issuance of the solicitation and opening of bids) of at least 30 calendar days is required, unless the Contracting Officer determines that a shorter period is reasonable.[15]

C. PREPARING THE BID

A bidder must take extreme care to ensure that its bid is completed in exact compliance with the terms of the IFB. Any *material* deviations from those terms (even if inadvertent) could result in rejection of the bid as nonresponsive. Moreover, as will be discussed below, mistakes in bids—particularly those not discovered until after bid opening or award of a contract—lead to significant problems and are not always correctable.

A typical checklist for ensuring that responsiveness and mistake problems (as well as the problem of submitting a late bid) are minimized should include the following:

(1) Be certain that the entire bid package—including all attachments and all amendments—is completed and returned to the procuring agency.

(2) Carefully follow all instructions to bidders contained in the solicitation.

(3) Check (and recheck) all price computations.

(4) Carefully note the due date on the IFB for submission of bids and the location to which bids must be transmitted.

(5) Make no suggestions or requests for changes in the terms of the IFB that could be construed as amending its terms (and result in a nonresponsive bid).

These and other elements of the bid preparation procedure are discussed below.

1. Complete Bid Package

Most IFBs state (usually on the first page) the total number of pages in the IFB. It is not unusual, especially in complex procurements, for pages or attachments to be inadvertently omitted. Thus, the solicitation should be carefully checked to ensure that *all* pages and *all* referenced attachments are included. Otherwise, a bidder could fail to fully understand the nature and extent of its obligation, and its bid could be determined nonresponsive if omitted pages or attachments contain material information regarding the solicitation.

2. Instructions To Bidders

Every solicitation contains basic instructions for bid preparation. These instructions are extremely important and should be strictly followed. Generally, to ensure compliance with these instructions, the prospective bidder should:

(a) Carefully read and examine *all* the provisions of the IFB, including the drawings, specifications, and standard terms and conditions.

(b) Print or type the bidder's *name* on the schedule and each continuation sheet on which an entry is made.

(c) Initial all *erasures or other changes* made in the bid.

(d) Include evidence of the authority of any *agent* who signs the bid.

(e) State each price *accurately* to avoid the grievous error of misplaced or erroneous decimals and figures.

(f) Commit to meet at least the *minimum requirements* of the specifications, even though the product to be provided may be superior in a number of respects.

(g) Commit to meet at least the *required delivery schedule*, even though there may be an agreement to deliver on an earlier date.

(h) Submit the bid in a *sealed envelope* (unless the agency is accepting bids through electronic commerce procedures) with the requisite number of copies (usually an original and two copies).

(i) Deliver the bid *on or before* the deadline to the *precise* place specified in the IFB.

A substantial number of bids are found to be nonresponsive because the foregoing rules are not strictly followed. If a bid is worth submitting, and if there is a strong desire to compete and "get the job," there really is no alternative to adhering to the above rules.

3. Other Aids

In addition to the information and instructions included in the bid package, a bidder may be aided in preparing a bid by (1) clarifications of any ambiguities or uncertainties in the specifications by the Contracting Officer, (2) prebid conferences—if scheduled by the procuring agency, (3) inspections of the jobsite (often these are required or allowed, particularly in construction contracts), and (4) Government-furnished models or samples, which are sometimes made available to assist bidders in understanding the specifications.[16]

These aids can be helpful depending on the particular circumstances. Where a prebid conference is held by the Government, it is good policy to attend (although attendance is normally not mandatory), take notes, and request minutes of the meeting from the Government. Where an onsite inspection is authorized by the terms of the solicitation, it is important for a bidder to comply, since failure to do so will impair the bidder's right to challenge errors or omissions that could have been discovered by a reasonable and timely inspection.

4. Formulation Of Price Quotations

After careful review of the bid package, instructions, and any aids outside the package, a bidder is ready to begin the preparation of a price quotation. The starting point is a production plan. For a supply contract, for example, this will normally involve consideration of (a) what materials, parts, and components must be purchased, (b) which manufacturing or assembly operations will be performed "in-house" and which will be subcontracted, and (c) what production time schedule will be required to meet the contract delivery date. Then, subcontract quotations will ordinarily be solicited to provide the bidder with fixed and binding quotations for the period that the bidder is required to keep its bid to the Government open. Thereafter, "in-house" production costs will be calculated and a theoretical price for the products to be furnished will be determined.

This theoretical price may be adjusted by a number of practical considerations. One may be an estimate of what competitors are likely to bid, based on their bidding history and their competitive advantages (or disadvantages) due to such factors as prior experience, "in-place" tooling, financial position, and relative transportation costs (i.e., how close their plant is to the delivery point). Another consideration could be the bidder's other work, which essentially affects the intensity of the bidder's need to get the contract. A third consideration may be production economies that the bidder may be able to achieve through joint production of several items or advance buying for stock.

When entering unit prices—or extended or total prices—on a bid, a bidder must state them accurately and exactly as required by the IFB. For example, a bid could be considered nonresponsive for failure to include (1) taxes, when required—even though the omitted taxes may be less than the difference between the lowest and the next lowest bid, (2) an entry in each price "blank" (note that "0," "n/c," or "no charge" is generally regarded as a price entry), (3) a list of subcontractors to be used on the project (where this is required by the IFB), or (4) a guaranteed maximum shipping weight or shipping dimensions (again, where required by the IFB). Submission of an "unbalanced" bid may result in rejection of the bid as nonresponsive. An unbalanced bid is defined as one that is "based on prices significantly less than cost for some work and prices which are significantly overstated in relation to cost for other work."[17]

Prompt payment discounts are not considered in the evaluation of bids. However, any discount offered will form a part of the award and will be taken by the Government if payment is made within the discount period specified by the bidder. As an alternative to indicating a discount in conjunction with the offer, bidders may prefer to offer discounts on individual invoices.[18]

5. Acknowledgment Of Amendments

Amendments to IFBs are frequently required to (a) make changes in items such as quantity, specifications, delivery schedules, or opening dates, or (b) correct a defective or ambiguous provision. Amendments are sent to everyone to whom IFBs have been furnished, and they are also displayed in the agency's bid room.[19]

Bidder instructions provide—and many decisions make clear[20]—that IFB amendments *must be acknowledged* by a bidder unless the amendments do not affect price, quantity, quality, or delivery terms by more than a trivial or negligible amount. And this is so even if the bidder—through no fault of its own—did not receive the amendment. But if the agency fails to mail or otherwise deliver to the bidder a copy of the amendment, the bid should not be rejected because the amendment was not acknowledged. The agency is obligated to provide amendments to all bidders.[21] The simplest, safest (and proper) manner of acknowledgment is to sign the acknowledgment form immediately and return it to the procuring agency. However, written acknowledgments, by telegram or otherwise, are sufficient so long as it is clear that the bidder has accepted the terms of the amended IFB. Oral acknowledgments—although sometimes allowed in the past—are not favored.

It is a good practice to double-check the issuance of amendments with the procuring activity prior to submission of any bid and to acknowledge receipt of *all* amendments promptly, regardless of how unimportant they may appear. Some amendments, it should be noted, require not merely acknowledgment but also a price quotation for additional items or requirements.

D. BID OPENING

Bid opening is a strictly regulated and formal ritual and a key step in protecting the integrity of the bidding system. From the time bids are received until they are displayed at the bid opening, the process is clothed in secrecy and tight security.

1. Initial Handling

All bids received before bid opening are required to be kept *unopened* in a locked box or safe.[22] Even information regarding the *number* of bids received or the *identity* of bidders cannot be disclosed prior to opening except to "need-to-know" Government employees. When samples are submitted with bids, they are handled in a similar manner.

Ordinarily, the applicable IFB number is written on the outside cover of the bid envelope. This identification helps to ensure that the bid is placed in the proper location for the opening. If the bid envelope, for some reason, does *not* adequately identify the IFB, the rules permit opening the envelope in advance (by an employee *specifically authorized* to do so) to identify the IFB, but if a sealed bid is *mistakenly* opened in advance, it must be resealed and the circumstances reported in writing. If the prematurely opened bid is read aloud before the scheduled bid opening, however, the bid opening should be postponed to allow the bidder time to revise its bid.[23]

2. Procedures

All bids (except those that are classified) are publicly opened. The opening will be held at the *precise* time and place specified in the IFB and, when possible, the most important terms of each bid will be read aloud.[24]

An abstract of the bids is then prepared, identifying the procurement, the bidders, the bid prices, and other appropriate information required for bid evaluation.[25] After the abstract is prepared, it is certified by the bid-opening officer, and copies of the bids are normally made available for public inspection.[26] When a bid is received late and can be considered for award under the late bid rules (discussed below in Section D.4), it need not be publicly opened. However, it should be included in the abstract of bids and made available for inspection.

3. Early Or Late Openings

The bid-opening officer decides when the stated time for opening has arrived and has the responsibility to announce it to those present.[27] In making his decision, he is guided by the Uniform Time Act of 1966,[28] which provides that *current local time is Standard Time*, even if a particular locality may then be operating under Daylight Savings Time. Thus, because Daylight Savings Time is the "advanced" time used in summer, 10 A.M. Daylight Savings Time, for example, would really be 9 A.M. Standard Time. These rules—even though they tend to be confusing—are strictly enforced, making it extremely important for bidders to note this distinction and to provide for timely submission.

On occasion, bids may be opened early due to an incorrect decision as to the proper time by the opening officer. A bid that is submitted thereafter will be considered late, even though submitted prior to the *original* bid-opening time unless it is clear that the bidder could not in any way have taken advantage of the earlier opening.[29]

Bids opened later than the time scheduled in the IFB, or intentionally postponed, may be properly considered, even without prior written notice, when such action is deemed to be in the Government's best interest and no bidder is prejudiced thereby.[30] For example, a postponement may be made by a Contracting Officer because of (a) inadequate bid preparation time, (b) a day off given to Government employees due to bad weather, or (c) the possibility of delay in receipt of bids due to flood, fire, accident, strike, or similar incident.

4. Late Bids

A recurring problem with sealed bids is late submission of bids.[31] A bid—or a bid modification—will not be considered for award unless it is received no later than the precise time specified in the IFB.[32] Although this rule is strictly applied, it has a number of *exceptions*. Under the FAR, a late bid will be considered if (1) it was sent by registered or certified mail not later than the fifth calendar day (as evidenced by a U.S. or Canadian postmark both on the envelope or wrapper and on the original receipt from the Postal Service) prior to the date specified for receipt of bids, (2) it was sent by mail (or telegram or facsimile, if authorized) and it is determined that the late receipt was due *solely* to mishandling by the Government after receipt at the procuring agency, or (3) the bid was sent by "U.S. Postal Service Express Mail Next Day Service–Post Office to Addressee" not later than 5 P.M. at the place of mailing two working days prior to the date specified for receipt of bids.[33]

Under the FAR, no exceptions apply to late hand-delivered bids.[34] This somewhat harsh rule in the FAR is designed to prevent any possible advantage or option to a late bidder. One exception developed in the case law, however, allows late hand-carried bids to be considered when the delay is the sole fault of the Government and the bidder could not have obtained any undue advantage because of the delay.[35]

The rules regarding late bids are strictly applied. Thus, even a bid received a few minutes (or seconds) later than the bid opening time announced by the officer in charge is deemed late and not eligible for award.

If the bid is delivered to the *wrong place,* it will also normally be rejected.[36] However, a bid will be considered for award despite this rule where improper Government action, such as misdirection by Government personnel, was the paramount cause for the late delivery and consideration of the bid would not compromise the integrity of the competitive bidding system.[37]

5. Telegraphic Bids & Modifications

Telegraphic bids are prohibited unless they are expressly authorized by the IFB.[38] Usually they are not authorized. This prohibition applies even though it may not be possible to submit a timely bid by any other means.

However, under the FAR, telegraphic bid *modifications* are permissible even without authorization in the IFB.[39] As with mailed or hand-carried bids, telegraphic modifications must be received on time unless they meet the conditions for exceptions for late bids. Thus, telegraphic bids (when permitted) or modifications received late in the bidding room may be considered for award if the Government (not the telegraph company) was the cause of the delay (for example, through mishandling or incorrect instructions).[40]

The telegraph company may sometimes telephone a telegram to the bid-opening officer or a person duly authorized by him, and later confirm it in writing. Under certain circumstances, such a bid may be considered if telephoned on or before the opening time, even if the written confirmation is received after bid opening.[41] If the written confirmation is inconsistent with the prior telephonic message, however, the modification will not be considered.[42] Where telex equipment is used at a Government installation to receive a telegram bid submitted electronically, the bid may be considered after opening, provided that it was sent and acknowledged on time even if it was not transcribed due to a malfunction of the Government's equipment—as long as the malfunction is the sole responsibility of the Government, and the content of the message, as well as its time of transmittal, is clearly established.[43]

6. Facsimile Bids & Modifications

Contracting Officers may authorize the use of facsimile equipment for the submission of bids and bid modifications. In deciding whether to permit the use of facsimile bids for a particular procurement, a Contracting Officer is required to consider a number of factors: (a) the anticipated bid size and volume, (b) the urgency of the requirement, (c) the frequency of price changes, (d) the availability, reliability, speed, and capacity of the receiving facsimile equipment, and (e) the adequacy of administrative procedures and controls for receiving, identifying, recording, and safeguarding facsimile bids and ensuring their timely delivery to the bid-opening location.

After the date set for bid opening in a solicitation in which the use of facsimile bids has been authorized, the Contracting Officer may request the apparently successful bidder to provide the complete original signed bid. Unless the solicitation authorizes bidders to use a facsimile machine, a bid or amendment acknowledgment submitted by facsimile will be rejected as nonresponsive.[44]

7. FACNET Bids & Modifications

In 1994, Congress required the establishment of a Federal Acquisition Computer Network (FACNET), a computer-based source of procurement information and communication readily accessible to Government and private sector users. FACNET, which will be implemented in phases over several years, requires agencies to develop electronic commerce procedures including, among other things, procedures to receive responses to solicitations electronically.[45] Some agencies have already undertaken initiatives to implement electronic commerce procedures, and provisions will be included in the FAR regarding FACNET procurements.

E. ELIGIBILITY FOR AWARD

To be eligible for award, a responsible bidder must have submitted the lowest, responsive bid. There are thus two matters to be concerned with—the *responsiveness of bids* and the *responsibility of bidders*.

Although responsibility determinations (which are discussed in Section E.2 below) are sometimes challenged, most bid disputes relate to the responsiveness of the low bid. An affirmative finding of bidder responsibility will virtually never be overruled. While responsiveness is determined as of the date of bid opening, a bidder's responsibility is determined as of the date of contract award. Therefore, it is possible for a bidder who is nonresponsible when its bid is submitted to receive award on the theory that the bidder will become responsible prior to award or in time to satisfactorily perform (for example, by acquiring necessary equipment, facilities, or personnel). Once a nonresponsive bid has been submitted, however, nothing may be done to make it responsive.

1. Responsiveness Of Bids

Simply stated, a responsive bid is one that contains a definite, unqualified offer to meet the material terms of the IFB.[46] In this context, a "material" term is one that could affect the *price, quantity, quality,* or *delivery* of the items being procured.[47]

Any right reserved in the bid that permits a bidder to change a price or any other provision *after* contract award renders the bid nonresponsive. Even a printed legend on a cover letter (for example, "price is subject to change without notice"), which is merely enclosed with (but not incorporated in) the bid package, can disqualify a bid.[48] Likewise, a statement in the bid that it is confidential and can only be viewed by agency officials may render the bid nonresponsive.[49] In addition, a bid guarantee—usually in the form of a bid bond as security that the bidder will not withdraw the bid during a specified period and will execute a contract if awarded—may be required and must be complied with for the bid to be responsive.[50]

a. Minor Informalities. Minor defects or informalities that have no effect (or merely a trivial effect) on price, quantity, quality, or delivery and that may be corrected without prejudice to other bidders may be waived by the Contracting Officer.[51]

For example, the FAR indicates the following minor informalities may be waived:[52] (a) submitting the wrong number of copies of the bid, (b) omitting a handwritten signature in the signature block on the bidding form if the bid otherwise indicates an intent of the bidder to be bound, and (c) failing to acknowledge receipt of an amendment if it is clear from the bid or otherwise that the amendment was in fact received. Other minor informalities that might be acceptable are (1) submitting a bid in an unsealed envelope, (2) failing to initial changes in bid prices where the intended price and the identity of the person making the change is clear, (3) failing to price items separately as required by the IFB when the bid binds the bidder to provide all items, and (4) failing to submit a bid bond in the precise form required by the IFB where the Government obtains the same protection in all material respects under the bond or guarantee actually submitted.

b. Bid Acceptance Period. If the IFB prescribes a minimum time that bids are required to remain firm or irrevocable, a bid offering a shorter time is nonresponsive.[53] If no minimum is stated, there will be an "automatic" bid acceptance period of 30 to 60 calendar days on the bid form *unless* the bidder inserts a longer or shorter time on the bid form. However, there can be a substantial drawback in offering a shorter time for acceptance. If the award is not made within the shorter period specified, the bidder may not be allowed to extend its bid acceptance period—because to do so would give the bidder an unfair advantage—i.e., its initial cost exposure would be for a shorter period of time than applicable to bidders offering the full "automatic" time.

c. Binding Legal Obligation. A bidder, whether an individual, corporation, or partnership, obviously must be legally bound by the bid so that there can be no question regarding the bidder's obligation to perform. Otherwise, a successful bidder could, if it chose, avoid performance after award without liability. Thus, a bidder must be identifiable and existing at the time of bid opening.[54]

Further, a bid may not be transferred or assigned by a bidder to another after it has been opened.[55] If this practice were permitted, a responsible bidder could have a nonresponsible bidder submit a bid and then have the bid assigned to the responsible bidder after opening *if* it wished to perform.

d. Firm Price. A bid is not responsive unless it offers a firm, definite price—that is, an "approximate" price is unacceptable because the bidder is not bound to a fixed amount. So, too, a bid that is subject to (a) freight rate or other increases, (b) a service charge on overdue accounts, or (c) prices charged by suppliers at the time of delivery is clearly nonresponsive.

e. Completeness. As already noted, the bid must address all material portions of the IFB because the bid, upon award, becomes the parties' contract. However, the required parts of the bid need not all be physically included if they are incorporated by reference. Nonetheless, a bidder takes some risk if it omits any required portion of the IFB, even if an omitted page or pages did not require an entry.

f. Ambiguities. Any ambiguity in the bid *price* will render the bid nonresponsive unless (1) the bid is low under any interpretation, (2) the ambiguity does not otherwise affect responsiveness, and (3) the bidder agrees to be bound by the Government's interpretation.[56] Because of this rule, it is important that bidders double-check their figures, the placement of periods or commas, and price extensions.

One kind of ambiguity that has historically plagued bidders and has often been fatal to an otherwise successful bid is a request, recommendation, or suggestion contained in the bid[57] or a letter of transmittal.[58] Such "requests" may result in rejection of a bid because frequently it cannot be determined whether they are mere requests that have no material bearing on the bid or *condition* bid acceptance. In this regard, the Comptroller General has held, for example, that a bid "requesting" progress payments was nevertheless responsive because the request was regarded as precatory and not as a condition.[59]

Requests, recommendations, and suggestions are most likely to arise in transmittal letters. Therefore, bidders should probably not include letters of transmittal when they submit their bids.

2. Responsibility Of Bidders

To be eligible for award, a bidder must be "responsible." Responsibility may be defined as the *apparent ability* to complete the requirements of the contract successfully. The FAR requires the Contracting Officer to make an *affirmative* finding of responsibility and not merely a finding that there is no evidence of nonresponsibility.[60]

a. Responsibility Determinations. To the extent that it is possible in sealed bidding, the process of determining bidder responsibility permits the Contracting Officer to use his *subjective* analysis of the bidder's potential. In making the determination of bidder responsibility, a Contracting Officer will usually ascertain whether the bidder has met the "general standards" of responsibility set forth in the FAR.[61] In other words, the Contracting Officer will consider whether the bidder (a) has adequate financial resources to perform the contract or the ability to obtain them, (b) has the ability to meet the delivery schedule, taking into consideration other commitments, (c) has a satisfactory record of performance on other contracts, (d) has a good record of integrity, (e) has the necessary organization, experience, accounting and operational controls, and technical skills, or the ability to obtain them, (f) has the necessary production, construction, and technical equipment and facilities, or the ability to obtain them, and (g) is otherwise qualified and eligible under applicable laws and regulations.

The standard listed as "(c)" above is becoming increasingly important.[62] A record of poor performance on a prior contract or contracts, if substantial and pervasive, could constitute the basis for finding a bidder nonresponsible. In evaluating a bidder's prior performance, a Contracting Officer may take into consideration (1) a termination for default (discussed in Chapter 16) on a prior contract, even if the default is being appealed, (2) prior delinquencies, such as a bad safety record or late deliveries on one or more contracts, (3) the tenacity and perseverance of the bidder in overcoming difficulties in other contracts, (4) the connection between the bidder and a parent corporation with a poor record of performance on past contracts, and (5) the bankruptcy of a predecessor corporation if there has been no change in management. A surety's inadequate assets may also cause a bidder to be determined nonresponsible.[63] Obviously, it is also appropriate for the Contracting Officer to consider all positive aspects (recent good performance and changed operational procedures, for example) in making his decision regarding prior performance.

Note that even if a bidder's prior performance record is favorable, the bidder could still be found to be nonresponsible if it is determined to lack *integrity*. Such a finding is normally associated with an indictment or conviction for a crime involving the bidder's conduct of its business. Here again, individual Contracting Officers are given considerable discretion in making determinations. Thus, it would not necessarily be inappropriate for one Contracting Officer to determine that a bidder is nonresponsible for lack of integrity even though other Contracting Officers have awarded contracts to that same bidder.[64]

b. Buy-Ins. In connection with responsibility, it should be noted that sometimes bidders deliberately submit bids that are so low that it is certain they will result in loss contracts. This practice—commonly known as "buying-in"—is not encouraged because it frequently leads to problems and contractor claims after award. However, if the bidder who "buys-in" has the financial capability of absorbing the loss and the low price of the bidder is not based on a misunderstanding of the IFB's requirements, award to the bidder is permissible.[65] When this occurs, the procuring agencies are advised to monitor the contractor's performance carefully to ensure that the contractor does not improperly recoup the loss through contract changes (discussed in Chapter 11).

c. Special Requirements. Sometimes an IFB will impose certain "special" requirements on bidders as a prerequisite to award, such as (a) particular experience (for example, "a minimum of five years of experience" in manufacturing a particular item), (b) specified federal, state, or local licenses, operating certificates, or security clearances (although such licenses, certificates, or clearances need not be in hand at the time of bid submission, they must be obtained before the beginning of performance), (c) performance within a given geographical area, (d) an adequate quality control plan, or (e) academic qualifications. These kinds of requirements are proper as long as they represent a legitimate Government need and will normally be enforced even if enforcement results in barring otherwise responsible competitors.[66]

d. Preaward Survey. A bidder's responsibility may be determined by the Contracting Officer from a variety of sources, including credit rating publications, trade or financial journals, business directories, the "List of Parties Excluded from Procurement Programs," the bidder's contacts (suppliers, subcontractors, and customers), banks, and trade associations. However, most often, the Contracting Officer relies on a *preaward survey*.

Such surveys are generally based on an analysis of pertinent financial, technical, and management reviews performed by experienced Government employees in their respective fields. It is always in a bidder's best interest to be cooperative and provide complete information to Government representatives when a preaward survey is requested. Past performance of Government contracts is a very important consideration, but should be based on the contractor's own performance—not on the performance of affiliates.[67]

F. MISTAKES IN BIDS

The term "mistake in bid" normally means a mistake made in the bid price, as opposed to a mistake in business judgment. A mistake in price may occur, for example, in the placement of a decimal or a comma, the calculation of the price, or the extension of unit prices. It may also refer to errors in other information required by the IFB—for example, the weight and dimensions of the item to be furnished, a certification, or a statement contained in descriptive literature. Much has been written about mistakes in bids.[68] The following subsections discuss the highlights of this area.

1. Preaward Mistakes

a. Apparent Clerical Errors. Trivial errors that do not have any material effect on the bids or the bidders may be corrected by the Contracting Officer prior to award.[69] Before making such correction, the bidder must furnish the Contracting Officer with a written or telegraphic verification of the bid intended.[70] Examples of such apparent mistakes are obvious discount errors (e.g., 1%, 10 days; 2%, 20 days; 5%, 30 days) or obvious reversal of "price f.o.b. destination" with "price f.o.b. factory."

b. Other Preaward Mistakes. Mistakes other than apparent clerical mistakes that are discovered after opening and prior to award are handled somewhat differently. If the bidder (1) requests permission to *withdraw* its bid because of a mistake, and (2) the evidence reasonably supports the existence of a mistake, the bidder will *normally* be allowed to withdraw. However, if there is also clear and convincing evidence of what the bidder actually intended, and if the bid—both as uncorrected and as corrected—is the *lowest* received, the Contracting Officer has the option of simply allowing the bid to be corrected and not allowing its withdrawal.[71] Under certain circumstances, a bidder may be allowed to withdraw its allegation of a mistake—if the integrity of the competitive bidding system will not be compromised.[72]

If the bidder (a) requests permission to *correct* a mistake in its bid, and (b) clear and convincing evidence establishes both the existence of a mistake and the bid actually intended, correction will *normally* be allowed. However, if correction would result in displacing any lower bids, the evidence of the mistake and the bid actually intended must be ascertainable from an examination of the bid and the solicitation (and not from other documents). Moreover, if the bidder can show only the existence of the mistake (and not the bid actually intended), the Government retains the option to permit only withdrawal of the bid—not its correction.[73]

c. Bid Verification. As part of his preaward screening of bids, the Contracting Officer is required to look for possible mistakes. If he believes there is a mistake in a bid, he has the further duty to seek *verification* of the bid from the bidder. The verification request must be sufficiently detailed to put the bidder on notice of the suspected mistake, and to assure the Contracting Officer that the bid as confirmed is without error or to elicit an allegation of mistake by the bidder. For example, the bidder should be advised, as is appropriate, of (1) the fact that its bid is so much lower than the other bids or the Government's estimate that it indicates a possibility of error, (2) important or unusual characteristics of the specifications, (3) changes in requirements from previous purchases of a similar item, or (4) such other data that may put the bidder on notice of the suspected mistake.[74]

It is improper, however, for the Contracting Officer to require an "on the spot" verification. The bidder must be given sufficient time to check the bid thoroughly prior to verification. If the bid is adequately verified, the Contracting Officer will consider it as originally submitted. If the bidder alleges mistake, the bid will be handled in the manner discussed above.

2. Postaward Mistakes

For obvious reasons, the Government is a good deal more reluctant to grant relief to a bidder who is awarded a contract and *then* claims a mistake in bid. Considerations of fairness to the other bidders, as well as the basic concept that a contractor should be obligated to live up to the terms of the contract (even if they turn out to be unprofitable), make this a necessity. But— under certain rather narrow circumstances—relief may be granted after award.[75]

If the mistake alleged for the first time after award is a *mutual mistake* (where the Government and the bidder/contractor have made the *same* mistake so that the contract does not express the agreement that the parties intended), the contract may be reformed to reflect the true intent of the parties. If a *unilateral* mistake—normally based upon the bidder/contractor's negligence or carelessness in preparing the bid—is alleged, relief will not be granted unless it can be shown that the Contracting Officer had *actual* or *constructive* notice of the probability of error prior to accepting the bid.

Verification of bids (discussed above)—if properly conducted— minimizes the number of unilateral mistake claims based upon *constructive* Contracting Officer awareness of the mistake. On the other hand, if award is made without adequate verification, despite the presence of an apparent error in the bid (a price far lower than the other prices or the Government estimate, for example), the Contracting Officer will be said to have *constructive* knowledge of the mistake—that is, even if he did not actually know of the mistake, he should have known of it. The bidder/contractor would be entitled to relief on the general theory that a party (in this case the Government) cannot "snap-up" an offer that it knows (or should know) is too good to be true. If, however, it is the practice in the industry involved to submit high bids without serious expectation of receiving an award (known as "highballing"), the clustering of high bids will not require the Contracting Officer to request verification.[76]

If the bidder/contractor can prove that the Contracting Officer was on actual or constructive notice of an error, the contract may either be *reformed* (to correct the mistaken contract price) or *rescinded* (to cancel the obligations of both parties).

G. PROTESTS

As discussed in Chapter 2, Section D.2, CICA altered the methods by which Government procurements are made. The Act also addressed the subject of procurement protests.[77] The Act broadened the power of the General Accounting Office (GAO) in the area of protest adjudication by the Comptroller General, and added (initially for a three-year trial period and then permanently) a new forum—the General Services Administration Board of Contract Appeals (GSBCA)—for deciding protests that relate to automatic data processing (ADP) contracts.[78] Now, an interested person (normally a disappointed bidder or offeror or other party having an *economic* interest in the procurement) may protest any decision or anticipated decision of the Contracting Officer in any of several forums: (1) the contracting agency that issued the solicitation, (2) the Comptroller General, (3) a federal court—the Court of Federal Claims and District Courts, and (4) in the case of ADP procurements, the GSBCA. The protest may relate to (a) a deficiency—or deficiencies—in the solicitation, (b) an improper award (anticipated or actual), or (c) any other defect in the recognized procurement procedures.[79]

1. Contracting Agency

In most circumstances, it is wise for a bidder to file a protest *first* with the contracting agency, even though it is understandably difficult for a Contracting Officer to reverse himself. If the protest is made *before* award, the Contracting Officer may not have committed himself, and an error in the IFB, an imperfection in the low bid, or a procedural defect may be obvious and easy to correct. *After* award, a protest at the contracting agency is less likely to succeed unless the matter is sufficiently significant to attract the attention of someone at a level considerably above the Contracting Officer.

a. Procedures. Uniform procedures and time limits apply to protests to contracting agencies. Protests based on solicitation improprieties that are apparent prior to bid opening (or the closing date for receiving proposals in competitive negotiation; see Chapter 4) must be filed before the bid opening or the time set for receipt of proposals. Any other type of protest must be filed no later than 10 days after the protest's basis is known or should have been known, whichever is earlier. Contracting agencies may, at their discretion, waive the time limit. Agency protests are normally submitted to the Contracting Officer.

Protests must contain the following information: (1) the name, address, and telephone number of the protester, (2) the solicitation or contract number, (3) a detailed statement of the legal and factual grounds for the protest, including copies of relevant documents, (4) a request for a ruling by the agency, and (5) a statement as to the form of relief requested. Failure to comply with these requirements may be grounds for dismissal.[80] The Contracting Officer will then advise all affected persons of the protest and give them an opportunity to respond. Thereafter—based on the arguments, documents, and other information received—he will either (a) decide the protest, (b) refer it to a superior in accordance with internal procedures, or (c) refer it to the Comptroller General (which will take it out of his and the agency's control).

If the protest is filed *before* award, no contract will be awarded until the protest is decided *unless* there is an urgency or unacceptable delay involved—in which case the Contracting Officer must document the need to award and notify all affected persons.[81] If the protest is filed *after* award, the Contracting Officer may direct the contractor to stop performance under the authority of the "Protest After Award" clause. If the contractor is permitted to resume work, the Contracting Officer may grant an equitable adjustment in the contract's delivery schedule and price.[82]

b. Remedies. The remedy *before* award is simple: corrective action will be taken if the problem lies with the IFB, or the contract will be awarded to the proper party—unless the agency decides it no longer needs the product (in which case the procurement would be canceled). *After* award, the Contracting Officer may void the contract (an unusual option), terminate the contract for the Government's convenience (see Chapter 17), or permit the improper award to stand if it is clearly in the best interest of the Government to do so.

2. Comptroller General

CICA gave the GAO (specifically, the Comptroller General) express statutory authority to deal with bid protests filed by "interested parties" or referred by an Executive Branch agency or a federal court.[83] Although this Act was the first federal law to give the Comptroller General express authority to decide bid protests for Government contracts, he did so for over 50 years on the basis of the GAO's *general* power under federal law to settle and adjudicate claims by and against the Government.[84] The Comptroller General's decisions in the bid protest area—both before and after CICA—are numerous. Current decisions, in full-text form as issued by the Comptroller General, are available in the COMPTROLLER GENERAL'S PROCUREMENT DECISIONS, a monthly periodical published by Federal Publications Inc.

As a result of CICA, the GAO extensively modified its bid protest regulations in 1991.[85] Failure to follow the procedures of these regulations, discussed below, may be fatal to an otherwise meritorious protest.[86]

a. Procedures. Under GAO's bid protest regulations, a protest may be filed with the Comptroller General (1) directly (without involving the contracting agency other than advising it), (2) by referral from the Contracting Officer, or (3) by an "appeal" from the contracting agency's decision on the protest. If filed directly or after the agency's decision, time is of the essence. The protest must be filed in writing *within 10 days* after the protester is on actual or constructive notice of the procuring agency's *initial* adverse action (for example, its award of the contract or its acquiescence in and active support of continued performance despite the protest). In any event, if the protest alleges some deficiency in the solicitation, it must be received *before* the opening of the bids.

After receiving a protest, GAO will contact the procuring agency involved (normally by telephone—followed by a confirming letter) within 24 hours to request a detailed report and copies of all pertinent documents. The letter will request that all interested parties be (a) notified of the protest, (b) furnished with copies of all nonproprietary documents, and (c) advised to contact the Comptroller General if they wish to comment on the merits of the protest. Such comments must be filed within 10 days of receiving the contracting agency's report. Hearings, although not a matter of routine, may also be held in certain circumstances. If requested and properly identified, all proprietary information will normally be protected against disclosure to unauthorized individuals. GAO accomplishes this through the issuance of a "protective order," which limits the release of particular documents to counsel for the protester and interested parties.

While a protest is pending before the Comptroller General, the procuring agency is prohibited from awarding a contract based on the protested procurement after the Contracting Officer has received notice of the protest. Nevertheless, the head of a procurement activity may authorize award despite the protest after notifying the GAO in writing of his finding that "urgent and compelling circumstances" will not permit waiting for the Comptroller General's decision.

The Comptroller General will issue a decision on the protest after (1) receiving the agency report, including all "relevant documents" (within 35 days after the GAO's notification to the agency of the protest), (2) a hearing on the merits if requested by the parties, and (3) receiving comments or posthearing briefs and any rebuttals thereto from all interested parties. The decision generally must be issued within 125 days after the protest is submitted to the Comptroller General. Tighter time limits apply if the protester invokes "express option" procedures. Reconsideration of the decision may be requested if a detailed statement of the factual and legal grounds for such reconsideration is filed within 10 days after they are known or should have been known. The Protest Time Chart presented in Figure 3-6 summarizes the more significant time limitations in a typical GAO bid protest.

b. Remedies. The Comptroller General may—if he determines that the protested solicitation, proposed award, or award does not comply with a procurement statute—*recommend* that the agency take such steps as (a) refraining from exercising contract options, (b) immediately recompeting the contract, (c) issuing a new solicitation, (d) terminating the contract, (e) awarding a contract that complies with the procurement statutes, or (f) any combination of the above.[87] In addition, the Comptroller General may *recommend* that the federal agency conducting the procurement pay to an appropriate prevailing party the costs of filing and pursuing the protest (including "reasonable" attorney fees and consultant and expert witness fees that do not exceed a statutory cap) and preparing the bid or proposal.[88] The Comptroller General's "recommendations" are almost always implemented.

3. Federal Courts

As indicated at the start of Section G, one possible forum for a bid protest is federal court.[89] One federal court forum (for preaward protests) is the Court of Federal Claims. The Federal District Courts may also play a minor role in protest adjudication.

Under the Federal Courts Improvement Act of 1982[90] (discussed more fully in Chapter 21), the Court of Federal Claims has authority to grant complete relief on any protest brought *before* a contract is awarded, and has the *exclusive* authority to grant declaratory judgments and injunctive relief in appropri-

Figure 3-6

GAO PROTEST TIME CHART

Action	Deadline [*Must be received by Comptroller General within the deadline]
1. Filing protest	
(a) For automatic suspension	* Before award or the later of 10 days after award or 5 days after debriefing (Comptroller General must also notify contracting agency of receipt of protest within that time)
(b) For consideration of the merits (may be filed at Comptroller General or contracting agency)	
(1) Deficiency in the IFB	* Before bid opening
(2) Other matters	* Within 10 days after basis of protest was or should have been known
2. Appeal of adverse contracting agency decision to Comptroller General	* 10 days after initial adverse agency action (protest to agency must have been filed on time)
3. Copy of protest to Contracting Officer	Within 1 day after filing of protest
4. Comptroller General notification of protest to contracting agency	Within 1 day after Comptroller General's receipt of protest
5. Request for express option	* Within 3 days after protest is filed
6. Comptroller General decision on whether to grant express option	Within 2 days of receipt of request (express option rarely granted)
7. Agency report due under express option	* Within 20 days after notice that express option invoked
8. Comments on agency report under express option	* Within 5 days after receipt of report
9. Decision issued on express option case	Within 65 days after filing of protest

Items 5–9: EXPRESS OPTION ONLY

continued

Fig. 3-6 / continued

10. Contracting agency report	*	35 days after notice of protest
11. Request for protective order	*	20 days after protest filed
12. Requests for exclusion of documents from protective order	*	2 days after receipt of protective order request
13. Request for documents	*	Concurrent with protest at Comptroller General
14. Request for additional documents	*	2 days after receipt of contracting agency report
15. Comptroller General decision on release of documents		5 days after receipt of contracting agency report
16. Request for hearing (optional)		As early as practicable (not later than promptly after receipt of agency report)
17. Hearing (at discretion of Comptroller General)		As soon as possible after parties receive agency report
18. Posthearing comments	*	Within 7 days of hearing unless Comptroller General sets a different time
19. Comptroller General decision		Within 125 days after filing of protest
20. Request for reconsideration	*	Within 10 days of receipt of decision
21. Claim for protest costs and bid or proposal preparation costs	*	Within 60 days after receipt of decision

ate protest cases.[91] As a result, the Court of Federal Claims presently considers, on a routine basis, preaward requests for temporary restraining orders, permanent injunctions, and declaratory judgments.

The Court of Federal Claims' bid protest jurisdiction can be exercised only if a complaint is filed with it *prior* to contract award.[92] However, once the court assumes jurisdiction over a protest, it cannot be deprived of this power by a subsequent award.[93]

The Comptroller General has the option of forwarding to the Court of Federal Claims for trial and adjudication any matter (for example, a preaward protest) that could also properly be decided by the court. Other matters (such as postaward protests) would continue to be decided by the Comptroller General in accordance with the GAO's standard procedures. In addition, the Comptroller General has been requested, on a number of occasions, to render advisory opinions for the Court of Federal Claims on preaward protests that are pending there. This procedure will likely continue, although there is some disagreement as to its usefulness among the court's judges.

Prior to the Federal Courts Improvement Act, District Courts exercised jurisdiction—under the so-called "*Scanwell* Doctrine" named after the case in which it originated[94]—to grant preaward and postaward injunctions in bid protest situations. As a result of language in the Act that gives the Court of Federal Claims "exclusive jurisdiction to grant declaratory judgments and such equitable and extraordinary relief as it deems proper, including but not limited to injunctive relief" for the purpose of affording "complete relief on any contract claim brought before the contract is awarded,"[95] District Court jurisdiction in the bid protest area has been questioned. Some courts have held that preaward bid protest actions can only be heard in the Court of Federal Claims,[96] but it has also been held that District Courts have *concurrent* jurisdiction with the Court of Federal Claims over bid protest suits filed before award.[97] Courts have also held that the language quoted above does not prevent a District Court from considering a disappointed bidder's postaward claim for injunctive relief.[98] Statutory amendments are needed to define more clearly the role of the Court of Federal Claims vis-à-vis the District Courts.[99]

4. GSBCA

As already mentioned, CICA gave the GSBCA authority to resolve protests involving the procurement of ADP equipment and services for Government agencies.[100] The nature of the products or services specified in the solicitation—rather than the products or services offered—determines whether the procurement is an ADP procurement.[101] The GSBCA, in carrying out this role, has adopted Rules of Procedure for such protests.[102] Full-text decisions of the GSBCA on protests as well as the board's rules are available from Federal Publications' BOARD OF CONTRACT APPEALS BID PROTEST DECISIONS monthly reporter service.

The GSBCA offers more full-blown protest procedures than those of GAO, but must issue a final decision within 65 days (unless it is determined by the board's chairman that a longer period is necessary). Unlike the Comptroller General's decisions on protests, which are recommendations to the procuring agency, the GSBCA's decisions are *binding* on the Government agency involved. Moreover, the board may suspend contract award or performance while a protest is pending and may award bid or proposal preparation costs—as well as attorney fees and consultant and expert witness fees—when a protest is sustained. The GSBCA's rules are complex, require strict adherence to many procedural requirements, and contain multiple pitfalls for the uninitiated.

H. CONTRACT AWARD

After bid opening, the Contracting Officer normally awards the contract to the *lowest, responsive, responsible* bidder. However, in some situations, he may elect to (1) award a contract for a *lesser* quantity than stated in the IFB, (2) award more than one contract for the items to be purchased (i.e., split the award), or (3) reject all bids—and then, if the Government has a continuing need for the item or items, resolicit.

1. Award Procedures

An award is made either by furnishing the successful bidder with an executed award document (the contract) or by written or electronic notice, if followed as soon as possible by the formal award.[103]

The Contracting Officer executes supply and service contracts by filling out the bottom of Standard Form 33 (see Figure 3-1 earlier in this chapter). In a similar manner, construction, alteration, or repair contracts solicited under Standard Form 1442 (see Figure 3-4) will be executed on the second page of the Standard Form.

For the purpose of determining whether a contract was awarded *within the acceptance period* (usually 60 or 90 days), the date the notice or executed award document was deposited in a mailbox or otherwise placed in the control of the U.S. Postal Service—and not the date it was received—is binding.[104] In rare circumstances, a contract may be awarded without following these formal procedures if a Contracting Officer (the only person authorized to commit the Government) indicates an award will be made and the bidder changes its position in reliance thereon.

Unsuccessful bidders must be notified within three days (either in writing or by electronic means) that the contract has been awarded, unless the procurement is classified.[105] If award is made to other than the low bidder, the reason must be explained. If requested, the Contracting Officer will provide unsuccessful bidders with the name and address of the successful bidder, the contract price, and the location where a copy of the abstract of offers is available for inspection.[106]

A *preaward* notice to unsuccessful bidders need *not* be given. This presents a practical problem in making a timely bid protest—since a protester stands a far better chance of prevailing *before* award than after. Therefore, after bid opening, it is most important for all bidders who may be eligible for award to keep abreast of developments—and to be attentive to indications that their bids may be rejected.

Award may be made for a *lesser quantity* of the items or units indicated under any given item unless (a) this is prohibited under the terms of the IFB or (b) the bid is on an all-or-nothing basis. Further, an award may be *split* between the low and the next low bidder when it is determined to be in the interest of industrial mobilization to have an additional source of supply.

2. Rejection Of All Bids

The right to reject all bids is expressly reserved by the Government when it is in the public interest to do so.[107] But rejection *after bid opening* must be for "cogent" and "compelling" reasons—for the obvious reason that all bids are then exposed. The two most common grounds for rejection of all bids after opening are (1) substantial savings to the Government (because quality requirements are overstated or prices bid are unreasonable, for example), and (2) specifications or other IFB provisions are deficient, ambiguous, overly restrictive, or not representative of the Government's needs.

The prospect of *substantial* savings to the Government justifies rejection of all bids and resolicitation. Small savings will not. Substantial savings are most often indicated when (a) a significantly lower bid is unacceptable because of being late, nonresponsive, or from a nonresponsible bidder, (b) the price or prices are unreasonable in relation to the Government's estimate or the Contracting Officer's general knowledge of market conditions or prior procurements, or (c) an *uncorrectable* mistake in bid indicates that the Government could have obtained a significantly lower bid. The determination of whether the savings would be substantial is usually within the discretion of the Contracting Officer. However, a nonbidder's asserted willingness to offer a lower price is not a proper basis for rejection of all bids on the ground that the bids received were unreasonably priced.[108]

With respect to the other common ground for rejection—specifications are deficient or are no longer representative of the Government's needs—care must be exercised to assure that such a ground is the *real* reason for rejection (i.e., not merely a subterfuge to deprive the low bidder of an award) and any deficiency in the specifications is *significant* and cannot be corrected by other means. Ideally, any specification defect or change in the Government's needs should be identified before bids are opened. But sometimes such faults or changes in plans cannot be corrected until after bid opening. The Contracting Officer has broad discretion in such matters, unless an abuse is clearly established.

There are several other, less common, but legitimate grounds for rejecting all bids. Some of these are (1) a critical need to negotiate a shorter delivery schedule has developed, (2) sufficient funds are not available to pay the contract price, (3) the goods or services are no longer required, or (4) it is determined that work can be performed in-house rather than by contract.

I. TWO-STEP SEALED BIDDING

Two-step sealed bidding is a hybrid method of procurement.[109] It is recommended for use by the Government to promote the maximum competition practicable—especially in procurements for complex and technical items—when (a) available specifications are not sufficiently definite or complete for competitive bidding but definite criteria do exist for evaluating technical proposals, (b) there is more than one technically qualified source available and there is sufficient time available to evaluate each source, and (c) a firm-fixed-price or fixed-price contract with economic price adjustment can be awarded.[110]

This method of procurement requires the Contracting Officer to work closely with technical personnel and to rely on their specialized knowledge in determining the technical requirements of the procurement and the criteria to be used for evaluating technical proposals. A principal objective of the two-step procedure is to permit the development of a sufficiently descriptive statement of the Government's requirements, including the development of a technical data package, so that subsequent procurements may be made by conventional sealed bidding.[111]

1. Step One: Request For Technical Proposals

This step is initiated by the issuance of a Request for Technical Proposals (RFTP). Under the FAR, the RFTP must contain certain minimum information, for example, (1) a description of the supplies or services required, (2) the evaluation criteria for selecting the winning technical proposal, (3) instructions not to include prices or price information with the technical proposal, (4) the technical proposal's due date and its requirements, (5) a statement of intent to use the two-step method, and (6) a statement that in the second step only bids based on technical proposals determined to be acceptable will be considered for award.[112] Each offeror submits a detailed description of what the offeror proposes to furnish to satisfy the Government's need. The technical proposals are evaluated—and frequently revised or modified—during the negotiations and discussions that follow. After negotiations, those offerors who have submitted technical proposals that the Government determines are "acceptable" are then invited to participate in step two. There is no consideration of cost or price during this step.

2. Step Two: Invitation For Bids

In step two of the procedure, IFBs are sent to those firms whose proposals were judged to be in the acceptable category.[113] Each acceptable offeror then submits a sealed bid based on its own technical proposal. Then, award—without further discussion, modification, or negotiation—is made to the offeror that submits the *lowest* price on a technical proposal determined to be acceptable under step one.

REFERENCES

1. Deficit Reduction Act of 1984, tit. VII of "Div. B," P.L. 98-369, 98 Stat. 494.

2. Note 1, supra, § 2711(a)(1).

3. See FAR 53.236-1.

4. FAR 14.202-4(b), 14.202-5(b).

5. FAR 10.004(b).

6. See Shnitzer, "Ambiguities in Invitations & Bids," Briefing Papers No. 68-6 (Dec. 1968), 1 BPC 359.

7. See FAR 14.208.

8. Comp. Gen. Dec. B-169368, 49 Comp. Gen. 713, 1970 CPD ¶ 39, 12 GC ¶ 201.

9. See FAR 14.404-1.

SEALED BIDDING   3-47

10. FAR 14.404-1(a). E.g., Ace-Federal Reporters, Inc., Comp. Gen. Dec. B-237414, 90-1 CPD ¶ 144; Baldino's Lock & Key Service, Inc., Comp. Gen. Dec. B-238808, 90-2 CPD ¶ 20; PBM Const., Comp. Gen. Dec. 242221.3 et al., 91-2 CPD ¶ 181.

11. See, e.g., Bonded Maintenance Co., Comp. Gen. Dec. B-235207, 89-2 CPD ¶ 51; US Rentals, Comp. Gen. Dec. B-238090, 90-1 CPD ¶ 367, 32 GC ¶ 213 (Note).

12. FAR 14.205-1(b).

13. FAR 14.205-1(d)(2).

14. FAR 14.205-4.

15. FAR 14.202-1. See 41 USC § 416(a).

16. See generally Arnavas & Ganther, "Preventive Preaward Actions," Briefing Papers No. 90-9 (Aug. 1990), 9 BPC 179.

17. FAR 52.215-16 ("Contract Award" clause). See Price Bros. Co., Comp. Gen. Dec. B-228524, 88-1 CPD ¶ 180.

18. FAR 14.407-3.

19. FAR 14.208(a).

20. See, e.g., Comp. Gen. Dec. B-178640, 53 Comp. Gen. 64, 1973 CPD ¶ 84, 15 GC ¶ 337. But see Warfield & Sanford, Inc., Comp. Gen. Dec. B-223976, 86-2 CPD ¶ 448.

21. See Comp. Gen. Dec. B-164154 (July 3, 1968); Comp. Gen. Dec. B-135641, 37 Comp. Gen. 785, 1958 CPD ¶ 57; Phillip Sitz Const., Comp. Gen. Dec. B-245941, 92-1 CPD ¶ 170, 34 GC ¶ 193.

22. FAR 14.401(a).

23. FAR 14.401(b); Bartomeli Co., Comp. Gen. Dec. B-246060, 92-1 CPD ¶ 170, 34 GC ¶ 173.

24. FAR 14.402-1(a).

25. FAR 14.403(a).

26. FAR 14.403(b).

27. Note 24, supra.

28. 15 USC § 260a.

29. Comp. Gen. Dec. B-96406 (Oct. 6, 1950). See also Comp. Gen. Dec. B-161638 (June 21, 1967), 9 GC ¶ 240.

30. See FAR 14.402-3.

31. See generally Shnitzer, "Late Bids & Proposals," Briefing Papers No. 84-11 (Nov. 1984), 6 BPC 437; Cibinic, "Late Bids and Proposals: I Hear You Knocking but You Can't Come In," 6 Nash & Cibinic Rep. ¶ 16 (Mar. 1992).

32. FAR 14.304-1, 52.214-7.

33. FAR 14.304-1(a).

34. See note 32, supra.

35. See, e.g., H.A. Kaufman Co., Comp. Gen. Dec. B-186941, 77-1 CPD ¶ 162; Computer Literacy World, Inc. v. Department of Agriculture, GSBCA 11767-P, 92-3 BCA ¶ 25112, 1992 BPD ¶ 140, 34 GC ¶ 350.

36. Comp. Gen. Dec. B-136606, 38 Comp. Gen. 234, 1958 CPD ¶ 93; George W. Kane, Inc., Comp. Gen. Dec. B-245382.2, 92-1 CPD ¶ 143, 34 GC ¶ 139.

37. See, e.g., Allstate Rent-A-Car Inc., Comp. Gen. Dec. B-225633, 87-1 CPD ¶ 458, 29 GC ¶ 171; Baeten Const. Co., Comp. Gen. Dec. B-210681, 83-2 CPD ¶ 203; Geiger Co., Comp. Gen. Dec. B-216502, 85-1 CPD ¶ 155.

38. FAR 14.301(b). See also Building Maintenance Specialists, Inc., Comp. Gen. Dec. B-215019, 84-1 CPD ¶ 690.

39. FAR 14.303(a).

40. FAR 14.304-1(a).

41. FAR 14.302(b).

42. Ibex, Ltd., Comp. Gen. Dec. B-240770, 90-2 CPD ¶ 483, 33 GC ¶ 36.

43. Compare Hydro Fitting Mfg. Corp., Comp. Gen. Dec B-183438, 54 Comp. Gen. 999, 75-1 CPD ¶ 331, 17 GC ¶ 263 with Record Elec. Inc., Comp. Gen. Dec. B-186848, 56 Comp. Gen. 4, 76-2 CPD ¶ 315, 18 GC ¶ 473.

44. FAR 14.301(c), 52.214-31; Recreonics Corp., Comp. Gen. Dec. B-246339, 92-1 CPD ¶ 249, 34 GC ¶ 278.

45. Federal Acquisition Streamlining Act of 1994, P.L. 103-355, § 9001 et seq. (Oct. 13, 1994) (to be codified at 41 USC § 426 et seq.; 10 USC § 2302c).

46. FAR 14.301(a). See Aidco, Inc., Comp. Gen. Dec. B-249736, 92-2 CPD ¶ 407, 35 GC ¶ 84. See generally Shnitzer, "Submitting a Responsive Bid," Briefing Papers No. 66-2 (Apr. 1966), 1 BPC 157.

47. FAR 14.404-2(e).

48. See FAR 14.404-2.

SEALED BIDDING 3-49

49. Warfield & Sanford, Inc., Comp. Gen. Dec. B-223244.2, 86-2 CPD ¶ 21, 28 GC ¶ 256.

50. FAR 14.404-2(j), 28.101-4. See Cibinic, "Bid Guarantees: The Tail's Still Wagging!," 6 Nash & Cibinic Rep. ¶ 36 (June 1992).

51. FAR 14.405. See Mack Trucks, Inc. v. U.S., 6 Cl. Ct. 68 (1984), 3 FPD ¶ 29; Corbin Superior Composites, Inc., Comp. Gen. Dec. B-236777.2, 90-1 CPD ¶ 2; JRW Enterprises, Inc., Comp. Gen. Dec. B-238236, 90-1 CPD ¶ 464; K Services, Comp. Gen. Dec. B-238744, 90-1 CPD ¶ 556; Pro Alarm, Inc., Comp. Gen. Dec. B-240137, 90-2 CPD ¶ 242, 32 GC ¶ 366.

52. FAR 14.405.

53. Comp. Gen. Dec. B-161628 (July 20, 1967).

54. Martin Co., Comp. Gen. Dec. B-178540, 74-1 CPD ¶ 234; General Chemical Services, Inc., Comp. Gen. Dec. B-241595, 91-1 CPD ¶ 94, 33 GC ¶ 104.

55. Comp. Gen. Dec. B-171959, 51 Comp. Gen. 145, 1971 CPD ¶ 63, 13 GC ¶ 407. But see J.I. Case Co., Comp. Gen. Dec. B-239178, 90-2 CPD ¶ 108, 32 GC ¶ 303.

56. See Comp. Gen. Dec. B-148648 (Apr. 19, 1962).

57. Comp. Gen. Dec. B-164345 (Oct. 2, 1968).

58. Comp. Gen. Dec. B-166685 (June 16, 1969), 11 GC ¶ 348.

59. Canadian Commercial Corp., Comp. Gen. Dec. B-207777, 83-1 CPD ¶ 16, 25 GC ¶ 43.

60. FAR 9.103, 9.105-2. See generally Shnitzer, "Responsibility of Bidders," Briefing Papers No. 72-4 (Aug. 1972), 2 BPC 187.

61. FAR 9.104-1.

62. See note 45, supra, § 1091 (to be codified at 41 USC § 405). See generally Cibinic, "Consideration of Past Performance in Contract Awards: 'What Is Past Is Prologue'," 6 Nash & Cibinic Rep. ¶ 8 (Feb. 1992); Pushkar, Lent & Hopkins, "Past Performance Evaluations," Briefing Papers No. 94-6 (May 1994).

63. Bundick Enterprises, Inc., Comp. Gen. Dec. B-239867.2, 90-2 CPD ¶ 402, 33 GC ¶ 24.

64. Comp. Gen. Dec. B-141138, 39 Comp. Gen. 468, 1959 CPD ¶ 98, 2 GC ¶ 5.

65. See, e.g., Hunter Outdoor Products, Comp. Gen. Dec. B-179922, 74-2 CPD ¶ 207; Hardie-Tynes Mfg. Co., Comp. Gen. Dec. B-237938, 90-1 CPD ¶ 347, 32 GC ¶ 158; All Clean, Inc., Comp. Gen. Dec. B-228608, 87-2 CPD ¶ 154, 28 GC ¶ 280; Margaret N. Cox, Comp. Gen. Dec.

3-50 GOVERNMENT CONTRACT GUIDEBOOK

B-232588, 88-2 CPD ¶ 605, 31 GC ¶ 55. See generally Virden & Gallatin, "Buying-In," Briefing Papers No. 84-3 (Mar. 1984), 6 BPC 309.

66. FAR 9.104-2. See Dacker & Co., Comp. Gen. Dec. B-220807 et al., 86-1 CPD ¶ 100, 28 GC ¶ 79.

67. See FAR 9.104-2.

68. See, e.g., Welch, "Mistakes in Bids," Briefing Papers No. 63-6 (Dec. 1963), 1 BPC 47; Berger, "Mistakes in Bids/Edition II," Briefing Papers No. 76-5 (Oct. 1976), 4 BPC 75.

69. FAR 14.406-2.

70. FAR 14.406-1, 14.406-2.

71. FAR 14.406-3(a), (b).

72. Duro Paper Bag Mfg. Co., Comp. Gen. Dec. B-221377.3, 86-1 CPD ¶ 165, 28 GC ¶ 105; DGS Contract Services, Inc., Comp. Gen. Dec. B-237157.2, 90-1 CPD ¶ 162.

73. FAR 14.406-3(c).

74. FAR 14.406-3(g). See Connelly Containers, Inc. v. U.S., 7 Cl. Ct. 423 (1985), 3 FPD ¶ 109.

75. FAR 14.406-4. See generally Gammon & Allen, "Postaward Relief for Mistakes in Bids," Briefing Papers No. 88-11 (Oct. 1988), 8 BPC 213.

76. Hankins Const. Co. v. U.S., 838 F.2d 1194 (Fed. Cir. 1988), 7 FPD ¶ 16, 30 GC ¶ 109.

77. Note 1, supra, § 2741, adding 31 USC §§ 3551–3556.

78. 40 USC § 759(f).

79. See generally Shnitzer, "How To Recognize a Protestable Issue," Briefing Papers No. 93-3 (Feb. 1993).

80. See FAR 33.103.

81. FAR 33.103(a), (b)(1).

82. FAR 52.233-3.

83. 31 USC § 3553.

84. 31 USC § 3526(a); Comp. Gen. Dec. A-10024 (Aug. 19, 1925).

85. 56 Fed. Reg. 3759 (Jan. 31, 1991). See generally Shnitzer, "The New GAO Bid Protest Rules," Briefing Papers No. 92-4 (Mar. 1992). See also 33 GC ¶ 47; 29 GC ¶ 385; 27 GC ¶ 3. For discussions of prior protest procedures, see generally Shnitzer, "GAO Bid Protests," Briefing Papers

No. 86-12 (Nov. 1986), 7 BPC 403; Shnitzer, "Handling Bid Protests Before GAO," Briefing Papers No. 70-3 (June 1970), 2 BPC 25; and Shnitzer, "Handling Bid Protests Before GAO/Edition II," Briefing Papers No. 77-4 (Aug. 1977), 4 BPC 141. See also Stamps, "Subcontractor GAO Protests," Briefing Papers No. 89-5 (Apr. 1989), 8 BPC 349.

86. E.g., Marconi Electronics Inc., Comp. Gen. Dec. B-218088.3, 85-1 CPD ¶ 289.

87. 31 USC § 3554(b).

88. 31 USC § 3554(c). See generally Shnitzer, "Bid or Proposal & Protest Costs Under CICA," Briefing Papers No. 88-12 (Nov. 1988), 8 BPC 229; Nash, "Recovery of Protest Costs: Confusing and Conflicting Rules," 6 Nash & Cibinic Rep. ¶ 58 (Oct. 1992).

89. See generally Victorino & Fleming, "Bid Protest Suits in Federal Courts," Briefing Papers No. 83-4 (Apr. 1983), 6 BPC 141.

90. P.L. 97-164, 96 Stat. 25.

91. 28 USC § 1491(a)(3).

92. U.S. v. John C. Grimberg Co., 702 F.2d 1362 (Fed. Cir. 1983), 1 FPD ¶ 89, 25 GC ¶ 96.

93. F. Alderete General Contractors, Inc. v. U.S., 715 F.2d 1476 (Fed. Cir. 1983), 2 FPD ¶ 26, 25 GC ¶ 275. See also Alabama Metal Products, Inc. v. U.S., 4 Cl. Ct. 530 (1984), 2 FPD ¶ 114; Standard Mfg. Co. v. U.S., 7 Cl. Ct. 54 (1984), 3 FPD ¶ 83.

94. Scanwell Laboratories, Inc. v. Shaffer, 424 F.2d 859 (D.C. Cir. 1970), 12 GC ¶ 64.

95. Note 91, supra.

96. E.g., Opal Mfg. Co. v. UMC Industries, Inc., 553 F. Supp. 131 (D.D.C. 1982), 24 GC ¶ 444; International London Fog Co. v. Defense Logistics Agency, No. 4-82-1334 (D. Minn., Dec. 22, 1982), 25 GC ¶ 98; London Fog Co. v. Defense Logistics Agency, No. 83-1399 (W.D. Pa., Oct. 30, 1983); J.P Francis & Assocs., Inc. v. U.S., 902 F.2d 740 (9th Cir. 1990), 32 GC ¶ 228.

97. E.g., Coco Bros. v. Pierce, 741 F.2d 675 (3d Cir. 1984), 26 GC ¶ 298; In re Smith & Wesson, 757 F.2d 431 (1st Cir. 1985), 27 GC ¶ 159. See generally Victorino & Fleming, "Bid Protest Suits in Federal Courts," Briefing Papers No. 83-4 (Apr. 1983), 6 BPC 141.

98. E.g., American District Telegraph v. Department of Energy, 555 F. Supp. 1224 (D.D.C. 1983), 25 GC ¶ 58.

99. E.g., Streamlining Defense Acquisition Laws: Report of the Advisory Law Panel (Jan. 1993) (recommending that District Courts no longer handle bid protests and that the jurisdiction of the Court of Federal

Claims be expanded to include all preaward and postaward protests). See also Nash, "Preaward Litigation: Court of Federal Claims or District Court?," 7 Nash & Cibinic Rep. ¶ 2 (Jan. 1993).

100. Note 1, supra, § 2713 (codified at 40 USC § 759(f)). See generally Tolle & Duffy, "GSBCA Bid Protests," Briefing Papers No. 87-4 (Mar. 1987), 7 BPC 497; Burgett, Duberstein & Sweeney, "ADP & Telecommunications Procurements: Recurring Issues," Briefing Papers No. 92-3 (Feb. 1992); Shnitzer, Government Contract Bidding, ch. 23 (Federal Publications Inc., 3d ed. 1987 & Supp.).

101. E.g., Electronic Genie, Inc., GSBCA 10571-P, 90-3 BCA ¶ 23045, 1990 BPD ¶ 143, 32 GC ¶ 230; Ace Federal Reporters, Inc. GSBCA 9136-P, 87-3 BCA ¶ 20211, 30 GC ¶ 90; Best Power Technology Sales Corp. v. Austin, 984 F.2d 1172 (Fed. Cir. 1993), 12 FPD ¶ 4, 35 GC ¶ 86.

102. GSBCA Rules of Procedure (Revised, Jan. 3, 1994). See 36 GC ¶ 16.

103. FAR 14.407-1; 41 USC § 253b(c).

104. Comp. Gen. Dec. B-158862, 45 Comp. Gen. 700, 1966 CPD ¶ 40, 8 GC ¶ 25.

105. FAR 14.408-1; 41 USC § 253b(c); 10 USC § 2305(b).

106. FAR 14.408-1(c).

107. 41 USC § 253b(b); FAR 14.404. See generally Cibinic, "Cancellation of Solicitations: Are Bids and Proposals Sweeter the Second Time Around?" 7 Nash & Cibinic Rep. ¶ 36 (July 1993).

108. Airborne Services, Inc., Comp. Gen. Dec. B-221894 et al., 86-1 CPD ¶ 523, 28 GC ¶ 186.

109. See generally Pasley, "Unconventional Methods of Procurement," Briefing Papers No. 69-4 (Aug. 1969), 1 BPC 397.

110. FAR 14.502.

111. FAR 14.501.

112. FAR 14.503-1.

113. FAR 14.503-2.

COMPETITIVE NEGOTIATION

4

A. Conditions Permitting Use

B. Requests For Proposals Or Quotations
   1. RFP vs. RFQ
   2. Standard Forms
   3. Soliciting Offers
   4. Amendments
   5. Preproposal Conferences
   6. Evaluation Factors
   7. Cancellation

C. Proposal Preparation & Submission
   1. Proposal Preparation
   2. Best Response
   3. Timeliness

D. Discussions
   1. Award Without Discussions
   2. Competitive Range Concept
   3. Scope Of Discussions

E. Best & Final Offers

F. Contract Types
   1. Fixed-Price Contracts
   2. Cost-Reimbursement Contracts
   3. Other Contract Types

G. Postaward Notice & Debriefing

H. Protests

As noted in Chapter 3, procurement by sealed bidding is one of the Government's two basic methods of contracting under the Competition in Contracting Act (CICA). When sealed bidding is not used, the procurement will be conducted by the use of competitive negotiation.[1]

Procurement by negotiation and the use of competitive proposals enables the Government—to the extent that it is possible in the federal procurement context—to select the successful contractor in a manner similar to that used in the commercial marketplace. That is, unlike sealed bidding—where the evaluation procedure is highly objective, and where award, if made at all, *must* be made to the responsible bidder submitting the lowest, responsive bid—competitive proposals permit the Contracting Officer to be considerably more subjective in determining the winning contractor. He is free to consider, among other things, the offeror's particular *experience* with what is being procured, the offeror's *technical and management capability*, available and reliable *cost information*, and the *contract type* the offeror is willing to accept in case of award.

Competitive proposals will be used where the appropriate conditions are present. Note particularly that, except for sole-source procurements, competitive proposals do not represent any reduction in competition. Indeed, the FAR requires that procurement by competitive proposals be conducted on a full and open competitive basis to the same extent as procurement by sealed bidding.[2] Moreover, if the procurement must be conducted on a sole-source basis, the Contracting Officer must justify this requirement and take steps, whenever possible, to avoid resort to subsequent noncompetitive procurements.

This chapter will discuss (a) the conditions permitting use of competitive proposals, (b) requests for proposals and requests for quotations, (c) the preparation and submission of proposals, (d) requirements regarding discussions with offerors submitting offers within the "competitive range," (e) "best and final" offers, (f) the varied contract types available, and (g) postaward procedures and protests.

A. CONDITIONS PERMITTING USE

Under the FAR, sealed bids will be used in a procurement if the following four conditions are present:[3]

(1) Time permits the solicitation, submission, and evaluation of sealed bids.

(2) Award will be made on the basis of price and other price-related factors.

(3) It is not necessary to conduct discussions with the responding offerors.

(4) There is a reasonable expectation of receiving more than one bid.

If any of these conditions is not present, the Contracting Officer may decide to procure through the use of competitive proposals. He need only provide a brief written explanation citing which of the four conditions has not been met. He need not give any additional documentation or justification.

Obviously, the CICA requirement for "full and open competition" continues in effect, and the Contracting Officer is admonished to use good judgment in selecting the procedure that best meets the needs of the Government.[4] Moreover, if sealed bids are not appropriate, "any combination of competitive procedures (e.g., two-step sealed bidding)" may be used.[5]

B. REQUESTS FOR PROPOSALS OR QUOTATIONS

The "jargon" in competitive proposal procurements varies somewhat from that in sealed bid procurements. Instead of a "bid" there is a "proposal," in place of a "bidder" is an "offeror," and rather than an "Invitation for Bids" (IFB) either a "Request for Proposals" (RFP) or a "Request for Quotations" (RFQ) is used.

1. RFP vs. RFQ

According to the FAR, RFPs and RFQs are used in negotiated acquisitions "to communicate Government requirements to prospective contractors and to solicit proposals or quotations from them."[6] Originally, there was a technical distinction between the terms "RFP" and "RFQ." An RFP was used to solicit firm offers which, upon acceptance, became binding contracts. An RFQ, on the other hand, was used only to "test the market" (i.e., to solicit quotations that were not offers but merely indications of what prices might be expected). For instance, if an agency wanted to decide whether to exercise an option at the price specified in a contract, it might first wish to determine if a lower price could be obtained through an independent procurement. For that purpose, it would issue an RFQ. But this distinction has become blurred over the years, and the terms RFP and RFQ—particularly at the subcontract level—are generally used interchangeably. Only occasionally is the difference any longer important. In one case, for example, a protest was based on the argument that a reasonable acceptance period for a quote had expired when the Government made the award. The Comptroller General denied the protest, finding that the quotation received in response to the RFQ was not an offer and therefore could not be accepted by the agency to create a binding contract. Consequently, the concept of a bid acceptance period did not apply to the case.[7]

2. Standard Forms

Standard forms are used for competitive proposals in much the same way as they are used for sealed bids (see Chapter 3, Section A.1). For example, a solicitation for supplies and services to be obtained through competitive proposals will be made—as for a sealed bid procurement—on Standard Form 33 (see Figure 3-1 in Chapter 3). Although the same form is used in both types of procurements, a prospective offeror can easily determine which method of procurement applies by looking at the form to see whether the IFB or RFP square has been checked. The Government's procedures for preparation of an RFP are detailed in the FAR.[8]

3. Soliciting Offers

Offers are solicited by the same method that is used in sealed bidding (see Chapter 3, Section B). That is, announcements are placed in appropriate publications, including the *Commerce Business*

Daily, and mailing lists or electronic notices are used. Moreover, an interested firm may request a copy of the RFP from the agency. Such requests must be honored by the agency. In denying a protest by an incumbent contractor (who had been inadvertently left off a new mailing list), the Comptroller General noted that the agency (a) properly synopsized the procurement in the *Commerce Business Daily*, (b) posted a notice regarding it at several locations, and (c) sent solicitation packages to 11 firms. These actions, it was held, gave the incumbent contractor *constructive notice* of the solicitation and placed on it the burden of obtaining a copy of the RFP.[9]

4. Amendments

If, after issuance of an RFP—but before the closing date for submission of proposals—it becomes necessary to (1) make a significant change in quantity, specifications, or delivery schedule, (2) make any changes in closing dates, or (3) correct a defect or ambiguity in the solicitation, any change must be accomplished by issuing an amendment to the RFP.[10] The FAR provides that if an amendment is necessary, the period of time remaining before closing and the possible need for extending this period because of the amendment must also be considered.[11]

Any information given to one prospective offeror concerning an RFP must be promptly furnished to all other prospective offerors as a solicitation amendment if the information would be necessary for the other offerors to submit their proposals or if the lack of the information could be prejudicial to a prospective offeror.[12] The information must be supplied whether or not a preproposal conference (discussed below) is to be held.

5. Preproposal Conferences

It is common, particularly in complex procurements, to hold preproposal conferences after an RFP has been issued but before the proposals are prepared. The purpose of such conferences is to brief the prospective offerors to make certain they understand the RFP's requirements and to give them an opportunity to obtain clarifications and explanations.[13] If a preproposal conference is held, it is prudent (although not mandatory) for prospective offerors to attend the conference because questions and answers are often transcribed and distributed to all attendees. If attendance is not possible, minutes of the meeting should be requested.

The conference will be conducted by the Contracting Officer or his representative and will be attended by Government technical and legal personnel as appropriate.[14] Note that conferees will be advised that (a) remarks and explanations at the conference shall not qualify the terms of the solicitation, and (b) the terms of the solicitation and specifications remain unchanged unless the solicitation is amended in writing.[15]

6. Evaluation Factors

Because multiple evaluation factors are permitted in competitive proposals, the RFP must adequately disclose all the significant *factors* and *subfactors* (both price-related and non-price-related) that will be considered and the *relative importance* of the combined technical factors and price.[16] As the Comptroller General has noted, "each offeror has a right to know whether the procurement is intended to achieve a minimum standard at the lowest cost or whether cost is secondary to quality."[17] This statement is based on the primary goal of Government contracts—competition. Competition would not be served if offerors were not given any idea of the relative values of technical excellence and price.

There will ordinarily not be any ground for questioning the type and number of evaluation factors, provided they are set forth in the RFP and reasonably relate to the purposes of the procurement.[18] The factors used depend on the particular circumstances. Evaluation factors, especially for procurements involving research and development, fall into three major categories: technical, management, and cost. Separate evaluations are generally conducted by independent groups within the Government procurement agency with respect to the offeror's technical and management proposals and the offeror's price proposal.

Negotiations are frequently held in two phases: (1) a preliminary qualification phase involving a review of the offeror's technical and management proposals to determine those offerors selected for further negotiation, and (2) subsequent discussions of the pricing proposals submitted by the qualified offerors. Such procedures attempt to segregate technical decisions from pricing decisions. However, in many instances, the award process may include a balancing of technical and pricing factors as a composite decision, assuming acceptable standards of technical and management performance are met by the prospective contractor.

The evaluation factors and their relative weights—as stated in the RFP—must be used in the actual evaluation on the theory that once all the offerors are informed of the criteria against which their proposals are to be evaluated, the procuring agency must adhere to those criteria (or inform all offerors of any changes made in the evaluation scheme).[19] Thus, it was held in one decision involving a protest of a contract awarded under an RFQ that all offers would have to be reevaluated where the relative weight of price was changed by the procuring agency from 30% to 50%.[20]

While the evaluation factors themselves and the relative importance assigned to them must be set forth in the RFP or RFQ, the precise numerical weights of each factor and/or subcriterion need not be indicated.[21] In this regard, an agency decision not to award a contract to the offeror whose proposal received the highest number of technical evaluation points has been held proper on the ground that point scores are not determinative of the outcome but are merely guides for agency decisionmaking.[22] In one procurement of office automation systems, the agency issued a solicitation stating that it was more concerned with obtaining superior technical features than in making award at the lowest price, and that award would be determined by comparing differences in the value of technical features with the differences in overall cost to the Government. The General Services Administration Board of Contract Appeals (GSBCA) ruled that an agency has considerable discretion in conducting a price/technical tradeoff, and all the agency needed to do in this case was present a reasoned analysis showing that the Government expected to receive benefits commensurate with the price premium it would have to pay.[23]

"Best value" source selection is now widely used in negotiated procurements. Under these procedures, an agency reserves the right to trade off cost or technical considerations in selecting the successful offeror according to specific evaluation criteria stated in the solicitation.[24]

7. Cancellation

The Government may cancel an RFP or RFQ after the submission of proposals but before award for the same basic reasons that justify cancellation of an IFB (see Chapter 3, Section H.2).[25] Cancellation may be proper even if there have been extensive negotiations with one of the offerors.[26] Note, however, that the GSBCA has cautioned that "solicitations should not be canceled save for the most pressing of reasons," and "when the most advantageous offer departs from the stated requirements of the solicitation...the solution is to amend rather than cancel the solicitation."[27]

Cancellation can be based on a variety of circumstances—for example: (a) the *changed needs* of the Government where the Government can realize substantial savings by a change not contemplated at the time of original solicitation,[28] (b) subsequent realization that the procurement was *not justified*,[29] (c) a *defective specification* included in the solicitation which so seriously affects the procurement that it cannot be cured by amendment,[30] or (d) a *lack of adequate competition* because of defects in the solicitation and a short response time.[31] Generally, the cancellation of an RFP or RFQ is difficult to challenge because cancellation is a matter of Contracting Officer discretion. Moreover, unlike rejection of all bids after bid opening in a sealed bid procurement, offers in a negotiated procurement have not been exposed. In one case, the Comptroller General found cancellation justified because the agency anticipated "drastic budget cuts" even though it had already notified the protester that it was the apparent successful offeror.[32]

C. PROPOSAL PREPARATION & SUBMISSION

1. Proposal Preparation

Obviously, the same care should be given to preparing the response to an RFP or RFQ as to the preparation of a bid (see

Chapter 3, Section C). As a checklist for preparing a proposal, contractors should, at a minimum, do all of the following:

(1) Ascertain whether the RFP or RFQ is complete with all required pages and attachments included.

(2) Review and carefully follow instructions for preparing and submitting the proposal or quotation.

(3) Seek clarification of the specifications or other requirements of the contract, if necessary.

(4) Take into consideration each aspect of the RFP or RFQ, including the technical requirements, production plan, subcontract quotations, and competitive factors.

2. Best Response

Sometimes, tactical considerations will motivate an offeror not to submit its best response initially based on the rationale that if the best is "saved" until a later stage in the negotiations, there will be a better opportunity for the offeror to fully (or more nearly) achieve its various technical and price objectives. This approach may have some validity, but it also has some potential shortcomings.

The most obvious danger is that the response will be considered to be outside the "competitive range" for the procurement (discussed below in Section D) and thus eliminated from further consideration. The other risk is that the Government may—as it is entitled to do—award a contract without any discussions with the offerors and without ever requesting best and final offers. This approach may be followed by the Government when (a) it is clear that acceptance of the most favorable initial proposal will result in a fair price, and (b) the RFP or RFQ contains a notice to offerors that award may be made without any discussion.[33]

3. Timeliness

Timeliness in the submission of an initial proposal is as important and strictly enforced as it is in sealed bidding. Failure to submit the initial proposal on the exact closing date will usually result in its rejection.

Late proposals are handled in the same manner as late bids or modifications in sealed bid procurements (see Chapter 3, Section D.4).[34] Formerly, the Government had discretion to consider late proposals when it was in the Government's best interests to do so. This exception no longer exists. The Contracting Officer is now required under the FAR to notify the offeror promptly, when it is clear a proposal was received late, that the proposal will not be considered.[35] The FAR also now recognizes that a late proposal (like a late sealed bid) will be considered if sent by "U.S. Postal Service Express Mail Next Day Service" to the Contracting Officer not later than 5 P.M. two working days (which excludes weekends and federal holidays) prior to the date specified for receipt of bids.[36]

The National Aeronautics and Space Administration FAR Supplement is more liberal in treating late proposals than the FAR provisions discussed above. Under those provisions, a late proposal may be considered if there is a probability of (1) a significant reduction in cost to the Government, or (2) technical improvement to the product, provided that (a) the offeror had an excusable reason for the delay, (b) the failure of the proposal to arrive on time is due solely to a delay in the mails for which the offeror was not responsible, or (c) only one proposal was received.[37]

Contracting Officers have the option of allowing offerors to submit *facsimile proposals*. In making the determination of whether to authorize the use of facsimile proposals, the Contracting Officer must consider the following factors: (a) anticipated proposal size and volume, (b) urgency of the requirement, (c) frequency of price changes, (d) availability, reliability, speed, and capacity of the receiving facsimile equipment, and (e) adequacy of administrative procedures and controls for receiving, identifying, recording, and safeguarding facsimile proposals and ensuring their timely delivery to the proposal opening location.[38]

D. DISCUSSIONS

1. Award Without Discussions

Normally, in competitive proposal procurements, written or oral discussions must be held with all offerors in the "competitive range."[39] However, award may be made *without* discussions on the basis of initial proposals if the solicitation stated that evaluation of proposals and award would be made without discussions unless determined to be necessary.[40] Such award may also be based on non-cost- or non-price-related factors provided the relative importance of the factors and any "significant subfactors" are listed in the solicitation.[41]

Note that an award without discussions can only be made if the offer is accepted *as submitted*. This rule is strictly applied. Virtually any discussion with any offeror will require that negotiations be held with all offerors within the competitive range. For instance, in one case, a contract was to be awarded on the basis of initial proposals, but the Contracting Officer allowed the offeror to substitute certain key personnel in the proposal. This was construed to constitute "discussions," thus requiring that discussions be held with the other offeror.[42]

An offeror cannot insist that the Contracting Officer accept its initial proposal, even if it appears that the proposal is technically the best and has the lowest price. Such a decision is solely within the discretion of the Contracting Officer.

Protests in this area are frequent and have resulted in holdings that an award to other than the low offeror is proper where (a) the low offeror's proposal was nonconforming[43] or (b) the urgency of the procurement provided justification.[44] Obviously, where discussions are held, they must be conducted on an equal basis or the award will be set aside.[45]

2. Competitive Range Concept

As mentioned above, unless award is made without discussions on the basis of initial proposals, written or oral discussions *must* be conducted with all responsible offerors within the "competitive range." The concept of competitive range is thus an important one.

In determining the competitive range, the Contracting Officer must basically consider (1) the merits of the technical proposal, (2) its price, and (3) the responsibility of the offeror. Responsiveness (discussed below) is usually *not* a factor to be considered unless the offeror specifically refuses to comply with one of the material requirements of the solicitation. Of course, in the event the proposal is not within the competitive range technically, it is not necessary to consider price, responsibility, or any other factors.

The general rule is that a proposal is in the competitive range "unless it is so technically inferior or out of line with regard to price that meaningful negotiations are precluded."[46] This requirement is based on the concept that the basic purpose of the competitive range is to include all proposals that have a reasonable chance of being selected for award. Thus, in one case, retaining a proposal within the competitive range even though it was initially deemed technically unacceptable was proper,[47] and excluding a proposal ranked as "marginal" based solely on technical considerations was in error in another case.[48]

a. Determining The Range. On major competitive procurements, it is common to have one agency team score the proposals from a technical standpoint and another team analyze the proposed cost or price. In this process, each part of the proposal is usually assigned a numerical score based on the agency's analysis. But it is not always necessary that proposals be so graded.

In establishing evaluation criteria and scoring, it is improper to base eligibility for the competitive range on a predetermined passing grade. Likewise, it is impermissible to exclude all proposals other than a specified number of the best proposals (for example, the three highest-scored proposals). Rather, the objective should be to include in the competitive range *all* proposals that have a chance of award. As stated in the FAR: "When there is doubt as to whether a proposal is in the competitive range, the proposal should be included."[49]

Although the Comptroller General will not disturb a determination of the competitive range where the Contracting Officer had a reasonable basis for the decision, there are logical limits on the Contracting Officer's discretion. To exclude a proposal, the Contracting Officer must find that it (a) is so high in cost or so technically inferior as to preclude any possibility of meaningful negotiation, or (b) requires such major revision as to amount to a total resubmission.[50]

Once an offer is included in the competitive range, the offer may still be dropped from the competition. If the proposal, after further submissions by the offeror, is deemed so insufficient that the Contracting Officer decides that the offeror will not be able to improve its proposal adequately, the offer may then be excluded.

b. Responsiveness-Responsibility Relationship. Under sealed bidding, a bid must be *responsive* to be eligible for award. That is, it must represent an unqualified undertaking to perform in accordance with the terms of the IFB. This is not so—in a technical sense—in the case of competitive proposals. The concept of competitive range, which is established to determine whether a proposal is or can be made acceptable, has taken the place of the test of responsiveness. On the other hand, the Government always has a right to insist that the requirements of the solicitation be met regardless of the method of procurement. Therefore, an offeror's refusal to agree to meet a given requirement can result in rejection of its proposal.

If the offeror disagrees with some aspect of the RFP, tactical considerations—as well as the nature and magnitude of the disagreement—will all enter into the decision of when to call the matter to the Government's attention. Thus, the problem may be raised prior to responding to the RFP, in the proposal, or when negotiations take place. Certainly, if the disagreement could result in an amendment to the RFP, the offeror should discuss it with a responsible official at an early stage in the procurement.

Contractor responsibility is as important a consideration in negotiated procurement as it is in sealed bidding. Consequently, if the Government finds an offeror to be nonresponsible prior to establishing the competitive range, the offeror may be excluded on that basis alone.

3. Scope Of Discussions

In the event that written or oral discussions are held with offerors within the competitive range (i.e., an award is not made on the basis of initial proposals), the scope, form, and content of the discussions are generally left to the discretion of the Contracting Officer.[51] These discussions need not take any particular form—they may be conducted by letter,[52] by telephone, or in face-to-face meetings—as long as they are "meaningful." A telephone discussion (and nothing more), if meaningful, would be adequate.

In his discussions with competitive offerors, a Contracting Officer should (1) point out *specific* deficiencies in the offer (a vague inquiry will not suffice),[53] (2) address *all* deficiencies and ambiguities in the offer, however characterized (i.e., he cannot select some deficiencies and omit others that could adversely affect the offeror's revised proposal),[54] and (3) advise the offeror of those aspects of the proposal which may be *acceptable but weak*.[55]

Full discussions obviously give offerors a better opportunity to support or revise their proposals and thereby help to achieve the full competition that remains the Government's goal even in a negotiated procurement. Negotiations should inform offerors within the competitive range of the areas in which their proposals are believed to be deficient so that they can have an opportunity to support or revise their proposals.[56] *Fairness* is the key concept. For example, in one case, the Government's failure to tell an offeror to bring its project director to discussions (where all other offerors were so advised) caused the negotiations to be defective.[57]

A Contracting Officer's discretion is not unlimited, however, as made clear in the FAR. For example, it is not proper for him to engage in the course of his discussions in what have become known as "auction techniques." These include (a) indicating to an offeror a price that must be met to obtain further consideration, or (b) informing the offeror that its price is not low in relation to another offer. On the other hand, it is considered permissible to inform an offeror that its price is thought by the Government to be "unrealistic" or "too high."[58]

In addition, the FAR prohibits what is referred to as "technical leveling" or "technical transfusion." It provides that discussions may not disclose (1) the strengths or weaknesses of competing offers or (2) any information from an offeror's proposal which would allow another offeror to improve his proposal.[59] Problems in this area are most pronounced in the procurement of research and development contracts, where the specifications are usually performance-oriented and the Government is interested primarily in the offerors' innovative and independent approaches. In these situations, it is likely that the discussions will be relatively limited to avoid technical transfusions. The Comptroller General has indicated approval of this approach.[60] Common sense must be used in determining whether technical leveling or transfusion have, in fact, occurred and (if either occurred) whether a new procurement is necessary. For example, the GSBCA denied a protest in which an offeror alleged that the disclosure of a list of non-complying products of other offerors by the contracting agency's attorney resulted in technical transfusion. It was held that the effects of the disclosure were minimized by the solicitation modification that had been issued and the large number of items that were being acquired (which made information about a few of them less significant).[61]

E. BEST & FINAL OFFERS

The FAR provides that at the conclusion of discussions, the Contracting Officer must establish a common cut-off date for the submission of best and final offers.[62] If *oral* notification of best and final offers is given, it must be confirmed in writing, and the written notification must advise the offerors that (a) discussions have been concluded, (b) they are being given the opportunity to submit a "best and final" offer, and (c) if any such offer is submitted, it must be received by the date and time specified.[63]

It is not necessary that best and final offers be limited to one round.[64] In some cases, two or more rounds may be required. For example, after the first round the number of units required by the Government may be changed, there may be additions to the work, the Contracting Officer may become aware of inadequacies in the specifications, or he may recognize that material advice has been given to one offeror but not to all offerors within the competitive range. In any of these (or similar) situations, an additional round of best and final offers will likely be necessary.

An offeror may not insist that another round of best and final offers be solicited, however. Thus, where an offeror has won the contract and the discussions do not affect price, quality, quantity, delivery, specifications, or performance (unless the price is reduced to the Government's advantage), further proposals are not required. In some cases, for instance, Contracting Officers may do little more than request the submission of a cost and pricing form, or visit the prevailing offeror's plant to verify statements in the final proposal.

If substantive negotiations take place *after* a best and final offer, however, the Contracting Officer is required to call for another round of offers or reestablish the competitive range, depending on how significant the change underlying the negotiations is. The key to what must be done lies in (a) the change's effect on price, quantity, quality, or other material aspects of the RFP and (b) the fairness to other offerors.[65]

F. CONTRACT TYPES

One of the principal advantages of competitive proposals is the flexibility provided in the type of contract that can be used. These contract types fall into two broad categories: (1) fixed-price and (2) cost-reimbursement. In contrast, in sealed bid procurements, only two variations of fixed-price contracts—the firm-fixed-price or fixed-price with economic price adjustment—may be used.

It is frequently not practical to use fixed-price contracts in competitive proposals because of some (often substantial) uncertainty in the design, the specifications, or the costs of performance. In these circumstances, an alternative contract form must be used, as illustrated below in the discussion of contract types set forth in the FAR. This discussion is supplemented by the chart appearing in Figure 4-1 later in this chapter. The Government has available to it many alternative types of contracts that can be used to accomplish its objectives (for example, maximizing incentive and reducing the cost of administration).

Note that the basic method of establishing profit objectives in Defense Department contracts is known as the "Weighted Guidelines Method." It involves consideration—on an objective basis—of various "profit factors" (contractor effort, risk, facilities investment, special factors). The method used in negotiating a profit objective will vary depending on the contract's type (cost, fixed-price, etc.) and objective (supplies, construction, research and development, or services).[66]

1. Fixed-Price Contracts

Under the FAR, a variety of fixed-price contracts are available to a Contracting Officer.[67] Such contracts are not subject to adjustment based on the contractor's cost experience (except where the contracts provide for escalation or incentive profit). They place the maximum risk on the contractor (while also promising the greatest potential for profit) and impose the minimum administrative burden on the Government.[68]

a. Firm-Fixed-Price. The firm-fixed-price (FFP) contract,[69] which was discussed earlier in Chapter 2, Section D.3, may provide for (a) a specific quantity without change (the most common), (b) a fixed quantity with an option for additional units, or (c) an indefinite quantity which could allow the Government to direct deliveries or performance at designated places and times. Other variations are also possible, namely one type of FFP contract—called a firm-fixed-price, level-of-effort term contract—which obligates the contractor to provide a certain level of effort for a specific period of time on work that can be stated only in general terms.[70]

b. Fixed-Price With Economic Price Adjustment. The Contracting Officer may also use a fixed-price contract with economic price adjustment.[71] This contract arrangement provides for a fixed price which may be adjusted either upward or downward based upon certain contingencies that are specifically defined in the contract. For example, the adjustment may be based on an increase or decrease in the national (or a local) wage or material index, the "wholesale price index," or some other appropriate standard. Normally, there should not be a ceiling or floor for the adjustment. Such contracts limit some of the contractor's risk, particularly in inflationary times, and may at the same time reduce the Government's overall cost because offerors need not provide a contingency for unanticipated increases in labor and material costs.

c. Fixed-Price Incentive. Another type of contract available under the general fixed-price category is the fixed-price incentive (FPI) contract.[72] Under this type of contract, the parties negotiate a target cost, a target profit, a price ceiling, and a formula for establishing the actual profit to be paid. For example, a contract formula could provide a sharing ratio of 70-30 for costs over or under the target cost (with the Government's share being the larger) and a price ceiling of 120%. The ceiling is the maximum amount the Government is obligated to pay. If actual costs then exceed the target cost by $100,000, the Government would pay $70,000, the contractor $30,000, and the contractor's profit would be reduced accordingly. An alternate form of FPI contract, where costs are uncertain at the outset, provides for successive targets based on cost experience during performance. The point at which new targets would be fixed would be stated in the contract.

d. Fixed-Price Redeterminable. Yet another type of fixed-price contract is known as the fixed-price redeterminable contract.[73] Such contracts provide for price redeterminations to be made at various times during contract performance. Redeterminable contracts are virtually never used by the Government.

2. Cost-Reimbursement Contracts

Cost-reimbursement-type contracts are used when the uncertainties involved in contract performance are of such magnitude that the cost of performance cannot be estimated with sufficient reasonableness to permit use of any type of fixed-price contract.[74] In addition, to use a cost-reimbursement contract, it is essential that (1) the contractor's accounting system be adequate for determining costs applicable to the contract, (2) appropriate surveillance by Government personnel during performance be maintained to give reasonable assurance that inefficient or wasteful methods are not being used, (3) it be shown not only that a cost-reimbursement contract is less costly than another type but also that the subject of the procurement could not practically be obtained without using such a contract, and (4) statutory limits on price or fee be taken into account.[75]

As with fixed-price contracts, the Contracting Officer has a variety of cost-reimbursement-type contracts available under the FAR. This type of contract substantially increases the Government's administrative costs and places little—if any—cost risk on the contractor. To control the costs and protect the Government to the maximum extent possible, the Contracting Officer (a) attempts to use a contract type that will increase the contractor's incentive to reduce and control costs, and (b) fixes an estimated cost of performance which the contractor cannot exceed without the Contracting Officer's express approval.[76] Thus, even in a cost-reimbursement contract, the Government's cost exposure is limited by the "ceiling" on costs. At the same time, however, the contractor is protected because it is not required to complete performance within the cost estimate. That is, the contractor is normally permitted to stop performance if the Government does not agree to allow the contractor to exceed the total estimated cost established when work was commenced. There are five types of cost-reimbursement contracts recognized in the FAR.

a. Cost. The Contracting Officer may choose a cost contract with no profit to the contractor.[77] Generally, this type of contract is used with nonprofit organizations.

b. Cost-Sharing. Where a research project is involved and some benefits may accrue to the contractor from that research, a cost-sharing contract may be used.[78] The sharing can be based on as simple a formula as a 50-50 allocation of costs to each party. Or, it may be based on some other ratio or formula. In any event, the contractor under a cost-sharing contract agrees to assume some of the cost performance and forgo any profit.

c. Cost-Plus-Incentive-Fee. A third type of cost-reimbursement contract is a cost-plus-incentive-fee (CPIF) contract.[79] Under this arrangement, a contractor is reimbursed for all allowable costs expended and is also given a profit that varies with the actual costs incurred. The contract usually contains a target cost, a target profit (known as the "target fee"), and a formula for determining the actual profit to be paid the contractor. The formula includes a minimum and maximum fee which represent the lower and upper limits on the profit a contractor may earn.

There are similarities and differences between the FPI contract discussed above in Section F.1 and a CPIF contract. For example, both contract types have a target cost, a target profit (or fee), and a formula for determining actual profit after contract performance. On the other hand, FPI and CPIF contracts differ in that under FPI contracts there is no guarantee of a minimum profit or a limit on the maximum profit that can be earned, and the contractor must complete performance and bear all costs incurred in excess of the price ceiling. In contrast, under a CPIF contract, the contractor is reimbursed all of its costs and does get at least a minimum fee even though there is a limitation on the maximum fee. And, the contractor does not have to complete performance beyond the amount set forth as the estimated cost of performance.

The Government may choose to include multiple incentives (i.e., incentives other than cost) in a CPIF contract. Structuring multiple incentives is a difficult task and often requires highly technical skills on the part of both the Government and the contractor. Nevertheless, an incentive to improve performance (for example, to increase speed, decrease waste, improve reliability) or advance the date of delivery can be factored into the profit formula.

d. Cost-Plus-Award-Fee. Another type of cost-reimbursement contract is a cost-plus-award-fee (CPAF) contract.[80] It is a variation of the CPIF incentive concept in that it allows the application of incentives in contracts that are not susceptible to factors such as precise measurement of cost efficiency and technical performance. The fee established consists of two parts: (1) a fixed amount that does not vary with performance and (2) an award amount in addition to the fixed amount sufficient to provide motivation for excellence in contract performance in areas such as quality, timeliness, ingenuity, and cost effectiveness. The amount of the award fee to be paid is based on a subjective evaluation by the Government of the quality of the contractor's performance, judged by the criteria set forth in the contract.

The determination of the amount of the award fee is final and cannot be challenged before the agency boards of contract appeals, although sometimes the determination is appealable to an official in the contracting agency. Despite its "finality," however, the Government's determination is subject to limited board review to decide whether it was arbitrary or capricious.[81] During the course of performance, the contractor is often given a "report card" on its performance and afforded an opportunity to comment on the quality of its performance and ultimately on the amount of award fee to which it is entitled.

e. Cost-Plus-Fixed-Fee. The fifth (and most common) type of cost-reimbursement contract is the cost-plus-fixed-fee (CPFF) contract (which was briefly mentioned in Chapter 2, Section D.3).[82] The CPFF contract provides for the reimbursement of all allowable costs expended by the contractor, as well as payment to the contractor of a fee that remains fixed regardless of the contractor's actual cost experience. CPFF contracts offer the contractor virtually complete insulation from financial risks and, at the same time, guarantee payment of a fixed fee. As a result, they tend to minimize the contractor's incentive to perform in a cost efficient manner. Their use is therefore not recommended if one of the alternative contract types is available. However, if the contingencies of contract performance are such that use of another contract type is not practical, CPFF contracts may provide the only feasible alternative available.

3. Other Contract Types

In addition to the fixed-price and cost-reimbursement contracts discussed above, the FAR recognizes some other contract types.

A *time-and-materials* contract[83] is a hybrid of the fixed-price and cost-reimbursement contract. It is used where labor is provided on an indefinite quantity, fixed-price basis and materials are provided on a cost-reimbursement basis. Profit is included in the labor rates, but no fee is allowed with regard to the materials.

A *labor-hour* contract[84] is nearly identical to a time-and-materials contract. It does not require, however, that the contractor provide the materials.

Letter contracts[85] are not a truly distinct contract type. They are merely an abbreviated form for entering into a contract quickly. A letter contract contemplates that a fixed-price or cost-reimbursement contract will be executed within 180 days of the preliminary letter document.

A *basic ordering agreement*[86] (BOA) is also not truly a contract type but, rather, an agreement as to the terms and conditions that will apply to placing orders in future contracts when specific procurement needs arise.

G. POSTAWARD NOTICE & DEBRIEFING

After a contract is awarded by giving notice, either in writing or by electronic means, to the successful offeror, the agency must notify the unsuccessful offerors within three days that their proposals were not accepted.[87] This notice must include (1) the number of prospective contractors solicited, (2) the number of proposals received, (3) the name and address of each offeror receiving an award, (4) the items, quantities, and unit prices of each award, unless impracticable, and (5) a general statement of the reasons why the offeror's proposal was not accepted, unless it is otherwise obvious.[88]

Because offerors generally spend substantial time and effort in preparing their proposals, and to discourage the filing of bid protests, agencies must *debrief* unsuccessful offerors that request a debriefing within three days after receiving notice of the award.[89] This debriefing must be held, to the maximum extent possible, within five days after receipt of the request by the agency, and should include a complete evaluation of the significant weak or deficient factors contained in the losing offeror's proposal.[90] The debriefing may not include a point-by-point comparison of the debriefed offeror's offer with other offers, however, or disclose proprietary or confidential information.[91] An adequate debriefing can provide the basis on which offerors may improve future proposals and assure the offerors that the selection was handled fairly and in accordance with the applicable regulations and the provisions of the solicitation.

COMPETITIVE NEGOTIATION 4-23

Figure 4-1
CONTRACT TYPES

CONTRACT TYPE	AWARDED BY	CONTRACTOR COST RISK	MANAGEMENT BURDEN	NOTEWORTHY CONDITIONS FOR USE	BEST SUITED FOR
Firm-Fixed-Price [Price remains unchanged, regardless of actual cost experience]	Sealed Bidding or Competitive Proposals	Highest	Low	There must be clear specifications and ability to set realistic price for entire contract period.	Situations where there is prior cost experience, particularly for standard or modified commercial items.
Fixed-Price With Economic Price Adjustment [Specific cost elements are subject to upward, or downward, adjustment]	Sealed Bidding or Competitive Proposals	Moderate	Moderate	Labor and market contingencies must be specified. Care must be taken to eliminate any contingency allowance from contract price base to extent that adjustment is provided.	Situations where serious doubt exists as to stability of specific economic conditions during contract performance.
Fixed-Price Incentive [Contains formula under which profit (or loss) varies based upon actual cost experience and/or performance]	Competitive Proposals	Moderate	Moderate to High	Incentive provisions must have meaningful effect on manner in which contractor manages work. Cost incentives may be combined with incentives related to performance levels and delivery time.	Situations where nature of supplies or services is such that contractor will be motivated to control costs, improve performance, or expedite delivery.
Fixed-Price With Redeterminations [Price adjustments are negotiated either (a) during contract period, or (b) retroactively]	Competitive Proposals	Moderate to Low	High	Contractor's accounting system must be adequate to support price adjustment negotiations.	Situations where it is possible to negotiate fair and reasonable prices for initial period, but not for entire contract term. Rarely used.
Cost-Plus-Fixed-Fee [Contractor is reimbursed for all "allowable" costs and receives fee that remains unchanged]	Competitive Proposals	Lowest—fee is not subject to change	High	Contractor's accounting system must be adequate to support allowability of costs (this applies to all cost *reimbursement* contracts).	Situations where performance uncertainties are so great that the cost of performance cannot be estimated accurately enough to permit use of any other contract type.

continued

10/94

4-24 GOVERNMENT CONTRACT GUIDEBOOK

Fig. 4-1 / continued

CONTRACT TYPE	AWARDED BY	CONTRACTOR COST RISK	MANAGEMENT BURDEN	NOTEWORTHY CONDITIONS FOR USE	BEST SUITED FOR
Cost-Sharing [Contractor and Government share costs of performance—no fee is paid]	Competitive Proposals	Low, but contractor receives no fee	High	Contractor must agree to absorb portion of costs.	Situations where contractors are willing to absorb portions of costs because of potential benefits (new products, patents, prestige, etc.), usually in connection with research and development work of highly undefined nature.
Cost [Contractor is reimbursed for all "allowable" costs, but receives no fee]	Competitive Proposals	Low, but contractor receives no fee	High	Contractor's accounting system must be adequate for determining costs applicable to contract, and contractor will be subject to surveillance to assure use of efficient methods and effective cost controls.	Situations involving research, development, or facilities work by non-profit organizations and schools.
Cost-Plus-Incentive-Fee [Contractor is reimbursed for all "allowable" costs, and receives fee that varies based upon actual cost experience and/or performance]	Competitive Proposals	Low, but contractor risks loss of fee	High	Cost and performance incentives must be not only desirable, but also administratively practical.	Situations where it is possible to motivate contractor through negotiation of target cost and fee adjustment formula.
Time & Materials and Labor-Hour [Contractor is reimbursed (a) for time expended, at a fixed rate; and (b) for materials (not in Labor-Hour), at cost plus handling charge]	Competitive Proposals	Low to Moderate	High	Adequate controls for close Government surveillance to prevent inefficiency and waste.	Situations where Government knows types of goods and/or services required, but cannot estimate extent or duration of the work (e.g. repair, maintenance, or emergency services).

10/94

H. PROTESTS

The FAR provides that protests involving award of a negotiated procurement, either before or after actual award of the contract, are pursued in substantially the same manner as they would be in a sealed bid procurement.[92] Thus, as discussed in Chapter 3, Section G, there are a number of forums available for protests.

REFERENCES

1. See generally Shnitzer, "Competitive Negotiation/Edition II," Briefing Papers No. 83-10 (Oct. 1983), 6 BPC 237; Shnitzer, "Competitive Negotiation," Briefing Papers No. 75-4 (Aug. 1974), 3 BPC 217.
2. FAR 6.101.
3. FAR 6.401(a).
4. FAR 6.101(b).
5. FAR 6.102(c).
6. FAR 15.402(a).
7. Haworth, Inc., Comp. Gen. Dec. B-241583.5, 91-1 CPD ¶ 398, 33 GC ¶ 150.
8. See FAR 15.402.
9. Rut's Moving & Delivery Service, Inc., Comp. Gen. Dec. B-228406, 88-1 CPD ¶ 139, 30 GC ¶ 85.
10. FAR 15.410.
11. FAR 15.410(b).
12. FAR 15.410(c).
13. FAR 15.409(a).
14. FAR 15.409(b).
15. FAR 15.409(c).
16. 41 USC § 253a; 10 USC § 2305a.
17. Comp. Gen. Dec. B-176223, 52 Comp. Gen. 161, 1972 CPD ¶ 85. See also Federal Properties of R.I., Inc., Comp. Gen. Dec. B-218192.2, 85-1 CPD ¶ 508.

18. FAR 15.605.

19. Genasys Corp., Comp. Gen. Dec. B-187811, 56 Comp. Gen. 835, 77-2 CPD ¶ 60.

20. Dynelectron Corp., Comp. Gen. Dec. B-187057, 77-1 CPD ¶ 95. See also Lithos Restoration Ltd., Comp. Gen. Dec. B-247003.2, 92-1 CPD ¶ 379 (agency's failure to score all evaluation factors qualitatively was improper), 34 GC ¶ 352.

21. FAR 15.605(e).

22. Grey Advertising, Inc., Comp. Gen. Dec. B-184825, 55 Comp. Gen. 1111, 76-1 CPD ¶ 325.

23. Lockheed Missiles & Space Co. v. Department of the Treasury, GSBCA 11776-P et al., 93-1 BCA ¶ 25401, 1992 BPD ¶ 155, 34 GC ¶ 399, affd., 4 F.3d 955 (Fed. Cir. 1993), 12 FPD ¶ 81, 35 GC ¶ 560.

24. E.g., S-V Co., Comp. Gen. Dec. B-248566.3, 92-2 CPD ¶ 131. See generally Kenney & Sweeney, "Best Value Procurement," Briefing Papers No. 93-4 (Mar. 1993); Shnitzer & Humphrey, "The Scope of the Source Selection Official's Discretion," Briefing Papers No. 94-5 (Apr. 1994).

25. FAR 15.608(b).

26. Infodyne Systems Corp., Comp. Gen. Dec. B-185481, 76-2 CPD ¶ 33.

27. C.M.P. Corp., GSBCA 9015-P, 87-3 BCA ¶ 20075, 29 GC ¶ 345.

28. LEK Corp., Comp. Gen. Dec. B-185214, 76-2 CPD ¶ 153.

29. NJE Corp., Comp. Gen. Dec. B-185787, 76-2 CPD ¶ 117.

30. Environmental Protection Agency, Comp. Gen. Dec. B-184194, 76-2 CPD ¶ 50.

31. Note 26, supra.

32. Source AV, Inc., Comp. Gen. Dec. B-241155, 91-1 CPD ¶ 75, 33 GC ¶ 71.

33. FAR 15.610(a).

34. FAR 15.412.

35. FAR 15.412(d).

36. FAR 15.412, 14.304.

37. NASA FAR Supp. 18-15.412.

38. FAR 15.402(i), (j).

39. FAR 15.610(b).

COMPETITIVE NEGOTIATION   4-27

40. 41 USC § 253b(d).

41. FAR 52.215-16.

42. University of S.C., Comp. Gen. Dec. B-240208, 90-2 CPD ¶ 249, 32 GC ¶ 371.

43. Sterling Machine Co., Comp. Gen. Dec. B-236585, 89-2 CPD ¶ 409.

44. Raytheon Co., Comp. Gen. Dec. B-240333, 90-2 CPD ¶ 384, 33 GC ¶ 52.

45. SeaSpace, Comp. Gen. Dec. B-241564, 91-1 CPD ¶ 179, 33 GC ¶ 165.

46. Comp. Gen. Dec. B-164434, 48 Comp. Gen. 314, 1968 CPD ¶ 78, 10 GC ¶ 511. See also Alanthus Data Communications Corp., Comp. Gen. Dec. B-206946, 83-1 CPD ¶ 147.

47. National Assn. of State Directors of Special Education, Inc., Comp. Gen. Dec. B-233296, 89-1 CPD ¶ 189, 31 GC ¶ 97 (Note).

48. HSI-CCEC, Comp. Gen. Dec. B-240610, 90-2 CPD ¶ 465.

49. FAR 15.609(a).

50. PRC Computer Center, Inc., Comp. Gen. Dec. B-178205, 75-2 CPD ¶ 35.

51. Note 39, supra. See generally Shnitzer, "Discussions in Negotiated Procurements," Briefing Papers No. 91-4 (Mar. 1991), 9 BPC 363.

52. Stewart-Warner Corp., Comp. Gen. Dec. B-235774, 89-2 CPD ¶ 314.

53. Data Preparation, Inc., Comp. Gen. Dec. B-233569, 89-1 CPD ¶ 300.

54. Dynelectron Corp., Comp. Gen. Dec. B-193604, 79-2 CPD ¶ 50.

55. See FAR 15.610(c).

56. Comp. Gen. Dec. B-162387, 47 Comp. Gen. 336, 1967 CPD ¶ 51. See also Set Corp., Comp. Gen. Dec. B-207936, 83-1 CPD ¶ 409; CRC Systems, Inc., Comp. Gen. Dec. B-207847, 83-1 CPD ¶ 462; Tracor Marine, Inc., Comp. Gen. Dec. B-207285, 83-1 CPD ¶ 604, 25 GC ¶ 285.

57. Management Systems Designers, Inc., Comp. Gen. Dec. B-244383.4, 91-2 CPD ¶ 518, 34 GC ¶ 87.

58. FAR 15.610(e)(2). See generally Nash, "Postscript II: The Meaning of 'Technical Leveling'," 7 Nash & Cibinic Rep. ¶ 15 (Mar. 1993).

59. FAR 15.610(d), (e)(1).

60. Ocean Design Engrg. Corp., Comp. Gen. Dec. B-181079, 74-2 CPD ¶ 249.

61. Falcon Microsystems, Inc., GSBCA 10910-P, 91-1 BCA ¶ 23461, 1990 BPD ¶ 344, 33 GC ¶ 55, reconsideration denied, 91-1 BCA ¶ 23537, 1990 BPD ¶ 407.

62. FAR 15.611(b)(3).

63. FAR 15.611(a), (b). See also Woodward Assocs., Inc., Comp. Gen. Dec. B-216714, 85-1 CPD ¶ 274.

64. See FAR 15.611(c).

65. Microlog Corp., Comp. Gen. Dec. B-237486, 90-1 CPD ¶ 227.

66. See DFARS 215.902.

67. FAR subpt. 16.2.

68. FAR 16.202.

69. FAR 16.202–16.202-2.

70. FAR 16.207–16.207-3.

71. FAR 16.203–16.203-4.

72. FAR 16.204.

73. FAR 16.205–16.205-4 (prospective price redetermination); FAR 16.206–16.206-4 (retroactive price redetermination).

74. FAR 16.301-2.

75. FAR 16.301-3.

76. FAR 16.301-1.

77. FAR 16.302.

78. FAR 16.303.

79. FAR 16.304.

80. FAR 16.305.

81. Burnside-Ott Aviation Training Center, ASBCA 43184, 94-1 BCA ¶ 26590, 36 GC ¶ 137.

82. FAR 16.306.

83. FAR 16.601.

84. FAR 16.602.

85. FAR 16.603–16.603-4.

86. FAR 16.703.

87. E.g., 41 USC § 253b(d).

COMPETITIVE NEGOTIATION 4-29

88. FAR 15.1001(c)(1).
89. 41 USC § 253b(e).
90. Note 89, supra.
91. 41 USC § 253b(e)(3).
92. FAR 15.1004.

COSTS

5

A. Cost Principles
1. Applicability
2. Allowability
3. Reasonableness
4. Allocability
5. Selected Costs

B. Cost Accounting Standards
1. Applicability
2. Contractor Obligations
3. Disclosure Statements
4. Individual Standards

C. Truth In Negotiations Act
1. Applicability
2. Exemptions & Waiver
3. "Cost Or Pricing Data" Defined
4. Submission Of Data
5. Certification Of Data
6. Liability For Defective Data

D. Government Audit Rights
1. Procuring Agencies
2. General Accounting Office
3. Inspectors General

The subject of *costs* is as important as any in Government contracts, and its importance is maximized by the many problems involved in measuring and monitoring a contractor's costs. For one thing, Government contracts require the application of several accounting concepts that are not used in the conduct of commercial businesses. For another, costs that might be perfectly proper when judged under Internal Revenue Service or private accounting criteria are sometimes considered unallowable under Government contracts. Such costs are generally unallowable because of the provisions of a particular contract and the regulations that govern Government contract costs—the cost principles and the Cost Accounting Standards. As one federal court has astutely observed, the Government's costs policies "are not liberal; they forbid allocation to Government contracts of some true costs of doing business."[1] Moreover, monitoring contract costs requires broad audit rights on the Government's part and disclosure requirements for contractors.

This chapter discusses four major areas involving Government contract costs: (1) the cost principles, explaining how they affect allowability; (2) the Cost Accounting Standards, dealing with their impact on the rules for estimating, accumulating, and reporting contractor costs; (3) defective pricing as it relates to the disclosure of cost information to the Government; and (4) the Government's audit rights with respect to contractor books and records.

For an in-depth treatment of this important subject in Government procurement, the reader's attention is directed to Federal Publications' monthly periodical, GOVERNMENT CONTRACT COSTS, PRICING & ACCOUNTING REPORT, which deals with the subject of costs as well as with the related areas of accounting and pricing.

A. COST PRINCIPLES

The "cost principles" are set out in Part 31 of the FAR. They are the primary means of defining the costs that will be considered "allowable" by the Government in the negotiation and administration of its contracts. Using these principles—which, to some extent, are based on historic cost accounting—the Government measures what it will pay a particular contractor under cost-reimbursement or incentive contracts and also determines the extent of pricing adjustments under fixed-price contracts. Cost principles establish basic guidelines for the allowability of costs, and they also delineate specific categories of allowable or unallowable costs.

1. Applicability

Cost principles assume their greatest importance with regard to the allowability of costs expended under cost-reimbursement- or incentive-fee-type contracts. With respect to these types of contracts, what the contractor is paid for performing is governed, in significant part, by FAR Part 31.

In fixed-price-type contracts, the parties agree at the outset on the price the Government will pay for the work to be performed. The cost principles come into play in connection with such contracts when changes to a contract are negotiated (see Chapters 11 and 13) or when a contract is terminated (see Chapters 16 and 17). For example, if the Government changes the work called for under the contract, or if it suspends or stops work, the contractor is entitled to the increased cost of performance. In these circumstances, the amount of recovery will be based on the applicable cost principles. The "Pricing of Contract Modifications" clause, which is required to be incorporated into all Department of Defense (DOD) fixed-price contracts, sets forth this requirement as follows: "When costs are a factor in any price adjustment under this contract, the contract cost principles and procedures in FAR part 31 and [DOD FAR Supplement] part 231, in effect on the date of this contract, apply."[2]

Although the extent to which cost principles come into play depends, in large part, on the type of contract that has been awarded—fixed-price or cost-reimbursement—it should be noted that FAR Part 31 requires incorporation of the principles into all contracts where "cost analysis is performed," and for the "determination, negotiation or allowance of costs when required by a contract clause."[3] "Cost analysis" involves the evaluation of a contractor's judgmental factors used in estimating costs. Therefore, in the case of all negotiated contracts, even firm-fixed-price ones, FAR Part 31 cost principles could apply if cost analysis is performed by the Government.

Regarding applicability, it should be noted at the start that FAR Part 31 actually contains four sets of cost principles for the following types of contracts:

(1) Contracts with commercial organizations (FAR Subpart 31.2, which to a large degree also governs construction and architect-engineer contracts[4]).

(2) Contracts with educational institutions (FAR Subpart 31.3[5]).

(3) Contracts with state, local, and federally-recognized Indian tribal governments (FAR Subpart 31.6).

(4) Contracts with nonprofit organizations (FAR Subpart 31.7).

By far the most important of the four sets of cost principles—and the one that will be the focus in this chapter—is the one appearing in FAR Subpart 31.2 governing *commercial organization contracts*. Not only is this set the most extensive of the four, it is also the one to which most contracts will be subject since it covers supply, service, and construction contracts. For all practical purposes, the FAR Subpart 31.2 cost principles are "the" cost principles.

Note also that the FAR is the primary source for cost principles, but not the only source. Individual agencies, although subject to the FAR, may deviate from the FAR cost principles in their own individual agency regulations. Such deviations, however, will be minimal because of the FAR's requirement for advance approval by a designated official. FAR 31.101 provides as follows:

> In recognition of differing organizational characteristics, the cost principles and procedures in the succeeding subparts [FAR Subparts 31.2 through 31.7] are grouped basically by organizational type; e.g., commercial concerns and educational institutions. The overall objective is to provide that, to the extent practicable, all organizations of similar types doing similar work will follow the same cost principles and procedures. To achieve this uniformity, in-

dividual deviations concerning cost principles require advance approval of the agency head or designee in the case of civilian agencies and the National Aeronautics and Space Administration, and by the Director of Defense Procurement, Office of the Under Secretary of Defense for Acquisition (USD(A)DP) in the case of the Department of Defense. Agency supplements and class deviations require advance approval by either the USD(A)DP or Civilian Agency Acquisition Council, as appropriate.

2. Allowability

FAR Subpart 31.2 sets forth a general rule on the allowability of Government contract costs, listing five factors for determining allowability:[6]

(a) The factors to be considered in determining whether a cost is allowable include the following:

(1) Reasonableness.

(2) Allocability.

(3) Standards promulgated by the [Cost Accounting Standards] Board, if applicable; otherwise, generally accepted accounting principles and practices appropriate to the particular circumstances.

(4) Terms of the contract.

(5) Any limitations set forth in this subpart.

The factors listed as "(1)," "(2)," and "(5)" form the basis for the remainder of the discussion of cost principles in this chapter. The "Standards" mentioned in factor "(3)" are discussed at length below in Section B. The "generally accepted accounting principles and practices appropriate to the particular circumstances" also mentioned in factor "(3)" and the "[t]erms of the contract" mentioned in factor "(4)" do not lend themselves to discussion because they depend on individual facts and circumstances.

3. Reasonableness

The criteria set forth to determine whether a cost is "reasonable" for purposes of allowability are somewhat vague and subjective. The FAR provides that a "cost is reasonable if, in its nature and amount, it does not exceed that which would be incurred by a prudent person in the conduct of competitive business."[7]

A contractor's incurred costs are *not* presumed to be reasonable but must be proved reasonable by the contractor. The presumption of reasonableness previously established by case law was abolished by regulation in 1987.[8] This rule applies also to estimates of future costs (or unidentifiable costs), where the contractor also has the legal burden of establishing the reasonableness of its estimate. Neither the Government's nor the contractor's estimate is entitled to a presumption in its favor.[9]

A second key concept in determining reasonableness is that the Government will not be allowed to engage in "second guessing" the contractor's judgment. It is the contractor's judgment that is considered, not that of the Government or of some hypothetical (and extremely efficient) contractor. Therefore, it is not enough for the Government to say that the costs should have or could have been expended in a different (or more advantageous) manner. As long as the contractor's decision involves the use of reasonable judgment, that judgment will not be overruled.

As a practical matter, the Government has had relatively little success in disallowing costs solely on the basis of unreasonableness. Where it has been successful, the Government has established that the contractor abused its discretion, such as where a contractor retained a large, unproductive work force for longer than was prudent under the circumstances,[10] and where a contractor incurred excessive promotional costs with regard to the preparation of an unsolicited proposal.[11] Most frequently, however, the Government will not be able to have a cost deemed unreasonable on the basis of the contractor's judgmental decision. The concept of reasonableness (as it applies to cost-reimbursement contracts) was summed up by the Armed Services Board of Contract Appeals as follows:[12]

> The contracting officer's function is not that of a boss over the contractor, telling him what he can and cannot buy, whom he shall employ and how much he is allowed to pay employees. True, the contract bestows upon the contracting officer the authority to disapprove for reimbursement the costs involved in the contractor's performance, but

unless he is able to demonstrate that the contractor's acts, or the costs he incurs, violate the terms of the contract or the guides found in [the cost principles], it is the contracting officer's duty to approve the contractor's acts and to approve the costs thereof for reimbursement.

A Contracting Officer may attempt to eliminate the need for reasonableness determinations by including a requirement in the contract that his approval be obtained before a cost is incurred by the contractor. However, unless specifically called for by the contract, such prior approval is not required. Moreover, Government attempts to control costs through this device have not been successful because the Government must specify and justify the basis for refusing approval.[13]

4. Allocability

As indicated above, "allocability" is a factor listed in FAR Subpart 31.2 for determining allowability.[14] In its simplest terms, allocation of costs is the process of assigning costs to cost objectives. The FAR cost principles contain the following definition of allocability:[15]

> A cost is allocable if it is assignable or chargeable to one or more cost objectives on the basis of relative benefits received or other equitable relationship. Subject to the foregoing, a cost is allocable to a Government contract if it—
>
> (a) Is incurred specifically for the contract;
>
> (b) Benefits both the contract and other work, and can be distributed to them in reasonable proportion to the benefits received; or
>
> (c) Is necessary to the overall operation of the business, although a direct relationship to any particular cost objective cannot be shown.

In determining questions of allocability, it is always necessary to assess whether an allocable cost should be charged as a direct cost or as an indirect cost. The FAR defines a *direct cost* as "any cost that can be identified specifically with a particular final cost objective."[16] The provision goes on to say that costs "identified specifically with the contract are direct costs of the contract and are to be charged directly to the contract," and that "[a]ll costs specifically identified with other final cost objectives of the contractor are direct costs of those cost objectives and are not to be charged to the contract directly or indirectly."

In accordance with this definition, costs that are incurred for materials, labor, or other purposes that are clearly necessary for performance of a particular contract are direct costs of the contract. Even if a cost expenditure should eventually be determined to have been unnecessary for contract performance, it will nonetheless be allocable as a direct charge if the contractor reasonably believed it was necessary when it made the decision to incur the cost.[17] The legal test is sometimes referred to as the "but for" test (i.e., would the cost have been incurred but for the existence of the contract).

The FAR also defines an *indirect cost* as "one not directly identified with a single, final cost objective, but identified with two or more final cost objectives or an intermediate cost objective."[18] The provision requires that "[i]ndirect costs shall be accumulated by logical cost groupings with due consideration of the reasons for incurring such costs," and advises that "[c]ommonly, manufacturing overhead, selling expenses, and general and administrative (G&A) expenses are separately grouped."[19]

Cost allocations are essentially a function of the contractor's own accounting system. In this regard, it is clear that selection of an accounting system is the prerogative of the contractor's management, as long as the system follows generally accepted accounting principles and the Cost Accounting Standards (if they apply). The Government, accordingly, may not disturb a contractor's otherwise proper method of keeping its books solely in order to obtain a financial advantage. For the Government to require a change in a contractor's accounting system, it must either direct the change prospectively, pursuant to a statute or regulation, or show that the contractor's system is clearly inequitable.[20]

5. Selected Costs

In addition to describing the general rule governing cost allowability (discussed above in Section A.2), the FAR cost principles also *select* particular costs for special treatment.[21] In all,

51 specific types of costs are treated in the cost principles. These "selected costs" must not only meet the general requirements for allowability, they must also meet special criteria. Thus, even if a particular cost expenditure is eminently reasonable and allocable, it will be deemed unallowable if it is labeled as such in the selected costs provisions.

Note that if a cost is not specifically treated as a selected cost, the FAR Subpart 31.2 cost principles make it clear that the omission does not imply that the cost is either allowable or unallowable because the selected costs portion of Subpart 31.2 is not intended to "cover every element of cost."[22] When a particular cost is not treated, the determination of allowability will be based on the cost principles in general, as well as on the treatment of similar or related selected items. When more than one provision of the selected costs provisions of FAR Subpart 31.2 are relevant to a contractor cost, (a) the cost is apportioned among the applicable provisions, and (b) the determination of allowability of each portion is based on the guidance contained in the applicable provision. Where such apportionment cannot be accomplished, the determination of allowability will be based on the guidance in the provision that "most specifically deals with, or best captures the essential nature of, the cost at issue."[23]

Summarized below are the 51 selected costs provisions of FAR Subpart 31.2, treated in the order in which they appear in the FAR. The italicized headings reflect the provisions' titles exactly as given in the FAR.

(1) *Public relations and advertising costs.*[24] The only advertising costs that are allowable are those that are solely for (a) the recruitment of personnel required for performance of the contract, (b) the procurement of scarce items needed for performance, or (c) the disposal of scrap or surplus materials required during performance. Certain public relations costs are allowable—for example, the costs of responding to inquiries on company policies. However, costs of ceremonies, such as corporate celebrations and new product announcements, are unallowable. On the other hand, costs of promoting aerospace exports and foreign selling costs (including trade shows) are generally allowable.

(2) *Automatic data processing equipment leasing costs.*[25] Lease costs for automatic data processing equipment are allowable

only if the contractor can demonstrate annually, based on facts existing at the time of the lease-purchase decision, that the costs are reasonable and necessary for the conduct of the contractor's business and do not give rise to a "material equity" (option to renew or purchase at a bargain price, for example) in the facilities. Contracting Officer approval is also necessary if the costs are to be allocated entirely or in large part to Government negotiated contracts. Otherwise, only the costs of ownership that would have been incurred are allowable. Other limitations exist similar to those for general rental costs (see Item 35 below).

(3) *Bad debts.*[26] These costs (including related collection and legal costs) are unallowable.

(4) *Bonding costs.*[27] Bonding costs are allowable if they are required by the terms of a contract or required by the contractor in its business and (a) they are incurred in accordance with sound business practice, and (b) the rates and premiums are reasonable under the circumstances.

(5) *Civil defense costs.*[28] The costs of protective measures against the possible consequences of an enemy attack are generally allowable if the measures are undertaken on the contractor's premises and are directed by civil defense authorities. Civil defense costs that take the form of capital assets acquired for civil defense purposes are allowable through depreciation, but contributions to local civil defense funds or projects are not allowable.

(6) *Compensation for personal services.*[29] Compensation for personal services—broadly defined as "all remuneration paid currently or accrued, in whatever form and whether paid immediately or deferred, for services rendered by employees to the contractor during the period of contract performance"—is generally allowable if reasonable for the work performed.[30] Special forms of compensation for personal services are singled out in the selected cost provision for individual treatment. Provisions cover (a) compensation resulting from labor-management agreements, (b) salaries and wages, (c) domestic and foreign differential pay, (d) bonuses and incentive compensation,[31] (e) severance pay, (f) backpay, (g) stock options, stock appreciation rights, and phantom stock plans,[32] (h) pension costs,[33] (i) deferred com-

pensation, and (j) fringe benefits.[34] The regulation specifically provides that the part of the cost of company-furnished automobiles that relates to personal use by employees (including travel to and from work) is unallowable compensation for services, regardless of whether the cost is reported as taxable income to the employees; employee rebates and purchase discounts on contractor-produced products or services are unallowable; in certain circumstances, agreed-upon payments of special compensation to employees upon termination of their employment (commonly referred to as "golden parachutes") or to induce employees to remain with their employer (commonly referred to as "golden handcuffs") are unallowable costs;[35] severance payments to foreign nationals employed under service contracts performed outside the United States may not exceed typical rates of severance pay to workers performing similar services in the United States; contractors must credit or refund to the Government its equitable share of excess or surplus assets that revert to a contractor as a result of the termination of a defined benefit pension plan; the allowability of costs associated with postretirement benefits (PRBs) other than pensions is conditional on contractor funding of PRB accruals; and the allowability of increased pension costs resulting from the withdrawal of assets from a pension fund and transfer to another employee benefit plan is conditional on the existence of an advance agreement stating the Government's equitable share in the gross amount withdrawn. Transition costs (those attributable to past service) are allowable subject to certain limitations. Finally, for defense contracts entered into after April 15, 1995, the amount of executive compensation that can be charged to the contract is limited to $250,000 per individual.[36]

(7) *Contingencies.*[37] With limited exceptions, the costs of "contingencies" (possible future events or conditions arising from present known or unknown causes) are generally unallowable on the theory that contingencies that can be reasonably foreseen and estimated are to be included in contractor estimates—and in the final contract price.

(8) *Contributions and donations.*[38] These costs (whether in the form of cash, property, or services) are unallowable because they are completely discretionary and not necessary to the conduct of a contractor's business, regardless of the recipient.

(9) *Cost of money.*[39] This includes facilities capital cost of money and cost of money as an element of the cost of capital assets under construction.[40] Cost of money is allowable if (a) the individual Standard of the Cost Accounting Standards dealing with the cost is followed for measuring, allocating, and costing the capital investment, (b) the estimated cost is specifically identified or proposed in cost proposals relating to the contract under which the cost is claimed, (c) adequate records are kept to support the cost, and (d) the contractor observes the cost principle on asset valuations resulting from business combinations (see Item 51 below).

(10) *Depreciation.*[41] Normal depreciation on a contractor's plant and equipment generally is allowable to the extent it is reasonable and allocable to the contract. It is generally limited (where the two figures are different) to the lesser of the amount used for federal income tax purposes and that used for financial statement purposes. However, the provision on asset valuations resulting from business combinations limits the allowability of depreciation, regardless of whether the contract is subject to the Cost Accounting Standards.

(11) *Economic planning costs.*[42] These indirect costs—covering expenses associated with general long-range management planning (i.e., planning for the future overall development of the contractor's business)—are allowable.

(12) *Employee morale, health, welfare, food service, and dormitory costs and credits.*[43] These costs are allowable, less any income generated therefrom, except that a contractor's food and dormitory operations may not deliberately be operated on a loss basis.

(13) *Entertainment costs.*[44] Entertainment costs (including costs of memberships in social, dining, and country clubs) are unallowable. These include the costs of amusement, diversion, and social activities, and any directly associated costs.

(14) *Fines, penalties, and mischarging costs.*[45] Fines and penalties are unallowable, unless they result from compliance with the terms of a contract or with the Contracting Officer's written instructions. Costs incurred in connection with or related to the mischarging of Government contract costs are unallowable where

COSTS   5-13

the costs are the result of the alteration or destruction of records or other false or improper charging or recording of costs.

(15) *Gains and losses on disposition of depreciable property or other capital assets.*[46] The general rule is that in computing contract costs, gains and losses from sales, retirements, or other depreciable property dispositions are to be included in the year when they occur as credits or charges to the cost grouping(s) in which the depreciation or amortization applicable to the assets was included. Special provisions cover involuntary conversions—such as when property is destroyed by fire, flood, and theft—and mass or extraordinary sales. No gain or loss is recognized as a result of the transfer of assets in a business combination.

(16) *Idle facilities and idle capacity costs.*[47] Idle facility costs are unallowable, except to the extent they are reasonably necessary to meet fluctuations in workload, or for a reasonable period if the facilities were necessary when acquired and have become idle due to unforeseeable causes. Idle capacity costs are allowable (normally as a part of overhead) if (a) they are necessary due to fluctuations of work, or (b) they were originally reasonable and are not currently subject to reduction.[48] Where a contract is terminated for the Government's convenience, idle facility and capacity costs are directly recoverable if they result from the termination.

(17) *Independent research and development and bid and proposal costs.*[49] Different rules regarding allowability apply to these costs.[50] Costs incurred are subject to allowability ceilings, but ceilings are being phased out for "major contractors" through fiscal year 1995.[51] Deferred costs are generally unallowable, but there are exceptions.

(18) *Insurance and indemnification.*[52] Reasonable insurance costs are generally allowable, subject to certain restrictions. Indemnification costs are allowable only if they are provided for in the contract.

(19) *Interest and other financial costs.*[53] Interest on borrowings (however represented) is unallowable. It should be noted, however, that the Contract Disputes Act provides for payment of interest on a successful contractor claim, irrespective of bor-

rowings, from the date that the Contracting Officer received the claim until payment is made pursuant to court or board of contract appeals order.[54]

(20) *Labor relations costs.*[55] Costs of maintaining satisfactory relations between the contractor and its employees are generally allowable.

(21) *Legislative lobbying costs.*[56] Generally, the costs of attempting directly to influence—or encouraging others to influence—legislative officials to favor or oppose legislation or other official actions are unallowable. Some activities involving lobbying are given special treatment, however.

(22) *Losses on other contracts.*[57] These costs are unallowable.

(23) *Maintenance and repair costs.*[58] Normal and extraordinary upkeep costs are generally allowable.

(24) *Manufacturing and production engineering costs.*[59] Costs involving such efforts as the following are allowable: (a) the development and deployment of pilot production lines and new or improved materials, systems, processes, methods, equipment, tools, and techniques for producing goods or services; (b) improving current production functions; and (c) material and manufacturing producibility analyses for production suitability and the optimization of manufacturing processes, methods, and techniques.[60]

(25) *Material costs.*[61] These costs, involving such things as raw materials and parts, are allowable, with some restrictions.

(26) *Organization costs.*[62] Organization costs are generally unallowable. Such expenditures include the costs of incorporating or forming a business entity and the costs of "resisting or planning to resist the reorganization of the corporate structure of a business or a change in the controlling interest in the ownership of a business." Once the business is functioning, however, the costs of normal operations (such as conducting shareholder meetings) are allowable as "other business expenses," discussed below.[63]

(27) *Other business expenses.*[64] When allocated on an equitable basis, these designated costs (as well as similar ones) are

allowable: (a) shareholder meetings and the incidental expenses connected with directors' and committee meetings, (b) registry and transfer charges involving ownership changes of securities issued by the contractor, (c) standard proxy solicitations, (d) reports to shareholders, and (e) required reports and forms for taxing and regulatory bodies.

(28) *Plant protection costs.*[65] Costs such as wages, uniforms, and equipment for plant protection personnel—along with the depreciation of plant protection capital assets and expenses necessitated by military requirements—are allowable.

(29) *Patent costs.*[66] Patent costs are allowable to the extent they are incurred as requirements of a Government contract. The costs of general counseling services related to patent matters are also allowable.

(30) *Plant reconversion costs.*[67] The costs of restoring or rehabilitating the contractor's facilities to their precontract condition are unallowable except for the cost of removing Government property and the restoration or rehabilitation costs caused by the removal.

(31) *Precontract costs.*[68] These costs are allowable even though incurred prior to the effective date of the contract if (a) they were incurred directly pursuant to the negotiation and in anticipation of contract award and (b) incurrence was necessary to comply with the proposed contract's delivery schedule.[69]

(32) *Professional and consultant service costs.*[70] The costs of professional and consultant services are allowable when they are reasonable in relation to the services rendered and when payment is not contingent on recovery of the costs from the Government. Such costs are *not* allowable, however, when they are incurred in connection with (a) most corporate organizations or reorganizations, (b) the defense of antitrust lawsuits, (c) the prosecution of claims against the Government or defending against Government claims, (d) defending or prosecuting certain lawsuits or appeals between two contractors, (e) patent infringement litigation, or (f) services to improperly obtain information or data protected by law, services to improperly influence the evaluation of proposals or the selection of sources for

contract award by the Government, services that violate a statute prohibiting improper business practices, or services inconsistent with the purpose and scope of the services contracted for. Legal fees incurred in performance of the contract are similarly allowable, but those incurred in "prosecution of a claim" are not (see Item 46, below).[71] This distinction has raised several problems of interpretation.[72]

In determining the allowability of professional and consultant service costs (including retainer fees), the Contracting Officer shall consider the following eight factors, among others:[73]

(1) The nature and scope of the service rendered in relation to the service required.

(2) The necessity of contracting for the service, considering the contractor's capability in the particular area.

(3) The past pattern of acquiring such services and their costs, particularly in the years prior to the award of Government contracts.

(4) The impact of Government contracts on the contractor's business.

(5) Whether the proportion of Government work to the contractor's total business is such as to influence the contractor in favor of incurring the cost, particularly when the services rendered are not of a continuing nature and have little relationship to work under Government contracts.

(6) Whether the service can be performed more economically by employment rather than by contracting.

(7) The qualifications of the individual or concern rendering the service and the customary fee charged, especially on non-Government contracts.

(8) Adequacy of the contractual agreement for the service....

(33) *Recruitment costs*.[74] These costs are generally allowable, provided that the size of the staff recruited is in keeping with workload requirements. However, "[e]xcessive compensation costs offered to prospective employees to 'pirate' them from another Government contractor are unallowable."[75] Excessive costs may include salaries, fringe benefits, or special emoluments that exceed standard industry practices or the contractor's customary compensation practices.

(34) *Relocation costs.*[76] The allowability of these costs depends on the nature of the particular cost. For costs listed as allowable, some general requirements must be met; in particular, the relocation must be for the employer's benefit and reimbursement to the employee must be in accordance with an established policy and practice of the employer that is consistently followed and designed to motivate employees to relocate promptly and economically. A number of costs are singled out as unallowable, such as losses on home sales and continuing mortgage principal payments on residences being sold.

(35) *Rental costs.*[77] The costs of renting or leasing real or personal property are generally allowable to the extent they are reasonable.[78] However, rental costs under a sale and leaseback arrangement are allowable only up to the amount the contractor would be allowed if the contractor retained title.[79]

(36) *Royalties and other costs for use of patents.*[80] Subject to some designated restrictions, royalties on a patent or amortization of the cost of buying a patent or patent rights necessary for proper contract performance are generally allowable.

(37) *Selling costs.*[81] These costs, which arise in marketing the contractor's products or services to particular customers, are allowable if they are reasonable and allocable.[82] In addition, costs of "broadly targeted and direct selling efforts and market planning" which involve a "significant effort to promote export sales" are allowable in certain circumstances. Expressly disallowed are contingent fees of the types prohibited by the "Covenant Against Contingent Fees" contract clause.

(38) *Service and warranty costs.*[83] Costs of fulfilling contract obligations to provide services such as installation, training, correcting defects, and replacing defective parts are allowable.

(39) *Special tooling and special test equipment costs.*[84] These costs are generally allowable if they are direct charges to the specific contract or contracts for which the tooling or equipment is acquired.[85]

(40) *Taxes.*[86] In general, federal, state, and local taxes required to be paid or accrued in accordance with generally accepted ac-

counting principles are allowable. However, there are a number of exceptions, the most important being federal income taxes.

(41) *Termination costs.*[87] As discussed in detail in Chapter 17, a contractor whose contract has been terminated by the Government for convenience is entitled to recover its costs of performance up to the date of the termination, as well as certain continuing costs, costs associated with the settlement of the contract, and profit on those costs. While the FAR provides that all Subpart 31.2 cost principles apply in termination situations, it singles out specific termination costs—such as common items, costs continuing after termination, initial costs, loss of useful value, rental under unexpired leases, alterations of leased property, settlement expenses, and subcontractor claims—for special treatment.[88]

(42) *Trade, business, technical, and professional activity costs.*[89] These costs—relating to memberships, subscriptions, and organizing, setting up, sponsoring, and attending meetings, symposia, seminars, and conferences—are generally allowable.

(43) *Training and education costs.*[90] Costs of preparing and maintaining non-college training programs (or sending employees to such programs) to increase job effectiveness are allowable. Part-time college and graduate school costs are also allowable. Full-time graduate school—but not undergraduate college—costs (excluding wages) are allowable if they are related to present or anticipated work. All of these programs, however, are subject to time and other limitations, including a requirement for refunding to the Government training and education costs for employees who resign, for reasons within their control, within 12 months of completing their training or education.

(44) *Transportation costs.*[91] Allowable transportation costs include freight, express, cartage, and postage charges relating to goods purchased, in process, or delivered.

(45) *Travel costs.*[92] Travel costs (including lodging, meals, and incidental expenses) incurred by contractor personnel while on official company business are generally allowable, subject to certain limitations contained in the FAR. A statutory provision that previously made unallowable contractor travel costs in ex-

cess of the rates permitted to Government employees was repealed in 1994.[93] Special criteria apply to corporate aircraft costs.[94]

(46) *Costs related to legal and other proceedings.*[95] In general terms, if the Federal Government or a state, local, or foreign government brings a "proceeding" against a contractor for violating or failing to comply with a law or regulation causing the contractor to defend a criminal or civil investigation, grand jury proceeding, criminal prosecution, civil action, or suspension, debarment, or other administrative proceeding—and the contractor is unsuccessful in the defense—the costs of the defense are unallowable.[96] Even if the contractor wins in certain proceedings, recovery is frequently limited to 80% of actual costs.

(47) *Deferred research and development costs.*[97] These costs—when the research and development effort is sponsored by (or required in performance of) a contract, and when the costs were incurred before award of a particular contract—are unallowable except when they are allowable as precontract costs (discussed above in Item 31).

(48) *Goodwill.*[98] Goodwill is defined as the unidentifiable intangible asset originating under the purchase method of accounting for a business combination when the price paid by the acquiring company exceeds the sum of the identifiable individual assets acquired less liabilities assumed, based on their fair values. Such costs are unallowable.[99]

(49) *Executive lobbying costs.*[100] Costs of attempting to improperly influence an officer or employee of the Executive Branch of the Federal Government to give consideration to or act regarding a regulatory or contract matter are unallowable.[101]

(50) *Costs of alcoholic beverages.*[102] These costs are unallowable.

(51) *Asset valuations resulting from business combinations.*[103] Increased costs due to the write-up of assets resulting from a business combination are disallowed by limiting amortizations, cost of money, and depreciations "to the total of the amounts that would have been allowed had the combination not taken place."

B. COST ACCOUNTING STANDARDS

In 1970, Congress passed a statute that provided for the establishment of the Cost Accounting Standards Board (CAS Board).[104] The statute directed the Board to devise cost accounting standards that would achieve uniformity and consistency in the cost accounting practices followed by prime contractors and subcontractors in estimating, accumulating, and reporting costs under certain negotiated prime and subcontract procurements. In addition, the CAS Board was directed to prepare regulations requiring contractors—as a condition of contracting with the Government—to (1) disclose in writing their cost accounting practices and (2) agree to a contract price adjustment in the event of noncompliance with applicable Cost Accounting Standards or inconsistent adherence to disclosed cost accounting practices.

The CAS Board carried out its mission with vigor, promulgating regulations establishing a number of individual Standards (which are collectively referred to as the Cost Accounting Standards) and requirements for contractor disclosure statements and contract price adjustments. The Board also promulgated regulations covering its own administration.

As the result of legislation enacted late in 1988, a new, independent CAS Board was created.[105] This legislation provides that all Standards, interpretations, modifications, rules, regulations, waivers, and exemptions promulgated by the first CAS Board "remain in effect unless and until amended, superseded or rescinded by the new Board," and gives the new Board exclusive authority to promulgate, amend, interpret, and rescind Cost Accounting Standards. The new Board is composed of the Administrator of the Office of Federal Procurement Policy, one representative each from the DOD and the General Services Administration, and two private sector members.

The CAS Board has promulgated a recodified set of rules and Cost Accounting Standards.[106] Where the CAS and FAR cost allocability provisions conflict, the CAS have been held to govern.[107]

1. Applicability

The CAS Board's Cost Accounting Standards and regulations apply to both defense and nondefense negotiated prime and subcontracts over $500,000.

Implementation of the CAS and contractor disclosure requirements are accomplished by including a notice in solicitations and a "Cost Accounting Standards" clause in contracts.[108] Thus, a prospective offeror will be advised in the solicitation as to whether or not the particular contract is subject to the CAS Board's requirements.

a. Exemptions & Waiver. The following categories of contracts and subcontracts are generally *exempt* from all CAS requirements: sealed bid contracts; negotiated contracts not exceeding $500,000; contracts with small businesses, foreign governments, or their agents; contracts where the price is set by law or regulation or is based on established catalog or market prices of commercial items sold in substantial quantities to the general public; fixed-price contracts or subcontracts (without cost incentives) for commercial items; contracts with educational institutions other than those to be performed by Federally Funded Research and Development Centers; contracts awarded to labor surplus area concerns pursuant to labor surplus area set-asides; certain contracts to be executed and performed outside the U.S.; and firm-fixed-price contracts and subcontracts awarded without submission of any cost data.[109]

In some instances, all or part of the CAS Board's Standards and requirements may be *waived* for a particular contractor or subcontractor. Generally, to obtain a waiver, the Contracting Officer (not the contractor) must demonstrate that the proposed contractor or subcontractor refused to accept a contract containing all or part of the CAS and that it is impractical to obtain the materials, supplies, or services from any other source.[110]

b. Types Of Coverage. There are two types of CAS coverage—"full" and "modified."[111] *Full* coverage applies to any contractor business unit that (a) receives a single CAS-covered contract or subcontract of $25 million or more or (b) received $25 million or more in net CAS-covered awards during its preceding cost accounting period, of which at least one award exceeded $1 million. A contractor subject to full coverage must follow all of the Cost Accounting Standards.

A business unit that receives a covered contract of less than $25 million may elect *modified* CAS coverage if (1) the covered contracts that it was awarded in the immediately preceding cost accounting period totaled less than $25 million, or (2) it did not receive at least one CAS-covered contract that exceeded $1 million. Modified coverage requires that the business unit comply with CAS 401, CAS 402, CAS 405, and CAS 406 (see Section B.4 below).

2. Contractor Obligations

The "Cost Accounting Standards" clause must be inserted in contracts subject to *full* coverage of the Cost Accounting Standards. The clause requires contractors to do all of the following:[112]

(1) Disclose in writing their cost accounting practices through completion of a "Disclosure Statement."

(2) Follow their disclosed practices consistently in estimating, accumulating, and reporting costs.

(3) Comply with all of the individual Cost Accounting Standards in effect on the contract award date.

(4) Agree to an adjustment of the contract price when the contractor fails to comply with existing Standards or its own disclosed practices.

Besides implementing the substantive content of the law, the "Cost Accounting Standards" clause also establishes the *price adjustment* procedure to be followed for adjusting a contract whenever a contractor departs from basic CAS policy by making an accounting change. The clause identifies several types of adjustments in various provisions. One provision permits an upward adjustment in contract price only when a new Standard is issued that has the effect of increasing the cost of a previously-awarded covered contract. Another requires downward adjustment, if appropriate, pursuant to a "voluntary" accounting change by the contractor, but does not permit upward ad-

COSTS 5-23

justment. A third provision entitles the contractor to an adjustment for a "voluntary" accounting change, without regard to increased costs to the Government, if the Contracting Officer finds the change to be "desirable" and "not detrimental to the interests of the Government." Finally, a fourth provision deals with the consequences of a failure to comply with the Standards or disclosed accounting practices, whether intentional or inadvertent. This liability is equal to the amount of the increased costs paid by the Government as a result of noncompliance.

3. Disclosure Statements

a. Requirements. Unless exempted from filing requirements, a contractor covered by the Cost Accounting Standards is obligated to file a "Disclosure Statement"—a written description of the contractor's cost accounting practices and procedures.[113] As indicated above, the "Cost Accounting Standards" clause for full-coverage contracts covers this requirement. Specifically, the contractor shall:[114]

> By submission of a Disclosure Statement, disclose in writing the Contractor's cost accounting practices...including methods of distinguishing direct costs from indirect costs and the basis used for allocating indirect costs. The practices disclosed for this contract shall be the same as the practices currently disclosed and applied on all other contracts and subcontracts being performed by the Contractor and which contain a Cost Accounting Standards (CAS) clause. If the Contractor has notified the Contracting Officer that the Disclosure Statement contains trade secrets and commercial or financial information which is privileged and confidential, the Disclosure Statement shall be protected and shall not be released outside of the Government.

There are certain Government responsibilities regarding Disclosure Statements. After including an appropriate notice in the solicitation for a proposed contract to indicate that the contract is subject to CAS Board requirements, the Contracting Officer must ensure that offerors submit required Disclosure Statements. The appropriate Government auditor is designated to conduct an initial review of Disclosure Statements. Thereafter, the cognizant Administrative Contracting Officer determines whether a Statement is adequate and notifies the contractor in case of any deficiency.

b. Time Of Submission. Currently, any contractor that, together with its segments, received net awards of negotiated prime contracts and subcontracts subject to coverage of the CAS totaling more than $25 million during its most recent cost accounting period (of which at least one award exceeded $1 million) must submit a completed Disclosure Statement before award of its first covered contract in the immediately following cost accounting period. In addition, a contractor business unit selected to receive a covered negotiated contract or subcontract of $25 million or more must submit a Disclosure Statement before award. If a Disclosure Statement is required, a separate Disclosure Statement must also be submitted for each segment of a company whose costs included in the total price of any CAS-covered contract or subcontract exceed $500,000, unless the contract or subcontract is exempt from CAS requirements or the segment's CAS-covered awards were less than 30% of total segment sales and less than $10 million in the most recently completed cost accounting period.[115] If the cost accounting practices are identical for more than one segment, only one Disclosure Statement clearly identifying each segment must be submitted.[116]

c. Form Of Submission. The standard Disclosure Statement is submitted on Form CASB-DS-1, a lengthy document, which can be obtained from the cognizant Administrative Contracting Officer. Offerors must file their Forms CASB-DS-1 with both the Administrative Contracting Officer (the original and one copy) and the cognizant auditor (one copy).[117]

The Form CASB-DS-1 is divided into a number of parts beginning with an overall accounting description of the contractor's business—including sales volume, proportion of Government business to total business, and type of cost system. The remaining parts deal with the contractor's treatment of (1) direct and indirect costs, (2) depreciation and capitalization, (3) other costs and credits, (4) deferred compensation and insurance costs, and (5) corporate system and group expenses.

The CASB-DS-1 Disclosure Statement emphasizes the concept of *full* disclosure. Such disclosure can avoid a deficient filing as well as subsequent compliance problems.

4. Individual Standards

The individual Cost Accounting Standards issued by the CAS Board are aimed primarily at assuring more uniform treatment of costs incurred by Government contractors. There is a close relationship between the CAS and the cost principles. For example, it was pointed out in Section A.2 above that one of the factors for determining cost allowability set forth in the FAR Subpart 31.2 cost principles is consideration of applicable CAS Board "Standards." Nonetheless, the CAS are not based on cost principles. The Cost Accounting Standards collectively represent the Government's view of acceptable cost accounting techniques. Thus, even though the Standards do not determine categories or individual items of cost that are allowable, it is more likely that the costs expended will be deemed allowable if the CAS are followed.[118]

Discussed briefly below are the 19 individual CAS promulgated by the CAS Board and set out in the Code of Federal Regulations.[119] As is the common practice, each Standard is designated as "CAS" followed by a three-digit number (corresponding to the sections in Title 48 of the Code of Federal Regulations where each Standard has been codified).

- CAS 401—*Consistency in Estimating, Accumulating, and Reporting Costs*. CAS 401 establishes the rule that a contractor's practices used in estimating costs for proposals must be consistent with the cost accounting practices the contractor uses in accumulating and reporting those costs.

- CAS 402—*Consistency in Allocating Costs Incurred for the Same Purpose*. CAS 402 requires that each type of cost be allocated to a contract only once, and only on one basis (i.e., only as a direct or as an indirect cost). However, CAS 402 does not require direct cost treatment for bid and proposal costs incurred to enhance chances of winning a follow-on contract.[120]

- CAS 403—*Allocation of Home Office Expenses to Segments*. CAS 403 establishes criteria for allocation of home office expenses to segments reporting directly to one home office, based on beneficial or causal relationship.

- CAS 404—*Capitalization of Tangible Assets*. CAS 404 requires contractors to establish and adhere to capitalization policies that satisfy criteria set forth in the Standard.[121]

- CAS 405—*Accounting for Unallowable Costs*. CAS 405 sets forth guidelines for early identification and treatment of unallowable costs.

- CAS 406—*Cost Accounting Period*. CAS 406 includes criteria for the selection of time periods to be used as cost accounting periods for cost estimating, accumulating, and reporting.

- CAS 407—*Use of Standard Costs for Direct Material and Direct Labor*. CAS 407 provides for the use of standard costs for estimating, accumulating, and reporting costs.

- CAS 408—*Accounting for Costs of Compensated Personal Absence*. CAS 408 is intended to assure that personal absence costs are assigned to the accounting period in which the related labor is performed and the related wage and salary costs are recognized.

- CAS 409—*Depreciation of Tangible Capital Assets*. CAS 409 establishes criteria for assigning depreciation costs to the proper cost accounting period and for consistent allocation to cost objectives.[122]

- CAS 410—*Allocation of Business Unit General and Administrative Expenses to Final Cost Objectives*. This Standard sets forth criteria for allocating the cost of management and administration—i.e., general and administrative expense—of a business unit based on beneficial or causal relationship.

- CAS 411—*Accounting for Acquisition Costs of Material*. CAS 411 provides methods for using material inventory records to determine acquisition costs.

- CAS 412—*Composition and Measurement of Pension Cost*. CAS 412 establishes the components of pension costs, the basis for measuring the amount of such costs, and the criteria for assignment to cost accounting periods.

- CAS 413—*Adjustment and Allocation of Pension Costs*. CAS 413 gives guidance for adjusting pension costs by measuring actuarial gains and losses and assigning them to accounting periods. If a pension plan is terminated, the Government has been held to be entitled to share in the proceeds reverting to a contractor from the termination.[123]

- CAS 414—*Cost of Money as an Element of the Cost of Facilities Capital*. CAS 414 provides for explicit recognition of the cost of money for facilities capital as an element of contract cost.

- CAS 415—*Accounting for the Cost of Deferred Compensation*. This Standard applies to the cost of all deferred compensation except for compensated personal absence and pension plan costs covered in CAS 408 and CAS 412.

- CAS 416—*Accounting for Insurance Costs*. CAS 416 provides criteria for measurement of insurance costs, assignment to accounting periods, and allocation to cost objectives.[124]

- CAS 417—*Cost of Money as an Element of the Cost of Capital Assets Under Construction*. CAS 417 provides for the determination of an imputed cost of money to be included in the capitalized cost of acquisition of assets constructed for a contractor's own use.

- CAS 418—*Allocation of Direct and Indirect Costs*. CAS 418 provides for consistent determination of direct and indirect costs. It does not apply to the allocation of indirect cost pools covered by other Standards.

- CAS 420—*Accounting for Independent Research and Development and Bid and Proposal Costs*. This Standard sets forth criteria for the accumulation of independent research and development and bid and proposal costs and their allocation to cost objectives.

In addition to the Standards, the CAS Board periodically has issued "Interpretations" as appendices to certain Standards. An Interpretation was added to CAS 401 and to CAS 402 in 1976, and one was added to CAS 403 in 1980. The Board also has published "Comments" concerning some of the factors that it considered in issuing Standards and Interpretations at the time they were issued. The 52 Comments can serve as legislative histories to aid in the understanding of uncertain or unclear provisions.

C. TRUTH IN NEGOTIATIONS ACT

In 1962, Congress passed a law known as the Truth in Negotiations Act (TINA).[125] The purpose of the Act was to put the Government on an equal footing with contractors in contract negotiations by requiring contractors to provide the Government with cost or pricing information relevant to the expected costs of contract performance. TINA, as amended, and the implementing procurement regulations[126] require prime contractors and subcontractors to *submit* cost or pricing data to the Government and to *certify* that, to the best of their knowledge and belief, the data submitted are accurate, complete, and current.[127] These rules have had a tremendous impact on the Government contractor: the slightest defect or omission in cost or pricing data submitted to the Government—even if unintentional—may lead to a reduction in the contract price[128] or even to a fraud investigation of the contractor.

1. Applicability

Although TINA originally applied only to DOD, the National Aeronautics and Space Administration, and the Coast Guard, Congress extended the coverage of the Act in 1985 to civilian agencies.[129] The Act now applies to any negotiated contract expected to exceed $500,000, a modification of a negotiated or sealed bid contract involving a price adjustment exceeding $500,000, the award of a subcontract exceeding $500,000 if the prime contractor and each higher-tier subcontractor are required to submit cost or pricing data, or the modification of a subcontract involving a price adjustment exceeding $500,000. The dollar threshold for TINA applicability may be adjusted every five years to account for inflation.[130]

When determining the threshold for application of the Act to a contract or subcontract modification, the price adjustment amount includes both increases *and* decreases totaling more than $500,000. For example, a $150,000 modification resulting from a reduction of $350,000 and an increase of $200,000 is a price adjustment exceeding $500,000.[131]

The head of the procuring activity may require cost or pricing data from a contractor where the price of the contract (or modification) is less than the established threshold amount only if the head determines in writing that the data are necessary for the evaluation by the agency of the reasonableness of the price of the contract. The agency may not require certified cost or pricing data to be submitted, however, for any contract, modification, or subcontract covered by a statutory exemption (discussed below).[132] When certified cost or pricing data are not required, the head of the activity may nevertheless require the submission of the minimum of data necessary to determine price reasonableness.[133]

2. Exemptions & Waiver

TINA exempts prime contracts, subcontracts, and contract modifications from the requirements of the Act where (1) the price negotiated is based on (a) adequate price competition, (b) established catalog or market prices of commercial items sold in substantial quantities to the general public, or (c) prices set by law or regulation, or (2) in the procurement of a commercial item, the procurement is conducted on a competitive basis and based upon adequate price competition. In addition, in exceptional cases, the head of the agency may waive TINA requirements.[134]

a. Adequate Price Competition. The first basis for exemption—"adequate price competition"—has spawned confusion over the years. Under the current FAR, price competition exists if (1) the Government solicits offers, (2) two or more responsible offerors that can satisfy the Government's requirements submit priced offers responsive to the solicitation, and (3) these offerors compete independently for a contract to be awarded to the responsible offeror submitting the lowest evaluated price.[135] Price competition is presumed to be adequate price competition except under narrowly defined circumstances delineated in the FAR.[136] Thus, assuming that at least two responsible offerors submit responsive offers, the key to finding price competition is whether the contract is to be awarded to the offeror submitting the "lowest evaluated price." This does not mean the "lowest price." According to the Comptroller General, "adequate price competition exists...where...price is a substantial, though not necessarily determinative factor in the prescribed evaluation criteria."[137]

Contracting Officers have been reluctant to implement the adequate price competition exemption over the years, often requiring the submission and certification of cost or pricing data where circumstances warranted an exemption. As a result, the DOD FAR Supplement currently instructs that the Contracting Officer "rarely should need to require the submission or certification of cost or pricing data on acquisitions where adequate price competition is expected (regardless of the type of contract anticipated)," as long as price is a substantial factor in the source selection criteria.[138]

b. Established Catalog Or Market Price. The "established catalog or market price" exemption pertains to commercial items that are sold regularly to other than Government customers. These items must be sold in "substantial quantities" to the "general public," without regard to the quantity of items that may be sold to the Federal Government.[139]

c. Price Set By Law Or Regulation. A price is "set by law or regulation," and hence exempt from the cost or pricing data submission requirement, if the price is set by "a governmental body."[140] This exemption applies chiefly to public utilities and has limited application to other contractors.

d. Commercial Item Procurements. In 1994, Congress added special exceptions to TINA for commercial item acquisitions. For commercial item procurements based on adequate price competition, cost or pricing data shall not be required. For commercial item procurements not based on adequate price competition (and not covered under another TINA exemption), the Contracting Officer initially should seek information on prices at which the same or similar items have been sold in the commercial market that is adequate for analyzing price reasonableness. If the Contracting Officer is unable to obtain such price reasonableness information, however, he may require the submission of cost or pricing data.[141]

e. Waiver. In exceptional cases, the head of an agency may waive cost or pricing data requirements for a particular procurement. The waiver must be in writing, and the authority to grant waivers cannot be delegated by the agency head.[142]

3. "Cost Or Pricing Data" Defined

TINA defines "cost or pricing data" as follows:[143]

> [T]he term "cost or pricing data" means all facts that, as of the date of agreement on the price of a contract (or the price of a contract modification), a prudent buyer or seller would reasonably expect to affect price negotiations significantly. Such term does not include information that is judgmental, but does include the factual information from which a judgment was derived.

The definition thus has three elements: (1) all *facts* (but not judgments), (2) existing at the *date of agreement* on price, (3) that are *significant* to price negotiations.

Under the above definition of cost or pricing data, the contractor must disclose as "facts" the data forming the basis for any judgment, projection, or estimate that is made. The nondisclosure of this data will render the submission incomplete or inaccurate.

The "date of price agreement" means the "handshake" date of price agreement between the parties, even though no legal contract may actually exist at that time. Data are required to be current as of the time of price agreement. Some "lag time" is inherent, however, between the time when data are submitted and the time of price agreement. The contractor's failure to update the data at the negotiations has been held to be a violation of the Act.[144] However, new or changed facts occurring *after* the "handshake" date need not be disclosed.

Information on which a contractor cannot reasonably have been expected to rely in formulating its price is not cost or pricing data because "prudent buyers and sellers" could not be expected to consider it "significant." For example, failure to disclose a vendor quote that was not seriously considered at the proposal stage would not constitute failure to disclose significant data.[145] The question in specific cases is whether "prudent buyers and sellers" would regard the quote as significant.

The concept of a "significant effect" on the price negotiations has been interpreted very broadly. For example, in one case it was held that $20,000 out of a target price of $15 million was "significant."[146] Moreover, it has been held that, in determining whether defective data have had a significant effect on the contract price, all defective pricing data must be considered cumulatively.[147] Thus, a defect that, standing alone, could not be considered sufficiently grave to warrant further action may be added to other defects (whether related or not) to cumulatively arrive at a significant defect. In addition, significance has been determined in absolute dollar terms rather than as a percentage of the total contract price.[148]

4. Submission Of Data

a. Form. Cost or pricing data must be submitted on Standard Form 1411, "Contract Pricing Proposal Cover Sheet," along with supporting attachments. The Form 1411 is set forth in the FAR,[149] and a reduced reproduction appears in Figure 5-1.

There are few definite rules regarding precisely what constitutes a proper submission of cost or pricing data. Obviously, the contractor must do more than merely make records available for Government inspection.[150] Data disclosed to an auditor but contradicted or not accurately represented in negotiations have also been held not to have been properly disclosed.[151] Moreover, the duty to furnish accurate and complete data—since it is imposed by statute—cannot be waived or modified by the Contracting Officer.[152] And, as a general rule, the contractor cannot escape liability by proving merely that the Government should have been aware that the data were defective.[153]

b. When Submitted. TINA requires that data be submitted *before the award* of a contract, subcontract, or contract modification expected to exceed the statutory price thresholds,[154] but the FAR requires that data be submitted or identified in writing by the time of *agreement on price*.[155] There will likely be more than one submission of data needed to comply with TINA and the regulations, including a submission with the initial proposal and the updating of the data during negotiations. Many contractors—out of an abundance of caution—will perform a "sweep" (an updating of all cost or pricing data after the conclusion of negotiations but prior to executing the "Certificate of Current Cost or Pricing Data") to ensure that all relevant data in the contractor's possession when negotiations were concluded

COSTS 5-33

Figure 5-1

STANDARD FORM 1411, "CONTRACT PRICING PROPOSAL COVER SHEET"

have, in fact, been submitted to the Government. Contractors customarily furnish any additional data discovered as a result of the sweep with their executed "Certificate." (Prudent prime contractors require their subcontractors to engage in similar sweeps and include any additional subcontractor data in their supplemental data submissions.)

c. Subcontractor Data. Prime contractors must obtain certified cost or pricing data before the award of any subcontract when (1) the subcontract is expected to exceed the applicable dollar threshold for TINA coverage and (2) the prime and each higher-tier sub have been required to submit data.[156] A subcontractor is *not* required to submit its cost or pricing data if *any* party in the chain above was not required to submit such data or if the subcontract price is based on one of the exemptions discussed in Section C.2 above. For modifications to subcontracts, the dollar threshold is the same as for modifications to prime contracts, and is based on the aggregate price adjustment, considering both increases and decreases (see Section C.1 above).[157] Under TINA, a subcontractor must certify that the cost or pricing data it submits are accurate, complete, and current.[158] A prime contractor is liable to the extent defective subcontractor data cause an increase in price, costs, or fee to the Government.[159]

d. Failure To Submit Data. The FAR provides guidance for the situation where required cost or pricing data are not submitted to a Contracting Officer.[160] If this occurs, the Contracting Officer "shall again attempt to secure the data." If the contractor persists in its refusal, the Contracting Officer must then withhold making the contract award or contract adjustment. If this happens, the Contracting Officer is required to forward the contract action to higher authority, together with details of the attempts made to resolve the matter, and a statement of the practicability of obtaining the supplies or services sought under the contract from another source.

5. Certification Of Data

TINA requires not only that contractors and subcontractors submit all cost or pricing data significant to price negotiations at the time of agreement on price, it also requires that they certify

> **Figure 5-2**
>
> **CERTIFICATE OF CURRENT COST
> OR PRICING DATA**
>
> This is to certify that, to the best of my knowledge and belief, the cost or pricing data (as defined in section 15.801 of the Federal Acquisition Regulation (FAR) and required under FAR subsection 15.804-2) submitted, either actually or by specific identification in writing, to the contracting officer or to the contracting officer's representative in support of _____* are accurate, complete, and current as of _____**. This certification includes the cost or pricing data supporting any advance agreements and forward pricing rate agreements between the offeror and the Government that are part of the proposal.
>
> Firm
>
> Signature
>
> Name
>
> Title
>
> Date of execution***
>
> * Identify the proposal, quotation, request for price adjustment, or other submission involved, giving the appropriate identifying number (e.g., RFP No.).
>
> **Insert the day, month, and year when price negotiations were concluded and price agreement was reached.
>
> ***Insert the day, month, and year of signing, which should be as close as practicable to the date when the price negotiations were concluded and the contract price was agreed to.

that, to the best of their knowledge and belief, the data submitted to the Government are *accurate, complete,* and *current*.[161] The FAR requires that the contractor do so in a prescribed "Certificate of Current Cost or Pricing Data."[162] The form of the Certificate, as set forth in the FAR, appears in Figure 5-2.

The FAR provision containing the Certificate states that only one Certificate must be submitted, and that it must be submitted "as soon as practicable after price agreement is reached." Thus, a Certificate should not be requested by the Government in the solicitation or furnished by the contractor with the proposal. The Certificate covers all cost or pricing data that are "reasonably available" at the "handshake" date.[163]

6. Liability For Defective Data

The "Price Reduction for Defective Cost or Pricing Data" contract clause implementing TINA states that if "any price, including profit or fee...was increased by any significant amount" because the contractor or subcontractor submitted data "that were not complete, accurate, and current as certified," the contract's "price or cost shall be reduced accordingly."[164] The contractor's liability is usually measured as the difference between the actual contract price based on the defective data and the price that would have been negotiated had accurate, complete, and current data been disclosed. Generally, the Government will receive this dollar-for-dollar reduction in the contract price as a matter of course unless the contractor presents evidence that the defective data did not have such an impact on the negotiated price.[165] In addition, if the contractor or subcontractor *knowingly* or *intentionally* submitted defective data, it may be liable for a wide variety of civil and criminal penalties, including fines, imprisonment, and suspension and debarment from contracting with the Government (see Chapter 7).[166] To recover under any of these theories, however, the Government must prove that it *relied* on the defective data.[167]

D. GOVERNMENT AUDIT RIGHTS

As discussed in detail below, the Government has the right to audit a contractor's price proposal *before* negotiations, as well as to audit the directly pertinent records, books, and other data of the contractor at any time up to three years *after* final payment under a contract. Indeed, it is a felony to try to "influence, obstruct or impede a federal auditor in the performance of official duties relating to a person receiving in excess of $100,000, directly or indirectly, from the United States in any one year period under a contract or subcontract."[168]

1. Procuring Agencies

The Defense Contract Audit Agency (DCAA) is the principal contract audit entity in the Federal Government. It performs all the contract audit functions for DOD.[169] In addition, it is used by most civilian agencies to perform contract audits, although some agencies use other federal audit assistance.[170] DCAA has been given subpoena power to secure contractor records, including federal tax return workpapers, but DCAA may not subpoena a contractor's own internal audit materials.[171]

DCAA headquarters are located in suburban Washington, D.C. In addition, it maintains regional offices in five U.S. cities and branch offices in approximately 150 cities located throughout the world.

a. Price Proposal Audits. At the proposal stage of a negotiated procurement, prior to the award of the contract, the Contracting Officer may request that Government auditors review the contractor's price proposal to ensure that the contractor's costs are developed consistently with the cost regulations.[172] The contractor should keep in mind that its rationale for (and documents used in developing) cost estimates may be subject to scrutiny by Government auditors. The auditors will typically inquire into the contractor's source documentation, the nature of its accounting system, and its compliance with cost principles. Usually, at the completion of the audit, the auditors will conduct an "exit interview" with the contractor and subsequently issue a written report to the Contracting Officer for his use in price negotiations.

b. Contract Settlement Audits. One of DCAA's more significant duties relates to the settlement of cost-reimbursement contracts. This process is initiated by the contractor's submission of a completion voucher and supporting documents (including a release of claims). The Government auditor then processes the completion voucher, concluding with the issuance of a contract audit closing statement. The final processing includes (a) completion of an audit of the contractor's operations and the costs related to the contract, (b) a final audit determination regarding the allowability of all costs claimed under the contract, and (c) a determination of the amount of fixed or incentive fee payable under the terms of the contract. DCAA also participates in the audit of contracts terminated for the Government's convenience. As programs are curtailed, this activity has become increasingly significant.

c. Cost Or Pricing Data Audits. The Government has both contractual and statutory rights to audit contractors who are subject to the cost or pricing data submission requirements discussed above in Section C.

(1) *Contract Audit Clauses.* The "Audit–Negotiation" clause[173] gives the Government the right to audit all books and records that are related to the negotiation, pricing, or performance of the contract, or that will permit adequate evaluation of cost or pricing data (this clearly includes performance costs). The purpose of this audit can only be to verify cost or pricing data. The "Audit–Sealed Bidding" clause[174] provides similar audit rights regarding the negotiation, pricing, or performance of modifications to contracts awarded by sealed bidding.

(2) *TINA.* A provision in this law[175] gives the agency the right—for three years after final payment—to audit all books and records related to contract negotiation, pricing, or performance, but only for the purpose of verifying the accuracy, completeness, and currency of cost or pricing data. TINA is self-executing (i.e., it needs no implementing contract clause), although the standard "Audit" clause does, in effect, implement it. A contractor that is unable to produce its records for a DCAA audit within the three-year period may be required to repay alleged overcharges to the Government because invoiced costs cannot be supported.[176]

Neither of these sources of Government audit rights gives agency officials the legal right to audit a contractor that is exempt from cost or pricing data requirements to determine the contractor's costs of performance, the adequacy of any uncertified data that may have been submitted, or whether the exemption was properly granted.

2. General Accounting Office

The role of the General Accounting Office (GAO) is to oversee the adequacy and effectiveness of agency procurement procedures, not to duplicate the work of contract audit agencies. Both may use the same data, but agency audit is restricted to the pricing of contracts, while the GAO's responsibility is much broader. GAO audits are undertaken on a selective basis; they are essentially "spot checks." GAO audit reports can be furnished to Congress and are also given to procuring agencies and contractors.[177]

The FAR provides[178] that the "Examination of Records by Comptroller General" clause[179] must be included in all negotiated contracts except small purchase contracts, contracts for utility services at established rates, and contracts with foreign contractors for which the contracting agency head authorizes omission. This clause is not required in sealed bid contracts; however, audits may still be conducted by certain federal agencies under the statutory powers provided in the Inspector General Act of 1978 (discussed below).

The clause gives the Comptroller General the right to inspect any "directly pertinent" records involving transactions related to "this" contract.[180] The clause also requires the contractor to insert a similar clause in all first-tier subcontracts that exceed the small purchase threshold (except for public utility services contracts at established rates), thus giving the Comptroller General the right to examine the records of subcontractors. Although the GAO's audit rights under this clause remain extensive, the U.S. Supreme Court has held that the concept of "directly pertinent" records does not extend to records involving a contractor's *indirect costs*, such as research and development, marketing, and distribution expenses, except to the extent they were allocated as attributable to a particular contract.[181]

In sealed bid contracts that are expected to exceed the TINA dollar threshold, the "Audit–Sealed Bidding" clause gives the GAO the same audit rights as those of the procuring agency with respect to the cost or pricing data submitted in the negotiation or performance of contract changes.[182]

3. Inspectors General

The Inspector General Act of 1978,[183] as amended, established an Office of Inspector General (IG) in many of the civilian federal executive agencies, as well as in the DOD.[184] IGs are authorized under the Act to conduct audits and investigations relating to "programs and operations" of their agencies to "prevent fraud and abuse." This mandate could be interpreted broadly enough to include contractor records not related to doing business with the Government. The IGs are also given broad subpoena powers for documents and other information necessary for them to fulfill their functions under the Act. The courts have generally taken a broad view of the IGs' subpoena powers.[185]

REFERENCES

1. Lockheed Aircraft Corp. v. U.S., 375 F.2d 786 (Ct. Cl. 1967), 9 GC ¶ 174.

2. DFARS 252.243-7001.

3. FAR 31.000.

4. See FAR 31.105.

5. This FAR Subpart refers to Office of Management and Budget, Circular A-21, "Cost Principles for Educational Institutions," as amended, 58 Fed. Reg. 39996 (July 26, 1993); see 35 GC ¶ 462. See also "Cost Principles for Educational Institutions—OMB Final Rule," 93-8 CP&A Rep. 15 (Aug. 1993); Keevan, Roth & Evans, "The Indirect Cost Controversy at Institutions of Higher Education," 91-8 CP&A Rep. 3 (Aug. 1991); Apatoff, Lawrence & Humphries, "Special Rules for Educational & Nonprofit Institutions," Briefing Papers No. 92-5 (Apr. 1992).

6. FAR 31.201-2.

7. FAR 31.201-3.

8. Note 7, supra (abolishing the rule of Bruce Const. Corp. v. U.S., 324 F.2d 516 (Ct. Cl. 1963)).

9. Stanley Aviation Corp., ASBCA 12292, 68-2 BCA ¶ 7081, 10 GC ¶ 424.

10. Stanwick Corp., ASBCA 18083, 76-2 BCA ¶ 12114, 19 GC ¶ 67.

11. General Dynamics Corp., ASBCA 13869, 70-1 BCA ¶ 8143, 12 GC ¶ 278.

12. J.A. Ross & Co., ASBCA 2326, 6 CCF ¶ 61801 (1955).

13. See, e.g., Michigan State Univ., ASBCA 12172, 68-1 BCA ¶ 6837.

14. For an examination of the differences between cost allowability and allocability, see Shapiro, "Allowability vs. Allocability Determinations: An Agenda for the CAS Board," 92-5 CP&A Rep. 17 (May 1992).

15. FAR 31.201-4.

16. FAR 31.202(a).

17. DeLong v. U.S., 175 F. Supp. 169 (Ct. Cl. 1959), 1 GC ¶ 478.

18. FAR 31.203(a).

19. FAR 31.203(b).

20. Litton Systems, Inc. v. U.S., 499 F.2d 392 (Ct. Cl. 1971), 13 GC ¶ 473.

21. FAR 31.205.

22. FAR 31.204.

23. FAR 31.204(c).

24. FAR 31.205-1. See also Aerojet-General Corp., ASBCA 13372, 73-2 BCA ¶¶ 10164, 10307, 16 GC ¶ 6.

25. FAR 31.205-2.

26. FAR 31.205-3.

27. FAR 31.205-4.

28. FAR 31.205-5.

29. FAR 31.205-6.

30. See generally Albertson, Jackson & Bruggeman, "Compensation Costs," Briefing Papers No. 90-11 (Oct. 1990), 9 BPC 219; Pettit & Victorino, "Personal Compensation Costs," Briefing Papers No. 84-6 (June 1984), 6 BPC 351; Featherstun & Narayen, "Executive Compensation Costs," 93-4 CP&A Rep. 3 (Apr. 1993).

31. Maxwell, "Bonus, Incentive & Stock Gain-Sharing Plans Under the Compensation Cost Principle (FAR 31.205-6(f)(i))," 92-4 CP&A Rep. 19 (Apr. 1992).

32. Grumman Aerospace Corp., ASBCA 34665, 90-1 BCA ¶ 22417, 32 GC ¶ 5; "ASBCA Finds Dividends on Restricted Stock Allowable Compensation Costs," 89-11 CP&A Rep. 16 (Nov. 1989).

33. See generally Lemmer, Davis & Pompeo, "Pension & Postretirement Benefit Costs: Recent Developments," Briefing Papers No. 92-6 (May

1992); Shanahan, "Accounting for Other Postretirement Benefits—Continuing Controversy," 91-12 CP&A Rep. 3 (Dec. 1991).

34. See generally Barger, "Employee Health Care Costs: The 'Compensation' Cost Principle (FAR 31.205-6)," 90-1 CP&A Rep. 15 (Jan. 1990); Porter & Porter, "Banked Vacation Under the 'Compensation' Cost Principle (FAR 31.205-6(m))," 91-6 CP&A Rep. 11 (June 1991).

35. Villet, "Golden Handcuffs & Parachutes—The 'Compensation' Cost Principle (FAR 31.205-6)," 89-3 CP&A Rep. 13 (Mar. 1989).

36. P.L. 103-335 (Sept. 30, 1994).

37. FAR 31.205-7.

38. FAR 31.205-8.

39. FAR 31.205-10.

40. See generally McGeehin & Kmieciak, "Recovery for Cost of Money," 92-10 CP&A Rep. 3 (Oct. 1992).

41. FAR 31.205-11.

42. FAR 31.205-12.

43. FAR 31.205-13.

44. FAR 31.205-14.

45. FAR 31.205-15.

46. FAR 31.205-16.

47. FAR 31.205-17.

48. See Knapp, "Idle Facilities & Idle Capacity Costs—Allowability & Allocability Issues (FAR 31.205-17)," 93-5 CP&A Rep. 13 (May 1993).

49. FAR 31.205-18.

50. See generally Chierichella, "IR&D Redux," 93-2 CP&A Rep. 3 (Feb. 1993); Chierichella, "IR&D vs. Contract Effort," 90-2 CP&A Rep. 3 (Feb. 1990); Victorino & Briggerman, "The IR&D/B&P/Selling Costs Dilemma," Briefing Papers No. 87-10 (Sept. 1987), 7 BPC 625.

51. FAC 90-13, 57 Fed. Reg. 44264 (Sept. 24, 1992). See Cibinic, "IR&D and B&P Advance Agreements and Ceilings: Gone and Slowly Fading Away," 6 Nash & Cibinic Rep. ¶ 62 (Nov. 1992).

52. FAR 31.205-19.

53. FAR 31.205-20. See also Tomahawk Const. Co., ASBCA 45071, 94-1 BCA ¶ 26312.

54. 41 USC § 611.

55. FAR 31.205-21. See generally Diamond & Cassidy, "The 'Lobbying' Cost Principles & Related Disclosure Requirements," 93-3 CP&A Rep. 3 (Mar. 1993).

56. FAR 31.205-22.

57. FAR 31.205-23.

58. FAR 31.205-24.

59. FAR 31.205-25.

60. See generally Stafford, "Classifying Manufacturing & Production Engineering (M&PE) Effort," 90-9 CP&A Rep. 3 (Sept. 1990).

61. FAR 31.205-26.

62. FAR 31.205-27.

63. See generally Villet, "The Organization Costs Cost Principle (FAR 31.205-27)," 91-7 CP&A Rep. 13 (July 1991).

64. FAR 31.205-28.

65. FAR 31.205-29.

66. FAR 31.205-30.

67. FAR 31.205-31.

68. FAR 31.205-32.

69. See generally Wiener, "The Allowability of Precontract Costs," 91-11 CP&A Rep. 3 (Nov. 1991); Hordell, "The Precontract Cost Principle (FAR 31.205-32)," 89-1 CP&A Rep. 13 (Jan. 1989).

70. FAR 31.205-33.

71. See, e.g., Bill Strong Enterprises, Inc., ASBCA 42946, 93-3 BCA ¶ 25961, appeal docketed, No. 94-1013 (Fed. Cir. Oct. 13, 1993); Hayes Intl. Corp., ASBCA 18847, 75-1 BCA ¶ 11076, 17 GC ¶ 157; R-D Mounts, Inc., ASBCA 17422, 75-1 BCA ¶ 11077, 17 GC ¶ 425.

72. See generally Cibinic, "Unallowable Claims Costs: When Is a Claim a Claim?," 7 Nash & Cibinic Rep. ¶ 48 (Sept. 1993); Vacketta, Yesner & Snyder, "Recovery of Legal Costs," Briefing Papers No. 93-12 (Nov. 1993); Stafford & Pompeo, "Costs of Prosecuting Claims—Bill Strong on Appeal," 94-6 CP&A Rep. 3 (June 1994).

73. FAR 31.205-33(d).

74. FAR 31.205-34.

75. FAR 31.205-34(c).

76. FAR 31.205-35.

77. FAR 31.205-36.

78. See generally McGeehin, "The Rental Cost Principle (FAR 31.205-36)," 89-2 CP&A Rep. 11 (Feb. 1989).

79. Talley Defense Systems, Inc., ASBCA 39878, 93-1 BCA ¶ 25521. See "Sale & Leaseback Arrangement Results in Rental Cost Disallowance," 92-1 CP&A Rep. 15 (Nov. 1992).

80. FAR 31.205-37.

81. FAR 31.205-38.

82. See generally Wimberly, "The 'Selling' Cost Principle (FAR 31.205-38)," 90-5 CP&A Rep. 17 (May 1990); Chierichella & Maxwell, "Foreign Selling Costs Under the Cost Principles (FAR 31.205-38(f), DFARS 231.205-38(c)(S-70))," 90-12 CP&A Rep. 11 (Dec. 1990).

83. FAR 31.205-39.

84. FAR 31.205-40.

85. See generally Hill, "The Special Tooling & Special Test Equipment Cost Principle (FAR 31.205-40)," 89-7 CP&A Rep. 15 (July 1989).

86. FAR 31.205-41.

87. FAR 31.205-42.

88. See generally Pettit, "Post-Termination Costs," Briefing Papers No. 73-3 (June 1973), 3 BPC 29; Pettit & Victorino, "Post-Termination Costs/Edition II," Briefing Papers No. 83-6 (June 1983), 6 BPC 171; Kulish & Holmes, "Maximizing Cost Recovery in Convenience Terminations: Part II," 90-3 CP&A Rep. 3 (Mar. 1990).

89. FAR 31.205-43.

90. FAR 31.205-44.

91. FAR 31.205-45.

92. FAR 31.205-46.

93. Federal Acquisition Streamlining Act of 1994, P.L. 103-355, § 2191, 108 Stat. 3243 (Oct. 13, 1994) (repealing 41 USC § 420).

94. See, e.g., General Dynamics Corp., ASBCA 31359, 92-1 BCA ¶ 24698, modified, 92-2 BCA ¶ 24922. See generally "ASBCA Rules on Allowability of Corporate Aircraft Costs," 92-6 CP&A Rep. 28 (June 1992).

95. FAR 31.205-47.

96. See generally Lovitky, "Defense of Fraud Proceedings Cost Principle (FAR 31.205-47)," 88-1 CP&A Rep. 11 (Nov. 1988); Schechter & Kelly, "The 'Proceedings' Cost Principle (FAR 31.205-47)," 91-3 CP&A Rep. 15 (Mar. 1991).

97. FAR 31.205-48.

98. FAR 31.205-49.

99. See generally Starrett, "The Goodwill Cost Principle (FAR 31.205-49)," 88-2 CP&A Rep. 11 (Dec. 1988).

100. FAR 31.205-50.

101. See generally Diamond & Cassidy, note 55, supra.

102. FAR 31.205-51.

103. FAR 31.205-52.

104. P.L. 91-379, 84 Stat. 796. See Wright, "Uniform Cost Accounting Standards," Briefing Papers No. 70-2 (Apr. 1970), 2 BPC 13.

105. P.L. 100-679, 102 Stat. 4055, 4058–4063 (codified at 41 USC § 422). See generally Gallagher & Chadwick, "Cost Accounting Standards: New Developments," Briefing Papers No. 89-6 (May 1989), 8 BPC 359.

106. 48 CFR ch. 99 (57 Fed. Reg. 14148, Apr. 17, 1992), replacing the CAS in FAR pt. 30 and 4 CFR pts. 331–420. See "CAS Recodification—OFPP Final Rule," 92-4 CP&A Rep. 37 (Apr. 1992); 34 GC ¶ 225.

107. U.S. v. Boeing Co., 802 F.2d 1390 (Fed. Cir. 1986), 5 FPD ¶ 93, 28 GC ¶ 297; compare Emerson Electric Co., ASBCA 30090, 87-1 BCA ¶ 19478, 29 GC ¶ 51.

108. FAR 30.201-4.

109. 48 CFR § 9903.201-1; 41 USC § 422(f).

110. 48 CFR § 9903.201-5; FAR 30.201-5.

111. See 48 CFR § 9903.201-2.

112. FAR 52.230-2. See also 48 CFR § 9903.201-4.

113. See Harry, "CAS Coverage & Disclosure Statement Filing Requirements," 88-11 CP&A Rep. 3 (Nov. 1988).

114. FAR 52.230-2, para. (a)(1).

115. 48 CFR § 9903.202-1(c).

116. Note 115, supra.

117. 48 CFR § 9903.202-5.

118. Dewey Electronics Corp., ASBCA 17696, 76-2 BCA ¶ 12146.

119. 48 CFR § 9904.401–.420.

120. Boeing Co. v. U.S., 862 F.2d 290 (Fed. Cir. 1988), 7 FPD ¶ 160, 30 GC ¶ 416.

121. See generally Shapiro, "CAS Board Staff Discussion Paper: Changing Capital Asset Values Resulting From Mergers & Business Combinations," 92-1 CP&A Rep. 15 (Jan. 1992); Keevan & Ruona, "Accounting for Business Combinations," 90-6 CP&A Rep. 3 (June 1990).

122. See generally Keevan & Ruona, "Accounting for Gains & Losses," 91-1 CP&A Rep. 3 (Jan. 1991).

123. NI Industries, Inc., ASBCA 34943, 92-1 BCA ¶ 24631, 34 GC ¶¶ 2, 227. See also "Government Shares in Pension Reversion After Plan Termination," 91-12 CP&A Rep. 15 (Dec. 1991); "Following Up," 92-4 CP&A Rep. 40 (Apr. 1992).

124. See generally Shapiro & Relly, "Retiree Health Care & the Cost Accounting Standards," 89-8 CP&A Rep. 3 (Aug. 1989).

125. P.L. 87-653, 76 Stat. 528 (originally codified at 10 USC § 2306(f)). See generally Pettit, "Truth in Negotiations–Part I," Briefing Papers No. 68-3 (June 1968), 1 BPC 305; Cuneo, Ackerly & Lane, "Truth in Negotiations–Part II," Briefing Papers No. 68-4 (Aug. 1968), 1 BPC 319; Boyd & Aylward, "Truth in Negotiations/Edition II," Briefing Papers No. 77-2 (Apr. 1977), 4 BPC 105; Morrison & Ebert, "Truth in Negotiations/Edition III," Briefing Papers No. 89-11 (Oct. 1989), 8 BPC 441. See also Knight & Ochs, "The Truth in Negotiations Act in Competitive Acquisitions," 92-6 CP&A Rep. 3 (June 1992).

126. See FAR 15.804 et seq.

127. 10 USC § 2306a(a); 41 USC § 254b(a).

128. 10 USC § 2306a(e); 41 USC § 254b(e). See also FAR 15.804-7, 52.215-22.

129. Act of July 18, 1984, tit. VII § 2712, 98 Stat. 1181.

130. Note 93, supra, §§ 1201, 1251 (amending 10 USC § 2306a, striking 41 USC § 254(d), and adding new section to be codified at 41 USC § 254b).

131. FAR 15.804-2(a)(1)(ii).

132. 10 USC § 2306a(c)(1); 41 USC § 254b(c)(1).

133. 10 USC § 2306a(c)(2); 41 USC § 254b(c)(2).

134. 10 USC § 2306a(b), (d); 41 USC § 254b(b), (d).

135. FAR 15.804-3(b)(1).

136. FAR 15.804-3(b)(2).

137. Serv-Air, Inc., Comp. Gen. Dec. B-189884, 78-2 CPD ¶ 223, affd. on reconsideration, 79-1 CPD ¶ 212, 21 GC ¶ 307.

138. DFARS 215.804-3. See also E.R. Spector, Deputy Asst. Secy. of Defense for Procurement, Memorandum, "Adequate Price Competition" (May 1, 1992).

139. 10 USC § 2306a(b); 41 USC § 254b(b).

140. FAR 15.804-3(d).

141. 10 USC § 2306a(d); 41 USC § 254b(d).

142. Note 139, supra.

143. 10 USC § 2306a(i); 41 USC § 254b(i).

144. American Bosch Arma Corp., ASBCA 10305, 65-2 BCA ¶ 5280, 8 GC ¶ 51, corrected, 66-2 BCA ¶ 5747.

145. See Plessey Industries, Inc., ASBCA 16720, 74-1 BCA ¶ 10603, 16 GC ¶ 362.

146. Sylvania Electric Products, Inc., ASBCA 13622, 70-2 BCA ¶ 8387, 12 GC ¶ 430; Sylvania Electric Products, Inc. v. U.S., 479 F.2d 1342 (Ct. Cl. 1973), 15 GC ¶ 250.

147. Note 144, supra.

148. Sylvania Electric Products, Inc. v. U.S., note 146, supra.

149. FAR 15.804-6(b)(2).

150. M-R-S Mfg. Co. v. U.S., 492 F.2d 835 (Ct. Cl. 1974), 16 GC ¶ 202.

151. See, e.g., McDonnell-Douglas Corp., ASBCA 12786, 69-2 BCA ¶ 7897, 11 GC ¶ 422.

152. Note 150, supra.

153. 10 USC § 2306a(e)(3)(B); 41 USC § 254b(e)(3)(B).

154. 10 USC § 2306a(a)(1); 41 USC § 254b(a)(1).

155. FAR 15.804-6(d).

156. 10 USC § 2306a(a)(1)(C); 41 USC § 254b(a)(1)(C). See generally Arnavas & Gildea, "Subcontractor Cost or Pricing Data/Edition II," Briefing Pa-

pers No. 93-8 (July 1993); Morrison & Ebert, "Subcontractor Cost or Pricing Data: Riddles, Mysteries, Quandaries & Ghosts," 93-12 CP&A Rep. 3 (Dec. 1993).

157. See FAR 15.804-2(a)(1)–(3).

158. 10 USC § 2306a(a)(2); 41 USC § 254b(a)(2).

159. FAR 15.804-7(e).

160. FAR 15.804-6(e).

161. Note 127, supra.

162. FAR 15.804-4(a).

163. FAR 15.804-4(b).

164. FAR 52.215-22, para. (a).

165. See, e.g., EDO Corp., ASBCA 41448, 93-3 BCA ¶ 26135, 35 GC ¶ 522; Aerojet General Corp., ASBCA 12873, 69-1 BCA ¶ 7585, 11 GC ¶ 396; Aydin Monitor Systems, NASABCA 381-1, 84-2 BCA ¶ 17297, 26 GC ¶ 153.

166. E.g., 31 USC § 231; 18 USC §§ 287, 1001.

167. See Mateer, "Defective Pricing—The Government's Burden of Proof," 93-9 CP&A Rep. 3 (Sept. 1993).

168. 18 USC § 1516. See generally Bond, O'Sullivan & Feldstein, "The New Crime of 'Obstruction of Federal Audit'," 89-4 CP&A Rep. 3 (Apr. 1989).

169. See DFARS 242.7005. See generally Arnavas, Gildea & Duquette, "DCAA Audits," Briefing Papers No. 94-9 (Aug. 1994).

170. See FAR 42.102(a).

171. 10 USC § 2313(b); U.S. v. Newport News Shipbldg. & Dry Dock Co., 737 F. Supp. 897 (E.D. Va. 1989), 31 GC ¶ 302; Martin Marietta Corp., ASBCA 31248 et al., 87-2 BCA ¶ 19875, 29 GC ¶ 205. See generally West & Kassel, "Access to Contractor Records/Edition II," Briefing Papers No. 88-5 (Apr. 1988), 8 BPC 113; Kipps & Brown, "DCAA Access to Records After Newport News," 89-3 CP&A Rep. 3 (Mar. 1989).

172. See FAR 15.805-5.

173. FAR 52.215-2.

174. FAR 52.214-26.

175. 10 USC § 2306a(g); 41 USC § 254b(g).

176. JANA, Inc. v. U.S., 936 F.2d 1265 (Fed. Cir. 1991), 10 FPD ¶ 70, cert. denied, 112 S. Ct. 869 (1992).

177. See generally Roe, "GAO Contract Audit Reports," Briefing Papers No. 65-2 (Apr. 1965), 1 BPC 107.

178. FAR 15.106-1.

179. FAR 52.215-1.

180. FAR 52.215-1, para. (b).

181. Bowsher v. Merck & Co., 460 U.S. 824 (1983), 25 GC ¶ 132.

182. FAR 52.214-26.

183. P.L. 95-452, 92 Stat. 1101 (codified at 5 USC app. §§ 1–12).

184. Fiscal Year 1983 National Defense Authorization Act, P.L. 97-252, § 1117, 96 Stat. 759.

185. U.S. v. Westinghouse Electric Corp., 788 F.2d 164 (3d Cir. 1986), 28 GC ¶ 135; Baranowski v. Environmental Protection Agency, 699 F. Supp. 1119 (E.D. Pa. 1988), affd., 902 F.2d 1558 (3d Cir. 1990). Compare Burlington Northern R.R. Co. v. Office of Inspector General, R.R. Retirement Bd., 983 F.2d 631 (5th Cir. 1993), 35 GC ¶ 192.

SOCIOECONOMIC CONSIDERATIONS

6

A. Small Business Preferences
1. Qualification
2. Contract Set-Asides
3. Certificates Of Competency
4. Subcontracting
5. Equal Access To Justice Act

B. Women-Owned Small Business Preferences

C. Labor Surplus Area Preferences
1. Qualification
2. Contract Set-Asides
3. Subcontracting

D. Nondiscrimination Requirements
1. Equal Employment Opportunity
2. Miscellaneous Requirements
3. Administration & Enforcement

E. Labor Standards Requirements
1. Walsh-Healey Act
2. Service Contract Act

F. Buy American Act Requirements

G. Environmental Protection Requirements

H. Drug-Free Workplace Requirements

Although the Government's primary interest in procuring goods and services is to obtain them on a competitive, least-cost basis, the Government has also implemented—through the procurement process—certain policies to ensure that various basic socioeconomic objectives are met. Thus, programs have been created that provide certain contracting *preferences* to small and small disadvantaged businesses, women-owned small businesses, and firms performing in labor surplus areas. In addition, contractors must comply with *requirements* arising under various laws, such as the federal environmental laws and labor standards statutes. This chapter discusses many of these preferences and requirements. It should be noted that under the Federal Acquisition Streamlining Act of 1994, lists of the laws and contract clauses that are (1) inapplicable to contracts (and subcontracts) for the procurement of commercial items and (2) inapplicable to procurements under the simplified acquisition threshold (formerly called the small purchase threshold) will be included in the FAR by October 1, 1995.[1]

A. SMALL BUSINESS PREFERENCES

The largest category of procurement preferences consists of those established for small businesses. The most noteworthy of the small business groups singled out for such preferences are small business concerns and small business concerns owned and controlled by socially and economically disadvantaged individuals. Both types of firms have been given special status in Government contracting under the Small Business Act.[2] Another small business group given preferred treatment is composed of women-owned small businesses (see Section B below).

The Office of Federal Procurement Policy issued a Policy Letter in 1991 which implemented already existing practices by establishing a Government-wide goal of awarding (a) 20% of the total value of all prime contract awards in each fiscal year to small business concerns and (b) 5% of the total value of all prime contracts and subcontracts in each fiscal year to small business concerns owned and controlled by socially and economically disadvantaged individuals.[3] The 5% goal for small disadvantaged businesses applies separately to prime contracts and subcontracts. The Policy Letter also established reporting requirements to facilitate monitoring whether the Government-wide goals are being achieved. In 1994, Congress established a Government-wide initiative that authorizes agencies to set-aside certain contracts for small disadvantaged businesses or to apply a 10% price evaluation preference for such businesses in unrestricted procurements.[4]

1. Qualification

Qualification for preferential procurement treatment as a *"small business concern"*—defined in the Small Business Act as "one which is independently owned and operated and which is not dominant in its field of operation"[5]—depends on where a firm meeting this definition falls in terms of the size standards established by the Small Business Administration (SBA).[6] As the Government agency that administers the Act, the SBA applies a variety of size standards to different industries in defining small business concerns. For example, in the construction industry, small business status is determined by the average annual receipts of the concern (generally not more than $17 million for the preceding three fiscal years, but only $7 million for certain special trades such as concrete work). On the other hand, for manufacturing industries, the number of employees of the concern and its affiliates determines whether it is a small business.[7] Nonmanufacturers are limited to 500 employees in order to be considered small.[8]

Whether a firm qualifies for preferences as a *"small business concern owned and controlled by socially and economically disadvantaged individuals"* (such a firm is accorded greater preference than an ordinary small business concern) depends on whether the firm falls within the Act's definition of the term: the firm (a) meets the Act's definition of "small business concern," (b) is at least 51% owned or controlled by socially and economically disadvantaged individuals, and (c) is under the control of such individuals for its management and daily business operations.[9]

2. Contract Set-Asides

The most common method by which the Government gives preference in its procurements to small business concerns is by setting aside or reserving all or part of a proposed procurement for exclusive participation by small business firms.[10] These set-asides can be total or partial. Each contract for supplies or services that has an anticipated value greater than $2,500 but not greater than $100,000 is also reserved exclusively for small business.[11]

a. Total Set-Asides. The entire amount of an individual procurement or class of procurements generally must be set aside for exclusive small business participation if there is a reasonable expectation that (1) offers will be received from at least two responsible small business concerns, and (2) awards will be made at reasonable prices.[12]

b. Partial Set-Asides. If the criteria for a total small business set-aside cannot be met, a portion of an individual procurement—not including construction—generally must be set aside for exclusive small business participation when, under the current FAR, (a) a procurement exceeding the small purchase threshold is severable into two or more economic production runs or reasonable lots, and (b) one or more small business concerns are expected to be able to furnish the set-aside work at a reasonable price.[13]

When the Government decides to effect a partial set-aside, the procurement is divided into a non-set-aside portion and a set-aside portion. Offers are first obtained on the non-set-aside portion from all interested firms, whether or not they are small business concerns. After the award prices for the non-set-aside portion have been determined, negotiations are conducted—exclusively with small business concerns—for the set-aside portion. However, to be eligible to participate in those negotiations, a small business concern must have submitted a responsive offer on the non-set-aside portion. As a general rule, awards of the set-aside portion are made at the highest unit price for each item awarded on the non-set-aside portion, adjusted to reflect transportation and other cost factors considered in evaluating offers on the non-set-aside portion.[14]

3. Certificates Of Competency

The SBA has statutory authority to certify the competency of any small business concern.[15] A Certificate of Competency (COC) is a written certification by the SBA that a particular small business has the capability to perform a specific Government contract. Contracting Officers must ordinarily accept COCs as establishing conclusively prospective contractors' capability, competency, capacity, credit, integrity, perseverance, and tenacity.[16] The COC program is thus another method—a procedural method—by which small business concerns are given special treatment in Government procurements.

If a Contracting Officer has substantial doubt as to the concern's ability to perform, the Contracting Officer and the SBA must make every effort to resolve the issue before the SBA takes final action on the COC. However, the determination of the SBA Central Office is conclusive and must be accepted by the Contracting Officer.[17] As a result, it is possible that a Contracting Officer could be forced to award a contract to a small business concern that he does not believe is capable of performing the contract.

4. Subcontracting

Another method for furthering the Government's preference for small and small disadvantaged businesses in procurements is by encouraging the use of such businesses as subcontractors.

a. By Private Firms. Except for contracts performed totally outside the U.S. and contracts for personal services, a clause requiring contractors—whether or not they are small business concerns—to seriously consider using small businesses as subcontractors is prescribed by the FAR for all contracts exceeding the small purchase threshold.[18] Specifically, the clause requires that the contractor agree to award subcontracts to small business concerns "to the fullest extent consistent with efficient contract performance."[19]

Note that under this clause, the prime contractor retains the right to determine for itself if a small business concern has the capability to perform a subcontract. Generally, the Government will not question the prime contractor's decision in this regard since the prime is responsible for defaults of its subcontractors. Nevertheless, if the prime contractor fails to make a "good faith" effort to meet its small business subcontracting goals as required by the Small Business Act, it could be assessed liquidated damages.[20]

Another amendment to the Small Business Act imposes even greater burdens on low offerors for large contracts.[21] Under it, as implemented by the FAR,[22] solicitations for supply contracts expected to exceed $500,000 and for construction contracts expected to exceed $1 million must contain a clause entitled "Small Business and Small Disadvantaged Business Subcontracting Plan" (note that separate versions of the clause are prescribed for negotiated and sealed bid contracts).[23] The clause requires the prospective contractor to submit a subcontracting plan outlining—in detail—the efforts the contractor will make to ensure that small business and small disadvantaged business concerns will have an equitable opportunity to compete for subcontracts. The plan must be approved by the Contracting Officer, and the approved plan will be included in the resulting contract.

b. By The SBA. One of the most important advantages available to a small disadvantaged contractor is the right to participate in the SBA's so-called "8(a) Program" (derived from § 8(a) of the Small Business Act[24]). Under this program, the SBA obtains contract awards from other agencies and subcontracts the work—in whole or in part—to small disadvantaged contractors.[25]

Eligibility to receive awards under the program is limited to a fixed period of time that the contractor negotiates with the SBA.[26] The regulations provide that to be considered economically disadvantaged for purposes of 8(a) Program participation, an individual must have a net worth of less than $250,000 (less than $750,000 for non-8(a) Programs).[27] They also require that to be eligible to participate in the 8(a) Program, a small business must have been in business for two full years and have demonstrated a "potential for success."[28] Any costs to the procuring agency in excess of the estimated fair market price anticipated under normal contracting procedures are required to be funded by the SBA.[29] Because the SBA is usually unable or unwilling to fund such extra costs, a "fair market price" is established through negotiation. The FAR further requires that acquisitions under the SBA's 8(a) Program be awarded on the basis of competition restricted to eligible program participants if (a) there is a reasonable expectation that at least two eligible participants will submit offers and the award can be made at a fair market price, and (b) the anticipated contract price will exceed $5 million for manufacturing and $3 million for all other contract opportunities.[30] In addition, the SBA may appeal a Contracting Officer's decision (1) not to make a particular acquisition available for award under the 8(a) Program, (2) on the terms and conditions of a sole-source acquisition to be awarded under the program, and (3) on the estimated fair market price.[31]

In form, the small disadvantaged business concern is a subcontractor to the procurement agency involved and the prime contractor is the SBA. However, as a practical matter, these two entities are engaged in a single contractual transaction, and all meaningful actions during performance, including disputes, are handled directly between the procuring agency and the small disadvantaged business concern.[32]

5. Equal Access To Justice Act

a. History. Closely associated with the preferences for small businesses in Government contracting is the Equal Access to Justice Act (EAJA). The original Act, which appeared as an amendment to the Small Business Act,[33] went into effect on October 1, 1981, for a three-year period, and permitted the award of attorney fees to prevailing private parties in certain actions against the Government.[34] Specifically, one section of the Act provided that a "court" could award to the "prevailing party" (other than the Government) the "fees and other expenses" incurred in a civil action brought by or against the Government whenever the Government's position in the action was not "substantially justified."[35] As indicated from the Act's definition of "party"—an individual having a net worth not exceeding $1 million or a firm having a net worth not exceeding $5 million (or fewer than 500 employees) at the time suit was filed[36]—the Act was a remedial statute that gave a preference to small businesses.

The EAJA originally provided that a "court" shall award legal fees to the prevailing party. Some agency boards of contract appeals initially held that they also had the authority to provide such relief, but this position was rejected by the Court of

Appeals for the Federal Circuit.[37] This disparity between the courts and the boards was resolved in the 1985 revisions to the Act, which expressly provided for boards to make awards under the EAJA precisely as a court would.[38]

The original 1984 legislation reauthorizing the EAJA, although passed by Congress, failed to become law because the President refused to sign it, and Congress could not override his veto.[39] Reauthorizing legislation was eventually passed and signed, however, in 1985.[40] The EAJA also became permanent at that time.[41]

b. Eligibility. A "party" entitled to recover fees and expenses—if the party prevails in an action in which the Government's position is not substantially justified—must qualify under the EAJA's net worth and size limitations. For individuals, the Act limits recovery to persons whose net worth did not exceed $2 million at the time the court action or board appeal was initiated. Eligible businesses must have a net worth of no more than $7 million and have no more than 500 employees.[42] Note that when a subcontractor's claim is brought in the name of the prime contractor, it is the net worth of the prime contractor that will be considered in determining the party's small business status.[43]

c. "Prevailing Party." In determining what constitutes a "prevailing party" in litigation against the Government, the boards have held that the small business (1) need not prevail on every claim,[44] (2) must prevail on a claim that is more than "de minimus,"[45] (3) cannot be a "prevailing party" if the matter is not litigated (even if it is negotiated to a successful conclusion),[46] and (4) can be a "prevailing party" if it prevails after mediation.[47]

d. Government Position Not "Substantially Justified." The EAJA provides that a court or board may not award attorney fees or expenses to an eligible, prevailing party if the Government's position in the litigation was "substantially justified."[48] Congress specifically provided in the 1985 amendments to the EAJA that "whether or not [an agency] position...was substantially justified shall be determined on the basis of the administrative record, as a whole, which is made in the adversary adjudication for which fees and other expenses are sought."[49]

Boards and courts have ruled that (a) to be substantially justified, the Government's litigation position must be "justified to a degree that would satisfy a reasonable person,"[50] (b) the Government has the burden of proving its position was justified,[51] (c) the Government's position was substantially justified where the case was a close one of first impression[52] and where the contractor recovered only 18% of its claim,[53] and (d) the Government's position was not substantially justified where the Government failed to recognize industry customs and practice;[54] where the Government, without explanation, failed to produce an important witness;[55] and where the Government's interpretation of the contract either ignored or rendered meaningless a significant portion of the contract's specifications.[56]

e. Amount Of Recovery. As to the amount of the award, boards have held that (1) attorney fees will be based upon prevailing market rates without regard to the actual fee arrangement used,[57] and (2) attorney fees and expenses will be based on the amount of effort expended on the successful portion of the claim rather than on a strict mathematical formula.[58]

B. WOMEN-OWNED SMALL BUSINESS PREFERENCES

The Government's offer of special consideration to women-owned small businesses has existed for some time. Under an Executive Order issued in 1979,[59] federal agencies were directed to take appropriate action to facilitate, preserve, and strengthen women's business enterprises and to ensure full participation by women in the free enterprise system.[60]

The FAR implements this directive by requiring the inclusion of a clause in all contracts expected to exceed the small purchase limitation—except contracts to be performed entirely outside the U.S. and contracts for personal services.[61] This clause, the "Utilization of Women-Owned Small Businesses" clause,[62] requires a contractor to use its "best efforts to give women-owned small businesses the maximum practicable opportunity to participate in the subcontracts it awards to the fullest extent consistent with the efficient performance of its contract."[63] The clause defines "women-owned small businesses" as businesses "that are at least 51 percent owned by women who are United States citizens and who also control and operate the business."[64]

In 1994, Congress specifically added women-owned small businesses to the set-aside programs for small and small disadvantaged businesses under the Small Business Act (see Section A above) and established a Government-wide goal of 5% participation by women-owned small businesses in prime contract and subcontract awards for each fiscal year.[65]

C. LABOR SURPLUS AREA PREFERENCES

The Government has established, and the FAR implements, a system of contracting preferences—primarily contract set-asides and subcontracting programs—that favor contractors who perform in labor surplus areas. A "labor surplus area" (LSA) is defined in the FAR as a "geographical area identified by the Department of Labor...as an area of concentrated unemployment or underemployment or an area of labor surplus."[66]

1. Qualification

Contractors qualify for LSA concern status if they and their first-tier subcontractors perform contract work substantially in a labor surplus area. A contractor has performed substantially in a labor surplus area if the manufacturing, production, or performance costs incurred under the contract in the labor surplus area exceed 50% of the contract price.[67] A contractor need not be a small business to qualify for LSA concern preferences.

2. Contract Set-Asides

Contracts may be entirely set aside for LSA concerns when there is a reasonable expectation that offers will be obtained from a sufficient number of responsible LSA concerns to ensure reasonable prices.[68] Whether the requisite conditions support a set-aside is within the discretion of the Contracting Officer, whose decision will not be overturned unless there is a clear showing of an abuse of discretion.[69]

LSA contract set-asides are required to be awarded by using sealed bids or competitive proposals restricted to eligible LSA concerns.[70] However, if before contract award the Contracting Officer determines that a set-aside would be detrimental to the public interest (because of unreasonable prices, for example), the set-aside may be withdrawn and the acquisition may be completed by unrestricted procurement procedures.[71]

3. Subcontracting

Under the FAR, in contracts that exceed the small purchase threshold but do not exceed $500,000, contractors are required to use their best efforts to subcontract with LSA concerns.[72] In contracts that exceed $500,000, contractors and their major subcontractors are required to take affirmative action to place subcontracts with LSA concerns.[73] Note, however, that these requirements are conditional and operate only when such subcontracting is (a) consistent with the efficient performance of the contract and (b) at prices no higher than those obtainable elsewhere.[74]

D. NONDISCRIMINATION REQUIREMENTS

As discussed below, prime contractors and subcontractors—both large and small—must comply with various statutes and regulations requiring equal employment opportunity and prohibiting discrimination in employment.

1. Equal Employment Opportunity

a. **"Equal Opportunity" Clause.** The primary clause for implementing the policy of equal employment opportunity under the FAR[75] is the "Equal Opportunity" clause[76] (promulgated under Executive Order 11246,[77] as amended). This clause—with some exceptions—must be incorporated into all prime contracts and subcontracts over $10,000.[78] However, if the contract is less than $10,000 but the contractor has been awarded contracts or subcontracts aggregating over $10,000 in any previous 12-month period, the clause must be included in the current contract.[79]

Under the "Equal Opportunity" clause, contractors are (1) prohibited from discriminating against any employee or applicant for employment on the basis of race, color, religion, sex, or national origin and (2) required to take affirmative action to ensure nondiscriminating employment practices.[80] Such affirmative action applies not only to hiring practices but to practices *related* to hiring—such as promotion, demotion or transfer, recruitment or recruitment advertising, layoff or termination, rates of pay or other forms of compensation, and selection for training or apprenticeship.[81]

b. Affirmative Action Plans. In addition to complying with the "Equal Opportunity" clause, supply or service contractors and subcontractors with (a) 50 or more employees and (b) either (1) nonexempt contracts or subcontracts of $50,000 or more or (2) Government bills of lading expected to exceed $50,000 in any 12-month period, are required to develop—within 120 days from the time performance of a contract begins—a written affirmative action program for each of their establishments, complete with detailed goals and timetables.[82] Construction contractors with nonexempt construction contracts must comply with contract terms and conditions specifying affirmative action requirements applicable to covered geographical areas or projects and applicable rules and regulations promulgated by the Secretary of Labor.[83]

2. Miscellaneous Requirements

Title VII of the Civil Rights Act of 1964,[84] Executive Order 11141,[85] the Federal Rehabilitation Act of 1973,[86] the Americans with Disabilities Act of 1990,[87] and the Vietnam Era Veterans Readjustment Assistance Act of 1974[88] also impose some nondiscrimination requirements on federal contractors. Title VII makes it unlawful for employers with 15 or more employees to discriminate on the basis of race, color, religion, sex, or national origin,[89] while Executive Order 11141 establishes a federal policy against discrimination on the basis of age. Although contract clauses prohibiting age discrimination are not required, the FAR requires agencies to bring this policy to the attention of contractors[90] and request compliance if valid complaints are made.[91]

In implementation of the Rehabilitation Act, the FAR directs that all Government contracts or subcontracts over $2,500 must contain an affirmative action clause stating that the contractor "shall not discriminate against any employee or applicant because of physical or mental handicap."[92] This clause need not be used, however, if the contract work is performed outside the U.S. by employees recruited outside the U.S., or if the clause terms have been waived by the contracting agency.[93] The Americans with Disabilities Act mandates strict personnel rules so that the disabled can be assured of fair employment practices (as well as changes in the physical makeup of some contractor facilities to provide reasonable work accommodations). To carry out the Vietnam Era Veterans Readjustment Assistance Act, the FAR directs that, in the absence of a waiver by the contracting agency, all contracts or subcontracts exceeding $10,000 contain a clause[94] requiring affirmative action to employ (and advance) qualified disabled veterans and veterans of the Vietnam War.[95]

3. Administration & Enforcement

The Office of Federal Contract Compliance Programs (OFCCP), operating under authority delegated by the Secretary of Labor, is responsible for the administration and enforcement of the Government's equal employment policies.[96] Complaints received by the Contracting Officer alleging violations of the Executive Order establishing these policies[97] and contractors' inquiries regarding their compliance status or their right to appeal enforcement sanctions[98] are referred to the OFCCP for resolution. If the OFCCP determines that a contractor has violated the policies of the Executive Order, regulations of the Secretary of Labor, or applicable contract clauses, it may impose the following sanctions:[99]

(1) Publication of the contractor's name.

(2) Cancellation, termination, or suspension of all (or part) of the contractor's contracts.

(3) Debarment of the contractor from future Government contracts (or extensions or modifications of existing contracts) until the contractor has established and carried out personnel and employment policies in compliance with Executive Order 11246 and the regulations of the Secretary of Labor.

(4) Referral to the Department of Justice or the Equal Employment Opportunity Commission for appropriate civil or criminal proceedings.

Title VII of the Civil Rights Act is enforced by the Equal Employment Opportunity Commission.[100] The Commission is authorized to investigate charges of discrimination, to secure voluntary compliance with the Act, and to initiate suit against the violating contractor if voluntary compliance fails. Under Title VII, an aggrieved person may also sue the contractor in U.S. District Court seeking an injunction or damages.[101]

E. LABOR STANDARDS REQUIREMENTS

Government contractors are required to comply with the labor standards imposed under various federal statutes,[102] notably the Walsh-Healey Act, the Service Contract Act, the Davis-Bacon Act, and the Contract Work Hours and Safety Standards Act. These statutes were enacted to prevent substandard wage rates and working conditions in the performance of Government contracts. Because two of these statutes—the Davis-Bacon Act and the Contract Work Hours and Safety Standards Act—pertain to construction contracts, they are discussed in detail in the last part of this book where matters relating specifically to Government construction contracting are treated (see Chapter 27). The other two statutes are discussed below.

1. Walsh-Healey Act

a. Coverage. The Walsh-Healey Act establishes labor standards for Government contracts in excess of $10,000 to manufacture or furnish materials, supplies, articles, and equipment.[103] The Act applies to prime contractors. However, if a subcontractor is performing the work of a prime contractor, it may be considered a *substitute* manufacturer or supplier and will then be subject to the Act.[104] The Act covers only those employees actually engaged in (or connected with) the manufacturing and supply process—not to office or custodial workers, executive-level personnel, or outside sales personnel.[105]

The Walsh-Healey Act contains a certification requirement.[106] Thus, the contractor must certify the following:

(a) Employees manufacturing or furnishing the contract items will be paid no less than the prevailing minimum wage for persons performing similar work (or in the particular industry) in the locality where the contract is to be performed (as determined by the Secretary of Labor).

(b) These employees (1) will be compensated at applicable overtime rates for work in excess of 40 hours in one week, (2) will not be required to perform under working conditions that are hazardous, unsanitary, or dangerous to health and safety, (3) are over 16 years of age, and (4) are not convict laborers.

Both statutory and regulatory *exemptions* are available under the Walsh-Healey Act. Statutorily exempted from the Act's requirements are supply contracts for specifically authorized "open market" purchases (commodities), perishables, agricultural products, and contracts made by the Secretary of Agriculture in purchasing agricultural products.[107] Regulatory exemptions are granted at the discretion of the Secretary of Labor where such exemptions would further justice and the public interest.[108] Examples of regulatory exemptions include contracts for public utility services and contracts for supplies manufactured outside the U.S., Puerto Rico, and the Virgin Islands.[109]

b. Administration & Enforcement. The Secretary of Labor is charged with the administration and enforcement of the Walsh-Healey Act.[110] Penalties for violating the Act include

(1) terminating the contract for default and charging the contractor for the excess costs of reprocurement, (2) debarring the contractor from contracting with the Government for up to three years, and (3) assessing damages in the amount of unpaid wages plus liquidated damages of $10 per day for each underaged worker or convict improperly employed. Penalties are collected by the Government on behalf of the employees by withholding payments on the contract or, if necessary, through court action.[111]

2. Service Contract Act

a. Coverage. Just as the Walsh-Healey Act covers supply contracts, the Service Contract Act establishes labor standards for contracts that are primarily for services.[112] The Service Contract Act applies to every Government contract over $2,500 when its principal purpose is to furnish services in the United States through the use of service employees, and the Act covers both contractors and subcontractors.[113]

The Act does not cover service contracts that are performed (a) exclusively by executive-level, administrative, or professional personnel, or (b) primarily by bona fide executive, administrative, or professional employees when service employees are only a minor factor in the performance of the contract.[114] In addition, the Act's coverage specifically excludes the following: (1) construction work covered by the Davis-Bacon Act (see Chapter 27), (2) supply contracts covered by the Walsh-Healey Act, (3) transportation contracts, (4) communications contracts, (5) contracts for public utility services, and (6) contracts for individual personal services.[115]

b. Administration & Enforcement. Administration and enforcement under the Service Contract Act is similar to the Walsh-Healey Act. Thus, contractors are required to comply with certain minimum wage levels and working conditions or face sanctions, such as the withholding of payments or debarment from contracting.[116] As with the other Acts, the Secretary of Labor is authorized to administer the Act and enforce its requirements.[117]

F. BUY AMERICAN ACT REQUIREMENTS

Another socioeconomic policy created by the Government and implemented in the procurement process is that expressed in the provisions of the Buy American Act.[118] The Act carries out the Government's preference for the use of American-made materials and the purchase of domestically-manufactured goods, establishing the requirement that acquisitions for public use be for materials, supplies, or articles substantially composed of domestic products.[119] In this regard, the Comptroller General has held that the fact that the manufacturer of a domestically manufactured end product is foreign-owned is not a factor to be considered in determining whether to apply the Buy American Act differential.[120]

Contracts for the construction, repair, or alteration of public buildings or public works within the United States also come within the provisions of the Buy American Act.[121] However, the Act does not apply to supply contracts if (1) what is acquired will be used outside the U.S., (2) the use of a domestic product is inconsistent with the public interest, or (3) a domestic product is not available in reasonable quality or quantity or at a reasonable cost.[122] Similarly, with respect to construction contracts, "domestic construction materials" need not be used when (a) the cost would be unreasonable, (b) the use of a particular domestic material is impracticable, or (c) the material is not mined, produced, or manufactured in the U.S. in sufficient and reasonably available commercial quantities of satisfactory quality.[123] "Domestic construction material" is defined as (1) an unmanufactured construction material that is mined or produced in the U.S. or (2) a manufactured construction material if (a) it is manufactured in the U.S., and (b) the cost of its U.S. components exceeds 50% of the cost of all its components.[124]

As noted above, materials and end products are exempt from the Buy American Act if they are not mined, produced, or manufactured in the U.S. in sufficient and reasonably available commercial quantities of a satisfactory quality. The FAR contains a list of nearly 100 items that fall into this category, including bauxite, nickel, rubber, graphite, petroleum, and spare parts for foreign equipment.[125] In addition, DOD and the National Aeronautics and Space Administration have determined that it is not in the public interest to apply Buy American Act restrictions to certain of their procurements[126] or to purchases from North Atlantic Treaty Organization countries or from Israel and Egypt.[127]

The Trade Agreements Act of 1979 waives the Buy American Act preference for products from signatory countries to the General Agreement on Tariffs and Trade (GATT).[128] Regulations implementing the Trade Agreements Act establish a policy—with certain exceptions—that agencies evaluate offers over designated amounts for an "eligible end product" without regard to the restrictions of the Buy American Act.[129] An "eligible end product" is an article that (a) is entirely the growth, product, or manufacture of the designated country or (b) consists in whole or in part of materials from another country and has been substantially transformed into a new and different article with a name, character, or use distinct from the article from which it was transformed.[130] The term includes services incidental to supply (except transportation services), provided the value of the incidental services does not exceed the value of the product itself. Service contracts as such are not included.[131]

Note finally that effective June 1990,[132] the Buy American Act applied to services (for the first time) and prohibited Government agencies from purchasing products and services from individuals or organizations of countries that have (1) signed but not abided by the GATT Agreement on Government Procurement, (2) signed and abided by the Agreement but discriminated against U.S. products and services not covered by the Agreement, and (3) not signed the Agreement and discriminated against U.S. products and services in their procurements. To fall within the last two categories, (a) the country's services and products must have been acquired in significant amounts by the U.S. Government, and (b) the country must have maintained a significant and persistent practice of discriminating against U.S. products, resulting in identifiable harm to U.S. businesses. The prohibition does not apply with respect to services procured and used outside the U.S. and its territories or to articles from, or citizens of, a "least developed country" under the Trade Agreements Act of 1979.

To assure compliance with the Buy American Act, the FAR requires use of a number of solicitation provisions and contract clauses.[133] Contractors who violate the Buy American Act—as well as subcontractors or suppliers with whom they are associated—may be debarred from contracting with the Government for a period of three years.[134]

G. ENVIRONMENTAL PROTECTION REQUIREMENTS

The federal procurement process has also been used to implement the Government's policy of improving environmental quality. Provisions have been included in the FAR[135] to help carry out the objectives contained in, for example, the Clean Air Act,[136] the Clean Water Act,[137] the Solid Waste Disposal Act,[138] and the National Environmental Policy Act.[139] As a result, Government agencies are required to conduct their procurement activities in a way that will effectively enforce these statutes.[140]

For example, procurement agencies are prohibited from entering into, renewing, or extending contracts over $100,000 with firms that intend to use facilities that the Environmental Protection Agency has listed as violating the Clean Air Act or the Clean Water Act.[141] Contractors are required to certify that they do not intend to use such a facility in the performance of their contracts.[142] In addition, a clause must be included in all Government contracts over $100,000 that requires contractors to (a) comply with all requirements of the Clean Air Act and the Clean Water Act relating to inspection, entry, monitoring, reports, and information, (b) use their best efforts to comply with Clean Air and Clean Water Act standards at facilities where the contract is performed, and (c) include the certification requirement in all nonexempt subcontracts.[143]

H. DRUG-FREE WORKPLACE REQUIREMENTS

In response to the increasing problem of illicit drug use, the Government has taken steps to counteract drug use among Government employees and in the Government contractor workplace. Legislation enacted in 1988 and amended in 1994 requires that, for contracts in excess of the simplified acquisition threshold (except for contracts for commercial items), contractors establish and maintain a drug-free workplace as a condition of maintaining their current contracts and eligibility for future contracts.[144] Provisions have been added to the FAR to implement this legislation, and a "Certification Regarding a Drug-Free Workplace" clause has been promulgated as well.[145]

Under the implementing regulations, contractors must certify that they will provide a drug-free workplace by taking the following steps:[146]

(1) Publishing a statement (a) notifying employees that the unlawful manufacture, distribution, dispensing, possession, or use of a controlled substance is prohibited in the contractor's workplace and (b) specifying the actions that will be taken against employees who violate that prohibition.

(2) Establishing an ongoing drug-free awareness program to inform employees about (a) the dangers of drug abuse in the workplace, (b) the contractor's drug-free workplace policy, (c) any available drug counseling, rehabilitation, and employee assistance programs, and (d) the possible penalties for drug abuse violations occurring in the workplace.

(3) Requiring that employees directly involved in performing a Government contract notify the contractor within five days of any criminal drug conviction for a violation occurring in the workplace.

(4) Notifying the Contracting Officer about any such conviction within 10 days after the contractor (a) received the above notice from the employee or (b) otherwise received actual notice from any employee convicted of a drug abuse violation in the workplace, either taking "appropriate personnel action" against the employee (up to and including termination) or requiring the employee to participate in an approved drug abuse assistance or rehabilitation program.

The regulations and legislation further provide that the Government can suspend payments or terminate contracts when contractors make false certifications, violate their certifications, or fail to make good faith efforts to provide a drug-free workplace.[147] However, the head of the contracting agency may waive these actions if necessary to prevent a severe, detrimental disruption of the agency's operations. The Office of Management and Budget has published a question-and-answer-style "guidance" to assist the public in meeting the requirements of the Drug-Free Workplace Act.[148]

Prior to enactment of the law described above, DOD issued a "Drug-Free Work Force" clause as part of its own procurement regulations requiring defense contractors to institute and maintain a program to achieve a drug-free work force.[149] This clause includes a requirement for drug testing by contractors of employees who hold "sensitive positions," a requirement that goes beyond what the legislation and FAR procurement regulations mentioned above require. The clause applies to all DOD contracts involving access to classified information and any other defense contract if the Contracting Officer determines it necessary for reasons of national security or for the purpose of protecting the health and safety of those using or affected by the contract's performance or end-product.

REFERENCES

1. P.L. 103-355, § 8003, 108 Stat. 3243 (Oct. 13, 1994). See generally Horowitz & Wickersty, "Socio-Economic Procurement Requirements," Briefing Papers No. 85-3 (Mar. 1985), 7 BPC 49.

2. P.L. 85-536, 72 Stat. 384, as amended (codified at 15 USC § 631 et seq.).

3. Office of Federal Procurement Policy, Policy Letter 91-1, 56 Fed. Reg. 11796 (Mar. 20, 1991).

4. P.L. 103-355, note 1, supra, § 7102.

5. 15 USC § 632(a).

6. See FAR 19.101.

7. See FAR 19.102.

8. Note 7, supra. See also Hordell & Lipman, "Small Business Size Appeals/Edition II," Briefing Papers No. 92-7 (June 1992).

9. See 15 USC § 637(d).

10. FAR subpt. 19.5.

11. 15 USC § 644(j); FAR 13.105.

12. FAR 19.502-2.

13. See FAR 19.502-3(a).

14. See FAR 52.219-7, para. (b)(3).

15. 15 USC § 637(b)(7).

16. See FAR 9.103, subpt. 19.6. See generally Efron & Muchmore, "Certificates of Competency," Briefing Papers No. 87-11 (Oct. 1987), 7 BPC 637.

17. See FAR 19.602-2, 19.602-3.

18. FAR 19.708(a).

19. FAR 52.219-8, para. (b).

20. FAR 19.705-7.

21. P.L. 95-507, 92 Stat. 1757.

22. FAR 19.708(b).

23. FAR 52.219-9.

24. 15 USC § 637(a).

25. See FAR subpt. 19.8.

26. See FAR 19.802; 13 CFR § 124.101 et seq. See also San Antonio General Maintenance, Inc. v. Abnor, 691 F. Supp. 1462 (D.D.C. 1987) (contractor who "graduates" from 8(a) Program is ineligible to bid on follow-on portion of 8(a) contract if Government decides contract should remain in 8(a) Program and be awarded to another small disadvantaged firm), 30 GC ¶ 71.

27. 13 CFR § 124.106.

28. 13 CFR § 124.107.

29. See FAR 19.806-4.

30. FAR 19.805-1.

31. FAR 19.810.

32. See Decorama Painting, Inc., ASBCA 25299, 81-1 BCA ¶ 14992; Kyle Engrg. Co., ASBCA 25168, 81-1 BCA ¶ 14990, 23 GC ¶ 18; North Chicago Disposal Co., ASBCA 25535, 81-1 BCA ¶ 14978, 23 GC ¶ 418.

SOCIOECONOMIC CONSIDERATIONS 6-23

33. P.L. 96-481, tit. II, 94 Stat. 2321.

34. See generally Tobin & Stiffler, "Recovering Legal Fees Under EAJA/ Edition II, Briefing Papers No. 91-7 (June 1991), 9 BPC 421. See also Pachter & Howarth, "Recovering Legal Fees Under EAJA," Briefing Papers No. 82-2 (Apr. 1982), 6 BPC 17, for a discussion of the Act shortly after it went into effect.

35. Note 33, supra, § 204.

36. Note 33, supra, § 204.

37. See, e.g., T.H. Taylor, Inc., ASBCA 26494-0, 83-1 BCA ¶ 16310; Stephens Assocs., PSBCA 933, 82-2 BCA ¶ 16043. Cf. Fidelity Const. Co. v. U.S., 700 F.2d 1379 (Fed. Cir.), 1 FPD ¶ 68, 25 GC ¶ 86, cert. denied, 464 U.S. 826 (1983).

38. 5 USC § 504(a)(1).

39. See 26 GC ¶ 347.

40. P.L. 99-80, 99 Stat. 183 (codified at 5 USC § 504, 28 USC § 2412).

41. Note 40, supra, § 6.

42. 5 USC § 504(b)(1)(B); 28 USC § 2412(d)(2)(B).

43. Teton Const. Co., ASBCA 27700, 87-2 BCA ¶ 19766, 29 GC ¶ 146.

44. Murphy Bros., Inc., DOTBCA 1836, 87-1 BCA ¶ 19500, 29 GC ¶ 146 (Note); Crown Laundry & Dry Cleaners, Inc., ASBCA 28889 et al., 87-3 BCA¶ 20034.

45. Yamas Const. Co., ASBCA 27366, 87-2 BCA ¶ 19695, 29 GC ¶ 146 (Note).

46. Preston-Brady Co., VABCA 1849-E, 89-3 BCA ¶ 22122.

47. Olson's Mechanical & Heavy Rigging, ENGBCA 5260-F et al., 90-1 BCA ¶ 22472.

48. 5 USC § 504(a)(1); 28 USC § 2412 (d)(1)(A).

49. 5 USC § 504(a)(1); 28 USC § 2412(d)(1)(B).

50. Pierce v. Underwood, 487 U.S. 552 (1988), 30 GC ¶ 311.

51. Cox Const. Co. v. U.S., 17 Cl. Ct. 29 (1989), 8 FPD ¶ 61.

52. JANA, Inc., ASBCA 32447, 89-2 BCA ¶ 21638; Insul-Glass Inc., GSBCA 9910-C(8223), 89-3 BCA ¶ 22223.

53. Russell Drilling Co., IBCA 2560-F, 90-1 BCA ¶ 22500.

54. Gracon Corp., IBCA 2582-F, 90-2 BCA ¶ 22550, 32 GC ¶ 147.

55. Sardis Contractors, ENGBCA 5256-F, 90-3 BCA ¶ 23010.

56. Hill Bros. Const. Co., ENGBCA 5673-F, 90-3 BCA ¶ 23249.

57. Margaret Howard, ASBCA 28648, 88-3 BCA ¶ 21040, 32 GC ¶ 147.

58. Salisbury & Dietz Inc., IBCA 2382-F, 89-3 BCA ¶ 21981, 31 GC ¶ 354 (Note). See also Community Heating & Plumbing v. Garrett, 12 FPD ¶ 75 (Fed. Cir. 1993) (method of computing fees where contractor obtained only partial judgment), 36 GC ¶ 45.

59. Exec. Order 12138, 44 Fed. Reg. 29637 (May 18, 1979).

60. See FAR 19.901.

61. FAR 19.902.

62. FAR 52.219-13.

63. FAR 52.219-13, para. (c).

64. FAR 52.219-13, para. (a).

65. 15 USC §§ 644(g), 637(d).

66. FAR 20.101.

67. Note 66, supra.

68. FAR 20.201-1. See FAR 52.220-2.

69. Friedrich Air Conditioning & Refrigeration Co., Comp. Gen. Dec. B-212777, 83-2 CPD ¶ 308.

70. FAR 20.204(a).

71. FAR 20.205(a).

72. FAR 20.301(a). See also the clause in FAR 52.220-3.

73. FAR 20.301(b). See also the clause in FAR 52.220-4.

74. FAR 20.301(a), (b).

75. FAR subpt. 22.8.

76. FAR 52.222-26.

77. 30 Fed. Reg. 12319 (Sept. 24, 1965).

78. See FAR 22.807.

SOCIOECONOMIC CONSIDERATIONS 6-25

79. See FAR 52.222-26, para. (a).
80. FAR 52.222-26, para. (b).
81. FAR 52.222-26, para. (b)(2).
82. FAR 22.804-1.
83. FAR 22.804-2.
84. P.L. 83-352, tit. VII, 78 Stat. 253 (codified at 42 USC § 2000e et seq., as amended).
85. 29 Fed. Reg. 2477 (Feb. 12, 1964).
86. P.L. 93-112, 87 Stat. 355 (codified at 29 USC § 793).
87. P.L. 101-336, 104 Stat. 327 (codified at 42 USC § 12101 et seq.). See generally Arnavas, Marsh & Ortman, "Employment Provisions of the Americans With Disabilities Act," Briefing Papers No. 92-9 (Aug. 1992).
88. P.L. 92-450, 86 Stat. 1074 (codified at 38 USC § 2012).
89. 42 USC § 2000e-2.
90. FAR 22.901.
91. FAR 22.902.
92. FAR 52.222-36, para. (a).
93. FAR 22.1408.
94. FAR 22.1302.
95. FAR 52.222-35.
96. See FAR 22.803.
97. FAR 22.808.
98. FAR 22.806.
99. FAR 22.809.
100. 42 USC § 2000e-5.
101. See note 100, supra.
102. See generally Speck, "Labor Standards in Government Contracts," Briefing Papers No. 67-3 (June 1967), 1 BPC 241.
103. Act of June 30, 1936, 49 Stat. 2036, as amended (codified at 41 USC § 35 et seq.).

104. See U.S. v. Davison Fuel & Dock Co., 371 F.2d 705 (4th Cir. 1967), 9 GC ¶ 130; Dept. of Labor Rulings and Interpretations No. 3, § 30.

105. 41 CFR § 50-201.102. See also West Byrd Inc., Comp. Gen. Dec. B-237515, 90-1 CPD ¶ 159, 32 GC ¶ 97; Commercial Energies, Inc., Comp. Gen. Dec. B-240148, 90-2 CPD ¶ 319, 33 GC ¶ 26.

106. 41 USC § 35.

107. 41 USC § 43.

108. 41 USC § 40.

109. See FAR 22.604-2.

110. See 41 USC § 38.

111. 41 USC §§ 36, 37.

112. P.L. 89-286, 79 Stat. 1034 (codified at 41 USC § 351 et seq.). See generally Ginsburg, Abrahams & English, "The Service Contract Act," Briefing Papers No. 90-7 (June 1990), 9 BPC 139.

113. 41 USC § 351.

114. 29 CFR § 4.113.

115. 41 USC § 356.

116. 41 USC § 352.

117. 41 USC § 353.

118. Act of March 3, 1933, 47 Stat. 1520 (codified at 41 USC § 10a et seq.). See generally Kenney, Burgett & Schroer, "Domestic Preference Provisions/Edition II," Briefing Papers No. 94-3 (Feb. 1994); Kenney & Duberstein, "Domestic Preference Provisions," Briefing Papers No. 89-3 (Feb. 1989), 8 BPC 299; Speck, "Buy American Act," Briefing Papers No. 70-6 (Dec. 1970), 2 BPC 85.

119. 41 USC § 10a.

120. Military Optic, Inc., Comp. Gen. Dec. B-245010.3, 92-1 CPD ¶ 78, 34 GC ¶ 204.

121. 41 USC § 10b.

122. See FAR 25.102(a).

123. See FAR 25.202.

124. FAR 25.201.

125. FAR 25.108(d).

SOCIOECONOMIC CONSIDERATIONS 6-27

126. FAR 25.103.
127. See, e.g., DFARS pt. 225.
128. P.L. 96-39, 93 Stat. 146 (codified at 19 USC § 2501 et seq.). See FAR subpt. 25.4.
129. FAR 25.402.
130. See FAR 25.401.
131. Note 130, supra.
132. Omnibus Trade and Competitiveness Act of 1988, P.L. 100-418, tit. VII (amending the Buy American Act).
133. See FAR 25.109, 25.205.
134. 41 USC § 10b(b); FAR 25.204.
135. See FAR subpt. 23.1.
136. 42 USC § 7401 et seq.
137. 33 USC § 1251 et seq.
138. 42 USC § 6901 et seq.
139. 42 USC § 4321 et seq.
140. FAR 23.103. See generally Hall & Davis, "Environmental Compliance at Federal Facilities," Briefing Papers No. 88-9 (Aug. 1988), 8 BPC 183; Hannah & Boehlert, "Environmental Requirements," Briefing Papers No. 75-2 (Apr. 1975), 3 BPC 185; Efron & Engel, "Government Indemnification for Environmental Liability," Briefing Papers No. 92-11 (Oct. 1992).
141. FAR 23.103(b).
142. FAR 23.105(a), 52.223-1.
143. FAR 23.105(b), 52.223-2.
144. Omnibus Drug Initiative Act of 1988, P.L. 100-690 § 5152 (codified at 41 USC § 701 et seq., as amended by P.L. 103-355, note 1, supra, §§ 4104, 8301).
145. FAR subpt. 23.5, 52.223-5, 52.223-6.
146. FAR 23.504.
147. FAR 23.506.

148. 55 Fed. Reg. 21679 (May 25, 1990); see 32 GC ¶ 181. See also Arnavas & Ganther, "The Drug Free Workplace," Briefing Papers No. 89-9 (Aug. 1989), 8 BPC 409.

149. DFARS 252.223-7004. See DFARS subpt. 223.5; 33 GC ¶ 372; 34 GC ¶ 425.

FRAUD AND ETHICAL CONSIDERATIONS

7

A. **Fraud**
   1. Civil False Claims Act
   2. "Qui Tam" Provisions
   3. Criminal False Claims Act
   4. False Statements Act
   5. Mail & Wire Fraud
   6. Program Fraud Civil Remedies Act
   7. Major Fraud Act

B. **Corruption**
   1. Anti-Kickback Enforcement Act Of 1986
   2. Bribery & Illegal Gratuities Statutes
   3. Procurement Integrity Act
   4. Byrd Amendment

C. **Enforcement**
   1. Inspectors General
   2. Department Of Justice
   3. Suspension & Debarment

The Government has continued its efforts to eliminate, or at least minimize, the adverse effects that fraudulent conduct by contractors can have on the integrity of the federal procurement process. The numerous civil and criminal investigations and prosecutions of Government contractors in recent years bear witness to the fact that fraud and misconduct is considered a major impediment to the conduct of proper procurement and will be vigorously combatted.

There are numerous statutes that the Government may employ to combat procurement fraud, including laws as diverse as the Racketeer Influenced and Corrupt Organizations Act, the Sherman Antitrust Act, or the law against improper conveyance of Government property.[1] As a procurement "streamlining" panel observed, in the main, these statutes properly serve their intended purposes:[2]

> The laws governing criminal and civil fraud, for example, represent carefully adjusted balances of public and private interests. Many of them have Civil War antecedents, and if redrafted today would, in all likelihood, emerge in starkly different form and vocabulary. With rare exception, however, they remain current and serve well.

This chapter provides an overview only of the most significant civil and criminal statutes—and penalties—that may arise in the procurement context. It also considers some of the predominant enforcement mechanisms used by the Government to attack fraud and corruption in the procurement process.

A. FRAUD

There are several criminal statutes under which the Government prosecutes procurement fraud. There are also several civil statutes that provide for heavy fines and administrative penalties for fraudulent conduct. The seven most important of these in the procurement context—(1) the civil False Claims Act, (2) the "qui tam" provisions of the civil False Claims Act, (3) the criminal False Claims Act, (4) the false statements provisions of the criminal False Claims Act (commonly called the False Statements Act), (5) the mail and wire fraud statutes, (6) the Program Fraud Civil Remedies Act, and (7) the Major Fraud Act of 1988—are discussed below.

1. Civil False Claims Act

The civil False Claims Act, as amended in 1986,[3] subjects to liability a person who, among other things:

(a) Knowingly presents, or causes to be presented to a Government official a false or fraudulent claim for payment or approval;

(b) Knowingly makes, uses, or causes to be made or used a false record or statement to get a false or fraudulent claim paid or approved;

(c) Conspires to defraud the Government by getting a false or fraudulent claim allowed or paid; or

(d) Knowingly makes, uses, or causes to be made or used a false record or statement to conceal, avoid, or decrease an obligation to pay or transmit money or property to the Government.

a. Key Definitions. The 1986 amendment to the civil False Claims Act clarified the definitions of "knowingly" and "claim" as used in the Act. A person acts "knowingly" if he has actual knowledge of the information or acts in deliberate ignorance (or in reckless disregard) of the truth or falsity of the information.[4] No proof of specific intent to defraud the Government is required. "Claim" is defined to include any request or demand for money or property "made to a contractor, grantee, or other recipient" if the Government provides or will reimburse any portion of the money or property requested or demanded.[5]

b. Burden Of Proof. The Government bears the burden of proof in civil prosecutions under the False Claims Act and, prior to the 1986 amendments, most courts required that violations be proved by "clear and convincing evidence." This deviation from the usual burden of proof by "a preponderance of the evidence" in civil cases was based both on the penal nature of the statute's remedies and on the historical use of the higher burden of proof in common law fraud cases. Today, however, the Act mandates that all essential elements of a civil false claims violation, including damages, be proved merely by "a preponderance of the evidence."[6]

c. Penalties. If liability is found under the civil False Claims Act, the Government may recover (1) between $5,000 and $10,000 for each false claim, (2) an amount equal to three times the amount of damages the Government sustained because of the false claim, plus (3) the costs to the Government of prosecution. Because penalties are imposed for *each* false claim presented, violation of the civil False Claims Act can lead to large fines that have been criticized as "unreasonable or excessive."[7]

The Act attempts to encourage cooperation by violators by providing for a *reduced* penalty of not more than two times the amount of damages sustained by the Government if, prior to the commencement of any criminal, civil, or administrative action, the person committing the violation (a) furnishes the Government with all information that person has about the violation (within 30 days of receiving the information) and (b) cooperates fully with any Government investigation.[8]

Consequential damages—those that do not flow directly and immediately from the proscribed act but only incidentally from its consequences or results—generally may not be collected under the civil False Claims Act. For example, in one early case that involved the sale of mislabeled aircraft bearings that the Government subsequently had to remove and replace, the Court of Appeals for the Fifth Circuit allowed the Government to recover twice the price of the bearings but not twice the cost of removal and replacement.[9] The replacement cost was eventually recovered, however, under a breach of warranty theory.

2. "Qui Tam" Provisions

"Qui tam" provisions have been part of the civil False Claims Act ever since its original passage.[10] These provisions allow private individuals to initiate civil false claims lawsuits on behalf of themselves and the Government and then keep a share of the Government's recovery. (The Government may take over prosecution of the action if it wishes to do so.) The law was unpopular and problematic for years, but it was reinvigorated by the 1986 amendments to the False Claims Act "to encourage any individual knowing of Government fraud to bring that information forward" by making such lawsuits more attractive and lucrative to a plaintiff.[11] The encouragement given appears to have had the desired effect. In the period between 1986 and the end of 1992, 407 "qui tam" lawsuits were filed, 75 were still under investigation, 150 had been dismissed, and 66 had been taken over by the Department of Justice. Of these 66, 37 had been settled for a total recovery to the Government of $147 million.[12]

a. Relators. When a private party files a "qui tam" suit in the name of the Government, the lawsuit is said to be brought "on relation of" the private party. Hence, the private party is referred to as the "relator." Relators may be natural persons or artificial persons such as corporations. Most "qui tam" suits are filed by employees against their former employers.[13] Some "qui tam" relators have continued working for their employers even after filing suits against them.[14] A law firm,[15] a nonprofit organization,[16] and Government employees[17] are among those that have filed suits pursuant to the amended "qui tam" provisions of the civil False Claims Act.

b. Limitations. There are statutory and other limitations on bringing "qui tam" suits. For example, (a) suits between members of the military, (b) suits against Government officials based on information already known to the Government, and (c) suits based on allegations that are the subject of a civil suit to which the Government is a party are excluded.[18] The most important restriction is the "original source" rule created by the 1986 False Claims Act amendments. If the allegations in the complaint are based on *public information* (such as information from a court or congressional hearing or a report in the media), then the relator must be the "original source" of the information—i.e., he must have direct and independent knowledge of the information—in order to file a "qui tam" action.[19]

c. Procedures. Procedures for initiating a "qui tam" action are detailed and specific and failure to comply with the procedural requirements can result in dismissal of the action.[20]

The action is initiated by filing a complaint. A copy of the complaint, together with disclosure of substantially all material evidence, must be furnished to the Government. The complaint is filed under seal and remains under seal for at least 60 days. During this period, the Government determines whether it will intervene in the matter.[21] If the Government proceeds, it has the primary responsibility for prosecuting the action.[22] The relator has the right to continue as a party to the action subject to a number of limitations.[23]

The Government may dismiss the action over the objections of the relator if the relator was notified by the Government of the filing of the motion to dismiss and if the court provided the relator with an opportunity for a hearing on the motion.[24] The Government may settle the action over the objections of the relator if the court determines, after a hearing, that the proposed settlement is "fair, adequate, and reasonable under all the circumstances."[25] At least one court has refused to approve a settlement agreed to by the Government and the defendant but objected to by the relator.[26]

If the Government elects not to proceed with the action, the relator has the right to conduct the trial. The Government may—if it shows good cause—still intervene at a later juncture in the proceedings.[27] If the Government does not intervene, the case may only be dismissed by the relator if the Government concurs in writing.[28]

d. Recovery. If the Government prosecutes the action and is successful, the relator will be awarded between 15% and 25% of any proceeds of the action or settlement, depending on the relator's contributions to prosecution of the action, plus an amount for reasonable attorney fees and costs.[29] If the Government does not proceed with the action and the relator proceeds alone to trial or settlement, it will receive between 25% and 30% of the proceeds of the action or settlement, plus an amount for reasonable expenses and reasonable attorney fees and costs.[30]

Obviously, the court may *reduce* a relator's reward if it finds that the relator planned and initiated the False Claims Act violation.[31] If the relator is convicted of criminal conduct arising out of its role in violating the Act, it must be dismissed from the civil action and may not receive any proceeds.[32]

3. Criminal False Claims Act

The criminal False Claims Act has been in existence in substantially the same form since Civil War days. It currently provides as follows:[33]

> Whoever makes or presents to any person or officer in the civil, military, or naval service of the United States, or to any department or agency thereof, any claim upon or against the United States, or any department or agency thereof, knowing such claim to be false, fictitious, or fraudulent, shall be imprisoned not more than five years and shall be subject to a fine in the amount provided in this title.

a. "Claim." The criminal False Claims Act does not define what is meant by the phrase "any claim upon or against the United States," and the Supreme Court has taken an ambivalent view of the scope of this critical language. In one case, the Court cautioned that the term "claim" must be strictly construed because the Act is a criminal statute.[34] Subsequently, the Court appeared to expand its view (in discussing the civil False Claims Act) of a "claim" to include any fraudulent *attempt* to cause the Government to pay out money.[35]

As a practical matter, any invoice or other demand for payment or property from the Government is a "claim," and it is probably a "false claim" if it contains any incorrect or misleading information relating to that demand for payment. Lower courts have found "claims" in some very obvious and some less than obvious transactions. Certainly an "invoice submitted for payment is a claim within the meaning of the statute."[36] Other "claims" include progress payment invoices,[37] documents evidencing expenses to be credited against funds advanced by the Government,[38] "claims" for reduction of liability to the United States,[39] inflated labor and equipment charges,[40] invoices claiming payment for higher quality goods,[41] bloated insurance claims,[42] excessive or fraudulent travel vouchers,[43] and fraudulent tax returns.[44]

b. Knowledge & Intent. Both the civil and the criminal False Claims Acts require that a person make a claim "knowing" that it is false or fraudulent.[45] The difference between the civil and criminal statutes are in the level of intent required. As noted above in Section A.1, specific intent to defraud is not a prerequisite to civil liability under the False Claims Act—reckless conduct may be enough. Similarly, a specific intent to defraud is not required under the criminal Act.[46] The Government must prove, however, that the defendant knew the claim was false, fictitious, or fraudulent. And, as in all criminal cases, the Government must prove its case "beyond a reasonable doubt."

Since mere "knowledge" of a false claim is sufficient for conviction, a number of courts have rejected defense arguments that the contractor "gave the Government its money's worth" and had no intent to cheat when it submitted a false claim. Such decisions have reasoned that the purpose of the criminal False Claims Act "would be frustrated if criminal prosecutions were limited to those instances 'where the defendant is motivated solely by an intent to cheat the government or to gain an unjust benefit.'"[47]

c. Presentation Against Government. A criminal false claim must be made or presented "upon or against the United States." The claim need not be presented *directly* to the Government to violate the Act, however. For example, submission of falsified invoices by a subcontractor to a prime contractor with the knowledge that the prime contractor will pass the cost on to the Government constitutes a claim "upon or against" the Government.[48]

d. Penalties. A person convicted under the criminal False Claims Act is subject to imprisonment for not more than five years and may also be fined. The Federal Sentencing Guidelines make jail sentences virtually mandatory, even for first offenders, if the false claim exceeds $2,000.[49] Under the alternative penalties that may be imposed under the "Sentence of Fine" statute, fines can range up to $250,000 per offense for individuals and $500,000 per offense for organizations.[50] Under defense contracts, the maximum fine per contract may not exceed $1 million.[51]

4. False Statements Act

The False Statements Act[52] is one of the most widely used federal laws in prosecuting criminal fraud cases against contractors, although it originally was not specifically intended for use in Government contract matters. It provides as follows:

> Whoever, in any matter within the jurisdiction of any department or agency of the United States knowingly and willfully falsifies, conceals or covers up by any trick, scheme, or device a material fact, or makes any false, fictitious or fraudulent statements or representations, or makes or uses any false writing or document knowing the same to contain any false, fictitious or fraudulent statement or entry, shall be fined not more than $10,000 or imprisoned not more than five years, or both.

a. Included Offenses. The False Statements Act creates three related offenses: (1) "concealment" of a material fact, (2) making "false statements" or representations, and (3) making "false writings." "Statements" include oral statements and written documents, both sworn and unsworn.[53] The numerous transactions and certifications involved in Government contracting can readily give rise to "statements" that could be prosecuted under the Act.

The Supreme Court has repeatedly stated that Congress intended the False Statements Act to be broadly and liberally interpreted.[54] Thus, when a single act violates more than one statute, the Government may prosecute under the False Statements Act, even in cases where a narrower and more specific statute could be applied.[55]

b. Elements. Conviction under the False Statements Act requires proof of a number of elements, depending, in part, on which offenses are charged. There are five basic elements that must be proved: (a) a statement was made, (b) the statement was false, (c) the person making the statement knew it was false, fictitious, or fraudulent when made, (d) the statement was material (i.e, it had a natural tendency to influence or was capable of influencing the Government's determination that was based on the statement[56]), and (e) the statement concerned a matter within the jurisdiction of a federal agency.

c. Penalties. The penalty for violating the False Statements Act is a fine of up to $10,000 and up to five years' imprisonment.[57] In addition, as for criminal false claims (see Section A.3.d above), the alternative "Sentence of Fine" statutory penalties may be imposed.[58]

5. Mail & Wire Fraud

The federal criminal statutes covering mail fraud[59] and wire fraud[60] prohibit the use of the mails or interstate (or foreign) telecommunications systems to further a "scheme to defraud." These broadly-worded statutes basically make illegal any activity that is covered by the false claims or false statements criminal statutes discussed above and involves use of the mails, telephone, telegraph, etc. "Schemes to defraud" charged under these statutes in the procurement context have involved, for example, (1) a scheme to obtain competitors' bid information and Government evaluations of competing proposals,[61] (2) defective pricing schemes to inflate vendor quotations used to compile contract proposals,[62] and (3) billing by a contractor for work never performed by a fictitious subcontractor.[63]

The penalty for each count of mail or wire fraud is a fine of up to $1,000 and up to five years' imprisonment. The penalties can mount rapidly because each separate mailing or wiring is an offense under the statutes. Alternative "Sentence of Fine" penalties may also be imposed (see Section A.3.d above).

6. Program Fraud Civil Remedies Act

In 1986, Congress passed the Program Fraud Civil Remedies Act[64] to establish an administrative remedy for relatively minor fraud cases. Because the dollar value of many false claims against the Government is small, and court dockets are overcrowded, the Government has not judicially pursued, under the civil False Claims Act, many small-dollar false claims cases. The Program Fraud Civil Remedies Act provides a means of resolving small-dollar fraud cases in which the cost of litigation would exceed the damages subject to recovery by the Government.

The administrative procedure established by the Act is limited to cases of fraud not exceeding $150,000. The statute allows federal agencies to sue contractors for false claims and certified written false statements in *administrative tribunals* instead of federal courts. The Act imposes a civil penalty of up to $5,000 for each violation and double the falsely claimed amount for claims paid by the Government.

Agencies designate an investigative official—usually the Inspector General—to conduct investigations into possible violations of the Act and report his findings to a reviewing official. If there is "adequate evidence" of liability, the reviewing official refers the matter to the Department of Justice, which reviews the charges and determines whether to litigate the case. Only if the Justice Department approves may the agency commence administrative proceedings, which include a hearing, appeal procedures, and limited judicial review.[65] The Government has thus far made infrequent use of this law to combat contractor fraud.[66]

7. Major Fraud Act

The Major Fraud Act of 1988[67] created a new crime called "major fraud against the United States." This crime covers any Government prime contractor (or subcontractor or supplier) who knowingly executes (or attempts to execute) any scheme to defraud the Government (or to obtain money or property from the Government by false or fraudulent pretenses, representations, or promises) in any procurement of property or services over $1 million.

Prosecution can be initiated up to seven years after the offense has been committed. The penalties for violation of the Major Fraud Act are up to 10 years' imprisonment and a

$1-million fine. However, the fine may increase to $5 million if (1) the Government's gross loss (or the defendant's gross gain) is $500,000 or more, or (2) the offense involves a conscious or reckless risk of serious personal injury. The maximum fine for a prosecution charging multiple counts is $10 million.

The Major Fraud Act also contains "whistleblower" protections and rewards. If a contractor discharges, demotes, suspends, threatens, harasses, or otherwise discriminates against an employee who (a) assists in a prosecution under the statute and (b) was not a participant in the unlawful activity that is the subject of the prosecution, the employee can file suit to obtain any relief needed to make him "whole" (including twice the amount of his back pay and any special damages, including litigation costs and reasonable attorney fees). The Attorney General may also pay up to $250,000 to whistleblowers who furnish information relating to a possible prosecution for a major fraud.[68]

B. CORRUPTION

Statutes other than those relating to fraud may also come into play in procurement investigations. Public corruption—such as bribery or improper Executive or Legislative Branch lobbying—is an increasing concern of Government investigators, as is commercial bribery in the form of kickbacks from subcontractors to contractors in connection with federal contracts or the misuse of confidential procurement information by Government or contractor employees. Corruption-related offenses are discussed in this section.

1. Anti-Kickback Enforcement Act Of 1986

The federal campaign against fraud, waste, and abuse in the contracting process has focused, with one notable exception, on prime contractors and their dealings with the Federal Government. The exception is the revitalized effort to control kickbacks—commercial bribes—paid by subcontractors, vendors, and suppliers to prime contractors, other subcontractors, or their representatives in return for varying sorts of favorable contractual treatment. The Anti-Kickback Enforcement Act of 1986[69] injected new life into the existing anti-kickback statute that had been characterized as "extraordinarily ambiguous" and filled with "loopholes, limitations, and relics of a bygone contracting era that has not kept pace with changes in contracting practices."[70] As a result of these changes, there has been more vigorous criminal and civil policing of both prime and subcontractors.

a. Prohibited Conduct. The 1986 Act expressly bans three categories or types of conduct. It forbids any person from:[71]

(1) Providing, attempting to provide, or offering to provide any kickback.

(2) Soliciting, accepting, or attempting to accept any kickback.

(3) Including (directly or indirectly) the amount of any prohibited kickback in the price charged by a subcontractor to a prime contractor or higher-tier subcontractor, or in the price charged by the prime contractor to the Government.

The term "kickback" (which was not defined in the earlier Act) includes "any money, fee, commission, credit, gift, gratuity, thing of value, or compensation of any kind which is provided, directly or indirectly, to a prime contractor, prime contractor employee, subcontractor, or subcontractor employee for the purpose of improperly obtaining or rewarding favorable treatment in connection with a prime contract or in connection with a subcontract relating to a prime contract."[72] The terms "money," "credit," and "thing of value" were intended to expand the definition of a "kickback" to allow the Government to prosecute more violators under the Act by making it clear that the Act reaches all forms of payment.[73]

Unlike the original Anti-Kickback Act, the 1986 Act extends to *any type* of Government contract, not just negotiated contracts, and adds a prohibition against *offers* and *attempts* to provide kickbacks as well as to executed kickbacks.[74]

b. Penalties. "Knowing and willful" violations of the Anti-Kickback Act are criminal and carry penalties of a fine and up to 10 years' imprisonment. "Knowing" violations are civil, for which the maximum penalty is twice the amount of each kickback involved in the violation and up to $10,000 for each occurrence of prohibited conduct.[75]

2. Bribery & Illegal Gratuities Statutes

The statutory federal crime of bribery is far more expansive than its common law counterpart. It applies to *all* federal public officials (not only judges and court officials) and it punishes parties on *both* sides of the transaction (not only the person offering the bribe). The illegal gratuities statute is also broad and bears many similarities to the bribery offense.

a. Bribery Statute. The bribery statute prohibits the giving and receiving of bribes. The elements of a bribery offense are (1) corruptly giving or offering a thing of value, (2) to a public official, (3) with the specific intent to influence an official act or to induce the public official to commit some fraud or violate an official duty. It is also a crime for the public official to ask for or accept a bribe.[76]

The bribery statute is written in very broad language. For example, the statute applies (a) when the prohibited acts are performed "directly or indirectly," and (b) when a person "gives, offers, or promises" something or "demands, seeks, receives, accepts, or agrees to receive or accept" something. Although the bribery statute does not require that the bribe actually be *paid* (only that it be offered, promised, asked for, or requested), there must be a clear "quid pro quo"—a clear connection between the thing of value offered or received and the official act.[77] The penalty for violation of the bribery statute is a fine of up to three times the monetary equivalent of the bribe and up to 15 years' imprisonment.

b. Illegal Gratuities Statute. The illegal gratuities statute,[78] like the bribery statute, is a criminal law that applies to offers and solicitations of gifts. The principal difference between bribery and illegal gratuities is the intent requirement. A higher degree of criminal intent is required under the bribery provisions.[79] The bribery statute requires a showing of corrupt intent on the part of the offeror and a showing that the gift is a "quid pro quo" made directly in return for an act by a Government official. The illegal gratuities provisions require only a showing of a wrongful purpose to offer or accept a thing of value "for or because of an official act."[80] In other words, the illegal gratuities provisions prohibit "rewards" or "gifts" to Government officials for acts they would perform even in the absence of the "reward." Moreover, the statute prohibits illegal offerings to *former* public officials as well as those currently in office.[81] The penalty for violation of the illegal gratuities statute is a fine and two years' imprisonment.

3. Procurement Integrity Act

Congress enacted what is commonly called the "Procurement Integrity Act" as part of the Office of Federal Procurement Policy Act Amendments of 1988.[82] The Act imposes extremely broad restrictions on the conduct of Government procurement officials and their contractor counterparts and represents an intensive effort on the part of Congress "to correct the seedy trade of favors and information" and thus restore the public's confidence in the procurement process.[83] The Act was designed to deter offers of gifts or gratuities to Government officials during procurements and the unauthorized release of procurement information from Government officials to companies competing for Government business. In addition, the Act restricts the ability of Government officials involved in a procurement to seek employment with a competing company, and imposes training and certification requirements on both contractor and Government procurement officials.

a. Prohibitions. The Act prohibits competing contractors and procurement officials, during the conduct of a federal agency procurement, from (1) soliciting, offering, or accepting future employment or business opportunities, (2) offering, giving, demanding, or receiving any money, gratuity, or other thing of value, or (3) soliciting, disclosing, or obtaining protected procurement-related information. The Act contains disclosure and certification requirements[84] for both contractors and Government officials, imposes postemployment restrictions on Government procurement officials, and has a recusal provision.

The Act states that former Government procurement officials who have participated "personally and substantially" in evaluating bids, selecting sources, or conducting negotiations for a particular procurement are prohibited from participating on behalf of a competing contractor in the performance of that procurement. This restriction, however, does not apply to subcontracts of $100,000 or less or to third- and lower-tier subcontracts.

Under the recusal provision, current Government officials may enter into otherwise prohibited discussions with competing contractors concerning future employment or business opportunity if they first disqualify themselves from that procurement and receive approval from the head of the procuring activity.[85]

b. Penalties. Individuals or companies that violate the Procurement Integrity Act face substantial administrative, civil, or criminal penalties. Administrative penalties include denial of all profits on the Government contract, termination of the contract for default, or "[a]ny other appropriate penalty."[86] A person who engages in prohibited conduct is subject to a civil fine not to exceed $100,000, and in the case of a company, not to exceed $1 million.[87] A Government official who discloses or promises to disclose any proprietary or source selection information faces a criminal fine and imprisonment not to exceed five years. Likewise, an employee of a contractor who solicits or obtains any proprietary or source selection information faces a criminal fine and imprisonment not to exceed five years.[88]

4. Byrd Amendment

The so-called "Byrd Amendment" to the 1990 Department of the Interior and Related Agencies Appropriations Act[89] places Government-wide restrictions on the use of federal funds for Legislative and Executive Branch lobbying. The Amendment was intended to deal with improper "influence peddling" by lobbyists on behalf of contractors and grantees. Since its enactment, the Byrd Amendment has been criticized as ambiguous, confusing, and unnecessary.[90]

a. Prohibitions. The Byrd Amendment prohibits contractors and subcontractors from using *"appropriated funds"* to pay any person for "influencing or attempting to influence" a Government official or employee or Member of Congress in connection with contract awards or extensions. The law also requires a contractor that requests or receives a federal contract to *disclose* the names and activities of persons the contractor is paying with its own funds to influence the award or extension of the contract.[91]

The prohibition does not apply to officers and employees performing liaison activities with Congress and executive agencies that are not directly related to a "federal action." There is another exception for professional or technical services rendered directly in the preparation, submission, or negotiation of any bid, proposal, or application for the federal contract or for meeting requirements imposed by or pursuant to law as a condition for receiving the federal contract.[92]

The Byrd Amendment imposes reporting requirements and penalties on those who pay lobbyists. The specifics of any payment of, or agreement to pay, any amount that would be prohibited if appropriated funds were used must be reported. The declaration must include a *certification* that the person has not made, and will not make, any prohibited payments.[93] Persons requesting or receiving subcontracts, subgrants, and the like also are required to file declarations. The declarations need not report (a) payments of "reasonable compensation" to regularly employed (at least 130 working days) officers and employees, (b) a request for or receipt of a contract that does not exceed $100,000, or (c) a request for or receipt of a loan or commitment that does not exceed $150,000. The certification and disclosure requirements apply even to contractors that are unsuccessful bidders or offerors.

b. Penalties. The Byrd Amendment provides that any person who makes a prohibited payment or fails to make the required disclosure may be subject to a civil penalty of not less than $10,000 and not more than $100,000, even if the violation was inadvertent.[94] Filing a declaration or amended declaration after the date required does not prevent the imposition of a penalty, nor does it prevent the Government from seeking any other remedy it may have for the same conduct.

C. ENFORCEMENT

Most of the criminal and civil penalties for improper procurement activities discussed above are enforced by the agency Inspectors General or by the Department of Justice. In addition, the Government can enforce its procurement laws through the administrative sanctions of suspension and debarment of contractors from contracting with the Government.

1. Inspectors General

In 1978, the Inspector General Act[95] became law and established the office of Inspector General (IG) within each of the civilian agencies engaged in procurement activities. In 1982, an Inspector General's office was established within the Department of Defense (DOD).[96]

As the Government's chief representatives in its efforts to reduce fraud, waste, and abuse, the Inspectors General have been provided with a broad mandate. The IGs are required to coordinate investigative activities with other state and federal agencies and devise and supervise programs to detect and prevent fraud and abuse in the agency's programs and operation.[97] The DOD Inspector General has an even more extensive range of duties and investigative responsibilities.[98] The work of the DOD IG is conducted in close conjunction with the Defense Contract Audit Agency (discussed earlier in Chapter 5, Section D).

During an investigation, an Inspector General of an agency has access to a wide range of material. The Inspector General Act provides the IGs access to all materials relating to a particular program or procurement that are available to the agency.[99] In addition, the Act gives the IGs power to subpoena all documents necessary to perform the functions assigned by the Act.[100]

2. Department Of Justice

The Department of Justice (DOJ) prosecutes all violations of federal criminal law.[101] In addition, DOJ may seek civil sanctions in the form of monetary damages and forfeitures under certain statutes. As a result of its broad enforcement authority, DOJ plays a major role in the Government's effort to eliminate fraud and abuse in federal contracts.

3. Suspension & Debarment

The administrative penalties of suspension and debarment are among the most aggressive enforcement mechanisms available to a Federal Government agency that has been the victim of either illegal or irresponsible behavior by a contractor. A procuring agency may debar or suspend current and potential contractors who engage in fraud or other unlawful activity from bidding on, entering into, or continuing to perform Government contracts. Under current procedures, an indictment alone is sufficient for suspension, and a conviction may be cause for debarment. These penalties are also among the most serious for contractors because they exclude both companies and individuals from doing business with the Government, usually on a Government-wide basis.[102]

a. Suspension. For a contractor facing indictment, or who has become the subject of a fraud investigation, the most immediate risk is suspension from Government contracting. Suspension is often a preliminary step to debarment and immediately excludes the contractor from procurement activities.[103] Unless otherwise stated, a suspension is effective on the date the notice of the suspension is issued.[104]

Suspensions are open ended in that they are imposed "pending the completion of investigation or legal proceedings."[105] However, unless an extension is requested, the suspension will normally be terminated if legal proceedings are not initiated within 12 months.[106]

A suspension may be imposed "on the basis of adequate evidence" when it has been determined that "immediate action is necessary to protect the Government's interest."[107] The grounds for suspension include (1) adequate evidence of certain improper conduct, (2) indictment on certain kinds of criminal charges, and (3) adequate evidence of any other serious cause affecting the present responsibility of a contractor.[108]

The FAR suspension procedures require notice to the contractor when the suspension comes into effect, *not before*. Still, it is not unusual for the Government to send the contractor a notice of proposed suspension. The contractor has 30 days in which to submit information in opposition to the suspension, but has no right to a presuspension hearing. In certain circumstances, a fact-finding hearing may be granted once the suspension is in effect, however.[109]

b. Debarment. Debarment precludes a contractor from receiving new contract awards for a specified time, usually not exceeding three years. The length of the debarment is "for a period commensurate with the seriousness of the cause."[110] Upon debarment, the contractor's name is placed on the "Parties Excluded from Procurement Programs" list, which is compiled, maintained, and distributed by the General Services Administration.[111] The period of debarment begins to run when the name of the contractor is published in the debarred bidders' list.[112]

The grounds for debarment may be either statutory or administrative, including (a) a criminal conviction or civil judgment for a procurement-related or other state or federal offense, (b) violation of the terms of a Government contract or subcontract so serious as to justify debarment, (c) or any other cause sufficiently serious to affect the present responsibility of the contractor.[113]

The FAR includes a list of mitigating factors that should be considered before any debarment decision is made.[114] For example, the debarring official should consider whether the con-

FRAUD AND ETHICAL CONSIDERATIONS 7-21

tractor (1) made timely disclosure of the violation, (2) has paid all civil and criminal fines, (3) has agreed to make restitution, (4) has cooperated fully with Government investigators, (5) has taken appropriate disciplinary actions against individuals involved in the violation, (6) has implemented (or agreed to implement) remedial measures, or (7) has effective standards of conduct and internal control systems in place at the time of the activity that constituted cause for debarment or has agreed to institute such procedures.[115]

The contractor must be afforded its rights of due process in any debarment action.[116] This includes the right to a fairly detailed statement of "reasons" for the proposed debarment and 30 days in which to present information in opposition to the proposed debarment.[117] A predebarment hearing need not be provided the contractor when the debarment is based on a conviction or civil judgment. The conviction or judgment alone constitutes sufficient cause of debarment.[118]

REFERENCES

1. 18 USC § 1961–1968; 15 USC § 1; 18 USC § 641.

2. Report of the DOD Acquisition Law Advisory Panel, "Streamlining Defense Acquisition Laws" (Jan. 1993).

3. 31 USC § 3729. See generally Spriggs & Babbin, "The False Claims Act," Briefing Papers No. 79-3 (June 1979), 5 BPC 41; Elmer, Beizer & Gourley, "Procurement Fraud Investigations," Briefing Papers No. 89-9 (Sept. 1989), 6 BPC 393; Smith, "Statutes Countering Contract Administration Fraud," Briefing Papers No. 87-5 (Apr. 1987), 7 BPC 529.

4. 31 USC § 3729(b).

5. 31 USC § 3729(c).

6. 31 USC § 3731(c).

7. See, e.g., note 2, supra (recommending that the civil False Claims Act be amended to allow a court to adjust the penalties when they are found to be disproportionate to the actual damages suffered by the Government).

8. 31 USC § 3729(a).

9. U.S. v. Aerodex, Inc., 469 F.2d 1003 (5th Cir. 1972).

10. 31 USC § 3730(b).

11. P.L. 99-562, 100 Stat. 3154 (1986).

12. Note 2, supra. See also, e.g., settlement agreements in U.S. ex rel. Taxpayers Against Fraud v. General Electric Co., No. C-90-7920 (S.D. Ohio, Apr. 23, 1993), 35 GC ¶ 276, and U.S. ex rel. Taxpayers Against Fraud v. Teledyne Industries, Inc., No. 90-4996 KN (C.D. Cal., Apr. 21, 1994), 36 GC ¶ 236.

13. E.g., U.S. ex rel. Stilwell v. Hughes Helicopters, Inc., 714 F. Supp. 1084 (C.D. Cal. 1989), 31 GC ¶ 212.

14. E.g., U.S. ex rel. Truong v. Northrop Corp., 728 F. Supp. 615 (C.D. Cal. 1989).

15. U.S. ex rel. Kreindler & Kreindler v. United Technologies Corp., 777 F. Supp. 195 (N.D.N.Y. 1991), 34 GC ¶ 138, affd. on other grounds, 985 F.2d 1148 (2d Cir. 1993), 35 GC ¶ 258.

16. U.S. ex rel. Carton v. Litton Industries, Inc., No. CV88-2276 (C.D. Cal. 1989).

17. U.S. ex rel. Erickson v. American Institute of Biological Services, 716 F. Supp. 908 (E.D. Va. 1989), 32 GC ¶ 157 (Note). Compare U.S. ex rel. Le Blanc v. Raytheon Co., 913 F.2d 17 (1st Cir. 1990), 32 GC ¶ 299 (Note). See also note 2, supra (suggesting limitations on authority of Government employees to bring "qui tam" suits and on "qui tam" suits based on contractor voluntary disclosures).

18. 31 USC § 3730(e)(1)–(3).

19. 31 USC § 3730(e)(4). See U.S. ex rel. Barajas v. Northrop Corp., 5 F.3d 407 (9th Cir. 1993), 35 GC ¶ 608, cert. denied, No. 93-1368 (U.S. Apr. 18, 1994).

20. U.S. ex rel. Erickson v. American Institute of Biological Services, note 17, supra.

21. 31 USC § 3730(b).

22. 31 USC § 3730(c)(1).

23. 31 USC § 3730(c)(2).

24. 31 USC § 3730(c)(2)(A).

25. 31 USC § 3730(c)(2)(B).

26. Gravitt v. General Electric Co., 680 F. Supp. 1162 (S.D. Ohio 1988), 30 GC ¶ 104.

27. 31 USC § 3730(c)(3).

FRAUD AND ETHICAL CONSIDERATIONS 7-23

28. 31 USC § 3730(b)(1).

29. 31 USC § 3730(d)(1).

30. 31 USC § 3730(d)(2).

31. 31 USC § 3730(d)(3).

32. Note 31, supra.

33. 18 USC § 287.

34. U.S. v. McNinch, 356 U.S. 595 (1958).

35. U.S. v. Neifert-White Co., 390 U.S. 228 (1968).

36. U.S. v. Wertheimer, 434 F.2d 1006 (2d Cir. 1970).

37. U.S. v. American Precision Products Corp., 115 F. Supp. 823 (D.N.J. 1953).

38. U.S. v. Duncan, 816 F.2d 153 (4th Cir. 1987).

39. U.S. v. Jackson, 845 F.2d 880 (9th Cir.), cert. denied, 488 U.S. 857 (1988).

40. U.S. v. White, 765 F.2d 1469 (11th Cir. 1985).

41. Imperial Meat Co. v. U.S., 316 F.2d 435 (10th Cir.), cert. denied, 375 U.S. 820 (1963).

42. U.S. v. Marrero, 904 F.2d 251 (5th Cir.), cert. denied, 111 S. Ct. 561 (1990).

43. U.S. v. Allery, 905 F.2d 204 (8th Cir.), cert. denied, 111 S. Ct. 531 (1990).

44. U.S. v. Dorotich, 900 F.2d 192 (9th Cir. 1990).

45. 31 USC § 3729(a); 18 USC § 287.

46. E.g., U.S. v. Maher, 582 F.2d 842 (4th Cir. 1978), cert. denied, 439 U.S. 1115 (1980). But see U.S. v. Martin, 772 F.2d 1442 (8th Cir. 1985).

47. U.S. v. Maher, note 46, supra.

48. U.S. v. Blecker, 657 F.2d 629 (4th Cir. 1981), 24 GC ¶ 6, cert. denied, 454 U.S. 1150 (1982).

49. U.S. Sentencing Commn., Sentencing Guidelines and Policy Statements for the Federal Courts § 2F1.1 (1987).

50. 18 USC § 3571.

51. P.L. 99-145, tit. IX, § 931, 99 Stat. 699 (1985).

52. 18 USC § 1001.

53. E.g., U.S. v. Massey, 550 F.2d 300 (5th Cir. 1977); U.S. v. Carrier, 654 F.2d 559 (9th Cir. 1981).

54. E.g., U.S. v. Rodgers, 466 U.S. 475 (1984). See, e.g., U.S. v. Fairchild, 990 F.2d 1139 (9th Cir. 1993) (refusal to sign false certification did not prevent conviction of contractor under Act), 35 GC ¶ 488.

55. U.S. v. Hartness, 845 F.2d 158 (8th Cir.), cert. denied, 488 U.S. 925 (1988).

56. E.g., U.S. v. Kwiat, 817 F.2d 440 (7th Cir.), cert. denied, 484 U.S. 984 (1987).

57. Note 52, supra.

58. Note 50, supra.

59. 18 USC § 1341.

60. 18 USC § 1343.

61. U.S. v. Stone, Cr. No. 90-00096 (E.D. Va. Mar. 21, 1990).

62. U.S. v. Litton Systems, Inc., Cr. No. 86-311 (E.D. Pa. July 15, 1986).

63. U.S. v. Busher, 817 F.2d 1409 (9th Cir. 1987).

64. P.L. 99-509, § 6101, 100 Stat. 1934 (codified at 31 USC § 3801 et seq.). See generally Bellman, "The Program Fraud Civil Remedies Act," Briefing Papers No. 88-4 (Mar. 1988), 8 BPC 97.

65. See, e.g., implementing regulations by DOD, 53 Fed. Reg. 39262 (Oct. 6, 1988); General Services Admin., 52 Fed. Reg. 45183 (Nov. 25, 1987); and Natl. Aeronautics and Space Admin., 54 Fed. Reg. 599 (Jan. 19, 1989).

66. See General Accounting Office Report AFMD 91-73 (Sept. 13, 1991) (between Oct. 1986 when Act became effective and Sept. 1990, 7 of 8 agencies reviewed by the General Accounting Office had referred only 41 cases to the Justice Department for permission to prosecute (which included 26 from the U.S. Postal Service) and only 3 of 15 resolved cases involved procurement fraud).

67. P.L. 100-700, 102 Stat. 4631 (codified at 18 USC § 1031).

68. 18 USC § 1031(g).

69. P.L. 99-634, 100 Stat. 3525 (codified at 41 USC §§ 51–58). See generally Arnavas, "The New Anti-Kickback Act," Briefing Papers No. 87-9 (Aug. 1987), 7 BPC 615.

70. H.R. Rep. No. 964 (pt. 1), 99th Cong., 2d Sess. 10 (1986).

71. 41 USC § 53.

72. 41 USC § 52(2).

73. S. Rep. No. 435, 99th Cong., 2d Sess. 10–11 (1986).

74. See note 73, supra, at 8; note 70, supra at 9.

75. 41 USC § 54.

76. 18 USC § 201(b)(1)–(4).

77. See, e.g., U.S. v. Brewster, 506 F.2d 62 (D.C. Cir. 1974); U.S. v. Johnson, 621 F.2d 1073 (10th Cir. 1980).

78. 18 USC § 201(c). See generally Kenney & Sweeney, "Gratutities," Briefing Papers No. 90-3 (Feb. 1990), 9 BPC 67.

79. U.S. v. Brewster, note 77, supra.

80. U.S. v. Evans, 572 F.2d 455 (5th Cir.), cert. denied, 439 U.S. 870 (1978); U.S. v. Niederberger, 580 F.2d 63 (3d Cir.), cert. denied, 439 U.S. 980 (1978).

81. 18 USC § 201(c)(1)(a).

82. P.L. 100-679, § 6, as amended in P.L. 101-189, § 814, and P.L. 101-510, § 815 (codified at 41 USC § 423). See generally Arnavas & Marsh, "The Procurement Integrity Act," Briefing Papers No. 91-9 (Aug. 1991), 9 BPC 453.

83. 134 Cong. Rec. S17071 (daily ed. Oct. 20, 1988) (statement of Sen. Glenn).

84. E.g., 41 USC § 423(e)(1). See FAR subpt. 3.104, 52.203-8.

85. 41 USC § 423(c)(2), (3).

86. 41 USC § 423(h).

87. 41 USC § 423(i).

88. 41 USC § 423(j).

89. P.L. 101-121, § 319, 103 Stat. 701 (codified at 31 USC § 1352). See generally Pushkar & Stoughton, "Restrictions on Consultant Services," Briefing Papers No. 90-6 (May 1990), 9 BPC 117.

90. Compare, e.g., Office of Management and Budget, proposed guidance on the Byrd Amendment, 57 Fed. Reg. 1772 (Jan. 15, 1992) (extending prohibitions on use of federal funds to influence federal actions to in-

clude "program lobbying" and disclosure requirements to include "third-party lobbying"), 34 GC ¶ 35, with note 2, supra (recommending repeal of lobbying restrictions because they duplicate existing requirements).

91. 31 USC § 1352(b).

92. 31 USC § 1352(b)(7)(e).

93. 31 USC § 1352(b)(2).

94. 31 USC § 1352(b)(7).

95. P.L. 95-452, 92 Stat. 1101 (codified at 5 USC app. §§ 1–12).

96. P.L. 97-252, § 1117, 96 Stat. 759.

97. 5 USC app. § 4.

98. 5 USC app. § 8(c); DOD Directive 5106.1 (Mar. 14, 1983).

99. 5 USC app. § 6(a)(1).

100. 5 USC app. § 6(a)(4).

101. 18 USC § 516.

102. See generally Toomey, Fisher & Shapiro, "Debarment & Suspension/Edition III," Briefing Papers No. 89-4 (Mar. 1989), 8 BPC 329; Johnson & DeVecchio, "Debarment & Suspension/Edition II," Briefing Papers No. 83-9 (Sept. 1983), 6 BPC 223; Dembling, "Debarment & Suspension," Briefing Papers No. 78-6 (Dec. 1978), 4 BPC 257.

103. See FAR 9.403, 9.407-1(b).

104. FAR 9.407-3(c)

105. FAR 9.407-1(b)(1).

106. FAR 9.407-4(b).

107. Note 105, supra.

108. FAR 9.407-2.

109. FAR 9.407-3.

110. FAR 9.406-4(a).

111. FAR 9.404.

112. Dimitrious A. Maurophilipos, GSBCA D-5, 80-1 BCA ¶ 14446, 22 GC ¶ 32. See also J.B. Kies Const. Co., Comp. Gen. Dec. B-250797, 93-1 CPD ¶ 127, 35 GC ¶ 485 (Note).

113. FAR 9.406-2.

114. FAR 9.406-1.

115. FAR 9.406-1(a).

116. Gonzales v. Freeman, 334 F.2d 570 (D.C. Cir. 1964), 6 GC ¶ 281(a).

117. FAR 9.406-3. See Arthur H. Padula, HUDBCA 78-284-D30, 79-2 BCA ¶ 13934, 21 GC ¶ 298.

118. FAR 9.406-3(d)(1).

Part III

PERFORMANCE

chapters

- **8** | Specifications
- **9** | Government Property
- **10** | Intellectual Property Rights
- **11** | Changes
- **12** | Delays
- **13** | Equitable Adjustment Claims
- **14** | Inspection And Warranty
- **15** | Payment

SPECIFICATIONS

8

A. Design vs. Performance Specifications
   1. Design Specifications
   2. Performance Specifications

B. Government's "Minimum Needs"

C. Specifications, Standards & Purchase Descriptions
   1. Specifications
   2. Standards
   3. Purchase Descriptions
   4. Deviations & Waivers

D. Qualified Products

E. Government Warranty Of Specifications
   1. The "Implied Warranty"
   2. Government Disclaimers

F. Contractor Compliance With Specifications
   1. Strict Compliance
   2. Minimum Compliance

G. Substantial Performance
   1. Construction Contracts
   2. Supply Contracts
   3. Service Contracts

H. Defective Specifications
   1. Impossibility Of Performance
   2. Notice
   3. Right To Stop Work

This chapter begins Part III of the book where the focus turns to contract performance. In addition to this chapter dealing with contract specifications, Part III contains chapters covering Government property (Chapter 9), intellectual property rights (Chapter 10), contract changes (Chapter 11), delays of contract work (Chapter 12), equitable adjustment claims arising from contract performance (Chapter 13), inspections and warranties (Chapter 14), and payment provisions that determine when and how contractors receive payment for contract performance (Chapter 15).

Specifications provide contractors with a description of the work that is required to be performed under the contract. Because they also establish a starting point for determining the rights and obligations of the parties, specification provisions are often of controlling importance in resolving questions involving the adequacy of contract performance. The FAR defines a "specification" as a "description of the technical requirements for a material, product, or service that includes the criteria for determining whether these requirements are met."[1]

This chapter will review, among other things, (a) the various types of specifications, (b) the Government's warranty when it furnishes the specifications that if the contractor complies with the specifications, an adequate result will follow, and (c) the problems of contractor compliance with specifications, especially defective specifications and the doctrine of substantial performance.

A. DESIGN vs. PERFORMANCE SPECIFICATIONS

Government specifications generally fall into one of two major groups— *design* and *performance*. How the specifications are categorized determines the parties' responsibilities and obligations under the contract.

In many contracts, the Government's requirements consist of a *combination* of performance and design specifications. Where this occurs, it is necessary to test each portion of the specifications to determine where the responsibility for contract problems should be placed.

1. Design Specifications

In design specifications, the Government states—in precise detail—the materials to be used and the mode and manner in which the work is to be performed.[2] These specifications incorporate text and drawings that set out requirements such as measurements, tolerances, testing procedures, quality control, and inspection procedures. With regard to design specifications, the Government accepts general responsibility for design and related omissions, errors, or deficiencies, not only in the specifications themselves but in the incorporated drawings as well.[3]

2. Performance Specifications

Performance specifications are normally less precise than their design counterparts. They describe the performance desired of the end product without specifically directing how the contractor should design or assemble the item.[4] For instance, such a specification might designate the performance characteristics desired (for example, a vehicle weighing no more than 5,000 pounds to attain a speed of 50 miles per hour in 10 seconds) and little else. Design, measurements, tolerances, and so forth are not stated or considered to be of particular importance in such specifications, as long as the performance requirements are met.

Consequently, when an item is purchased under a performance specification, the contractor accepts responsibility for design, engineering, and achievement of the stated performance requirements. The contractor has general discretion regarding the detail of the work, but the end item is subject to the Government's right of final inspection. In some instances, the Government also reserves the right to approve or reject proposed plans and methods before the work is performed. When this is done, it is frequently accomplished through submission of bid or preproduction samples.[5]

B. GOVERNMENT'S "MINIMUM NEEDS"

The Armed Services Procurement Act requires that the head of an agency shall "develop specifications in such manner as is necessary to obtain full and open competition...and include restrictive provisions or conditions only to the extent necessary to satisfy the needs of the agency or as authorized by law."[6] The FAR definition of "specification" explains that "[s]pecifications shall state only the Government's actual minimum needs and be designed to promote full and open competition, with due regard to the nature of the supplies or services to be acquired."[7]

The reference to "minimum needs" is important (and sometimes troublesome), since the underlying concept of the competitive bidding process—to foster full and open competition—requires specifications that precisely and fully define the supplies or services being procured, yet are not unduly restrictive. A specification that exceeds the Government's minimum needs by containing unnecessary requirements improperly restricts competition since it may prevent one or more bidders from submitting responsive bids. It is necessary, therefore, to strike an equitable balance between these two somewhat opposing goals. In the absence of clear and convincing evidence that the agency's judgment is unreasonable, an agency's determination of the Government's minimum needs and the best method of obtaining those needs will not be overturned.[8]

Clear and unambiguous specifications are particularly important in procurement by sealed bidding because there is virtually no opportunity for extensive prebid discussion and because competition is based on price alone. As stated by the General Accounting Office (GAO) in one decision:[9]

> The full and free competition required cannot be obtained unless the invitation and the specifications are sufficiently definite to permit the preparation and evaluation of bids on a common basis.... There can be no legal competition unless bidders are competing on a common basis; no intelligent bidding for a contract unless all bidders know what the contract requirements will be.

The preparation of specifications is primarily a function of the individual procuring agency, since the agency is uniquely knowledgeable regarding what will meet its minimum requirements in a given instance.[10] At times, however, it has been held that items or requirements specified by the Government improperly restricted competition, as where ordering a deluxe model automobile exceeded the Government's minimum needs,[11] and where a restriction to the product of one manufacturer was not required for interchangeability.[12]

C. SPECIFICATIONS, STANDARDS & PURCHASE DESCRIPTIONS

There are—within the two major categories of design and performance discussed above in Section A—a number of standard *types* of specifications available to the military and civilian procuring agencies. They are briefly described below. In addition, the term "specification" can be viewed as encompassing the terms "standard" and "purchase description." The FAR distinguishes the three terms, yet treats them all together in Part 10.

1. Specifications

a. Federal Specifications. A federal specification is a specification issued or controlled by the General Services Administration (GSA) and listed in the "Index of Federal Specifications, Standards and Commercial Item Descriptions."[13] Federal specifications are used by all agencies acquiring supplies or services covered by such specifications.[14] In 1994, however, Congress directed the heads of federal agencies to ensure "to the maximum extent practicable" that requirements for the procurement of supplies or services are stated in terms of functions to be performed, performance required, or essential physical characteristics. Agencies are to state their specifications in terms that "enable and encourage" offerors to supply commercial items. The new statutory preference for commercial items is intended to minimize reliance on Government-unique specifications.[15]

b. Military Specifications. A military specification ("milspec") is a specification issued by the Department of Defense (DOD) for mandatory use by DOD activities. The "Department of Defense Index of Specifications and Standards" lists unclassified federal and military specifications and standards, related standardization documents, and voluntary standards approved for use by DOD.[16] In June 1994, however, the Secretary of Defense directed the simplification of the way the Pentagon buys goods and key components for military systems and ordered the replacement of milspecs with commercial and performance standards wherever possible and the use of milspecs only as a last resort.[17] Congress later established a statutory preference for the acquisition of commercial items in the Armed Services Procurement Act.[18]

c. Industry Specifications. Specifications prepared by technical or industry associations may be approved for use by federal agencies.

Government specifications published in an index will normally not be furnished with a solicitation unless (a) the nature and complexity of the items makes it necessary to enable prospective contractors to make a competent initial evaluation of the solicitation, (b) the Contracting Officer believes that it would be difficult for prospective contractors to obtain the documents containing the specifications in time to respond to the solicitation, or (c) the specifications are requested by a prospective contractor who has not previously bid on the item. Specifications and standards not listed in the indexes will normally be furnished with the solicitation.[19] When this is not feasible (because of the bulk of the documents, the limited number of copies available, or some other good reason), agency regulations generally provide that prospective contractors will be informed when and where they may be obtained or examined.[20]

2. Standards

The FAR defines a "standard" as "a document that establishes engineering and technical limitations and applications of items, materials, processes, methods, designs, and engineering practices."[21] Thus, standards are not complete specifications in themselves. They are criteria considered essential to achieve uniformity in materials or products or interchangeability of parts used in those products.[22] Government standards are categorized in the same manner as specifications (i.e., federal or military). However, a particular contract may cite a "voluntary standard," which is defined by the FAR as "a standard established by a private sector body and available for public use."[23]

3. Purchase Descriptions

a. Definition. According to the FAR, a "purchase description" is "a description of the essential physical characteristics and functions required to meet the Government's minimum needs."[24] A purchase description may be used when no applicable specification is required. The FAR provides that purchase descriptions should not specify a particular product (or a particular feature of a product peculiar to one manufacturer) and thereby prevent consideration of a product manufactured by another, unless the particular product or feature is essential to the Government's requirements and similar products would not meet the minimum requirements for the item.[25] Moreover, where services are being procured, the purchase description should outline to the greatest degree practicable the specific services that the contractor is expected to perform.[26]

b. Brand Name Or Equal. An alternate type of purchase description is one that identifies one or more commercial products by brand name and make or model or part number (or other appropriate nomenclature),[27] followed by the words "or equal." A "brand name or equal" purchase description must set forth those salient physical, functional, or other characteristics of the named products that are essential to the needs of the Government (for example, where interchangeability of parts is required, this requirement should be identified as a salient characteristic).[28] The salient characteristics are the critical features of a "brand name or equal" procurement, because no item can be considered acceptable unless it meets all the salient characteristics, and no item can be rejected as nonconforming unless it fails to comply with one or more of them. Failure to set forth the salient characteristics restricts competition and requires cancellation of the solicitation.[29] Similarly, the inclusion of too many or unnecessary salient characteristics may also restrict competition and require cancellation of the solicitation.[30]

When an "or equal" specification is used, there are varying and shifting degrees of responsibility. If the contractor furnishes the brand name product precisely as specified, the responsibility for its proper performance falls on the Government. If, however, the contractor elects to manufacture or otherwise furnish an "equal" product, it is its responsibility to ensure that the product it furnishes is, in fact, the equal of the specified brand name product.[31]

In construction contracts, the standard "Material and Workmanship" clause provides that specification references to material by "trade name, make, or catalog number shall be regarded as establishing a standard of quality and shall not be construed as limiting competition."[32] However, in one case, a specification requirement for calcium silicate insulation did not establish a standard of quality but had to be complied with exactly even though other materials of equal or superior quality may have been available.[33]

c. Foreign Purchase Descriptions. The FAR provides that agencies engaged in the procurement of supplies or services for use outside the United States may use purchase descriptions of foreign governments or foreign industry associations, unless precluded by law.[34] The description must satisfy the agency's actual minimum requirements.

4. Deviations & Waivers

A *deviation* is an authorization—granted *before* the fact—to depart from a designated specification requirement. If an existing Government specification does not meet an agency's needs, deviations may be authorized by the agency under strictly limited conditions.[35]

A *waiver*, on the other hand, applies *after* work has been completed. It is an administrative action that authorizes acceptance of an item which, although not in full compliance with a particular requirement, is nevertheless considered acceptable. In most cases, waivers are only granted for items already manufactured and submitted for acceptance. However, Government actions—short of an express waiver of specifications—may be construed as a constructive waiver.[36] "Blanket" waivers for units still to be manufactured are normally not available.[37]

D. QUALIFIED PRODUCTS

The Government sometimes finds it necessary to conduct tests *in advance* of any procurement action to determine if a product is available that will meet specification requirements. In such cases, the specifications may require qualification of the contractor's product—performed independently and in advance of any specific procurement action. Under the FAR, a "qualification requirement" is "a Government requirement for testing or other quality assurance demonstration that must be completed before award of a contract."[38] A Qualified Products List (QPL) is a list of products that have been examined, tested, and have satisfied all applicable qualification requirements.[39] Similarly, a Qualified Manufacturers List (QML) (or Qualified Bidders List (QBL)) is a list of manufacturers (or bidders) that have had their products examined and tested and that have satisfied all applicable qualification requirements.[40]

Suppliers who furnish evidence that their products have successfully passed qualification are eligible for award even though not yet included on the QPL.[41] The lists are always kept open for inclusion of products from additional suppliers.

Whenever qualified products are to be procured by the Government as end items or as components of end items, the product, manufacturer, or source must be qualified at the time of contract award, whether or not the product, manufacturer, or source is actually included on a QPL, QML, or QBL. The solicitation will contain the "Qualification Requirements" clause[42] which requires the offeror to insert the item name and test number (if known) of each qualified product. If qualified products are procured as components of end items, the Contracting Officer must assure that the product or source meets the qualification requirements at the time of award of the prime contract.[43]

Synopses of proposed procurements involving qualified products are published in the *Commerce Business Daily* (see Chapter 2, Section D.4).[44] However, qualification of a product is likely to be time consuming. A manufacturer that does not submit its product for qualification until publication of the synopsis—or issuance of the solicitation—is likely to find there is insufficient time remaining to qualify its products. Thus, it is important that manufacturers interested in having their products qualified do so well in advance of the procurement. Requests for qualification of products should be forwarded to the specification-preparing activity identified in the specification.

E. GOVERNMENT WARRANTY OF SPECIFICATIONS

As noted above in Section A.1, when the specifications furnished to the contractor are the "design" type, the Government accepts responsibility for any errors or defects they contain.[45] This responsibility is the same regardless of whether the Government actually prepares the documents or adopts specifications and drawings prepared by the contractor or others.[46]

1. The "Implied Warranty"

The basic "implied warranty" applicable to a Government specification is that, if the specification is followed, a satisfactory product will result.[47] This concept is derived from a case decided by the Supreme Court in 1918.[48] At issue was a contract in which part of the work consisted of relocating a sewer line. After the sewer had been rebuilt in accordance with the Government specifications, during a heavy rain, a dam—that was not shown in the drawings—forced excess water into the new section causing it to break in several places. The Government insisted that the contractor was obligated to repair the sewer at the contractor's expense, but the Supreme Court disagreed, noting first that the terms in the contract "prescribing the character, dimensions and location of the sewer imported a warranty that, if the specifications were complied with, the sewer would be adequate." The Court then stressed that where the contractor is required to build in accordance with specifications prepared by the owner, the contractor cannot be held responsible for defects in the plans. Furthermore, this implied warranty of the specifications cannot be "overcome by the general clauses" in the contract requiring the contractor to examine the site or check the plans.

The implied warranty concept has been extended beyond construction contracts. In a supply contract case, for example, where the Government rejected a product based on defects caused by Government-specified shipping containers, the Court of Claims, in ruling for the contractor, stated that "when the Government, through one of its important agencies, orders the production of a specified thing by a specified means, it would be a rare instance when the supplier could reasonably be expected to investigate for himself whether compliance with the specifications would, in fact, produce the desired result."[49] Obviously, under this rationale, the Government's warranty obligations will apply even where a defective design prepared by its design contractor is found lacking under a subsequent production contract. Although the Government could seek indemnification from the design contractor, its liability to the production contractor is clear.

However, the Government's designation of a sole source for an item is a representation only that the requirements can be met by use of the item—not that the item will necessarily be properly manufactured or delivered on time.[50]

2. Government Disclaimers

The Government will sometimes attempt to avoid the implied warranty of adequacy of its specifications by including disclaimers or other exculpatory language in its contracts. Such provisions are enforceable, but they are usually given a narrow interpretation by agency boards of contract appeals and the federal courts.

For instance, in one board case, it was held that labeling a specification "advisory" did not defeat the contractor's right to rely on its accuracy.[51] Similarly, where the Government stated that the specifications were provided only for the contractor's "guidance" and also required the contractor to ensure that the specifications were "adequate for the intended purpose," a board nonetheless held that the contractor had the right to rely on their accuracy.[52]

On the other hand, as the Court of Claims rather picturesquely put it: "You can engage a contractor to make snowmen in August, if you spell it out clearly [that] you are not warranting there will be any subfreezing weather in that month."[53] On this theory, disclaimers have been held enforceable (and thus have shifted the risk of adequacy of the specifications to the contractor) if (1) the risks can be reasonably determined, (2) the Government discloses all available information, and (3) the disclaimer gives clear notice that potential problems exist.[54]

F. CONTRACTOR COMPLIANCE WITH SPECIFICATIONS

1. Strict Compliance

The FAR succinctly sets forth the Government's general policy regarding a contractor's obligation to comply with the specifications, requiring that agencies ensure that "[s]upplies or services tendered by contractors meet contract requirements."[55] Many decisions have agreed that the Government is indeed entitled to strictly enforce compliance with a contract's requirements.[56] Thus, the Government has no obligation to accept nonconforming supplies or services, and it will generally not do so, unless there are circumstances (for example, reasons of economy or urgency) where acceptance of the nonconforming supplies or services is in its best interests.[57] This principle applies even though the nonconforming items might be "better,"[58] and even though strict compliance is really unnecessary from a technical standpoint.[59] However, one recognized exception to this rule is where the removal of completed work that does not conform to specifications but is nevertheless adequate would amount to "economic waste."[60]

2. Minimum Compliance

Although the Government is entitled to strict compliance with contract requirements, the contractor also has the right to perform in a minimum manner—provided the contract's requirements are satisfied. Stated another way: "A contractor is entitled to use the least expensive means of achieving contract performance provided the means selected are a reasonable choice."[61] Therefore, if the specifications permit alternate methods of performance, the contractor may use any of the alternatives. If the Contracting Officer denies the contractor that right, specifying that one particular mode of performance must be followed, the contract will be deemed "changed" and—if the facts justify it—the contractor will be entitled to an equitable adjustment in the contract price or time of performance (or both).[62]

G. SUBSTANTIAL PERFORMANCE

The doctrine of "substantial performance" by the contractor—which basically prohibits a default termination of the contract by the Government (see Chapter 16) if a contractor's performance deviates only in *minor* respects from the contract requirements—may initially appear to conflict with the Government's right to insist upon strict contract compliance. It is best understood when it is considered as a limitation on the Government's right to terminate a contract where strict compliance has not been obtained—and not as a limitation on any other Government contract rights.

1. Construction Contracts

The concept of substantial performance has long been associated with construction contracts. It provides that if a construction project is essentially complete, but minor deficiencies that do not unduly interfere with the facility's purpose are still present, the Government may not (a) terminate the contract for default[63] or (b) assess liquidated damages after the date of substantial completion.[64] The Government may still insist on subsequent completion of the project if practical,[65] but if completion is not practical, or if it is simply not desired, then the Government is entitled to a credit for the reasonable value of the unperformed work.[66]

For a construction contractor to be shielded from default by the substantial performance doctrine, it must demonstrate two things. First, a high percentage of completion must be shown. Second, it must be demonstrated that the project is available for its intended use.

A "high percentage" of completion is necessarily a subjective concept and will be determined on a case-by-case basis. In one case involving a ship repair project, the Armed Services Board of Contract Appeals held that a contract could be properly terminated (despite alleged 99% completion), because two forced air draft blowers were "so bad they had to be rebalanced" and one had a noisy fan that could not be fixed in four days.[67] Similarly, a post office alteration and landscaping contract was deemed properly terminated for default because only 85% to 95% completion had been achieved, and two "essential areas" remained incomplete by a revised completion date.[68] Under other circumstances, however, percentages of 86%[69] and 92%[70] have been deemed adequate for substantial performance.

Regarding the second required element—that the project is available for its intended use—much again depends on a subjective evaluation based on the nature of the overall project and the nature of the as yet incomplete work. Therefore, in one case where it was essential to have reliable air conditioning for the operation of sensitive radio equipment, substantial completion did not occur—even though the remainder of the work was finished—until the air conditioning was functional.[71]

2. Supply Contracts

In 1966, the Court of Claims applied the doctrine of substantial performance to supply contracts.[72] It set forth four rather strict requirements that must be met for a supply contractor to avert a default termination. The court held that (1) the supplies must be timely delivered, (2) the supplies must substantially conform to the contract requirements, (3) the contractor must reasonably believe that the goods comply with the contract requirements, and (4) the nonconformance must be minor and correctable within a reasonable time. Note that, for the doctrine to apply, the nonconforming goods must be delivered in compliance with the contract's delivery schedule. The doctrine has no application where delivery is not made on time.[73]

3. Service Contracts

In determining whether a service contract has been substantially performed, the courts and boards of contract appeals have looked to (a) the degree of completion of the work and (b) the quality of the work performed. Generally, a service contract can be default terminated only when the number of individual defaults have *cumulated* to the point where it can be said the contract has not been substantially performed.[74] For example, failures to substantially perform a service contract have included (1) a janitorial service contractor's failure to clean various areas of a hospital for days at a time[75] and (2) failure by a property manager to submit required reports, hire qualified personnel, or clean houses in preparation for resale of Government-owned properties as required by the contract.[76] On the other hand, where, under a repair service contract that generated approximately 200 calls a month, the contractor failed in 20 instances to respond to repair requests within the required 10-hour limit, the contractor was found to have substantially complied with the contract.[77]

H. DEFECTIVE SPECIFICATIONS

The term "defective specifications" usually refers to a defect or inconsistency in the specifications so severe that performance of the contract as stated cannot be attained by *any* contractor—or can be obtained only at an *exorbitant cost*. Defective specifications (like the doctrine of substantial performance discussed above in Section G) can be a special *defense* for contractors. If the defective specifications make performance impossible or commercially senseless,[78] the contractor may be excused from a contract default or delay and may be entitled to recover the costs it incurred in attempting to perform (see Chapter 16). The contractor may also allege that defective specifications caused a "constructive change" to the contract entitling the contractor to an equitable adjustment of the contract's price or schedule (see Chapter 11, Section F.2), or that the faulty specifications constituted a breach of the contract entitling the contractor to damages.

The legal theory of these defenses and claims, as discussed earlier in this chapter in Section E, is that the Government impliedly warrants that its specifications, if followed, will result in an item that can be produced and performance requirements that can be achieved. Therefore, when the Government specifications are defective and cause the contractor problems, the general rule is that the Government is liable—under an *implied warranty* theory—for any resulting delay or expense caused to the contractor.[79]

1. Impossibility Of Performance

a. Types Of Impossibility. There are two types of impossibility—actual impossibility and practical impossibility. The former is based on technical grounds; the latter on economic ones.

Actual impossibility exists when the contract cannot be performed according to its terms—by the contractor or by any other contractor—because (a) the contract's specifications are erroneous, (b) the contract's performance requirements can, in no event, be met, or (c) the contractor would be obliged to go beyond the state of the art to attain the contract requirements.[80] For example, in a case involving the manufacture of halogen lamps, where the Government specifications required that each lamp have a perfectly flat holding ledge, the board found that, given the current state of the art, flat holding ledges could not be produced without prior research and study effort. It therefore held that the specifications were impossible to perform.[81]

Practical impossibility (sometimes called "impracticability") involves situations where performance is not possible within the basic objectives of the contract. Normally, this would be shown by demonstrating that the work—although attainable—could be performed only with extreme difficulty, expense, injury, or loss.[82] For example, in a construction contract situation, the Court of Claims found that the contractor experienced no difficulty in achieving 90% soil compaction, but that 95% compaction was impossible as a practical matter.[83] The court noted that it was achieved only after great effort and the use of a variety of special equipment, and that, even then, progress was slow and the work was greatly delayed by the 95% requirement. In another case, a contractor was permitted to recover for attempting to meet a portion of a specification that was a practical impossibility to achieve—even though the contract subsequently was properly terminated for default for failure to deliver on time.[84]

If cost is the key issue, a contractor must demonstrate not merely a loss—even a significant one—but that it would be *economically unrealistic* to further perform.[85] Thus, boards of contract appeals have rejected practical impossibility arguments where specified aluminum was available only by special order and at extra cost,[86] where the cost of cement under the supply contract had increased,[87] where the price of gold for lapel buttons had increased by 200%,[88] and where the costs of fuel increased by 45% as a result of Iraq's invasion of Kuwait.[89] In these cases, the boards held that the increased costs were not so excessive or unreasonable as to amount to commercial impracticability.

b. Allocation Of Risk. Allocation of risk is another important concept when discussing impossibility. The question of which party *assumed the risk* of performance has to be determined at the same time that impossibility is being considered because it is the key to deciding who will prevail.

The *Government* assumes the risk—and must thus bear the consequences of impossibility—if it, for example, furnishes the contract specifications and breaches its implied warranty of suitability because they are impossible to perform,[90] or has superior knowledge regarding performance difficulties that are likely to be encountered by the contractor during the course of its work but makes no disclosure.[91]

The *contractor* assumes the risk of performance (and thus cannot recover even if the work is, in fact, impossible) if, for example, the risks of performance are obvious,[92] the contractor has superior knowledge regarding performance problems that might be encountered,[93] or the contractor furnished the design that ultimately proved to be impossible to perform.[94]

2. Notice

A prerequisite for contractor recovery due to defective specifications is that timely notice be given to the Government of the difficulties being encountered.[95] There are two reasons for this requirement. First, notice records (quite effectively) when and to what extent the contractor actually experienced performance problems. Second, it gives the Government a timely opportunity to consider the proper form of corrective action (for example, the Government might well be willing to consider a waiver of an impossible or otherwise erroneous requirement).

Thus, in one case where the contractor delayed for over three months in notifying the Government of the problem it was facing (while it sought to resolve the problem itself), and then attempted to charge the Government with the delay, the Court of Claims denied relief, noting that "[i]f, within the reasonable time after discovery of the conflict, [the contractor] had apprised the Navy of the matter, then, clearly, the time spent in reaching a solution could have been characterized as a Government-caused delay."[96]

3. Right To Stop Work

If (1) the Government provides specifications that are so deficient that performance of the work is impossible—that is, the defects are not merely minor and correctable, and (2) the provisions of the contract's "Disputes" clause allow it, the contractor may stop work and will not be deemed in breach of contract.[97] This conclusion is based on the rationale that the contractor's work stoppage is excused since the reason for discontinuing performance is beyond the control and without the fault or negligence of the contractor. Note that, under any circumstances, stoppage of work by the contractor is a drastic action and must be given very careful consideration. A wrong decision usually results in a default termination of the contract.

REFERENCES

1. FAR 10.001.

2. Blake Const. Co., GSBCA 3590, 73-1 BCA ¶ 9819.

3. Aerodex, Inc., ASBCA 7121, 1962 BCA ¶ 3492, 5 GC ¶ 173.

4. In-Trol Div., Aseeco Corp., GSBCA 4495, 76-2 BCA ¶ 12085; note 3, supra.

5. See note 3, supra; Blount Bros. Const. Co., ASBCA 6172, 1962 BCA ¶ 3300, 4 GC ¶ 515.

6. 10 USC § 2305(a). See also 41 USC § 253a(a).

7. Note 1, supra.

8. Allen Organ Co.–Reconsideration, Comp. Gen. Dec. B-231473.2, 88-2 CPD ¶ 196, 30 GC ¶ 330; Comp. Gen. Dec. B-175633, 52 Comp. Gen. 219, 1972 CPD ¶ 93.

9. Comp. Gen. Dec. B-141803, 39 Comp. Gen. 570, 1960 CPD ¶ 15, 2 GC ¶ 140.

10. FAR 10.002.

11. 15 Comp. Gen. 974 (1936).

12. Comp. Gen. Dec. B-161080, 47 Comp. Gen. 175, 1967 CPD ¶ 39, 9 GC ¶ 376.

13. Note 1, supra.

14. FAR 10.006(a).

15. Federal Acquisition Streamlining Act of 1994, P.L. 103-355, § 8203, 108 Stat. 3243 (Oct. 13, 1994).

16. Note 1, supra.

17. Secy. of Defense William Perry, Memorandum to the Secretaries of the Military Departments (June 29, 1994).

18. 10 USC ch. 140 (added by P.L. 103-355, note 15, supra, §§ 8103, 8104).

19. FAR 10.008(a).

20. See, e.g., DFARS 210.011.

21. Note 1, supra.

22. Note 1, supra.

23. Note 1, supra.

24. Note 1, supra.

25. FAR 10.004(b)(2).

26. FAR 10.004(b)(4).

27. Note 1, supra.

28. FAR 10.004(b)(3).

29. E.g., Comp. Gen. Dec. B-136941, 38 Comp. Gen. 345, 1958 CPD ¶ 105.

30. E.g., Comp. Gen. Dec. B-157726, 45 Comp. Gen. 462, 1966 CPD ¶ 11, 8 GC ¶ 110.

31. Note 3, supra.

32. FAR 52.236-5, para (a).

33. CPF Underground Utilities Inc., ASBCA 33436, 87-1 BCA ¶ 19596, 29 GC ¶ 156. See also J.L. Malone & Assocs., Inc. v. U.S., 879 F.2d 841 (Fed. Cir. 1989), 8 FPD ¶ 94, 31 GC ¶ 291.

34. FAR 10.004(d).

35. FAR 10.007.

36. See Cibinic, "Constructive Waiver of Specifications," 6 Nash & Cibinic Rep. ¶ 43 (July 1992).

37. Canadian Commercial Corp., ASBCA 17187, 76-2 BCA ¶ 12145.

38. FAR 9.201.

39. Note 38, supra.

40. Note 38, supra.

41. FAR 9.202(c), 9.206-1(c).

42. FAR 52.209-1.

43. FAR 9.206-1(d).

44. See FAR 9.204.

45. See Air Tech Remsel Corp., ASBCA 19948, 76-2 BCA ¶ 11919.

46. North American Phillips Co. v. U.S., 358 F.2d 980 (Ct. Cl. 1966), 8 GC ¶ 222; Dynalectron Corp., ASBCA 11766, 69-1 BCA ¶ 7595, 11 GC ¶ 487.

47. See Allen & Villet, "Implied Warranty of Specifications," Briefing Papers No. 91-8 (July 1991), 9 BPC 439.

48. U.S. v. Spearin, 248 U.S. 132 (1918). See also R.C. Hedreen Co., ASBCA 20599, 77-1 BCA ¶ 12328; Huber, Hunt & Nichols, Inc., GSBCA 4311, 75-2 BCA ¶ 11457, 17 GC ¶ 409.

49. Hollingshead Corp. v. U.S., 111 F. Supp. 285 (Ct. Cl. 1953).

50. Alabama Dry Dock & Shipbldg. Corp., ASBCA 39215, 90-2 BCA ¶ 22855.

51. Celesco Industries Co., ASBCA 18370, 76-1 BCA ¶ 11766, 18 GC ¶ 255.

52. Bethlehem Steel Corp., ASBCA 13341, 72-1 BCA ¶ 9186, 14 GC ¶ 193.

53. Rixon Electronics, Inc. v. U.S., 536 F.2d 1345 (Ct. Cl. 1976), 18 GC ¶ 287.

54. Arvin Industries, Inc., ASBCA 15215, 71-2 BCA ¶ 9143, 14 GC ¶ 67.

55. FAR 46.102(b).

56. See, e.g., Red Circle Corp. v. U.S., 398 F.2d 836 (Ct. Cl. 1968), 10 GC ¶ 316; California Reforestation, AGBCA 87-226-1 et al., 89-1 BCA ¶ 21301, 32 GC ¶ 159; Caddell Const. Co., GSBCA 9196 (7991)-REIN et al., 91-1 BCA ¶ 23478, 33 GC ¶ 73 (Note).

57. FAR 46.407(c).

58. R&M Mechanical Contractors, Inc., DOTCAB 75-51, 76-2 BCA ¶ 12084; Mech-Con Corp., GSBCA 8415, 88-3 BCA ¶ 20889, 30 GC ¶ 251.

59. Reynolds Tile & Terrazzo Corp., ASBCA 20362, 76-2 BCA ¶ 12004; R.B. Wright Const. Co., ASBCA 31967 et al., 90-1 BCA ¶ 22364, affd., 919 F.2d 1569 (Fed. Cir. 1990), 9 FPD ¶ 164, 33 GC ¶ 57.

60. Granite Const. Co. v. U.S., 962 F.2d 998 (Fed. Cir. 1992), 11 FPD ¶ 42, 34 GC ¶ 293. See Cibinic, "Economic Waste: When 'Just As Good' Is Good Enough," 6 Nash & Cibinic Rep. ¶ 28 (May 1992).

61. Wil-Freds, Inc., DOTCAB 75-10, 76-2 BCA ¶ 11959.

62. Mann Const. Co., AGBCA 444, 76-1 BCA ¶ 11710; N.G. Adair, Inc., ASBCA 25961, 83-2 BCA ¶ 16887.

63. J.F. Kane Contracting Co., GSBCA 2005, 66-2 BCA ¶ 5992.

64. Paul A. Teegarden, IBCA 419-1-64, 65-2 BCA ¶ 5011.

65. Note 63, supra.

66. E.S. Good, Jr., ASBCA 10514, 66-1 BCA ¶ 5362, 8 GC ¶ 433.

67. General Ship & Engine Works, Inc., ASBCA 19243, 79-1 BCA ¶ 13657, 21 GC ¶ 143.

68. Skipper & Co., PSBCA 445, 79-2 BCA ¶ 13984.

69. Mr.'s Landscaping & Nursery, HUDBCA 75-6, 76-2 BCA ¶ 11968, 18 GC ¶ 350.

70. Note 64, supra.

71. Electronic & Missile Facilities Co., ASBCA 10077, 66-1 BCA ¶ 5493.

72. Radiation Technology, Inc. v. U.S., 366 F.2d 1003 (Ct. Cl. 1966), 8 GC ¶ 489.

73. SCM Corp., ASBCA 19941, 75-2 BCA ¶ 11508. See also T.C. Wilson, Inc., ASBCA 26035, 83-1 BCA ¶ 16149.

74. E.g., Pride Unlimited, Inc., ASBCA 17778, 75-2 BCA ¶ 11436, reconsideration denied, 75-2 BCA ¶ 11631.

75. Note 74, supra.

76. Decatur Realty Sales, HUDBCA 75-26, 77-2 BCA ¶ 12567.

77. ITRA Coop Assn., GSBCA 7974, 90-1 BCA ¶ 22410, 31 GC ¶ 382.

78. See generally Pettit, "Impossibility of Performance," Briefing Papers No. 63-1 (Mar. 1963), 1 BPC 13; Pettit, "Impossibility of Performance/Edition II," Briefing Papers No. 66-5 (Oct. 1966), 1 BPC 199; Martell & Meagher, "Impossibility of Performance/Edition III," Briefing Papers No. 88-7 (June 1988), 8 BPC 151.

79. U.S. v. Spearin, note 48, supra.

80. See, e.g., F.P. Lathrop Const. Co., ASBCA 25800, 83-2 BCA ¶ 16790.

81. GTE Sylvania, DOTCAB 78-57, 79-2 BCA ¶ 14069, 21 GC ¶ 512.

82. See, e.g., Natus Corp. v. U.S., 371 F.2d 450 (Ct. Cl. 1967), 9 GC ¶ 41.

83. Tombigbee Constructors v. U.S., 420 F.2d 1037 (Ct. Cl. 1970), 12 GC ¶ 144.

84. Clay Bernard Systems Intl., Ltd., ASBCA 25382, 88-3 BCA ¶ 20856, 30 GC ¶ 252.

85. Note 82, supra; Nedlog Co., ASBCA 26034, 82-1 BCA ¶ 15519.

86. Lee Mfg. & Engrg. Co., ASBCA 22187, 79-1 BCA ¶ 13814.

87. Jalaprathan Cement Co., ASBCA 21248, 79-2 BCA ¶ 13927. See also Transatlantic Financing Corp. v. U.S., 259 F. Supp. 725 (D.D.C. 1965), affd., 363 F.2d 312 (D.C. Cir. 1966).

88. HLI Lordship Industries, Inc., VABCA 1785, 86-3 BCA ¶ 19182, 28 GC ¶ 217 (Note).

89. Southern Dredging Co., ENGBCA 5843, 92-2 BCA ¶ 24886, 34 GC ¶ 307.

90. Note 81, supra.

91. Midvale-Heppenstall Co., ASBCA 7525, 65-1 BCA ¶ 4629, 7 GC ¶ 117. But see Hobbs Const. & Development, Inc., ASBCA 34890, 91-2 BCA ¶ 23755, 33 GC ¶ 154.

92. Consolidated Avionics Corp., ASBCA 6315 et al., 1963 BCA ¶ 3888, 6 GC ¶ 37.

SPECIFICATIONS 8-23

93. See National U.S. Radiator Corp., ASBCA 3792, 59-2 BCA ¶ 2386, 1 GC ¶ 774.

94. Austin Co., ASBCA 4255, 61-1 BCA ¶ 2927, 3 GC ¶ 266.

95. Suffolk Environmental Magnetics, Inc., ASBCA 17593, 74-2 BCA ¶ 10771, 16 GC ¶ 380.

96. Kings Electronics Co. v. U.S., 341 F.2d 632 (Ct. Cl. 1965), 7 GC ¶ 95.

97. Seven Sciences, Inc., ASBCA 21079, 77-2 BCA ¶ 12730, 19 GC ¶ 377; L.J. Casey Co., AGBCA 75-148, 76-2 BCA ¶ 12196, 18 GC ¶ 490.

GOVERNMENT PROPERTY

9

A. Overview
1. Definitions
2. Neutralizing The Competitive Advantage
3. Standard Contract Clauses
4. Title

B. Government Obligations
1. Furnishing Property
2. Timely Delivery
3. Suitability Of Property
4. Suitability Of Data & Information

C. Contractor Obligations
1. Mitigation Of Damages
2. Notice To Government
3. Maintenance & Repair

D. Contractor Remedies
1. Recovery Of Extra Costs
2. Performance Time Extension

E. Risk Of Loss
1. Competitive, Fixed-Price Contracts
2. Other Contracts

The performance of many Government contracts involves Government property—the subject treated in this chapter. For example, contractors may be *required* or *permitted* to use Government property in the performance of the contract. Or the contract's purpose may be *rehabilitating* Government property—for instance, the overhaul of aircraft engines or the maintenance of vehicles. Regardless of the situation, important rights and obligations—both for the Government and the contractor—come into play when Government property is involved.

A. OVERVIEW

One entire part of the FAR—Part 45—has been set aside for the subject of Government property. The part prescribes policies and procedures for providing Government property to contractors; contractors' use and management of Government property; and reporting, redistributing, and disposing of contractor inventory. Its most notable provisions, however, deal with one category—Government-furnished property (GFP).[1]

1. Definitions

a. Government Property. "Government property" is defined in the FAR as "all property owned by or leased to the Government or acquired by the Government under the terms of the contract."[2] It includes both GFP and contractor-acquired property.

Government property may be *real* or *personal*, and it may be *tangible* or *intangible*. Tangible property will usually fall into one of five categories: (1) material, (2) special tooling, (3) special test equipment, (4) property designed for military operations, and (5) facilities used for production, maintenance, research, development, or test purposes. Intangible Government property will most likely take the form of data or information required for contract performance.

b. Government-Furnished Property. The FAR defines GFP as "property in the possession of or directly acquired by the Government and subsequently made available to the contractor."[3] Simply stated, GFP is whatever property the Government's solicitation describes as property that will be furnished to the contractor, together with related data and information that may reasonably be required for the intended use of the property. The solicitation should describe the property in sufficient detail to permit evaluation by prospective contractors.[4]

Any type of property can be GFP—not only equipment, material, hardware, and the like (as well as related data), but drawings, patterns, models, parts, and microfilms. Even property that is *not* specifically listed in the contract as GFP can qualify as GFP if compliance with some portion of the contract provisions *in fact* requires that property be furnished by the Government.[5]

2. Neutralizing The Competitive Advantage

According to the "Policy" provision of FAR Part 45, contractors are ordinarily expected to furnish all materials and equipment required to perform Government contracts. However, when contractors are in possession of Government property, the contracting agencies must do all of the following:[6]

>(a) Eliminate to the maximum practical extent any competitive advantage that might arise from using such property;
>
>(b) Require contractors to use Government property to the maximum practical extent in performing Government contracts;
>
>(c) Permit the property to be used only when authorized;
>
>(d) Charge appropriate rentals when the property is authorized for use on other than a rent-free basis;
>
>(e) Require contractors to be responsible and accountable for, and keep the Government's official records of Government property in their possession or control...;
>
>(f) Require contractors to review and provide justification for retaining Government property not currently in use; and

(g) Ensure maximum practical reutilization of contractor inventory...within the Government.

The most important responsibility of contracting agencies is the one listed in Paragraph (a) of the above quote. A contractor in possession of Government production and research property could obviously gain an advantage over its competitors if that property could be used on a new contract. It is the Government's policy to eliminate that advantage.[7] On the other hand, a Government agency is not *required* to furnish Government facilities for contract performance to permit inadequately equipped firms to bid on a procurement.[8] In addition, a contractor's proposal based on using GFP—not promised since it was not available—will be rejected.[9]

a. Sealed Bid Procurements. In sealed bid procurements, the competitive advantage that might otherwise be enjoyed by a contractor from the use of existing Government production and research property is eliminated by adding an evaluation factor to each bid that involves such use. An amount equal to the rent that would *otherwise* have been charged for use of the property is added to the bid. And where use of an evaluation factor is not practical, rent is actually charged for the use.[10]

A Government bid invitation may require bidders in possession of GFP to execute a written agreement with the Government agency for payment of a fair rental value for the property *prior to* the bid-opening date.[11] If the Government reasonably expects that GFP will be needed to perform the contract, its solicitation should provide for furnishing the GFP. It is improper to award a contract without mentioning GFP—which should have been foreseen as required for performance—and then modify the contract after award to provide for the GFP.[12]

The advantages enjoyed by small business firms in Government procurements (see Chapter 6) do *not* include a right to demand that Government property be furnished. The Government has no obligation to furnish GFP to a small business firm to enable it to bid at a reasonable price. Therefore, if a bid price submitted by a small business is unreasonably high because it includes the cost of expensive tooling to be acquired by the bidder, the bid will be rejected.[13]

b. Negotiated Procurements. In negotiated procurements—except when the Contracting Officer determines that the choice of contractors would *not* be affected—the competitive advantage of GFP is eliminated by use of an evaluation factor.[14] The basic evaluation factor used is one that is equal to the rent that would otherwise have been charged for the use of the property.[15]

c. Other Costs & Savings. If the Government will incur direct and measurable *costs* as a result of furnishing production and research property, an evaluation factor will be set forth in the solicitation to reflect the costs.[16] The factor will be either in the form of a dollar amount or a formula. For example, the estimated cost of rehabilitating the property for use will be added to bid prices. And the costs of shipping the GFP to the prospective contractors will be considered in evaluating offers.[17] Even where more than one—but *not all*—likely competitors have GFP available for use in performing a contract, an evaluation factor must be set forth in the solicitation.[18] On the other hand, if measurable *savings* to the Government will result directly from the use of GFP, a dollar amount representing those savings will be employed in the evaluation of bids and proposals. For example, savings from allowing a contractor to use and maintain idle tools, rather than the Government incurring the cost of maintaining them, will be deducted from bid prices.[19]

3. Standard Contract Clauses

FAR Part 45 contains a section that prescribes the six "principal" contract clauses dealing with Government property.[20] Three of the clauses deal with special situations—(1) the "Property Records" clause,[21] which covers the situation when the contract provides for the contracting office to maintain the Government's official Government property records (in other situations, the contractor's records of Government property will be the Government's official records);[22] (2) the "Identification of Government-Furnished Property" clause[23] applicable to fixed-price construction contracts providing for the Government to furnish Government property f.o.b. railroad cars at a specific destination or f.o.b. truck at the project site; and (3) the "Liability for Government Property (Demolition Services)" clause,[24] which applies to solicitations and contracts for the dismantling, demolition, or removal of improvements.

The other clauses all deal with GFP. One, the "Government Property (Fixed-Price Contracts)" clause,[25] is the general clause used in solicitations and contracts when a fixed-price contract is contemplated, and it contains alternate provisions. Another, the "Government Property (Cost-Reimbursement, Time-and-Material, or Labor-Hour Contracts)" clause[26] is for use in solicitations and contracts when a cost-reimbursement, time-and-material, or labor-hour contract is contemplated. It also contains an alternate provision. Still another clause is the "Government-Furnished Property (Short Form)" clause,[27] used in solicitations and contracts not involving educational or nonprofit organizations when a fixed-price, time-and-material, or labor-hour contract is contemplated and the acquisition cost of the GFP involved in the contract is $100,000 or less.

Of these six principal clauses, those dealing with Government-furnished property are the most significant. These clauses are similar in that they all cover the major issues regarding GFP (discussed in the sections below)—title, Government and contractor obligations, and risk of loss. For purposes of illustration, the basic "Government Property (Fixed-Price Contracts)" clause is set forth in Figure 9-1.

4. Title

Title to Government property remains in the Government unless the contract specifically provides otherwise. If the contract is silent on the subject, the silence is invariably regarded as meaning that the Government retains title.[28] Normally, however, the contract will expressly state that title to all Government property shall remain in the Government. Such language appears in the FAR contract clauses dealing with GFP that were mentioned above in Section A.3 (see, for example, Paragraph (c) of the clause set forth in Figure 9-1).

It should also be noted that the Government may take title to property acquired by the contractor. For example, if progress

Figure 9-1

"GOVERNMENT PROPERTY (FIXED-PRICE CONTRACTS)" CLAUSE
(FAR 52.245-2)

(a) *Government-furnished property.* (1) The Government shall deliver to the Contractor, for use in connection with and under the terms of this contract, the Government-furnished property described in the Schedule or specifications together with any related data and information that the Contractor may request and is reasonably required for the intended use of the property (hereinafter referred to as "Government-furnished property").

(2) The delivery or performance dates for this contract are based upon the expectation that Government-furnished property suitable for use (except for property furnished "as-is") will be delivered to the Contractor at the times stated in the Schedule or, if not so stated, in sufficient time to enable the Contractor to meet the contract's delivery or performance dates.

(3) If Government-furnished property is received by the Contractor in a condition not suitable for the intended use, the Contractor shall, upon receipt of it, notify the Contracting Officer, detailing the facts, and, as directed by the Contracting Officer and at Government expense, either repair, modify, return, or otherwise dispose of the property. After completing the directed action and upon written request of the Contractor, the Contracting Officer shall make an equitable adjustment as provided in paragraph (h) of this clause.

(4) If Government-furnished property is not delivered to the Contractor by the required time, the Contracting Officer shall, upon the Contractor's timely written request, make a determination of the delay, if any, caused the Contractor and shall make an equitable adjustment in accordance with paragraph (h) of this clause.

(b) *Changes in Government-furnished property.* (1) The Contracting Officer may, by written notice, (i) decrease the Government-furnished property provided or to be provided under this contract, or (ii) substitute other Government-furnished property for the property to be provided by the Government, or to be acquired by the Contractor for the Government, under this contract. The Contractor shall promptly take such action as the Contracting Officer may direct regarding the removal, shipment, or disposal of the property covered by such notice.

(2) Upon the Contractor's written request, the Contracting Officer shall make an equitable adjustment to the contract in accordance with paragraph (h) of this clause, if the Government has agreed in the Schedule to make the property available for performing this contract and there is any—

continued

Fig. 9-1 / continued

(i) Decrease or substitution in this property pursuant to subparagraph (b)(1) above; or
(ii) Withdrawal of authority to use this property, if provided under any other contract or lease.

(c) *Title in Government property.* (1) The Government shall retain title to all Government-furnished property.

(2) All Government-furnished property and all property acquired by the Contractor, title to which vests in the Government under this paragraph (collectively referred to as "Government property"), are subject to the provisions of this clause. However, special tooling accountable to this contract is subject to the provisions of the Special Tooling clause and is not subject to the provisions of this clause. Title to Government property shall not be affected by its incorporation into or attachment to any property not owned by the Government, nor shall Government property become a fixture or lose its identity as personal property by being attached to any real property.

(3) Title to each item of facilities and special test equipment acquired by the Contractor for the Government under this contract shall pass to and vest in the Government when its use in performing this contract commences or when the Government has paid for it, whichever is earlier, whether or not title previously vested in the Government.

(4) If this contract contains a provision directing the Contractor to purchase material for which the Government will reimburse the Contractor as a direct item of cost under this contract—

(i) Title to material purchased from a vendor shall pass to and vest in the Government upon the vendor's delivery of such material; and

(ii) Title to all other material shall pass to and vest in the Government upon—

(A) Issuance of the material for use in contract performance;
(B) Commencement of processing of the material or its use in contract performance; or
(C) Reimbursement of the cost of the material by the Government, whichever occurs first.

(d) *Use of Government property.* The Government property shall be used only for performing this contract, unless otherwise provided in this contract or approved by the Contracting Officer.

(e) *Property administration.* (1) The Contractor shall be responsible and accountable for all Government property provided under this contract and shall comply with Federal Acquisition Regulation (FAR) Subpart 45.5, as in effect on the date of this contract.

continued

Fig. 9-1 / continued

(2) The Contractor shall establish and maintain a program for the use, maintenance, repair, protection, and preservation of Government property in accordance with sound industrial practice and the applicable provisions of Subpart 45.5 of the FAR.

(3) If damage occurs to Government property, the risk of which has been assumed by the Government under this contract, the Government shall replace the items or the Contractor shall make such repairs as the Government directs. However, if the Contractor cannot effect such repairs within the time required, the Contractor shall dispose of the property as directed by the Contracting Officer. When any property for which the Government is responsible is replaced or repaired, the Contracting Officer shall make an equitable adjustment in accordance with paragraph (h) of this clause.

(4) The Contractor represents that the contract price does not include any amount for repairs or replacement for which the Government is responsible. Repair or replacement of property for which the Contractor is responsible shall be accomplished by the Contractor at its own expense.

(f) *Access.* The Government and all its designees shall have access at all reasonable times to the premises in which any Government property is located for the purpose of inspecting the Government property.

(g) *Risk of loss.* Unless otherwise provided in this contract, the Contractor assumes the risk of, and shall be responsible for, any loss or destruction of, or damage to, Government property upon its delivery to the Contractor or upon passage of title to the Government under paragraph (c) of this clause. However, the Contractor is not responsible for reasonable wear and tear to Government property or for Government property properly consumed in performing this contract.

(h) *Equitable adjustment.* When this clause specifies an equitable adjustment, it shall be made to any affected contract provision in accordance with the procedures of the Changes clause. When appropriate, the Contracting Officer may initiate an equitable adjustment in favor of the Government. The right to an equitable adjustment shall be the Contractor's exclusive remedy. The Government shall not be liable to suit for breach of contract for—

(1) Any delay in delivery of Government-furnished property;

(2) Delivery of Government-furnished property in a condition not suitable for its intended use;

(3) A decrease in or substitution of Government-furnished property; or

(4) Failure to repair or replace Government property for which the Government is responsible.

continued

> *Fig. 9-1 / continued*
>
> (i) *Final accounting and disposition of Government property.* Upon completing this contract, or at such earlier dates as may be fixed by the Contracting Officer, the Contractor shall submit, in a form acceptable to the Contracting Officer, inventory schedules covering all items of Government property (including any resulting scrap) not consumed in performing this contract or delivered to the Government. The Contractor shall prepare for shipment, deliver f.o.b. origin, or dispose of the Government property as may be directed or authorized by the Contracting Officer. The net proceeds of any such disposal shall be credited to the contract price or shall be paid to the Government as the Contracting Officer directs.
>
> (j) *Abandonment and restoration of Contractor's premises.* Unless otherwise provided herein, the Government—
> (1) May abandon any Government property in place, at which time all obligations of the Government regarding such abandoned property shall cease; and
> (2) Has no obligation to restore or rehabilitate the Contractor's premises under any circumstances (e.g., abandonment, disposition upon completion of need, or upon contract completion). However, if the Government-furnished property (listed in the Schedule or specifications) is withdrawn or is unsuitable for the intended use, or if other Government property is substituted, then the equitable adjustment under paragraph (h) of this clause may properly include restoration or rehabilitation costs.
>
> (k) *Communications.* All communications under this clause shall be in writing.
>
> (l) *Overseas contracts.* If this contract is to be performed outside of the United States of America, its territories, or possessions, the words "Government" and "Government-furnished" (wherever they appear in this clause) shall be construed as "United States Government" and "United States Government-furnished," respectively.

payments—payments made to the contractor as the work progresses—are provided for by the contract, title to all materials acquired or produced by the contractor for the performance of the contract immediately vests in the Government under the standard "Progress Payments" clause.[29] The Government may also acquire title to "special tooling" (tooling of a specialized nature limited to the development or production of particular supplies) in negotiated contracts by use of the "Special Tooling" clause in contracts that require use of such tooling.[30]

B. GOVERNMENT OBLIGATIONS

1. Furnishing Property

The "Government Property "clauses mentioned in Section A.3 above recognize that the Government has the duty to provide GFP (see, for example, Paragraph (a)(1) of the clause in Figure 9-1). The Government's failure to furnish the tangible GFP promised entitles the contractor to an equitable adjustment in the contract price for its increased costs.[31] A failure to supply written "data and information" required to be furnished by the Government also entitles the contractor to an equitable price adjustment.[32] In addition, the data must be provided by a reasonable method—merely allowing a contractor to hunt through voluminous files for the data is not sufficient. The contractor is entitled to an equitable adjustment for searching out for itself the information the Government was obligated to furnish.[33] Of course, if a failure to furnish GFP delays performance of the contract, the time for performance should also be extended.

Sometimes the only way the Government can adequately furnish a contractor with the required "data and information" is by providing personal assistance—such as the services of engineers employed by the firms that originally furnished the GFP to the Government. Such people may have valuable information about new developments in the industry which can only be obtained, as a practical matter, by person-to-person contact. The contract may, however, give a Government official discretion to determine whether the services of engineers will be furnished. In exercising that discretion, the official involved may not withhold his approval arbitrarily—he must exercise his authority reasonably. In one case, where a Government official provided fewer engineering services than reasonably required—thus furnishing less than the promised data and information—a contractor was entitled to an equitable adjustment for the increased costs of obtaining the needed data and information itself.[34]

2. Timely Delivery

The "Government Property" clauses also contemplate timely delivery of GFP to the contractor (see, for example, Paragraph (a)(2) of the clause in Figure 9-1). Equitable adjustments in performance time and contract price for Government delays in delivery of GFP are fairly routine under the standard "Government Property" clauses.[35] If the contract contains a standard "Government Property" clause, the contractor need not even make a formal demand for the GFP.[36] Moreover, even in the absence of a contract clause, the Government may be liable to a contractor for damages when it has not been diligent in making deliveries on time. The theory of recovery in such situations is that the Government breached its contract.[37]

Government delay in furnishing GFP can be a shield, as well as a sword, for the contractor. For example, where the delay causes a contractor's failure to perform, that failure will be considered excusable, and the contractor will have the same right to recover the costs incurred in attempting to perform as if the contract had been terminated for the Government's convenience.[38] To recover for delayed delivery of GFP or to have an excuse for default, however, the contractor must demonstrate that the delay actually *affected* its performance.[39] And, of course, a contractor cannot claim an equitable adjustment for a delay in delivery of GFP for which the contractor is responsible.[40]

A contractor may justifiably suspend *other* operations when the delivery of GFP is delayed—even if the operations are not *directly* affected by the Government's delay in furnishing property—if it would serve no purpose to perform those other operations in the absence of the GFP. In one case where a contract involved the use of two different kinds of cloth needed at the same time for sewing operations, it served no purpose to cut one of the two cloths when the other was not available because of Government delay in delivery of GFP.[41]

3. Suitability Of Property

The standard "Government Property" clause will contain language similar to that found in Paragraph (a)(2) of the clause in Figure 9-1, which provides that contract performance is based on the "expectation that Government-furnished property suitable for use (except for such property furnished 'as-is') will be delivered to the Contractor." This provision constitutes a warranty on the Government's part.[42] It will not lightly be read out of a contract nor weakened by Government disclaimers of responsibility.[43]

However, if the Government states *clearly and unmistakably* in the contract that it does not represent the condition, quality, or completeness of the GFP, it can escape from liability if the GFP causes difficulties to the contractor.[44] In addition, if the contract states that property will be furnished "as is," such property is *expressly* excepted from the suitability-for-use provisions, and a contractor has no right to an equitable adjustment for repairs or replacement of "as is" GFP[45] unless the enforcement of the "as is" disclaimer would be *unconscionable* under the circumstances (for example, when the use of that disclaimer is not justified because the Government knew the poor condition of the property and should have disclosed its condition in the contract's solicitation[46]).

"Suitability for use" is a question of fact to be determined on the basis of the unique circumstances of each situation. Thus, where GFP is furnished for use in a production contract, it must be suitable from a mass production manufacturing standpoint, taking into consideration the background of price and delivery schedules.[47] On the other hand, suitable for use does not necessarily mean ready for immediate use without any work by the contractor. For instance, where it was clear in a contract that boxes to be furnished by the Government might not be assembled, the contractor could not complain that it had to assemble the boxes before it could use them.[48] However, GFP that is suitable for use does not have to be inventoried as to all parts and components, or broken down or restructured by the contractor. A visual inspection is all that should be necessary,[49] unless there is a specific provision in the contract requiring the contractor to test the GFP.[50]

Paragraph (a)(3) of the clause in Figure 9-1 specifically contemplates an equitable adjustment in the contract where repair or return of the property is necessary because the "Government-furnished property is received by the Contractor in a condition not suitable for the intended use."[51] Even if the contract does not contain a "Government Property" clause, however, the contractor may nevertheless be entitled to an equitable adjustment for increased costs under the standard contract "Changes" clause[52] (see Chapter 11). Or, if there is no contractual remedy, the contractor can be granted relief on a breach of contract basis.[53]

4. Suitability Of Data & Information

The warranty of suitability of data and information relating to the Government property provided by the Government to the contractor is *separate and distinct* from the comparable warranty relating to property itself. Accordingly, even if the contract contains a specific disclaimer of the warranty of suitability of the equipment, a contractor may, nonetheless, recover under the standard "Government Property" clause for unsuitability of data and information relating to the equipment. In one case where the Government stipulated that certain Government-furnished tools would be furnished "as is," it nevertheless had the duty to supply, in suitable form, the related data and information necessary to make the tools operable. The Government's failure to carry out that duty entitled the contractor to an equitable adjustment for the costs incurred in making the tools functional without the benefit of the promised information.[54]

When hardware or equipment is unsuitable for use, the fact of unsuitability is ordinarily easy to determine. It is therefore not difficult to calculate the increased costs of necessary repairs. However, more problems may be presented by unsuitable data or information because the damage incurred by the lack of good data is more subtle and not susceptible to easy proof.

Even in the absence of the "Government Property" clause in a contract, a contractor will be entitled to an equitable adjustment under the "Changes" clause for increased costs that result from erroneous data or information supplied by the Government.[55] Moreover, an equitable adjustment will be granted not only when the data are clearly erroneous,[56] but also when the data are incomplete, not applicable, grossly inaccurate, or require lengthy study to be intelligible.[57]

C. CONTRACTOR OBLIGATIONS

1. Mitigation Of Damages

The standard "Government Property" clause provides that if GFP is unsuitable for use, the Government may require the contractor to make repairs or modifications at Government expense (see, for example, Paragraph (a)(3) of the clause in Figure 9-1). Obviously, in making those repairs, the contractor must act *reasonably* and mitigate damages to the extent practicable. A contractor will not be reimbursed for expenses incurred unreasonably—such as fruitless efforts to make equipment meet faulty specifications.[58]

2. Notice To Government

Under the standard "Government Property" clauses, the contractor must notify the Government when GFP is furnished late or is unsuitable for use. With respect to *delay*, the standard "Government Property" clause provides—in language similar to that found in Paragraph (a)(4) of the Figure 9-1 clause—that the Contracting Officer shall make a determination of the delay in performance caused by the GFP delivery delay "upon the Contractor's timely written request." Similarly, with respect to *suitability* for use, the clause requires the contractor to notify the Contracting Officer that the property is unsuitable "upon receipt" of that property (see Paragraph (a)(3) of the Figure 9-1 clause).

Contractors should comply with these provisions. Prompt notice is always wise for the protection of the contractor's interests and to enable the Government to take prompt corrective action.

Moreover, notice requirements will be enforced against the contractor when delay in the giving of notice results in *prejudice* to the Government[59] (for example, when the Government could have substituted suitable property—and avoided any increased costs to the contractor—if prompt notice had been given). However, the contractor's claim is not barred if it gives notice as soon as it is reasonably aware of the nature of the defect—even if considerable time has passed since the GFP was received.[60] Thus, in one case where a contractor delayed in giving notice of defects in certain GFP cloth because it reasonably attributed the defects to the chemical treatment of the cloth (which would come out in the cleaning and pressing), the delay did not preclude consideration of the merits of its claim.[61] The primary requirement is that notice be given as soon as the contractor is *reasonably* aware of the defect.[62] Depending on the facts in a particular case, a contractor may also be able to argue that the Government had actual or constructive knowledge of the faulty GFP—even though the contractor failed to notify the Government promptly.

3. Maintenance & Repair

Under the FAR, contractors must meet certain minimum requirements for the care, maintenance, and use of Government property they possess, including, in many cases, the establishment of a written "property control system."[63] Those requirements, while strict, are not unreasonable. For example, a contractor's obligation to maintain GFP does not extend to performing a major overhaul of the property.[64] Contractors are, however, "directly responsible and accountable" for Government property in the possession and control of subcontractors.[65] In the end, it is a fact question whether particular work exceeds what would be required as normal maintenance.[66]

These maintenance and repair requirements are reflected in the standard "Government Property" clauses mentioned in Section A.3 above. Paragraph (e)(2) of the clause set out in Figure 9-1, for example, requires the contractor to "establish and maintain" a program for the "use, maintenance, repair, protection, and preservation of Government property." Moreover, the program is to be administered in accordance with "sound industrial practice" *and* the applicable provisions of the FAR.

D. CONTRACTOR REMEDIES

1. Recovery Of Extra Costs

In general, a contractor will be able to recover the extra costs caused by the Government's failure to deliver GFP, delay in delivering GFP, or furnishing of unsuitable GFP (including data and information).[67] Recoverable costs for unsuitable GFP include (1) costs of making an inventory of and replacing the defective GFP, (2) costs of abnormal (but necessary) requisitioning, purchasing, receiving, stocking, and handling of parts and components, (3) costs of repair necessary to correct the GFP, (4) costs of obtaining replacement parts, and (5) all other costs reasonably necessary to make the GFP workable.[68] In short, any *reasonable* expenses caused by the Government's actions should be recoverable.[69]

When unsuitable or delayed GFP disrupts the contractor's *work*, the contractor may also recover the resulting costs of the work delays and disruption.[70] For example, a contractor may recover for the increased costs of engineering efforts, labor inefficiencies, idle time, and overtime that result from unsuitable or late GFP.[71] Disruption costs may add up to very substantial sums and may even exceed basic costs. But as long as they can be shown to have been caused by the Government, an equitable adjustment is allowable.[72]

2. Performance Time Extension

If the Government delays in providing GFP, fails to deliver it, or furnishes unsuitable GFP, the contractor may be entitled to a compensating extension of the contract's performance schedule. Such a time extension can be of crucial importance where the contract might otherwise be terminated for default for failure to perform on time, or where the contractor might be held liable for liquidated damages due to otherwise untimely performance.[73]

E. RISK OF LOSS

1. Competitive, Fixed-Price Contracts

A contractor under a competitively awarded, fixed-price contract will ordinarily be held liable for loss or damage to GFP while it is in the contractor's possession. Paragraph (g) of the clause set forth in Figure 9-1 expressly provides that the contractor "assumes the risk of, and shall be responsible for, any loss or destruction of, or damage to, Government property" provided under the contract. The liability imposed can be significant, and it applies regardless of the contractor's lack of fault.[74]

In practical effect, then, the risk of loss or damage imposed under the clause requires a contractor receiving GFP under a fixed-price contract to insure the property.[75]

There are some *limitations* on the risk assumed by the contractor. First, a contractor will not be liable for damage or defects caused by *design deficiencies* for which the Government is responsible; rather, the contractor will be entitled to an equitable adjustment for the increased costs caused by the design deficiencies.[76] Second, if the Government fails to advise a contractor of the *peculiarities* of the GFP, the contractor will not be liable for damage that occurs to the GFP because of those peculiarities. For instance, a contractor was not liable where the Government failed to advise the contractor that a winch had a tendency to build up cable, causing the cable to snap.[77] Third, the standard clause itself provides that a contractor is not responsible for *reasonable wear and tear* to the GFP, or for property *consumed in performance* of the contract (see Paragraph (g) of the Figure 9-1 clause). A *reasonableness* test will be applied to the manner in which the contractor protected the GFP.[78]

2. Other Contracts

The risk-of-loss provisions used in fixed-price contracts awarded on the basis of price competition or established prices discussed above differ from the risk-of-loss provisions that apply when the contract is a *negotiated* fixed-price contract for which the price is *not* based on (a) adequate price competition, (b) established catalog or market prices, or (c) prices set by law or regulation. The FAR prescribes the use of "Alternate I" of the "Government Property (Fixed-Price Contracts)" clause, which sets forth a different Paragraph (g), entitled "Limited Risk of Loss." This paragraph provides considerably less burdensome risks for the contractor.[79]

Under the Alternate I Paragraph (g), a contractor is *not* liable for loss, destruction, or damage to the GFP *except as specifically* provided in Paragraph (g) or elsewhere in the particular contract. The contractor is liable for loss or damage to Government property that results from (1) willful misconduct or lack of good faith of any of the contractor's *managerial* personnel or (2) failure, due to willful misconduct or lack of good faith of the contractor's *managerial* personnel, to establish and administer a program or system for the control, protection, preservation, maintenance, and repair of GFP.[80]

Managerial (not merely rank and file) employees must be involved for the contractor to be liable under this alternate risk-of-loss paragraph. The paragraph also places a considerable burden on the contractor to establish that loss or damage (a) did *not* result from its failure to maintain an approved program or system, or (b) occurred during a period when an approved program or system for control of the property was being maintained. The "Government Property" clauses for other types of contracts (see Section A.3 above) also contain "Limited Risk of Loss" provisions.[81]

REFERENCES

1. See generally Allen & Stockton, "Government Property," Briefing Papers No. 94-4 (Mar. 1994); vom Baur, "Government-Furnished Property," Briefing Papers No. 69-3 (June 1969), 1 BPC 385.

2. FAR 45.101.

3. Note 2, supra.

4. FAR 45.303-2.

5. Drexel Dynamics Corp., ASBCA 9502, 66-2 BCA ¶ 5860.

6. FAR 45.102.

7. FAR subpt. 45.2. See Raytheon Co., ASBCA 14617, 71-1 BCA ¶ 8691, 13 GC ¶ 213.

8. Southwest Marine, Inc., Comp. Gen. Dec. B-192251, 78-2 CPD ¶ 329.

9. Bristol Electronics, Inc., Comp. Gen. Dec. B-190341, 78-2 CPD ¶ 122.

10. FAR 45.201(a).

11. James R. Parks Co., Comp. Gen. Dec. B-186699, 76-2 CPD ¶ 360.

12. Midland Maintenance, Inc., Comp. Gen. Dec. B-184247, 76-2 CPD ¶ 127.

13. Note 9, supra.

14. FAR 45.201(a).

15. FAR 45.202-1.

16. FAR 45.202-3(a).

17. Ensign Bickford Co., Comp. Gen. Dec. B-180844, 74-2 CPD ¶ 97.

18. E-Systems, Inc., Comp. Gen. Dec. B-191346, 79-1 CPD ¶ 192.

19. FAR 45.202-3(c).

20. FAR 45.106.

21. FAR 52.245-1.

22. See FAR 45.105.

23. FAR 52.245-3.

24. FAR 52.245-6.

25. FAR 52.245-2.

26. FAR 52.245-5.

27. FAR 52.245-4.

28. Wiebe Const. Co., ASBCA 19678, 76-2 BCA ¶ 11920; Basic Const. Co., ASBCA 21140, 76-2 BCA ¶ 12153.

29. See FAR 52.232-16, para. (d).

30. See FAR 52.245-17, para. (b).

31. See note 5, supra.

32. See note 5, supra.

33. Buffington Const. Co., ASBCA 9720, 1964 BCA ¶ 4506.

34. New York Shipbldg. Corp., ASBCA 10819, 67-1 BCA ¶ 6242.

35. See, e.g., A. Dubois & Sons, Inc., ASBCA 5176, 60-2 BCA ¶ 2750, 2 GC ¶ 519; Fairchild Industries, Inc., ASBCA 15272, 74-1 BCA ¶ 10551; Kestrel Corp., ASBCA 17968, 74-1 BCA ¶ 10555, 16 GC ¶ 234. See also C.W. Vincent, Inc., ASBCA 7995, 65-1 BCA ¶ 4728, 7 GC ¶ 210 (contractor granted equitable adjustment under "GFP" clause where Government delayed giving permission to remove needed material from Government stockpile).

36. Woodside Screw Machine Co., ASBCA 6936, 1962 BCA ¶ 3308, 4 GC ¶ 363.

GOVERNMENT PROPERTY   9-21

37. Ozark Dam Constructors v. U.S., 130 Ct. Cl. 354 (1955).

38. Note 36, supra.

39. Meridian Industries, Inc., ASBCA 18340, 76-1 BCA ¶ 11866; Disan Corp., ASBCA 21323, 78-2 BCA ¶ 13528.

40. Mid-States Mfg. Co., ASBCA 6344, 1962 BCA ¶ 3544, 5 GC ¶ 152; Republic Electronic Industries Corp., ASBCA 7994, 1963 BCA ¶ 3874, 6 GC ¶ 154.

41. A. Dubois & Sons, Inc., note 35, supra.

42. N. Summergrade & Sons, ASBCA 11916, 68-2 BCA ¶ 7221; Singer-General Precision, Inc., ASBCA 15372, 72-2 BCA ¶ 9640, 14 GC ¶ 493; Stanwick Corp., ASBCA 11613, 72-1 BCA ¶ 9285.

43. Thompson Ramo Wooldridge v. U.S., 361 F.2d 222 (Ct. Cl. 1966), 8 GC ¶ 263; FMC Corp., ASBCA 14658, 72-1 BCA ¶ 9238; AAA Engrg. & Drafting Co., ASBCA 21326, 77-1 BCA ¶ 12454, 19 GC ¶ 279; Hart's Food Service, Inc., ASBCA 30756, 89-2 BCA ¶ 21789, 31 GC ¶ 271 (Note).

44. Rixon Electronics, Inc. v. U.S., 536 F.2d 1345 (Ct. Cl. 1976), 18 GC ¶ 287; note 5, supra.

45. L.T. Industries, Inc., ASBCA 12832, 69-1 BCA ¶ 7534; Carrollton Mfg. Co., ASBCA 14136, 69-2 BCA ¶ 7967; Baifield Industries v. U.S., 1 FPD ¶ 75 (Fed. Cir. 1983) (unpublished), 25 GC ¶ 108.

46. See G.W. Galloway Co., ASBCA 16656, 73-2 BCA ¶ 10270, 15 GC ¶ 476.

47. Topkis Bros. Co. v. U.S., 297 F.2d 536 (Ct. Cl. 1961), 3 GC ¶ 615.

48. MAPAC, Inc., ASBCA 19271, 74-2 BCA ¶ 10790.

49. International Aircraft Services, Inc., ASBCA 8389, 65-1 BCA ¶ 4793; Logicon, Inc., ASBCA 39683, 90-2 BCA ¶ 22786, 32 GC ¶ 211.

50. Republic Electronic Industries Corp., note 40, supra.

51. See Keco Industries, Inc., ASBCA 11468, 66-2 BCA ¶ 5899.

52. Sutton Const. Co., ASBCA 8405, 1963 BCA ¶ 3762, 6 GC ¶ 111; Seaview Electric Co., ASBCA 6966, 61-2 BCA ¶ 3151, 4 GC ¶ 159; Field Engrg. Corp., ASBCA 10124, 66-2 BCA ¶ 5959, 9 GC ¶ 228; Volt Technical Corp., VACAB 701, 69-2 BCA ¶ 7809.

53. Koppers/Clough v. U.S., 201 Ct. Cl. 344 (1973), 15 GC ¶ 234.

54. Note 5, supra.

55. Hayes Intl. Corp., ASBCA 9750, 65-1 BCA ¶ 4767, 7 GC ¶ 254; Chris Berg, Inc., ASBCA 8382, 1964 BCA ¶ 4040.

56. Fort Sill Assocs., ASBCA 7482, 1963 BCA ¶ 3869, 6 GC ¶ 155; Chris Berg, Inc., note 55, supra.

57. Hayes Intl. Corp., note 55, supra; AAA Engrg. & Drafting Co., note 43, supra.

58. See Frost Engrg. Development Corp., ASBCA 9416, 65-1 BCA ¶ 4762.

59. Reeves Instrument Co., ASBCA 11534, 68-2 BCA ¶ 7078, 10 GC ¶ 415.

60. Lockheed Aircraft Corp., ASBCA 9396, 65-1 BCA ¶ 4689.

61. Capici Coat Shop, Inc., ASBCA 9196, 1964 BCA ¶ 4484.

62. National Roofing & Painting Corp., ASBCA 10245, 66-1 BCA ¶ 5409.

63. FAR subpt. 45.5, 45.502(a).

64. Lake Service Corp., ASBCA 9422, 1964 BCA ¶ 4265, 7 GC ¶ 150.

65. FAR 45.502(a), (c).

66. See Rheem Mfg. Co., ASBCA 3445, 56-2 BCA ¶ 145, affd., 153 Ct. Cl. 465 (1961). See also American Hydrotherm Corp., ASBCA 5678, 60-1 BCA ¶ 2617, 2 GC ¶ 352.

67. Note 60, supra.

68. International Aircraft Services, Inc., note 49, supra.

69. International Aircraft Services, Inc., note 49, supra.

70. International Aircraft Services, Inc., note 49, supra.

71. Sun Shipbldg. & Drydock Co., ASBCA 11300, 68-1 BCA ¶ 7054, 11 GC ¶ 196; Power Eqpt. Corp., ASBCA 5904, 1964 BCA ¶ 4025, 6 GC ¶ 79; Lake Union Drydock Co., ASBCA 3073, 59-1 BCA ¶ 2229, 1 GC ¶ 504.

72. Lake Union Drydock Co., note 71, supra; International Aircraft Services, Inc., note 49, supra.

GOVERNMENT PROPERTY   9-23

73. See Carl W. Schutter Industries Co., ASBCA 3867, 59-2 BCA ¶ 2390, 2 GC ¶ 25; Indian Affiliates, Inc., IBCA 1861, 86-2 BCA ¶ 18749, 29 GC ¶ 9 (Note); Bogue Electric Mfg. Co., ASBCA 25184, 86-2 BCA ¶ 18925, 29 GC ¶ 9 (Note).

74. See American Photographic Industries, Inc., ASBCA 29995, 86-1 BCA ¶ 18738, 29 GC ¶ 9.

75. Fraass Surgical Mfg. Co. v. U.S., 571 F.2d 34 (Ct. Cl. 1978), 20 GC ¶ 129; Chromalloy American Corp., ASBCA 19885, 76-2 BCA ¶ 11997, 18 GC ¶ 367.

76. B.J. Lucarelli & Co., ASBCA 8768, 65-1 BCA ¶ 4655.

77. See Stauerei-Vereinigung, GmbH, ASBCA 7802, 1964 BCA ¶ 4361.

78. Elmore Moving & Storage, Inc. v. U.S., 845 F.2d 1001 (Fed. Cir. 1988), 7 FPD ¶ 52, 30 GC ¶ 194; E.L. David Const. Co., ASBCA 32823, 89-3 BCA ¶ 21954, 31 GC ¶ 232.

79. See FAR 52.245-2, alternate I.

80. Note 79, supra, para. (g)(3).

81. E.g., FAR 52.245-5, para. (g) (cost-reimbursement contracts); FAR 52.245-2, alternate II, para. (g) (contracts with nonprofit institutions).

INTELLECTUAL PROPERTY RIGHTS

10

A. Patents
 1. Title vs. License
 2. Current Government Policy
 3. FAR Coverage
 4. Patent Infringement
 5. Contractor Indemnification Of Government
 6. Contractor Notice & Assistance

B. Technical Data
 1. The Regulations
 2. Types Of Government Rights
 3. Government Policy
 4. DOD Policy & Procedures
 5. Enforcing Data Rights

C. Copyright

The Federal Government has for some time been engaged in a continuing debate with contractors regarding the proper policies to adopt with respect to contractors' *intellectual property*. This dialogue has centered primarily on the treatment to be accorded *patents* and *technical data*, and it involves considerations that must take into account the rights of the Government, the contractor, and third parties.

This chapter reviews the Government's intellectual property policies, particularly as they relate to work performed under research and development (R&D) contracts. The focus will be on (1) *patents*, especially the problems of infringement and indemnification, (2) contractors' rights with respect to their *technical data*, and (3) *copyright* policy under Government contracts.

A. PATENTS

The debate referred to above between contractors and the Government concerns a most basic question: who should retain title to patents resulting from work performed under R&D contracts—the Government or the R&D contractors?

1. Title vs. License

The two schools of thought in this area are divided between (a) those who favor a *title* policy under which the Government would retain title to any patent resulting from an invention first conceived or reduced to practice under an R&D contract (the phrase "reduced to practice" is meant to include the construction of at least a functioning model of the invention), and (b) those who favor a *license* policy under which the contractor/inventor retains full title to the patent for commercial purposes, while conveying a nonexclusive, nontransferable, paid-up (royalty-free) license to the Government to use the invention for Government purposes.

The basic rationale in support of these divergent positions is obvious. On the one hand, it is logical to require a contractor to turn over to the Government title to inventions that are a direct result of publicly-funded work. On the other hand, it is equally true that innovation is greatly enhanced by providing contractors with the economic incentive of a monopoly position. All things being equal, contractors are more likely to develop innovative technology when title to any resulting patents will remain in their possession.

2. Current Government Policy

The Government's current position is basically the *license* policy with regard to R&D contracts. For many years, the allocation of patent rights varied throughout federal agencies, depending on the needs of each agency. In 1980, Congress passed a law that added provisions covering patent rights in inventions made with federal assistance to Title 35 of the United States Code.[1] The law granted small business firms, universities, and other nonprofit scientific or educational organizations the right to retain title to inventions derived under federally-funded R&D contracts and grants.[2] The Government acquires a nonexclusive, irrevocable, paid-up license to use the subject invention for its own purposes.[3] Further, under the statute, the Government may *modify* the rights of the contractor or grantee only where (a) national security is threatened, (b) the contractor is operating a Government-owned research or production facility, or (c) other exceptional circumstances exist.[4] Although this law created a uniform Government policy and new opportunities for small businesses and nonprofit organizations, it did not change Government policy for *other* contractors.

However, in February 1983, President Reagan issued a memorandum directing the heads of all departments and agencies to extend the benefits of the 1980 law to all R&D contractors, including large businesses and profitmaking organizations.[5] The major premises underlying the 1983 memorandum are as follows: (1) patented processes or products developed under federal programs have significant *commercial* value, (2) properly used, they can improve *industrial productivity* and the overall *national economy*, and (3) allowing the *contractor* to retain title is the best incentive for developing an invention's commercial potential. Under the memorandum, the Government will continue to retain at least a royalty-free license in all subject inventions. An exception can be made to waive *all* Government rights when (a) it is necessary to obtain an agreement with a uniquely qualified contractor, or (b) the contract involves co-sponsored, cost-sharing, or joint venture R&D, and the contractor is making a substantial contribution of funds, facilities, or equipment to the work performed.

In an age when much of the new technology is being developed with private funds, this patent policy allows federal agencies to have the flexibility they need to contract for R&D work on terms that contractors will accept and that will promote participation of technologically sophisticated contractors in Government programs. For example, the Government supports basic research in computer technology with the active cooperation of firms that developed their own technological base. These firms would be reluctant to apply their expertise if the Government could acquire a royalty-free license to all inventions made under the R&D program. Note, however, that because patent policy for large businesses and profitmaking institutions is established by presidential decree and not by statute, it is subject to *change* by later administrations or *preemption* by existing or future statutes.

3. FAR Coverage

The Government policy set forth in the presidential memorandum discussed above—promoting the commercialization of patentable results of federally-funded research by granting to all contractors, regardless of size, the title to patents made in whole or in part with federal funds in exchange for royalty-free use by or on behalf of the Government—is reflected in the FAR and the various FAR "Patent Rights" clauses appearing in contracts.[6]

a. Contractor Title. The "Patents Rights" clause requires the contractor to disclose to the Government in writing any "subject invention"—that is, "any invention of the Contractor conceived or first actually reduced to practice in the performance of work under this contract."[7] After the required disclosure, the contractor may *elect* to retain title to the invention (unless an agency's statutory requirements necessitate a different policy set forth in that agency's supplement to the FAR).[8]

The FAR allows agencies to alter the general rules of granting title to inventions to the contractor in the following circumstances: (1) when the contractor is not located in the United States or is subject to the control of a foreign government, (2) when the contract is for the operation of certain Government-owned contractor-operated Department of Energy facilities, (3) in "exceptional circumstances" when a restriction on contractor title rights will better serve the FAR policy objectives, and (4) when granting title in an invention would endanger national security.[9]

b. Government License. When the contractor elects to retain title, the Government retains a "nonexclusive, nontransferable, irrevocable, paid-up license to practice or have practiced for or on behalf of the United States the subject invention throughout the world."[10] That license gives the Government the right to allow other contractors, including competitors, to produce the item for sale to the Government. When the Government is the only or the major consumer of the invention, the license the Government retains under the "Patent Rights" clause could deprive the contractor of much of the benefit of its title in the invention.

4. Patent Infringement

One of the basic rights of a patent holder is the right to prevent, or enjoin, others from the unauthorized use, sale, or production of the patent holder's invention. Where the patent infringer is a Government contractor (or the Government), however, the right of a patent holder to seek an injunction against the infringer has been significantly altered.

Government contractors are protected by statute from suits by other contractors for patent infringement.[11] The statute provides that suit in the United States Court of Federal Claims against the Government is the exclusive remedy for a patent owner who claims its patented invention has been infringed either by the Government or by someone acting for the Government. Therefore, the patent holder must proceed against the *Government* (not the contractor), and it may sue to enforce its rights only in the Court of Federal Claims.

The statute also provides that the Government may be liable for "reasonable and entire compensation" (i.e., for money damages) for the "unauthorized use" of a patent, but will not be liable for the tort of "patent infringement." This means that the patent holder may not seek the remedy of *injunctive* relief against the Government but is limited to *monetary* compensation (usually equivalent to a fair licensing fee).[12] More importantly, the Government (or its contractor) may continue to use the patented invention once "reasonable compensation" has been paid. Therefore, under this statutory scheme, the contract work may proceed uninterrupted even when an infringement has occurred, while the patent holder may seek its limited remedy of monetary compensation for the infringement.

To implement the statutory policy in this area, an "Authorization and Consent" clause is included in most Government contracts. These clauses are normally broad and generally provide that the Government gives its authorization and consent to a contractor to use any invention covered by a United States patent in the performance of its contract. This authorization also extends to subcontracts performed under a prime contract. The broadest of the standard clauses is the clause prescribed for R&D contracts (or contracts where R&D is the primary purpose of the contract) that are to be performed in the United States.[13] That clause is reproduced from the FAR in Figure 10-1.

Figure 10-1

"AUTHORIZATION AND CONSENT" CLAUSE
(FAR 52.227-1, Alternate I)

(a) The Government authorizes and consents to all use and manufacture of any invention described in and covered by a United States patent in the performance of this contract or any subcontract at any tier.

(b) The Contractor agrees to include, and require inclusion of, this clause, suitably modified to idemnify the parties, in all subcontracts at any tier for supplies or services (including construction, architect-engineer services, and materials, supplies, models, samples, and design or testing services expected to exceed $25,000); however, omission of this clause from any subcontract, under or over $25,000, does not affect this authorization and consent.

Thus, if a court finds that the "Authorization and Consent" clause applies, the court will normally dismiss a claim of patent infringement brought against the contractor-infringer.[14] On occasion, however, a *lack* of authorization and consent has been found, as in one case where the court concluded that a refuse collection contractor used patented equipment when it was not required to do so, either by the specifications or by the Contracting Officer.[15]

5. Contractor Indemnification Of Government

The Government may be liable for damages caused by an infringement of a patent by a Government contractor, or the Government may pass the liability on to the infringing contractor by means of a "Patent Indemnity" clause in the contract.[16] Under such a clause, the contractor agrees to indemnify the Government for any damages suffered by the Government as a result of the contractor's infringement of a patent. "Patent Indemnity" clauses are usually not considered to be appropriate for inclusion in R&D contracts, however, because they would tend to restrain the creativity of contractors performing such work. In *construction, service,* and *supply* contracts of a commercial type, however, Government policy requires that the ultimate liability for patent infringement be placed on the contractor.[17] These contracts routinely include both an "Authorization and Consent" clause and a "Patent Indemnity" clause. However, a "Patent Indemnity" clause is not mandatory in negotiated contracts (except those involving construction), but may be used in certain circumstances.[18]

6. Contractor Notice & Assistance

The "Notice and Assistance Regarding Patent and Copyright Infringement" clause requires contractors to report to the Contracting Officer "promptly and in reasonable written detail" all notices or claims of patent (or copyright) infringement that are made against them as a result of their contract work.[19] Under the clause, contractors must also—if a claim or suit is ultimately brought against the Government—assist the Government in its defense and furnish it with all available documentation pertaining to the claim.

B. TECHNICAL DATA

The subject of technical data stimulates divergent views, more than the subject of patents does.[20] Some hold the strong feeling that the Government should have unlimited rights to such data, particularly where it came into existence under a publicly-funded contract. However logical this approach might initially appear, its enforcement presents some practical problems.

1. The Regulations

Currently, Government contractors must be aware of two different sets of rules for data rights—those found in the FAR governing civilian agency procurements and those found in the Department of Defense (DOD) FAR Supplement (DFARS) for defense agency procurements. There are differences between the two sets of rules.

The FAR provisions[21] are drafted from the perspective of agencies predominantly involved in the procurement of commercial products. These provisions, in general, are simpler and easier to comprehend than their DFARS counterparts. The general approach of the FAR provisions is to require delivery of only the minimum data essential to the use and maintenance of the contract product.

The DFARS provisions[22] are basically governed by a statute that authorizes the Secretary of Defense to (a) prescribe regulations governing technical data rights and (b) outline what those regulations are to contain.[23] The DFARS provisions approach data rights from the perspective of defense agencies generally concerned with large systems that are developed and built to unique military requirements and have no close counterpart in the commercial market. Accordingly, the DFARS provisions do not use commercially familiar terminology and are complicated in nature. Similarly, although both the FAR and the DFARS set forth specific procedures for contractors to follow to protect data delivered to the Government, the DFARS requirements (discussed briefly below in Section B.4.b) are more complex.

The ultimate goal for the treatment of technical data (and computer software) in Government contracts is the development of a *uniform* set of rules for all procurements that would be contained in the FAR.

2. Types Of Government Rights

Three basic types of standard Government licenses in contractors' technical data have evolved. First, the Government may insist on *Unlimited Rights* to technical data, thus gaining the right to use, reproduce, modify, or disclose the data as it wishes. Use of this technique, of course, runs the risk of deterring knowledgeable contractors from bidding on the contract since they would naturally be reluctant to disclose technical information that may contain their trade secrets. Second, the Government may obtain *no rights* by providing that the contractor may withhold data—for example, when the contractor is merely providing a standard commercial item and the Government does not need the data to use the item. Third, the Government may require delivery of technical data, but permit the use of restrictive legends on the data and agree to hold such information in confidence. This third technique provides the Government with *Limited Rights* to use and release the data in certain circumstances, but not for commercial purposes or in competitive procurements.[24] This technique may present the Government with potential administrative problems, however.

Another type of data rights, *Government Purpose License Rights*, applies only to defense contracts and provides an intermediate level of negotiated Government rights between limited rights and unlimited rights (see Section B.4 below). In addition, Contracting Officers may tailor data rights to the specific procurement by negotiation, and agencies may develop differing rights in their FAR supplements.[25]

3. Government Policy

The basic Government policy on rights in technical data as stated in the FAR is that the rules of all procurement agencies and their implementation by Government personnel should "strike a balance between the Government's need and the contractor's legitimate proprietary interest" in the data.[26] This policy encourages the development and availability of innovative technology for Government use by preserving private proprietary rights, while recognizing that it is often necessary for Government agencies "to carry out their missions and programs, to acquire or obtain access to many kinds of data produced during or used in the performance of their contracts."[27]

4. DOD Policy & Procedures

a. Policy. DOD's policy is to acquire only such technical data rights as are essential to meet Government needs.[28] DOD recognizes three standard types of Government rights in technical data:[29] (1) "Unlimited Rights" in data developed exclusively with Government funds, data resulting directly from R&D work that is specified as an element of performance under a Government contract, and data in several other specified categories; (2) "Limited Rights" in properly marked technical data developed exclusively at private expense; and (3) "Government Purpose License Rights," which are negotiated rights regarding data developed with "mixed funding" (part Government, part private) to which the Government otherwise would obtain unlimited rights. "Government Purpose License Rights" are intended to encourage commercial use of technologies developed under Government contracts.

If the Government obtains "Unlimited Rights" in data, it obtains the right to use, duplicate, or disclose the technical data, in whole or in part, in any manner and for any purpose whatsoever, including the right to distribute the data to competitors to enable them to produce the same or similar equipment. If the Government obtains "Government Purpose License Rights," a developer gives the Government the right to use, duplicate, and disclose the data (and have or permit others to do so) for Government purposes only.[30] This category of rights includes the right to use a data package for the needs of the Government, such as developing a second source of supply for the Government's future needs. It does not include the right to permit another company to make itself a competitor of the developer for customers in the commercial marketplace.

b. Procedures. The DFARS sets forth specific procedures to be followed by contractors to secure data rights protection. If a contractor intends to deliver technical data to the Government on other than an "Unlimited Rights" basis, it must identify those items or processes in its proposal.[31] This list serves as the basis for identifying all technical data restrictions on the Government, unless the Contracting Officer challenges the validity of the contractor's assertions.[32] If the contractor asserts that the data were developed with "mixed funding," then the Contracting Officer and contractor will negotiate, before contract award if possible, the respective rights of the parties in the data.[33]

To preserve "Limited Rights" in data, the contractor must mark that data with a restrictive legend.[34] The following information must appear in the legend: (a) the contract number and contractor name, (b) the date the data will be subject to unlimited rights (if applicable), and (c) an indication (by circling, underscoring, etc.) of the specific data to which the legend applies.[35] The legend must appear on each piece of data submitted to the Government for which "Limited Rights" are claimed, and the Government must include the legend on all reproductions of the data. A similar marking requirement applies to data submitted subject to "Government Purpose License Rights."[36]

If a contractor—through inadvertence or otherwise—submits data without a restrictive legend, the data will be considered to have been submitted with unlimited rights.[37] However, the contractor may—within six months—add a restrictive legend if it (1) demonstrates that the omission was inadvertent, (2) establishes that the use of a marking is authorized, and (3) relieves the Government of liability with regard to the data.[38] The six-month limit applies to the delivery of each item of data and not delivery of the final package.[39] The prior release of the data by the Government prevents the use of this corrective procedure—since the data are then considered to be in the public domain.[40]

Note, however, that merely using the correct legend will not result in protection of information not *otherwise* entitled to protection. Therefore, the Government is perfectly free to use an idea generally known in the trade, even though the idea was submitted to the Government as a trade secret.[41] On the other hand, merely because design and development are part of the contractor's obligations under a contract does not necessarily mean that a particular item was developed at Government expense. The contractor may still show that it previously developed the item.[42]

The DFARS (and the FAR) also contain "validation" procedures that the Government may use to review or challenge restrictive markings on data. The Contracting Officer accomplishes a prechallenge review by requesting the contractor to furnish a written justification for any restriction asserted, which the Contracting Officer then reviews.[43] If the Contracting Officer determines that a challenge to the restrictive marking is warranted, he sends a written notice to the contractor setting forth the grounds for the challenge and giving the contractor 60 days in which to justify "by sufficient evidence" the current validity of the restrictive marking.[44] The Contracting Officer then issues a final appealable decision on the validity of the restrictive marking.[45]

5. Enforcing Data Rights

Misuse of proprietary contractor data related to a Government contract can occur either in a procurement or outside the procurement process. There are essentially three remedies available to a contractor for data misuse by the Government: (a) an injunction (and declaratory relief), (b) a "bid protest" remedy, or (c) money damages.[46] An injunction to stop the data disclosure can only be obtained from a court. If the data misuse occurs in connection with a Government contract solicitation, the contractor may file a bid protest seeking either to rewrite the solicitation or stay the procurement action. Finally, if the misuse has occurred or cannot be prevented, monetary compensation—based on a theory of breach of contract or unconstitutional taking of property, for example—may be available from the Government.[47]

C. COPYRIGHT

Copyright protection extends to any original work of authorship in any tangible medium of expression. Generally, the owner of a copyright has the exclusive rights, among others, to (1) reproduce the copyrighted work and (2) prepare derivative works.[48] Thus, copyrighted material is not available to the general public without the permission of the copyright owner through a license or other conveyance. Computer software, for example, which may be delivered by a contractor in connection with a Government contract, is often published and copyrighted.[49]

The general Government policy is to preserve contractors' rights under the copyright laws while ensuring that the Government's use of copyrighted material will not be considered an infringement of the copyright.[50] Under the FAR, contractors are normally authorized, without the permission of the Government, to establish claims to copyrights to technical or scientific articles based on or containing data first produced in the performance of a Government contract containing the "Rights in Data–General" clause[51] and published in academic, technical, or professional journals and similar works.[52] Otherwise, the permission of the Contracting Officer is required.[53] The FAR states that assent will normally be given, but lists several broad grounds on which the Contracting Officer may deny the request.[54]

DOD takes the position that—unless a work is designated a "special work"—a contractor may copyright any work of authorship first generated under a contract as long as the contractor grants to the Government a royalty-free license to use the work for Government purposes.[55] Where the primary purpose of the contract is the creation of a "special work" (such as an audiovisual work or departmental history), however, the Government retains ownership and control of the work.[56]

The DOD standard "Rights in Technical Data and Computer Software" clause also provides that—unless written approval of the Contracting Officer is obtained—the contractor shall not include in any work generated under the contract any copyrighted material not owned by the contractor without acquiring a nonexclusive license for the benefit of the Government in the copyrighted work.[57]

The exclusive remedy for copyright infringement against the Government is to sue for reasonable compensation in the U.S. Court of Federal Claims.[58]

REFERENCES

1. Patent and Trademark Amendments of 1980, P.L. 96-517, 94 Stat. 3019 (codified at 35 USC § 200 et seq.). See generally Vacketta & Holmes, "Patent Rights Under Government Contracts," Briefing Papers No. 83-12 (Dec. 1983), 6 BPC 273.

2. 35 USC § 202(a).

3. 35 USC § 202(c).

4. Note 3, supra.

5. President's Memorandum to the Heads of Executive Departments and Agencies, "Government Patent Policy" (Feb. 18, 1983).

6. See, e.g., FAR 27.302(a), 52.227-11 ("Patent Rights–Retention by Contractor (Short Form)" clause), 52.227-12 ("Patent Rights–Retention by Contractor (Long Form)" clause).

7. E.g., FAR 52.227-12, para. (a).

8. FAR 27.302(b).

9. Note 8, supra. See also FAR 52.227-13 ("Patent Rights–Acquisition by the Government" clause).

10. FAR 52.227-11, para. (b); FAR 52.227-12, para. (b).

11. 28 USC § 1498.

12. E.g., De Graffenried v. U.S., 25 Cl. Ct. 209 (1992), 11 FPD ¶ 15 (patent holder's recovery for Government's unauthorized use of patented device may be based on what license terms reasonably should have been negotiated by the Government), 34 GC ¶ 130.

13. FAR 52.227-1, alternate I. See FAR 27.201-2.

14. See, e.g., Molinaro v. Watkins-Johnson CEI Div., 359 F. Supp. 467 (D. Md. 1973).

15. Carrier Corp. v. U.S., 534 F.2d 244 (Ct. Cl. 1976), 18 GC ¶ 71.

16. FAR 52.227-3.

17. FAR 27.203-1.

18. FAR 27.203-3.

19. FAR 52.227-2, para. (a).

20. See generally Taylor & Burgett, "Rights in Data and Software," Briefing Papers No. 88-3 (Feb. 1988), 8 BPC 63; Vacketta & Holmes, "Govern-

INTELLECTUAL PROPERTY RIGHTS 10-15

ment Rights in Technical Data," Briefing Papers No. 84-12 (Dec. 1984), 6 BPC 455; Pasley, "Technical Data Dialogue," Briefing Papers No. 67-5 (Oct. 1967), 1 BPC 267.

21. FAR subpt. 27.4.

22. DFARS subpt. 227.4 (interim regulations). See generally Simchak & Vogel, "A Few Words of Advice: Protecting Intellectual Property When Contracting With the Department of Defense According to the October 1988 Regulations," 23 Pub. Cont. L.J. 2 (Winter 1994).

23. 10 USC § 2320. See also P.L. 102-190, § 807 (1992) (establishing Government-industry committee to recommend final DOD data rights rules); Nash, "The New DOD Policy on Technical Data and Computer Software," 8 Nash & Cibinic Rep. ¶ 22 (Apr. 1994).

24. See, e.g., FAR 52.227-14 ("Rights in Data–General" clause), para. (g)(1).

25. E.g., FAR 27.403, 27.404(e)(2), 27.408.

26. FAR 27.402(b).

27. FAR 27.402(a).

28. DFARS 227.402-71.

29. DFARS 227.402-72.

30. DFARS 227.401.

31. DFARS 227.403-70(a). See also DFARS 252.227-7013 ("Rights in Technical Data and Computer Software" clause), para. (j).

32. DFARS 227.403-70(b).

33. DFARS 227.403-70(b)(3).

34. DFARS 252.227-7018 ("Restrictive Markings on Technical Data" clause).

35. DFARS 252.227-7013, para. (b)(3).

36. DFARS 252.227-7013, para. (b)(2).

37. DFARS 227.403-72(c).

38. Note 37, supra.

39. Comp. Gen. Dec. B-169077, 50 Comp. Gen. 271, 1970 CPD ¶ 97, 12 GC ¶ 449.

40. Comp. Gen. Dec. B-174517 (May 24, 1972).

41. Frodge v. U.S., 204 Ct. Cl. 812 (1974). See also Comp. Gen. Dec. B-177436, 53 Comp. Gen. 161, 1973 CPD ¶ 95, 15 GC ¶ 397.

42. Dowty Decoto, Inc. v. Department of the Navy, 883 F.2d 774 (9th Cir. 1989), 31 GC ¶ 371.

43. DFARS 227.403-73.

44. DFARS 252.227-7037 ("Validation of Restrictive Markings on Technical Data" clause), para. (d).

45. DFARS 252.227-7037, para. (f).

46. See generally Victorino & McQuade, "Enforcing Data Rights," Briefing Papers No. 91-10 (Sept. 1991), 9 BPC 471.

47. E.g., Research, Analysis & Development, Inc. v. U.S., 8 Cl. Ct. (1985), 3 FPD ¶ 142; Radioptics, Inc. v. U.S., 621 F.2d 1113 (Ct. Cl. 1980), 24 GC ¶ 204 (Note).

48. 17 USC § 101.

49. See generally Nash, "Copyright of Computer Programs: How Much Protection Is Possible?," 6 Nash & Cibinic Rep. ¶ 65 (Nov. 1992).

50. See, e.g., 10 USC § 2320(a)(1); 41 USC § 418a(a).

51. FAR 52.227-14.

52. FAR 27.404(f).

53. FAR 27.404(f)(1).

54. FAR 27.404(f)(1)(ii).

55. DFARS 227.403-76(c).

56. Note 55, supra; DFARS 252.227-7020 ("Rights in Data–Special Works" clause).

57. DFARS 252.227-7013, 227.403-76(e).

58. 28 USC § 1498(b). See, e.g., Steve Altman Photography v. U.S., 18 Cl. Ct. 267 (1989), 8 FPD ¶ 134, 32 GC ¶ 8.

CHANGES

11

A. Standard "Changes" Clauses
   1. Fixed-Price Contracts
   2. Cost-Reimbursement Contracts

B. Changes Authority
   1. Non-Contracting Officers
   2. Changes Outside Contract's "Scope"

C. Contractor's Duty To Proceed
   1. Scope Of Duty
   2. Effect Of Failure To Proceed

D. Value Engineering
   1. Value Engineering Change Proposals
   2. Administration

E. Formal Change Orders
   1. Origination
   2. Procedures

F. Constructive Changes
   1. Development Of The Doctrine
   2. Types Of Constructive Changes

With the exception of terminating contracts, probably the most important action the Government takes regarding its contracts is to make "changes" in them. Not surprisingly, changes—whether made formally or "constructively" (through the Government's acts)—are the most frequent source of disputes between the Government and the contractor that arise in connection with contract performance.

This chapter examines the subject of changes. For an in-depth treatment of this same subject beyond the scope of this chapter, the reader may consult Nash, GOVERNMENT CONTRACT CHANGES (Federal Publications Inc., 2d ed. 1989 & Supp.).

A. STANDARD "CHANGES" CLAUSES

The FAR sets forth several standard "Changes" clauses.[1] Which clause is used depends on the nature of the contract in which it appears. For purposes of examining these standard clauses, it is best to treat those used in fixed-price contracts separately from those used in cost-reimbursement contracts—a distinction made in the FAR.

1. Fixed-Price Contracts

The basic standard "Changes–Fixed-Price" clause set forth in the FAR for fixed-price contracts is the one designated for use in supply contracts.[2] Alternate provisions for this clause are given so that it can be tailored for use in other fixed-price contracts.[3] This basic standard "Changes" clause for fixed-price contracts is set forth in Figure 11-1.

As Paragraph (a) of the Figure 11-1 clause indicates, the clause empowers the Contracting Officer to "at any time, by written order...make changes within the general scope of this contract" in the (1) drawings, designs, or specifications, (2) method of shipment or packing, or (3) place of delivery. Under Paragraph (b), if such changes *increase* the contractor's costs, the contractor is entitled to a contract price increase, and if they *delay* the contractor's performance, the contractor is entitled to

> **Figure 11-1**
>
> **"CHANGES–FIXED-PRICE" CLAUSE**
> (FAR 52.243-1)
>
> (a) The Contracting Officer may at any time, by written order, and without notice to the sureties, if any, make changes within the general scope of this contract in any one or more of the following:
> (1) Drawings, designs, or specifications when the supplies to be furnished are to be specially manufactured for the Government in accordance with the drawings, designs, or specifications.
> (2) Method of shipment or packing.
> (3) Place of delivery.
>
> (b) If any such change causes an increase or decrease in the cost of, or the time required for, performance of any part of the work under this contract, whether or not changed by the order, the Contracting Officer shall make an equitable adjustment in the contract price, the delivery schedule, or both, and shall modify the contract.
>
> (c) The Contractor must assert its right to an adjustment under this clause within 30 days from the date of receipt of the written order. However, if the Contracting Officer decides that the facts justify it, the Contracting Officer may receive and act upon a proposal submitted before final payment of the contract.
>
> (d) If the Contractor's proposal includes the cost of property made obsolete or excess by the change, the Contracting Officer shall have the right to prescribe the manner of the disposition of the property.
>
> (e) Failure to agree to any adjustment shall be a dispute under the Disputes clause. However, nothing in this clause shall excuse the Contractor from proceeding with the contract as changed.

an extension of the contract completion date. On the other hand, if the changes *decrease* the cost of or time for performance, the contract price will be decreased or the completion time shortened.

The clause, in Paragraph (c), requires the contractor to assert a changes claim to the Contracting Officer within 30 days from the date of receipt of the change order. This requirement will usually be waived when the Government is not prejudiced by the failure to give timely notice (for example, when it is reasonably certain that the Government would not have acted differently if notice had been given).[4] Indeed, the clause provides, in Paragraph (c), that the Contracting Officer may receive and act on a changes claim asserted at any time prior to *final payment*. But a claim asserted after the Government has made its final payment under the contract will almost certainly be barred.[5] Final payment, of course, occurs after the contractor has completed performance. The last payment check is usually accompanied by a voucher marked "Final Payment."

The standard construction contract "Changes" clause set forth in the FAR for use in fixed-price contracts[6] is even broader in scope than the supply contract clause. For example, the construction contract "Changes" clause gives the Contracting Officer the right to order a change within the general scope of the contract that accelerates the performance of the work.[7] The construction contract clause contains a provision similar to that discussed above relating to the time within which the contractor must assert a changes claim after receipt of a change order.[8]

2. Cost-Reimbursement Contracts

A distinctive feature of cost-reimbursement contracts is that the primary obligation of the contractor is not to complete the contract but rather to work until the funds allotted to it have been expended. Thus, the contractor has no obligation to proceed with contract performance until additional funds are furnished by the Government. In this situation, a claim for additional compensation under the "Changes" clause is essentially only a claim for additional fees or costs subject to sharing under a cost-plus-incentive-fee contract (see Chapter 4, Section F.2).

The Government sometimes provides for cost ceilings in cost-reimbursement contracts. Because the ceilings apply only to work called for by the original contract, any additional work ordered should fall under the "Changes" clause, entitling the contractor to the normal equitable adjustment, unless the contract specifically provides otherwise.[9]

The greatest difficulty in a cost-reimbursement contract is defining what constitutes a "change." This is because such contracts are frequently awarded for research and development projects where it is not possible to describe the work with a high degree of precision. For example, the work statement may only contain a description of the end objective that is to be achieved by the contractor. In such cases, the best measurement for determining whether a change has occurred is to examine the work contemplated by the parties when they negotiated the estimated costs of the contract. Work papers, negotiations notes, and engineering appraisals of what methods normally would have been followed are useful in filling in the gaps in the work statement.[10]

Under the FAR, the basic standard "Changes–Cost-Reimbursement" clause used when supplies are being procured is set forth in Figure 11-2 on the following page.[11] It also has alternate provisions for specific types of procurements.[12]

The "Limitation of Cost" and "Limitation of Funds" clauses mentioned in Paragraph (e) of the Figure 11-2 clause provide the primary means for limiting the total amount of costs that will be paid under a cost-reimbursement contract. The standard "Limitation of Cost" clause applicable to most cost-reimbursement contracts that are fully funded states that the Government is not obligated to reimburse the contractor for money expended in excess of the cost limitation set forth in the contract.[13] Moreover, the clause specifically provides that changes to the contract fall within the overall limitation of costs as set forth in the contract schedule.[14] This clause has been held to bar recovery of the cost of changes in excess of the contract's estimated cost,[15] but not for cardinal changes beyond a contract's scope (see Section B.2 below).[16] Therefore, even though some exceptions exist,[17] a contractor must exercise great care not to perform changed work that causes its total costs to exceed the cost estimate stated in the contract.

The similar standard "Limitation of Funds" clause is used in cost-reimbursement contracts that are incrementally funded.[18] This clause has the same provision regarding changes as the "Limitation of Cost" clause. Thus, the contractor must take the same care not to exceed the estimated cost in performing changed work.

Besides the "Limitation" clauses, "Technical Direction" clauses should also be mentioned in connection with cost-reimburse-

Figure 11-2

"CHANGES–COST-REIMBURSEMENT" CLAUSE
(FAR 52.243-2)

(a) The Contracting Officer may at any time, by written order, and without notice to the sureties, if any, make changes within the general scope of this contract in any one or more of the following:
(1) Drawings, designs, or specifications when the supplies to be furnished are to be specially manufactured for the Government in accordance with the drawings, designs, or specifications.
(2) Method of shipment or packing.
(3) Place of delivery.

(b) If any such change causes an increase or decrease in the estimated cost of, or the time required for, performance of any part of the work under this contract, whether or not changed by the order, or otherwise affects any other terms and conditions of this contract, the Contracting Officer shall make an equitable adjustment in the (1) estimated cost, delivery or completion schedule, or both; (2) amount of any fixed fee; and (3) other affected terms and shall modify the contract accordingly.

(c) The Contractor must assert its right to an adjustment under this clause within 30 days from the date of receipt of the written order. However, if the Contracting Officer decides that the facts justify it, the Contracting Officer may receive and act upon a proposal submitted before final payment of the contract.

(d) Failure to agree to any adjustment shall be a dispute under the Disputes clause. However, nothing in this clause shall excuse the Contractor from proceeding with the contract as changed.

(e) Notwithstanding the terms and conditions of paragraphs (a) and (b) above, the estimated cost of this contract and, if this contract is incrementally funded, the funds allotted for the performance of this contract, shall not be increased or considered to be increased except by specific written modification of the contract indicating the new contract estimated cost and, if this contract is incrementally funded, the new amount allotted to the contract. Until this modification is made, the Contractor shall not be obligated to continue performance or incur costs beyond the point established in the Limitation of Cost or Limitation of Funds clause of this contract.

ment contract changes. Procuring agencies often use "Technical Direction" clauses to clarify and define the relationship between Government and contractor technical personnel in cost-reimbursement contracts.[19] Such clauses—which are closely related to the "Changes" clause—serve to (1) give the Government the right to direct the course of the work as it proceeds, (2) define the role of Government technical personnel during contract performance, and (3) establish a rule that orders of Government technical personnel will not constitute changes without the approval of the Contracting Officer.

B. CHANGES AUTHORITY

All standard "Changes" clauses provide that changes may be issued by the "Contracting Officer." Unlike the general rule in the commercial world that a company may be bound by the acts of agents with *apparent* authority, in Government procurement, the Government may only be bound by the actions of employees with *actual authority*. Therefore, whether the Government representative who ordered a change had the actual authority to do so is often an issue in changes claims. This places the burden on contractors to make certain that the person ordering the change has actual authority. As discussed below, arguments involving waiver, ratification, and constructive knowledge are available in instances where actual authority is at issue—but these concepts are usually difficult to prove and are not good substitutes for exercising care before carrying out a Government direction. (See Chapter 2, Section D.7.)

On the other hand, the Contracting Officer's authority to make changes is limited by the "Changes" clause to changes that are "within the general scope of the contract." Legally, a change outside the scope of the contract is a new procurement that the Contracting Officer is not authorized to order and the contractor is not obligated to perform.

1. Non-Contracting Officers

Much litigation involving changes concerns the authority of Government employees who have *not* been officially designated as "Contracting Officers" to legally commit the Government to contract changes. Generally, such non-Contracting Officers have only limited authority to represent the Contracting Officer—for example, to inspect supplies being manufactured for the Government. They do not have the authority to order or authorize changes.[20] (However, statements, acts, or inaction by these employees may be deemed "constructive changes" that can nevertheless bind the Government.[21] The subject of constructive changes is discussed in Section F below.)

In construction contracts, the limits on the authority of the Contracting Officer's representatives and inspectors are usually covered in detail at the preconstruction conference between Government and contractor representatives and confirmed in writing. However, only the Contracting Officer generally has the authority to *order* changes.

Implied authority to order changes may be found if non-Contracting Officers are placed in a position of responsibility. For example, a project officer with authority to certify payment vouchers, receive progress reports, and perform inspections and final acceptance was been held in one case to have the implied authority to order a change when expeditious action was required.[22]

Another possibility is that the Contracting Officer may be held to have *ratified* the order of someone lacking actual authority. For instance, where a Contracting Officer normally relied on an inspector and was in constant communication with him, knowledge of the inspector's order to change the work was *imputed* to the Contracting Officer. The result was that ratification of the inspector's order by the Contracting Officer was found.[23] The FAR provides a formal procedure for ratification of unauthorized commitments by Government representatives where the resulting contract or agreement would otherwise have been proper if made by an appropriate Contracting Officer.[24] However, it is extremely risky for a contractor to assume that such exceptions will be made to the general rule that only the Contracting Officer is authorized to order changes.

Closely related to the concept of ratification is the theory of *constructive notice* and *acquiescence* to the extra work being performed by the contractor. For instance, in one case, after signing a modification to remove sections of a sidewalk, a sidewalk repair contractor began experiencing difficulties because the pavers in the sidewalk were very firmly attached. The contractor was forced to use a more expensive method to remove the pavers. This extra effort was observed without objection by the Government's architect-engineer, but the architect-engineer never informed the Contracting Officer. Under these circumstances, it was held that the Government had constructive knowledge of the removal method used by the contractor and had acquiesced to it, thus entitling the contractor to additional compensation.[25]

When someone *other than* the Contracting Officer orders a contractor to perform work that the contractor believes constitutes a contract change, the contractor should (1) promptly inform the Contracting Officer *before* performing the work, or (2) if such notice is impractical (because of time or distance), promptly write a letter to the Contracting Officer—with a copy to the person ordering the change—which describes the change, names the person ordering it, states that the contractor is proceeding with the work, and advises that a formal claim will be filed as soon as sufficient information is available. If the Contracting Officer then agrees with the order, or fails to countermand it, it will be treated as having been issued by the Contracting Officer—thus protecting the contractor's right to recover for the changed work.

2. Changes Outside Contract's "Scope"

A Contracting Officer has no authority to order what are called "cardinal changes"—that is, changes that have the effect of making the work as performed *not* essentially the same work the parties bargained for when the contract was awarded.[26] Such cardinal changes are outside the scope of the "Changes" clause and constitute a breach of the contract by the Government.[27]

In determining whether a change is "within the general scope of the contract," the *character* of the change is far more important than the *amount* by which the change increases performance costs.[28] Nor are the *number* of contract changes generally determinative of whether the contract has been altered beyond its scope.[29] For example, multiple changes to a hospital construction contract which altered many of the materials used in its construction were found in one case to be within the scope of the contract because the hospital was not different in its size or performance after the changes were effected.[30]

As a practical matter, contractors generally welcome changes and frequently perform cardinal changes as ordered and are compensated under the "Changes" clause without any further comment. However, if the contractor does not want to comply with the change order—and if it is certain that the change is outside the scope of the "Changes" clause—it can refuse to perform the change. Of course, the contractor in that case takes the risk that its characterization of the change as a cardinal change will be upheld. If the contractor's assertion that the Government breached the contract by ordering a cardinal change—which the contractor refused to follow—is found to be correct by a court or board of contract appeals, the contractor should be able to receive damages. If the contractor is wrong, a termination of the contract for default could result.

C. CONTRACTOR'S DUTY TO PROCEED

1. Scope Of Duty

The typical "Changes" clause specifically provides that although a contractor may dispute an adjustment for a change, "nothing in this clause shall excuse the Contractor from proceeding with the contract as changed" (see Paragraph (e) of the Figure 11-1 clause and Paragraph (d) of the Figure 11-2 clause). Moreover, the standard "Disputes" clause prescribed by the FAR requires the contractor to "proceed diligently with performance of this contract, pending final resolution of any request for relief, claim, appeal, or action arising under the contract, and comply with any decision of the Contracting Officer."[31] This duty to continue performance applies only to claims "arising under" a contract—for example, claims for equitable adjustments based on contract changes—it does *not* apply to orders to perform cardinal changes (see Section B.2 above). However, contracting agencies are authorized, in unusual circumstances, to require a contractor to continue performance pending final resolution on a claim "relating to" the contract—that is, pending resolution of a claim for breach of contract.[32] This means that—where the contract contains such a provision—the contractor must proceed as directed even though the change ordered is a cardinal change or is deemed another type of breach of contract. It should be reemphasized, however, that a contractor runs a risk in not proceeding with performance merely because it believes that an order goes beyond the authority of the Contracting Officer—such a contractor is either very brave or extremely imprudent.

A more important exception to the contractor's duty to proceed arises when the contractor is unable to obtain clear direction from the Contracting Officer regarding the course of action the Government wants the contractor to follow. For example, when the contractor discovers that the specifications are defective and informs the Government of the problem, the contractor is entitled to withhold performance until it receives a meaningful response to its reasonable request.[33]

Another exception to the duty to proceed is when the Government's action leaves the contractor in an untenable position. For example, one contractor was excused from continuing performance after the Government used faulty testing methods in rejecting the items delivered by the contractor.[34]

2. Effect Of Failure To Proceed

The Government's remedy is drastic when a contractor refuses to perform pending resolution of a disputed changes claim (assuming the Government had authority to direct the contractor to proceed). If the contractor refuses to follow the directions of the Contracting Officer, its contract may be default terminated (see Chapter 16). For example, in one case where a contractor refused to follow the Contracting Officer's directive to remove and replace a tile floor, instead abandoning the work and refusing to proceed except at Government expense and by a method of installation specified by the Government, the Court of Claims held that such an election was "not open" to the contractor under the "Disputes" clause.[35]

The wisest course for a contractor to follow, if it believes the Contracting Officer's directive is wrong, is to immediately request the Contracting Officer's superior to review the matter but to continue working pending a decision from this higher authority. If the contractor follows the directive of the Contracting Officer, it will not lose any of its rights to an equitable adjustment.[36]

D. VALUE ENGINEERING

Under the typical "Changes" clause, a contractor has no monetary incentive to submit a change proposal suggesting a method of *reducing* the cost of performance. If such a change is ordered, the contract price will be reduced by the full cost saved, plus the contractor's profit on such cost. As a result, the contractor is penalized by a reduction in profit for suggesting a method of saving money for the Government.

To avoid this result and encourage contractors to make suggestions for performing contracts more economically, the Government developed the concept of "value engineering," which permits contractors to share in savings resulting from their suggestions.[37] The Government encourages the use of value engineering through its regulations and contract clauses, and in fact the use of "Value Engineering" clauses is mandatory in a great number of Government contracts.[38] The most widely used clauses for implementing the concept are the "Value Engineering" clause for supply and service contracts,[39] and the "Value Engineering–Construction" clause, which is for use in most construction contracts.[40]

1. Value Engineering Change Proposals

"Value Engineering" clauses contemplate the use of value engineering change proposals (VECPs). Submission of these cost savings proposals under the clauses is generally left entirely up to the contractor. However, if a contractor's VECP is submitted and accepted, the "Value Engineering" clause provides for the contractor to share in (a) the savings generated on the contract being performed—"instant contract savings," (b) savings on concurrent contracts for essentially the same items—"concurrent contract savings," (c) savings on future contracts—"future contract savings," and (d) savings of the Government in operation, maintenance, logistic support, or Government property resulting from the value engineering change—"collateral savings."[41] Note that for "concurrent contract savings" and "future contract savings" under the "Value Engineering" clause used in supply and service contracts, the contractor may share in savings generated under contracts awarded to *other* contractors—as well as under additional contracts it performs. The "Value Engineering–Construction" clause provides for contractor sharing only in "instant contract savings." Both clauses specify what the contractor's share of net savings will be. Under the supply and service clause, the range is from 15% to 50%.[42] Under the construction clause, the range is from 45% to 75%.[43]

The most common VECPs by contractors are suggestions for reducing costs by modifying the specifications or drawings to allow the use of simpler methods, less expensive materials or components, or other changes to the work that will not adversely affect the product or construction.

2. Administration

It is important that a contractor identify its proposal as a VECP—so that the proposal is not considered merely a gratuitous suggestion for which no reward is expected. Many disputes have arisen regarding whether a Contracting Officer accepted a VECP or issued a change order independent of the proposal.[44] Clearly, if the change order is issued after the submission of the proposal, there is a presumption that the two are connected—and the Government will have a difficult task to overcome this presumption.[45] On the other hand, no value engineering change share will be granted for what is, in essence, a Government concept.[46]

The VECP must relate directly to the work required to be done on the contract. Government officials have no authority to purchase unsolicited suggestions that are not submitted under an existing contract.[47] Nor can a contractor enforce a "Value Engineering" clause that was improperly included in its contract.[48]

The decision of a Contracting Officer to adopt or reject a contractor's VECP is *not* subject to litigation under the Contract Disputes Act (CDA).[49] However, *other* disputes arising under the clause may be routinely appealed by the contractor.[50] For example, the Contracting Officer's determination that (1) a proposal was not intended to be a value engineering change proposal, (2) a change ordered was not the result of the contractor's proposal, or (3) the proposal did not relate directly to the work done on the contract, would be subject to appeal by the contractor. The proper method of determining the contractor's share of savings has also been the subject of appeals.[51]

E. FORMAL CHANGE ORDERS

1. Origination

The impetus for a change can originate with either the Government or the contractor, depending on the circumstances involved. Changes based on revised requirements usually originate with the Government, whereas those involving a better (or different) way to perform the work most frequently originate with the contractor. In either case, an exchange of information between the Government and the contractor will be necessary before the change is adopted.

a. Contractor-Proposed Changes. Some Government agencies prescribe formal procedures that a contractor must follow in suggesting changes. The Department of Defense (DOD), for example, requires contractors to submit "detailed information...for evaluation of the technical, cost, and schedule effects of implementing the change."[52] DOD also issues military standards which furnish details concerning processing changes, deviations (approvals to depart from performance or design requirements for a specific number of units or period of time), and waivers.[53]

b. Government-Originated Changes. Many changes are originated by the Government procuring agency. Typically, the

Government originates a change by requesting the contractor to document the details of the proposed change. For example, DOD uses a clause entitled "Engineering Change Proposals"[54] (set forth in Figure 11-3), which provides that the Contracting Officer may request the contractor to submit an engineering change proposal containing the information pertinent to the change proposed by the Government. The proposal must set forth a "not to exceed" or "not less than" price for the change and delivery adjustment. A word of caution is necessary here. A contractor is generally not entitled to be reimbursed for the cost of preparing such a proposal if the change is not later ordered.[55]

Figure 11-3

"ENGINEERING CHANGE PROPOSALS" CLAUSE
(DFARS 252.243-7000)

(a) The Contracting Officer may ask the Contractor to prepare engineering change proposals for engineering changes within the scope of this contract. Upon receipt of a written request from the Contracting Officer, the Contractor shall prepare and submit an engineering change proposal in accordance with the instructions of _____*, in effect on the date of contract award.

(b) The Contractor may initiate engineering change proposals. Contractor inititated engineering change proposals shall include a "not to exceed" price** or a "not less than" price** and delivery adjustment. If the Contracting Officer orders the engineering change, the increase shall not exceed nor the decrease be less than the "not to exceed" or "not less than" amounts.***

(c) When the price** of the engineering change is $500,000 or more, the Contractor shall submit
  (1) A completed [Standard Form] 1411, Contract Pricing Proposal Cover Sheet, and
  (2) At the time of agreement on price**, a signed Certificate of Current Cost or Pricing Data.

*Insert MIL-STD-480 or MIL-STD-481
**Use a term suitable for the type of contract
***In cost reimbursement type contracts, replace this sentence with the following: "Change orders issued under the Changes clause of this contract are not an authorization to exceed the estimated cost in the schedule unless there is a statement in the change order, or other contract modification, increasing the estimated cost."

2. Procedures

When a decision has been made to change contract work, the Contracting Officer is responsible for preparing and issuing the necessary documents to the contractor and deciding on the form of the documents. The Contracting Officer uses Standard Form 30, "Amendment of Solicitation/Modification of Contract."[56] Most importantly, the Contracting Officer decides whether the change can be issued in *bilateral* or *unilateral* form.

a. Bilateral Change Orders. Although the "Changes" clause speaks in terms of unilateral orders of the Contracting Officer, most Government agencies attempt to avoid the use of unilateral changes. The agencies have found that a contractor's original estimate of the eventual cost of the change is frequently low, with the result that the actual cost of the change is higher than anticipated by the Contracting Officer. Thus, the Government's policy is to make every effort to negotiate the price of a proposed change at the time it is being considered, and to issue the change as a bilateral amendment to the contract.[57]

b. Unilateral Change Orders. It is not always possible to enter into a bilateral agreement on a change. For example, additional work may be necessary—such as prototype manufacturing—to determine the specific nature of the change. More often, the parties are unable to agree on the price of the change. In these circumstances, the Contracting Officer may issue a unilateral change order.[58] When it is too soon to know the ramifications of the change, the unilateral order will contain no mention of the price or time impact of the change, and the contractor will later submit a proposal for equitable adjustment.

c. Timing. There is no limitation upon the time during which a change can be ordered. The typical "Changes" clauses state that a change can be made "at any time"—i.e., at any time after the contract is signed and before final payment.[59]

F. CONSTRUCTIVE CHANGES

A "constructive" change is any action or inaction by the Contracting Officer or other Government representative (who has the authority to order changes) that is not a formal change order but has the effect of requiring the contractor to perform additional work beyond the contract's requirements. Although the Government may believe that the action was proper under the terms of the contract, if the contractor's view that the extra work was not required by the contract ultimately prevails, the action will be construed as a constructive change (or a breach of contract), and the contractor will be entitled to compensation for the extra costs it incurred.

1. Development Of The Doctrine

Before the enactment of the Contract Disputes Act of 1978, the boards of contract appeals only had jurisdiction over claims "arising under" the contract (i.e., claims that could be resolved by some "remedy-granting" clause of the contract, such as the "Changes" clause). Contractor claims based on Government conduct that could be characterized as a contract breach were outside the boards' authority. Therefore, the boards developed the doctrine of "constructive" changes to provide authority to the boards to decide these breach of contract claims[60]—meaning that although the Government did not use the procedures of the "Changes" clause when requiring the extra work, the results of the Government conduct were the same as if a change had been issued.

The importance of the constructive changes doctrine has diminished since the boards were given authority by the CDA to hear any claim connected with a contract.[61] (See Chapter 18, Section A.) The boards no longer need the constructive changes doctrine to enlarge their jurisdiction. Nonetheless, the constructive changes doctrine retains some vitality.[62] Whether a contractor characterizes its claim as a "change" or as a "breach of contract" can still have an effect, for example, on the contractor's duty to proceed with contract performance, on the amount of the contractor's recovery (equitable adjustment versus contract damages), and on the contractor's notice obligations.

2. Types Of Constructive Changes

Regardless of the type of Government conduct that forms the basis of a constructive changes claim, for the Government to be held liable for the cost of the extra work, the contractor must establish the following three elements: (1) the act of the Government can be traced, in some way, to a Government employee with authority to order the additional work (see Section B.1 above), (2) the "extra" work done exceeded the requirements of the contract, and (3) depending on the specific contract involved, the contractor gave the proper notice to the Government of the Government action that the contractor believed constituted a constructive change.[63]

There are five major types of Government conduct that may result in constructive changes. They are examined below.

a. Contract Interpretation. An extremely common type of constructive change occurs when the Government, during contract administration, interprets the contract to require work that is more costly than the work contemplated by the contractor. There are two fundamental steps in interpreting a contract: (a) determining the meaning of contract language when the contractor's and the Government's interpretations differ and (b) determining which party should bear the risk of misinterpretation of the contract when the rules of interpretation provide no clear solution to the problem. To accomplish the first step, the court or board will attempt to ascertain the intent of the parties at the time they entered into the contract. Because, in most litigated cases, the parties were not of a single mind when they agreed to the contract, it will be necessary to use principles of contract interpretation to resolve the issue.[64] The second step—which party should bear the risk of misinterpretation when the intent of the parties cannot be ascertained—will require the application of risk allocation principles by the board or court. For example, the legal doctrine of *contra proferentem* requires that an ambiguity in a contract must be construed against the party that drafted the contract—in Government contracts, that is typically the Government.[65]

It should be added that in looking at the language of the contract, the boards and courts interpret words and phrases that are peculiar to the field of Government contracts in accordance with their meaning in that field. For example, the proper and common interpretation of "equitable adjustment" means that Government contractors are chargeable with the knowledge that an equitable adjustment under the "Changes" clause will include profit but not anticipatory profits.[66] This rule means, of course, that the contractor must be knowledgeable regarding the special terms that are used in this field in order to interpret its contract correctly; common usages of the particular trade in question must also be understood.[67]

Even if its contract interpretation is reasonable, a contractor cannot recover if the interpretation arises from an ambiguity that is clear on the face of the contract (i.e., a "patent" ambiguity). This rule is based on concepts of fair dealing which require that a contractor that intentionally submits a low bid—with the goal of claiming ambiguities during contract performance to obtain price increases—not be rewarded for its duplicity.[68] Therefore, a bidder has a duty to request clarification before bidding if there is a major patent discrepancy, obvious omission, or significant conflict in the contract provisions, including drawings and specifications.[69] For example, a bidder on a contract for building construction had a duty to call to the attention of the Contracting Officer the failure of the specifications to provide any method for draining water from the building's roof—an obvious error.[70]

On the other hand, a bidder confronted with complex drawings and specifications is not required to seek out subtleties and inferences and inquire about each of them.[71] Of necessity, the facts and circumstances of each case must be considered to determine whether the bidder should have requested clarification.[72]

b. Interference & Failure To Cooperate. A constructive change can also arise when the Government increases the contractor's cost of performance by actively interfering with the progress of the work or by failing to cooperate with the contractor. Each contracting party has as *implied duty* to cooperate with the other contracting party. Thus, relief on the basis of constructive change has been granted to contractors where the Government (1) improperly disapproved first articles,[73] (2) inspected overly restrictively and thereby caused extra work,[74] (3) restricted the contractor to two methods of performance even though the contract provided for three,[75] (4) insisted on delivery under threat of termination despite the existence of an excusable cause of delay,[76] and (5) limited the number of security clearances available for the employees of a security services contractor.[77]

c. Defective Specifications. The constructive change theory has also been applied where the specifications are defective or call for performance that cannot be attained (see Chapter 8), and the contractor incurs additional expense in attempting to comply with the specifications. Equitable adjustments have frequently been granted in such cases. Indeed, the defective specifications-type of constructive change is implicitly incorporated in the construction contract "Changes" clause.[78]

In one case, a contractor was allowed to recover its costs of *trying* to perform under an impossible specification—even though the contractor inexcusably *failed* to perform the contract (failed to deliver supplies) after the specification was corrected.[79] Similarly, a Government demand that drainage facilities be constructed by a construction contractor as a condition for relaxing the moisture content specification for concrete aggregate—which could not be achieved by standard industry procedures—was a constructive change.[80] To recover under this theory, the contractor must show both that the specifications are defective and that the defects caused the additional work claimed.[81]

d. Nondisclosure Of Vital Information. The fourth type of constructive change occurs when the Government has information that it knows the contractor will need to achieve satisfactory performance but fails to disclose it to the contractor, resulting in extra effort and expense by the contractor. The nondisclosure of that vital information is a contract "change" in the sense that it should have been given to the contractor at the outset. It follows that the equitable adjustment for this type of constructive change should cover all costs resulting from nondisclosure of the information.

The elements of the Government's duty to disclose information to the contractor are (a) the Government's possession of important information,[82] (b) the contractor's lack of the information and inability to obtain it through normal investigation,[83] and (c) Government knowledge (actual or imputed) that the contractor does not have the information.[84]

The leading case on the subject of duty to disclose was decided by the Court of Claims. It arose when the Government issued a competitive solicitation for the production of a chemical compound without revealing the production method disclosed by a recently completed research and development contract. The court held that the Government had a duty to share the information with prospective contractors rather than let them "flounder on their own" since the balance of knowledge was so clearly on its side.[85]

The information that the Government has a duty to disclose usually relates to the work to be performed. Such information is often technical in nature—for example, that prior contractors had the same difficulties encountered by the contractor,[86] or that the roads at a facility had load limitations.[87] Other types of information may also be so important to the project that the Government should disclose it. For example, in one case, the Government had a duty to disclose that it intended to award other contracts at the construction site where those awards made labor difficult to obtain and directly affected the way the work was performed.[88]

e. Acceleration. The fifth type of constructive change occurs when the contractor is ordered or induced to incur additional costs to accelerate the work to complete performance prior to the time the contract requires.[89] The essence of constructive acceleration is an act or order of the Contracting Officer that forces the contractor to perform earlier than it would have been required to perform had the contract schedule been properly adjusted to reflect excusable delays (see Chapters 12 and 26). The theory is that each time a contractor incurs an excusable delay, it becomes entitled to a commensurate extension of the contract schedule. Therefore, if the Contracting Officer does not recognize these schedule changes but instead demands performance in accordance with the original (or any shorter) schedule, his action will be treated as a constructive acceleration.

Notice to the Contracting Officer that an excusable delay has occurred is particularly important to a successful recovery for acceleration. This is because the Contracting Officer cannot be held to have ordered an acceleration if he had no knowledge of the delay and hence no knowledge of the contractor's entitlement to a revised schedule. An order to meet the contract schedule without knowledge of excusable delays is more properly characterized as an order to meet the contract obligations as they are believed to exist.[90] The proper response by the contractor to such an order is to request a time extension for excusable delay.

Direct orders of the Contracting Officer to accelerate are constructive changes, even if there is a clause in the contract allowing such orders when the contractor is behind schedule.[91] In addition, a so-called *"request"* to accelerate the work is tantamount to an order to accelerate. For example, a resident engineer's request that a contractor speed up performance was deemed an acceleration order where, at the initiative of the Government, the work was performed in a manner different from that required by the contract.[92]

If it is not clear whether "urgings" by the Government are firm requests to accelerate, the contractor should not accelerate performance until it has asked for and obtained clarification of the Contracting Officer's instructions. Indeed, procrastination by the Contracting Officer in responding to a contractor's request for a time extension due to unusually severe weather—resulting in performance under more adverse conditions than originally anticipated—was construed in one case as a constructive acceleration.[93]

REFERENCES

1. FAR 43.205.

2. FAR 52.243-1.

3. See, e.g., FAR 52.243-1, alternate IV (for fixed-price contracts for transportation services).

4. Mil-Pak Co., ASBCA 19733, 76-1 BCA ¶ 11725; Eggers & Higgins, VACAB 537, 66-1 BCA ¶ 5525, 9 GC ¶ 206.

5. Gulf & Western Industries, Inc., ASBCA 22204, 79-1 BCA ¶ 12706, 21 GC ¶ 130; Etowah Mfg., ASBCA 23521, 80-1 BCA ¶ 14438.

6. FAR 52.243-4.

7. See FAR 52.243-4, para. (a)(4).

8. See FAR 52.243-4, para. (e).

9. Chemical Const. Corp., IBCA 946-1-72, 73-1 BCA ¶ 9892.

10. H.K. Ferguson Co., ASBCA 2826, 57-1 BCA ¶ 1293.

11. FAR 52.243-2.

12. See, e.g., FAR 52.243-2, alternate V (for cost-reimbursement contracts involving research and development requirements).

13. FAR 52.232-20, para. (d).

14. FAR 52.232-20, para. (g).

15. Breed Corp., ASBCA 14523, 72-1 BCA ¶ 9304; American Electronics Laboratories, Inc., ASBCA 26042, 84-2 BCA ¶ 17468.

16. Recon Systems Inc., IBCA 1214-9-78, 79-2 BCA ¶ 14058, 21 GC ¶ 409.

17. See also Breed Corp. v. U.S., 223 Ct. Cl. 702 (1980) (Government waived rights under clause by inducing contractor to perform additional work with knowledge of contractor's overrun position); but cf. Hughes Aircraft Corp. ASBCA 24601, 83-1 BCA ¶ 16396, 25 GC ¶ 318.

18. FAR 52.232-22.

19. See, e.g, NASA FAR Supp. 18-52.242-70.

20. Mil-Spec Contractors, Inc. v. U.S., 835 F.2d 865 (Fed. Cir. 1987), 6 FPD ¶ 164, 30 GC ¶ 23.

21. Jordan & Nobles Const. Co., GSBCA 8349 et al., 91-1 BCA ¶ 23659, 33 GC ¶ 107.

22. Urban Pathfinders, Inc., ASBCA 23134, 79-1 BCA ¶ 13709, 21 GC ¶ 122.

23. Southwestern Sheet Metal Works, Inc., ASBCA 22748, 79-1 BCA ¶ 13744, 21 GC ¶ 304. See also Parking Co. of America, GSBCA 7654, 87-2 BCA ¶ 19823, Reliable Disposal Co., ASBCA 40100, 91-2 BCA ¶ 23895, 33 GC ¶ 164.

24. FAR 1.602-3.

25. Alta Const. Co., PSBCA 1334, 87-1 BCA ¶ 19491.

26. E.g., Freund v. U.S., 260 U.S. 60 (1922); Akon, Inc., ENGBCA 5593, 90-3 BCA ¶ 23250 (cardinal change exists only where work performed was "a different undertaking" from work bargained for).

27. Edward R. Marden Corp. v. U.S., 442 F.2d 364 (Ct. Cl. 1971), 13 GC ¶ 205; Air-A-Plane Corp. v. U.S., 408 F.2d 1030 (Ct. Cl. 1969), 11 GC ¶ 95; Brand S Roofing, ASBCA 24688, 82-1 BCA ¶ 15717, 24 GC ¶ 122. See also Indian & Native American Employment & Training Coalition, Comp. Gen. Dec. B-216421, 85-1 CPD ¶ 432.

28. Axel Electronics, Inc., ASBCA 18990, 74-1 BCA ¶ 10471, 16 GC ¶ 147. See also Bruce-Andersen Co., ASBCA 35791, 89-2 BCA ¶ 21871, 31 GC ¶ 287.

29. Air-A-Plane Corp. v. U.S., note 27, supra; Coley Properties Corp., PSBCA 291, 75-2 BCA ¶ 11514, 18 GC ¶ 138; Reliance Ins. Co. v. U.S., 20 Cl. Ct. 715 (1990), 9 FPD ¶ 92, affd., 931 F.2d 863 (Fed. Cir. 1991), 10 FPD ¶ 47, 33 GC ¶ 153.

30. Aragona Const. Co. v. U.S., 165 Ct. Cl. 382 (1964), 6 GC ¶ 193. See also Perry & Wallis, Inc. v. U.S., 427 F.2d 722 (Ct. Cl. 1970), 12 GC ¶ 256.

31. FAR 52.233-1, para. (i).

32. 41 USC § 605(b). See FAR 33.213.

33. Monitor Plastics Co., ASBCA 11187, 67-2 BCA ¶ 6408, 10 GC ¶ 42.

34. Puma Chemical Co., GSBCA 5254, 81-1 BCA ¶ 14844.

35. Stoeckert v. U.S., 391 F.2d 639 (Ct. Cl. 1968), 10 GC ¶ 145.

36. Dynamics Corp. of America v. U.S., 389 F.2d 424 (Ct. Cl. 1968), 10 GC ¶ 58.

37. See generally Connelly, "Value Engineering," Briefing Papers No. 94-7 (June 1994); Tracy & Tieder, "Defense Department Value Engineering," Briefing Papers No. 74-5 (Oct. 1974), 3 BPC 151.

38. FAR 48.102. See generally Office of Management and Budget Circular A-131, 58 Fed. Reg. 31056 (June 14, 1993); 35 GC ¶ 354.

39. FAR 52.248-1.

40. FAR 52.248-3.

41. FAR 48.001. See FAR 52.248-1, para. (b) and FAR 52.248-3, para. (b).

42. See FAR 52.248-1, para. (f).

43. See FAR 52.248-3, para. (f).

44. E.g., John J. Kirlin, Inc. v. U.S., 827 F.2d 1538 (Fed. Cir. 1987), 6 FPD ¶ 109, 29 GC ¶ 300. See generally Nash, "'Value Engineering' Clauses: Read Them Carefully!," 8 Nash & Cibinic Rep. ¶ 18 (Mar. 1994).

45. American Standard Inc., DOTCAB 71-1, 72-1 BCA ¶ 9433, 14 GC ¶ 354; Thompson Aircraft Tire Corp., ASBCA 144-32, 71-2 BCA ¶ 8981, 13 GC ¶ 436; North American Rockwell Corp., ASBCA 14485, 71-1 BCA ¶ 8733, 13 GC ¶ 361; McDonnell Douglas Astronautics Co., ASBCA 19971, 76-2 BCA ¶ 12117, 19 GC ¶ 63. See also Gulf Apparel Corp., ASBCA 27784, 89-2 BCA ¶ 21735, 31 GC ¶ 211.

46. Traylor Bros., Inc., ENGBCA 5305 et al., 89-2 BCA ¶ 21679.

47. Grismac Corp. v. U.S., 556 F.2d 494 (Ct. Cl. 1977), 19 GC ¶ 250.

48. Charles Baseler Co., ASBCA 22669, 78-2 BCA ¶ 13483, 20 GC ¶ 431.

49. FAR 52.248-1, para. (e)(3); FAR 52.248-3, para. (e)(3).

50. Covington Industries Inc., ASBCA 12426, 68-2 BCA ¶ 7286, 11 GC ¶ 24; North American Rockwell Corp., note 45, supra.

51. Fermont Div., Dynamics Corp. of America, ASBCA 22250, 79-2 BCA ¶ 14086, 22 GC ¶ 10; Turco Products, ASBCA 20290, 75-2 BCA ¶ 11442, 17 GC ¶ 400; Antaya Bros., ASBCA 19390, 75-2 BCA ¶ 11403, 17 GC ¶ 420.

52. DFARS 243.205-70.

53. Military Standard 480 (MIL-STD-480); Military Standard 481 (MIL-STD-481). See also DOD Instruction 5000.2, pt. 9 (Feb. 23, 1991).

54. DFARS 252.243-7000.

55. Blinderman Const. Co., ASBCA 24127, 80-2 BCA ¶ 14804; Greenhut Const. Co., ASBCA 14354, 70-1 BCA ¶ 8209; Century Industries Corp., ASBCA 3873, 58-2 BCA ¶ 1933. Cf. Campos Const. Co. VABCA 3019, 90-3 BCA ¶ 23108, 32 GC ¶ 267.

56. FAR 43.301.

57. FAR 43.102(b), 43.103(a).

58. FAR 43.103(b).

59. Hedin Const. Co. v. U.S., 347 F.2d 235 (Ct. Cl. 1965), 7 GC ¶ 329.

60. See generally vom Baur, "Constructive Change Orders," Briefing Papers No. 65-5 (Oct. 1965), 1 BPC 139; vom Baur, "Constructive Change Orders/Edition II," Briefing Papers No. 73-5 (Oct. 1973), 3 BPC 59.

61. 41 USC §§ 605(a), 607(d).

62. See generally Vacketta & Mullen, "Constructive Change Orders/Edition III," Briefing Papers No. 92-13 (Dec. 1992).

63. E.g., FAR 52.243-4, para. (d). See Imbus Roofing Co., GSBCA 10430, 91-2 BCA ¶ 23820; Niko Contracting Co., IBCA 2368, 91-1 BCA ¶ 23321.

64. See generally Pettit, "Interpretation of Government Contracts," Briefing Papers No. 65-6 (Dec. 1965), 1 BPC 147.

65. E.g., U.S. v. Turner Const. Co., 819 F.2d 283 (Fed. Cir. 1987), 6 FPD ¶ 66, 29 GC ¶ 190.

66. General Builders Supply Co. v. U.S., 409 F.2d 246 (Ct. Cl. 1969), 11 GC ¶ 160. See also Wallace C. Boldt, General Contractor, Inc., ASBCA 24862, 83-2 BCA ¶ 16765, 26 GC ¶ 38.

67. Gholson, Byars & Holmes Const. Co. v. U.S., 351 F.2d 987 (Ct. Cl. 1965), 7 GC ¶ 506.

68. Beacon Const. Co. v. U.S., 314 F.2d 501 (Ct. Cl. 1963), 5 GC ¶ 133.

69. Blount Bros. Const. Co. v. U.S., 346 F.2d 962 (Ct. Cl. 1965), 7 GC ¶ 300; Mountain Home Contractors v. U.S., 425 F.2d 1260 (Ct. Cl. 1970), 12 GC ¶ 199; R&G Roofing Co., ASBCA 22172, 78-1 BCA ¶ 12879, 20 GC ¶ 24, affd., 218 Ct. Cl. 739 (1978), 21 GC ¶ 37; Assurance Co., ASBCA 25254, 83-2 BCA ¶ 16908; Walsky Const. Co., ASBCA 27099, 83-2 BCA ¶ 16771, 25 GC ¶ 303.

70. Gall Landau Young Const. Co., ASBCA 21549, 77-1 BCA ¶ 12515, 19 GC ¶ 367.

71. Southwestern Sheet Metal Works, Inc., note 23, supra; W.P.C. Enterprises, Inc. v. U.S., 323 F.2d 874 (Ct. Cl. 1963), 5 GC ¶ 480; Santa Fe, Inc., VABCA 1783, 83-1 BCA ¶ 16322.

72. L. Rosenman Corp. v. U.S., 390 F.2d 711 (Ct. Cl. 1968), 10 GC ¶ 107; Brezina Const. Co. v. U.S., 449 F.2d 372 (Ct. Cl. 1971), 13 GC ¶ 438.

73. Winfield Mfg. Co., ASBCA 34901, 88-1 BCA ¶ 20353, 30 GC ¶ 14.

74. Harris System Intl., Inc., ASBCA 33280, 88-2 BCA ¶ 20641, 30 GC ¶ 161.

75. Long Services Corp., PSBCA 1606, 87-3 BCA ¶ 20109, 29 GC ¶ 301.

76. Alley-Cassetty Coal Co., ASBCA 33315, 89-3 BCA ¶ 21964, 32 GC ¶ 352 (Note).

77. Old Dominion Security, ASBCA 40062, 91-3 BCA ¶ 24173, 33 GC ¶ 236.

CHANGES 11-27

78. FAR 52.243-4, para. (d).

79. Laka Tool & Stamping Co. v. U.S., 650 F.2d 270 (Ct. Cl. 1981), 23 GC ¶ 30. See also Clay Bernard Systems Intl., ASBCA 25382, 88-3 BCA 20856, 30 GC ¶ 252.

80. Guy F. Atkinson Co., ENGBCA 4771, 88-2 BCA ¶ 20714, 30 GC ¶ 192.

81. E.g., Lionsgate Corp., ENGBCA 5391 et al., 91-1 BCA ¶ 23368.

82. Cf. Bethlehem Corp. v. U.S., 462 F.2d 1400 (Ct. Cl. 1972) (disclosure is required if the information is available within the same procuring activity—even if it is at different location than procuring office), 14 GC ¶ 296 with Unitec, Inc., ASBCA 22025, 79-2 BCA ¶ 13923 (disclosure is not required if information is known to another unrelated Government agency but not to the procuring agency), 22 GC ¶ 19.

83. H.N. Bailey & Assocs. v. U.S., 499 F.2d 376 (Ct. Cl. 1971) (Government is not obligated to volunteer information in its files if contractor can reasonably be expected to seek and obtain the facts elsewhere), 13 GC ¶ 439; Ambrose-Augusterfer Corp. v. U.S., 394 F.2d 536 (Ct. Cl. 1968), 10 GC ¶ 263; Bermite Div., ASBCA 19211, 77-2 BCA ¶ 12675; Arnold M. Diamond, Inc., ASBCA 22733, 78-2 BCA ¶ 13477 (patent status of item or process is information that is reasonably available to bidders in commercial channels), 20 GC ¶ 417.

84. See generally Victorino, Southern & Soyars-Berman, "Government Failure To Disclose," Briefing Papers No. 92-10 (Sept. 1992).

85. Helene Curtis Industries v. U.S., 312 F.2d 744 (Ct. Cl. 1963), 5 GC ¶ 70.

86. See Federal Electric Corp., ASBCA 13030, 69-2 BCA ¶ 7792, 11 GC ¶ 449; Telline Radio Inc., ASBCA 20564, 78-1 BCA ¶ 12915, 20 GC ¶ 118; Nab-Lord Assocs., PSBCA 318 et al., 77-2 BCA ¶ 12802, 20 GC ¶ 83; Numax Electronics, Inc., ASBCA 29080, 90-1 BCA ¶ 22280.

87. R.G. Pitts, Inc., ASBCA 37816, 89-3 BCA ¶ 22245.

88. J.A. Jones Const. Co. v. U.S., 390 F.2d 886 (Ct. Cl. 1968), 10 GC ¶ 114.

89. See generally Bruner, Sand & Allen, "Acceleration/Edition II," Briefing Papers No. 81-2 (Apr. 1981), 5 BPC 175.

90. Mechanical Utilities, Inc., ASBCA 7466, 1962 BCA ¶ 3556, 5 GC ¶ 235.

91. Yukon Const. Co., ASBCA 10859, 67-1 BCA ¶ 6334, 10 GC ¶ 86.

92. Hyde Const. Co., ASBCA 8393, 1963 BCA ¶ 3811, 6 GC ¶ 32. See Tombigbee Contractors v. U.S., 420 F.2d 1037 (Ct. Cl. 1970), 12 GC ¶ 144. But see Welmetco, Ltd., ASBCA 23213 et al., 84-2 BCA ¶ 17395.

93. Barrett Co., ENGBCA 3877, 78-1 BCA ¶ 13075, 20 GC ¶ 190.

DELAYS

12

A. **Compensable Delays**
   1. Standard Contract Clauses
   2. Recovery For Constructive Suspensions
   3. Types Of Constructive Delays

B. **Excusable Delays**
   1. Standard Clause
   2. Elements & Proof
   3. Enumerated Causes Of Excusable Delay
   4. Unenumerated Causes Of Excusable Delay

The effect of a delay in contract performance on the contractor and the Government depends on the cause of the delay and the contract clause involved. Generally, the Government agrees in the contract—through the "Government Delay of Work" clause (for supply and service contracts) or the "Suspension of Work" clause (for construction contracts)—to compensate the contractor in both time and money for the delays the Government causes. On the other hand, the contractor is responsible for both the time and cost of delays that the contractor causes or are within its control. If the delay was caused by events beyond the control of the contractor, however, typically the contractor will be excused for the delay in performance (under the contract's "Default" clause), but the contractor must bear the additional costs caused by the delay.

The subject of delays and interruptions in contract performance has historically been of great significance in construction contracts. In fact, contract clauses dealing with this subject were first developed for use in such contracts. Because of its importance in construction contracting, the subject of construction delays is treated in Chapter 26 in Part VII of this book, the part that is is devoted entirely to the peculiarities of construction contracting.

However, the subject is also of importance to other kinds of contracts, particularly to supply contracts. A significant number of contracts are of this type, and a frequent cause of problems during the performance of such contracts is a delay or interruption in delivery of the contract end items.

A. COMPENSABLE DELAYS

1. Standard Contract Clauses

The "Government Delay of Work" clause[1] set forth in Figure 12-1 is required to be included in fixed-price contracts for most types of supplies and is optional for use in fixed-price service contracts.[2] As indicated in the text of Paragraph (a) of the clause, this clause covers suspensions of work that are caused by the Government but occur without an express order from the

> **Figure 12-1**
>
> **"GOVERNMENT DELAY OF WORK" CLAUSE**
> (FAR 52.212-15)
>
> (a) If the performance of all or any part of the work of this contract is delayed or interrupted (1) by an act of the Contracting Officer in the administration of this contract that is not expressly or impliedly authorized by this contract, or (2) by a failure of the Contracting Officer to act within the time specified in this contract, or within a reasonable time if not specified, an adjustment (excluding profit) shall be made for any increase in the cost of performance of this contract caused by the delay or interruption and the contract shall be modified in writing accordingly. Adjustment shall also be made in the delivery or performance dates and any other contractual term or condition affected by the delay or interruption. However, no adjustment shall be made under this clause for any delay or interruption to the extent that performance would have been delayed or interrupted by any other cause, including the fault or negligence of the Contractor, or for which an adjustment is provided or excluded under any other term or condition of this contract.
>
> (b) A claim under this clause shall not be allowed (1) for any costs incurred more than 20 days before the Contractor shall have notified the Contracting Officer in writing of the act or failure to act involved, and (2) unless the claim, in an amount stated, is asserted in writing as soon as practicable after the termination of the delay or interruption, but not later than the day of final payment under the contract.

Contracting Officer—so-called "constructive suspensions" of work. In the event of a Government delay of the work, an adjustment in the contract price and schedule will be made for any increased costs or time caused by the delay.

In supply and service contracts, *ordered* suspensions are covered by the "Stop Work Order" clause,[3] which is optional for use in negotiated supply, services, or research and development contracts.[4] This clause provides that the Contracting Officer may require the contractor, by written order, to stop all or any part of the work. If the stop work order is later canceled, the Contracting Officer shall make an equitable adjustment in the delivery schedule or contract price or both if the work stoppage resulted in increased costs and performance time for the contractor.[5] If the stop work order is not canceled and the contract work is terminated, the Contracting Officer shall allow the reasonable costs resulting from the work stoppage.[6]

2. Recovery For Constructive Suspensions

To recover additional money under the "Government Delay of Work" clause, the contractor must prove that the delay was for an *unreasonable* period of time. Generally, if the entire delay was caused by the Government, the contractor can be compensated for the entire period. If, however, the cause of the delay was due to the Government's exercise of a contractual right, or both parties contributed to the delay, the contractor may be compensated for only part of the delay or may receive no price increase at all.[7] The terms of the clause itself add other limitations: (a) no contract adjustment will be made for any delay to the extent that performance would have been delayed by any other cause (including the fault or negligence of the contractor), (b) no cost will be allowed that was incurred more than 20 days before the contractor notified the Government in writing of the cause of the delay, (c) the claim must be asserted in a specific amount as soon as practicable after the delay in the work ends, and (d) no allowance for profit will be granted.

Arguably, one other limitation in the "Government Delay of Work" clause—that no contract adjustment will be made "for which an adjustment is provided or excluded under any other term or provision of this contract"—indicates that where a delay claim for an equitable adjustment could be brought under the contract's "Changes" clause (or "Government Property" or other clause), then the use of these other clauses is preferred.[8]

3. Types Of Constructive Delays

Some of the types of delays that frequently arise in the performance of fixed-price supply contracts are examined in the sections below.

a. Delays Involving Changes. The largest number of Government-caused delays occur in connection with changes in the work that are ordered under the authority of the standard "Changes" clause (see Chapter 11 for a discussion of contract changes). Ordering of changes can result in two types of delays. First, there may be a delay between the time the contractor is advised that the Government is planning to make a change and the time the contractor is finally given all the necessary technical information and told to proceed with the changed work. Second, even after the change is received, it may so increase the volume of work or so disorganize the contractor's planned sequence of operations for accomplishing the original work that completion of the entire work is delayed.

The first type, delays in ordering changes, is one for which an equitable adjustment can be made under the "Government Delay of Work" clause. The second type of delay in connection with changes—resulting from an increase in the volume of work or disruption and disorganization of the contractor's planned operations—is one for which a contract adjustment can be made under the "Changes" clause.

b. Delays Involving Faulty Specifications. Closely related to delays in connection with contract changes are interruptions in work that occur when the Government gives the contractor inadequate or faulty plans or specifications governing the performance of work. The general rule in these situations is that the Government is liable—under an "implied warranty" theory (see Chapter 8, Section E)—for excess time or expense caused to the contractor as a result of the defective specifications.

c. Delays In Furnishing Property. The Government's failure to timely furnish materials or equipment for a contractor's use in performing the work may delay the contractor's performance. As mentioned in Chapter 9, Section D, this type of delay for which the Government is responsible can result in an equitable adjustment under the "Government Property" clause as well.

d. Delays In Approval Or Inspection Of Work. When the contract provides that the contractor must obtain Government approvals before proceeding with the work or some part of the work, or where the contract requires Government inspection of the work, such approvals or inspections must occur within a reasonable time. An unreasonable delay in approval or inspection may be compensable.

B. EXCUSABLE DELAYS

As noted at the beginning of this chapter, the contract language typically allocates the risks of performance delays between the parties, depending on who is responsible for the events that delay the performance. When the events that delay performance are beyond the control of the contractor, the contractor is usually excused from nonperformance. The purpose of the "excusable delay" contract provisions is to protect the contractor from sanctions for late performance. Such sanctions typically include termination of the contract for default, the assessment of the excess costs of reprocurement or completion, actual damages, or liquidated damages (see Chapter 16).

1. Standard Clause

The standard "Default (Fixed-Price Supply and Service)" clause (see Chapter 16, Figure 16-1) lists a number of causes of delay that—provided they are beyond the control and without the fault or negligence of the contractor—will excuse the contractor's failure to perform on time:[9]

(1) Acts of God (also referred to as a *force majeure* in legal terminology) or of the public enemy.

(2) Acts of the Government in either its sovereign or contractual capacity.

(3) Fires.

(4) Floods.

(5) Epidemics.

(6) Quarantine restrictions.

(7) Strikes.

(8) Freight embargoes.

(9) Unusually severe weather.

(10) Subcontractor or supplier delays at any tier arising from unforeseeable causes beyond the control of and without the fault or negligence of both the contractor and the subcontractor or supplier.

An extension of time—but not a price increase—will generally be granted if a contractor's performance is delayed by one of these occurrences.[10]

2. Elements & Proof

The mere occurrence of an event that qualifies as an excusable delay does not *automatically* entitle the contractor to an extension of time. The contractor must establish (a) that the occurrence of the event that caused the delay was unforeseeable, beyond the contractor's control, and without its fault or negligence,[11] (b) that the delay prevented timely completion of the contract,[12] and (c) the number of days of relief to which the contractor is entitled.[13]

The contractor has the burden of showing not only that the cause of the delay was excusable, but also that the contractor had no control over it.[14] For example, a contractor could not claim a strike as an excusable delay when the strike resulted from the contractor's own unfair labor practices.[15] The contractor must also establish the extent to which its job performance was delayed by the event[16] and make reasonable efforts to mitigate the effect of a delay or prevent delay where possible.[17]

3. Enumerated Causes Of Excusable Delay

Discussed below are several of the causes of excusable delay specifically enumerated in the "Default" clause and listed above in Section B.1 that may arise in the performance of a supply or service contract.

a. Government Sovereign Acts. The Government is not accountable for any actions taken in its "sovereign" capacity—that is, for public acts that are not directed to the contractor—and thus is not liable for delays caused by such acts.[18] The rationale for the Government's immunity from liability for its sovereign acts was explained long ago by the Court of Claims as follows: "Whatever acts the Government may do, be they legislative or executive, so long as they be public and general, cannot be deemed specially to alter, modify, obstruct or violate the particular contract into which it enters with private persons."[19]

The contractor is normally held to have *assumed the risk* that its contract performance may be delayed by a sovereign act, unless the Government expressly promises to the contrary in the contract. Some examples of sovereign acts are (1) the imposition, alteration, and removal of price controls,[20] (2) devaluation of the dollar,[21] (3) cancellation of a Government loan,[22] and (4) suspension of contract performance as required by statute due to a protest of a contract award.[23]

b. Government Contractual Acts. Acts of the Government in its "contractual" capacity are also potential causes of excusable delay. Such acts of the Government must be directed to the specific contractor[24] and must be wrongful to excuse the contractor from any resulting delay.[25] For example, the following Government actions have been found to cause excusable delays: (a) failure to respond to the contractor's request for clarification,[26] (b) payment delays,[27] (c) unreasonable delays in approving contractor drawings, equipment, materials or subcontractors,[28] (d) failure to accept or reject a "first article" within a reasonable time,[29] (e) improper and unreasonable Government inspections,[30] (f) formal or constructive suspensions of work (see Section A above), (g) defective specifications or drawings (see Chapter 8), (h) late or defective Government-furnished property (see Chapter 9), and (i) failure to disclose vital information.[31] Because many of these actions can also be treated as actual or constructive changes to the contract (see Chapter 11), if the contractor is granted relief for these actions under the "Changes" clause, there is no need to rely on the contract's excusable delay provisions.

c. Weather. Although weather is obviously of greater concern to a construction contractor than to a supply contractor (see Chapter 26, Section B.1), weather can also cause delays in the performance of a supply contract. For example, a severe storm can cause loss of electric power needed to perform, or can damage a contractor's production facilities.

Note that the weather must be *unusually* severe to justify a time extension.[32] "Unusually severe weather" means adverse weather that at the time of year in which it occurred is unusual for the place in which it occurred. For example, in one case involving a contract to wash aircraft on an out-of-doors wash rack, the contractor was excused for delay where winter weather caused the cleaner to freeze.[33]

Like other causes of excusable delay, unusually severe weather only excuses *delay*—it does not generally excuse performance of the contract. The general rule is that unusually severe weather only relieves the contractor from completing performance for a *temporary* period equivalent to the delay caused by the weather.[34]

d. Subcontractor Delays. One of the most frequent causes of delayed performance by supply or construction contractors is the failure of suppliers or subcontractors to deliver material or perform in a timely manner. The "Default" clause's excusable delay provisions strictly limit the extent to which such delays are excusable, however. To be excusable, a delay of a subcontractor or supplier at any tier must be beyond the control and without the fault or negligence of *both* the contractor and all the intervening subcontractors. Thus, a prime contractor cannot cite delay of a subcontractor as an excusable delay *unless* the subcontractor delay is itself excusable.[35] A supplier's failure to perform may be excusable if the supplier was the sole source for materials or supplies, for example.[36] On the other hand, under the "Default" clause for supply contracts, the contractor is obligated to attempt to obtain other sources when a subcontractor has been excusably delayed.[37] For example, when an oil embargo prevented a contractor's supplier from delivering petroleum products, the contractor's default was held *not* excusable because the contractor neglected to make inquiry of other potential suppliers.[38]

4. Unenumerated Causes Of Excusable Delay

The causes of delay listed in the "Default" clause (and set forth above in Section B.1) are not intended to be exclusive. A contractor can also rely on another unspecified event that was beyond its control and occurred without its fault or negligence as a ground for excusable delay. However, the courts and boards of contract appeals typically take a restrictive view of such claims, finding that the event was foreseeable or within the contractor's control. For example, delays due to financial difficulties,[39] breakdown of equipment,[40] or shortage of material[41] during performance are usually not excusable.

REFERENCES

1. FAR 52.212-15. See generally McWhorter, "Suspension of Work/Edition II," Briefing Papers No. 76-2 (Apr. 1976), 4 BPC 15; McWhorter, "Suspension of Work," Briefing Papers No. 66-6 (Dec. 1966), 1 BPC 215.

2. FAR 12.505(d).

3. FAR 52.212-13.

4. FAR 12.505(b).

5. FAR 52.212-13, para. (b).

6. FAR 52.212-13, paras. (c), (d).

7. E.g., Tri-Cor, Inc. v. U.S., 458 F.2d 112 (Ct. Cl. 1972), 14 GC ¶ 209; E.H. Marhoefer Co., DOTCAB 70-17, 71-1 BCA ¶ 8791.

8. See, e.g., Piracci Const. Co., GSBCA 3477, 74-2 BCA ¶¶ 10799, 10800, 16 GC ¶¶ 287, 446.

9. FAR 52.249-8, paras. (c), (d). See also Gubin, "Default Excuses," Briefing Papers No. 69-5 (Oct. 1969), 1 BPC 411.

10. Albina Marine Iron Works v. U.S., 79 Ct. Cl. 714 (1934); Nogler Tree Farm, AGBCA 81-104-1, 81-2 BCA ¶ 15315, 23 GC ¶ 427.

11. E.g., Atlas Mfg. Co., ASBCA 15177, 71-2 BCA ¶ 9026.

12. E.g., George A. Fuller Co., ASBCA 9590 et al., 1964 BCA ¶ 4396, 6 GC ¶ 498.

13. E.g., Robert P. Jones Co., AGBCA 391, 76-1 BCA ¶ 11824.

14. Note 11, supra.

15. See Transit Warehouse Corp., ASBCA 16761, 72-2 BCA ¶ 9696.

16. E.g., Williamsburg Drapery Co., ASBCA 5484 et al., 61-2 BCA ¶ 3111, 3 GC ¶ 470, affd., 369 F.2d 729 (Ct. Cl. 1966).

17. Harris & Covington Hosiery Mill, Inc., ASBCA 260, 4 CCF ¶ 60806 (1949).

18. Horowitz v. U.S., 267 U.S. 458 (1925). See generally Latham, "Government Interference and Sovereign Acts," Briefing Papers No. 76-3 (June 1976), 4 BPC 31; Nash, "Postscript: The Sovereign Power of Congress to Abrogate Contract Terms," 7 Nash & Cibinic Rep. ¶ 45 (Aug. 1993).

19. Jones v. U.S., 1 Ct. Cl. 383 (1865).

20. Dyer & Dyer, Inc., ENGBCA 3429, 74-1 BCA ¶ 10636, 16 GC ¶ 326; J.B. McGrary Co. v. U.S., 114 Ct. Cl. 12 (1949); Northern Va. Electric Co., ASBCA 21446, 80-1 BCA ¶ 14239, 22 GC ¶ 39.

21. Zena Co., ASBCA 18239, 75-1 BCA ¶ 11024; Marcel Watch Corp., GSBCA 3558, 72-2 BCA ¶ 9651, 14 GC ¶ 441.

22. Southland Mfg. Corp., ASBCA 10519, 69-1 BCA ¶ 7714, 9 GC ¶ 311.

23. Port Arthur Towing Co., ASBCA 37516, 90-2 BCA ¶ 22857.

24. Sundswick Corp. v. U.S., 75 F. Supp. 221 (Ct. Cl.), cert. denied, 334 U.S. 827 (1948).

25. E.g., George T. Johnson v. U.S., 618 F.2d 751 (Ct. Cl. 1980).

26. Henry Spen & Co., ASBCA 16296, 74-2 BCA ¶ 10651.

27. See RHJ Corp., ASBCA 9922, 66-1 BCA ¶ 5361.

28. See, e.g., Patti Const. Co., ASBCA 8423, 1964 BCA ¶ 4225.

29. See, e.g., Remsel Industries, Inc., ASBCA ¶ 5899,61-1 BCA ¶ 2909, 3 GC ¶ 1195. See also Tree Best Reforestors, Inc., AGBCA 82-266-3, et al., 83-1 BCA ¶ 16290, 25 GC ¶ 213. See generally Ewing, Lawrence & Zenner, "First-Article Contracts," Briefing Papers No. 93-6 (May 1993).

30. Paul G. Maddox, ASBCA 11712, 67-2 BCA ¶ 6415.

31. See, e.g., Cryo-Sonics, Inc., ASBCA 11483, 66-2 BCA ¶ 5890.

32. See generally Crowell & Dees, "The Weather," Briefing Papers No. 65-4 (Aug. 1965), 1 BPC 129.

33. Albert J. Jansen, ASBCA 6245 et al., 60-2 BCA ¶ 2793, 3 GC ¶ 20(3).

34. Note 33, supra.

35. Note 11, supra.

36. Southwest Engrg. Co., DOTCAB 70-26, 71-1 BCA ¶ 8818. See also Federal Television Corp., ASBCA 9863, 1964 BCA ¶ 4392, 6 GC ¶ 423.

37. FAR 52.249-8, para. (d).

38. Free-Flow Packaging Corp., GSBCA 3992, 75-1 BCA ¶ 11105, 17 GC ¶ 197.

39. E.g., In re Boston Shipyard Corp., 886 F.2d 451 (1st Cir. 1989), 32 GC ¶ 71; Ace Electronics Assocs., Inc., ASBCA 13899, 69-2 BCA ¶ 7922.

40. Vereinigte Osterreichische Eisen und Stahlwerke Aktiengesellschaft, IBCA 327, 1962 BCA ¶ 3503, 4 GC ¶ 563(c).

41. Aargus Poly Bag, GSBCA 4314, 76-2 BCA ¶ 11927, 18 GC ¶ 394.

EQUITABLE ADJUSTMENT CLAIMS

13

A. Basic Rules Of Computation
   1. Added Work
   2. Deleted Work
   3. Overhead & Profit

B. Proving The Equitable Adjustment Amount
   1. Actual Cost Data
   2. "Total Cost" Method
   3. "Jury Verdict" Method

C. Claim Preparation Costs

D. Interest
   1. Interest On Claims
   2. Interest On Borrowings

E. Notice Of Claims

In 1969, the Court of Claims noted that "the meaning of 'equitable adjustment' has become, so to speak, a 'trade usage' for those engaged in contracting with the Federal Government."[1] This term is so well known because of its significance and importance in determining the measure of a contractor's recovery on a claim against the Government under the contract—typically under a contract's "Changes" clause for problems arising during performance (see Chapter 11), but under other contract clauses as well (see, for example, the discussions of the "Government Delay of Work" clause in Chapter 12 and the "Government Property" clause in Chapter 9). This chapter will review some of the basic rules that relate to negotiations and agreements concerning equitable adjustment claims,[2] emphasizing claims under the "Changes" clause.

A. BASIC RULES OF COMPUTATION

Although there are variations depending upon the type of contract, the typical "Changes" clause does not offer precise guidance regarding how an equitable adjustment allowed under the clause is to be computed. For example, the "Changes" clause set forth in the FAR for fixed-price supply contracts states that the following is to take place if a change occurs:[3]

> If any such change causes an increase or decrease in the cost of, or the time required for, performance of any part of the work under this contract, whether or not changed by the order, the Contracting Officer shall make an equitable adjustment in the contract price, the delivery schedule, or both, and shall modify the contract.

A basic rule of repricing changed work, however, is that the positions of both parties must be considered. That is, (1) the contractor must be "kept whole" when the Government modifies a contract, and (2) the Government's pricing position must be preserved in the portion of the work not affected by the change. To achieve these goals, one authority suggests that the adjustment process be broken down into three component parts.[4] First, the proper amount of costs attributable to *work added* by the change order must be ascertained. Second, deductions must be made for any costs directly attributable to *work deleted* by the change order. Third, *overhead and profit* increments must be applied to the costs directly attributable to the change. These steps will be discussed below. As an aid to understanding the computation of equitable adjustments, concrete examples illustrating the situations most commonly encountered are given in Figure 13-1 later in this chapter.

The question of who has the burden of proof in these matters was nicely summed up by the Claims Court when it stated:[5]

> The burden for establishing the amount of a total equitable adjustment is allocated to the party claiming the benefit of the adjustment.... In fulfilling this burden of proof, the party must establish both the reasonableness of the costs claimed and their causal connection to the event on which the claim is based.... As in other civil actions, the standard used to determine whether the burden has been met is the "preponderance of the evidence" test.

1. Added Work

When a contractor is able to prove that it is entitled to an equitable adjustment because of additional work, the new work is normally priced at its *reasonable cost* to the contractor. This general rule is subject to two considerations: (a) the timing of the pricing, and (b) determining what are the reasonable costs. (As noted in Chapter 5, Section A, the FAR cost principles typically apply to the pricing of equitable adjustments.)

Timing is important because most equitable adjustment negotiations are conducted *before* the costs are actually incurred. The general rule, consistently applied in these cases, is that *estimated costs* are a proper source of determining the reasonable amount of an adjustment if they constitute the most accurate information existing at the time of the pricing action.[6] If the pricing negotiations take place *after* some—or all—of the additional costs have already been incurred, the *actual cost* information that has been accumulated by the contractor may be used for determining the value of the new work performed. It has been stated that these actual or historical costs are the best measure of reasonable costs where the work has been performed.[7]

Actual costs may be used in testing what are "reasonable" costs for the additional work. These costs (as opposed to the "reasonable value" of the additional work to the Government) will be presumed to be the proper measure of recovery for the contractor. In connection with actual costs, the Court of Claims noted the following:[8]

> Equitable adjustments...are simply corrective measures utilized to keep a contractor whole when the Government modifies a contract. Since the purpose underlying such adjustments is to safeguard the contractor against increased costs engendered by the modification, it appears patent that the measure of damages cannot be the value received by the Government, but must be more closely related to and contingent upon the altered position in which the contractor finds himself by reason of the modification.

2. Deleted Work

When the Government deletes work from the contract—and the work has not yet been performed by the contractor—the Government is entitled to a *downward* adjustment in the contract price equal to the amount of cost the contractor *would have incurred* had the work been performed. Note that in attempting to fairly ascertain these costs, the basis used will, if possible, be cost information current at the time the change is ordered (as opposed to the contractor's original estimate of the cost of the deleted work).[9] Other measures may be used if appropriate. In one case, the sales price of certain deleted work rather than its fair market value was determined to be the proper measure of the adjustment.[10] Note also that, if the contractor is in a loss position because its original estimate was erroneously low, it will be forced to bear the loss that it would have borne had the change not been issued.[11]

The Government has the obligation of proving the amount of the deduction to which it is entitled in these situations. The rationale behind this requirement is one of fairness—as expressed by the Court of Claims, "[j]ust as the contractor has that task when an upward adjustment is sought under the Changes clause, so the [Government] has the laboring oar, and bears the risk of failure of proof, when a decrease is at issue."[12] This obligation can present problems to the Government since proof in this area is often fragmentary and difficult to ascertain.

3. Overhead & Profit

A contractor is entitled to overhead and profit as part of an equitable adjustment that increases the contract price. Similarly, the Government may reduce the overhead and profit on changes that decrease the contractor's costs.

a. Overhead. The normal rules governing contract costs (see Chapter 5) apply to determining how a contractor's overhead rate—and the types and amounts of costs included—will be determined. In normal accounting practice, indirect costs are charged as a percentage of direct costs reflecting the contractor's cost experience over a period of time. In many cases, therefore—especially where the change can be easily factored into the contractor's performance—a board or court may determine that the direct costs in an equitable adjustment bear the standard amount of overhead.[13] If the parties can demonstrate that a change (or series of changes) has caused an abnormal alteration in overhead, however, the boards and courts—when the contractor is working under a firm-fixed-price contract—have considerable flexibility in determining the proper overhead adjustment to be made.[14] In the case of significantly large changes, it is sometimes a better practice for the parties to negotiate a specific dollar amount that reflects the actual indirect cost impact.

b. Profit. Profit is also an integral part of the equitable adjustment. As the Armed Services Board of Contract Appeals (ASBCA) has noted, "[w]ithout the payment of a profit which is fair under the circumstances, the Government would be getting something for nothing and the contractor would not truly be made whole."[15] The type of work required to be performed under the change, as well as the risks involved in the changed work, must be considered in determining the amount of profit to which a contractor is entitled in the equitable adjustment. Frequently—particularly where the change has not had a significant cost impact—the parties may simply agree that the same profit percentage that applied to the original contract will apply to the change. However, if the changed work is more complex than the original work or entails a higher degree of risk, the profit factor may be increased accordingly.[16] The opposite result could also be warranted where the changed work is less demanding or risky.[17]

The FAR provides direction for a "structured" profit analysis method considering specific factors in computing the profit to which a contractor may be entitled[18]—called the "weighted guidelines" method in the Department of Defense FAR Supplement.[19] The FAR states that if a change involves a relatively small dollar amount and the same type and mix of work as the basic contract, the basic contract profit rate may be applied.[20]

Because an understanding of the computation of equitable adjustments can best be gained by examining concrete examples, Figure 13-1, set forth on the following pages, provides four illustrations of the situations most commonly encountered— three covering added work and one covering deleted work.[21]

B. PROVING THE EQUITABLE ADJUSTMENT AMOUNT

The contractor has the burden of proving the amount of an equitable adjustment for increased work (and the Government has the burden of proving the amount of a downward adjustment for decreased work). In the discussion in Section A, above, it was assumed that the costs expended (or deleted) as a result of the change were known. Under perfect conditions, the contractor would—through its internal accounting procedures—establish a *separate account* for the changed work and accumulate all costs attributable to the change order in an organized and precise manner. Unfortunately, particularly where a "constructive change" (see Chapter 11, Section F) causes additional work, costs are not always segregated in a manner that allows their easy computation. For this reason, the agency boards of contract appeals and the courts have set forth some basic principles as to the type of information that is acceptable to prove the amount of the equitable adjustment. The Claims Court commented on these methods as follows:[22]

EQUITABLE ADJUSTMENT CLAIMS 13-7

Figure 13-1

EQUITABLE ADJUSTMENT CALCULATIONS

Example 1: Substitution of Small Purchased Component

Factors

(a) Lump sum firm-fixed-price contract for 1,000 units

(b) Change substituting Component B for Component A (both purchased)

(c) Component A: Original estimate — $10.00 per unit
    Vendor price (firm purchase order) — $13.00 per unit

(d) Component B: Quotations from
    Vendor 1 — $ 7.50 per unit
    Vendor 2 — $ 8.50 per unit
    Vendor 3 — $11.00 per unit

(e) Vendor 1 found not responsible and disqualified

(f) Overhead rate for most recent period — 10%

(g) Profit rate used in pricing original contract — 8%

Pricing Technique

(a) [Added Work (Component B) - Deleted Work (Component A)] + Overhead + Profit

(b) [$8.50 - $13.00] + 10% + 8%

(c) - ($4.50 + .45 + .40) = -$5.35 per unit

(d) Total Adjustment: $5,350.00 Deduction

Explanation

Here the parties have available firm information on what the work would have cost if the change had not been issued (firm purchase order on Component A) and good pricing information on the new work (competitive quotations on Component B). Current overhead rates and the contract profit rate are acceptable for use in a relatively small change such as this.

Example 2: Substitution of Large Purchased Component

Factors

(a) Lump sum firm-fixed-price contract for 1,000 units

(b) Change substituting Component B for Component A (both purchased)

continued

Fig. 13-1 / continued

    (c) Component A: Original estimate $100.00 per unit
                                   Vendor price (firm
                                        purchase order) $ 90.00 per unit
                                    Vendor claims $27,420.00 from contractor, based on 70 completed units and costs incurred on balance of work of $12,000 plus 60% overhead and 10% profit

    (d) Component B: Vendor quotation $175.00 per unit
                                    Government estimate $140.00 per unit
                                    based on quotations to another contractor from Vendor 2 ($150.00 per unit) and Vendor 3 ($175.00 per unit) for quantities of 100 units and theory that a lower price should be obtainable for larger quantity involved in this contract

    (e) Overhead rate: For contractor's most recent
                                    period   10%
                                    Government auditor forecast
                                    for year in question   9%

    (f) Profit rate: Used in original contract   8%
                                    Government computation for
                                    purchased items   4%

Pricing Technique

    (a) [Added Work (Component B) - Deleted Work (Component A)] + Overhead + Profit

    (b) [$140.00 - ($90.00 - $27.42)] + 9% + 4%

    (c) $77.42 + $6.97 + $3.38 = $87.77 per unit

    (d) Total Adjustment: $87,770.00

Explanation

Here the parties have available firm information on (1) the amount the work would have cost had it not been changed (the firm purchase order on Component A) and (2) the vendor's termination claim. This allows a precise calculation of the amount to be deleted. They have a dispute over the amount to be added, but the contractor is in a weak position with only one quotation. The Government evidence of competitive quotations for the component is stronger and, in addition, the Government theory that some price reduction is justified for larger quantities is sound. The change is of large enough size to justify more detailed analysis of overhead and profit than in Example 1, and the Government figures indicate that such analysis has been made. The lower profit figure used by the Government is in accordance with the "weighted guidelines" theory that less profit is proper on purchased items.

continued

Fig. 13-1 / continued

Example 3: Substitution of Large In-House Assembly

Factors

(a) Lump sum firm-fixed-price contract for 1,000 units

(b) Change substituting Assembly B for Assembly A (both assembled in-house)

(c) Assembly A: Contractor's original estimate
    Labor 20 hrs. @ $4.25 $ 85.00
    Material $ 15.00
    Contractor's postchange estimate
    Labor 12 hrs. @ $4.10 $ 49.20
    Material (vendor prices) $ 17.70

(d) Assembly B: Contractor estimate
    Labor 40 hrs. @ $4.10 $164.00
    Material $ 36.00
    Government estimate
    Labor 30 hrs. @ $4.10 $123.00
    Material $ 32.00

(e) Overhead rate (applicable to labor only):
    Original estimate   90%
    Current estimate   100%

(f) Profit rate: Used in contract   11%
    Contractor proposal   15%

Pricing Technique

(a) [Added Work (labor & material for Component B) − Deleted Work (labor & material for Component A)] + Overhead + Profit

(b) [($143.50 (35 hrs. @ $4.10) + $34.00) − ($82.00 (20 hrs. @ $4.10) + $17.70)] + 100% of labor + 13% of total costs

(c) [$177.50 − $99.70] + 100% of ($143.50 − $82.00) + 13% of ($77.80 + $61.50)

(d) $77.80 + $61.50 + $18.11 = $157.41 per unit

(e) Total Adjustment: $157,410.00

Explanation

Here the adjustment must be based on estimates since there is little firm pricing information. With regard to Assembly A, the best estimate of the number of labor hours is the estimate made prior to the change (estimates made after a change is ordered tend to be suspect). The labor rate, however, should be based on the most current information and the $4.10 rate is the most current one. The material should also be based on current informa-

continued

Fig. 13-1 / continued

tion—in this case, on the existing purchase order prices. With regard to Assembly B, only the labor rate is based on actual data. Both the labor hours and material amount are based on estimates and the figure used is a compromise between the contractor and Government estimates. The most current overhead rate is the one that should be used and the contractor is entitled to a higher rate of profit than the contract rate on the grounds that the change affects an assembly where there is a higher than normal content of in-house work (the converse of the principle followed in Example 2).

Example 4: Substitution of Component Purchased at Second Tier

Factors

(a) Lump sum firm-fixed-price contract for 1,000 units

(b) Change substituting Component B for Component A (both purchased from second-tier subcontractor)

(c) Component A: Original estimate of contractor — $ 80.00
Purchase order price of contractor — $100.00
Original estimate of subcontractor — $120.00
Purchase order price of subcontractor — $ 90.00
Component B: Contractor's estimate — $170.00
Contractor's last three purchases
quantity 100 — $180.00
quantity 400 — $160.00
quantity 250 — $150.00

(d) Overhead rate projected for contract period — 6%

(e) Profit rate used in original contract — 6%

(f) Subcontractor overhead rate — 10%

(g) Subcontractor profit rate — 10%

Pricing Technique

(a) [Added Work (Component B) - Deleted Work (Component A)] + Overhead + Profit

(b) [$140.00 - ($90.00 + 10% + 10%)] + 6% + 6%

(c) $31.10 ($140.00 - $108.90) + $1.87 + $1.98 = $34.95 per unit

(d) Total Adjustment: $34,950.00

continued

EQUITABLE ADJUSTMENT CLAIMS 13-11

Fig. 13-1 / continued

Explanation

Here the parties have good purchasing history on the added part (Component B). This history indicates that prices are following a downward trend, and the substantially larger purchase on this contract would also indicate a lower price. A negotiated amount of $140.00 reflects this trend. The deleted part (Component A) is made by a second-tier subcontractor (a sub-sub). The contractor is entitled to negotiate an equitable adjustment for this component with the subcontractor pursuant to the *Changes* clause in the subcontract. This adjustment should be made at the amount the subcontractor would have paid the sub-sub (the subcontractor's purchase order price) plus the subcontractor's overhead and profit. Since this amount is the amount the contractor is entitled to receive from the subcontractor as a result of the change, it represents the actual amount saved by the contractor as a result of the change. It is therefore the proper amount to be used in computing the cost of the deleted component. The contractor's current overhead rate and contract profit rate are also applicable to this change and can be accepted because they are quite low. Note that this calculation is proper *only* if the change can be ordered under the *Changes* clause in the sub-sub contract. Hence, if Component B were bought from a *different* sub-sub, a different calculation would be used.

A contractor must prove its costs using the best evidence available under the circumstances. The preferred method is through the submission of actual cost data.... In maintaining cost data, a contractor should segregate costs associated with the change where it is feasible to do so, and especially where the contractor can anticipate submitting a large claim....

Where actual cost data is not available, estimates of the costs may be used. Such estimates should be prepared by competent individuals with adequate knowledge of the facts and circumstances. Estimates should also be supported with detailed substantiating data.... The expert testimony of individuals familiar with the facts is helpful in verifying the validity of estimates.

The three major methods for proving equitable adjustment claims are discussed below.

1. Actual Cost Data

The most desirable (and most exact) proof of the amount of an equitable adjustment is the actual cost data in the contractor's books and records. Actual costs are most likely to be available where (a) a formal change order has been issued, (b) the contractor initiated the accounting procedures necessary to identify all costs that directly relate to the change, and (c) the changed work has been completed. However, this method cannot always be used. For example, as noted above, where the change is "constructive" in nature, the contractor typically does not recognize the existence of the change until after a number—perhaps all—of the costs related to it have been incurred without being segregated by the contractor's accounting system. Moreover, even where contractors (particularly small businesses) recognize the existence of a change, their accounting systems may not permit them to separate the costs of the change from the costs incurred pursuant to regular performance under the contract. In these other situations, alternative methods of proving the equitable adjustment amount must be used.

2. "Total Cost" Method

The "total cost" basis of computing the amount of an equitable adjustment is used, with some reluctance, where no alternative method of computation is available. Under the total cost method, the total cost of the work performed is used as a base, and from it is subtracted the original estimate of the work the contractor made during the bidding or negotiation of the contract. The remainder represents the amount of the equitable adjustment (i.e., the amount attributable to the change). The validity of this method of adjustment is inherently suspect because it assumes that (1) all costs expended by the contractor in excess of the original estimate were caused by the change and not by other non-Government-related causes, and (2) the contractor's original estimate was correct and reasonable. For these reasons, the Court of Claims indicated that it would use the total cost basis only as a last resort[23] or would reject its use outright.[24]

The ASBCA has set forth a number of factors to be considered in determining if the total cost basis should be used in a particular instance involving contract changes.[25] These include examining whether (a) the contractor was experienced and competent, (b) the original contract price was reasonable and realistic, (c) actual incurred costs were significantly in excess of the contract price, (d) the contractor performed with a reasonable degree of efficiency and economy, and (e) the contractor's increased costs resulted from the changes. As a general rule, however, the use of the total cost method is only appropriate if there is no other method of proof available to the parties.[26]

Under some circumstances, a *modified* total cost method may be used to determine the proper amount of an equitable adjustment for a contract change. Under the modified method, the amounts that could be attributed to underbidding, contractor inefficiency, or unrelated contractor costs (i.e., costs not incurred because of the change) are excluded from the equitable adjustment, and whatever available evidence the contractor has of the specific costs incurred is examined. In all likelihood, an expert witness would be required in complex cases to estimate the amount of the costs for which the Government should be responsible.[27] The Court of Claims commented favorably on this computation method,[28] since—when properly used—it minimizes a number of dangers inherent in the total cost approach.

3. "Jury Verdict" Method

The third major method for computing the amount of an adjustment is popularly known as the "jury verdict" method. Under this method, after the board or court considers the evidence of the actual costs the contractor expended, the opinions of experts, and other evidence in the case—much as a jury does—the board or court determines the amount to which the contractor is entitled. The jury verdict method was first used by the Court of Claims in a case where the contractor's claimed costs could not be substantiated in detail by the contractor's records, and the court, as a result, was obligated to consider the testimony of expert witnesses in reaching what it termed a "jury verdict."[29] More recently, the Claims Court said the following about the jury verdict approach:[30]

> Where a court or a board of contract appeals sitting as the finder of fact is confronted with competent but conflicting evidence on what is a reasonable amount for an equitable adjustment, it may employ what is referred to as the "jury verdict approach." The court may adopt the jury verdict approach where, (1) there is clear proof that

the contractor was injured, (2) there is no more reliable method for computing damages, and (3) the evidence adduced is sufficient for the court to make a fair and reasonable approximation of the damages.

Although the jury verdict method attempts to consider the costs that directly relate to a change, it involves a considerable amount of subjectivity and speculation. For this reason, it is also not a preferred method for determining equitable adjustment amounts. However, it is recognized that the ascertainment of an equitable adjustment is not an exact science, and the ASBCA has noted that "all that is required is adequate evidence from which a fair and reasonable approximation of the dollar amount of adjustment can be made."[31] Thus, a total cost approach has been used as the basis for a jury verdict,[32] and a contractor has been allowed a jury verdict recovery based on the Government's cost estimate.[33] Nevertheless, the method will be used cautiously where there is a lack of concrete evidence of costs and estimating techniques on which to base a decision. This attitude is reflected by the fact that "jury verdict" equitable adjustments are generally not in the amount requested by the contractor but are for a significantly lower figure.[34] Note that in no event will the jury verdict method be used when there is a lack of some substantial evidence of the validity of the contractor's claim.[35]

C. CLAIM PREPARATION COSTS

Obviously, every equitable adjustment claim requires preparation. In some instances, this may amount to little more than a brief review of the cost records that relate to the changed work. In complicated cases, however, a significant amount of effort—on the part of the contractor's administrative staff as well as its attorneys, engineers, and other consultants—may be required to prepare and present a complete claim to the Contracting Officer. If the Contracting Officer denies the claim, the contractor will incur additional costs in litigating the claim before a board or court. Unfortunately, the answer to the question of when these claim preparation costs are recoverable from the Government is not clear.

The FAR cost principles state that the costs of attorney fees—and those of other experts—are *not* allowable when they are incurred in connection with the "prosecution of claims or appeals against the Federal Government" or in "[d]efense against Federal Government claims or appeals."[36] While it is clear that the cost of preparing a claim under the Contract Disputes Act (CDA) is not recoverable,[37] the issue is less clear in other, preliminary situations.

For instance, it was long considered that the prohibition against recovery of claim preparation costs did not apply to costs incurred in presenting a claim *before* the Contracting Officer reached his final decision.[38] This position was based on the logic that the Contracting Officer's decision offered an easily identifiable dividing line. That is, costs incurred *prior to* its issuance could be considered to have been incurred in the performance of the work—and hence were allowable. Costs incurred *after* issuance were considered costs of prosecuting a claim—and hence were unallowable. Through time this distinction has blurred.[39] However, in one decision by the ASBCA, the cost of an attorney's fee for preparation of an equitable adjustment proposal for an ordered change was allowable because (1) the contractor's claim was meritorious on its face, and (2) the controversy "never became so disputatious as to reach the level of a claim against the Government."[40] The Court of Claims later distinguished this case denying claim preparation costs (including an attorney's fee) where the claim related to a constructive change, the claim was presented after completion of all the work, and the costs bore no "beneficial nexus" to either contract administration or production.[41] The costs were therefore unallowable costs of prosecuting a claim against the Government.

Thus, if costs incurred in claim preparation are to be deemed allowable, (a) they must be related to an obviously meritorious claim—preferably a Government-ordered change where there is no doubt about contractor entitlement, and (b) the claim must be presented to the Contracting Officer prior to the completion of performance.[42]

In connection with claim preparation costs, it should be noted that the Equal Access to Justice Act (discussed more fully in Chapter 6, Section A.5) provides for the award of attorney fees and expenses to eligible individuals and small business firms who prevail in certain suits involving the Government, unless the Government can show that its position was "substantially justified."[43]

D. INTEREST

Another aspect of nearly all claims involving equitable adjustments—and one that has also been the subject of varied and somewhat inconsistent treatment—is the payment of interest.

1. Interest On Claims

If negotiations between the contractor and the Contracting Officer over the amount of the equitable adjustment fail, the contractor must process its claim under the "Disputes" clause of the contract, seeking a final decision of the Contracting Officer on the claim and then litigating any denied claim before a board of contract appeals or Court of Federal Claims. Under the CDA, if the contractor is successful, it is entitled to interest on the claim from the date a proper claim is submitted to the Contracting Officer until payment pursuant to order of a court or board.[44] Even if the Contracting Officer agrees—after receipt of a claim conforming to the requirements of the Act—that all or part of the claimed amount is payable, the contractor is entitled to interest. For example, in one case where a Contracting Officer allowed part of a claim but denied part, and the contractor appealed the denied portion of its claim to the ASBCA, the board held that the contractor was entitled to interest on both the disputed and *undisputed* portions.[45]

Interest accrues under the CDA even if the claim is finally settled by the Contracting Officer, with the result that no final decision is ever issued.[46] However, if interest is not mentioned in the settlement negotiations or agreement, the contractor may be considered to have *waived* or *abandoned* its interest claim.[47] Moreover, because the CDA provides that interest begins to accrue on the date of receipt of the claim by the Contracting Officer, interest will be paid from that date without regard to the fact that some of the costs may be incurred later.[48]

Interest under the CDA is simple interest that accrues at a variable rate specified by the Secretary of the Treasury for each six-month period during which the claim was pending.[49]

2. Interest On Borrowings

Contractors have argued—with some logic—that their extra costs that result from a Government change to the contract or some other action must be financed either through borrowings, through the use of equity capital, or through a combination of the two. Therefore, they should be permitted to recover interest paid to finance changed work. The FAR cost principles, however, specifically disallow the recovery of interest on borrowings (however represented).[50]

E. NOTICE OF CLAIMS

A contractor has an obligation, under all versions of the standard "Changes" clause, to notify the Contracting Officer of any changes claim. Specifically, the contractor must "assert its right to an adjustment" within 30 days of the receipt of a change order.[51] In addition, the construction contract "Changes" clause implicitly requires notice of constructive changes.[52] The "Changes" clause notice requirements have never been strictly enforced, however, and may be waived in appropriate circumstances.[53]

Notice of a claim by the Government for a downward equitable adjustment in the contract price is not governed by any "Changes" clause language, but such claims may be considered untimely if not asserted within a "reasonable" time.[54] In addition, there is a six-year statute of limitations governing all Government claims against contractors, unless the Government claim is asserted for defensive purposes.[55]

REFERENCES

1. General Builders Supply Co. v. U.S., 409 F.2d 246 (Ct. Cl. 1969), 11 GC ¶ 160.

13-18 GOVERNMENT CONTRACT GUIDEBOOK

2. See generally Witte, "Principles of Equitable Adjustment," Briefing Papers No. 71-2 (Apr. 1971), 2 BPC 95.

3. FAR 52.243-1, para. (b).

4. Nash, Government Contract Changes, ch. 16 (Federal Publications Inc., 2d ed. 1989 & Supp.).

5. Delco Electronics Corp. v. U.S., 17 Cl. Ct. 302 (1989), 8 FPD ¶ 85, 32 GC ¶ 284 (Note), 33 GC ¶ 22 (Note).

6. See, e.g., Ensign-Bickford Co., ASBCA 6214, 60-2 BCA ¶ 2817, 3 GC ¶ 333.

7. Bruce Const. Corp. v. U.S., 342 F.2d 516 (Ct. Cl. 1963), 5 GC ¶ 554.

8. Note 7, supra. See also Montoya Const. Co., ASBCA 34691, 89-1 BCA ¶ 21575.

9. Bruce Anderson Co., ASBCA 29412, 89-2 BCA ¶ 21872. See also Plaza Maya Ltd. Partnership, GSBCA 9086, 91-1 BCA ¶ 23425.

10. JEM Development Corp., DOTBCA 1961, 88-3 BCA ¶ 21022, 30 GC ¶ 333.

11. Nielson Co. v. U.S., 141 Ct. Cl. 793 (1958).

12. Nager Electric Co. v. U.S., 442 F.2d 936 (Ct. Cl. 1971), 13 GC ¶ 211.

13. E.g., Kenmore Garment Co., ASBCA 14142, 71-1 BCA ¶ 8768, 13 GC ¶ 339.

14. E.g., Lionsgate Corp., ENGBCA 5425, 90-2 BCA ¶ 22730.

15. New York Shipbldg. Co., ASBCA 16164, 76-2 BCA ¶ 11979.

16. American Pipe & Steel Corp., ASBCA 7899, 1964 BCA ¶ 4058.

17. Varo, Inc., ASBCA 15000, 72-2 BCA ¶ 9719, 15 GC ¶ 80.

18. FAR 15.902, 15.905.

19. DFARS 215.971.

20. FAR 15.903(f).

21. Note 4, supra, at Figure 16-1.

22. Note 5, supra. See also Brasfield & Gorrie, Inc., GSBCA 8605, 89-2 BCA ¶ 21673.

23. Oliver-Finnie Co. v. U.S., 279 F.2d 498 (Ct. Cl. 1960), 2 GC ¶ 342.

24. McGraw & Co. v. U.S., 131 Ct. Cl. 501 (1955).

EQUITABLE ADJUSTMENT CLAIMS 13-19

25. Tenney Engrg., Inc., ASBCA 7352, 1962 BCA ¶ 3471, 5 GC ¶ 42. See also Claude Wood Co., AGBCA 83-106-3, 83-1 BCA ¶ 16543. Compare Hewitt Contracting, ENGBCA 4596, 83-2 BCA ¶ 16816.

26. E.g., J.D. Hedin Const. Co. v. U.S., 347 F.2d 235 (Ct. Cl. 1965), 7 GC ¶ 329; WRB Corp. v. U.S., 183 Ct. Cl. 409 (1968), 10 GC ¶ 183.

27. E.g., Servidone Const. Corp. v. U.S., 931 F.2d 860 (Fed. Cir. 1991), 10 FPD ¶ 48 33 GC ¶ 149, affg., 19 Cl. Ct. 346 (1990), 9 FPD ¶ 12, 32 GC ¶¶ 143 (Note), 284 (Note).

28. Boyajian v. U.S., 423 F.2d 1231 (Ct. Cl. 1970), 12 GC ¶ 173. See also Parsons of Cal., ASBCA 20867, 82-1 BCA ¶ 15659.

29. Western Contracting Corp. v. U.S., 144 Ct. Cl. 318 (1958), 1 GC ¶ 20.

30. Note 5, supra. Compare Dawco Const., Inc. v. U.S. 930 F.2d 872 (Fed. Cir. 1991), 10 FPD ¶ 40 (indicating that use of jury verdict method is inappropriate unless contractor can prove that it could not have accumulated actual cost data on the changed work), 33 GC ¶ 136.

31. Henry Products Co., ASBCA 16128, 73-2 BCA ¶ 10348.

32. E.W. Eldridge, Inc., ENGBCA 5268, 90-3 BCA ¶ 23080, 32 GC ¶ 284.

33. Freeman General, Inc. v. U.S., 918 F.2d 188 (Fed. Cir. 1990), 9 FPD ¶ 154, 32 GC ¶ 365.

34. E.g., Environmental Protection Inspection & Consulting, Inc., ASBCA 41264, 91-1 BCA ¶ 23637.

35. S.W Electronics & Mfg. Corp., ASBCA 20698, 77-2 BCA ¶ 12631, 20 GC ¶ 27.

36. FAR 31.205-33(d), 31.205-47(f).

37. E.g., Coastal Dry Dock & Repair Corp., ASBCA 36754, 91-1 BCA ¶ 23324.

38. Lake Union Drydock Co., ASBCA 3073, 59-1 BCA ¶ 2229.

39. Power Eqpt. Corp., ASBCA 5904, 1964 BCA ¶ 4025, 6 GC ¶ 79; Baifield Industries, ASBCA 18057, 77-1 BCA ¶ 12348.

40. Allied Materials & Eqpt. Co., ASBCA 17318, 75-1 BCA ¶ 11150.

41. Singer Co., Librascope Div. v. U.S., 568 F.2d 695 (Ct. Cl. 1977), 20 GC ¶ 21.

42. See, e.g., Bill Strong Enterprises, Inc. ASBCA 42946 et al., 93-3 BCA ¶ 25961, 35 GC ¶ 540, appeal docketed, No. 94-1013 (Fed. Cir., Oct. 13, 1993).

43. 5 USC § 504(a)(1); 28 USC § 2412(d).

44. 41 USC § 611.

45. Oxwell, Inc., ASBCA 25703, 81-2 BCA ¶ 15392.

46. E.g., Brookfield Const. Co. v. U.S., 661 F.2d 159 (Ct. Cl. 1981), 23 GC ¶ 390.

47. E.g., River City Contractors, DOTBCA 2073, 91-1 BCA ¶ 23531, 33 GC ¶ 120; Mann Const. Co., IBCA 1280-7-79, 82-1 BCA ¶ 15481.

48. Servidone Const. Corp. v. U.S., 10 FPD ¶ 48 (Fed. Cir. 1991), 33 GC ¶ 149, affg., 19 Cl. Ct. 346 (1990), 9 FPD ¶ 12, 32 GC ¶¶ 143 (Note), 284 (Note).

49. Note 44, supra; J.F. Shea Co. v. U.S., 754 F.2d 338 (Fed. Cir. 1985), 3 FPD ¶ 104.

50. FAR 31.205-20. E.g., Tomahawk Const. Co., ASBCA 45071, 94-1 BCA ¶ 26312 (1993).

51. See, e.g., FAR 52.243-1, para. (c) and FAR 52.243-4, para. (e).

52. FAR 52.243-4, paras. (b), (d).

53. E.g., Chimera Corp., ASBCA 18690, 76-1 BCA ¶ 11901, 18 GC ¶ 325; Max Blau & Sons, Inc., GSBCA 9827, 91-1 BCA ¶ 23626; Imbus Roofing Co., GSBCA 10430, 91-2 BCA ¶ 23820.

54. E.g., Roberts v. U.S., 357 F.2d 938 (Ct. Cl. 1966), 8 GC ¶ 154; Lindwall Const. Co., ASBCA 23148, 79-1 BCA ¶ 13822, 21 GC ¶ 198.

55. 28 USC § 2415; 41 USC § 605(a).

INSPECTION AND WARRANTY

14

A. Government Inspection Rights
1. Regulations
2. Standard Contract Clauses

B. Inspection Procedures
1. Contractor Inspection
2. Time Of Inspection
3. Place Of Inspection
4. Costs Of Inspection
5. Manner Of Inspection

C. Rejection & Correction
1. Rejection Notice
2. Contractor Correction

D. Acceptance
1. Effect
2. Method Of Acceptance
3. Government's Postacceptance Rights

E. Warranties
1. Express Warranties
2. Implied Warranties

The Government—like any buyer—is entitled to receive what it bargains for when it makes a purchase under a contract. A major mechanism for ensuring that this occurs is through quality assurance measures—*inspection* and *warranty* provisions that are included in Government contracts.[1] With regard to inspection, this chapter discusses (a) the Government's *inspection rights* under the regulations and contract clauses dealing with inspection, (b) inspection *procedures*, (c) Government *rejection* and contractor *correction* of defective work, and (d) the effect, methods, and limits on the Government's final *acceptance* of the contract work. In addition, this chapter briefly examines *warranty* coverage under Government contracts.

A. GOVERNMENT INSPECTION RIGHTS

1. Regulations

In a part titled "Quality Assurance,"[2] the FAR provides specific guidance with respect to the inspection of contractor supplies and services. The FAR indicates that inspection is the primary means of assuring quality and that the intensity of the inspection process may vary considerably depending on the contractor involved in the procurement and the nature of the supplies being procured.[3] Once the Government accepts contract items its rights are limited, so careful inspection during contract performance or before acceptance is critical.

While the Government retains the ultimate right to determine the type and extent of quality assurance, the FAR demonstrates a policy of relying on contractors—as opposed to the Government—for the inspection of the contract work. The FAR also establishes standard inspection requirements in contract clauses as a means of assuring quality.[4] Moreover, it recognizes that "higher-level" contract quality requirements apply to contracts for complex and critical items or when necessitated by technical requirements of the contract.[5]

2. Standard Contract Clauses

The standard FAR "Inspection" clauses set forth the basic rules and procedures for quality assurance, acceptance of the contract work by the Government, and the parties' rights and obligations regarding inspection. Separate clauses are prescribed in the FAR for different categories of contracts.[6] Because it is the most commonly used of the various "Inspection" clauses, the "Inspection of Supplies—Fixed-Price" clause[7] is set forth in Figure 14-1.

Figure 14-1

"INSPECTION OF SUPPLIES–FIXED-PRICE" CLAUSE
(FAR 52.246-2)

(a) Definition. "Supplies," as used in this clause, includes but is not limited to raw materials, components, intermediate assemblies, end products, and lots of supplies.

(b) The Contractor shall provide and maintain an inspection system acceptable to the Government covering supplies under this contract and shall tender to the Government for acceptance only supplies that have been inspected in accordance with the inspection system and have been found by the Contractor to be in conformity with contract requirements. As part of the system, the Contractor shall prepare records evidencing all inspections made under the system and the outcome. These records shall be kept complete and made available to the Government during contract performance and for as long afterwards as the contract requires. The Government may perform reviews and evaluations as reasonably necessary to ascertain compliance with this paragraph. These reviews and evaluations shall be conducted in a manner that will not unduly delay the contract work. The right of review, whether exercised or not, does not relieve the Contractor of the obligations under the contract.

(c) The Government has the right to inspect and test all supplies called for by the contract, to the extent practicable, at all places and times, including the period of manufacture, and in any event before acceptance. The Government shall perform inspections and tests in a manner that will not unduly delay the work. The Government assumes no contractual obligation to perform any inspection and test for the benefit of the Contractor unless specifically set forth elsewhere in this contract.

continued

Fig. 14-1 / continued

(d) If the Government performs inspection or test on the premises of the Contractor or a subcontractor, the Contractor shall furnish, and shall require subcontractors to furnish, without additional charge, all reasonable facilities and assistance for the safe and convenient performance of these duties. Except as otherwise provided in the contract, the Government shall bear the expense of Government inspections or tests made at other than the Contractor's or subcontractor's premises; *provided*, that in case of rejection, the Government shall not be liable for any reduction in the value of inspection or test samples.

(e) (1) When supplies are not ready at the time specified by the Contractor for inspection or test, the Contracting Officer may charge to the Contractor the additional cost of inspection or test.
(2) The Contracting Officer may also charge the Contractor for any additional cost of inspection or test when prior rejection makes reinspection or retest necessary.

(f) The Government has the right either to reject or to require correction of nonconforming supplies. Supplies are nonconforming when they are defective in material or workmanship or are otherwise not in conformity with contract requirements. The Government may reject nonconforming supplies with or without disposition instructions.

(g) The Contractor shall remove supplies rejected or required to be corrected. However, the Contracting Officer may require or permit correction in place, promptly after notice, by and at the expense of the Contractor. The Contractor shall not tender for acceptance corrected or rejected supplies without disclosing the former rejection or requirement for correction, and, when required, shall disclose the corrective action taken.

(h) If the Contractor fails to promptly remove, replace, or correct rejected supplies that are required to be removed or to be replaced or corrected, the Government may either (1) by contract or otherwise, remove, replace, or correct the supplies and charge the cost to the Contractor or (2) terminate the contract for default. Unless the Contractor corrects or replaces the supplies within the delivery schedule, the Contracting Officer may require their delivery and make an equitable price reduction. Failure to agree to a price reduction shall be a dispute.

(i)(1) If this contract provides for the performance of Government quality assurance at source, and if requested by the Government, the Contractor shall furnish advance notification of the time (i) when Contractor inspection or tests will be performed in accor-

continued

Fig. 14-1 / continued

dance with the terms and conditions of the contract and (ii) when the supplies will be ready for Government inspection.

(2) The Government request shall specify the period and method of the advance notification and the Government representative to whom it shall be furnished. Requests shall not require more than 2 workdays of advance notification if the Government representative is in residence in the Contractor's plant, nor more than 7 workdays in other instances.

(j) The Government shall accept or reject supplies as promptly as practicable after delivery, unless otherwise provided in the contract. Government failure to inspect and accept or reject the supplies shall not relieve the Contractor from responsibility, nor impose liability on the Government, for nonconforming supplies.

(k) Inspections and tests by the Government do not relieve the Contractor of responsibility for defects or other failures to meet contract requirements discovered before acceptance. Acceptance shall be conclusive, except for latent defects, fraud, gross mistakes amounting to fraud, or as otherwise provided in the contract.

(l) If acceptance is not conclusive for any of the reasons in paragraph (k) hereof, the Government, in addition to any other rights and remedies provided by law, or under other provisions of this contract, shall have the right to require the Contractor (1) at no increase in contract price, to correct or replace the defective or nonconforming supplies at the original point of delivery or at the Contractor's plant at the Contracting Officer's election, and in accordance with a reasonable delivery schedule as may be agreed upon between the Contractor and the Contracting Officer; *provided*, that the Contracting Officer may require a reduction in contract price if the Contractor fails to meet such delivery schedule, or (2) within a reasonable time after receipt by the Contractor of notice of defects or nonconformance, to repay such portion of the contract as is equitable under the circumstances if the Contracting Officer elects not to require correction or replacement. When supplies are returned to the Contractor, the Contractor shall bear the transportation cost from the original point of delivery to the Contractor's plant and return to the original point when that point is not the Contractor's plant. If the Contractor fails to perform or act as required in (1) or (2) above and does not cure such failure within a period of 10 days (or such longer period as the Contracting Officer may authorize in writing) after receipt of notice from the Contracting Officer specifying such failure, the Government shall have the right by contract or otherwise to replace or correct such supplies and charge to the Contractor the cost occasioned the Government thereby.

The "Inspection of Supplies—Fixed-Price" clause set forth in Figure 14-1 contains the following four important elements: (1) a requirement that the contractor provide and maintain an *inspection system* acceptable to the Government, (2) a reservation of the Government's right to *inspect* the contractor's work during the *course of contract performance or before acceptance*, (3) a reservation of the Government's right to require the contractor to *correct or replace* nonconforming work or to *reduce* the contract price to reflect the decreased value of the nonconforming work, and (4) a reservation of the Government's right to correct or replace nonconforming work at the *contractor's expense* or to *default terminate* the contract if the contractor fails to correct the work as directed. This clause, which contains provisions similar to those found in all of the various "Inspection" clauses, provides the framework for the discussion in this chapter.

B. INSPECTION PROCEDURES

1. Contractor Inspection

Paragraph (b) of the "Inspection of Supplies—Fixed-Price" clause requires the contractor to "provide and maintain an inspection system acceptable to the Government." This contract requirement is supplemented by a FAR provision that emphasizes that the contractor retains the principal obligation for product quality and must (a) control the quality of the supplies tendered, (b) offer to the Government only supplies that conform to the contract specifications, (c) ensure that its suppliers and subcontractors have adequate quality control systems, and (d) in some instances maintain substantiating evidence of conformance.[8] Paragraph (b) of the clause specifically requires the contractor to "prepare records evidencing all inspections made under the system and the outcome." And it further directs that such records must be "kept complete and made available to the Government during contract performance and for as long afterwards as the contract requires."

The FAR sets forth three levels of inspection: (1) inspection only by the contractor, (2) standard inspection (as prescribed by the standard "Inspection" clauses), and (3) higher-level quality inspection.[9] The level of inspection that applies depends on the extent of quality assurance needed by the Government for the acquisition involved. For example, the Government relies on inspection only by the contractor when purchasing commercial, noncritical items. Higher-level quality inspection requirements (which are imposed through a special contract clause, the "Higher-Level Contract Quality Requirement (Government Specification)" clause[10]) typically apply to complex and critical items and require the contractor to comply with a Government-specified inspection or quality control system.

2. Time Of Inspection

Under Paragraph (c) of the Figure 14-1 clause, the Government reserves the right to inspect and test the contract supplies "at all places and times, including the period of manufacture, and in any event before acceptance." This gives the Government flexibility in terms of when it may conduct inspections, but its discretion in this regard is not unlimited. The clause also states that the Government "shall perform inspections and tests in a manner that will not unduly delay the work." Note that not all delay is unreasonable—some delay should properly be anticipated by a contractor in any system of inspection.[11] Moreover, if the contractor is already experiencing production difficulties at the time the Government inspection is conducted, the contractor cannot place the blame for its delay on the Government's inspection procedures.[12] However, if the Government unreasonably delays the contract work, the contractor may be entitled to an extension of time in the contract schedule (excusable delay) and the recovery of delay costs (see Chapter 12).[13]

Although the clause contemplates that inspection by the Government shall generally take place prior to acceptance, the FAR contains a provision under which a "Certificate of Conformance" (providing contractor certification that the supplies comply with the contract's requirements) may be used as the sole basis for the Government acceptance when (1) small losses would be incurred in the event of a defect, or (2) the contractor's reputation or past performance provides assurance that the supplies or services will be acceptable and any defective work would be corrected without contest.[14] However, even where this procedure is followed, the Government still retains its right to conduct inspections if it wishes to do so.[15]

3. Place Of Inspection

The Figure 14-1 clause states simply, in Paragraph (c), that Government inspection may be conducted "at all places." The FAR is more specific in that it requires each contract to designate the place or places where the Government reserves the right to perform the inspections it considers necessary to determine that the supplies conform to the contract requirements.[16] It further requires that inspection be performed "at source" where (a) inspection at any other place would necessitate uneconomical disassembly or destructive testing, (b) considerable loss would result from the manufacture and shipment of unacceptable supplies or delay in making corrections, (c) special required instruments, gauges, or facilities are available only at source, (d) performance at any other place would destroy or require replacement of costly packing and packaging, (e) a higher-level contract quality requirement is included in the contract, (f) Government inspection *during* contract performance is essential, (g) the supplies are destined for overseas shipment, or (h) it is determined for other reasons to be in the Government's interest.[17] "At source" inspections may occur at a subcontractor's facility.[18] Conversely, inspection "at destination" is usually appropriate for off-the-shelf commercial items or when necessary testing equipment is only available at the Government destination.[19]

4. Costs Of Inspection

Paragraph (d) of the "Inspection of Supplies—Fixed-Price" clause set out in Figure 14-1 requires—if the Government inspects on the premises of the contractor or a subcontractor—that "the Contractor shall furnish...without additional charge, all reasonable facilities and assistance for the safe and convenient performance of these duties." Conversely, if inspection is conducted at a point other than the premises of the contractor or a subcontractor, "the Government shall bear the expense." A contractor would be entitled to reimbursement (regardless of where inspection was conducted) if it incurred additional costs in furnishing the Government with *special* inspection equipment.[20]

5. Manner Of Inspection

As noted above in Section B.2, the Government must conduct its inspections to avoid undue delay in the contract work. There are other limitations on the Government's inspection rights. The Government may not exercise its inspection rights in a way that interferes with the contractor's performance—for example, by excessive supervision or numbers of inspectors[21] or by interrupting the contractor's employees' ability to accomplish their tasks.[22] Similarly, inspection and test procedures used by the Government must be consistent with the contract specifications.[23] It is improper, for example, for the Government to use an unspecified test that does not reasonably measure contract compliance[24] or to use a test that increases the level of performance.[25]

C. REJECTION & CORRECTION

As noted in Chapter 8, the Government has the right to insist on strict compliance with its specifications and may reject work that does not so comply. Paragraph (f) of the "Inspection of Supplies—Fixed-Price" clause (see Figure 14-1) provides the Government with alternative remedies in the event that supplies are found to be defective. The Government may either (1) *reject* the nonconforming contract items or (2) direct the contractor to *correct* the defect. Nonconforming supplies under the clause are supplies that "are defective in material or workmanship" or otherwise do not conform to the contract's requirements. The FAR directs Contracting Officers to reject supplies (or services) when the nonconformance "adversely affects safety, health, reliability, durability, performance, interchangeability of parts or assemblies, weight or appearance (where a consideration), or any other basic objective of the specification."[26] Otherwise, and if it can be accomplished within the delivery schedule, the Contracting Officer "ordinarily" should give the contractor "an opportunity to correct or replace" the nonconforming items.[27]

1. Rejection Notice

a. Timing. Notice of rejection must be given to a contractor "promptly."[28] If timely notice is not furnished, acceptance may be implied as a matter of law.[29] Thus, in one case it was held that the Government had—by implication—accepted almost 3,000 dozen eggs when it retained them for more than two months after inspection without communication of rejection to the contractor.[30] In a second case, a five-month delay was deemed unreasonable (and hence the equivalent of acceptance) where the Government knew of a defect shortly after the item's receipt, and its failure promptly to reject prejudiced the contractor.[31] Also, in another case, a five-day delay was judged unreasonable in light of the perishable nature of the contract item—shrimp.[32] On the other hand, lengthy delays in notice may be reasonable where the delay was necessary and there was no prejudice to the contractor.[33]

b. Form. The FAR does not set forth any specific format for a notice of rejection, except to require that the notice include the reasons for rejection.[34] Nor is it necessary for the notice to be in writing unless (a) rejection has occurred at a point other than the contractor's plant, (b) the contractor continues to offer nonconforming supplies or services, or (c) performance is inexcusably overdue.[35]

Although the rejection notice may state the nature of the defect in general terms,[36] the notice should (1) fairly apprise the contractor of the defect, (2) repel any inference of Government waiver of the defect, and (3) assert—at least by implication—that there has been a violation of the Government's rights.[37] The notice of rejection may be found improper if the Government does not inform the contractor of the defects that caused the rejection and there is time remaining in the contract delivery schedule to correct the defects.[38]

2. Contractor Correction

As noted above, if the Contracting Officer elects reject the tender, the contractor must be given an opportunity to correct the defects if that can be accomplished within the contract delivery schedule.[39] Conversely, where it is evident that the corrections could not be properly made within the contract period, the Government is under no such obligation.[40] If the Contracting Officer orders correction instead of issuing a rejection notice, however, the contractor is entitled to a reasonable time within which to make the correction without regard to the original delivery schedule.[41] In any event, if (a) the defects are relatively minor and can be corrected within a reasonable time, (b) the contractor reasonably believed that the supplies would be accepted, and (c) they were delivered *prior to* the contract delivery date, the contractor must be given a reasonable period of time *beyond* the delivery date to make such corrections.[42]

Under Paragraph (h), if the contractor fails "promptly" to correct or replace rejected work, the Government may either (1) remove, replace, or correct the rejected supplies at the *contractor's expense*, (2) *terminate* the contract for default and *reprocure* the supplies at the contractor's expense pursuant to its rights under the contract's "Default" clause (see Chapter 16), or (3) *retain* the nonconforming items and *reduce* the contract price based on the difference in value between the work as delivered and the work contemplated by the contract.[43]

D. ACCEPTANCE

Depending on the terms of the particular contract, acceptance of contractor supplies may occur prior to, at the time of, or after delivery. Where acceptance is accomplished at a point other than destination, the supplies cannot be reinspected at destination for acceptance purposes but may be examined at destination for quantity, damage in transit, and possible substitution or fraud.[44]

1. Effect

Paragraph (k) of the "Inspection of Supplies—Fixed-Price" clause set out in Figure 14-1 expressly provides that acceptance of the contract work by the Government is *conclusive*, "except for latent defects, fraud, gross mistakes amounting to fraud, or as otherwise provided in the contract." Thus, in the absence of one of the exceptions (which are discussed below in Section D.3), the Government is bound by its acceptance whether it was made with actual knowledge of the defects in the supplies[45] or without such knowledge.[46]

Acceptance of the supplies by the Government is an acknowledgment that the tendered items conform to the contract quality and quantity requirements.[47] Acceptance is important because it (a) limits the Government's rights against the contractor with respect to patent (obvious) defects in the work, (b) entitles the contractor to payment of the contract price, (c) usually transfers the risk of loss of the work from the contractor to the Government, and (d) starts the running of any warranty period.

Although the Government always has the initial right to insist upon strict compliance with contract requirements, the FAR permits it to accept nonconforming supplies if there are "circumstances (e.g., reasons of economy or urgency) when acceptance...is...in the Government's best interest."[48] If this is done, the contract (except in the case of extremely minor defects) must be modified to provide for an equitable price reduction or other consideration.[49]

2. Method Of Acceptance

The method of acceptance is not specified in the "Inspection" clause. Acceptance can be either *formal* or *implied*. Government agencies typically prescribe the use of standard forms to document formal acceptance by the agency. Acceptance can also be implied, however. One form of implied acceptance—late rejection—was discussed above in Section C.1.

Implied acceptance may also occur where the Government does any act inconsistent with the contractor's continued ownership of the supplies. This most frequently occurs through the Government's *retention* or *use* of the goods. For instance, in one case, the Government was found to have impliedly accepted a boiler where, among other things, it operated the boiler for its own purposes for over 80 days, selected the employees to operate the boiler, and controlled when the boiler would be operated.[50] Implied acceptance has also been found where the Government lost the items delivered to it,[51] altered the nature of the supplies,[52] and merely used the items without altering their

INSPECTION AND WARRANTY 14-13

nature.[53] The contractor must usually show implied acceptance by the totality of the circumstances rather than just one event.[54]

3. Government's Postacceptance Rights

As stated in Section D.1 above, the Government's acceptance of contractor supplies is final unless one of the four following circumstances is present: (1) the particular defect was *latent*, (2) *fraud* was involved, (3) there were *gross mistakes* amounting to fraud, or (4) a *contract term* specifically provides otherwise. The presence of one of these circumstances gives the Government broad postacceptance rights, including the right to retract acceptance.

a. Latent Defects. A "latent" defect is one that existed at the time of acceptance and "could not be discovered by ordinary and reasonable care or by a reasonable inspection."[55] A defect that can be readily discovered by an ordinary examination or test is patent, not latent, and a failure to conduct the examination or test properly does not make the defect latent.[56] Similarly, if the Government *knows* of the defects at the time of acceptance—even if the defects might not have been discovered by a reasonable inspection—the defects are not latent.[57]

It is the Government's obligation to prove that the defect was latent, and this is a heavy burden. The Government must demonstrate (a) that the defect was in existence at the time of delivery, (b) what kind of examination or test would have revealed the defect, and (c) whether the Government could reasonably be expected to use that type of inspection.[58] Thus, dimensional defects, readily discoverable by measurements, were determined not to be latent,[59] and the lack of specified hardness of a grinding wheel was held not latent since a simple test would have revealed the hardness.[60] On the other hand, 16 undersized bolts holding a derrick, which could have been discovered by turning the bolts with a special tool, were deemed to constitute a latent defect where there were 11,967 bolts in the structure.[61]

Unless the contract provides otherwise, the contractor is liable for latent defects discovered at any time after final acceptance—even after expiration of a separate warranty period.[62] However, if the Government continues to use contract items after it discovers—or should have discovered—a latent defect, it may be held to have impliedly reaccepted those items.[63]

b. Fraud & Gross Mistakes. The Government may also revoke acceptance if the contractor, with the *intent* to deceive the Government, makes a statement or representation it knows to be untrue, and the Government accepts the contract items in reliance on that misstatement or misrepresentation.[64] In addition to revoking its acceptance of the contractor's supplies, such fraud on the part of the contractor would entitle the Government to prosecute the contractor under the civil or criminal fraud statutes (see Chapter 7).[65]

"Gross mistakes amounting to fraud" is similar to fraud except that the Government does not have to prove that the contractor had a specific intent to deceive.[66] It has been described as "a mistake so serious or uncalled for as not to be reasonably expected, or justifiable, in the case of a responsible contractor for the items concerned."[67] This concept has been applied somewhat more frequently to revoke acceptance than has the fraud theory. For example, it has been used where a contractor failed to tell the Contracting Officer and a Government inspector of a change in material in a previously approved component,[68] and in a case where a contractor incorrectly certified that certain contract items were identical to ones previously tested and approved by the Government.[69] However, gross mistake was not found in a case where the contractor failed to conform precisely to the specifications but did not suspect that the change would have any adverse effect on the product being furnished to the Government.[70]

c. Other Contract Terms. The last exception to the finality of Government acceptance is if the contract separately provides that the contractor will be liable for any defects discovered after acceptance. A "Certificate of Conformance" clause[71] or a "Warranty" clause, for example, usually extend the contractor's liability for defects beyond acceptance. In one case where the standard "Inspection" clause was supplemented by a special clause that stated that final acceptance of the work would not be binding or conclusive if the contractor "has otherwise departed from the terms of the contract," it was held that the contractor's failure to provide a particular hoist was such a departure and that the Contracting Officer could order its correction after accepting the item.[72]

E. WARRANTIES

Warranties—another means of assuring the quality of contract performance—can, under some circumstances, increase the *scope* and the *duration* of a contractor's liability for the goods it provides the Government.[73] The FAR defines a "warranty" as "a promise or affirmation given by a contractor to the Government regarding the nature, usefulness, or condition of the supplies or performance of services furnished under the contract."[74] There are two types of warranties—*express* and *implied*—that may apply to Government contracts. A general description of each and a discussion of their effect is given below.

1. Express Warranties

a. Regulations. The FAR states that the "principal purposes of a warranty in a Government contract are (1) to delineate the rights and obligations of the contractor and the Government for defective items and services and (2) to foster quality performance."[75] The FAR sets forth five factors that must be considered by the Government in determining whether to include a warranty provision in a given contract.[76] In general terms, the factors are:

(1) Nature and use of the supplies or services—their complexity and function, the difficulty of detecting defects prior to acceptance, and the potential harm to the Government that could result if there are defects.

(2) Cost—the contractor's charge for accepting deferred liability and the cost of Government administration and enforcement.

(3) Administration and enforcement—the Government's ability to enforce the warranty.

(4) Trade practice—whether or not the contract item is customarily warranted in the trade.

(5) Reduced requirements—the possibility of reducing Government inspection in light of the warranty.

The FAR also instructs that a warranty should (a) survive acceptance, (b) provide a stated period of time or use, or the occurrence of a specified event, after acceptance for the correction of defects, and (c) provide benefits commensurate with cost of the warranty to the Government.[77]

The FAR provides that the *duration* of the warranty must be clearly specified, and that factors such as the nature of the item, its shelf life and estimated useful life, and trade practice must all be considered.[78] The period specified, however, should not extend the contractor's liability for defects beyond a reasonable time after acceptance by the Government.[79]

The FAR also provides that the warranty clause shall specify a reasonable time for furnishing *notice* to the contractor regarding the discovery of defects.[80] This time period should be determined after considering the time period that is likely to be required for the Government to discover and report to the contractor the existence of the defect, as well as the time required to discover and report defective replacements.[81]

b. Standard Contract Clauses. The FAR contains several "Warranty" clauses providing for express warranties in various kinds of contracts.[82] For purposes of illustration, one of these clauses, the "Warranty of Supplies of a Noncomplex Nature" clause for fixed-price contracts,[83] is set forth in Figure 14-2.

c. Government's Remedies. If there is a breach of warranty, the Contracting Officer has alternative remedies available under the "Warranty" clauses for supply contracts. He may either (a) require the contractor to *correct or replace* the nonconforming supplies (or parts) or (b) *retain* the nonconforming supplies and *reduce* the contract price (see, e.g., Paragraph (c) of the clause in Figure 14-2). Moreover, the FAR provides that, when appropriate, the Contracting Officer can include in the

Figure 14-2

"WARRANTY OF SUPPLIES OF A NONCOMPLEX NATURE" CLAUSE
(FAR 52.246-17)

(a) *Definitions.* "Acceptance," as used in this clause, means the act of an authorized representative of the Government by which the Government assumes for itself, or as an agent of another, ownership of existing supplies, or approves specific services as partial or complete performance of the contract.

"Correction," as used in this clause, means the elimination of a defect.

"Supplies," as used in this clause, means the end item furnished by the Contractor and related services required under the contract. The word does not include "data."

(b) *Contractor's obligations.* (1) Notwithstanding inspection and acceptance by the Government of supplies furnished under this contract, or any condition of this contract concerning the conclusiveness thereof, the Contractor warrants that for......................[*Contracting Officer shall state specific period of time after delivery, or the specified event whose occurrence will terminate the warranty period; e.g., the number of miles or hours of use, or combinations of any applicable events or periods of time*]—

(i) All supplies furnished under this contract will be free from defects in material or workmanship and will conform with all requirements of this contract; and

(ii) The preservation, packaging, packing, and marking, and the preparation for, and method of, shipment of such supplies will conform with the requirements of this contract.

(2) When return, correction, or replacement is required, transportation charges and responsibility for the supplies while in transit shall be borne by the Contractor. However, the Contractor's liability for the transportation charges shall not exceed an amount equal to the cost of transportation by the usual commercial method of shipment between the place of delivery specified in this contract and the Contractor's plant, and return.

(3) Any supplies or parts thereof, corrected or furnished in replacement under this clause, shall also be subject to the terms of this clause to the same extent as supplies initially delivered. The warranty, with respect to supplies or parts thereof, shall be equal in duration to that in paragraph (b)(1) of this clause and shall run from the date of delivery of the corrected or replaced supplies.

(4) All implied warranties of merchantability and "fitness for a particular purpose" are excluded from any obligation contained in this contract.

continued

Fig. 14-2 / continued

(c) *Remedies available to the Government.* (1) The Contracting Officer shall give written notice to the Contractor of any breach of warranties in paragraph (b)(1) of this clause within...... *[Contracting Officer shall insert specific period of time; e.g., "45 days of the last delivery under this contract," or "45 days after discovery of the defect"].*

(2) Within a reasonable time after the notice, the Contracting Officer may either—

(i) Require, by written notice, the prompt correction or replacement of any supplies or parts thereof (including preservation, packaging, packing, and marking) that do not conform with the requirements of this contract within the meaning of paragraph (b)(1) of this clause; or

(ii) Retain such supplies and reduce the contract price by an amount equitable under the circumstances.

(3)(i) If the contract provides for inspection of supplies by sampling procedures, conformance of suppliers or components subject to warranty action shall be determined by the applicable sampling procedures in the contract. The Contracting Officer—

(A) May, for sampling purposes, group any supplies delivered under this contract;

(B) Shall require the size of the sample to be that required by sampling procedures specified in the contract for the quantity of supplies on which warranty action is proposed.

(C) May project warranty sampling results over supplies in the same shipment or other supplies contained in other shipments even though all of such supplies are not present at the point of reinspection; *provided,* that the supplies remaining are reasonably representative of the quantity on which warranty action is proposed; and

(D) Need not use the same lot size as on original inspection or reconstitute the original inspection lots.

(ii) Within a reasonable time after notice of any breach of the warranties specified in paragraph (b)(1) of this clause, the Contracting Officer may exercise one or more of the following options:

(A) Require an equitable adjustment in the contract price for any group of supplies.

(B) Screen the supplies grouped for warranty action under this clause at the Contractor's expense and return all nonconforming supplies to the Contractor for correction or replacement.

(C) Require the Contractor to screen the supplies at locations designated by the Government within the continental United States and to correct or replace all nonconforming supplies.

(D) Return the supplies grouped for warranty action under this clause to the Contractor (irrespective of the f.o.b. point or the point of acceptance) for screening and correction or replacement.

continued

INSPECTION AND WARRANTY 14-19

Fig. 14-2 / continued

(4)(i) The Contracting Officer may, by contract or otherwise, correct or replace the nonconforming supplies with similar supplies from another source and charge to the Contractor the cost occasioned to the Government thereby if the Contractor—
(A) Fails to make redelivery of the corrected or replaced supplies within the time established for their return; or
(B) Fails either to accept return of the nonconforming supplies or fails to make progress after their return to correct or replace them so as to endanger performance of the delivery schedule, and in either of these circumstances does not cure such failure within a period of 10 days (or such longer period as the Contracting Officer may authorize in writing) after receipt of notice from the Contracting Officer specifying such failure.
(ii) Instead of correction or replacement by the Government, the Contracting Officer may require an equitable adjustment of the contract price. In addition, if the Contractor fails to furnish timely disposition instructions, the Contracting Officer may dispose of the nonconforming supplies for the Contractor's account in a reasonable manner. The Government is entitled to reimbursement from the Contractor, or from the proceeds of such disposal, for the reasonable expenses of the care and disposition of the nonconforming supplies, as well as for excess costs incurred or to be incurred.
(5) The rights and remedies of the Government provided in this clause are in addition to and do not limit any rights afforded to the Government by any other clause of this contract.

warranty's terms other remedies for breach of warranty, such as repair of replacement of the defective item by the Government at the contractor's expense.[84] The Government, of course, has the burden of proving a warranty breach.[85]

The remedies available to the Government under the "Warranty" and "Inspection" clauses are *cumulative*. Unless the contract specifications provide otherwise, a contractor's liability for latent defects and defects resulting from fraud and gross mistake (under the contract's "Inspection" clause, see Section D.3 above) will continue to apply *after* the expiration of the time period set forth in the contract's "Warranty" clause.[86] Most "Warranty" clauses contain language that they override the finality of acceptance under the "Inspection" clause.[87] See, for example, Paragraph (c)(5) of the clause in Figure 14-2 stating that the "rights and remedies of the Government provided in this clause are in addition to and do not limit any rights afforded to the Government by any other clause of this contract."

2. Implied Warranties

The Uniform Commercial Code (UCC) provides the two *implied* warranties of *quality* that apply to the sale of supplies: (1) the implied warranty of merchantability—that is, that the supplies will be fit for the ordinary and usual purposes for which such goods are sold and (2) the implied warranty of fitness for a particular purpose.[88] The UCC also permits the exclusion of these warranties by clear language in the contract.[89]

The FAR states that where express warranties are included in a contract (except contracts for commercial items), all implied warranties of merchantability and fitness for a particular purpose "shall be negated"[90] (see also Paragraph (b)(4) of the "Warranty" clause in Figure 14-2). Moreover, because the "Inspection of Supplies—Fixed-Price" clause provides that acceptance is conclusive unless "otherwise provided in the contract" (see Paragraph (k) of the clause in Figure 14-1), courts and boards of contract appeals have held—in cases involving contracts containing such language—that final acceptance by the Government bars Government claims based on the implied warranties since they are not "contained" in the contract.[91] On the other hand, if no such language is included in the contract, there is nothing to bar the Government from taking advantage of implied warranties—and it has done so.[92]

REFERENCES

1. See generally Victorino & Ivey, "The 'Inspection' Clause," Briefing Papers No. 88-10 (Sept. 1988), 8 BPC 199; Bruner, "Inspection Under Fixed-Price Supply Contracts," Briefing Papers No. 71-4 (Aug. 1971), 2 BPC 119.

2. FAR pt. 46.

3. FAR 46.201.

4. FAR 46.202-2.

INSPECTION AND WARRANTY   14-21

5. FAR 46.202-3. See generally Zupa, Southern & Livingston, "Quality Assurance Requirements," Briefing Papers No. 93-13 (Dec. 1993).

6. FAR subpt. 46.3.

7. FAR 52.246-2.

8. FAR 46.105.

9. FAR 46.202-1, 46.202-2, 46.202-3.

10. FAR 52.246-11.

11. See, e.g., Russell R. Gannon Co., ASBCA 6664, 1962 BCA ¶ 3335, 4 GC ¶ 513.

12. Emeco Corp., ASBCA 4101, 59-2 BCA ¶ 2300, 1 GC ¶ 622.

13. E.g., Maintenance Engrs., ASBCA 17474, 74-2 BCA ¶ 10690.

14. FAR 46.504.

15. FAR 46.504(b)(2).

16. FAR 46.401(b).

17. FAR 46.402.

18. FAR 46.405.

19. FAR 46.403.

20. Corbetta Const. Co., ASBCA 5045, 60-1 BCA ¶ 2613, 2 GC ¶ 375.

21. E.g., Roberts v. U.S., 174 Ct. Cl. 940 (1966); G.W. Galloway Co., ASBCA 16656, 73-2 BCA ¶ 10270, 15 GC ¶ 476.

22. E.g., G.A. Karnavas Painting Co., NASABCA 28, 1963 BCA ¶ 3633, 5 GC ¶ 74.

23. Kahn Communications, Inc., ASBCA 27461, 86-3 BCA ¶ 19249, 29 GC ¶ 8.

24. E.g., Tester Corp., ASBCA 21312, 78-2 BCA ¶ 13373, 20 GC ¶ 399, affd., 227 Ct. Cl. 648 (1981); Technical Ordnance, Inc., ASBCA 34748, 89-2 BCA ¶ 21818, 31 GC ¶ 214.

25. E.g., Southwest Welding & Mfg. Co. v. U.S., 413 F.2d 1167 (Ct. Cl. 1969), 11 GC ¶ 358.

26. FAR 46.407(c).

27. FAR 47.407(b).

28. FAR 46.407(g).

29. Note 28, supra.

30. Cudahy Packing Co. v. U.S., 109 Ct. Cl. 833 (1948).

31. Mastic-Tar Co., ASBCA 7272, 1962 BCA ¶ 3365, 4 GC ¶ 383.

32. Mazur Bros. & Jaffe Fish Co., VACAB 512, 65-2 BCA ¶ 4932.

33. E.g., Mann Chemical Laboratories, Inc. v. U.S., 182 F. Supp. 40 (D. Mass. 1960) (seven-month delay in rejection of water purification tablets was reasonable because test took that long and defective tablets were dangerous), 2 GC ¶ 221; D. Gerald Bing, ASBCA 5394, 61-1 BCA ¶ 2904 (delay resulted from contractor trying to change the mind of the Contracting Officer), 3 GC ¶ 173.

34. Note 28, supra.

35. Note 28, supra.

36. F.W. Lang Co., ASBCA 2677, 57-1 BCA ¶ 1334.

37. See UCC §§ 2-602(1), 2-606.

38. See, e.g., Space Dynamics Corp., ASBCA 12085, 69-1 BCA ¶ 7662, 11 GC ¶ 341.

39. FAR 46.407(b).

40. E.g., Filtron Co., DCAB ESSA-3, 69-2 BCA ¶ 8039.

41. E.g., Bailfield Industries, Div. A-T-O, Inc., ASBCA 14582, 72-2 BCA ¶ 9676, 15 GC ¶ 25.

42. Radiation Technology, Inc. v. U.S., 366 F.2d 1003 (Ct. Cl. 1966), 8 GC ¶ 489.

43. See, e.g., Valley Asphalt Corp., ASBCA 17595, 74-2 BCA ¶ 10680.

44. FAR 46.503.

45. McQuagge v. U.S., 197 F. Supp. 460 (W.D. La. 1961), 3 GC ¶ 616.

46. H.P. Carney, ASBCA 8222 et al., 1964 BCA ¶ 4149.

47. FAR 46.501.

48. FAR 46.407(c).

49. FAR 46.407(f).

50. John C. Kohler Co. v. U.S., 498 F.2d 1360 (Ct. Cl. 1974), 16 GC ¶ 267.

INSPECTION AND WARRANTY 14-23

51. Replac Corp., ASBCA 7275, 1962 BCA ¶ 3527, 5 GC ¶ 10.

52. Waterbury Cos., ASBCA 6634, 61-2 BCA ¶ 3158, 4 GC ¶ 89.

53. Bell & Flynn, ASBCA 11038, 66-2 BCA ¶ 5855, 9 GC ¶ 167.

54. See, e.g., K-Square Corp., NASABCA 1271-23, 76-1 BCA ¶ 11867.

55. Geranco Mfg. Corp., ASBCA 12376, 68-1 BCA ¶ 6898, 10 GC ¶ 239. See also Cross-Aero Corp., ASBCA 14801, 71-2 BCA ¶ 9075, 14 GC ¶ 74.

56. Herley Industries, Inc., ASBCA 13727, 71-1 BCA ¶ 8888, 13 GC ¶ 353.

57. Note 25, supra; Hercules Engrg. & Mfg. Co., ASBCA 4979, 59-2 BCA ¶ 2426, 2 GC ¶ 68.

58. See note 56, supra; Santa Barbara Research Center, ASBCA 27831, 88-3 BCA ¶ 21098, 31 GC ¶ 118.

59. Hercules Engrg. & Mfg. Co., note 57, supra.

60. Action Diamond Tool Co., ASBCA 625, 5 CCF ¶ 61271 (1951).

61. Kaminer Const. Corp. v. U.S., 488 F.2d 980 (Ct. Cl. 1973), 12 GC ¶ 171.

62. Federal Pacific Electric Co., IBCA 334, 1964 BCA ¶ 4494, 6 GC ¶ 473.

63. Frosty Morn Meats, Inc., ASBCA 4221, 58-1 BCA ¶ 1746.

64. Dale Ingram, Inc., ASBCA 12152, 74-1 BCA ¶ 10436; Catalytic Engrg. & Mfg. Corp., ASBCA 15257, 72-1 BCA ¶ 9342, 14 GC ¶ 202.

65. See 18 USC §§ 287, 1001; 31 USC § 231. See U.S. v. Aerodex, Inc., 469 F.2d 1003 (5th Cir. 1972), 15 GC ¶ 29.

66. Catalytic Engrg. & Mfg. Corp., note 64, supra.

67. Catalytic Engrg. & Mfg. Corp., note 64, supra.

68. Catalytic Engrg. & Mfg. Corp., note 64, supra.

69. Boston Pneumatics Inc., GSBCA 3122, 72-2 BCA ¶ 9682, 14 GC ¶ 468.

70. Stewart Avionics Inc., ASBCA 15512, 75-1 BCA ¶ 11253.

71. FAR 46.504, 52.246-15.

72. Rexach-HRH Const. Corp., VACAB 966, 71-2 BCA ¶ 9052, 13 GC ¶ 461.

73. See generally Arnavas & Latham, "Supply Contract Warranties," Briefing Papers No. 84-7 (July 1987), 6 BPC 365.

74. FAR 46.701.

75. FAR 46.702(a).

76. FAR 46.703(a)-(e).

77. FAR 46.702(b).

78. FAR 46.706(b)(3).

79. Note 78, supra.

80. FAR 46.706(b)(4).

81. Note 80, supra.

82. E.g., FAR 52.246-17 ("Warranty of Supplies of a Noncomplex Nature" clause), 52.246-18 ("Warranty of Supplies of a Complex Nature" clause), 52.246-19 ("Warranty of Systems and Equipment Under Performance Specifications or Design Criteria" clause), 52.246-20 ("Warranty of Services" clause), 52.246-21 ("Warranty of Construction" clause).

83. FAR 52.246-17.

84. FAR 46.706(b)(2).

85. E.g., Vi-Mil, Inc., ASBCA 16820, 75-2 BCA ¶ 11435, 18 GC ¶ 7.

86. Note 62, supra.

87. E.g., Gresham & Co., ASBCA 13812, 70-1 BCA ¶ 8318, revd. on other grounds, 470 F.2d 542 (Ct. Cl. 1972). Cf. Instruments for Industry, Inc. v. U.S., 496 F.2d 1157 (2d Cir. 1974), 16 GC ¶ 294.

88. UCC §§ 2-314, 2-315.

89. UCC § 2-316.

90. FAR 46.706(b)(1)(iii).

91. Republic Aviation Corp., ASBCA 9934, 66-1 BCA ¶ 5482; Trio-Tech Inc., VACAB 598, 68-1 BCA ¶ 6828, 10 GC ¶ 147.

92. E.g., Reeves Soundcraft Corp., ASBCA 9030, 1964 BCA ¶ 4317 (contract did not contain "Inspection" clause so implied warranty of fitness for a particular purpose applied), 6 GC ¶ 406.

PAYMENT

15

A. Contract Payments
   1. Standard Contract Clauses
   2. Partial Payments
   3. Prompt Payment Act Requirements

B. Contract Financing
   1. Progress Payments
   2. Advance Payments
   3. Other Financing Methods

C. Government Withholding

D. Government Debt Collection Through Offset
   1. Applicability Of Debt Collection Act
   2. Regulations

15-2 GOVERNMENT CONTRACT GUIDEBOOK

Obviously, contractors are critically interested in when they will receive payment from the Government and how much they will be paid. As a general rule, and depending on the terms of the contract, when the contractor *performs the contract*, in whole or in part, it is entitled to payment from the Government. Payment may also be available from the Government in some situations to assist the contractor in *financing* completion of the contract work. If the Government believes that the contractor has not performed its contractual obligations, however, the Government may interrupt or *withhold* payments it otherwise owes the contractor. Similarly, if the Government believes that the contractor owes the Government money, it may *"offset"* those amounts against other funds due the contractor. This chapter explores these and other payment issues.

A. CONTRACT PAYMENTS

1. Standard Contract Clauses

The FAR provides for the use of different "Payment" clauses depending on the nature of the contract.[1] Two of the most often-used clauses are the (1) "Payments" clause[2] for fixed-price supply contracts (this clause is also authorized for use in fixed-price service contracts and contracts for nonregulated communication services) and (2) the "Payments Under Fixed-Price Construction Contracts" clause.[3] Both of these clauses provide for payment of the contract price on the completion of the work and the submission by the contractor of proper invoices.

In its first sentence, the "Payments" clause for fixed-price supply contracts, which is set forth in full in Figure 15-1, provides that the Government shall pay the contractor "upon the submission of the proper invoices or vouchers" the stipulated prices "for supplies delivered and accepted or services rendered and accepted." If this clause is the only payment provision in the contract, the supply contractor must finance all of its work and expenses until its first, substantial delivery is made and accepted. This means that the supply contractor will have to use its working capital to pay subcontractors, material suppliers, vendors, employees, and other creditors. Special facilities and equipment may have to be purchased with the contractor's own funds to perform the contract—all before receiving any payment from the Government. Often, there will be a substantial interval between the incurrence of such costs and the receipt of payment.

Figure 15-1

"PAYMENTS" CLAUSE
(FAR 52.232-1)

The Government shall pay the Contractor, upon the submission of proper invoices or vouchers, the prices stipulated in this contract for supplies delivered and accepted or services rendered and accepted, less any deductions provided in this contract. Unless otherwise specified in this contract, payment shall be made on partial deliveries accepted by the Government if—
   (a) The amount due on the deliveries warrants it; or
   (b) The Contractor requests it and the amount due on the deliveries is at least $1,000 or 50 percent of the total contract price.

The standard "Payments Under Fixed-Price Construction Contracts" clause is set forth in Figure 15-2 on the following page. Paragraph (h) of that clause requires the Government to pay the contractor the contract price after "(1) Completion and acceptance of all work; (2) Presentation of a property executed voucher; and (3) Presentation of release of all claims against the Government." Note that this clause is much longer than the "Payments" clause in Figure 15-1. It contains special provisions regarding the retention of a percentage of progress payment amounts (Paragraph (e) of the Figure 15-2 clause) and the ownership of material and work covered by progress payments (Paragraph (f) of the Figure 15-2 clause).

2. Partial Payments

The Government is authorized to make partial payments "for accepted supplies and services that are only a part of the contract requirements."[4] The "Payments" clause in Figure 15-1 also authorizes payment for "partial deliveries accepted by the Government" where warranted or where the contractor requests it

Figure 15-2

"PAYMENTS UNDER FIXED-PRICE CONSTRUCTION CONTRACTS" CLAUSE
(FAR 52.232-5)

(a) The Government shall pay the contractor the contract price as provided in this contract.

(b) The Government shall make progress payments monthly as the work proceeds, or at more frequent intervals as determined by the Contracting Officer, on estimates of work accomplished which meets the standards of quality established under the contract, as approved by the Contracting Officer. The Contractor shall furnish a breakdown of the total contract price showing the amount included therein for each principal category of the work, which shall substantiate the payment amount requested in order to provide a basis for determining progress payments, in such detail as requested by the Contracting Officer. In the preparation of estimates the Contracting Officer may authorize material delivered on the site and preparatory work done to be taken into consideration. Material delivered to the Contractor at locations other than the site may also be taken into consideration if—
  (1) Consideration is specifically authorized by this contract; and
  (2) The Contractor furnishes satisfactory evidence that it has acquired title to such material and that the material will be used to perform this contract.

(c) Along with each request for progress payments, the contractor shall furnish the following certification, of payment shall not be made:
  I hereby certify, to the best of my knowledge and belief, that—
  (1) The amounts requested are only for performance in accordance with the specifications, terms, and conditions of the contract;
  (2) Payments to subcontractors and suppliers have been made from previous payments received under the contract, and timely payments will be made from the proceeds of the payment covered by this certification, in accordance with subcontract agreements and the requirements of chapter 39 of Title 31, United States Code; and
  (3) This request for progress payments does not include any amounts which the prime contractor intends to withhold or retain from a subcontractor or supplier in accordance with the terms and conditions of the subcontract.

continued

Fig. 15-2 / continued

_____
(Name)

_____
(Title)

_____
(Date)

(d) If the Contractor, after making a certified request for progress payments, discovers that a portion or all of such request constitutes a payment for performance by the Contractor that fails to conform to the specifications, terms, and conditions of this contract (hereinafter referred to as the "unearned amount"), the Contractor shall—

(1) Notify the Contracting Officer of such performance deficiency; and

(2) Be obligated to pay the Government an amount (computed by the Contracting Officer in the manner provided in 31 U.S.C. 3903(c)(1)) equal to interest on the unearned amount from the date of receipt of the unearned amount until—

(i) The date the Contractor notifies the Contracting Officer that the performance deficiency has been corrected; or

(ii) the date the Contractor reduced the amount of any subsequent certified request for progress payments by an amount equal to the unearned amount.

(e) If the Contracting Officer finds that satisfactory progress was achieved during any period for which a progress payment is to be made, the Contracting Officer shall authorize payment to be made in full. However, if satisfactory progress has not been made, the Contracting Officer may retain a maximum of 10 percent of the amount of the payment until satisfactory progress is achieved. When the work is substantially complete, the Contracting Officer may retain from previously withheld funds and future progress payments that amount the Contracting Officer considers adequate for protection of the Government and shall release to the Contractor all the remaining withheld funds. Also, on completion and acceptance of each separate building, public work, or other division of the contract, for which the price is stated separately in the contract, payment shall be made for the completed work without retention of a percentage.

(f) All material and work covered by progress payments made shall, at the time of payment, become the sole property of the Government, but this shall not be construed as—

(1) Relieving the Contractor from the sole responsibility for all material and work upon which payments have been made or the restoration of any damaged work; or

continued

Fig. 15-2 / continued

(2) Waiving the right of the Government to require the fulfillment of all of the terms of the contract.

(g) In making these progress payments, the Government shall, upon request, reimburse the Contractor for the amount of premiums paid for performance and payment bonds (including coinsurance and reinsurance agreements, when applicable) after the Contractor has furnished evidence of full payment to the surety. The retainage provisions in paragraph (e) of this clause shall not apply to that portion of progress payments attributable to bond premiums.

(h) The Government shall pay the amount due the contractor under this contract after—
(1) Completion and acceptance of all work;
(2) Presentation of a properly executed voucher; and
(3) Presentation of release of all claims against the Government arising by virtue of this contract, other than claims, in stated amounts, that the Contractor has specifically excepted from the operation of the release. A release may also be required of the assignee if the Contractor's claim to amounts payable under this contract has been assigned under the Assignment of Claims Act of 1940 (31 U.S.C. 3727 and 41 U.S.C. 15).

(i) Notwithstanding any provision of this contract, progress payments shall not exceed 80 percent on work accomplished on undefinitized contract actions. A "contract action" is any action resulting in a contract, as defined in FAR Subpart 2.1, including contract modifications for additional supplies or services, but not including contract modifications that are within the scope and under the terms of the contract, such as contract modifications issued pursuant to the Changes clause, or funding and other administrative changes.

and the amount due is at least $1,000 or 50% of the contract price. Partial contract payments are not technically a method of contract "financing" because they depend on delivery and acceptance of contract items.[5] They can, however, reduce a contractor's need for financing by providing interim payments during contract performance.

3. Prompt Payment Act Requirements

Late payment by the Government may threaten the contractor's financial stability, may force the contractor to borrow additional money to finance performance, and may even convince the contractor to refuse to do further business with the Government. To correct the practice of many federal agencies of paying contractors late, Congress passed the Prompt Payment Act[6] in 1982 (and amended it in 1988[7]) to provide that the Government pay *interest penalties* for late payments.

a. Interest Penalties. As illustrated by the Figure 15-1 and Figure 15-2 clauses, payment is generally due from the Government on the submission of invoices or vouchers or the completion of work. Under the Prompt Payment Act, the Government's due date for making a payment (if the contract does not specify a particular date) is 30 days after the Government *receives* a *proper invoice* for the amount due. The 30 days is computed from the later of the dates (1) the person or place designated by the agency in the contract to first receive an invoice actually receives a proper invoice from the contractor or (2) the seventh day after delivery or performance of the contract property or services unless actual acceptance by the Government is earlier or the contract specifies a longer period.[8]

Interest begins accruing the day after the required payment date and ends on the date when payment is made. Interest is computed at the rate established for interest on Contract Disputes Act claims in effect at the time the payment became late,[9] and the interest penalty compounds every 30 days.[10] The Prompt Payment Act specifically provides that the date of payment by the Government is the date of the check, not the date the contractor receives the check.[11] If the Government fails to pay interest due, it may be liable for an additional penalty.[12]

b. "Proper" Invoices. Interest does not begin to accrue until the contractor submits a "proper" invoice to the Government. The FAR provides a checklist of information a proper invoice must contain.[13] If the invoice is defective, the Government has seven days after receipt of the invoice to alert the contractor and explain the deficiencies.[14]

c. Applicability Of The Act. The Prompt Payment Act generally applies, according to one board of contract appeals judge, where the Government simply "cannot get its act together" to pay the contractor on time.[15] It applies to Government delay in paying *undisputed* invoices. It does not apply where the contractor's entitlement is in dispute or where there are questions regarding the contractor's compliance with the contract's requirements, for example.[16] The Act also does not apply to Government delays in acting on change orders or requests for equitable adjustment,[17] or to delays in payments made solely for financing purposes (such as advance payments or progress payments based on cost).[18] It does apply, however, to partial or periodic deliveries of supplies or performance of services[19] and to progress payments and retainage due under construction contracts.[20] Construction contractors must include with each progress payment request a certification and substantiation of the amount requested, however (see Paragraph (c) of the Figure 15-2 clause).

B. CONTRACT FINANCING

To facilitate performance by its contractors, the Government provides several financing techniques. There are three basic methods of contract financing: (1) progress payments, (2) advance payments, and (3) other methods, such as private financing and Government loan guarantees.[21] To minimize risk on the part of the Government, the regulations also provide that when a contractor requests financing, the Contracting Officer should consider the financing methods in the following order of preference—(a) private financing, (b) "customary" progress payments, (c) loan guarantees, (d) "unusual" progress payments, and (e) advance payments.[22]

1. Progress Payments

One of the most important and frequently used ways in which the Government assists contractors in financing their contracts is to make periodic progress payments as contract performance proceeds. Progress payments may be based on either the costs incurred in performance or on a percentage or stage of completion.[23] Under the FAR, progress payments based on a percentage or stage of completion are typically used only in construction contracts (see, for example, the "Payments Under Fixed-Price Construction Contracts" clause in Figure 15-2) and are *not* governed by the FAR's financing provisions. Similarly, progress payments are not payments made to contractors under typical cost-reimbursement contracts.[24] Progress payments are payments under fixed-price contracts that are based on the contractor's *incurred costs* and are limited by the contract price.[25]

An important point about progress payments is that the Government may not make progress payments if they were not provided for in the contract as awarded, *unless* the contractor agrees to an appropriate price reduction or to furnish other valuable consideration (for example, a promise to do additional work) to the Government. The value received by the Government should approximate the amount by which the contract price would have been reduced if the progress payments had been required in the original contract.[26]

a. Standard Contract Clause. The FAR provides that Contracting Officers generally should not provide for progress payments on contracts of less than $1 million, unless the contract is a small business contract of at least $100,000.[27] If the Gov-

---

Figure 15-3

"PROGRESS PAYMENTS" CLAUSE
(FAR 52.232-16)

Progress payments shall be made to the Contractor when requested as work progresses, but not more frequently than monthly in amounts approved by the Contracting Officer, under the following conditions:

(a) *Computation of amounts.* (1) Unless the Contractor requests a smaller amount, each progress payment shall be computed as (i) 80 percent of the Contractor's cumulative total costs under this contract, as shown by records maintained by the Contractor for the purpose of obtaining payment under Government contracts, plus (ii) progress payments to subcontractors (see paragraph (j) below), all less the sum of all previous progress payments made by the Government under this contract. Cost of money that would be allowable under 31.205-10 of the Federal Acquisition Regulation shall be deemed an incurred cost for progress payment purposes.

continued

Fig. 15-3 / continued

(2) The following conditions apply to the timing of including costs in progress payment requests:

(i) The costs of supplies and services purchased by the Contractor directly for this contract may be included only after payment by cash, check, or other form of actual payment.

(ii) Costs for the following may be included when incurred, even if before payment, when the Contractor is not delinquent in payment of the costs of contract performance in the ordinary course of business:

(A) Materials issued from the Contractor's stores inventory and placed in the production process for use on this contract.

(B) Direct labor, direct travel, and other direct in-house costs.

(C) Properly allocable and allowable indirect costs.

(iii) Accrued costs of Contractor contributions under employee pension or other postretirement benefit, profit sharing, and stock ownership plans shall be excluded until actually paid unless—

(A) The Contractor's practice is to contribute to the plans quarterly or more frequently; and

(B) The contribution does not remain unpaid 30 days after the end of the applicable quarter or shorter payment period (any contributions remaining unpaid shall be excluded from the Contractor's total costs for progress payments until paid).

(iv) If the contract is subject to the special transition method authorized in Cost Accounting Standard (CAS) 410, Allocation of Business Unit General and Administrative Expense to Final Cost Objective, General and Administrative expenses (G&A) shall not be included in progress payment requests until the suspense account prescribed in CAS 410 is less than—

(A) Five million dollars; or

(B) The value of the work-in-process inventories under contracts entered into after the suspense account was established (only a pro rata share of the G&A allocable to the excess of the inventory over the suspense account value is includable in progress payment requests under this contract).

(3) The Contractor shall not include the following in total costs for progress payment purposes in subparagraph (a)(1)(i) above:

(i) Costs that are not reasonable, allocable to this contract, and consistent with sound and generally accepted accounting principles and practices.

(ii) Costs incurred by subcontractors or suppliers.

(iii) Costs ordinarily capitalized and subject to depreciation or amortization except for the properly depreciated or amortized portion of such costs.

(iv) Payments made or amounts payable to subcontractors or suppliers, except for—

(A) Completed work, including partial deliveries, to which the Contractor has acquired title; and

continued

Fig. 15-3 / continued

(B) Work under cost-reimbursement or time-and-material subcontracts to which the Contractor has acquired title.

(4) The amount of unliquidated progress payments may exceed neither (i) the progress payments made against incomplete work (including allowable unliquidated progress payments to subcontractors) nor (ii) the value, for progress payment purposes, of the incomplete work. Incomplete work shall be considered to be the supplies and services required by this contract, for which delivery and invoicing by the Contractor and acceptance by the Government are incomplete.

(5) The total amount of progress payments shall not exceed 80 percent of the total contract price.

(6) If a progress payment or the unliquidated progress payments exceed the amounts permitted by subparagraphs (a)(4) or (a)(5) above, the Contractor shall repay the amount of such excess to the Government on demand.

(b) *Liquidation.* Except as provided in the Termination for Convenience of the Government clause, all progress payments shall be liquidated by deducting from any payment under this contract, other than advance or progress payments, the unliquidated progress payments, or 80 percent of the amount invoiced, whichever is less. The Contractor shall repay to the Government any amounts required by a retroactive price reduction, after computing liquidations and payments on past invoices at the reduced prices and adjusting the unliquidated progress payments accordingly. The Government reserves the right to unilaterally change from the ordinary liquidation rate to an alternate rate when deemed appropriate for proper contract financing.

(c) *Reduction or suspension.* The Contracting Officer may reduce or suspend progress payments, increase the rate of liquidation, or take a combination of these actions, after finding on substantial evidence any of the following conditions:

(1) The Contractor failed to comply with any material requirement of this contract (which includes paragraphs (f) and (g) below).

(2) Performance of this contract is endangered by the Contractor's (i) failure to make progress or (ii) unsatisfactory financial condition.

(3) Inventory allocated to this contract substantially exceeds reasonable requirements.

(4) The Contractor is delinquent in payment of the costs of performing this contract in the ordinary course of business.

(5) The unliquidated progress payments exceed the fair value of the work accomplished on the undelivered portion of this contract.

continued

Fig. 15-3 / continued

(6) The Contractor is realizing less profit than that reflected in the establishment of any alternate liquidation rate in paragraph (b) above, and that rate is less than the progress payment rate stated in subparagraph (a)(1) above.

(d) *Title.* (1) Title to the property described in this paragraph (d) shall vest in the Government. Vestiture shall be immediately upon the date of this contract, for property acquired or produced before that date. Otherwise, vestiture shall occur when the property is or should have been allocable or properly chargeable to this contract.

(2) "Property," as used in this clause, includes all of the below-described items acquired or produced by the contractor that are or should be allocable or properly chargeable to this contract under sound and generally accepted accounting principles and practices.

(i) Parts, materials, inventories, and work in process;

(ii) Special tooling and special test equipment to which the Government is to acquire the title under any other clause of this contract;

(iii) Nondurable (i.e., noncapital) tools, jigs, dies, fixtures, molds, patterns, taps, gauges, test equipment, and other similar manufacturing aids, title to which would not be obtained as special tooling under subparagraph (ii) above; and

(iv) Drawings and technical data, to the extent the Contractor or subcontractors are required to deliver them to the Government by other clauses of this contract.

(3) Although title to property is in the Government under this clause, other applicable clauses of this contract, e.g., the termination or special tooling clauses, shall determine the handling and disposition of the property.

(4) The Contractor may sell any scrap resulting from production under this contract without requesting the Contracting Officer's approval, but the proceeds shall be credited against the costs of performance.

(5) To acquire for its own use or dispose of property to which title is vested in the Government under this clause, the Contractor must obtain the Contracting Officer's advance approval of the action and the terms. The Contractor shall (i) exclude the allocable costs of the property from the costs of contract performance, and (ii) repay to the Government any amount of unliquidated progress payments allocable to the property. Repayment may be by cash or credit memorandum.

(6) When the Contractor completes all of the obligations under this contract, including liquidation of all progress payments, title shall vest in the Contractor for all property (or the proceeds thereof) not—

continued

Fig. 15-3 / continued

(i) Delivered to, and accepted by, the Government under this contract; or

(ii) Incorporated in supplies delivered to, and accepted by, the Government under this contract and to which title is vested in the Government under this clause.

(7) The terms of this contract concerning liability for Government-furnished property shall not apply to property to which the Government acquired title solely under this clause.

(e) *Risk of loss.* Before delivery to and acceptance by the Government, the Contractor shall bear the risk of loss for property, the title to which vests in the Government under this clause, except to the extent the Government expressly assumes the risk. The Contractor shall repay the Government an amount equal to the unliquidated progress payments that are based on costs allocable to property that is damaged, lost, stolen, or destroyed.

(f) *Control of costs and property.* The Contractor shall maintain an accounting system and controls adequate for the proper administration of this clause.

(g) *Reports and access to records.* The Contractor shall promptly furnish reports, certificates, financial statements, and other pertinent information reasonably requested by the Contracting Officer for the administration of this clause. Also, the Contractor shall give the Government reasonable opportunity to examine and verify the Contractor's books, records, and accounts.

(h) *Special terms regarding default.* If this contract is terminated under the Default clause, (i) the Contractor shall, on demand, repay to the Government the amount of unliquidated progress payments and (ii) title shall vest in the Contractor, on full liquidation of progress payments, for all property for which the Government elects not to require delivery under the Default clause. The Government shall be liable for no payment except as provided by the Default clause.

(i) *Reservations of rights.* (1) No payment or vesting of title under this clause shall (i) excuse the Contractor from performance of obligations under this contract or (ii) constitute a waiver of any of the rights or remedies of the parties under the contract.

(2) The Government's rights and remedies under this clause (i) shall not be exclusive but rather shall be in addition to any other rights and remedies provided by law or this contract and (ii) shall not be affected by delayed, partial, or omitted exercise of any right, remedy, power, or privilege, nor shall such exercise or any single

continued

Fig. 15-3 / continued

exercise preclude or impair any further exercise under this clause or the exercise of any other right, power, or privilege of the Government.

(j) *Progress payments to subcontractors.* The amounts mentioned in (a)(1)(ii) above shall be all progress payments to subcontractors or divisions if the following conditions are met:

(1) The amounts included are limited to (i) the unliquidated remainder of progress payments made plus (ii) for small business concerns any unpaid subcontractor requests for progress payments that the Contractor has approved for current payment in the ordinary course of business.

(2) The subcontract or interdivisional order is expected to involve a minimum of approximately 6 months between the beginning of work and the first delivery, or, if the subcontractor is a small business concern, 4 months.

(3) The terms of the subcontract or interdivisional order concerning progress payments—

(i) Are substantially similar to the terms of the clause at 52.232-16, Progress Payments, for any subcontractor that is a large business concern, or that clause with its *Alternate I* for any subcontractor that is a small business concern;

(ii) Are at least as favorable to the Government as the terms of this clause;

(iii) Are not more favorable to the subcontractor or division than the terms of this clause are to the Contractor;

(iv) Are in conformance with the requirements of paragraph 32.504(e) of the Federal Acquisition Regulation, and

(v) Subordinate all subcontractor rights concerning property to which the Government has title under the subcontract to the Government's right to require delivery of the property to the Government if (A) the Contractor defaults or (B) the subcontractor becomes bankrupt or insolvent.

(4) The progress payment rate in the subcontract is the customary rate used by the Contracting Agency, depending on whether the subcontractor is or is not a small business concern.

(5) The parties agree concerning any proceeds received by the Government for property to which title has vested in the Government under the subcontract terms, that the proceeds shall be applied to reducing any unliquidated progress payments by the Government to the Contractor under this contract.

(6) If no unliquidated progress payments to the Contractor remain, but there are unliquidated progress payments that the Contractor has made to any subcontractor, the Contractor shall be subrogated to all the rights the Government obtained through the terms required by this clause to be in any subcontract, as if all such rights had been assigned and transferred to the Contractor.

continued

Fig. 15-3 / continued

(7) The Contractor shall pay the subcontractor's progress payment request under subdivision (j)(1)(ii) above, within a reasonable time after receiving the Government progress payment covering those amounts.

(8) To facilitate small business participation in subcontracting under this contract, the Contractor agrees to provide progress payments to small business concerns, in conformity with the standards for customary progress payments stated in Subpart 32.5 of the Federal Acquisition Regulation. The Contractor further agrees that the need for such progress payments shall not be considered as a handicap or adverse factor in the award of subcontracts.

(k) *Limitations on Undefinitized Contract Actions.* Notwithstanding any other progress payment provisions in this contract, progress payments may not exceed 80 percent of costs incurred on work accomplished under undefinitized contract actions. A "contract action" is any action resulting in a contract, as defined in Subpart 2.1, including contract modifications for additional supplies or services, but not including contract modifications that are within the scope and under the terms of the contract, such as contract modifications issued pursuant to the Changes clause, or funding and other administrative changes. This limitation shall apply to the costs incurred, as computed in accordance with paragraph (a) of this clause, and shall remain in effect until the contract action is definitized. Costs incurred which are subject to this limitation shall be segregated on Contractor progress payment requests and invoices from those costs eligible for higher progress payment rates. For purposes of progress payment liquidation, as described in paragraph (b) of this clause, progress payments for undefinitized contract actions shall be liquidated at 80 percent of the amount invoiced for work performed under the undefinitized contract action as long as the contract action remains undefinitized. The amount of unliquidated progress payments for undefinitized contract actions shall not exceed 80 percent of the maximum liability of the Government under the undefinitized contract action or such lower limit specified elsewhere in the contract. Separate limits may be specified for separate actions.

ernment will provide progress payments based on costs in the fixed-price contract, the "Progress Payments" clause set forth in Figure 15-3 is included in the contract.[28]

b. Amount. The regulations set forth "customary" limits on the percentage of incurred costs for which progress payments may be made. Currently, under the FAR, the customary rate is 80% of the "total costs of performing the contract" for large businesses and 85% for small businesses.[29] Progress payments made at higher rates are considered "unusual" progress payments.[30]

Under Paragraph (a)(2) of the "Progress Payments" clause, and with the exception of some specified "incurred costs," the contractor may bill the Government only *actual paid costs*. Under Paragraph (a)(3) of the clause, contractors must exclude from their progress payment billings costs that are not "reasonable, allocable to this contract, and consistent with sound and generally accepted accounting principles and practices," costs that are ordinarily capitalized and subject to depreciation or amortization, and costs incurred by subcontractors and suppliers. In addition, to encourage the contractor to provide progress payments to subcontractors, the Government will reimburse contractors for the total amount of "customary" progress payments made to subcontractors (see Paragraph (j) of the Figure 15-3 "Progress Payments" clause).[31]

c. Title To Property. To assure some security for the progress payments made, the "Progress Payments" clause (Paragraph (d)) provides that the Government has title to all property "allocable or properly chargeable" to the contract. This includes, for example, materials, inventories, work-in-process, special tooling and testing equipment, and other nondurable items necessary to perform the contract. The contractor may dispose of such property only with the consent of the Contracting Officer. The "title" provisions of the clause have caused difficulty regarding the scope of the Government's interest in contractor property in tax cases,[32] for example, and bankruptcy proceedings.[33]

d. Suspension Or Reduction Of Payments. Paragraph (c) of the Figure 15-3 "Progress Payments" clause gives the Contracting Officer express authority to reduce or suspend progress payments in six specified circumstances. For example, if the Contracting Officer finds there is "substantial evidence" the contractor has failed to comply with a material contract requirement, failed to make adequate progress, or is delinquent in paying subcontractors or suppliers, he can suspend or reduce progress payments. Suspension of progress payments is also justified if the contractor's financial condition is such that it is unlikely the contract can be completed.[34] Not surprisingly, progress payments may also be suspended or reduced where there is substantial evidence that the contractor's progress payment request is based on fraud.[35]

However, where the parties execute the contract with the understanding that it will be financed solely by progress payments on a cost basis, the Government's unjustified failure to make prompt progress payments excuses any duty of further performance of the work by the contractor.[36] Of course, in that case, the contractor must establish that the Government's failure to make progress payments was the *primary* cause of the contractor's inability to continue performance.[37] If—despite the Government's unjustified suspension of progress payments—the contractor is able to continue performance by borrowing funds, the Government will be liable for interest charges incurred, as well as any other additional costs incurred as a result of that suspension.[38]

2. Advance Payments

Where no other financing is available, the Government may agree to make advance payments to a contractor—advances paid before the contractor acquires any materials for or does any work under a contract.[39] Although authorized by statute,[40] advance payments entail substantial risk for the Government and so are made only "sparingly" and where the head of the agency determines in writing that advance payments are in the public interest.[41]

As a practical matter, very few contractors will be eligible to receive advance payments. The FAR identifies several types of contracts that may be targeted for advance payments, such as experimental research and development contracts with nonprofit institutions, contracts with financially weak contractors whose technical ability is considered essential, or highly classified contracts.[42]

If advance payments are authorized, the contract must contain the "Advance Payments" clause.[43] Under this clause, advance payments are made only at such times as the contractor's financial necessity dictates, and must be approved by a special "administering office" of the Government.[44] The contract clause also requires that advance payments be deposited in a special bank account and that withdrawals from that account must be countersigned by a Government official.[45] The use of the funds is restricted to paying allowable costs incurred for purposes of the contract.[46] Finally, the clause requires the contractor to pay interest on the advance payments made.[47]

3. Other Financing Methods

a. Loan Guarantees. Guaranteed loans are available only to "borrowers performing contracts related to national defense."[48] Loan guarantees are made by Federal Reserve Banks on behalf of designated "guaranteeing agencies" to enable contractors to obtain financing from private sources under contracts for the acquisition of supplies or services for the national defense.[49]

b. Private Financing. Contractors may finance a Government contract much the same way they would finance a commercial contract—by obtaining financing through a commercial bank or financial institution. Commercial financing is, in fact, the method of financing preferred by the Government.[50] Because a private financing institution typically requires a contractor to assign to it the proceeds of the contract to be financed as security for any funds advanced, the Government imposes restrictions on these transactions. If contract proceeds are to be assigned in exchange for a loan, the contractor must comply with the Anti-Assignment Act and its implementing regulations.[51]

The Act prohibits the assignment of Federal Government contracts (and the assignment of claims against the Federal Government). An attempt to transfer an interest in a Government contract, such as the contract proceeds, may result in a declaration that the contract is null and void.[52] However, to encourage private financing of Government contracts, a transfer of contract proceeds is exempt from the Act's prohibitions where the proceeds exceed $1,000 and "are assigned to a bank, trust company, or other financing institution" for the purpose of facilitating performance of the contract.[53] To effect a valid assignment under the Act, however, the contractor must strictly comply with the regulatory procedures set forth in the FAR.[54]

C. GOVERNMENT WITHHOLDING

The Government is entitled to withhold payment to a contractor in certain circumstances generally having to do with the contractor's failure to perform. As noted in Section B.1.d above, the Government may suspend progress payments, for example, for contractor nonperformance. Similarly, Paragraph (e) of the "Payments Under Fixed-Price Construction Contracts" clause (see Figure 15-2) directs the Contracting Officer to hold 10% of payments due the contractor as retainage to protect the Government unless the Contracting Officer finds that "satisfactory progress was achieved." The Government is also entitled to withhold payment to contractors that fail to meet certain obligations under various labor statutes.[55]

D. GOVERNMENT DEBT COLLECTION THROUGH OFFSET

The Government can interrupt or reduce payments to a contractor when the Government seeks to use funds otherwise due the contractor under the contract to offset (also called "setoff") debts of the contractor allegedly arising either under the affected contract or independently. The Government has a "longstanding common law right to offset contract debts against contract payments."[56]

1. Applicability Of Debt Collection Act

Although the Government has a common law right to administrative offset, under the Debt Collection Act of 1982, the Government may not collect debts by offset unless it follows certain *procedures*—such as notice to the debtor, providing the debtor an opportunity to inspect agency records and decisions relating to the claim, and permitting the debtor an opportunity to negotiate a repayment agreement with the agency.[57] For many years, there was controversy in the courts and boards of contract appeals over whether the Government had to comply with Debt Collection Act procedures before collecting contract debts through offset. The controversy was largely resolved in 1993 by the Court of Appeals for the Federal Circuit, which ruled that the Act does not apply to the use of contract funds to satisfy claims relating either to the same contract or to a different contract.[58] The decision did not address, however, whether the Debt Collection Act procedures apply to the Government's use of contract funds to offset noncontract debts.

2. Regulations

The FAR contains procedures governing the Government's ascertainment and collection of contract debts. Under the regulations, the Government cannot issue a demand for payment until the Contracting Officer issues a final decision on the debt under the contract's "Disputes" clause.[59] The demand for payment must include notice to the contractor that it may request a deferment of collection if immediate payment is not practicable or the amount is disputed.[60] Debt deferral is more likely if the contractor has appealed the Contracting Officer's debt decision under the Contract Disputes Act or the contractor is a small business or financially weak.[61] If, within 30 days, payment is not completed and deferment is not requested, the Government may begin withholding contractor funds to offset the debt.[62]

REFERENCES

1. See FAR 32.111.
2. FAR 52.232-1.
3. FAR 52.232-5.
4. FAR 32.102(d).
5. Note 4, supra.

PAYMENT 15-21

6. 31 USC § 3901 et seq., as amended. See FAR subpt. 32.9; Office of Management and Budget Circular A-125, "Prompt Payment" (Rev.), 54 Fed. Reg. 52700 (Dec. 21, 1989).

7. P.L. 100-496, 102 Stat. 2455 (1988). See Rosen, McGrath & Davis, "Prompt Payment Act Amendments of 1988," Briefing Papers No. 90-4 (Mar. 1990), 9 BPC 87.

8. 31 USC § 3901(a)(4); FAR 32.905(a).

9. 31 USC § 3902(a), (b).

10. 31 USC § 3902(e). E.g., Professional Design Constructors, GSBCA 7937 et al., 91-1 BCA ¶ 23363.

11. 31 USC § 3901(a)(5).

12. 31 USC § 3902(c)(3); FAR 32.907-1.

13. FAR 32.905(e).

14. Note 13, supra.

15. Nash Janitorial Service, Inc., GSBCA 6935, 84-1 BCA ¶ 17201 (Lieblich, J. concurring).

16. FAR 32.905(a)(1)(ii). See also Ross & McDonald Contracting, GmbH, ASBCA 38154 et al., 94-1 BCA ¶ 26316 (interest does not accrue even if Government payment delay involves dispute unrelated to invoices), 35 GC ¶ 682.

17. E.g., Koehring Cranes & Excavators, Inc., ASBCA 41008, 91-1 BCA ¶ 23551.

18. Office of Management and Budget Circular A-125, note 6, supra, §§ 1.f, 7.c. See also FAR 32.907-2. See generally Nash, "Application of the Prompt Payment Act to Interim Payments on Cost Reimbursement Contracts," 6 Nash & Cibinic Rep. ¶ 26 (Apr. 1992).

19. 31 USC § 3903(a)(5). See Northrop Worldwide Aircraft Services, Inc. v. Department of the Treasury, GSBCA 11162-TD et al., 92-2 BCA ¶ 24765, 34 GC ¶ 336.

20. 31 USC § 3903(a)(6) (Government has 14 days to make construction contract progress payments).

21. See FAR 32.102. See generally Chierichella, Oliver, Everhart & Villet, "Financing Government Contracts," Briefing Papers No. 86-7 (June 1986), 7 BPC 311.

22. FAR 32.106.

23. See FAR 32.102(b), (e).

24. FAR 32.500.

25. FAR 32.501-3.

26. See FAR 32.501-4.

27. FAR 32.502-1.

28. FAR 32.502-4, 52.232-16.

29. FAR 32.501-1(a). Cf. DFARS 232.501-1 (establishing different rates for Department of Defense and National Aeronautics and Space Administration contracts).

30. FAR 32.501-1(b).

31. FAR 32.504.

32. Mitchell Aero, Inc. v. City of Milwaukee, 168 N.W.2d 183 (Wis. 1969).

33. E.g., Welco Industries, Inc. v. U.S., 790 F.2d 90 (Fed. Cir. 1986), 5 FPD ¶ 9.

34. E.g., Electro Optical Mechanisms, Inc., ASBCA 20422, 79-2 BCA ¶ 14118, 22 GC ¶ 157.

35. 10 USC § 2307(h); 41 USC § 255(g).

36. R.H.J. Corp., ASBCA 9922, 66-1 BCA ¶ 5361; Drain-A-Way Systems, GSBCA 6473, 83-1 BCA ¶ 16202, 25 GC ¶ 67.

37. Valda Const. Co., ASBCA 18550, 74-2 BCA ¶ 10705.

38. Sun Electric Corp., ASBCA 13031, 70-2 BCA ¶ 8371; Aerojet-General Corp., ASBCA 17171, 74-2 BCA ¶ 10863, 16 GC ¶ 482. Cf. Consumers Oil Co., ASBCA 24172, 86-1 BCA ¶ 18647, 28 GC ¶ 64 (Note).

39. See FAR subpt. 32.4.

40. 41 USC § 255; 10 USC § 2307.

41. FAR 32.402(b), (c).

42. FAR 32.403.

43. FAR 52.232-12.

44. See FAR 52.232-12, para. (a).

45. FAR 52.232-12, para. (b).

46. FAR 52.232-12, para. (c).

47. FAR 52.232-12, para. (f).

48. FAR 32.300. See 50 USC app. § 2091.

49. FAR 32.102(c), subpt. 32.3.

50. FAR 32.106(e).

51. 31 USC § 3727; 41 USC § 15; FAR 32.8. See generally Vickery & Paalborg, "Assignment of Claims Act," Briefing Papers No. 87-3 (Feb. 1987), 7 BPC 483.

52. 41 USC § 15.

53. Note 52, supra. See FAR 32.802.

54. FAR 32.805, 52.232-23 ("Assignment of Claims" clause).

55. E.g., Davis-Bacon Act, 40 USC § 276a et seq.; Service Contract Act, 41 USC § 351 et seq.

56. Cecile Industries, Inc. v. Cheney, 995 F.2d 1052 (Fed. Cir. 1993), 12 FPD ¶ 58, 35 GC ¶ 410. See generally Barletta, "Contract Debts," Briefing Papers No. 92-8 (July 1992).

57. 31 USC § 3701 et seq.

58. Cecile Industries, Inc. v. Cheney, note 56, supra, overturning DMJM/Norman Engrg. Co., ASBCA 28154, 84-1 BCA ¶ 17226, 26 GC ¶ 102. See generally Cibinic, "Withholding, Offset, and Debt Collection: A Double Whammy for the Debt Collection Act," 7 Nash & Cibinic Rep. ¶ 44 (Aug. 1993).

59. FAR 32.608(c).

60. FAR 32.610.

61. FAR 32.613(b), (e).

62. FAR 32.612.

Part IV

TERMINATIONS

chapters

16 | Termination For Default

17 | Termination For Convenience

TERMINATION FOR DEFAULT

16

A. **Standard "Default" Clauses**

B. **Bases For Termination**
   1. Failure To Deliver Or Perform
   2. Failure To Make Progress
   3. Failure To Perform Other Contract Provisions
   4. Anticipatory Breach Of Contract

C. **The Termination Decision**
   1. Contracting Officer Discretion
   2. Improper Motive Or Grounds
   3. Notices

D. **Contractor Defenses**
   1. Excusable Delay
   2. Waiver Of Due Date

E. **Government Remedies**
   1. Excess Costs Of Reprocurement
   2. Other Remedies
   3. Liquidated Damages

F. **Contesting Default Terminations**
   1. Procedures
   2. Contractor Remedies

16-2   GOVERNMENT CONTRACT GUIDEBOOK

This part of the book (Part IV)—entitled "Terminations"—deals with the situation where a Government contract ends sooner than anticipated. There are two types of terminations that can arise under Government contracts: "termination for default" (examined in this chapter, Chapter 16) and "termination for convenience" of the Government (examined in Chapter 17).

Termination for default is undoubtedly the most traumatic experience that can befall a Government contractor. Not only does termination (unless successfully contested by the contractor) put an end to performance of the contract and, in all probability, to the contractor's hopes for profit on the contract, it also subjects the contractor to possible liability for the Government's extra costs of having the contract completed by another contractor. In addition, the termination is a negative entry on the contractor's record that could prevent the contractor from receiving future contract awards (see Chapter 3, Section E.2).

Thus, termination of a contract for default is to be assiduously avoided, and—should it occur—to be challenged if at all possible. This chapter explores the subject of default termination as provided for under standard Government contract "Default" clauses. Specifically, it examines (a) the standard "Default" clauses for fixed-price contracts, (b) contractor actions that can lead to default termination, (c) the termination decision by the Government, (d) contractor defenses to default termination, such as excusable delay or waiver by the Government, (e) the Government's remedies after a valid termination of a contract for default, and (f) how contractors can contest default terminations. For an in-depth discussion of this subject, readers should refer to Pettit, Vacketta, and Anthony, GOVERNMENT CONTRACT DEFAULT TERMINATION (Federal Publications Inc. 1991 & Supp.).

A. STANDARD "DEFAULT" CLAUSES

Default terminations are provided for in Government contracts under standard clauses set forth in the FAR.[1] Two of these clauses are set forth as figures in this chapter to aid in the discussion—Figure 16-1 contains the "Default (Fixed-Price Supply and Service)" clause used for most fixed-price supply and service contracts,[2] while Figure 16-2 (beginning on page

16-5) contains the "Default (Fixed-Price Construction)" clause used for most construction contracts.[3]

Figure 16-1

"DEFAULT (FIXED-PRICE SUPPLY AND SERVICE)" CLAUSE
(FAR 52.249-8)

(a)(1) The Government may, subject to paragraphs (c) and (d) below, by written notice of default to the Contractor, terminate this contract in whole or in part if the Contractor fails to—

(i) Deliver the supplies or to perform the services within the time specified in this contract or any extension;

(ii) Make progress, so as to endanger performance of this contract (but see subparagraph (a)(2) below); or

(iii) Perform any of the other provisions of this contract (but see subparagraph (a)(2) below).

(2) The Government's right to terminate this contract under subdivisions (1)(ii) and (1)(iii) above, may be exercised if the Contractor does not cure such failure within 10 days (or more if authorized in writing by the Contracting Officer) after receipt of the notice from the Contracting Officer specifying the failure.

(b) If the Government terminates this contract in whole or in part, it may acquire, under the terms and in the manner the Contracting Officer considers appropriate, supplies or services similar to those terminated, and the Contractor will be liable to the Government for any excess costs for those supplies or services. However, the Contractor shall continue the work not terminated.

(c) Except for defaults of subcontractors at any tier, the Contractor shall not be liable for any excess costs if the failure to perform the contract arises from causes beyond the control and without the fault or negligence of the Contractor. Examples of such causes include (1) acts of God or of the public enemy, (2) acts of the Government in either its sovereign or contractual capacity, (3) fires, (4) floods, (5) epidemics, (6) quarantine restrictions, (7) strikes, (8) freight embargoes, and (9) unusually severe weather. In each instance the failure to perform must be beyond the control and without the fault or negligence of the Contractor.

(d) If the failure to perform is caused by the default of a subcontractor at any tier, and if the cause of the default is beyond the control of both the Contractor and the subcontractor, and without the fault or negligence of either, the Contractor shall not be liable

continued

> *Fig. 16-1 / continued*
>
> for any excess costs for failure to perform, unless the subcontracted supplies or services were obtainable from other sources in sufficient time for the Contractor to meet the required delivery schedule.
>
> (e) If this contract is terminated for default, the Government may require the Contractor to transfer title and deliver to the Government, as directed by the Contracting Officer, any (1) completed supplies, and (2) partially completed supplies and materials, parts, tools, dies, jigs, fixtures, plans, drawings, information, and contract rights (collectively referred to as "manufacturing materials" in this clause) that the Contractor has specifically produced or acquired for the terminated portion of this contract. Upon direction of the Contracting Officer, the Contractor shall also protect and preserve property in its possession in which the Government has an interest.
>
> (f) The Government shall pay contract price for completed supplies delivered and accepted. The Contractor and Contracting Officer shall agree on the amount of payment for manufacturing materials delivered and accepted and for the protection and preservation of the property. Failure to agree will be a dispute under the Disputes clause. The Government may withhold from these amounts any sum the Contracting Officer determines to be necessary to protect the Government against loss because of outstanding liens or claims of former lien holders.
>
> (g) If, after termination it is determined that the contractor was not in default, or that the default was excusable, the rights and obligations of the parties shall be the same as if the termination had been issued for the convenience of the Government.
>
> (h) The rights and remedies of the Government in this clause are in addition to any other rights and remedies provided by law or under this contract.

The "Default" clause for fixed-price supply and service contracts provides that when a contractor fails to deliver required supplies or to perform services within the *time* set forth in the contract (see Paragraph (a)(1)(i) of the Figure 16-1 clause), the Government may terminate the contract *immediately*. However, for any other default of a fixed-price supply or service contract, the Contracting Officer must notify the contractor of its deficiencies and give the contractor 10 days to correct them. This notice is called a "cure notice," and it is required where the contract schedule has not expired (and more than 10 days remain before the contract's due date). Only if the contractor fails to cure the problems delineated in the cure notice can the Contracting Officer terminate the contract for default. The "Default" clause for construction contracts (Figure 16-2) makes no provision for pretermination cure notices.

Figure 16-2

"DEFAULT (FIXED-PRICE CONSTRUCTION)" CLAUSE
(FAR 52.249-10)

(a) If the Contractor refuses or fails to prosecute the work or any separable part, with the diligence that will insure its completion within the time specified in this contract including any extension, or fails to complete the work within this time, the Government may, by written notice to the Contractor, terminate the right to proceed with the work (or the separable part of the work) that has been delayed. In this event, the Government may take over the work and complete it by contract or otherwise, and may take possession of and use any materials, appliances, and plant on the work site necessary for completing the work. The Contractor and its sureties shall be liable for any damage to the Government resulting from the Contractor's refusal or failure to complete the work within the specified time, whether or not the Contractor's right to proceed with the work is terminated. This liability includes any increased costs incurred by the Government in completing the work.

(b) The Contractor's right to proceed shall not be terminated nor the Contractor charged with damages under this clause, if—
(1) The delay in completing the work arises from unforeseeable causes beyond the control and without the fault or negligence of the Contractor. Examples of such causes include (i) acts of God or of the public enemy, (ii) acts of the Government in either its sovereign or contractual capacity, (iii) acts of another Contractor in the performance of a contract with the Government, (iv) fires, (v) floods, (vi) epidemics, (vii) quarantine restrictions, (viii) strikes, (ix) freight embargoes, (x) unusually severe weather, or (xi) delays of subcontractors or suppliers at any tier arising from unforeseeable causes beyond the control and without the fault or negligence of both the Contractor and the subcontractors or suppliers; and
(2) The Contractor, within 10 days from the beginning of any delay (unless extended by the Contracting Officer), notifies the Contracting Officer in writing of the causes of delay. The Contracting Officer shall ascertain the facts and the extent of delay. If, in the judgment of the Contracting Officer, the findings of fact warrant such action, the time for completing the work shall be extended.

continued

> *Fig. 16-2 / continued*
>
> The findings of the Contracting Officer shall be final and conclusive on the parties, but subject to appeal under the Disputes clause.
>
> (c) If, after termination of the Contractor's right to proceed, it is determined that the Contractor was not in default, or that the delay was excusable, the rights and obligations of the parties will be the same as if the termination had been issued for the convenience of the Government.
>
> (d) The rights and remedies of the Government in this clause are in addition to any other rights and remedies provided by law or under this contract.

B. BASES FOR TERMINATION

Terminations for default are much more common in supply contracts than in construction contracts. Reflecting this fact, the "Default" clause for supply and service contracts is more specific in stating the bases for default termination than is the clause for construction contracts. The standard clause used in supply and service contracts recites (see Paragraph (a) of the Figure 16-1 clause) that the Government has the right to terminate for default if the contractor fails to (1) *deliver* the contract supplies or perform the services *on time*, (2) *make progress* so as to endanger performance of the contract, or (3) *perform* any of the *other provisions* of the contract. On the other hand, the standard construction contract "Default" clause merely states that the Government may terminate the contract if the contractor "refuses or fails to prosecute the work or any separable part, with the diligence that will insure its completion within the time specified in [the] contract including any extension, or fails to complete the work within this time" (see Paragraph (a) of the Figure 16-2 clause). In addition, although not explicitly set forth in either "Default" clause, express or implied *repudiation* of the contract also constitutes a basis for default termination.

1. Failure To Deliver Or Perform

Paragraph (a)(1)(i) of the clause in Figure 16-1 provides that a contract may be terminated for default if the contractor fails to "[d]eliver the supplies or perform the services within the time specified in [the]. contract or any extension." This provision has traditionally been viewed as giving the Government the right to terminate a contract if (a) the contractor fails to deliver on the date specified, or (b) the contractor fails to comply with the specifications set forth in the contract. Thus, if the contractor fully complies with the specifications but fails to deliver on the date required, the contract may be terminated for default. Conversely, if the contractor delivers the items specified or performs the services required on time, but fails to comply with the specifications, the contract may also be terminated. Contractors are expected to perform in strict conformance with contract delivery schedules and contract specifications.

a. Timely Delivery. It has usually been held that time is "of the essence" in any Government contract containing fixed dates for performance. Thus, when a contractor fails to make timely delivery, the Government ordinarily may terminate the contract for default *immediately* and *without notice* after the close of business on the exact day specified in the delivery schedule.[4] Thus, a supply or service contractor is in danger of having its contract terminated for default as soon as the scheduled date for delivery has passed.[5] In fact, even an untimely delivery made before the Government had a reasonable opportunity to issue a termination notice has been found not to bar a default termination action.[6]

Even where a contract calls for deliveries in increments— with different dates specified for each increment—the Government has the right to terminate the *entire* contract (or the remaining undelivered quantities if some deliveries have been made and accepted) on the contractor's failure to make timely delivery of *any* increment.[7] It is only when a delinquent performance is *severable* that the right to terminate the entire contract for that delinquency does not arise. If a contract is found to be severable or divisible, the Government may only terminate those portions of the contract that are in default.[8]

A contract is not severable merely because delivery is required in increments or installments.[9] In addition, where it appears that the parties have intended to make payment of consideration depend on acceptable delivery of *all* items, a contract will be viewed as entire and not severable. For example, when a contract for delivery of several articles is to be paid in a lump sum, the contract will usually be held indivisible.[10]

b. Compliance With Specifications. As noted in Chapter 8, Section F, the Government is entitled to insist on strict compliance with contract specifications. Many default terminations have been upheld in connection with contractors' deviations from specifications. Thus, default terminations have been upheld where deviations (1) were minor in nature,[11] (2) were otherwise in accordance with commercial practice,[12] and (3) resulted in products as good as or better than the specified ones.[13]

Of course, the Government may not terminate in the absence of *objective* and *enforceable* performance standards.[14] And, a termination for default may not be upheld if the contractor's performance is deemed *substantially complete* (see Chapter 8, Section G, for a complete analysis of this "substantial performance" doctrine). Even though a contract has been substantially completed, however, a contractor cannot refuse to complete or correct work that is practical to perform. The Government may terminate a contract for default on the basis of such a refusal.[15]

2. Failure To Make Progress

A termination for failure to make progress may occur when the contractor fails to progress satisfactorily toward completion of performance—despite the fact that the final performance date has not yet arrived.[16] This basis for default termination is recognized in both the Figure 16-1 and Figure 16-2 clauses.

Paragraph (a)(1)(ii) of the "Default" clause for fixed-price supply and service contracts lists failure to make progress so as to endanger contract performance as a separate basis for default (see Figure 16-1). Unlike default terminations for untimely delivery, however, a contractor is entitled—under Paragraph (a)(2) of the clause—to notice and 10 days to cure the default *before* the Government may terminate the contract for default for failure to make progress.[17] The fixed-price construction contract clause does not require the Government to give the contractor any notice before terminating the contract for failure to "prosecute the work...with the diligence that will insure its completion within the time specified" (see Paragraph (a) of the Figure 16-2 clause).

A cure notice must specify the progress failures in sufficient detail to enable the contractor to effectively cure them unless the contractor already has been made aware of the failures.[18] In other words, the adequacy of the notice will be judged in light of all prior communications between the parties. For example, in one case, a cure notice merely stated that it was "apparent from the status of testing that you are failing to make progress as will permit delivery under the contract." The board of contract appeals held that the notice was adequate because the contractor was fully aware—from constant communications with a Government representative on the job—of the specific difficulties to which the notice referred.[19]

A termination for failure to make progress will be upheld if it is reasonably certain that the contractor—on the date of termination—was incapable of completing the contract within the time prescribed by the contract. For example, in a case where 60% of the scheduled time had elapsed but only 15% of the work had been completed, it was held that a termination for failure to make progress was proper.[20]

The Government has the heavy burden of demonstrating that a contractor's performance endangered completion of the contract. That burden has been described as requiring "convincing proof that [the contractor] had placed timely performance beyond his reach."[21] The mere failure of the contractor to assure the Government that the completion date will be met does not justify default termination.[22] However, certain indicators have been recognized as satisfying the Government's burden of proof. Thus, terminations for failure to make progress have been upheld where the contractor (a) failed to meet progress "milestones" (stages in production called for by the contract),[23] (b) delayed in effecting an agreement with an important supplier,[24] (c) failed to maintain necessary materials and supplies while attempting to secure cheaper prices than offered by suppliers,[25] or (d) lost or failed to employ key personnel.[26]

3. Failure To Perform Other Contract Provisions

The "Default" clause for fixed-price supply and service contracts set forth in Figure 16-1 provides, as a third specific ground for default termination, that the Government may terminate the contract if the contractor fails to perform "any of the other provisions of [the] contract" (see Paragraph (a)(1)(iii) of the Figure 16-1 clause). As with terminations for failure to make progress, the "Default" clause requires that a cure notice be given prior to a termination on this ground. Default termination based on a contractor's breach of other contract provisions has occurred where a contractor refused to provide cost records,[27] submitted fraudulent test reports,[28] and did not furnish required payment bonds.[29]

Note that a variety of other contract clauses apart from the "Default" clause—such as clauses that regulate the contractor's business or labor practices—may provide *independent* bases for terminating the contract if those provisions are breached by the contractor.[30]

4. Anticipatory Breach Of Contract

Although not expressly set forth in either the supply and service contract or the construction contract "Default" clauses, repudiation of the contract, whether express or implied, may also be a basis for default termination. The Government retains this common-law right under Paragraph (h) of the Figure 16-1 clause and Paragraph (d) of the Figure 16-2 clause. An "anticipatory breach" occurs "whenever there is a positive, definite, unconditional, and unequivocal manifestation of intent, by words or conduct, on the part of a contractor of his intent not to render the promised performance when the time fixed therefor by the contract shall arrive."[31]

A termination for anticipatory breach or repudiation of the contract will be found in two situations: (1) where it is evident from the circumstances that the contractor is totally unable to perform, although willing to do so, or (2) where the contractor—

before performance is due—makes a positive, definite, unconditional, and unequivocal statement that the contractor will not perform in accordance with the contract's terms. Examples of anticipatory breach include a contractor's closing of a plant accompanied by statements that the contractor did not intend to continue with performance,[32] and a contractor's conceded inability to correct serious product deficiencies within the delivery schedule.[33] However, where a contractor simply expressed disagreement with the Government's interpretation of the scope of work required by the contract but never indicated it would not perform the work if required to do so by the Government, it was held that there was not unequivocal evidence of a refusal to perform.[34]

Because a termination of a contract for anticipatory breach is not based on the "Default" clause, a cure notice is not required.[35]

The doctrine of anticipatory repudiation is closely connected to the contractor's duty to proceed (under the standard "Disputes" clause) with contract performance pending resolution of a contract dispute.[36] A refusal to proceed with performance pending resolution of a dispute may constitute a repudiation of the contract justifying default termination.[37] However, there are some exceptions to this rule. For example, a contractor is justified in refusing to continue performance where the Government materially breaches the contract by failing to pay the contractor,[38] for example, or by ordering work clearly in excess of what is required by the contract.[39]

C. THE TERMINATION DECISION

Although the Government has the *right* under the "Default" clause to terminate the contract when the contractor fails to perform, the Government does not have to exercise that right. If, for example, the Government needs the supplies or work and the delinquent contractor is likely to provide them before any other contractor, the Contracting Officer may allow contract performance to proceed. Thus, a Contracting Officer will generally weigh all options carefully—taking into account practical and business factors as well as alternatives to termination—before taking action against a defaulting contractor.

1. Contracting Officer Discretion

The FAR requires Contracting Officers to consider various *factors* in arriving at a default termination decision—such as the contractor's excuses for its failure, the availability of the supplies or services from other sources, the need for the supplies or services balanced against the time it would take to obtain them from the contractor or from another source, and the effect a termination would have on the contractor's other contracts.[40] The FAR also gives *alternatives* to default termination that the Government can pursue—such as permitting the defaulting contractor to continue performance by means of a subcontract or executing a no-cost termination settlement agreement.[41] If the Contracting Officer fails to give reasoned consideration to the factors listed in the FAR, the default termination may be overturned on appeal.[42] However, failure to consider one or more of the FAR factors will not necessarily invalidate a default termination if the termination was otherwise proper.[43]

Note that the "Default" clauses refer to action by the "Government" rather than by the "Contracting Officer." In this regard, it has been held that the termination decision is to be made by responsible officials of the Government, not necessarily limited to a Contracting Officer.[44] Indeed, a Contracting Officer can change his mind about terminating a contract for default after consulting the using agency.[45] But the procuring agency must exercise the discretion granted to it by the contract in deciding whether to terminate a contract. For example, termination based on the instructions of a U.S. Senator has been deemed improper.[46]

2. Improper Motive Or Grounds

A default termination is a drastic sanction that requires strict accountability by the Government for its termination action.[47] The default proceeding has been recognized essentially as a *forfeiture* so that every reasonable presumption is against the forfeiture.[48] Thus, the Government has the burden of sustaining its contention that there was a basis for default termination.[49]

The Government's right to terminate a contract for default has generally been upheld if valid grounds for the default termination exist at the time the termination notice is issued.[50] In fact, it has been held that in such a situation the right to terminate for default cannot be waived unless the Government receives adequate consideration for forgoing default termination.[51] However, a default termination may be held improper—even though valid grounds exist for the termination—if the *motivation* for the termination was improper.[52]

Sometimes the basis for the default termination referenced in the Government's termination notice or the cure notice is not legally supportable, but other grounds for default exist. For example, a particular defect in a contractor's product—cited in the termination notice—may be found not to exist, but the product is defective in other respects. In such a situation, the termination will usually be upheld unless the Government's error in incorrectly specifying the basis for the default action has *prejudiced* the contractor.[53] Prejudice is most often seen where the termination of a supply contract should have been for failure to make progress, but the Government erroneously based the termination on a failure to deliver. Prejudice is found in this sort of situation because the Government often neglects to give the contractor the required cure notice—thus depriving the contractor of the right to cure the default.[54]

Obviously, if the Government fails to specify whether a termination is for default or for convenience, it may be precluded from later asserting that the termination was for default.[55] Therefore, the Government must take care first in determining whether grounds for a default termination exist and then in asserting those grounds if it is appropriate to do so.

3. Notices

The Government's failure to issue the notices required by the "Default" clause or other relevant regulations may also invalidate the Government's termination decision. As noted earlier in Section A, under the Figure 16-1 clause (see Paragraph (a)(2)), a 10-day "cure notice" demanding that the contractor cure the failure is only required when the Government seeks to terminate a contract *prior to* the scheduled date of delivery or performance. A cure notice is not required if the delivery or performance schedule has expired, the contractor has repudiated performance, or less than 10 days remain before performance is due.[56] Failure to issue a "cure notice" when required will invalidate the default termination.

When a termination for default "appears appropriate," the Contracting Officer "should, if practicable," notify the contractor of the possibility of termination and request the contractor to "show cause" why the contract should not be terminated for default.[57] Although "show cause notices" are often sent to tardy contractors, the Government is not legally obligated to send such a notice or to wait the entire 10 days (or other period specified) before terminating the contract for default.[58]

When the Contracting Officer decides that termination is proper after complying with all the procedures set forth in the FAR, he must notify the contractor in writing.[59] Although the FAR lists the information that should be included in a "termination notice," the Government's omission of some of the required information will not invalidate a termination decision unless the omission prejudices the contractor.[60]

D. CONTRACTOR DEFENSES

When faced with termination of a contract for default, the contractor may be able to avoid the termination if it can show either (a) that contract performance is not late because the contractor encountered an excusable delay that extended the contract's schedule or (b) even though performance is late, the Government nevertheless waived the contract's due date.

1. Excusable Delay

Both the supply and service contract "Default" clause set out in Figure 16-1 (see Paragraphs (c) and (d)) and the construction contract "Default" clause in Figure 16-2 (see Paragraph (b)) provide examples of some recognized causes of delay that may excuse a contractor's failure to perform on time. The subject of excusable delay—including the types of delays enumerated in the clauses that may excuse a contractor from the sanction of default termination for late performance—is discussed in some detail in Chapter 12, Section B, and Chapter 26, Section B.

In addition, other delaying events that are not enumerated in the "Default" clauses may also be grounds for excusing a contractor's failure to deliver or perform on time (see Chapter 12, Section B.4). Perhaps the most common of these types of excusable delay is a *constructive change* in the scope or nature of performance brought about by the Government's action or inaction. (Constructive changes are discussed in detail in Chapter 11.) Other common Government-caused excusable delays are (1) delays in awarding a contract such that the contractor does not have a reasonable time to prepare for the start of performance,[61] (2) payment delays,[62] (3) unreasonable delays in approving contractor drawings, equipment, materials, or subcontractors,[63] (4) failure to accept or reject a "first article" within a reasonable time,[64] (5) improper and unreasonable Government inspections,[65] (6) formal or constructive suspensions of work (see Chapters 12 and 26), (7) defective specifications or drawings (see Chapter 8), (8) late or defective Government-furnished property (see Chapter 9), and (9) failure to disclose vital information.[66]

2. Waiver Of Due Date

Although a handy and much-used label, the Government's so-called "waiver" of a scheduled delivery date is more properly characterized as the Government's "election" to allow a contractor to continue with performance despite the fact that the contractor will not be able to deliver on time.[67] If the contractor fails to perform on or before the due date, the Government must—within a reasonable time—elect whether to terminate the contract for default or permit performance to continue. The Government is entitled to a period of "forbearance"—that is, a sufficient time to determine what to do. However, if the Government does not exercise its right to terminate within a reasonable time, and if the contractor relies on the Government's inaction and continues to perform the contract and incur costs, the Government may lose its right to terminate the contract.

Waiver is a more significant defense in supply contract defaults than in construction contract defaults primarily because a construction contractor is paid for partially completed acceptable work even if the contract is terminated, while a supply contractor that continues with performance while in default usually incurs costs that will not be recovered if the Government later terminates. Thus, continued performance of a construction contract after the completion date typically will not support a claim of waiver.[68]

a. Forbearance vs. Waiver. The forbearance period only lasts for a *reasonable* time. What is a reasonable time for the Government to decide whether or not to terminate depends on the circumstances of each case. Certainly, the forbearance period should be sufficient to allow the Government to investigate and determine whether there is excusable cause for the default and whether it wishes to allow the contractor to continue performance.[69] Once the forbearance period is passed, however, the Government's failure to terminate the contract constitutes a waiver of the delivery date that excuses the contractor's default.

It is frequently difficult to say when the forbearance period ends and a waiver of the default has occurred. In one unusual case, the Armed Services Board of Contract Appeals held that the Government should have terminated a contract as soon as the delivery time expired because—as a result of extensive discussions with the contractor and investigations before the delivery date—the Government had all the information it needed and knew the contractor was relying on its inaction.[70]

More commonly, however, mere inaction on the part of the Government after the delivery date has passed will not be construed as a waiver of default.[71] In fact, Government agencies often expressly inform delinquent contractors that the agencies' forbearance should *not* be considered a waiver of the Government's right to terminate.[72]

On the other hand, where Government action manifests an intent to have the contractor continue performance, the Government will be deemed to have waived the default. This can happen, for example, where the Government (a) actually directs a contractor to continue performance,[73] (b) enters into negotiations for or issues a change order or amendment to the contract,[74] (c) accepts a late delivery,[75] or (d) assists the contractor in locating a subcontractor.[76]

Although the facts and circumstances of each case must be considered, the Government has generally been held to a high standard of fairness for purposes of determining whether a waiver of a due date has taken place. If the Government no longer needs the supplies contracted for, a termination for default will be given especially close scrutiny.[77] Also, the more the contractor relies on lack of Government action and diligently continues with performance, the shorter the time the Government will be allowed to forbear terminating—perhaps only a week or 10 days.[78] However, if the contractor makes little or no effort to continue to perform, the period of forbearance may extend for a long time—perhaps as long as two years.[79] Moreover, even when a contractor continues to perform, the contractor usually must show that it did so in reliance on the Government's failure to terminate.[80]

b. Termination After Waiver. After "waiving" the delivery date, the Government can *revive* its right to terminate for default by establishing a new delivery schedule either unilaterally or by agreement with the contractor. If the contractor agrees to a new delivery schedule, the contractor will not be permitted to later complain that the new schedule allowed it less than a reasonable time to perform.[81] However, when the Government unilaterally establishes a new delivery schedule, it must set a *specific* date and notify the contractor of it.[82] The new performance date must take into consideration the capabilities of the particular contractor and be reasonably possible for the contractor to meet.[83]

Of course, if a contractor abandons or is clearly incapable of performance after a waiver, the contract may be terminated for default without notice.[84] Likewise, termination for default is proper if the contractor delivers nonconforming supplies after waiver of the contract delivery date.[85]

E. GOVERNMENT REMEDIES

The principal remedies for the Government on default termination of a contract are provided in the standard "Default" clauses for fixed-price contracts. Where the Government properly terminates a contract for default, it is entitled to charge the contractor the "excess costs" of reprocurement (see, e.g., Paragraph (b) of the Figure 16-1 clause and Paragraph (a) of the Figure 16-2 clause ("increased costs")).[86] This remedy provides the Government with a short-cut method of obtaining the contract work or items from a new source and charging the defaulted contractor for any increase in the cost of the reprocured work or items.

The standard "Default" clauses also provide that the Government's right to recover the excess costs of reprocurement is "in addition to any other rights and remedies provided by law or under this contract" (see Paragraph (h) of the Figure 16-1 clause and Paragraph (d) of the Figure 16-2 clause). Thus, the Government may recover its actual damages, recoup unliquidated progress payments, or confiscate project-related inventory *in addition to* or *instead of* excess reprocurement costs.

Finally, liquidated damages may also be assessed against the defaulted contractor if the contract contains a "Liquidated Damages" clause that meets the basic requirements of enforceability. The Government may assess liquidated damages as an alternative to termination in the case of default by the contractor or as a substitute for actual damages for delayed or incomplete work.

1. Excess Costs Of Reprocurement

a. Measure Of Excess Costs. The standard measure of excess costs is the difference between the contract price of the terminated contract and the price the Government is required to pay to the reprocurement contractor for the quantity of supplies or services called for under the terminated contract or for completion of unfinished work remaining under the terminated contract. To assess excess costs against the defaulted contractor, the Government must show that the reprocurement contract has been performed and that complete payment has been made.[87]

In addition to the difference in price between the terminated contract and the reprocured contract, excess reprocurement cost assessments may include the additional costs necessary for contract completion, such as (a) the cost to the Government of installing and then removing defective items,[88] (b) recovery of interest,[89] and (c) the administrative costs of reprocuring the supplies.[90]

b. Similarity Of Repurchase. The supply and service contract "Default" clause requires that the reprocured items or services be "similar to those terminated" (see Figure 16-1, Paragraph (b)). Although not expressly stated in the construction contract "Default" clause, in completing a terminated contract, the Government cannot make "material" changes in the work.[91] A question often arises about whether the reprocured supplies or work are sufficiently similar to the supplies or work ordered under the terminated contract to permit the Government to recover the difference in the cost between the two contracts. To be similar, the supplies need not be identical.[92] Generally, reprocured supplies will be considered similar to the supplies required by the terminated contract if any differences could have been ordered under the "Changes" clause, but any additional costs attributable to such changes will be deducted from the excess cost assessment.[93]

If, however, the changes result in a relaxation of the specifications or time for performance to such an extent that the original contractor could have met the relaxed specifications or later delivery date, the reprocurement contract cannot serve as a basis for the assessment of excess costs.[94] For example, where a reprocurement contractor was allowed to use new materials that the Government had refused to allow the defaulted contractor to use, assessment of excess costs was held improper because the contract items could have been supplied by the defaulted contractor had that contractor been given permission to use those materials.[95]

Generally, the burden is on the defaulted contractor to show that such changes have invalidated the excess cost assessment.[96] Usually, the excess costs will, at most, be reduced by the amount the changes increased the repurchase price—as, for example, when reprocurement of a smaller quantity has increased the unit prices of the supplies.[97]

Of course, if the Government reprocures *more* than the quantity called for under the terminated contract, the Government cannot charge the defaulted contractor for the *extra* units.[98] But, normally, unless the defaulted contractor can show that the unit prices were increased because of the larger quantity, the unit prices paid on the reprocurement contract will be the basis for the excess cost assessment—up to the quantity required under the terminated contract.[99]

c. Government Duty To Mitigate. In carrying out its reprocurement after a default termination, the Government has an obligation to limit the amount of excess costs as much as it reasonably can. Questions about whether the Government has met this obligation have arisen principally in two areas: (1) the timeliness of the reprocurement and (2) the method of reprocurement.

If the Government delays unreasonably in reprocuring—and the delay prejudices the defaulted contractor—the excess costs incurred may not be fully charged to the defaulted contractor.[100] For example, in one case, at a time when the principal material components of certain supplies were subject to rapid price inflation, undue delay by the Government in reprocuring the supplies resulted in a substantial reduction in the excess costs the Government was permitted to charge the defaulted contractor.[101]

If, in a reprocurement, the Government does not solicit bids from *all* the firms that bid on the original contract, it may be barred from assessing the excess costs incurred against the defaulted contractor unless it can prove that a lower price could not have been obtained had it done so.[102] However, if the Government can show an emergency or public exigency that required it to limit the reprocurement competition to those suppliers (or even a single source) able to make accelerated deliveries, it will satisfy its duty of mitigation.[103]

The Government must also accept completed supplies offered by the defaulted contractor if they meet contract requirements.[104] In fact, the defaulted contractor cannot *automatically* be excluded from the reprocurement. The default termination most likely will preclude award of the reprocurement to the defaulted contractor, however, on the ground that the contractor cannot be determined to be a responsible bidder.[105] If awarded the contract, the defaulted contractor may not receive more than the initial contract price for the reprocurement.[106] The Government's duty to mitigate may also require it to consider obtaining the items called for under the terminated contract under an existing, indefinite quantity contract rather than awarding a new contract.[107]

A failure by the Government to mitigate excess reprocurement costs does not necessarily mean that the defaulted contractor cannot be charged any excess costs. Frequently, the assessment is merely *reduced* by basing the charge to the defaulted contractor on the difference between the original contract price and the next lowest bid for that contract.[108]

d. Government Completion Of Work. The Government can decide to complete the contract itself (see, for example, Paragraph (a) of the Figure 16-2 clause) rather than repurchase from another contractor. In that event, the excess costs are based on the expenses the Government incurs in completing the contract.[109] Of course, the Government still retains its obligation to mitigate the expenses it incurs. And, if the work could have been done at a lower cost by an outside contractor, the Government cannot base its excess cost assessment on its in-house expenses.[110] Completion of the contract work by the Government is more common in construction contracts than in supply contracts.

2. Other Remedies

The "Default" clauses specifically reserve to the Government "any other rights and remedies provided by law or under [the] contract."[111] Some of the other remedies provided by the contract typically include recovery of unliquidated progress payments and transfer of title to the Government of completed contract items and manufacturing materials.[112]

The Government may also pursue other remedies provided by law, such as maintaining an action for breach of contract on the contractor's default. Common-law damages for breach of contract are available in addition to or instead of the excess costs of reprocurement. The breach of contract damages available to the Government in the case of default are the same as those available to the Government following a contractor's delay (although the damages may be limited to the extent the contract contains a "Liquidated Damages" clause that covers such damages).[113] Remedies apart from those provided under the "Default" clauses are only infrequently pursued—probably because the measure of proof required tends to be greater than it would be under the clause.

3. Liquidated Damages

If the default terminated contract contains a "Liquidated Damages" clause, those damages may be assessed against the contractor until the Government obtains completion of the contract work.[114] Liquidated damages are in addition to the excess costs of reprocurement. The "Liquidated Damages" clause used in fixed-price supply and service contracts provides that—in the case of a termination for default—the contractor shall be liable for liquidated damages (as well as excess costs) "until the time the Government may reasonably obtain delivery or performance of similar supplies or services."[115] In construction contracts, liquidated damages—in the event of termination for default—can extend until the time reasonably required to complete the work.[116] If the Government does not reprocure the contract items or complete the contract work, it cannot recover any liquidated damages from the defaulted contractor.[117] On the other hand, the Government's waiver of its right to terminate a contract for default does not also waive its right to assess liquidated damages for late completion of the contract.[118]

The "Liquidated Damages" clause requires the contractor to pay the Government a specific amount for each calendar day of delay. The stipulated amount of the liquidated damages is set at the time the contract is entered into and is the parties' estimate of the extent of loss that one party's breach of the contract would cause to the other. This stipulated amount serves as a substitute for actual damages caused by late performance. To be enforceable, the rate of liquidated damages used must be reasonable and not punitive. A contract may include an overall *maximum dollar amount* or *period of time* (or both) during which damages may be assessed to ensure that liquidated damages assessments are not unreasonable.[119]

Government policy is to use a "Liquidated Damages" clause in a contract when *both* (1) the time of delivery or performance is such an important factor that the Government may reasonably expect to suffer damages if the delivery or performance is delinquent, and (2) the extent or amount of actual damages would be difficult or impossible to ascertain or prove.[120] "Liquidated Damages" clauses are regularly used in construction contracts (see Chapter 26, Section C) and occasionally used in supply or service contracts. When used in supply contracts, "Liquidated Damages" clauses must meet the same standards and criteria as those used in construction contracts.

F. CONTESTING DEFAULT TERMINATIONS

1. Procedures

A contractor that believes its contract has been improperly terminated for default can contest that action by filing a claim with the Contracting Officer under the "Disputes" clause of the contract (see Chapter 19). If the Contracting Officer denies the claim, the contractor may appeal to the appropriate agency board of contract appeals or file suit in the U.S. Court of Federal Claims.[121] The procedures used in these forums are explained in detail in Chapters 20 and 21.

Sometimes a contractor chooses not to contest the default termination after receiving the Government's notice of termination (because, for example, the Government does not immediately proceed with a reprocurement and the contractor believes it will not be liable for excess costs). If the Government later completes the contract and assesses excess costs against the contractor, however, the contractor may wish to contest both the excess costs assessment and the underlying termination decision. Most tribunals will allow the contractor to challenge the propriety of the termination as well as the propriety of the reprocurement procedure by making a timely appeal from the assessment of excess costs.[122] In one case, although a contractor did not appeal from either the default termination or the excess cost assessment, the contractor was permitted to challenge both those actions when the contractor appealed from the assessment of *other* damages (the Government's cost of removing Government-furnished property).[123] However, in another case, a contractor that did appeal a default termination—but failed to prosecute the appeal so that it was dismissed with prejudice—was barred from later contesting the propriety of the termination when the contractor appealed from the excess cost assessment.[124]

2. Contractor Remedies

If a board or court determines that the contractor was actually not in default or the default was excusable, the termination for default will be converted into a termination for convenience (see Paragraph (g) of the Figure 16-1 clause and Paragraph (c) of the Figure 16-2 clause). Similarly, before the appeal is even decided, the Contracting Officer can convert the termination for default into one for the Government's convenience.

The contractor's recovery under a convenience termination may be significant. For example, under a convenience termination, the contractor is eligible to recover its costs of performance, some "continuing costs," settlement expenses, and a reasonable profit on completed work. For a more detailed discussion of the contractor's rights when a termination for default is converted into a termination for convenience, see Chapter 17.

Should the contractor be unsuccessful in contesting the propriety of the default termination itself, the contractor may still be able to challenge the excess costs assessment and achieve a reduction or elimination of those costs. Furthermore, in the case of a construction contract, even if a default termination is upheld, the contractor can recover under the contract's "Changes" and "Differing Site Conditions" clauses for work performed prior to the termination.[125] Similarly, in a supply contract, a contractor has been allowed to recover the costs of attempting to comply with impossible specification requirements—although the contract was later properly terminated for failing to meet revised specifications.[126]

REFERENCES

1. See, e.g., FAR 49.504.

2. FAR 52.249-8.

3. FAR 52.249-10.

4. DeVito v. U.S., 413 F.2d 1147 (Ct. Cl. 1969), 11 GC ¶ 307; General Ship & Engine Works, Inc., ASBCA 19243, 79-1 BCA ¶ 13657, 21 GC ¶ 143; Boston Pneumatics, Inc., ASBCA 14671, 71-1 BCA ¶ 8751. See also Franklin E. Penny Co. v. U.S., 524 F.2d 668 (Ct. Cl. 1975), 17 GC ¶ 458.

5. R.E.C. Corp., ASBCA 21357, 79-2 BCA ¶ 13961, 22 GC ¶ 14.

6. Nuclear Research Assocs., Inc., ASBCA 13563, 70-1 BCA ¶ 18237, 12 GC ¶ 165.

7. Raytheon Service Co., ASBCA 14746, 70-2 BCA ¶ 8390, 12 GC ¶ 417; Woodside Screw Machine Co., ASBCA 6936, 1962 BCA ¶ 3308, 4 GC ¶ 363.

8. Capitol City Const. Co., DOTCAB 74-29, 75-1 BCA ¶ 11012, 17 GC ¶ 122; R.E. Lee Electric Co., ASBCA 6195, 61-1 BCA ¶ 3002, 3 GC ¶ 377.

9. Delmar Mills, Inc., ASBCA 6138, 61-1 BCA ¶ 2910; Green Street, Inc., ASBCA 3137, 59-1 BCA ¶ 2089; Norrington v. Wright, 115 U.S. 188 (1855).

10. Telecommunication Consultants, ASBCA 13801, 69-2 BCA ¶ 7925.

11. Werner G. Smith, Inc., AGBCA 383, 75-1 BCA ¶ 10922; Arrow Lacquer Corp., ASBCA 4667, 58-2 BCA ¶ 2003; Acme Litho Plate Graining, Inc., ASBCA 2878, 56-2 BCA ¶ 1091.

12. E.g., Newark Boneless Meat Prods., Inc., ASBCA 22132, 78-2 BCA ¶ 13229.

13. E.g., Tri-M Builders, AGBCA 83-225-1 et al., 87-3 BCA ¶ 19972; Acme Litho Plate Graining, Inc., note 11, supra.

14. Mid-American Engrg. & Mfg., ASBCA 20939, 78-1 BCA ¶ 12870, 20 GC ¶ 29.

15. J.F. Kane Contracting Co., GSBCA 2005, 66-2 BCA ¶ 5992; Joe Dougherty Const. Co., GSBCA 1412, 65-2 BCA ¶ 4904.

16. See generally Speidel, "Default for Failure To Make Progress," Briefing Papers No. 64-5 (Oct. 1964), 1 BPC 87.

17. But see Lee Maintenance Co., PSBCA 522, 79-2 BCA ¶ 14067 (obligation to give contractor full 10-day period was "preempted" by contractor's threatening Government employees with physical harm), 21 GC ¶ 404.

18. Halifax Engrg., Inc v. U.S., 915 F.2d 689 (Fed. Cir. 1990), 9 FPD ¶ 137, 32 GC ¶ 347; Valley Contractors, ASBCA 9397, 1964 BCA ¶ 4071.

19. Midwest Engrg. & Const. Co., ASBCA 5801, 1962 BCA ¶ 3289, 4 GC ¶ 340.

20. W.B. Branin Const. Co., AGBCA 313, 73-1 BCA ¶ 9887. See also Olympic Painting Contractors, ASBCA 15773, 72-2 BCA ¶ 9549; Electronic Industries, Inc., ASBCA 11706, 66-2 BCA ¶ 5883. Cf. Pipe Tech, Inc., ENGBCA 5959 et al., 94-2 BCA ¶ 26649, 36 GC ¶ 191.

21. Norfolk Air Conditioning Service & Eqpt. Corp., ASBCA 14080, 71-1 BCA ¶ 8617, 13 GC ¶ 243. See also G.A. Karnavas Painting Co., ASBCA 19569, 76-1 BCA ¶ 11837, 18 GC ¶ 254; Flora Const. Co., ASBCA 9818, 67-1 BCA ¶ 6099.

22. Ener-Tech Automated Control Systems, Inc., ASBCA 31527, 89-3 BCA ¶ 22091, 31 GC ¶ 275.

23. AAR Corp., ASBCA 16486, 74-2 BCA ¶ 10653, 16 GC ¶ 382.

24. Marmac Industries, Inc., ASBCA 11861, 69-2 BCA ¶ 8067, 12 GC ¶ 240, affd. on reconsideration, 70-2 BCA ¶ 8421, 12 GC ¶ 404.

25. Kaufman DeDell Printing, Inc., ASBCA 19268, 75-1 BCA ¶ 11042, 17 GC ¶ 167; Alabama Bridge & Iron Co., ASBCA 6124, 61-1 BCA ¶ 2970, 3 GC ¶ 298(f).

26. Cal-Pacific Foresters, AGBCA 250, 70-1 BCA ¶ 8088.

27. American Business Systems, GSBCA 5140, 80-2 BCA ¶ 14461.

28. Michael C. Avino, Inc., ASBCA 31752, 89-3 BCA ¶ 22156, 31 GC ¶ 303.

29. Al's Enterprises, Ltd., PSBCA 13576, 70-1 BCA ¶ 8080.

30. E.g., FAR 52.203-3 ("Gratuities" clause), 52.222-6 ("Davis-Bacon Act" clause). See Kelso v. Kirk Bros. Mechanical Contractors, Inc., 16 F.3d 1173 (Fed. Cir. 1994), 13 FPD ¶ 26, 36 GC ¶ 283. See generally Cibinic, "Default Termination for Failure To Comply with 'Other Provisions': Requiring Contractors To Do the Complete Job," 8 Nash & Cibinic Rep. ¶ 24 (Apr. 1994).

31. Mission Valve & Pump Co., ASBCA 13552, 69-2 BCA ¶ 8010. See also Sunox, Inc., ASBCA 30025, 85-2 BCA ¶ 18077, 28 GC ¶ 92; Big Three Contracting Corp., ASBCA 20929, 79-1 BCA ¶ 13601. But see Scott Aviation, ASBCA 40776, 91-3 BCA ¶ 24123, 33 GC ¶ 317; M.V.I. Precision Machining, Ltd., ASBCA 37393, 91-2 BCA ¶ 23898, 33 GC ¶ 317 (Note); Martin Suchan, ASBCA 22521, 83-1 BCA ¶ 16323, 25 GC ¶ 167.

32. Southland Mfg. Corp., ASBCA 10519, 67-1 BCA ¶ 6128.

33. Wacline, Inc., ASBCA 8725, 1963 BCA ¶ 3903.

TERMINATION FOR DEFAULT 16-27

34. Norfolk Air Conditioning Service & Eqpt. Corp., note 21, supra.

35. E.g., Fairfield Scientific Corp., ASBCA 21151, 78-1 BCA ¶ 13082, affd. on reconsideration, 78-2 BCA ¶ 13429; Great Northern Forestry Service, AGBCA 85-260-1 et al., 90-2 BCA ¶ 22668.

36. See "Disputes" clause, FAR 52.233-1, para. (h).

37. E.g., Lon E. Nelson, AGBCA 80-179-1, 86-3 BCA ¶ 19077; Kirk Casavan, AGBCA 76-192, 78-2 BCA ¶ 13459.

38. E.g., H.E. & C.F. Blinee Contracting Co., ENGBCA 4174, 83-1 BCA ¶ 16388. Cf. U.S. v. DeKonty Corp., 922 F.2d 826 (Fed. Cir. 1991), 10 FPD ¶ 2 (Government's merely putting payment to the contractor "on hold" did not justify abandonment of the contract), 33 GC ¶ 37.

39. Malone v. U.S., 849 F.2d 1441 (Fed. Cir. 1988), 7 FPD ¶ 73 (Contracting Officer insisted improperly that a painting contractor repaint houses after 70% of the work had been done), 30 GC ¶ 314.

40. FAR 49.402-3(f).

41. FAR 49.402-4.

42. E.g., JAMCO Constructors, VABCA 3271 et al., 94-1 BCA ¶ 26405 (exercise of discretion involves more than pro forma checkoff of factors set forth in the FAR), 35 GC ¶ 705, reconsideration denied, 94-2 BCA ¶ 26792, 36 GC ¶ 258; Walsky Const. Co., ASBCA 41541, 94-1 BCA ¶ 26264, 35 GC ¶ 605, reconsideration denied, 94-2 BCA ¶ 26698.

43. E.g., Michigan Joint Sealing, Inc., ASBCA 41477, 93-3 BCA ¶ 26011; Lafayette Coal Co., ASBCA 32174, 89-3 BCA ¶ 21963, 31 GC ¶ 243.

44. Schlesinger v. U.S., 390 F.2d 702 (Ct. Cl. 1969), 10 GC ¶ 129.

45. Nuclear Research Corp. v. U.S., 814 F.2d 647 (Fed. Cir. 1987), 6 FPD ¶ 34, 29 GC ¶ 114.

46. Note 44, supra. See also Fairfield Scientific Corp. v. U.S., 611 F.2d 854 (Ct. Cl. 1979), 21 GC ¶ 515; Square Const. Co., ENGBCA 3494, 76-1 BCA ¶ 11747, 18 GC ¶ 114.

47. H.N. Bailey & Assocs. v. U.S., 449 F.2d 387 (Ct. Cl. 1971), 13 GC ¶ 503; J.D. Hedin Const. Co. v. U.S., 408 F.2d 424 (Ct. Cl. 1969), 11 GC ¶ 125.

48. Tri-State Tool Co., ASBCA 16300, 73-1 BCA ¶ 9886, 15 GC ¶ 170. See also Monitor Systems, ASBCA 14261, 71-1 BCA ¶ 8885, 13 GC ¶ 368.

49. G.A. Karnavas Painting Co., note 21, supra.

50. See, e.g., General Instruments Corp., ASBCA 9790, 67-1 BCA ¶ 6086, 9 GC ¶ 409; Quality Granite Const. Co., ASBCA 43846, 93-3 BCA ¶ 26703, 36 GC ¶ 27.

51. Comp. Gen. Dec. B-172266, 1971 CPD ¶ 34, 50 Comp. Gen. 769, 13 GC ¶ 266.

52. Darwin Const. Co. v. U.S., 811 F.2d 593 (Fed. Cir. 1987), 6 FPD ¶ 19, 29 GC ¶ 66. See generally Cibinic, "Default Terminations: To Be or Not To Be?," 2 Nash & Cibinic Rep. ¶ 33 (June 1988).

53. Cross-Aero Corp., ASBCA 14801, 71-2 BCA ¶ 9075, 14 GC ¶ 74.

54. See, e.g., Nanofast, Inc., ASBCA 12545, 69-1 BCA ¶ 7566.

55. See, e.g., Stroud Realty, HUDBCA 75-13, 76-1 BCA ¶ 11770, 18 GC ¶ 191.

56. FAR 49.607(a). See, e.g., Bendix Corp., GSBCA 4352, 77-2 BCA ¶ 12656, 19 GC ¶ 344.

57. FAR 49.402-3, 49.607(b).

58. Kan-Du Tool & Instrument Corp., ASBCA 23466, 79-2 BCA ¶ 13907, 21 GC ¶ 287. See Aargus Poly Bag, GSBCA 4314, 76-2 BCA ¶ 11927, 18 GC ¶ 394. Cf. Udis v. U.S., 7 Cl. Ct. 379 (1985), 3 FPD ¶ 105, 27 GC ¶ 155.

59. FAR 49.402-3(g).

60. E.g., Philadelphia Regent Builders, Inc. v. U.S., 634 F.2d 569 (Ct. Cl. 1980), 22 GC ¶ 454.

61. Valley Contractors, note 18, supra.

62. See RHJ Corp., ASBCA 9922, 66-1 BCA ¶ 5361.

63. See, e.g., Patti Const. Co., ASBCA 8423, 1964 BCA ¶ 4225.

64. See, e.g., Remsel Industries, Inc., ASBCA 5899, 61-1 BCA ¶ 2909, 3 GC ¶ 195. See also Tree Best Reforestors, Inc., AGBCA 82-266-3 et al., 83-1 BCA ¶ 16290, 25 GC ¶ 213. See generally Ewing, Lawrence & Zenner, "First-Article Contracts," Briefing Papers No. 93-6 (May 1993).

65. Paul G. Maddox, ASBCA 11712, 67-2 BCA ¶ 6415.

66. See, e.g., Cryo-Sonics, Inc., ASBCA 11483, 66-2 BCA ¶ 5890. See generally Victorino, Southern & Soyars-Berman, "Government Failure To Disclose," Briefing Papers No. 92-10 (Sept. 1992).

67. See generally Pettit, "Waiver of Delivery Date," Briefing Papers No. 71-6 (Dec. 1971), 2 BPC 151. See also DeVito v. U.S., note 4, supra.

68. See Olson Plumbing & Heating Co., ASBCA 17965, 75-1 BCA ¶ 11203, 17 GC ¶ 427. But see Corway, Inc., ASBCA 20683, 77-1 BCA ¶ 12357, 19 GC ¶ 172.

69. Standard Electronics Corp., ASBCA 14753, 73-2 BCA ¶ 10137, 16 GC ¶ 100. See also Cecile Industries, Inc., ASBCA 24600 et al., 83-2 BCA ¶ 16842, 26 GC ¶ 10.

70. Amecon Div., Litton Systems, Inc., ASBCA 19867, 77-1 BCA ¶ 12329.

71. Lapp Insulator Co., ASBCA 13303, 70-1 BCA ¶ 8219, 12 GC ¶ 341. But see Flexonics Div., Universal Oil Products Co., ASBCA 18485, 74-1 BCA ¶ 10525, 16 GC ¶ 209.

72. See, e.g., P.J. Hydraulics, Inc., ASBCA 16310, 72-2 BCA ¶ 9524, 14 GC ¶ 398.

73. See Lemesany Roofing & Insulation Co., IBCA 533-12-65, 67-2 BCA ¶ 6413.

74. New Jersey Mfg. Co., ASBCA 15216, 72-1 BCA ¶ 9420; Monitor Plastics Corp., ASBCA 11187, 67-2 BCA ¶ 6408, 10 GC ¶ 42. See Kings Pt. Mfg. Co., ASBCA 27201, 85-2 BCA ¶ 18043.

75. See Phil Rich Fan Mfg. Co., ASBCA 12770, 71-1 BCA ¶ 8694, 13 GC ¶ 395. See also Multi Electric Mfg. Inc., ASBCA 30055, 85-1 BCA ¶ 17878.

76. J.J. Seifert Machine Co., ASBCA 41398, 91-2 BCA ¶ 23705, 33 GC ¶ 195 (Note).

77. Flexonics Div., Universal Oil Products Co., note 71, supra.

78. Devito v. U.S., note 4, supra.

79. Security Parachute Co., ASBCA 20334, 76-1 BCA ¶ 11722.

80. Olson Plumbing & Heating Co. v. U.S., 602 F.2d 950 (Ct. Cl. 1979), 21 GC ¶ 344.

81. Systems & Industry Optical, ASBCA 21635, 79-2 BCA ¶ 13966, 21 GC ¶ 388.

82. International Telephone & Telegraph Corp., ITT Defense Communications Div. v. U.S., 509 F.2d 541 (Ct. Cl. 1975).

83. L.W. Foster Sportswear Co., ASBCA 5754, 1962 BCA ¶ 3364, 4 GC ¶ 404.

84. Discount Co. v. U.S., 554 F.2d 435 (Ct. Cl. 1977), 19 GC ¶ 261; Ace Electronics Assocs., Inc., ASBCA 11496, 67-2 BCA ¶ 6456.

85. See Bendix Corp., note 56, supra.

86. See generally Crowell & Johnson, "Excess Reprocurement Costs," Briefing Papers No. 67-6 (Dec. 1967), 1 BPC 281.

87. Whitlock Corp. v. U.S., 141 Ct. Cl. 758 (1958).

88. Jung Ah Industrial Co., ASBCA 22632, 79-1 BCA ¶ 13643, 21 GC ¶ 91.

89. Telectro Systems Corp., ASBCA 21976, 78-2 BCA ¶ 13480, 21 GC ¶ 6; Read Plastics, Inc., GSBCA 4159-R, 77-2 BCA ¶ 12859, 20 GC ¶ 9.

90. FAR 49.402-7. But see Birken Mfg. Co., ASBCA 32651, 88-1 BCA ¶ 20385, 30 GC ¶ 12.

91. See U.S. v. California Bridge & Const. Co., 245 U.S. 337 (1917).

92. United Microwave Co., ASBCA 9420, 65-1 BCA ¶ 4641, 8 GC ¶ 115.

93. Consolidated Airborne Systems, Inc. v. U.S., 348 F.2d 941 (Ct. Cl. 1965), 7 GC ¶ 337; Anglers Co., GSBCA 4230, 77-1 BCA ¶ 12319, 19 GC ¶ 219; National Robe Co., ASBCA 11227, 67-1 BCA ¶ 6365; Skiatron Electronics & Television Corp., ASBCA 9564, 65-2 BCA ¶ 5098, 8 GC ¶ 37.

94. F.R. Schultz Const. Co., AGBCA 455, 79-2 BCA ¶ 13890, 21 GC ¶ 263; Sterling Tool, Inc., ASBCA 19790, 75-2 BCA ¶ 11577, 18 GC ¶ 153.

95. Federal Identification Co., ASBCA 9117, 1964 BCA ¶ 4191, 8 GC ¶ 29.

96. U.S. v. Warsaw Elevator, 213 F.2d 517 (2d Cir. 1954); Guenther Systems, Inc., ASBCA 16238, 73-1 BCA ¶ 9868, 15 GC ¶ 97.

97. Consolidated Airborne Systems, Inc. v. U.S., note 93, supra.

98. Onus Co., ASBCA 16706, 72-2 BCA ¶ 9722, 15 GC ¶ 62.

99. F.P. Pla Tool & Mfg. Co., ASBCA 19073, 75-1 BCA ¶ 11091, 17 GC ¶ 185; San Antonio Const. Co., ASBCA 8110, 1964 BCA ¶ 4479, 8 GC ¶ 33.

100. Calmont Industries, Inc., ASBCA 10376, 65-2 BCA ¶ 5180, 9 GC ¶ 119.

101. Rayco, Inc., ENGBCA 4792, 88-2 BCA ¶ 20671, 30 GC ¶ 238. See also Continental Chemical Corp., GSBCA 4483, 76-2 BCA ¶ 11948, 18 GC ¶ 438; Hiltemp Wires Co., ASBCA 11638, 67-1 BCA ¶ 6252.

102. See Dillon Total Maintenance, Inc. v. U.S., 218 Ct. Cl. 732 (1978), 21 GC ¶ 48. See also Pastushin Aviation Co., ASBCA 21243 et al., 82-1 BCA ¶ 15639.

103. Vari-Ohm Electronics, Inc., ASBCA 12875, 69-2 BCA ¶ 7782.

104. Junkunc Bros., American Lock Co., ASBCA 12042, 68-1 BCA ¶ 7059, 10 GC ¶ 368.

105. Marimac Industries, Inc., ASBCA 12158, 72-1 BCA ¶ 9249.

106. Churchill Chemical Corp. v. U.S., 602 F.2d 358 (Ct. Cl. 1979), 21 GC ¶ 306.

107. Century Tool Co., GSBCA 4006, 76-2 BCA ¶ 12030, 18 GC ¶ 409; Hyland Electrical Supply Co., ASBCA 19270, 75-2 BCA ¶ 11466, 17 GC ¶ 483.

108. Zero Temp, Inc., ASBCA 21590, 78-1 BCA ¶ 13212; T.M. Industries, ASBCA 18729, 77-1 BCA ¶ 12452.

109. Collins Electronics, Inc., ASBCA 15956, 72-2 BCA ¶ 9542, 14 GC ¶ 415.

110. Brent L. Sellick, ASBCA 21869, 78-2 BCA ¶ 13510, 21 GC ¶ 12.

111. See generally Williamson & Medill-Jones, "Government Damages for Default," Briefing Papers No. 89-7 (June 1989), 8 BPC 377.

112. See, e.g., FAR 52.232-16, para. (d); FAR 52.249-8, para. (e).

113. E.g., Tester Corp. v. U.S., 1 Cl. Ct. 370 (1982), 1 FPD ¶ 15, 25 GC ¶ 10.

114. See FAR 12.202(c).

115. FAR 52.212-4, para. (b).

116. See FAR 52.212-5, para. (b).

117. Hydro Flex Inc., ASBCA 20352, 77-1 BCA ¶ 12353, 19 GC ¶ 378.

118. McDonough Const. Co. of La., DOTCAB 76-10, 78-1 BCA ¶ 12930, 20 GC ¶ 114.

119. FAR 12.202(b).

120. FAR 12.202(a).

121. See 28 USC § 1491(a)(2), amended by Federal Courts Administration Act of 1992, P.L. 102-572, § 907. See generally Nash, "Postscript: Appealing a Default Termination," 7 Nash & Cibinic Rep. ¶ 3 (Jan. 1993).

122. D. Moody Co. v. U.S., 5 Cl. Ct. 70 (1984), 2 FPD ¶ 150; Airco, Inc., IBCA 1074-8-75, 76-1 BCA ¶ 11822, 18 GC ¶ 209; Fulford Mfg. Co., ASBCA 2143, 6 CCF ¶ 61815 (1955).

123. Pantronics Inc., ASBCA 20982, 78-2 BCA ¶ 13285, 20 GC ¶ 377.

124. Bullock Intl., Inc., ASBCA 44210, 93-2 BCA ¶ 25692.

16-32 GOVERNMENT CONTRACT GUIDEBOOK

125. Sosa y Barbero Constructores, S.A., ENGBCA PCC-57, 89-2 BCA ¶ 21754, 31 GC ¶ 194.

126. Laka Tool & Stamping Co. v. U.S., 650 F.2d 270 (Ct. Cl. 1981), 23 GC ¶ 271. See also Clay Bernard Systems Intl., Ltd., ASBCA 25382, 88-3 BCA ¶ 20856.

TERMINATION FOR CONVENIENCE

17

A. Government's Convenience Termination Right
   1. Standard "Termination For Convenience" Clause
   2. Scope Of Right

B. Termination Procedures
   1. Government's Obligations
   2. Contractor's Obligations

C. Constructive Termination
   1. Conversion Of Improper Default Termination
   2. Cancellation Of Contract, Award, Or Work

D. Contractor Recovery
   1. Settlement Proposals
   2. Settlement Principles & Limitations
   3. Special Termination Costs
   4. Settlement Expenses
   5. Subcontractor Claims
   6. Profit
   7. Loss Adjustments

E. Partial Terminations
   1. Partial Termination vs. Deductive Change
   2. Contractor Recovery

In the commercial marketplace, a buyer is not normally allowed to cancel a contract simply because his needs change. An attempt to do so could be regarded by the seller as a breach of contract entitling him to recover damages from the buyer, including anticipated profit. This is not the case in a Government contract, for most Government contracts contain a "Termination for Convenience of the Government" clause. The "Termination for Convenience" clause permits the Government to cancel a contract without cause—that is, cancel a contract simply because the Government's needs change and regardless of contractor fault.

This chapter explores the unusual power of the Government under the "Termination for Convenience" clause to escape from its contractual obligations. Specifically, it examines (1) the standard "Termination for Convenience" contract clause and the scope of the Government's right under that clause, (2) the termination procedures set forth in the clause and the regulations that apply to both the Government and the contractor, (3) constructive terminations for convenience, (4) what a contractor can expect to recover in the termination settlement, and (5) partial terminations.

A. GOVERNMENT'S CONVENIENCE TERMINATION RIGHT

The Government's reservation in its contracts of the right to terminate the contracts for convenience arose primarily to provide the Government a means to discontinue contracts that are made obsolete by technological and other developments or that are otherwise no longer advantageous to the Government. In exchange for the privilege of being able to terminate a contract with relative ease, the Government agrees to make the contractor "whole"; that is, to reimburse the contractor for all reasonable and allocable costs incurred in connection with performance, as well as a reasonable profit on work done. The contractor is also entitled to recover certain post-termination costs and settlement expenses. The contractor may not, however, recover its *anticipated profits* (profits it had reasonably expected to earn on the terminated portion of the contract).

1. Standard "Termination For Convenience" Clause

The right of the Government to terminate a contract for its own convenience is embodied in standard "Termination for Convenience of the Government" clauses.[1] Typical of these is the FAR "Termination for Convenience of the Government (Fixed-Price)" clause, designated for use in fixed-price contracts expected to exceed $100,000.[2] This clause is set forth in Figure 17-1.

Figure 17-1

"TERMINATION FOR CONVENIENCE OF THE GOVERNMENT (FIXED-PRICE)" CLAUSE
(FAR 52.249-2)

(a) The Government may terminate performance of work under this contract in whole or, from time to time, in part if the Contracting Officer determines that a termination is in the Government's interest. The Contracting Officer shall terminate by delivering to the Contractor a Notice of Termination specifying the extent of termination and the effective date.

(b) After receipt of a Notice of Termination, and except as directed by the Contracting Officer, the Contractor shall immediately proceed with the following obligations, regardless of any delay in determining or adjusting any amounts due under this clause:

(1) Stop work as specified in the notice.

(2) Place no further subcontracts or orders (referred to as subcontracts in this clause) for materials, services, or facilities, except as necessary to complete the continued portion of the contract.

(3) Terminate all subcontracts to the extent they relate to the work terminated.

(4) Assign to the Government, as directed by the Contracting Officer, all right, title, and interest of the contractor under the subcontracts terminated, in which case the Government shall have the right to settle or to pay any termination settlement proposal arising out of those terminations.

(5) With approval or ratification to the extent required by the Contracting Officer, settle all outstanding liabilities and termination settlement proposals arising from the termination of subcontracts; the approval or ratification will be final for purposes of this clause.

(6) As directed by the Contracting Officer, transfer the title and deliver to the Government (i) the fabricated or unfabricated parts, work in process, completed work, supplies, and other material pro-

continued

Fig. 17-1 / continued

duced or acquired for the work terminated, and (ii) the completed or partially completed plans, drawings, information, and other property that, if the contract had been completed, would be required to be furnished to the Government.

(7) Complete performance of the work not terminated.

(8) Take any action that may be necessary, or that the Contracting Officer may direct, for the protection and preservation of the property related to this contract that is in the possession of the Contractor and in which the Government has or may acquire an interest.

(9) Use its best efforts to sell, as directed or authorized by the Contracting Officer, any property of the types referred to in subparagraph (6) above; *provided,* however, that the Contractor (i) is not required to extend credit to any purchaser and (ii) may acquire the property under the conditions prescribed by, and at prices approved by, the Contracting Officer. The proceeds of any transfer or disposition will be applied to reduce any payments to be made by the Government under this contract, credited to the price or cost of the work, or paid in any other manner directed by the Contracting Officer.

(c) After expiration of the plant clearance period as defined in Subpart 45.6 of the Federal Acquisition Regulation, the Contractor may submit to the Contracting Officer a list, certified as to quantity and quality, of termination inventory not previously disposed of, excluding items authorized for disposition by the Contracting Officer. The Contractor may request the Government to remove those items or enter into an agreement for their storage. Within 15 days, the Government will accept title to those items and remove them or enter into a storage agreement. The Contracting Officer may verify the list upon removal of the items, or if stored, within 45 days from submission of the list, and shall correct the list, as necessary, before final settlement.

(d) After termination, the Contractor shall submit a final termination settlement proposal to the Contracting Officer in the form and with the certification prescribed by the Contracting Officer. The Contractor shall submit the proposal promptly, but no later than 1 year from the effective date of termination, unless extended in writing by the Contracting Officer upon written request of the Contractor within this 1-year period. However, if the Contracting Officer determines that the facts justify it, a termination settlement proposal may be received and acted on after 1 year or any extension. If the Contractor fails to submit the proposal within the time allowed, the Contracting Officer may determine, on the basis of information available, the amount, if any, due the Contractor because of the termination and shall pay the amount determined.

continued

Fig. 17-1 / continued

(e) Subject to paragraph (d) above, the Contractor and the Contracting Officer may agree upon the whole or any part of the amount to be paid because of the termination. The amount may include a reasonable allowance for profit on work done. However, the agreed amount, whether under this paragraph (e) or paragraph (f) below, exclusive of costs shown in subparagraph (f)(3) below, may not exceed the total contract price as reduced by (1) the amount of payments previously made and (2) the contract price of work not terminated. The contract shall be amended, and the Contractor paid the agreed amount. Paragraph (f)(3) below shall not limit, restrict, or affect the amount that may be agreed upon to be paid under this paragraph.

(f) If the Contractor and the Contracting Officer fail to agree on the whole amount to be paid because of the termination of work, the Contracting Officer shall pay the Contractor the amounts determined by the Contracting Officer as follows, but without duplication of any amounts agreed on under paragraph (e) above:

(1) The contract price for completed supplies or services accepted by the Government (or sold or acquired under subparagraph (b)(9) above) not previously paid for, adjusted for any saving of freight and other charges.

(2) The total of—

(i) The costs incurred in the performance of the work terminated, including initial costs and preparatory expense allocable thereto, but excluding any costs attributable to supplies or services paid or to be paid under subparagraph (f)(1) above;

(ii) The cost of settling and paying termination settlement proposals under terminated subcontracts that are properly chargeable to the terminated portion of the contract if not included in subdivision (i) above; and

(iii) A sum, as profit on subdivision (i) above, determined by the Contracting Officer under 49.202 of the Federal Acquisition Regulation, in effect on the date of this contract, to be fair and reasonable; however, if it appears that the Contractor would have sustained a loss on the entire contract had it been completed, the Contracting Officer shall allow no profit under this subdivision (iii) and shall reduce the settlement to reflect the indicated rate of loss.

(3) The reasonable costs of settlement of the work terminated, including—

(i) Accounting, legal, clerical, and other expenses reasonably necessary for the preparation of termination settlement proposals and supporting data;

(ii) The termination and settlement of subcontracts (excluding the amounts of such settlements); and

continued

Fig. 17-1 / continued

(iii) Storage, transportation, and other costs incurred, reasonably necessary for the preservation, protection, or disposition of the termination inventory.

(g) Except for normal spoilage, and except to the extent that the Government expressly assumed the risk of loss, the Contracting Officer shall exclude from the amounts payable to the Contractor under paragraph (f) above, the fair value, as determined by the Contracting Officer, of property that is destroyed, lost, stolen, or damaged so as to become undeliverable to the Government or to a buyer.

(h) The cost principles and procedures of Part 31 of the Federal Acquisition Regulation, in effect on the date of this contract, shall govern all costs claimed, agreed to, or determined under this clause.

(i) The Contractor shall have the right of appeal, under the Disputes clause, from any determination made by the Contracting Officer under paragraph (d), (f), or (k), except that if the Contractor failed to submit the termination settlement proposal within the time provided in paragraph (d) or (k), and failed to request a time extension, there is no right of appeal. If the Contracting Officer has made a determination of the amount due under paragraph (d), (f), or (k), the Government shall pay the Contractor (1) the amount determined by the Contracting Officer if there is no right of appeal or if no timely appeal has been taken, or (2) the amount finally determined on an appeal.

(j) In arriving at the amount due the Contractor under this clause, there shall be deducted—

(1) All unliquidated advance or other payments to the Contractor under the terminated portion of this contract;

(2) Any claim which the Government has against the Contractor under this contract; and

(3) The agreed price for, or the proceeds of sale of, materials, supplies, or other things acquired by the Contractor or sold under the provisions of this clause and not recovered by or credited to the Government.

(k) If the termination is partial, the Contractor may file a proposal with the Contracting Officer for an equitable adjustment of the price(s) of the continued portion of the contract. The Contracting Officer shall make any equitable adjustment agreed upon. Any proposal by the Contractor for an equitable adjustment under this clause shall be requested within 90 days from the effective date of termination unless extended in writing by the Contracting Officer.

continued

> *Fig. 17-1 / continued*
>
> (l) (1) The Government may, under the terms and conditions it prescribes, make partial payments and payments against costs incurred by the Contractor for the terminated portion of the contract, if the Contracting Officer believes the total of these payments will not exceed the amount to which the Contractor will be entitled.
>
> (2) If the total payments exceed the amount finally determined to be due, the Contractor shall repay the excess to the Government upon demand, together with interest computed at the rate established by the Secretary of the Treasury under 50 U.S.C. App. 1215(b)(2). Interest shall be computed for the period from the date the excess payment is received by the Contractor to the date the excess is repaid. Interest shall not be charged on any excess payment due to a reduction in the Contractor's termination settlement proposal because of retention or other disposition of termination inventory until 10 days after the date of the retention or disposition, or a later date determined by the Contracting Officer because of the circumstances.
>
> (m) Unless otherwise provided in the contract or by statute, the Contractor shall maintain all records and documents relating to the terminated portion of this contract for 3 years after final settlement. This includes all books and other evidence bearing on the Contractor's costs and expenses under this contract. The Contractor shall make these records and documents available to the Government, at the Contractor's office, at all reasonable times, without any direct charge. If approved by the Contracting Officer, photographs, microphotographs, or other authentic reproductions may be maintained instead of original records and documents.

So important is the right of convenience termination that even when a contracting agency improperly neglects to include a clause covering the right in a contract, it may be held that it was incorporated into the contract as a matter of law.[3] On the other hand, as the Court of Claims observed, if the convenience termination clause is properly absent or inapplicable, the clause will not be read into the contract, and the contractor's "recovery is to be measured by its anticipated profits from the contract."[4]

2. Scope Of Right

The "Termination for Convenience" clause permits the Government to terminate a contract for convenience—either in whole or in part—when termination is "in the Government's interest" (see Paragraph (a) of the Figure 17-1 clause). Although this right is very broad, it is not without limits. The courts and boards have traditionally held that a termination for convenience is conclusive unless the contractor can prove that the Government acted in *bad faith* or *abused its discretion*. Thus, termination of a requirements contract was held to be improper when it was part of an attempt by a Government agency to effectively debar or suspend a contractor from Government business without following regulatory procedures.[5] The bad faith/abuse of discretion test is very difficult for a contractor to meet, however. An allegation of bad faith must be supported by "well-nigh irrefragable proof" that the Government acted with specific intent to injure the contractor.[6] Similarly, to show an abuse of discretion, the contractor must show that a Contracting Officer's decision to terminate had no reasonable relation to the Government's best interest.[7]

In addition, the Government may not use the "Termination for Convenience" clause to "dishonor with impunity its contractual obligations" (including its obligation to pay the contractor's anticipated profits) unless there has been some *change in circumstances* between the time of award of the contract and the time of termination.[8] For example, the Government may not terminate a requirements contract to take advantage of another contractor's lower price—of which the Government was aware before award.[9] Not all courts and boards have recognized the "changed circumstances" rule—or they have interpreted it very narrowly—in challenges to convenience terminations, however.[10]

B. TERMINATION PROCEDURES

The FAR (in conjunction with the "Termination for Convenience" clause) sets forth procedures to be followed by the Contracting Officer when terminating a contract for convenience (as it does for default terminations, see Chapter 16). It also describes the duties of the contractor after receiving a notice of termination.

1. Government's Obligations

a. Written Notice. The FAR directs the Contracting Officer to issue a detailed, written notice to terminate a contract for convenience.[11] Often, the Contracting Officer who terminates the contract—either for default or for convenience—will be designated as a Termination Contracting Officer (TCO), and will be a different individual than the Contracting Officer who awarded the contract (commonly called the Procuring Contracting Officer) or the one who administered performance (the Administrative Contracting Officer).

Under the FAR, the termination notice should include the following:[12]

(1) A statement that the contract is being terminated for the convenience of the Government.

(2) The effective date of the termination.

(3) The extent of the termination (i.e., whether the entire contract—or only a designated portion—is being terminated).

(4) Any special instructions regarding work-in-process or other matters.

(5) Recommended actions the contractor should take to minimize the impact of the termination on personnel, especially if the termination will result in a significant reduction in the contractor's work force.

b. Post-Termination Duties. After issuance of the termination notice, the FAR directs and authorizes the TCO to enter into a settlement agreement with the contractor. Specifically, the TCO should (a) examine the contractor's settlement proposal and negotiate a complete settlement, (b) if necessary to expedite settlement, request assistance from specially qualified personnel on legal, accounting, or contractual matters, (c) hold a conference with the contractor to develop a program for effecting the settlement, including the attendance of subcontractors if appropriate, and covering topics such as the status of any continuing work, the principles to be followed in settling subcontractor settlement proposals, arrangements for transfer of title and delivery to the Government of material or inventories, the accounting review of settlement proposals, time schedules for settlement negotiations, and the actions taken by the contractor to minimize the impact of the termination on its employees.[13]

2. Contractor's Obligations

A written notice of a termination for convenience usually includes detailed and specific procedures for the contractor to follow, including direction to follow the procedures contained in the "Termination for Convenience of the Government" clause in the contract (see, for example, Paragraph (b) of the Figure 17-1 clause).[14] Failure to follow these instructions exactly can result in disallowance of costs incurred. The notice and clause generally require that the contractor—

(1) Stop work immediately on the terminated portion of the contract and stop placing subcontracts.

(2) Terminate all subcontracts related to the terminated portion of the prime contract.

(3) Immediately advise the TCO of any special circumstances precluding stoppage of work.

(4) Perform the continued portion of the contract if the termination is partial and submit any request for equitable adjustment promptly.

(5) Take any action necessary to protect property in the contractor's possession in which the Government has or may acquire an interest.

(6) Promptly notify the TCO of any legal proceedings growing out of any subcontract or other commitment related to the terminated portion of the contract.

(7) Settle subcontractors' claims arising out of the termination, obtaining any required approvals and ratifications from the TCO.

(8) Promptly submit (within one year from the effective date of the termination) a settlement proposal, supported by appropriate schedules.

(9) Dispose of termination inventory, as directed and authorized by the TCO.

C. CONSTRUCTIVE TERMINATION

In addition to intentional terminations for convenience that are effected by written notice to the contractor from the Contracting Officer, a convenience termination may be deemed to have taken place by operation of law. These so-called "constructive terminations" can come about either by (1) conversion of an improper termination for default into a termination for convenience or (2) cancellation of a contract, award, or work.

1. Conversion Of Improper Default Termination

As discussed in Chapter 16, Section F.2, the typical "Default" clause provides that if a termination for default is determined to be erroneous—because the contractor actually was not in default or because the default was excusable, for example—the default termination will be converted to a convenience termination.[15] The contractor's recovery then will be the same as if the contract had been terminated for convenience (see Section D below).

2. Cancellation Of Contract, Award, Or Work

The most common constructive termination occurs when the Government takes action to cancel a contract or prevent the contractor from continuing performance but does not use the "Termination for Convenience" clause. The court or board reviewing the Government's action will apply the clause "constructively" to limit the contractor's recovery (that is, to prevent the contractor from recovering its anticipated profits). For example, if the Government wrongfully cancels an award as a result of an award controversy, the remedy is to convert the Government's mistaken cancellation into a termination of the contract for the Government's convenience.[16]

A constructive termination can also be based on "equitable estoppel." That is, the Government may not be allowed to repudiate or fail to extend a contract when (a) its prior actions were inconsistent with such repudiation or failure to extend, and (b) the contractor changed its position in reliance on those actions. For example, the Government was barred in one case from denying the existence of a contract for the full advertised quantity of boxes because it failed to notify an apparent low bidder of a late bid that it had decided to accept, thereby limiting the apparent low bidder to award of an uneconomical quantity.[17] Likewise, the assurance—by an authorized Government representative at a bidder's conference—that the Government would exercise its option to renew a two-month contract for an entire year entitled a contractor to recover the substantial preparatory costs the contractor incurred in reliance on the promise of the one-year extension.[18] In the first case, the Government's action was deemed a termination for convenience of the major quantity awarded to the late bidder. In the second, the contractor was permitted to file a termination for convenience claim based on the Government's failure to renew the contract for an additional year.

The constructive termination doctrine has been applied, in particular, to "requirements" contracts. These are contracts in which the quantity is not definite, but the Government agrees to order from the contractor all its requirements of specified goods or services for a designated period. The Government has the obligation to use due care in establishing the *estimated* quantities on which bids for requirements contracts are based. If the Government does not use due care in calculating the estimates, the contractor may be entitled to relief—by way of a constructive partial termination—when the actual requirements are less than estimated.[19]

Similarly, a constructive termination can occur if estimated requirements are not realized because of the Government's own actions after the requirements contract is awarded. For example, a constructive, partial termination of a painting contract was held to have taken place when the Government had some of the required painting done by its own employees.[20]

D. CONTRACTOR RECOVERY

When a contract is terminated for convenience, the contractor may recover (1) the costs of performance incurred up to the time of termination, (2) certain "continuing costs" (post-termination costs), (3) settlement expenses, and (4) under a fixed-price contract, an allowance for profit for work performed (unless the contract would have been performed at a loss) or, under a cost-reimbursement contract, a portion of the fee. However, the Government's "overriding objective" in a termination settlement should be to make the contractor "financially whole for all the direct consequences" of the termination.[21]

1. Settlement Proposals

a. Form & Content. The contractor is required to "submit a final termination settlement proposal to the Contracting Officer...promptly, but no later than 1 year from the effective date of termination" (see Paragraph (d) of the clause in Figure 17-1). If the contractor fails to submit a settlement proposal within one year, the contractor may be barred from any recovery.[22] When a termination for default is converted into a termination for convenience by agreement of the parties, the one-year period starts on the date of the contract modification effecting that conversion.[23]

The settlement proposal is the method by which a contractor demonstrates its legal and equitable entitlement to recovery. The FAR enumerates certain forms to be employed by contractors for the submission of settlement proposals and also sets out the text of the forms themselves.[24] The settlement proposal is subject to audit by the Government and thus should present not only the contractor's costs, but also an explanation of how they were incurred and computed. For terminated fixed-price contracts, *estimated* costs may be used if actual, standard, or average costs are not available and the method of estimating has been approved by the TCO.[25]

b. Settlement Basis. In addition to the general guidance in the FAR regarding settlement agreements,[26] the FAR provides special principles for settlements involving fixed-price contracts[27] and cost-reimbursement contracts.[28] The principles for fixed-price contracts are the more detailed and are particularly noteworthy for describing two major bases for settlement proposals.[29] The two bases are the "inventory basis," which is preferred, and the "total cost" basis.

Under the *inventory* method, the contractor's costs are allocated to inventory items such as raw materials, purchased parts, work-in-process, and tooling. Other appropriate charges—such as initial and administrative costs and the costs of settling with subcontractors—are added. The aggregate costs are then augmented by profit (or adjusted for loss), and any credits owing to the Government—for example, unliquidated progress payments—are deducted to arrive at a net settlement amount.

The *total cost* method measures total costs incurred without allocating costs to particular items of inventory. This method is appropriate for use only when the inventory method is not practical or will unduly delay settlement—for example, when the contractor's accounting system does not adequately establish the unit costs of work-in-process and finished products.[30] Settlement expenses, profit, loss, and credits are handled in the same manner as in the inventory method.

c. No-Cost Settlement. If the contractor has incurred no costs pertaining to the terminated portion of the contract—and no credits owing to the Government—the parties may execute a no-cost settlement agreement.[31] Use of such agreements is also, on occasion, the only practical way in which disputes involving settlements can be resolved.

2. Settlement Principles & Limitations

a. "Fair Compensation". The FAR provides that the FAR cost principles are to be used in determining termination settlement costs "subject to the general principles" in the FAR regarding the TCO's negotiation of settlement agreements.[32] These "general principles" emphasize that the TCO should exercise his "business judgment" to achieve the general goal of "fair compensation." Specifically, the FAR provides:[33]

(a) A settlement should compensate the contractor fairly for the work done and the preparations made for the terminated portions of the contract, including a reasonable allowance for profit. Fair compensation is a matter of judgment and cannot be measured exactly. In a given case, various methods may be equally appropriate for arriving at fair compensation. The use of business judgment, as distinguished from strict accounting principles, is the heart of a settlement.

(b) The primary objective is to negotiate a settlement by agreement. The parties may agree upon a total amount to be paid the contractor without agreeing on or segregating the particular elements of costs or profit comprising this amount.

(c) Cost and accounting data may provide guides, but are not rigid measures, for ascertaining fair compensation. In appropriate cases, costs may be estimated, differences compromised, and doubtful questions settled by agreement....

According to the General Services Administration Board of Contract Appeals, under the FAR:[34]

the objective of a termination for convenience settlement is to provide the contractor with "fair compensation" both for the work that has been completed prior to termination and for preparations made for terminated portions of the contract, including a reasonable allowance for profit.... To this end, the cost standards of the FAR, in part 31, are applied in accordance with principles of business judgment and fairness...with the ultimate objective of making the contractor "whole."

This concept was stressed by the Department of Transportation Board when it observed: "A contractor is not supposed to suffer as the result of a termination for convenience of the Government, nor to underwrite the Government's decision to terminate."[35] Thus, in convenience terminations, a board or court may permit recovery for costs ordinarily not allowed under the cost principles if, in the exercise of its discretion, it would be equitable to do so.[36]

b. General Limitations. In addition to the specific limitations on the amount of a contractor's recovery in a convenience termination that are discussed in Sections D.3 through D.7 below, there are some general limitations that must be mentioned at the start.

In a *fixed-price contract*, the sum of (a) the contractor's recovery in the termination settlement—exclusive of settlement expenses—and (b) the payments made under the contract may not exceed the contract price.[37] Another important limitation is the prohibition against recovery of anticipatory profits (profits the contractor hoped to earn on the terminated portion of the contract), noted earlier in this chapter. In addition, the contractor may not recover consequential damages (damages that arise from special circumstances not ordinarily predictable).[38] These limitations to a contractor's recovery apply even if the termination was a "constructive" termination for convenience (see Section C above)[39] or if the "Termination for Convenience" clause was omitted from the contract.[40]

In *cost-reimbursement contracts*, unless the contractor has been notified by the Contracting Officer that the estimated cost of the contract has been increased, the Government is not obligated to reimburse the contractor for any costs in excess of the estimated cost. This limitation—set forth in the standard "Limitation of Cost" contract clause[41]—applies even to costs incurred as a result of a convenience termination.

As noted above, the *cost principles* found in FAR Part 31 are used to determine the contractor's allowable costs in a termination settlement.[42] (See Chapter 5, Section A for a discussion of those cost principles.) Thus, some costs incurred by the contractor before termination may not be allowable under the cost principles. It is often stated that the effect of a termination for convenience is to convert a fixed-price contract into a cost-reimbursement contract as to the work performed up to the effective date of the termination.[43]

3. Special Termination Costs

When a contract is terminated for convenience, the recovery of some types of costs often proves problematic for the contractor, even with the guidance of the FAR Part 31 cost principles. For example, startup or precontract costs are frequently disproportionate to the number of items completed at the time of termination, and the costs of equipment and facilities may be rendered useless upon termination. Some of these special termination costs are discussed below.

a. Precontract Costs. A contractor may incur costs allocable to contract performance prior to the effective date of the contract. These can be recovered if (a) they were incurred directly pursuant to the negotiation of, and in anticipation of the award of, the contract, and (b) their incurrence was necessary to meet the delivery schedule of the proposed contract.[44] The standard applied is one of good faith and reasonable business judgment.[45]

Examples of precontract costs that have been allowed are capital improvements to production facilities,[46] labor costs incurred in training employees in the skills necessary to perform a contract,[47] costs of planning for anticipated production under a forthcoming contract,[48] and depreciation costs for equipment during the period of preparation for performance.[49]

b. Initial Costs. Because of inexperience, contractors often incur abnormally high labor, material, and administrative costs at the start of a contract due to necessary organizational activities, waste, and inefficiency. These preliminary costs will be amortized only to the extent that units have been completed. Therefore, the FAR provides for recovery of nonrecurring costs arising in the early stages that are not fully absorbed because of the termination.[50]

c. Termination Inventory Costs. Items of physical property that are purchased, supplied, manufactured, furnished, or otherwise acquired for performance of the contract—and that are properly allocable to the terminated portion of the contract—are considered termination inventory. The costs of termination inventory are generally recoverable as part of the termination settlement subject to the allowability requirements of the cost principles.[51] The TCO directs the disposition of the inventory and may require the contractor to transfer title and deliver to the Government or sell any material included in the inventory.[52]

The risk of loss of the inventory prior to transfer of title to the Government is on the contractor.[53] Even after title has passed to the Government, the contractor is responsible for the protection and preservation of the property still in the contractor's possession (see Paragraph (b)(8) of the Figure 17-1 clause).[54]

The contractor is also obliged to retain and pay for items reasonably usable on its other work—referred to as "common items."[55] However, if the contractor has no other work and—despite earnest efforts—is unable to obtain other work, the contractor need not retain the common items if the contractor would suffer a loss by doing so.[56]

If the termination inventory is defective (does not conform to contract specifications), the costs of producing the defective work may be recoverable, even though the contractor is not normally paid for defective work under a fixed-price contract. Neither the "Termination for Convenience" clause nor the regulations disallow the costs of defective work.[57] The Government may be entitled to an offset to correct the defective work, however.[58]

d. Post-Termination Costs. Before the termination of a contract, the contractor may have committed itself to various costs that, due to the termination, the contractor is prevented from absorbing through payments under the contract. Costs that cannot be discontinued after the effective date of the termination—"continuing costs"—are generally recoverable if the contractor exercises reasonable efforts to discontinue them as soon as possible.[59] The following examples of continuing costs have been allowed:

(1) Costs incurred after termination related to deactivating, reassigning, returning, and relocating employees.[60]

(2) Severance pay for terminated employees if such pay is required by law, labor agreements, or established company policy.[61]

(3) Costs of completing components or items if necessary to avoid their total loss.[62]

(4) Costs of taking inventory and preparing parts and materials for storage or transportation.[63]

(5) Costs of replacing or repairing machinery, tools, or equipment worn out or broken down before the termination.[64]

(6) Costs of dismantling, restoring, rearranging, or relocating plant facilities or equipment.[65]

(7) Depreciation costs of a facility especially constructed for contract performance.[66]

Unabsorbed overhead costs—the indirect costs that would have been absorbed through labor or other direct charges under the contract if the contract had not been terminated—generally have not been considered recoverable when the entire contract is terminated. Such continuing overhead costs have usually been considered costs of the contractor's ongoing business—not costs of the terminated contract.[67] However, where an erroneous termination for default effectively barred a contractor from obtaining new Government business, continuing overhead costs were allowed—after the termination was converted to one for convenience—for a reasonable period (three months) in which the contractor could have wound up its business.[68]

Another generally allowable post-termination cost is *rental expense* under unexpired leases—provided the contractor makes a reasonable effort to terminate or reduce the cost of the lease.[69] In addition, *loss of useful value* of special tooling, machinery, and equipment—not reasonably capable of being used in other work—is fully recoverable.[70] *Interest on borrowings* accruing after termination, however, is generally not recoverable.[71]

Finally, as indicated above, damages arising from special circumstances that are not ordinarily predictable or that are speculative in nature cannot be recovered. For example, a contractor cannot recover for loss of bonding capacity or impaired reputation and credit.[72]

4. Settlement Expenses

Settlement expenses are direct charges for the contractor's preparation of the termination settlement claim. Normally, such expenses would be considered indirect or overhead costs, but the FAR requires that they be removed from the indirect cost category and charged directly to the settlement claim.[73] Examples of settlement expenses that are generally allowable include the following:[74]

(a) Accounting, legal, clerical, and similar costs reasonably necessary for (1) preparing and presenting to the TCO settlement claims and supporting data and (2) the termination and settlement of subcontracts.

(b) Reasonable costs for the storage, transportation, protection, and disposition of property acquired or produced for the contract.

(c) Indirect costs related to salary and wages incurred in connection with settlement—normally limited to payroll taxes, fringe benefits, occupancy costs, and immediate supervision costs.

Most disputes concerning settlement expenses will involve one of three questions. Were the expenses reasonably necessary or related to the termination action? Has the contractor proven that the expenses were incurred?[75] Were the expenses reasonable in amount?

Note that only accounting, legal, clerical, and similar costs of preparing and presenting settlement claims to TCOs are recoverable. Generally, if a contractor is dissatisfied with what the TCO allows and appeals to a board or to the Court of Federal Claims, the costs of that litigation cannot be recouped.[76] Nor will the cost of contesting a termination for default—including litigation costs—be allowed even the default termination is determined to be improper and converted to a termination for convenience.[77] (However, a successful small business litigant may be able to recover attorney fees and expenses under the Equal Access to Justice Act (see Chapter 6, Section A.5).)

A more likely way for a contractor to recover accounting, legal, and similar costs is to show that they were incurred in attempting to *negotiate* a settlement of a termination claim—even though those negotiations took place *after* an appeal or suit had been filed.[78] For example, expenses of preparing materials for negotiations are allowable even though those same materials are also used in appealing to a board of contract appeals.[79]

The costs of reasonable attempts to persuade the Contracting Officer of the correctness of the contractor's claim will be allowed, but the contractor will not be reimbursed for continuing such efforts after it should be apparent that the contractor is "beating a dead horse."[80] Even if—on appeal—a termination claim is otherwise denied, the expenses of preparing the claim will be allowed if the contractor had a *reasonable* expectation that the claim would be allowed when the contractor prepared it.[81]

Contemporary records, memoranda, and diary entries maintained by employees, accountants, and attorneys that indicate time spent on termination activities will usually be accepted as adequate proof of termination settlement expenses.[82] Again, however, such activities must be reasonably necessary to the termination settlement. Excessive expenditures of time by attorneys or accountants will be deducted in arriving at an allowable amount for such expenses.[83]

Because settlement expenses are not considered costs of performing the contract work but are instead related to the contractor's obligation under the "Termination for Convenience" clause to prepare and submit a termination settlement proposal, they are not subject to the price ceiling on other costs or to any loss adjustment (see Section D.2.b and D.7).

5. Subcontractor Claims

Prime contractors are responsible for reviewing, negotiating, and settling—subject to Government approval or ratification—claims of their immediate (first-tier) subcontractors.[84] The FAR states that prime contractors "should" include a "Termination for Convenience" clause in their subcontracts "for their own protection" and provides a suggested clause.[85]

A subcontractor claim that is negotiated and approved by the Government is a proper cost to be included in the prime contractor's settlement proposal.[86] Allowability of a settlement with a subcontractor *after* initiation of litigation between the prime and subcontractor depends on a determination whether the risk and expense of the litigation justified the prime contractor's decision to settle.[87] Judgments or arbitration awards obtained by subcontractors against the prime contractor will be allowed if the contractor's actions in connection with the subcontracts and the defense of the subcontractors' suits were reasonable.[88]

6. Profit

Unless completion of a fixed-price contract would have resulted in a loss, a contractor may recover a "fair and reasonable" sum for profit on "costs incurred in the performance of the work terminated" (see Paragraph (f)(2) of the Figure 17-1 clause). The FAR specifies various factors to be considered in determining a fair profit, such as the difficulty of the work and the efficiency of the contractor.[89] However, the contractor's usual rate of profit may be the standard used for measuring allowable profit.[90] Nonetheless, since determination of an appropriate profit factor is somewhat judgmental and speculative, it is important for a contractor to present convincing proof that (1) the contractor was not performing the contract at a loss, and (2) the contractor's expected profit was realistic in light of past experience and the peculiarities of the contract.

Profit is not allowed on a contractor's settlement expenses as such.[91] Similarly, the contractor's payments to subcontractors for settlement of their termination claims may not be considered in determining the profit allowed the contractor (although the contractor's efforts in settling subcontractor proposals may be considered in arriving at the overall rate of profit allowed).[92] The rationale for these limitations is that settlement efforts and disposition of subcontractor claims involve little risk to the contractor—compared to performance of the contract.

7. Loss Adjustments

As indicated in Section D.6 above, if completion of a fixed-price contract would have resulted in a loss, a contractor cannot recover a profit in a termination settlement. Indeed, the FAR requires that the contractor's recovery—exclusive of settlement expenses—be reduced by a percentage equal to the percentage of loss the contractor would have suffered on the entire contract if it had been completed, and the FAR spells out a detailed procedure for applying this "loss formula."[93] The theory behind this rather harsh policy is that a contractor should not be better off as a result of a termination for convenience than the contractor would have been if the contract had been completely performed.[94]

The key element in determining whether a contractor would have suffered a loss on the contract is the estimated cost to complete the terminated work. A proper computation of the estimated cost to complete should take into account the increase in efficiency of workers and other cost efficiencies that would have occurred had the contract performance progressed.

Of course, if the loss was caused by the Government, the loss adjustment will not be made.[95] In addition, if the contractor can show that it is entitled to an equitable adjustment because of a change that occurred during performance, the price increase may convert the contract into a profitable one.[96]

E. PARTIAL TERMINATIONS

A termination for convenience need not terminate the entire contract. Partial terminations are possible (see, e.g., Paragraph (a) of the clause in Figure 17-1). On receipt of a notice of a partial termination—which should specify the extent of the termination—the contractor is required to take similar actions with regard to the terminated portion of the contract as in the case of a complete termination. Of course, if the termination is only partial, the contractor is obligated to continue performance on the work that has not been terminated.

1. Partial Termination vs. Deductive Change

Both the "Termination for Convenience of the Government" clause and the "Changes" clause in the contract permit the Government to delete work. The procedure the Government elects to use is important where the contract is for a fixed price because the different pricing formulas used by the two clauses may have a significant effect on the amount of compensation allowed the contractor.

As indicated in Chapter 11, use of the "Changes" clause is appropriate only when the change ordered by the Government is within the scope of the contract. Generally, a major deletion of the work called for by the contract will be effected by a partial termination, while a minor deletion may be accomplished by a deductive change.[97] However, deletion of as little as 5% of the work has been held to require application of partial termination procedures.[98]

Although the Contracting Officer's designation of his action as a change or partial termination will be given some weight,[99] the purposes for which the deletions are made—rather than the label used—will control.[100] The Armed Services Board of Contract Appeals has held that partial terminations "are more appropriate for a reduction of the number of units or supplies to be delivered, elimination of identifiable items of work, reduction in the quantity of work required under the contract, or similar reductions in contract tasks."[101]

2. Contractor Recovery

The standard "Termination for Convenience" clause provides that, in case of a partial termination, the contractor is to be paid the contract price for work not terminated, except that the contractor may request an equitable adjustment in the price of the nonterminated work (see, e.g., Paragraph (k) of the clause in Figure 17-1). As in the case of a complete termination, anticipated profits on the terminated portion or consequential damages are not recoverable in a partial termination.[102]

The equitable adjustment provided for by the clause is supposed to compensate for any additional costs incurred by the contractor in performing the work *not* terminated as a result of the partial termination. Usually, actual costs incurred are used as the basis for the equitable adjustment, subject to a loss adjustment if the contractor would have lost money in performing the entire contract.[103] The adjustment should not increase the contractor's profit margin or reverse a loss position.[104] (See the discussion of equitable adjustments in Chapter 13.)

If the deletion of work takes place under the "Changes" clause, the contractor will be paid the original contract price less the *actual* cost—rather than the bid price—of the deleted work and the profit reasonably attributable to that work.[105] Since the "Changes" clause requires deletion from the original contract price only of the profit attributable to the cost of the work deleted,[106] a contractor may be able to retain a substantial part of its anticipated profit. However, if the deletion is treated as a partial termination, the contractor will be allowed only a reasonable profit on the work actually performed.[107]

Under a deductive change, the contractor must absorb the same amount of loss the contractor would have sustained if the original contract had been performed completely. But—under the loss adjustment formula applied to a termination—the reduction in recovery on account of the loss is proportional to the amount of reduction in the work.[108] Thus, in a partial termination, the contractor bears only a part of the loss. Finally, while settlement costs are recoverable under a termination for convenience, similar costs of preparing and presenting a claim under the "Changes" clause are *not* allowable.[109]

Under a supply contract, the reduction in quantity resulting from a partial termination may reduce production efficiency due to a "loss of learning." For example, where a contract for 68 aircraft was reduced to 53 by partial termination, it was held that the unit price for the original quantity of 68 aircraft was too low for the reduced quantity. That conclusion was based on the "well recognized learning curve principle." The result was that the contract unit price based on 68 aircraft was adjusted to what would have been a proper unit price for only 53 aircraft.[110]

The reduction in quantity caused by a partial termination usually has a similar effect on material costs. That is, the unit cost of material for a larger volume is likely to be lower than for a smaller volume. Such increased unit costs are recoverable as part of the equitable adjustment for the partial termination.[111]

An increase in the overhead expense borne by the nonterminated work due to a partial termination is likewise recoverable. It is recognized that if the same plant and supervisory staff required to produce the original contract quantity are necessary to produce the reduced number of units following a partial termination, the contractor should be compensated for the greater overhead allocable to each unit.[112]

REFERENCES

1. See FAR 49.502.

2. FAR 52.249-2.

3. G.L. Christian & Assocs. v. U.S., 312 F.2d 418 (Ct. Cl. 1963), 5 GC ¶ 57; Blue Ridge Leasing Co., ENGBCA 4666, 82-1 BCA ¶ 15734, 24 GC ¶ 231. Cf. Johnson v. U.S., 15 Cl. Ct. 169 (1988), 7 FPD ¶ 92, 30 GC ¶ 349.

4. North Star Aviation Corp. v. U.S., 458 F.2d 64 (Ct. Cl. 1971), 13 GC ¶ 520.

5. Art Metal-U.S.A., Inc. v. Solomon, 473 F. Supp. 1 (D.D.C. 1978), 20 GC ¶ 442. See OAO Corp., GSBCA 10186-P, 1989 BPD ¶ 234, 90-1 BCA ¶ 22332, 32 GC ¶ 270 (Note). But see Salsbury Industries v. U.S., 905 F.2d 1518 (Fed. Cir. 1990), 9 FPD ¶ 86, 32 GC ¶ 244; Embrey v. U.S., 17 Cl. Ct. 617 (1989), 8 FPD ¶ 95, 31 GC ¶ 268; Nationwide Roofing & Sheet Metal Co. v. U.S., 14 Cl. Ct. 733 (1988), 7 FPD ¶ 56; Special Waste, Inc., ASBCA 36775, 90-2 BCA ¶ 22935; East Bay Auto Supply, Inc., ASBCA 32893, 89-2 BCA ¶ 21634, 31 GC ¶ 124; Automated Services, Inc., DOTBCA 1753, 87-1 BCA ¶ 19459.

6. SMS Data Products Group, Inc. v. U.S., 19 Cl. Ct. 612 (1990), 9 FPD ¶ 32. See also KAL M.E.I Mfg. & Trade Ltd., ASBCA 40597, 92-1 BCA ¶ 24411; Kalvar Corp. v. U.S., 543 F.2d 1298 (Ct. Cl. 1976), cert. denied, 434 U.S. 830 (1977); Knotts v. U.S. 121 F. Supp. 630 (Ct. Cl. 1954).

7. E.g., National Factors, Inc. v. U.S., 492 F.2d 1383 (Ct. Cl. 1974), 16 GC ¶ 135; Viktoria Transport GmbH & Co., ASBCA 30371, 88-3 BCA ¶ 20921, 31 GC ¶ 51 (Note); Vibra-Tech Engrs. v. U.S., 567 F. Supp. 484 (D. Colo. 1983), 25 GC ¶ 355.

8. Torncello v. U.S., 681 F.2d 756 (Ct. Cl. 1982), 24 GC ¶ 367. See also Maxima Corp. v. U.S., 847 F.2d 1549 (Fed. Cir. 1988), 7 FPD ¶ 60; Tamp Corp., ASBCA 25692, 84-2 BCA ¶ 17460.

9. Torncello v. U.S., note 8, supra.

10. E.g., Vec-Tor, Inc., ASBCA 25807 et al., 84-1 BCA ¶ 17145, 26 GC ¶ 154 (Note), reconsideration denied, 85-1 BCA ¶ 17755, affd., 4 FPD ¶ 61 (Fed. Cir. 1985) (unpublished); Federal Data Corp., DOTBCA 2389, 91-3 BCA ¶ 24063. See generally Cibinic, "Termination for Convenience of the Government: Another Chink in the Boilerplate," 2 Nash & Cibinic Rep. ¶ 43 (July 1988).

11. FAR 49.102. See also FAR 52.249-2, para. (a).

12. FAR 49.102(a), 49.601-2.

13. FAR 49.105.

14. FAR 49.104.

15. See, e.g., FAR 52.249-8, para. (g); FAR 52.249-10, para. (c).

16. E.g., Trilon Educational Corp. v. U.S., 578 F.2d 1356 (Ct. Cl. 1978), 20 GC ¶ 341; G.C. Casebolt Co. v. U.S., 421 F.2d 710 (Ct. Cl. 1970), 12 GC ¶ 119.

17. Emeco Industries, Inc. v. U.S., 485 F.2d 652 (Ct. Cl. 1973), 15 GC ¶ 428. See also Aydin Corp., ASBCA 35054, 89-1 BCA ¶ 21206, 30 GC ¶ 377.

18. Manloading & Mgmt. Assocs., Inc. v. U.S., 461 F.2d 1299 (Ct. Cl. 1972), 14 GC ¶ 241.

19. See, e.g., Pied Piper Ice Cream, Inc., ASBCA 20605, 76-2 BCA ¶ 12148, 19 GC ¶ 31; Integrity Mgmt. Intl., Inc., ASBCA 13289, 75-1 BCA ¶ 11235, 17 GC ¶ 343; Grover Contracting Corp., GSBCA 4115, 75-2 BCA ¶ 11550, 18 GC ¶ 65. But see Art Anderson Assocs., ASBCA 27807, 84-1 BCA ¶ 7225.

20. Henry Angelo & Sons, Inc., ASBCA 15082, 72-1 BCA ¶ 9356, 14 GC ¶ 246. But see Biener GmbH v. U.S., 17 Cl. Ct. 802 (1989), 8 FPD ¶ 107; PHP Healthcare Corp., ASBCA 39207, 91-1 BCA ¶ 23647.

21. American Electric, Inc., ASBCA 16635, 76-2 BCA ¶ 12151, citing American Machine & Foundry Co., ASBCA 8862, 65-1 BCA ¶ 4654. See generally Martell & Featherstun, "Convenience Termination: More Selected Problems," Briefing Papers No. 91-13 (Dec. 1991), 9 BPC 529; Pettit & Vacketta, "Convenience Termination: Selected Problems," Briefing Papers No. 90-12 (Nov. 1990), 9 BPC 245; Gubin, "Termination Settlements," Briefing Papers No. 63-3 (July 1963), 1 BPC 21.

22. Do-Well Machine Shop, Inc. v. U.S., 870 F.2d 637 (Fed. Cir. 1989), 8 FPD ¶ 33, 31 GC ¶ 116; R.D. Mounts, Inc., ASBCA 17667, 74-2 BCA ¶ 10740, 16 GC ¶ 319. Cf. Harris Corp., ASBCA 37940, 89-3 BCA ¶ 22145, 31 GC ¶ 284. See generally Nash, "Termination for Convenience: The Strict Notice Requirement," 4 Nash & Cibinic Rep. ¶ 37 (June 1990).

23. Space Dynamics Corp., ASBCA 25106, 81-2 BCA ¶ 15205.

24. See FAR 49.602. See FAR subpt. 53.3.

25. FAR 49.206-1(c).

26. FAR 49.109.

27. FAR subpt. 49.2.

28. FAR subpt. 49.3.

29. FAR 49.206-2.

17-28 GOVERNMENT CONTRACT GUIDEBOOK

30. FAR 49.206-2(b). See, e.g., Manuel M. Liodas, Trustee, ASBCA 12829, 71-2 BCA ¶ 9015, 13 GC ¶ 459.

31. See FAR 49.109-4.

32. FAR 49.113.

33. FAR 49.201.

34. Richerson Const. Inc. v. General Services Admin., GSBCA 1161, 93-1 BCA ¶ 25239.

35. Kasler Electric Co., DOTCAB 1425, 84-2 BCA ¶ 17374.

36. E.g., American Electric, Inc., note 21, supra; note 35, supra; Codex Corp. v. U.S., 226 Ct. Cl. 693 (1981), 23 GC ¶ 239; Huskie Oil NPR Operations, Inc., IBCA 1792, 86-1 BCA ¶ 18568.

37. FAR 49.207; Okaw Industries, Inc., ASBCA 17863, 75-2 BCA ¶ 11571, 17 GC ¶ 391.

38. FAR 49.202.

39. Nolan Bros., Inc. v. U.S., 405 F.2d 1250 (Ct. Cl. 1969), 11 GC ¶ 46; Dairy Sales Corp. v. U.S., 593 F.2d 1002 (Ct. Cl. 1979), 21 GC ¶ 114.

40. Note 3, supra.

41. FAR 52.232-20.

42. Note 32, supra.

43. E.g., Southland Mfg. Corp., ASBCA 16830, 75-1 BCA ¶ 10994, 22 GC ¶ 7 (Note), reconsideration denied, 75-1 BCA ¶ 11272.

44. FAR 31.205-32.

45. North American Rockwell Corp., ASBCA 15863, 72-2 BCA ¶ 9490, 14 GC ¶ 372.

46. General Electric Co., ASBCA 4865, 60-2 BCA ¶ 2705, 2 GC ¶ 502.

47. American Packers, Inc., ASBCA 14275, 71-1 BCA ¶ 8846.

48. Note 45, supra.

49. Ted J. Grimsrud, ASBCA 7971, 1962 BCA ¶ 3562, 5 GC ¶ 224.

50. FAR 31.205-42.

51. See, e.g., FAR 31.205-26(e).

52. See W.H. Kruger, ASBCA 33081, 89-1 BCA ¶ 21442.

TERMINATION FOR CONVENIENCE 17-29

53. FAR 49.204(b).

54. Best Lumber Sales, ASBCA 16737, 72-2 BCA ¶ 9661, 14 GC ¶ 474.

55. FAR 31.205-42(a).

56. Note 43, supra.

57. See, e.g., Caskel Forge, Inc., ASBCA 7638, 1962 BCA ¶ 3318, 4 GC ¶ 258; Riverport Industries, Inc. ASBCA 30888, 87-2 BCA ¶ 19876, 29 GC ¶ 281 (Note).

58. E.g., Air Cool, Inc., ASBCA 32838, 88-1 BCA ¶ 20399, 30 GC ¶ 25; Aydin Corp., EBCA 355-5-86, 89-3 BCA ¶ 22044. Cf. New York Shipbldg., ASBCA 15443, 73-1 BCA ¶ 9852, 15 GC ¶ 85.

59. FAR 31.205-42(b). See generally Pettit & Victorino, "Post-Termination Costs/Edition II," Briefing Papers No. 83-6 (June 1983), 6 BPC 171; Pettit, "Post-Termination Costs," Briefing Papers No. 73-3 (June 1973), 3 BPC 29.

60. Systems Development Corp., ASBCA 16947, 73-1 BCA ¶ 9788, 15 GC ¶ 121; Nolan Bros. Inc., ENGBCA 2680, 67-1 BCA ¶ 6095.

61. Trustees of Columbia Univ., ASBCA 15578, 73-1 BCA ¶ 9777; Telecomputing Services, Inc., ASBCA 10644, 68-1 BCA ¶ 7023, 10 GC ¶ 298. See FAR 31.205-6(g).

62. Kinn Electronics Corp., ASBCA 16440, 72-1 BCA ¶ 9288.

63. Amplitronics, Inc., ASBCA 20545, 76-1 BCA ¶ 11760, 18 GC ¶ 373; Condec Corp., ASBCA 14234, 73-1 BCA ¶ 9808, 15 GC ¶ 295.

64. Nolan Bros. Inc. v. U.S., 437 F.2d 1371 (Ct. Cl. 1971), 13 GC ¶ 108.

65. Baifield Industries, ASBCA 20006, 76-2 BCA ¶ 12096; Building Maintenance Specialists, Inc., DOTCAB 71-4, 71-2 BCA ¶ 8954; Q.V.S. Inc., ASBCA 7513, 1963 BCA ¶ 3699, 5 GC ¶ 277. But see C.W. McGrath, Inc., GSBCA 4586, 77-1 BCA ¶ 12379, 19 GC ¶ 127.

66. Sundstrand Turbo Div. of Sundstrand Corp. v. U.S., 389 F.2d 406 (Ct. Cl. 1968), 10 GC ¶ 70; Lowell O. West Lumber Sales, ASBCA 10879, 67-1 BCA ¶ 6101.

67. Pioneer Recovery Systems Inc., ASBCA 24658, 81-1 BCA ¶ 15059; KDI Precision Products, Inc., ASBCA 21522, 79-1 BCA ¶ 13640; Henry Spen & Co., ASBCA 20766, 77-2 BCA ¶ 12784, 20 GC ¶ 4; Chamberlain Mfg. Corp., ASBCA 16877, 73-2 BCA ¶ 10139; Technology, Inc., ASBCA 14083, 71-2 BCA ¶ 8956, 13 GC ¶ 397.

68. Note 43, supra.

69. FAR 31.205-42(e).

70. FAR 31.205-42(d).

71. FAR 31.205-20. See, e.g., Breed Corp., ASBCA 15163, 87-3 BCA ¶ 19999.

72. H.J. Const. Co., ASBCA 18521, 75-1 BCA ¶ 11171, 17 GC ¶ 265. See also K&M Const., ENGBCA 3542, 76-1 BCA ¶ 11847.

73. FAR 31.205-42(g).

74. FAR 31.205-42(g)(1).

75. H&H Reforestation, AGBCA 86-305-1, 87-3 BCA ¶ 20154.

76. Lieb Bros., Inc., ASBCA 10007, 74-1 BCA ¶ 10509.

77. A.C.E.S., Inc., ASBCA 21417, 79-1 BCA ¶ 13809, 21 GC ¶ 236.

78. Acme Process Eqpt. Co. v. U.S., 347 F.2d 538 (Ct. Cl. 1965), 7 GC ¶ 370; Douglas Corp., ASBCA 14998, 70-1 BCA ¶ 8338, 13 GC ¶ 86.

79. Baifield Industries, note 65, supra; E.A. Cowen Const., Inc., ASBCA 10669, 66-2 BCA ¶ 6060.

80. Henry Spen & Co., note 67, supra.

81. Engineered Systems, Inc., ASBCA 18241, 74-1 BCA ¶ 10492, 16 GC ¶ 160. But see Dairy Sales Corp. v. U.S., note 39, supra.

82. Cryo-Sonics, Inc., ASBCA 13219, 70-1 BCA ¶ 8313, 12 GC ¶ 351; Douglas Corp., ASBCA 8566, 69-1 BCA ¶ 7578, 11 GC ¶ 239.

83. E.g., Kleinschmidt Div., SCM Corp., ASBCA 22089, 78-2 BCA ¶ 13363, 20 GC ¶ 367.

84. FAR 49.108, 49.107(c).

85. FAR 49.108-2.

86. See FAR 31.205-42(h).

87. Boeing Co., ASBCA 10524, 67-1 BCA ¶ 6350, 10 GC ¶ 464; Lockheed-Georgia Co., ASBCA 8652, 1964 BCA ¶ 4325, 8 GC ¶ 85.

88. FAR 49.108-5.

89. FAR 49.202(b).

90. Keco Industries, Inc., ASBCA 8900, 1963 BCA ¶ 3891, 6 GC ¶ 293.

91. FAR 49.202(a).

92. Note 91, supra.

93. FAR 49.203.

94. Power Generators, Inc., ASBCA 7607, 1962 BCA ¶ 3358, 4 GC ¶ 377; Caskel Forge, Inc., note 57, supra.

95. Western States Painting Co., ASBCA 13843, 69-1 BCA ¶ 7616.

96. Allied Specialties Co., ASBCA 10335, 67-2 BCA ¶ 6657, 10 GC ¶ 23.

97. J.W. Bateson Co. v. U.S., 308 F.2d 510 (5th Cir. 1962), 4 GC ¶ 510; Fred A. Arnold, ASBCA 7761, 1962 BCA ¶ 3508, 5 GC ¶ 85.

98. Kakos Nursery, Inc., ASBCA 10989, 66-2 BCA ¶ 5733, 9 GC ¶ 350.

99. Richardson Camera Co., ASBCA 11930, 68-1 BCA ¶ 6990, 10 GC ¶ 438.

100. Nolan Bros. Inc., note 60, supra. See also Lucas Aul, Inc., ASBCA 37803, 91-1 BCA ¶ 23609, 33 GC ¶ 170.

101. Celesco Industries, Inc., ASBCA 22251, 79-1 BCA ¶ 13604, 21 GC ¶ 495. See also R&R Enterprises, IBCA 2417, 89-2 BCA ¶ 21708, 31 GC ¶ 184 (Note).

102. Note 49, supra.

103. E.g., Button & Winfield & Beasley, ASBCA 17281, 73-1 BCA ¶ 9780.

104. Fairchild Stratos Corp., ASBCA 9169, 67-1 BCA ¶ 6225; Power Generators, Inc., note 94, supra.

105. Bruce Const. Corp. v. U.S., 324 F.2d 516 (Ct. Cl. 1963), 5 GC ¶ 554.

106. Admiral Corp., ASBCA 8634, 1964 BCA ¶ 4161, 8 GC ¶ 219.

107. Note 38, supra.

108. Power Generators, Inc., note 94, supra; Skidmore, Owings & Merrill, ASBCA 5115, 60-1 BCA ¶ 2570, 2 GC ¶ 273.

109. N.P.D. Contractors, Inc., ASBCA 14789, 71-1 BCA ¶ 8862.

110. International Aircraft Services, Inc., ASBCA 8389, 65-1 BCA ¶ 4793.

111. FAR 31.205-26.

112. Henry Spen & Co., note 67, supra; Dunbar Kapple, Inc., ASBCA 3631, 57-2 BCA ¶ 1448.

Part V

DISPUTES AND REMEDIES

chapters

18 | The Disputes Process
19 | The Claim And Contracting Officer Decision
20 | Appeal To Board Of Contract Appeals
21 | Federal Court Proceedings

Part V

THE DISPUTES PROCESS

18

A. **Contract Disputes Act Overview**
   1. History
   2. Coverage

B. **Standard "Disputes" Clause**

C. **The Disputes Path**
   1. Contracting Officer
   2. Board of Contract Appeals
   3. Court Of Federal Claims
   4. Appellate Review

D. **Other Remedies**
   1. Alternative Dispute Resolution
   2. Extraordinary Contractual Relief

Most Government contracts are performed and paid for in satisfactory fashion. It is only on rare occasions that serious disagreements between the contracting parties arise. Even in those instances, the parties can normally achieve a more-or-less satisfactory resolution of their problems through informal discussions and negotiations.

When unresolved disputes do occur, however, the contract contains a mechanism—the "Disputes" clause—that allows the contract work to continue while an orderly settlement of the dispute is sought. If a mutually acceptable settlement cannot be attained, the Contracting Officer is given the power to decide the issue unilaterally. A contractor that disagrees with the Contracting Officer's decision has the option to take the matter to the appropriate agency board of contract appeals or to the Court of Federal Claims. Thereafter, an appeal can be heard by the Court of Appeals for the Federal Circuit. Beyond the Federal Circuit, significant issues with a far-ranging impact on procurement policies may ultimately be decided by the Supreme Court.

This chapter introduces Part V of this book on "Disputes and Remedies." It outlines the disputes procedures that are provided by the Contract Disputes Act of 1978 (CDA) and implemented in Government contracts through the "Disputes" clause, and that are discussed in greater detail in the chapters that follow. This chapter summarizes the path a Government contract dispute may take from the time a claim is filed with the Contracting Officer until the dispute is resolved, and includes this information in chart form. Finally, although most Government contract disputes are resolved in accordance with CDA procedures, this chapter briefly examines two other remedies that may be used by contractors—alternative dispute resolution and extraordinary contractual relief.

A. CONTRACT DISPUTES ACT OVERVIEW

1. History

For years, the resolution of Government contract disputes was governed by a patchwork quilt of statutes and contract clauses that limited the types of legal or equitable relief contractors could obtain from the Government and the procedures for obtaining that relief.[1] In 1978, Congress restructured the disputes process in the CDA, setting forth a standard procedure to be used by all executive agencies.[2] Among other things, the CDA (1) increased the authority of the Contracting Officer to settle disagreements and the agency boards of contract appeals to determine the merits of disputes, (2) broadened the types of claims that are subject to the disputes process and made Government claims against contractors subject to the process, (3) set time limitations on the issuance of Contracting Officer decisions on contractor claims, (4) created accelerated and expedited schedules for the resolution of small claims, (5) provided contractors with a choice of forum for challenging an adverse Contracting Officer decision (appeal to the appropriate agency board of contract appeals or filing suit in the Court of Claims (now called the Court of Federal Claims)), and (6) gave both the Government and contractors the right to appeal adverse board or Court of Claims decisions. All of these procedures were designed to avoid what Supreme Court Justice Douglas referred to as "vexatious and expensive and, to the contractor oftentimes, ruinous litigation."[3]

The disputes process is continually evolving through amendments to the CDA and reorganization of the judicial system. For example, the Federal Courts Improvement Act of 1982[4] replaced the trial division of the Court of Claims with the U.S. Claims Court, gave the Claims Court "exclusive" jurisdiction to grant declaratory and injunctive relief, and established the Court of Appeals for the Federal Circuit to hear appeals from the boards of contract appeals as well as from the Claims Court. The Federal Courts Administration Act of 1992[5] changed the name of the Claims Court to the Court of Federal Claims, gave the Court of Federal Claims jurisdiction to decide nonmonetary Government contract disputes (thus making court and board jurisdiction under the CDA almost identical), and provided that a defect in the certification of a contractor's claim does not deprive the boards or the Court of Federal Claims of jurisdiction over that claim. More recently, the Federal Acquisition Streamlining Act of 1994[6] altered, among other things, the dollar threshold in the CDA for claim certification.

2. Coverage

One of the most important changes made by the CDA was the extension of the disputes process to all claims of either party "relating to" a contract.[7] Before enactment of the CDA, only claims "arising under" the provisions of a Government contract were subject to the jurisdiction of the agency boards of contract appeals. Therefore, boards did not have the authority to hear breach of contract claims against the Government because breach claims were considered to arise "outside" the contract's terms. The contractor had to sue the Government in court for breach of contract. The CDA established that all claims "relating to" a contract are subject to the disputes procedure regardless of whether relief is available under the contract's terms.

Although the pre-CDA jurisdictional separation of claims alleging "breach of contract" and claims "arising under" the contract was resolved by the CDA, the term "arising under the contract" still has some legal significance. For example, the contractor's duty to proceed with performance pending resolution of the dispute (see Chapter 19, Section C.3), the amount of the contractor's recovery, or the contractor's notice obligations (see, e.g., Chapter 11, Section F) may be affected by whether the remedy sought by the contractor is based on a contract clause.

a. Excluded Contracts. Although the CDA broadened the coverage of the disputes process, it did not extend it to all Government contracts or procurement actions. The CDA applies to "any express or implied contract" entered into by "an executive agency" of the United States for "(1) the procurement of property, other than real property in being; (2) the procurement of services; (3) the procurement of construction, alteration, repair or maintenance of real property; or (4) the disposal of personal property."[8] The statutory exclusions have been narrowly construed, however. For example, the CDA does not apply to contracts implied in law[9] or contracts for subsidized shipbuilding under the Merchant Marine Act of 1936,[10] but it does provide jurisdiction in connection with lease agreements for real property and the sale of timber.[11]

b. Excluded Claims. In addition, not all controversies that may arise during the performance of a Government contract are subject to the procedures of the CDA. In implementing the CDA, the FAR gives the Contracting Officer authority "to decide or resolve all claims arising under or relating to a contract subject to the Act," but this authority "does not extend to—(a) a claim or dispute for penalties or forfeitures prescribed by statute or regulation that another Federal agency is specifically authorized to administer, settle, or determine; or (b) the settlement, compromise, payment, or adjustment of any claim involving fraud."[12] Claims for relief that have been held to be outside the Contracting Officer's jurisdiction because they involve "penalties or forfeitures" within the purview of "another Federal agency" include, for example, labor-related disputes.[13] Claims involving suspected fraud also may not be decided by the Contracting Officer but must be referred to "the agency official responsible for investigating fraud."[14] In board of contract appeals cases, Government counterclaims based on allegations of fraud must also be dismissed[15] and are typically severed from the disputes process and proceed to litigation in the appropriate forum (see Chapter 7).

B. STANDARD "DISPUTES" CLAUSE

The "Disputes" clause prescribed by the FAR[16] implements the CDA. This clause, set forth in Figure 18-1 beginning on the next page, is referred to throughout the chapters in this part—Part V—of the book (the language appearing in brackets in the clause updates the clause to conform to changes to the CDA made by the Federal Acquisition Streamlining Act of 1994 but not yet incorporated in the FAR at the time of publication of this book). The clause defines the term "claim" (see Paragraph (c) of the clause), describes how claims are submitted and certified by the contractor (see Paragraph (d)), imposes an obligation on the Contracting Officer to decide the claim within certain time limits and states that the claim "shall be final unless the Contractor appeals or files a suit as provided" in the CDA (see Paragraphs (e) and (f)), permits the parties to agree to use alternative means of dispute resolution to resolve their dispute (see Paragraph (g)), provides for the payment to the contractor of interest on any amounts found due the contractor (see Paragraph (h)), and requires the contractor to proceed with contract performance pending final resolution of the dispute (see Paragraph (i)). Most of these subjects are discussed in the subsequent chapters in this part of the book.

Figure 18-1

"DISPUTES" CLAUSE
(FAR 52.233-1)

(a) This contract is subject to the Contract Disputes Act of 1978 (41 U.S.C. 601–613).

(b) Except as provided in the Act, all disputes arising under or relating to this contract shall be resolved under this clause.

(c) "Claim," as used in this clause, means a written demand or written assertion by one of the contracting parties seeking, as a matter of right, the payment of money in a sum certain, the adjustment or interpretation of contract terms, or other relief arising under or relating to this contract. A claim arising under a contract, unlike a claim relating to that contract, is a claim that can be resolved under a contract clause that provides for the relief sought by the claimant. However, a written demand or written assertion by the Contractor seeking the payment of money exceeding [$100,000] is not a claim under the Act until certified as required by subparagraph (d)(2) below. A voucher, invoice, or other routine request for payment that is not in dispute when submitted is not a claim under the Act. The submission may be converted to a claim under the Act, by complying with the submission and certification requirements of this clause, if it is disputed either as to liability or amount or is not acted upon in a reasonable time.

(d)(1) A claim by the Contractor shall be made in writing and submitted to the Contracting Officer for a written decision. A claim by the Government against the Contractor shall be subject to a written decision by the Contracting Officer.

(2)(i) Contractors shall provide the certification specified in subparagraph (d)(2)(iii) of this clause when submitting any claim—
 (A) Exceeding [$100,000]; or
 (B) Regardless of the amount claimed, when using—
  (1) Arbitration conducted pursuant to 5 U.S.C. 575–580; or
  (2) Any other alternative means of dispute resolution (ADR) technique that the agency elects to handle in accordance with the Administrative Dispute Resolution Act (ADRA).
 (ii) The certification requirement does not apply to issues in controversy that have not been submitted as all or part of a claim.
 (iii) The certification shall state as follows: "I certify that the claim is made in good faith; that the supporting data are accurate and complete to the best of my knowledge and belief; that the amount requested accurately reflects the contract adjustment for which the Contractor believes the Government is liable; and that I am duly authorized to certify the claim on behalf of the Contractor."

continued

Fig. 18-1 / continued

(3) The certification may be executed by any person duly authorized to bind the Contractor with respect to the claim.

(e) For Contractor claims of [$100,000] or less, the Contracting Officer must, if requested in writing by the Contractor, render a decision within 60 days of the request. For Contractor-certified claims over [$100,000], the Contracting Officer must, within 60 days, decide the claim or notify the Contractor of the date by which the decision will be made.

(f) The Contracting Officer's decision shall be final unless the Contractor appeals or files a suit as provided in the Act.

(g) At the time a claim by the Contractor is submitted to the Contracting Officer or a claim by the Government is presented to the Contractor, the parties, by mutual consent, may agree to use ADR. When using arbitration conducted pursuant to 5 U.S.C. 575–580, or when using any other ADR technique that the agency elects to handle in accordance with the ADRA, any claim, regardless of amount, shall be accompanied by the certification described in subparagraph (d)(2)(iii) of this clause, and executed in accordance with subparagraph (d)(3) of this clause.

(h) The Government shall pay interest on the amount found due and unpaid from (1) the date the Contracting Officer receives the claim (certified, if required); or (2) the date that payment otherwise would be due, if that date is later, until the date of payment. With regard to claims having defective certifications, as defined in (FAR) 48 CFR 33.201, interest shall be paid from the date that the Contracting Officer initially receives the claim. Simple interest on claims shall be paid at the rate, fixed by the Secretary of the Treasury as provided in the Act, which is applicable to the period during which the Contracting Officer receives the claim and then at the rate applicable for each 6-month period as fixed by the Treasury Secretary during the pendency of the claim.

(i) The Contractor shall proceed diligently with performance of this contract, pending final resolution of any request for relief, claim, appeal, or action arising under the contract, and comply with any decision of the Contracting Officer.

C. THE DISPUTES PATH

This section provides an overview of the disputes process and the roles of the various "decisionmakers" in the process. As an aid to the discussion that follows, Figure 18-2 (which appears later in this chapter) illustrates the remedy routes—and time limitations—that are encountered from the time a claim is filed with the Contracting Officer until it is finally disposed of, possibly, by the Court of Appeals for the Federal Circuit, or even, in highly unusual instances, by the Supreme Court.

1. Contracting Officer

The disputes process begins with the presentation of a claim by the contractor to the Contracting Officer or by the transmission of a Government claim to the contractor. The Contracting Officer has two primary roles in the disputes process: to *settle* disagreements and to render *decisions* on contractor and Government claims. The FAR provides that Contracting Officers are authorized "to decide or settle all claims arising under or relating to a contract subject to the [CDA]."[17] In addition, it is the Government's policy "to try to resolve all contractual issues in controversy by mutual agreement at the contracting officer's level."[18] Thus, one of the Contracting Officer's primary functions when a disagreement arises between the Government and the contractor is to settle the matter through a negotiated settlement agreement that is binding on both parties. If negotiation fails, however, the Contracting Officer's second duty is to issue, under the contract's "Disputes" clause, a decision on a contractor's claim, usually within 60 days. If the decision is adverse to the contractor, the contractor may appeal the Contracting Officer's decision to the board of contract appeals (within 90 days) or file suit against the Government in the Court of Federal Claims (within one year).

2. Board Of Contract Appeals

As noted in Chapter 2, Section A.2, the boards of contract appeals serve as the administrative forums for deciding the merits of claims that the parties have been unable to resolve at the Contracting Officer level. The CDA broadened the authority of the boards by specifically giving each agency board jurisdiction "to decide any appeal from a decision of a contracting officer...relative to a contract made by its agency."[19] In exercising this jurisdiction, an agency board is authorized "to grant any relief that would be available to a litigant asserting a contract claim in the

United States Court of Federal Claims."[20] Accordingly, the boards—in addition to carrying out their traditional role of deciding disputes arising under the contract—are able to (1) modify, reform, or rescind contracts in the case of bid mistakes, and (2) decide the merits of cases involving breach of contract theories. These powers were not available to the boards before the CDA.

3. Court Of Federal Claims

The CDA gives the contractor the option of appealing an adverse Contracting Officer's decision to the board *or* filing suit directly in the Court of Federal Claims.[21] Since the Federal Courts Administration Act of 1992 expanded the jurisdiction of the Court of Federal Claims to include nonmonetary Government contract disputes,[22] the jurisdictions of the boards and the court with respect to Government contracts have been virtually identical. The pretrial, trial, and decision procedures used by the two forums differ, however. The court's procedures are generally more formal than the boards' procedures.

4. Appellate Review

The Court of Appeals for the Federal Circuit acts as the reviewing authority in cases that are appealed (by either party) after receipt of an adverse decision from a board or the Court of Federal Claims.[23] The contractor or the Government has 60 days after the date of entry of the judgment or order to file an appeal of a Court of Federal Claims decision and 120 days to file an appeal of a board decision. The Supreme Court reviews Government contract cases decided by the Federal Circuit only when they, at least potentially, would have far-reaching precedential effect.

D. OTHER REMEDIES

Although the chapters in this part of the book focus on the administrative and judicial procedures available to the parties under the CDA to determine their legal rights and duties in connection with Government contract disputes, these procedures

Figure 18-2

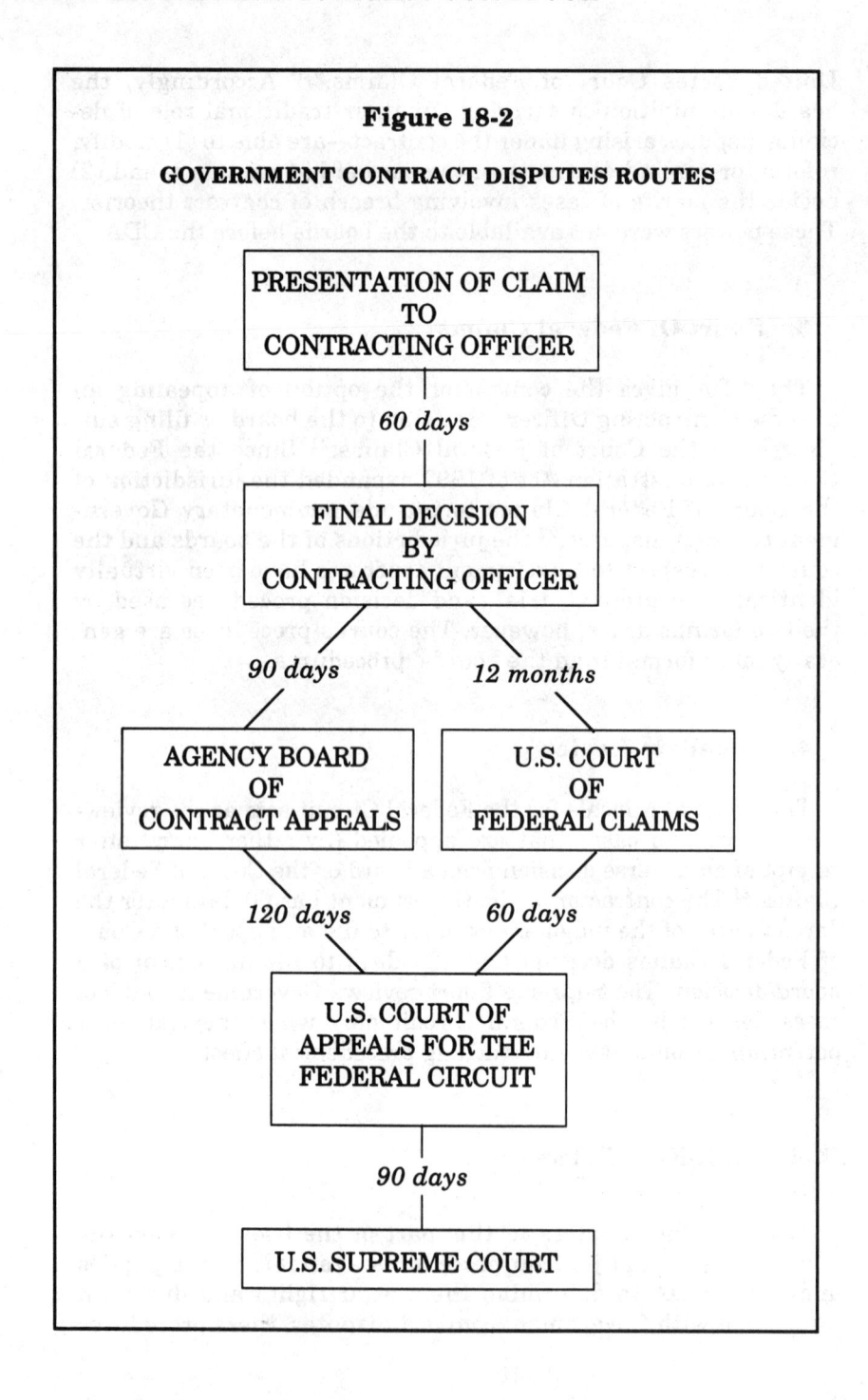

GOVERNMENT CONTRACT DISPUTES ROUTES

```
        PRESENTATION OF CLAIM
                 TO
        CONTRACTING OFFICER
                  |
               60 days
                  |
         FINAL DECISION
                BY
        CONTRACTING OFFICER
              /        \
         90 days      12 months
            /              \
   AGENCY BOARD         U.S. COURT
        OF                  OF
  CONTRACT APPEALS    FEDERAL CLAIMS
            \              /
         120 days       60 days
              \          /
         U.S. COURT OF
         APPEALS FOR THE
         FEDERAL CIRCUIT
                  |
               90 days
                  |
         U.S. SUPREME COURT
```

are not always the parties' sole recourse. For example, two alternatives—alternative dispute resolution (ADR) and extraordinary contractual relief—may also be available in certain circumstances.

1. Alternative Dispute Resolution

Efforts are increasingly being made to encourage parties involved in a Government contract dispute to forgo formal litigation whenever possible and instead resolve their dispute through alternative methods, such as minitrials, arbitration, use of settlement judges, and mediation. In 1987, the United States Administrative Conference, finding that Government contract appeals have become too expensive and time consuming, made several recommendations encouraging the increased use of ADR techniques. In 1990, Congress passed the Administrative Dispute Resolution Act,[24] which authorizes federal agencies to use ADR mechanisms to resolve Government contract claims.

Among other things, this statute amends the CDA to allow a contractor and a Contracting Officer to select "any alternative means of dispute resolution" or "other mutually agreeable procedures" to resolve a claim.[25] The statute also contains a "sunset" provision stating that federal agencies' authority to engage in ADR proceedings under the amended CDA will cease to be effective on October 1, 1999 (except for proceedings pending on that date).[26] In addition, the President issued an Executive Order to require Government lawyers to explore the use of ADR procedures,[27] and the FAR has been amended to encourage the use of such procedures.[28] Both the Court of Federal Claims and the boards of contract appeals encourage and support the use of ADR methods,[29] although the use of such methods is voluntary.[30]

2. Extraordinary Contractual Relief

Extraordinary contractual relief to facilitate the national defense is authorized by Public Law (P.L.) 85-804, enacted in 1958.[31] It gives the President the power to authorize federal departments and agencies to enter into contracts, or into amendments or modifications of contracts, "without regard to other provisions of law relating to the making, performance, amendment, or modification of contracts, whenever he deems that such action would facilitate the national defense."[32] Thus, if the conditions set forth in the statute and implementing Executive Orders and regulations are met, a Government contractor may obtain financial or other forms of relief even though the Government has *no legal obligation* to grant the relief, and even if the relief would otherwise be *prohibited*. The rationale behind P.L. 85-804 is that granting aid on a limited basis to selected contractors—even though no legal obligation to do so exists—will ultimately benefit the country as a whole.

Despite the broad scope of potential relief offered by P.L. 85-804, the statute has been used relatively infrequently. For example, during the 1980s, on average, the various agencies with authority to grant P.L. 85-804 relief disposed of fewer than 80 requests per year. This contrasts with the millions of dollars in legal claims submitted annually by contractors to Contracting Officers and the thousands of cases disposed of annually by boards and the Court of Federal Claims under the "Disputes" clause.

Readers desiring additional information on this subject should refer to the EXTRAORDINARY CONTRACTUAL RELIEF REPORTER published (with annual supplements) by Federal Publications Inc.

a. Agency Implementation. By Executive Order, 12 federal agencies have been authorized to grant the contractual relief made available by P.L. 85-804: (1) the Department of Defense (DOD), including the Army, Navy, Air Force, and Defense Logistics Agency, (2) the Department of Treasury, (3) the Department of the Interior, (4) the Department of Agriculture, (5) the Department of Commerce, (6) the Department of Energy, (7) the General Services Administration, (8) the National Aeronautics and Space Administration, (9) the Department of Transportation, (10) the Tennessee Valley Authority, (11) the Government Printing Office, and (12) the Federal Emergency Management Agency.[33] This authority was subsequently delegated by some of the agencies to Contract Adjustment Boards (CABs) to decide on the merits of petitions for relief.[34] Six CABs are in existence: the Air Force CAB, the Army CAB, the Navy CAB, the Department of Transportation CAB, the Department of Energy CAB, and the National Aeronautics and Space Administration CAB.

Membership on the CABs consists of a chairman and from two to six individuals who function as CAB members on a part-time basis in addition to their normal duties as Government employees (usually in the procurement field).

The designated agencies have implemented P.L. 85-804 in their regulations. Within DOD, for example, there are regulations containing extensive guidance and instructions with regard to the procedural aspects of seeking contractual relief under the statute.[35] The other involved agencies have developed similar regulations. By far, however, DOD remains the most active source of relief under P.L. 85-804.

b. Types Of Relief. Three main types of relief are potentially available under P.L. 85-804. The Government may make advance payments to contractors, grant several types of contract adjustments, or exercise certain "residual powers."

(1) *Advance Payments*—Advance payments may be made—although a contract does not authorize them—when doing so will facilitate the national defense.[36] Advance payments are essentially loans made to contractors that would otherwise face extreme difficulty in completing contracts that are essential to the United States. Advance payments under P.L. 85-804 will generally be authorized only in extraordinary situations.

(2) *Contract Adjustments*—The Government may also, under P.L. 85-804, grant three types of contract adjustments even though a contractor has no legal right to such relief: (a) contract "amendments without consideration" (modifications of contracts by the Government to provide some measure of relief to the contractor without receiving anything of value in return), (b) correction of mistakes, and (c) formalization of informal commitments.[37] According to the FAR, there are two bases for an amendment without consideration—essentiality or Government action.[38] "Essentiality" means that either (1) the contractor's existence as a continued source of supply to the Government or (2) the contractor's continued performance under a defense contract is considered essential to the national defense.[39] Essentiality will usually be found where the item under contract is urgently needed, the contractor is suffering a loss under the contract, and the Government cannot afford the delay involved in procuring the item from an alternate source. "Government

action" normally involves a situation where the Government—although not legally liable—interferes in some way with a contractor's performance, and considerations of fairness dictate that an adjustment be made in the contract's terms. The Government interference must result in financial loss to the contractor (not merely in a reduction in the contractor's profit).[40]

Amendments without consideration most frequently involve an increase in the contract price; however, they sometimes also extend the contract's performance period, relax specification requirements, waive the payment of liquidated damages, or allow other forms of assistance to the contractor.[41] When price increases are granted, payments are closely monitored by the Contracting Officer to make certain that the funds are used in a manner that will ensure complete contract performance. In most cases, a contractor—as a condition of payment—will be required to waive any claims the contractor may have against the Government under the contract.[42]

A contract adjustment may also be made in the case of certain contract mistakes.[43] Such adjustments can be made—so long as the adjusted contract price does not exceed the next lowest acceptable proposal price in a negotiated procurement—if (a) a mistake results in a contract provision that fails to express the intent of the parties, (b) a mistake on the contractor's part was so obvious that it should have been apparent to the Contracting Officer, or (c) there is a material mutual mistake in the contract.[44] Under any of these situations, the contract may be amended or modified to correct or mitigate the effect of the mistake. (This authority is *in addition to* the ordinary relief for contract mistakes discussed in Chapter 3, Section F.)

The third case in which amendments without consideration may be granted is to formalize informal commitments.[45] These problems are most often the result of a contractor's taking some action based on an instruction or directive from an unauthorized Government official—but they encompass any situation where the contractor's performance is not covered by a formal contract or modification. As the FAR notes, where a contractor relies in good faith on the apparent authority of a Government official and provides services or supplies without having the proper contract coverage, "[f]ormalizing commitments under such circumstances normally will facilitate the national defense by assuring such persons that they will be treated fairly and paid expeditiously."[46]

(3) *Residual Powers*—Finally, agencies also have "residual powers" to grant any other relief not otherwise prohibited by the statute. According to the FAR, "residual powers" includes all authority under P.L. 85-804 except contract adjustments and advance payments.[47] This relief alternative is normally exercised only by an agency head or his deputy. Under these residual powers, contractors have been indemnified against unusually hazardous risks, granted guaranteed loans, and compensated by the Government for property acquired during military operations.[48]

c. Procedures. If a contractor's petition for extraordinary contractual relief does not exceed $50,000, the contractor may secure relief below the Secretarial level in the agency. Normally, authority to decide the merits of petitions for relief involving less than $50,000 is vested in the head of the procuring activity. But if an adjustment exceeding $50,000 is sought, or if an advance payment is being requested, approval must come from the Secretarial level of the involved agency.[49] (Where a CAB has been established, it represents the agency head and may grant any relief that the head is authorized to grant.)

A contractor's petition for a contract adjustment should be prepared in accordance with the directions given in the FAR. It should normally be filed with the Contracting Officer.[50] The Contracting Officer will analyze the petition and the supporting data and make a recommendation to the head of the procuring activity. The head of the procuring activity (or other appropriate official) will conduct whatever investigation he believes necessary—including holding a brief nonadversary hearing in some cases—and then either grant or deny the petition or forward it to the CAB, with his views, for final action.

The CAB reviews the file and also conducts an informal hearing if it deems it necessary to do so. After fully considering the petition, the CAB renders its decision and prepares a memorandum finally disposing of the case. The CAB's decision is final; that is, a contractor has no right of appeal to any other administrative tribunal or court.

REFERENCES

1. See, e.g., Wunderlich Act, 41 USC §§ 321, 322; Federal Procurement Regulation 1-7.102-12.

2. P.L. 95-563, 92 Stat. 2383 (codified at 41 USC § 601 et seq.). See generally Pettit, Anthony, Joseph & Vacketta, "Contract Disputes Act of 1978," Briefing Papers No. 79-2 (Apr. 1979), 5 BPC 15; Perlman & Goodrich, "Contract Disputes Procedures," Briefing Papers No. 82-6 (Dec. 1982), 6 BPC 79.

3. S&E Contractors v. U.S., 406 U.S. 1 (1972), 14 GC ¶ 182.

4. P.L. 97-164, 96 Stat. 25 (1982). See White, "The New Government Contract Courts," Briefing Papers No. 83-11 (Nov. 1983), 6 BPC 257.

5. P.L. 102-572, 106 Stat. 4506 (1992). See generally Schaengold, Brams & Lerner, "Choice of Forum for Contract Claims: Court vs. Board," Briefing Papers No. 92-12 (Nov. 1992).

6. P.L. 103-355, § 2301 et seq., 108 Stat. 3243 (Oct. 13, 1994).

7. 41 USC § 605(a). See also 41 USC § 607(d).

8. 41 USC § 602(a). See, e.g., U.S. v. Triple A Machine Shop, Inc., 857 F.2d 579 (9th Cir. 1988), 31 GC ¶ 9; Forman v. U.S., 767 F.2d 875 (Fed. Cir. 1985), 4 FPD ¶ 26, 27 GC ¶ 225.

9. E.g., Coastal Corp. v. U.S., 713 F.2d 728 (Fed. Cir. 1983), 2 FPD ¶ 17.

10. Delta Steamship Lines v. U.S., 3 Cl. Ct. 559 (1983), 2 FPD ¶ 38.

11. E.g., Alvin, Ltd. v. U.S. Postal Service, 816 F.2d 1562 (Fed. Cir. 1987), 6 FPD ¶ 49, 29 GC ¶ 157; Seaboard Lumber Co. v. U.S., 903 F.2d 1560 (Fed. Cir. 1990), 9 FPD ¶ 72, 32 GC ¶ 190.

12. FAR 33.210; 41 USC § 605(a).

13. See, e.g., Prime Roofing, Inc., ASBCA 25836, 81-2 BCA ¶ 15203 (Davis-Bacon Act wage classification); Imperator Carpet & Interiors, Inc., GSBCA 6167, 81-2 BCA ¶ 15266 (Service Contract Act violations).

14. FAR 33.209.

15. E.g., Comada Corp. ASBCA 26599 et al., 83-2 BCA ¶ 16681; Warren Beaves, DOTCAB, 1324, 83-1 BCA ¶ 16232, 25 GC ¶ 82; Fidelity Const. Co., DOTCAB 1113, 80-2 BCA ¶ 14819, 25 GC ¶ 82 (Note), affd., 700 F.2d 1379 (Fed. Cir. 1983), 1 FPD ¶ 68, 25 GC ¶ 86.

16. FAR 52.233-1.

17. FAR 33.210.

18. FAR 33.204.

19. 41 USC § 607(d).

20. Note 19, supra.

21. 41 USC § 609(a)(1).

22. P.L. 102-572, tit. IX, § 907(b), 106 Stat. 4506 (1992).

23. See 41 USC § 607(g).

24. P.L. 101-552, 104 Stat. 2736 (1990). See generally Cibinic, "The Administrative Dispute Resolution Act: Making a Mountain Out of a Molehill," 6 Nash & Cibinic Rep. ¶ 34 (June 1991); Arnavas & Duffy, "Alternative Dispute Resolution," Briefing Papers No. 88-8 (July 1988), 8 BPC 167.

25. 41 USC § 605(d).

26. 41 USC § 605(e).

27. Exec. Order 12778, 55 Fed. Reg. 55195 (Oct. 25, 1991).

28. FAR 33.204; FAR 52.233-1, para. (g).

29. See, e.g., ASBCA 1993 Annual Report (Feb. 25, 1994) (from 1987–1993, the ASBCA received 73 requests for ADR covering 137 appeals and involving use of summary trial with binding decision method, settlement judge approach, and minitrial technique).

30. See, e.g., Court of Federal Claims, General Order No. 13 and "Notice to Counsel on Alternative Dispute Resolution Techniques" (Apr. 15, 1987); FAR 33.214.

31. 50 USC §§ 1431–1435. See generally Doke, "Extraordinary Relief Under P.L. 85-804," Briefing Papers No. 66-3 (June 1966), 1 BPC 171.

32. 50 USC § 1431.

33. Exec. Order 10789, 23 Fed. Reg. 8897 (Nov. 14, 1958).

34. See FAR 50.202.

35. See DFARS pt. 250.

36. 50 USC § 1431. See FAR 32.405.

37. FAR 50.302.

18-18 GOVERNMENT CONTRACT GUIDEBOOK

38. FAR 50.302-1.

39. FAR 50.302-1(a).

40. FAR 50.302-1(b).

41. E.g., Murdock Machine & Engrg. Co. v. U.S., 873 F.2d 1410 (Fed. Cir. 1989), 8 FPD ¶ 57, 31 GC ¶ 163.

42. E.g., Cincinnati Electronics Corp., ACAB 1185, 3 ECR ¶ 71 (1975).

43. FAR 50.302-2.

44. FAR 50.302-2(a).

45. FAR 50.302-3.

46. Note 45, supra.

47. See FAR 50.400.

48. See ECR Current Materials Volume, "Explanation," p. 1021 (Dec. 1991).

49. See FAR 50.201, 50.203.

50. FAR 50.303.

THE CLAIM AND CONTRACTING OFFICER DECISION

19

A. Contractor Claims vs. Government Claims
B. Asserting A "Claim"
    1. Early Notice To Contracting Officer
    2. Definition Of "Claim"
    3. Need For Preexisting Dispute
    4. Sum Certain
    5. Claim Certification

C. Contracting Officer's Decision
    1. Content
    2. Timing
    3. Contractor's Duty To Proceed

D. Contractor's Decision To Appeal Or Bring Suit
    1. Practical Considerations
    2. Binding Election Of Forum

The subject of this chapter is the first steps in the disputes process—the submission of a "claim" to the Contracting Officer and the Contracting Officer's "decision" on that claim. Not every request by a contractor to the Government qualifies as a "claim," nor does every communication from the Contracting Officer to the contractor on a subject in disagreement constitute a "decision" under the Contract Disputes Act (CDA) and the contract's "Disputes" clause. This chapter examines (a) the two types of claims that may begin the disputes procedures—contractor claims or Government claims, (b) the manner in which a claim is asserted, (c) the rules relating to issuance of a final decision by the Contracting Officer on the claim, and (d) when the Contracting Officer's decision on the claim is adverse to the contractor, the factors and consequences of the contractor's decision to litigate the dispute in a board of contract appeals or the Court of Federal Claims. The actual litigation process in a board or the court is discussed in the remaining two chapters in this part of the book.

A. CONTRACTOR CLAIMS vs. GOVERNMENT CLAIMS

The claim that begins the disputes process is usually a contractor claim. As discussed in Chapter 18, Section A.2, this may be a claim "arising under" some remedy-granting clause of the contract—such as the "Changes" clause or the "Suspension of Work" clause—for more money or more time to complete the contract. Or the contractor may allege a claim "relating to the contract," such as a breach of the contract by the Government or for relief based on a bid mistake.

The Government may also assert a claim against the contractor. For example, it may seek reimbursement of excess costs caused by defective performance, recovery of overpayments made to the contractor, a reduction in the contract price caused by defective pricing or failure to comply with the Cost Accounting Standards, or an assessment of liquidated damages.

Sometimes it is difficult to distinguish between "contractor claims" and "Government claims." For example, a question involving cost allowability is often resolved in the context of a claim asserted by the Government in the form of a formal notice to the contractor of cost disallowance. The contractor may, however, also file a "claim" with the Contracting Officer seeking an interpretation, in the form of a Contracting Officer's final decision, of the cost allowability issue. Whether the claim is characterized as a "contractor claim" or a "Government claim" can be important for two main reasons: (1) the filing of a contractor claim triggers the Contracting Officer's obligation to make a timely decision and begins the running of interest (see Sections B and C below) and (2) contractor claims over $100,000 must be certified (the certification requirement does not apply to Government claims; see Section B.5 below). Both contractor and Government claims, however, must be the subject of a Contracting Officer's decision (or, in the case of a contractor claim, be deemed denied by the Contracting Officer) before the parties can litigate their dispute before a board or the Court of Federal Claims.[1]

B. ASSERTING A "CLAIM"

The submission of a claim to the Contracting Officer initiates the disputes process. As mentioned above, the contractor's claim triggers the Contracting Officer's obligation to make a timely decision on the claim and begins the running of interest on the claim amount. Thus, whether and when a "claim" has arisen is of basic importance.

1. Early Notice To Contracting Officer

It is good business practice for a contractor to make the Contracting Officer aware—as soon as the *probability* of a claim appears—that a contract performance, price, or schedule adjustment may be requested. (Some contract clauses discussed elsewhere in this book—such as the "Government Property" clause (see Chapter 9, Section C) and the "Changes" clause (see Chapter 13, Section E)—*require* notice to the Contracting Officer.) Keeping the Contracting Officer and his advisors informed of contract problems can sometimes mean the difference between quick settlement of a dispute and long, expensive litigation. Notice (a) enables the Government to take early remedial action if it wishes to do so, and (b) makes the Government aware of the problem, negating the possibility of any later assertion that it was not told of the contractor's difficulties. Notice may consist of a short, written statement by the contractor, or it may arise from meetings between contractor and Government personnel or from visits to inspect the jobsite or manufacturing facility.

A contractor's initial request for relief is not considered a formal "claim" until the contractor complies with the requirements of the CDA and the "Disputes" clause and demands specific relief from the Government (see Sections B.2 through B.5 below). Nevertheless, during this early stage in the disputes process, the parties may—if any possibility of settlement exists—continuously consider and negotiate the potential "claims" that have been presented. Sometimes, dividing a claim into its technical and monetary components will aid settlement. That is, the parties may initially discuss the merits of the contractor's claim from a factual and technical point of view without considering its dollar impact on performance. Later, if the extent of Government liability is agreed upon, the financial aspects of the case can be considered. As stated in the FAR, it is the Government's policy "to try to resolve all contractual issues in controversy by mutual agreement at the contracting officer's level" and "prior to the submission of a claim."[2]

2. Definition Of "Claim"

The CDA contains no definition of "claim." It merely specifies two requirements for a claim: (1) all claims by a contractor "shall be in writing and submitted to the contracting officer for a decision," and (2) all contractor claims over $100,000 must be certified.[3] The "Disputes" contract clause, however, defines a claim as "a written demand or written assertion by one of the contracting parties seeking, as a matter of right, the payment of money in a sum certain, the adjustment or interpretation of contract terms, or other relief arising under or relating to this contract" (Paragraph (c) of the clause in Figure 18-1 in Chapter 18).[4] Thus, the contractor's claim must meet certain requirements (in addition to being certified when required, see Section

B.5 below). It must (a) be in writing, (b) request monetary relief in a sum certain (if monetary relief is the essence of the claim), and (c) demand a final decision.

3. Need For Preexisting Dispute

The "Disputes" clause also states, however, that a "voucher, invoice, or other routine request for payment that is not in dispute when submitted is not a claim under the [CDA]."[5] This language has caused some controversy in the boards and courts. In 1991, the Court of Appeals for the Federal Circuit addressed the extent to which a request for payment must be in dispute before it can be considered a valid claim under the CDA. The court held that the contractor's submission to the Contracting Officer of an initial cost proposal seeking compensation for additional costs incurred as a result of a Government change order was not a proper "claim" because "[u]nilateral cost proposals or correspondence suggesting disagreement during negotiations, while they may ultimately lead to a dispute, do not, for purposes of the [CDA], satisfy the clear requirement that the request be in dispute."[6] Thus, requests for equitable adjustments (before they are disputed by the Government) are not "claims" even if properly certified.[7] However, the parties need not completely abandon negotiations for a matter to be considered "in dispute."[8] A critical element in determining whether a submission constitutes a CDA claim is whether the contractor—expressly or impliedly—*requests a decision*.[9]

4. Sum Certain

The requirement that a monetary claim must be for a "sum certain" has also entangled contractors and the Government. For example, in one case, a board of contract appeals found that a claim for a sum certain that reserved the right to include additional line items and to otherwise "modify the presentation" was, in fact, simply a "predicate for negotiations" and not a proper CDA claim.[10] Nor did a "claim" exist where the contractor's counsel sent a letter to the Air Force saying that his client had been damaged in a yet-to-be-determined amount that approximated $1 million.[11] The amount of the claim need not be a definite sum if it can be derived from obvious mathematical computations, however.[12]

5. Claim Certification

The "Disputes" clause states that "a written demand or written assertion by the Contractor seeking the payment of money exceeding [$100,000] is not a claim under the Act until certified" (see Paragraph (c) of the Figure 18-1 clause in Chapter 18). The CDA provides as follows:[13]

> For claims of more than $100,000, the contractor shall certify that the claim is made in good faith, that the supporting data are accurate and complete to the best of his knowledge and belief, that the amount requested accurately reflects the contract adjustment for which the contractor believes the government is liable, and that the certifier is duly authorized to certify the claim on behalf of the contractor.

If a claim in excess of $100,000 is not properly certified, the CDA provides that the Contracting Officer has no obligation to render a final decision if, within 60 days after receipt of the claim, he notifies the contractor, in writing, of the reasons why the attempted certification is defective.[14] However, a defective certification does not deprive a court or board of jurisdiction over the claim so long as the defect is corrected prior to the entry of final judgment by the court or board.[15] Nor is interest on the claim affected, since interest on a corrected claim still accrues from the date that the Contracting Officer initially received the claim.[16]

a. Who Signs The Certification. Although the rules regarding who may sign a claim certification were previously complex and strictly construed, the CDA now provides that the certification "may be executed by any person duly authorized to bind the contractor with respect to the claim" (see also Paragraph (d)(3) of the "Disputes" clause in Figure 18-1).[17]

b. Content Of Certification. The FAR specifies mandatory language for the claim certification.[18] The certification contains four assertions: (1) the claim is made in good faith, (2) the supporting data are accurate and complete to the best

THE CLAIM AND CONTRACTING OFFICER DECISION 19-7

of the contractor's knowledge and belief, (3) the amount requested accurately reflects the contract adjustment for which the contractor believes the Government is liable, and (4) the certifier is duly authorized to certify the claim on behalf of the contractor (see Paragraph (d)(2)(iii) of the Figure 18-1 "Disputes" clause).

The meaning of "good faith" is that the principal claim has not been improperly increased for negotiation purposes by the inclusion of claims that have no merit. Absent very compelling circumstances, a board of contract appeals (at the time of claim submission) will not examine the facts surrounding a compliant certification to determine whether, in fact, a contractor's representations were made "in good faith."[19]

"Accurate" data means that the facts as stated in the claim are true. The accuracy of the facts is presumably certified as of the date of the certificate. However, if a claim has been otherwise properly certified, its amount may be revised without the need to recertify so long as (a) the amount certified was honestly believed due at the time of certification, and (b) the basic substance of the claim remains unchanged.[20] "Complete" data means that the contractor has presented sufficient underlying information to allow the Contracting Officer to reach an informed decision on the claim.[21] This information must relate not only to the amount of the claim, but also to the contractor's entitlement to it.

The purpose of the third part of the certification is to ensure that contractors do not submit overstated or artificially inflated claims to the Government. This does not require unqualified certainty that the amount claimed is correct, so long as the contractor reasonably believes that it has a right to recover the amount requested.

The contractor's certification should recite the exact words set forth in the regulation. The FAR states that a certification that "alters or otherwise deviates from the language" set forth in the regulation will be considered defective.[22] A defective certification can result in rejection of the certification and the need to correct the certification.[23] Therefore, the safest course for contractors is to use the regulatory language without change.

C. CONTRACTING OFFICER'S DECISION

If the Contracting Officer and the contractor are unable to dispose of their dispute through a negotiated settlement agreement, the Contracting Officer must issue a decision (called a "final decision") under the "Disputes" clause on the contractor's claim. The Contracting Officer's decision is the final rejection of the contractor's claim by the Government and the first step in the litigation process. The Contracting Officer's decision—whether an express or deemed decision—is a jurisdictional prerequisite to the contractor's filing an appeal to a board of contract appeals or a suit on the claim in the Court of Federal Claims as provided in the CDA.[24] The boards and courts are similarly without jurisdiction to consider a Government claim or counterclaim absent a valid Contracting Officer's final decision on the claim or counterclaim and an appeal of that decision by the contractor.[25]

1. Content

The FAR contains detailed guidance regarding the Contracting Officer's duties with respect to deciding claims. It provides that when a claim—by or against a contractor—cannot be settled by agreement, the Contracting Officer must (1) review the pertinent facts, (2) secure assistance from his legal and other advisors, (3) coordinate with other Government offices to the extent necessary, and (4) prepare a written decision.[26]

The final decision should include (a) a description of the claim or dispute, (b) reference to pertinent contract provisions, (c) a statement of the factual areas of agreement or disagreement, (d) a statement of the Contracting Officer's decision with supporting rationale, and (e) a demand for payment when the decision finds that the contractor is indebted to the Government.[27] By presenting his decision in some detail, the Contracting Officer will aid in eliminating undisputed matters from litigation. On the other hand, the CDA states that specific findings of fact are not required and will not be binding in subsequent litigation.[28] In any event, Contracting Officer decisions vary drastically in form and content. Some are lengthy and detailed, others short and abrupt. Much depends on the complexity of the issues presented and the inclinations of the individual Con-

THE CLAIM AND CONTRACTING OFFICER DECISION   19-9

tracting Officer. Regardless of its length or detail, the decision should be set forth in a logical and understandable manner. This may discourage further litigation since it could convince the contractor that its position is incorrect. A well-reasoned decision could also have a favorable impression on a board or court, which—although not bound by any statements in the decision—will review and consider it along with other appeal documents.

The Contracting Officer's decision must also include a paragraph containing language such as the following notifying the contractor of its appeal rights (the language appearing in brackets in the FAR quote below updates the quote to conform to changes to the CDA made by the Federal Acquisition Streamlining Act of 1994 but not yet incorporated in the FAR at the time of publication of this book):[29]

> This is the final decision of the Contracting Officer. You may appeal this decision to the agency board of contract appeals. If you decide to appeal, you must, within 90 days from the date you receive this decision, mail or otherwise furnish written notice to the agency board of contract appeals and provide a copy to the Contracting Officer from whose decision the appeal is taken. The notice shall indicate that an appeal is intended, reference this decision, and identify the contract by number. With regard to appeals to the agency board of contract appeals, you may, solely at your election, proceed under the board's small claims procedure for claims of [$50,000] or less or its accelerated procedure for claims of [$100,000] or less. Instead of appealing to the agency board of contract appeals, you may bring an action directly in the United States Court of Federal Claims...within 12 months of the date you receive this decision.

This paragraph notifies the contractor (1) that the document is a final decision of the Contracting Officer and (2) of its right of appeal. Without this paragraph—or equivalent language—a contractor could argue that the Contracting Officer's communication did not start the time period for filing an appeal or suit,[30] or be forced to treat all significant communications from the Contracting Officer as final decisions to be certain to protect its appeal rights. The standard paragraph eliminates uncertainty in the matter and provides a clear date for determining when the contractor must file a notice of appeal or complaint.

Note that the Contracting Officer's decision will not be considered "final" if there is a reasonable likelihood that he is reconsidering his decision.[31] Nor can there be a "final decision" if the parties continue to engage in negotiations.[32]

The FAR requirements for the Contracting Officer's decision are important. Failure of the decision to comply with the requirements will stay the running of the appeal period.[33]

2. Timing

Before the CDA, contractors sometimes complained of lengthy—and unnecessary—delays in the issuance of Contracting Officers' decisions on their claims. Therefore, the CDA established specific time limits for the issuance of decisions.

If the contractor's claim does not exceed $100,000, the CDA requires that the decision must be issued within 60 days after the Contracting Officer receives a written request from the contractor that a decision be rendered or within a reasonable time after receipt of the claim if the contractor does not make such a request.[34] If the claim exceeds $100,000, the Contracting Officer must either (a) issue a decision within 60 days after receiving a certified claim or (b) notify the contractor within that period of the time within which a decision will be issued.[35] The FAR provides that the decision of a Contracting Officer on submitted claims must be issued "within a reasonable time" taking into account the size and complexity of the claim, the adequacy of the contractor's supporting data, and any other relevant factors.[36]

In the event of undue delay on the Contracting Officer's part, the CDA also allows a contractor to request "the tribunal concerned" (the board or court) to *direct* the Contracting Officer to issue a decision within a specified time period.[37] If the Contracting Officer fails to act within the period of time ordered, the CDA makes it clear that his failure may be deemed to be a decision denying the claim that authorizes the contractor to commence an appeal to the board or a suit in the Court of Federal Claims.[38] This is a codification of the boards' practice in pre-CDA decisions to routinely treat an unreasonable failure to issue a timely Contracting Officer decision as the equivalent of an adverse final decision.

3. Contractor's Duty To Proceed

A unique feature of Government contracting is the requirement that even while the parties are contesting some aspect of contract performance, the contractor must continue with its performance under the contract as directed by the Contracting Officer. The "Disputes" clause provides that the contractor "shall proceed diligently with performance of this contract, pending final resolution of any request for relief, claim, appeal, or action arising under the contract, and comply with any decision of the Contracting Officer" (Paragraph (i) of the clause in Figure 18-1). If the contractor refuses or fails to proceed in accord with the Contracting Officer's decision, the contract may be terminated for default.

The phrase "arising under the contract" limits this obligation to proceed to disputes not involving breach of contract claims. Therefore, the FAR provides an alternate clause for use in contracts where "continued performance is necessary pending resolution of any claim arising under or relating to the contract."[39] The alternate language requires the contractor to proceed with performance regardless of the nature of the claim in dispute.

D. CONTRACTOR'S DECISION TO APPEAL OR BRING SUIT

The CDA gives only contractors, not the Government, the right to challenge Contracting Officer decisions. It also provides them a choice of forum in which to do so. Under the Act, contractors may either appeal the Contracting Officer's decision to a board of contract appeals or bypass the boards and bring an action against the Government directly in the Court of Federal Claims.[40] The contractor chooses a forum by filing a Notice of Appeal at the board (within 90 days) or by filing a complaint (within one year) in the Court of Federal Claims.

1. Practical Considerations

A contractor will receive a reasonably expeditious and just decision regardless of the forum in which it chooses to litigate its claim. Both forums provide essentially the same jurisdiction, discovery procedures, and remedies, and may hold hearings at locations that are convenient to the parties. However, a number of factors should be considered in deciding which forum to select.[41] Because litigation before a board of contract appeals is somewhat less formal than litigation in court, resolution of the dispute by a board will probably be less expensive, speedier, and afford greater flexibility in the conduct of the proceedings. In addition, pursuant to the CDA, each board has procedures for the accelerated and expedited processing of small claims.[42] A contractor may also wish to consider the presence or absence of precedent in the chosen forum on issues similar to those in the contractor's case.

2. Binding Election Of Forum

Initiating an action at a board or the Court of Federal Claims is an election of remedies that will *bar* a later action in the other tribunal if the first tribunal had jurisdiction.[43] If the contractor retrieves its Notice of Appeal from the board before the board has docketed it, however, the contractor's election to appeal to a board is not binding since, in effect, it never really filed its Notice.[44] A contractor may also appeal different claims under a single contract to different forums,[45] although the Court of Federal Claims may order consolidation of the cases or transfer the suit to the agency board involved.[46]

REFERENCES

1. 41 USC § 605(a). See Sharman Co. v. U.S., 2 F.3d 1564 (Fed. Cir. 1993), 12 FPD ¶ 73, 35 GC ¶ 668.

2. FAR 33.204.

3. 41 USC §§ 605(a), 605(c)(1).

4. See also FAR 33.201.

5. FAR 52.233-1, para. (c). See also FAR 33.201.

6. Dawco Const. Co. v. U.S., 930 F.2d 872 (Fed. Cir. 1991), 10 FPD ¶ 40, 33 GC ¶ 136. See also James R. Roane Const. Co., ASBCA 43603, 92-2 BCA

THE CLAIM AND CONTRACTING OFFICER DECISION 19-13

¶ 24802, 34 GC ¶ 318 (Note). See generally Dover & Pollack, "Invoking the Contract Disputes Act—Potential Pitfalls," Briefing Papers No. 90-8 (July 1990), 9 BPC 163.

7. Reflectone, Inc. v. Secretary of the Navy, 34 F.3d 1031 (Fed. Cir. 1994), 13 FPD ¶ 76. See also Essex Electro Engrs. Inc. v. U.S., 960 F.2d 1576 (Fed. Cir. 1992), 11 FPD ¶ 50, 34 GC ¶ 319; DEL Mfg. Co., ASBCA 43801 et al., 93-1 BCA ¶ 25394.

8. Transamerica Ins. Corp. v. U.S., 973 F.2d 1572 (Fed. Cir. 1992), 11 FPD ¶ 117, 34 GC ¶ 551; Holmes & Narver Services, Inc., ASBCA 40111, 92-3 BCA ¶ 25052.

9. Cibinic, "No Dispute—No Claim: The Impasse Requirement," 7 Nash & Cibinic Rep. ¶ 40 (July 1993).

10. McElroy Machine & Mfg. Co., ASBCA 39416, 92-3 BCA ¶ 25107. See also Boeing Co. v. U.S., 26 Cl. Ct. 872 (1992), 11 FPD ¶ 115, 34 GC ¶ 559; Granite State Mfg. Inc., ASBCA 43313, 93-2 BCA ¶ 25695.

11. San Antonio Foam Fabricators, ASBCA 36637, 88-3 BCA ¶ 21058, 31 GC ¶ 58. See also T.J.D. Services, Inc. v. U.S., 6 Cl. Ct. 257 (1984), 3 FPD ¶ 42.

12. E.g., Dillingham Shipyard, ASBCA 27458, 84-1 BCA ¶ 16984 (1983), 28 GC ¶ 198 (Note).

13. 41 USC § 605(c)(1), as amended by the Federal Acquisition Streamlining Act of 1994, P.L. 103-355, § 2351, 108 Stat. 3243 (Oct. 13, 1994).

14. FAR 33.211(e).

15. 41 USC § 605(c)(6), as amended by Federal Courts Administration Act of 1992, P.L. 102-572, 106 Stat. 4506 (Oct. 29, 1992). See generally Nash, "Contract Disputes Act Claims: Improvements in the Rules," 7 Nash & Cibinic Rep. ¶ 1 (Jan. 1993).

16. 41 USC § 611.

17. 41 USC § 605(c)(7). See FAR 33.207(e). For a discussion of the law on certification prior to enactment of the Federal Courts Administration Act of 1992, which revised the certification requirements of the CDA, see generally Ivey, "Claim Certification," Briefing Papers No. 91-11 (Oct. 1991), 9 BPC 489; Nash, "Postscript: Contractor Certification of Claims," 6 Nash & Cibinic Rep. ¶ 49 (Aug. 1992).

18. FAR 33.207(c).

19. Blount Const. Group of Blount Inc., ASBCA 38998, 92-3 BCA ¶ 25163, 34 GC ¶ 503. But see Arnold M. Diamond, Inc., ASBCA 40885, 93-2 BCA ¶ 25680.

20. J.F. Shea Co. v. U.S., 4 Cl. Ct. 46 (1983), 2 FPD ¶ 70; Armada/Hoffler Const. Co., DOTBCA 2437 et al., 93-1 BCA ¶ 25446, 34 GC ¶ 638;

Transco Contracting Co., ASBCA 28620, 85-2 BCA ¶ 17977, 27 GC ¶ 307; Rocky Mountain Constructors, Inc., AGBCA 82-256-1, 83-2 BCA ¶ 16704, 25 GC ¶ 363 (Note); Computer Sciences Corp., ASBCA 27275, 83-1 BCA ¶ 16452, 25 GC ¶ 147 (Note).

21. See McDonnell Douglas Corp., ASBCA 23826, 80-2 BCA ¶ 14807, 24 GC ¶ 421 (Note). But see Westclox Military Products, ASBCA 25592, 81-2 BCA ¶ 15270, 24 GC ¶ 106.

22. FAR 33.201.

23. FAR 33.207(f).

24. Federal Electric Corp., ASBCA 24002, 82-2 BCA ¶ 15862; L.T.D. Builders, ASBCA 27030, 82-2 BCA ¶ 15997.

25. American Mfg. Co. of Tex., ASBCA 25816, 83-2 BCA ¶ 16608; B.D. Click Co., ASBCA 25972, 83-2 BCA ¶ 16888. See also ITT Corp., ASBCA 27802, 83-2 BCA ¶ 16773.

26. FAR 33.211(a).

27. FAR 33.211(a)(4)(i)–(iv), (vi).

28. 41 USC § 605(a).

29. FAR 33.211(a)(4)(v).

30. E.g., VEPCO, Inc., ASBCA 26993, 82-2 BCA ¶ 15824, 26 GC ¶ 37 (Note); Marine Instrument Co., ASBCA 41964, 91-3 BCA ¶ 24289, 33 GC ¶ 287.

31. Royal Intl. Builders Co., ASBCA 42637, 92-1 BCA ¶ 24684.

32. Defense Systems Corp., ASBCA 42939 et al., 92-3 BCA ¶ 25439; P.J. Dick Contracting, Inc. v. General Services Admin., GSBCA 11646 et al., 92-2 BCA ¶ 24847.

33. See, e.g., Aargus Truck & Automotive Supply, Inc., ASBCA 26857, 82-2 BCA ¶ 16122, 24 GC ¶ 421 (Note), 28 GC ¶ 357 (Note); Virginia Polytechnic Inst., NASABCA 1281-17, 82-2 BCA ¶ 16072, 24 GC ¶ 421 (Note).

34. 41 USC § 605(c)(1). See FAR 33.211(c)(1).

35. 41 USC § 605(c)(2). See FAR 33.211(c)(2); Boeing Co. v. U.S., 26 Cl. Ct. 257 (1992), 11 FPD ¶ 54, 34 GC ¶ 271; Orbas & Assocs. v. U.S., 26 Cl. Ct. 647 (1992), 11 FPD ¶ 94.

36. FAR 33.211(d). See 41 USC § 605(c)(3).

37. 41 USC § 605(c)(4). See FAR 33.211(f).

38. 41 USC § 605(c)(5). See also Algernon Blair Inc., ASBCA 27079, 83-2 BCA ¶ 16660.

THE CLAIM AND CONTRACTING OFFICER DECISION 19-15

39. FAR 33.215. See also FAR 33.213.

40. 41 USC § 609(a).

41. See generally Schaengold, Brams & Lerner, "Choice of Forum for Contract Claims: Court vs. Board," Briefing Papers No. 92-12 (Nov. 1992).

42. 41 USC §§ 607(f), 608. See, e.g., ASBCA R. 12.

43. E.g., Bonneville Assocs. v. U.S., 30 Fed. Cl. 85 (1993), 12 FPD ¶ 116, 36 GC ¶ 58; National Neighbors, Inc. v. U.S., 839 F.2d 1539 (Fed. Cir. 1988), 7 FPD ¶ 13, 30 GC ¶ 86; Tuttle/White Constructors, Inc. v. U.S., 656 F.2d 644 (Ct. Cl. 1981), 23 GC ¶ 408.

44. Blake Const. Co. v. U.S., 13 Cl. Ct. 250 (1987), 6 FPD ¶ 121, 30 GC ¶ 84.

45. See, e.g., American Nucleonics Corp., ASBCA 27894, 83-1 BCA ¶ 16520, 25 GC ¶ 245; Fort Vancouver Plywood Co. v. U.S., 860 F.2d 409 (Fed. Cir. 1988), 7 FPD ¶ 141, 31 GC ¶ 11.

46. 41 USC § 609(d).

APPEAL TO BOARD OF CONTRACT APPEALS

20

A. Initial Steps
  1. Notice Of Appeal
  2. Docketing
  3. Representation
  4. Complaint
  5. Answer
  6. Rule 4 File

B. Discovery

C. Subpoenas

D. Motions

E. Abbreviated Proceedings
  1. Submission Without Hearing
  2. Small Claims Procedures

F. Hearings
  1. Prehearing Conference
  2. Location & Date
  3. Conduct
  4. Posthearing Briefs

G. Decision
  1. Reconsideration
  2. Judicial Review

This chapter reviews the procedures of an administrative appeal—that is, the appeal by the contractor of the Contracting Officer's decision on the claim to the agency board of contract appeals. The procedures of the Armed Services Board of Contract Appeals (ASBCA)—the largest and busiest of all the boards—are used as a model. The procedures of the ASBCA are found in its Rules of Practice.[1] They are typical of the rules of the various other boards.

A. INITIAL STEPS

1. Notice Of Appeal

The mechanism that initiates an appeal to a board of contract appeals is the filing of a Notice of Appeal by the contractor of the Contracting Officer's decision. Under the ASBCA's procedures, this notice is filed directly with the board, and a copy is given to the Contracting Officer.[2] Under the Contract Disputes Act (CDA), this notice must be filed no later than *90 days* after the contractor receives the Contracting Officer's decision.[3] Two points should be made with regard to the content and timing of the Notice of Appeal.

a. Content. First, the Notice of Appeal need not be a formal legal document nor set forth the reasons in support of the contractor's disagreement with the Contracting Officer's decision. Just a short statement indicating an intent to appeal the decision will suffice, even if it is inartfully phrased.[4] Thus, simply stating "We hereby appeal the Contracting Officer's decision dated ___with regard to contract number___" is sufficient. Boards are liberal in construing a document as a Notice of Appeal on the theory that all contractors (including those who do not have access to legal assistance) are entitled to a fair hearing on the merits of their dispute. But, obviously, the Notice of Appeal must make clear whether the contractor intends to appeal to a board or to sue in the Court of Federal Claims.[5]

b. Timing. Second, the liberality of the boards in finding the content of appeal notices legally sufficient does not extend

APPEAL TO BOARD OF CONTRACT APPEALS

to the 90-day period within which the Notice of Appeal must be filed. The 90-day limitation is an express jurisdictional requirement of the CDA,[6] and, as such, it may not be extended or waived by any board.[7] Therefore, regardless of how meritorious a contractor's excuse may be, a board will hold that it has no option but to dismiss the appeal if the notice is filed more than 90 days after receipt of the Contracting Officer's decision.

Although an appeal is considered to have been "filed" when it is placed in the United States (or foreign) mails, an appeal sent by way of a commercial carrier is not "filed" until it is received by the board.[8] In addition, if the Contracting Officer indicates—within the 90-day appeal period—a willingness to reconsider the final decision, the requirement to appeal within 90 days of receiving the decision is nullified.[9]

2. Docketing

Once the appeal notice has been received by the board, it is "docketed." This simply means that it is assigned a number, and a notice to that effect is sent to both parties. Under ASBCA procedures, the docketing notice sent to the appellant (the contractor) includes a copy of the ASBCA Rules and information about alternative dispute resolution procedures (see Chapter 18, Section D.1).[10]

3. Representation

The majority of appellants appearing before the boards of contract appeals are represented by attorneys, as they would be in most other substantial litigation. Representation by an attorney is not an absolute requirement, however, and a number of appellants pursue their appeals by themselves (i.e., *pro se*) without legal representation. The ASBCA Rules expressly permit this type of representation, stating that an "individual appellant may appear before the Board in person, a corporation by one of its officers; and a partnership or joint venture by one of its members."[11] Thus, in appeals involving smaller companies—particularly if the dollar amount in controversy is also rather small—it is not uncommon for an appellant to appear *pro se* before the board. Although the ASBCA Rules allow *pro se* representation, they make no special concessions for *pro se* parties; contractors proceeding *pro se* have the same legal obligations to prove their cases that apply to any other party.

The Government is always represented in board proceedings by at least one attorney from the department or agency involved.[12] For example, if an Air Force contract is the subject of the appeal, an Air Force attorney (either military or civilian) will represent the Government. In significant cases, it is common for both sides to be represented by more than one attorney.

4. Complaint

According to the ASBCA Rules, the appellant's complaint (referred to, together with the other legal documents, as "pleadings") must be filed within 30 days after the appellant receives notice that the appeal has been docketed.[13] The content and form of complaints can vary dramatically. Some are lengthy, legalistic, and detailed; others—particularly if filed by *pro se* appellants—may be terse and informal. The ASBCA Rules state that the complaint must set forth "simple, concise and direct statements" of each of the appellant's claims, as well as "the basis, with appropriate references to contract provisions, of each claim and the dollar amount claimed, to the extent known."[14]

The well-prepared complaint should state (1) the key facts surrounding the claim and (2) the underlying legal theories that support it. The ASBCA Rules permit an appellant to designate its Notice of Appeal as a complaint "if it otherwise fulfills the requirements of a complaint."[15] Although this is a convenient alternative procedure to filing a complaint, it should be avoided whenever possible because the Notice of Appeal does not usually express the claim in suitable terms.

5. Answer

Under the ASBCA Rules, the Government must respond to the appellant's allegations within 30 days from receipt of the complaint.[16] The answer must consist of "simple, concise and direct statements" of the Government's defenses to each claim asserted by the appellant.[17] Most frequently, the Government's answer admits or denies each of the allegations of the complaint—in the order in which they are presented—and informs the board of the defenses on which the Government is relying.

The ASBCA Rules also allow the Government to present any affirmative defenses that may be available to it.[18] For instance, in a given case, the Government may admit that a contract change did take place but deny further Government liability on the ground that the appellant had previously agreed to a contract modification in full compensation for the change (known in legal terms as an "accord and satisfaction"). The accord and satisfaction argument would be referred to as the Government's affirmative defense.

In some cases, the answer may deny an allegation made in the appellant's complaint "for lack of sufficient information on which to form a belief." This indicates to the board—and to the appellant—that the Government does not have a contrary version of the facts alleged by appellant, but nonetheless still requires that the allegation be fully proven.

6. Rule 4 File

Rule 4 of the ASBCA Rules requires the Contracting Officer—within 30 days after receiving the docketing notice—to assemble and transmit to the board "an appeal file consisting of all documents pertinent to the appeal."[19] These documents (known popularly as the "Rule 4 file") include (a) the Contracting Officer's decision, (b) the contract and all pertinent specifications, amendments, plans, and drawings, (c) all relevant correspondence, (d) any relevant transcripts, affidavits, or statements, and (e) any additional information considered relevant to the appeal.[20]

The Contracting Officer must arrange these Rule 4 documents chronologically, and must (if practicable) number, tab, and index them. Legible facsimiles or authenticated copies of documents may be used.[21] Copies of the Rule 4 file (except for the contract documents that are presumably already in the appellant's possession) must also be furnished to the appellant by the Contracting Officer during this 30-day period.[22] The appellant, within 30 days after receiving the Rule 4 documents, may transmit to the board (with two copies to the Government) any documents not contained in the file that the appellant considers relevant to the appeal.[23]

Rule 4 states that, if neither party objects, the documents contained in the file *automatically* become part of the record upon which the board will render its decision.[24] In such cases, the documents in the file are treated as authentic and genuine, although the presiding ASBCA judge has discretion to accord them whatever weight he deems appropriate in the course of deciding the appeal.

Either party may object to the inclusion of a particular document or documents in the Rule 4 file. If an objection is made (this should ordinarily be done well in advance of the hearing), the document will be removed from the Rule 4 file and the party who introduced it will have the opportunity to offer it into evidence as would be done with any other non-Rule 4 documents.[25]

As a practical matter, the Rule 4 materials are an important source of information in all contract appeals. In some cases (particularly those involving *pro se* appellants), they may be the *sole* source of documentary evidence relating to the dispute.

B. DISCOVERY

Discovery, as a general concept, can be defined as a pretrial procedure designed to promote full disclosure of all relevant facts related to a case.[26] As recognized in the ASBCA Rules, there are four major methods of discovery available to the parties in board proceedings: (1) taking depositions—either through oral examination or written questions, (2) submitting written interrogatories (questions) to the other party, (3) requesting the other party to produce documents, and (4) asking the other party to admit or deny the truth of relevant facts (called "requests for admissions").[27] The party that initiates an oral deposition will be required to bear the cost even though the other party also asks questions at the deposition.[28] A Government audit is another discovery device.[29]

The ASBCA Rules provide that discovery procedures may commence after the appeal has been docketed and the complaint filed.[30] The Rules emphasize that the parties are encouraged to engage in *voluntary* discovery procedures.[31] Thus, the presiding judge does not normally become directly involved unless disagreements or disputes arise between the parties.

If the parties are unable to agree to voluntary discovery, they may apply to the board for orders (a) directing that responses to discovery requests be made, or (b) limiting the scope, method, time, or place of discovery activity. Moreover, the board may make any other orders it considers necessary to protect either party from "annoyance, embarrassment, or undue burden or expense."[32] Although the ASBCA's Rules are silent regarding specific board powers to enforce its discovery orders, the ASBCA and other boards have authority under their Rules—and under the related Federal Rules of Civil Procedure, which govern proceedings in United States District Courts[33]—to issue orders penalizing parties that do not comply with discovery orders. For failing to comply with discovery orders, boards have refused to allow parties to introduce evidence[34] and have dismissed appeals.[35]

If used properly, discovery enables both parties to be fully informed about the material facts surrounding the appeal. It should eliminate to a large extent the "surprise" aspect that formerly characterized some proceedings. This does not mean, however, that every aspect of the other side's case is discoverable. On the contrary, some information may be *privileged* from disclosure. Although many privileges exist in the law, in the Government contracting context, two have particular importance. These are (1) the *attorney-client* privilege, which prevents certain communications made to an attorney from being inquired into during discovery proceedings or at trial, and (2) the *executive* privilege, which shields from disclosure confidential advisory opinions and recommendations whose disclosure would be injurious to the deliberative or consultative functions of the Government.[36] In addition, trial preparation materials—if they come under what is known as the *attorney work product* rule—are also protected to a limited extent from disclosure to the other party.[37]

C. SUBPOENAS

Somewhat related to discovery is the right of a board to issue subpoenas. Subpoenas may require (a) a witness to testify at a deposition or a hearing, or (b) the production by the witness—at the deposition or hearing—of books and records as designated in the subpoena. Under the ASBCA Rules, the board is authorized to issue a subpoena on written request of either party or on the board's own initiative.[38]

A showing of reasonable scope and general relevance to the appeal must be made for issuance of the subpoena.[39] A board may refuse to issue a subpoena if the party requesting it has not used reasonable prehearing discovery procedures to narrow the information being sought to relevant material.[40] Compliance with the subpoena is enforceable by application of the presiding ASBCA judge to a U.S. District Court for an order requiring compliance.[41]

Because the witnesses in contract appeals are usually already under the control of one of the parties, subpoenas are less often needed than in other forms of litigation. Even third parties will usually testify at a party's request without the need to issue a subpoena. Subpoenas offer an alternative in instances where voluntary cooperation is not forthcoming, however.

D. MOTIONS

Motions have become increasingly important in board proceedings. The full range of motions filed in court proceedings (see Chapter 21, Section B.5) are now common in board practice. Particularly important is the motion for summary judgment, which, if granted, results in disposition of the appeal without a hearing. The boards apply the same criteria in deciding motions for summary judgment as do the courts—that is, whether there are material facts in issue and, if not, whether the moving party is entitled to judgment as a matter of law.[42]

E. ABBREVIATED PROCEEDINGS

Usually, appeals are decided after both parties have the opportunity to present their evidence and arguments at a hearing. There are alternative methods for processing appeals, however, that require less time and less expense.

1. Submission Without Hearing

The ASBCA (like all other boards) provides that *either* party may elect to waive a hearing and to submit its case on the record before the board.[43] This simplified procedure is normally chosen in cases involving relatively small and uncomplicated claims where the dollar amount in controversy would likely be exceeded by the time and expense of preparing for, and appearing at, a hearing. Under this procedure, affidavits, depositions, answers to interrogatories, and the like may be used to supplement the documentary evidence in the Rule 4 file. In addition, the board may allow the parties to engage in oral argument and to submit briefs in support of their positions.

It is most important to note the admonition in the ASBCA Rules regarding a case submitted on the record: "Submission of a case without hearing does not relieve the parties from the necessity of proving the facts supporting their allegations or defenses."[44] Thus, while submitting an appeal for a decision without a hearing may offer a convenient and less expensive alternative to appearing at and conducting a hearing, a party's case—to succeed—must nevertheless be planned and submitted to the board in a complete and persuasive manner.

2. Small Claims Procedures

Under the CDA, contractors may—if their claims fall within certain prescribed amounts—elect to have decisions issued by a board within either four or six months after such elections are made.[45] Decisions within four months occur under the so-called "expedited procedure." Decisions within six months take place under the "accelerated procedure."

a. **Expedited Appeals.** An appellant with a claim of $50,000 or less may elect to use the expedited procedure. Under this procedure, the board must decide the case within 120 days of the appellant's election.[46] The expedited procedure requires the cooperation of both parties and the judge. For example, within 15 days after receiving the appellant's election notice, the judge must contact both parties (frequently through a telephone conference call) and (1) identify the issues, (2) establish a simplified procedure appropriate to the particular appeal involved, (3) determine whether either party wants a hearing and, if so, fix a time and place for it, (4) require the Government to furnish all the additional documents relevant to the appeal, and (5) establish an expedited schedule for resolution of the appeal.[47] Pleadings and discovery will be allowed only to the extent that they are consistent with the requirement to issue a decision within the four-month period.[48]

Written decisions in expedited appeals are rendered by a single administrative judge and are short, containing only summary findings of fact and conclusions of law.[49] Moreover, if there has been a hearing, the presiding judge may—if he believes it appropriate—render an oral decision in the appeal at the conclusion of the hearing.[50] Decisions in expedited appeals are not published, are of no precedential value, and may not (in the absence of fraud) be appealed.[51]

b. **Accelerated Appeals.** If the amount of the claim is less than $100,000, an appellant may elect to have a decision rendered by the board within 180 days after the election is made.[52] Accelerated proceedings follow a pattern similar to expedited proceedings. The parties will be encouraged to the extent possible—consistent with adequate presentation of their factual and legal positions—to waive pleadings, discovery, and briefs. Moreover, the board is given discretion to shorten time periods prescribed or allowed elsewhere in the ASBCA Rules.[53]

Written decisions in accelerated proceedings are rendered by the presiding judge with the concurrence of a vice chairman of the board.[54] Such decisions are published, may be appealed in the normal manner, and are valid precedent.

c. **Advantages & Disadvantages.** The most obvious advantage of the expedited and accelerated procedures is that they ensure the contractor a speedy decision in small claims appeals. On the other hand, because of the curtailed time schedule, there is little opportunity for either party to conduct discovery with regard to the other party's case. The time limits that the boards will likely impose make it difficult to prepare any but the most simple claims. Also, if the appeal is from a termination for default, an election of the accelerated or expedited procedure may limit a later claim for termination for convenience costs (see Chapter 17) to $50,000 (expedited procedure) or $100,000 (accelerated procedure).[55] For these reasons, most appeals continue to be processed in accordance with the boards' normal procedures.

F. HEARINGS

If the parties have not chosen to have the appeal decided on the written record and the appellant has not elected either of the small claims procedures, a hearing will be scheduled and conducted in accordance with normal procedures of the board. These procedures, as illustrated in the ASBCA's Rules, are discussed below.

1. Prehearing Conference

The ASBCA Rules provide that the board, "upon its own initiative, or upon the application of either party," may arrange for a prehearing conference.[56] Prehearing conferences can serve to (a) make parties aware of the board's Rules and procedures, (b) ensure that the pretrial discovery process is conducted in timely fashion, (c) resolve problems or disagreements between counsel, and (d) facilitate efficient scheduling of pretrial procedures and the trial itself. Specifically, the ASBCA's Rules mention six areas for potential discussion:[57]

> (1) simplification, clarification, or severing of the issues;

> (2) the possibility of obtaining stipulations, admissions, agreements and rulings on admissibility of documents, understandings on matters already of record, or similar agreements that will avoid unnecessary proof;

(3) agreements and rulings to facilitate discovery;

(4) limitation of the number of expert witnesses, or avoidance of similar cumulative evidence;

(5) the possibility of agreement disposing of any or all of the issues in dispute; and

(6) such other matters as may aid in the disposition of the appeal.

While a prehearing conference is obviously most important in a complex appeal involving multiple issues, it may also be useful in less complicated proceedings.

Depending on the magnitude of the appeal, the prehearing conference can be a rather formal proceeding with an agenda and a transcript prepared by a court reporter, or a more casual meeting between the parties and the ASBCA judge. The ASBCA Rules specifically provide for the use of telephone conference calls,[58] and this device—particularly when all of the parties are not located in the Washington, D.C., area where the ASBCA is located—has proven to be both efficient and economical. Regardless of the type of conference, its results, including any rulings and orders, will be put in writing by the presiding judge and will form a part of the record of the appeal.[59]

2. Location & Date

The ASBCA Rules provide that hearings "will be held at such places determined by the Board to best serve the interests of the parties and the Board."[60] Thus, although the ASBCA and the other boards are all located in and around Washington, D.C., hearings may be conducted in other locations. Indeed, nearly 75% of all ASBCA trials are held outside of the Washington area.

Generally, the presiding judge will request the parties to confer and agree on a mutually convenient hearing site (usually the locale where the work was performed and where the majority of witnesses and their attorneys are located). Assuming that the parties' choice is reasonable, the judge normally schedules the hearing as agreed. If there is no logical central place for the hearing (i.e., the witnesses and their counsel are located throughout the country), the hearing will likely be held in Washington. The board also usually requests the parties to suggest a mutually agreeable hearing date, and will—assuming the suggested date is reasonable—set the hearing as agreed.

A formal notice, indicating the time and place of the hearing, is sent by the board's Recorder's Office to both parties. The parties must be given at least 15 days' notice of the time and place set for the hearing.[61] An unexcused absence of a party from the hearing will not be occasion for delay—the hearing will proceed and the case will be regarded as being submitted on the record by the absent party.[62]

3. Conduct

The ASBCA Rules contemplate that hearings "shall be as informal as may be reasonable and appropriate under the circumstances."[63] This statement, however, can be misleading. The typical board hearing is conducted before a single ASBCA judge in a manner similar to a federal civil trial held without a jury, and the evidence presented by the parties must—subject to the presiding judge's discretion—be admissible under the Federal Rules of Evidence.[64] Therefore, while some procedural concessions may be made in the case of *pro se* appellants, the parties should be prepared to present and prove their cases as they would in any other federal litigation.

Both parties initially present brief opening statements, and then the appellant—who usually has the "burden of proof"—presents its witnesses. Each witness is subject to cross-examination by Government counsel and may also be questioned by the judge. Once the appellant has concluded its presentation, the Government witnesses testify under the same conditions. At the conclusion of both parties' testimony, each party presents whatever rebuttal evidence it deems appropriate.

Hearings vary greatly in length and formality depending on the complexity of the issues presented, the dollar amount involved, and the personalities and tactics of the attorneys and witnesses. Some hearings are concluded in a matter of hours, while others continue for weeks or months. Nevertheless, a common factor in all hearings is that the successful party is the one who builds a logical factual case through documentation and testimony.

4. Posthearing Briefs

Shortly after the trial has been concluded, a verbatim transcript of the hearing is distributed to the parties.[65] The ASBCA Rules provide that posthearing briefs may be submitted by the parties "upon such terms as may be directed by the presiding administrative judge...at the conclusion of the hearing."[66] Normally—at the hearing's conclusion—the parties and the judge will agree on a suitable schedule (for example, 45 days after receipt of the transcript) for submission of briefs (and, in more complex cases, reply briefs). Once the judge has received the transcript and briefs, he is able to begin the process of deciding the appeal.

G. DECISION

In reaching his decision on the appeal, the judge will review (1) the Rule 4 appeal file (see Section A.6 above), (2) any additional documentary evidence introduced at trial, (3) the transcript of the hearing, and (4) the posthearing briefs. After this review and a consideration of the proper legal precedents, the judge prepares a draft opinion. This opinion is then circulated to one of the ASBCA's three vice chairmen and the board's chairman. Thus, as opposed to expedited or accelerated proceedings where only one or two judges participate, three judges take part in deciding a standard ASBCA case. In fact, if one of the three judges *dissents* from the majority's conclusions, two additional judges will participate.

If the appeal is unusually difficult or of significant precedential importance, the ASBCA's chairman may refer the decision to the board's Senior Deciding Group.[67] This procedure is used sparingly.

In the "standard" appeal, a majority vote determines the winning party. As a practical matter, discussions, modifications, and compromises accompany the circulation of a draft opinion. Since changes and accommodations are frequently made, dissenting opinions are rare. However, in the event that the presiding judge cannot attain a majority vote for his views, the appeal is reassigned to another judge to write a majority opinion, and the original judge becomes a dissenter.

Once the presiding judge's opinion has been prepared in final form and signed by the participating judges, it is distributed to the parties, made available to the public, and published.[68] All board decisions—except those issued under expedited procedures—are commercially published in *Boards of Contract Appeals Decisions*.[69] In addition, THE GOVERNMENT CONTRACTOR, published weekly by Federal Publications Inc., provides analysis and discussion of significant board decisions.

1. Reconsideration

Under the ASBCA Rules, either party may—within 30 days after receipt of the board's decision—file a motion for reconsideration of either the entire decision or certain portions of it.[70] A motion for reconsideration should not simply reargue the points and issues considered by the board. Rather, it should attempt to point out some significant fact or facts that were overlooked or misinterpreted by the board, or indicate some newly discovered evidence not available during the original hearing that could cause the board to reevaluate its decision. An error in a decision that is irrelevant to the basis for the decision is not a valid ground for a motion for reconsideration.[71]

Both parties will be given the opportunity to submit briefs in support of their positions, and—although not common—there may be oral argument before the board. Although the boards retain the inherent right to correct errors in their decisions regardless of when brought to their attention, the 30-day requirement is generally enforced according to its terms.[72]

Motions for reconsideration are overwhelmingly denied, unless they can point objectively to some factual or mathematical error in the decision. As a result, experienced attorneys generally forgo filing such motions, particularly if they intend to seek judicial review of the board's decision.

2. Judicial Review

The Court of Appeals for the Federal Circuit has exclusive jurisdiction to review contractor or Government appeals from board of contract appeals decisions.[73] The procedures and standards of review of the Federal Circuit in appeals of board decisions are discussed in the next chapter—Chapter 21—in Section C.

REFERENCES

1. See DFARS app. A.

2. ASBCA R. 1(a).

3. 41 USC § 606. See, e.g., McMann Bros. Const. Co., ASBCA 30688, 85-2 BCA ¶ 18064; William F. Wilke, Inc., ASBCA 29928, 85-1 BCA ¶ 17917; KIME Plus, Inc., ASBCA 46580 (Aug. 29, 1994).

4. See ASBCA R. 2.

5. Stewart-Thomas Industries, Inc., ASBCA 38773, 90-1 BCA ¶ 22481, 32 GC ¶ 7.

6. 41 USC § 606.

7. Cosmic Const. Co. v. U.S., 687 F.2d 1389 (Fed. Cir. 1982), 1 FPD ¶ 53, 25 GC ¶ 67.

8. North Coast Remanufacturing, Inc., ASBCA 38599, 89-3 BCA ¶ 22232; Associate Engrg. Co., VABCA 2673, 88-2 BCA ¶ 20709, 30 GC ¶ 160. See also Tyger Const. Co., ASBCA 36100 et al., 88-3 BCA ¶ 21149, 30 GC ¶ 344.

9. M.G. Technology Corp., ASBCA 35249, 88-3 BCA ¶ 21185; Nash Janitorial Service, Inc., GSBCA 7338, 88-2 BCA ¶ 20809, 30 GC ¶ 172, reconsideration denied, 89-2 BCA ¶ 21615. But see Colfax, Inc., AGBCA 89-159-1, 89-3 BCA ¶ 22130.

10. ASBCA R. 3.

11. ASBCA R. 26.

12. See ASBCA R. 27.

13. ASBCA R. 6(a).

14. Note 13, supra.

15. Note 4, supra.

16. ASBCA R. 6(b).

17. Note 16, supra.

18. Note 16, supra.

19. ASBCA R. 4(a).

20. Note 19, supra.

21. ASBCA R. 4(c).

22. Note 19, supra.

23. ASBCA R. 4(b).

24. ASBCA R. 4(e). See also Hawaiian Dredging & Const. Co., ASBCA 25594, 84-2 BCA ¶ 17290; X-Tyal Intl. Corp., ASBCA 24353 et al., 84-2 BCA ¶ 17251, 26 GC ¶ 189.

25. ASBCA R. 4(e).

26. Gulf & Western Industries Inc., ASBCA 21090, 78-1 BCA ¶ 12988. See Arnavas, "Discovery Before Contract Appeal Boards," Briefing Papers No. 80-3 (June 1980), 5 BPC 103.

27. ASBCA R. 14, 15.

28. Duckels Const., Inc., AGBCA 89-1-218-1, 90-3 BCA ¶ 22955, 32 GC ¶ 196.

29. Inslaw, Inc., DOTBCA 1609 et al., 88-1 BCA ¶ 20368, 30 GC ¶ 44.

30. ASBCA R. 14(b).

31. ASBCA R. 14(a).

32. Note 31, supra. See also Federal Data Corp., DOTBCA 2381 et al., 91-3 BCA ¶ 24057; Aerospatiale Helicopter Corp., DOTBCA 1905 et al., 89-1 BCA ¶ 21502, 31 GC ¶ 57; Automar IV Corp., DOTBCA 1867, 88-3 BCA ¶ 20854, 30 GC ¶ 254.

33. Fed. R. Civ. P. 26–37. See Able Contracting Co., ASBCA 27411, 85-2 BCA ¶ 18017.

34. Charles G. Williams Const., Inc., ASBCA 33766, 89-2 BCA ¶ 21733, 32 GC ¶ 270 (Note); Coastal Structures, Inc., DOTBCA 1670 et al., 88-3 BCA ¶ 20956, 30 GC ¶ 233 (Note); Ralph Const., Inc., ASBCA 35633, 88-2 BCA ¶ 20731, 30 GC ¶ 195; Integrity Mgmt. Intl., ASBCA 18289, 75-1 BCA ¶ 11235, 17 GC ¶ 343.

35. Metadure Corp., ASBCA 23121 et al., 82-1 BCA ¶ 15496. See 48 CFR § 6101.15(g) (GSBCA R. 15(g)). But see Aerospatiale Helicopter Corp., DOTBCA 1905 et al., 89-3 BCA ¶ 21897.

36. See Ingalls Shipbldg. Div., Litton Systems, Inc., ASBCA 17717, 73-2 BCA ¶ 10205, 16 GC ¶ 28.

37. See Hickman v. Taylor, 329 U.S. 495 (1947).

38. ASBCA R. 21(a).

39. ASBCA R. 21(c)(2).

40. Noslot Cleaning Services, Inc., IBCA 2554, 90-3 BCA ¶ 23234, 32 GC ¶ 270.

41. ASBCA R. 21(g).

42. Grumman Aerospace Corp., ASBCA 35185, 92-3 BCA ¶ 25059. See generally Arnavas & Ferrell, "Motions Before Contract Appeals Boards," Briefing Papers No. 86-9 (Aug. 1986), 7 BPC 357.

43. ASBCA R. 11. See also ASBCA R. 8.

44. ASBCA R. 11.

45. 41 USC §§ 607(f), 608.

46. 41 USC § 608; ASBCA R. 12.1(a).

47. ASBCA R. 12.2(a)(2).

48. ASBCA R. 12.2(b).

49. ASBCA R. 12.2(c).

50. Note 49, supra.

51. ASBCA R. 12.2(d).

52. 41 USC § 607(f); ASBCA R. 12.3.

53. ASBCA R. 12.3(a).

54. ASBCA R. 12.3(b).

55. Transportes Especiales De Automoviles, S.A.(T.E.A.S.A.), ASBCA 40658, 91-1 BCA ¶ 23292; Silangan Manpower Services, ASBCA 35304, 88-2 BCA ¶ 20554; Alice Roofing & Sheet Metal Works, Inc., ASBCA 31605, 85-3 BCA ¶ 18510, 28 GC ¶ 64.

56. ASBCA R. 10(a).

57. Note 56, supra.

58. Note 56, supra.

59. ASBCA R. 10(b).

60. ASBCA R. 17.

61. ASBCA R. 18.

62. ASBCA R. 19.

63. ASBCA R. 20(a).

64. Note 63, supra. See also Arnavas & Latham, "Evidence Before Contract Appeal Boards," Briefing Papers No. 81-3 (June 1981), 5 BPC 185.

65. ASBCA R. 24.

66. ASBCA R. 23.

67. Note 1, supra; ASBCA Charter, para. 4.

68. ASBCA R. 28.

69. Published by Commerce Clearing House, Inc., 4025 W. Peterson Ave., Chicago, IL 60646.

70. ASBCA R. 29.

71. Cherokee Const. Co., ASBCA 36360, 90-2 BCA ¶ 22754.

72. See, e.g., General Time Corp., ASBCA 21211 et al., 85-1 BCA ¶ 17842, 27 GC ¶ 82 (Note); CWC Inc., ASBCA 28847, 85-1 BCA ¶ 17876, 27 GC ¶ 82.

73. 41 USC § 607(g)(1).

FEDERAL COURT PROCEEDINGS

21

A. History

B. Court Of Federal Claims
 1. Complaint
 2. Answer
 3. Pretrial Orders & Conferences
 4. Discovery
 5. Motions
 6. Trial
 7. Post-Trial Briefs
 8. Decision

C. Court Of Appeals For The Federal Circuit
 1. Review Of Board Decisions
 2. Review Of Court Of Federal Claims Decisions
 3. Procedures

As already noted in Chapter 18, Section C, two federal courts play key roles in the Government contract disputes process—the Court of Federal Claims and the Court of Appeals for the Federal Circuit. Under the Contract Disputes Act (CDA), contractors have the right of "direct access" to the Court of Federal Claims to challenge an unfavorable Contracting Officer decision. Appeal to the appropriate agency board of contract appeals was their sole recourse prior to the CDA. The Court of Appeals for the Federal Circuit serves as the reviewer of decisions by the boards or the Court of Federal Claims rendered under their CDA jurisdiction, regardless of whether the contractor or the Government seeks review. This chapter, the last in Part V, discusses these two courts and their procedures and roles in the contract disputes process.

A. HISTORY

In the Federal Courts Improvement Act of 1982,[1] Congress eliminated the Court of Claims—a federal court that had been in existence since 1855 and that, through its trial and appellate divisions, had been *the* federal court for resolving Government contract disputes.[2] In place of the Court of Claims, the 1982 Act established two new federal courts, the U.S. Court of Appeals for the Federal Circuit and the U.S. Claims Court.[3] The Claims Court has since been renamed the "Court of Federal Claims" pursuant to the Federal Courts Administration Act of 1992.[4]

The Court of Appeals for the Federal Circuit basically assumed the role of the Court of Claims' appellate division. It has jurisdiction over appeals from decisions of the boards of contract appeals and the Court of Federal Claims in CDA cases.[5]

The Court of Federal Claims replaces the former Court of Claims trial division. Contractors may appeal a Contracting Officer's decision directly to this court.[6] Moreover, to afford complete relief on any contract claim brought *before* the contract is awarded, the 1982 Act provided that the Court of Federal Claims has "exclusive jurisdiction to grant declaratory judgments and such equitable and extraordinary relief as it deems proper, including but not limited to injunctive relief."[7] The former

Court of Claims did not have authority to issue declaratory judgments and injunctions, and the reference in the 1982 Act to "exclusive jurisdiction" is intended to eliminate any inference that the boards of contract appeals may exercise similar injunctive powers under the CDA. In addition to renaming the court, the Federal Courts Administration Act of 1992 eliminated a source of controversy regarding the Court of Federal Claims' jurisdiction over nonmonetary claims by expressly giving the court jurisdiction over disputes "concerning termination of a contract, rights in tangible or intangible property, compliance with cost accounting standards, and other nonmonetary disputes."[8]

B. COURT OF FEDERAL CLAIMS

1. Complaint

If, after receipt of an adverse Contracting Officer's decision on its claim, a contractor decides to bypass the boards of contract appeals and bring an action directly on the claim in the Court of Federal Claims, the action must be brought no later than *one year* after the contractor receives the Contracting Officer's final decision.[9] Failure to file a complaint with the Clerk of the Court[10] within the 12-month period will result in dismissal of the complaint. The court has recognized as timely a facsimile complaint that was received before the 12-month deadline where the original arrived late.[11] Even if the contractor has attempted an *untimely* appeal to a board and the appeal has been dismissed for untimeliness, the contractor can still bring an action in the Court of Federal Claims if 12 months have not passed since receipt of the Contracting Officer's decision.[12] However, until a board has determined that an appeal is untimely, it is premature for a contractor to sue in the court.[13]

The court's Rules of Practice specify the form and content of the complaint. The complaint should contain a clear and concise statement of the claim, the basis of the court's jurisdiction, and a specific demand for relief.[14] The Clerk of the Court handles distribution of the complaint to the Government.

2. Answer

In Court of Federal Claims cases, the Government is represented by attorneys from the Civil Division of the Department of Justice, usually assisted by an agency attorney. The Government is required to file an answer to the contractor's complaint within 60 days after receipt of the complaint.[15] The answer serves the same function as it would in a board proceeding (see Chapter 20, Section A.5). It normally contains a series of admissions or denials of the allegations contained in the complaint, and it allows the court to ascertain, in broad terms, the issues involved in the case. Sometimes answers contain *counterclaims*—affirmative allegations of contractor liability to the Government. If a counterclaim is filed, the contractor must file a *reply* within 20 days after receiving the counterclaim.[16]

3. Pretrial Orders & Conferences

The Court of Federal Claims uses extremely detailed pretrial orders to a significant extent. The orders are used for different purposes, but they are generally very specific and require the parties to provide each other—and the court—with the particulars regarding the case's significant legal and factual issues. For example, a typical order will direct both parties to furnish the court with (1) exhibits, (2) a statement of uncontested facts, (3) a list of witnesses with a brief summary of their testimony, and (4) a memorandum setting forth the basic facts that each party hopes to establish.[17]

The court's Rules also provide for the issuance of a pretrial order that will detail all agreements reached, orders made, or actions taken at pretrial conferences.[18] Pretrial conferences are normally held shortly after the initial pleadings have been filed (to schedule pretrial proceedings, discovery, and the like), as well as close to the time of trial in order to make specific and detailed preparations for trial.[19]

The Rules provide that if a party fails or refuses to comply with a pretrial order, appropriate sanctions may be applied.[20] These range from (a) recommending the entering of judgment by default against the disobedient party to (b) ordering that the facts pertaining to the matter in default be taken as established. The court can also require the disobedient party to pay the reasonable expenses incurred because of the noncompliance—including attorney fees.

4. Discovery

The Court of Federal Claims Rules provide for discovery on much the same terms, through the same methods, and with the same limitations as provided in the Federal Rules of Civil Procedure governing civil litigation in the U.S. District Courts.[21] The court allows (1) interrogatories, (2) depositions, (3) requests for admissions, and (4) requests for the production of documents (all of which are also available under board rules; see Chapter 20, Section B). Like the boards of contract appeals, the Court of Federal Claims may impose sanctions if a party fails to obey an order to provide discovery.[22] One such sanction is dismissal of the party's claim, although there are limits on how the court exercises this discretion.[23] The Court of Federal Claims may issue subpoenas to witnesses ordering them to appear and testify or produce records. The court's subpoena power is similar to that of a U.S. District Court.[24]

The Rules also provide the court with a unique discovery power. The court may gather information on its own by issuing a "call" to a department or agency of the United States for information, papers, or computations that it deems necessary. Requests for calls may be initiated solely by the court or on the motion of a party. The head of the department or agency may refuse to comply with a call when, in his opinion, compliance would be injurious to the public interest.[25]

5. Motions

Motions practice at the Court of Federal Claims is essentially similar in scope to that at the boards. Motions are simply requests to the court to take or refrain from taking certain actions.[26] Motions may be (a) dispositive (for example, a motion for summary judgment or a motion for judgment on the pleadings[27]), in which case a ruling granting the motion would dispose of the case without further proceedings, or (b) procedural (for example, a motion for an extension of time to file a pleading).

6. Trial

Many Court of Federal Claims trials are held in Washington, D.C., where the court is headquartered. However, the court's Rules state simply that the trial shall be held "at a location selected by the court,"[28] and the court is expressly authorized to hear cases where the witnesses reside.[29] Trials—as is the case in board proceedings—are held before a single judge. They are similar to federal civil trials without a jury in the manner in which they are conducted.

The Court of Federal Claims is required to hold proceedings in accordance with the Federal Rules of Evidence.[30] Since there is no jury in Court of Federal Claims proceedings, there is a bias toward the admissibility of evidence, as is also true in board proceedings.

7. Post-Trial Briefs

After the testimony of the parties has been heard by the assigned judge (in essentially the same manner as in a board hearing), the judge will instruct the parties on filing post-trial briefs. The Court of Federal Claims Rules are quite specific as to the form of briefs,[31] which are limited in length "except by leave of the court on motion."[32] Normally, the contractor files the initial brief and the Government files an opposing brief.

8. Decision

Decisions of the Court of Federal Claims are rendered by a single judge (normally the one who presided at the trial).[33] The judge states his findings of fact and conclusions of law separately.[34] Judgment in accordance with the decision is entered by the Clerk of the Court.[35] Motions for a new trial or rehearing or to alter or amend a judgment must be filed within 10 days of the judgment.[36]

The text of opinions issued by the Court of Federal Claims are published by various sources, notably FEDERAL COURT PROCUREMENT DECISIONS, published by Federal Publications Inc., which contains the full text of all opinions issued for procurement cases since the court began operating in 1982.

C. COURT OF APPEALS FOR THE FEDERAL CIRCUIT

The Court of Appeals for the Federal Circuit has jurisdiction over appeals from final decisions of the Court of Federal Claims and from final decisions of the boards of contract appeals under the CDA.[37] The party wishing review of a board decision must file a Petition for Review with the Clerk of the Federal Circuit within 120 days.[38] A party appealing an unfavorable decision of the Court of Federal Claims must file a Notice of Appeal with the Clerk of the Court of Federal Claims within 60 days of entry of the court's judgment or order.[39]

For the Government to appeal an adverse board decision, it must obtain the approval of both the agency head and the Attorney General.[40] Prior to the CDA, only the contractor was permitted to appeal an adverse board decision; the Government could not appeal. Now both parties may challenge the decision on an equal basis. A Government appeal of a Court of Federal Claims decision requires only the approval of the Attorney General.

1. Review Of Board Decisions

The standards to which the Federal Circuit must adhere when it is reviewing a board decision are set forth in the following language from the CDA:[41]

> [T]he decision of the agency board on any question of law shall not be final or conclusive, but the decision on any question of fact shall be final and conclusive and shall not be set aside unless the decision is fraudulent, or arbitrary, or capricious, or so grossly erroneous as to necessarily imply bad faith, or if such decision is not supported by substantial evidence.

a. Law vs. Fact Distinction. The distinction between law and fact is central to the Federal Circuit's review process. If a question is one of law, the board's decision on the question can freely be changed—although the Federal Circuit has stated that "some deference" is given to the boards' "expertise in interpreting contract regulations."[42] However, if a question is one of fact, the court cannot set aside a board decision on the question unless (a) the decision is tainted by fraud, arbitrariness, caprice, or gross error, or (b) the decision is not supported by substantial evidence.

It is not always a simple task to distinguish between factual and legal issues. Basically, a question of law involves an issue concerning the rules that are applied by a board to decide the matter (for example, whether a contract clause should be given a particular interpretation). A question of fact, on the other hand, is one relating to the events that actually took place (for example, whether a contractor had actual knowledge of the conditions at a worksite).

b. Substantial Evidence Test. Although the CDA provides two grounds for overturning factual findings of boards—where findings are (1) "fraudulent, or arbitrary, or capricious, or so grossly erroneous as to necessarily imply bad faith" or (2) are "not supported by substantial evidence"—for all intents and purposes, the Federal Circuit conducts its factual review pursuant to the "substantial evidence" standard. As a practical matter, therefore, the sole question to be pursued in determining the finality of a factual aspect of a board decision is whether, when the entire record is carefully considered, that finding is supported by substantial evidence. This approach allows the court to exercise considerable discretion. In one decision, substantial evidence was characterized as "evidence which could convince an unprejudiced mind of the truth of the facts to which the evidence is directed."[43]

Even though it has considerable discretion in reviewing board decisions, the Federal Circuit may not substitute its own judgment for that of a board in deciding whether substantial evidence to support a decision exists. As the U.S. Supreme Court has recognized in connection with the substantial evidence standard, a court may not—even as to matters not requiring special expertise—set aside a board's "choice between two fairly conflicting views, even though the Court would justifiably have made a different choice had the matter been before it [from the start]."[44]

2. Review Of Court Of Federal Claims Decisions

The Federal Circuit freely reviews Court of Federal Claims decisions for errors of law but will not set aside findings of fact unless they are "clearly erroneous."[45] This is the same standard that all U.S. Courts of Appeals apply in reviewing decisions of U.S. District Courts.[46] As a practical matter, the "clearly erroneous" standard is similar to the "substantial evidence" standard applied to board decisions, although the Federal Circuit has indicated that board findings may be accorded greater deference under the "substantial evidence" test than Court of Federal Claims findings under the "clearly erroneous" test.[47]

3. Procedures

The procedures used in the Court of Appeals for the Federal Circuit are governed by its Rules of Practice, which supplement the Federal Rules of Appellate Procedure that apply to all U.S. Courts of Appeals. The major features of this process are discussed below.

a. Filings & Record. A party (the appellant) that is dissatisfied with a board or court decision initiates the appeal of that decision by filing a Petition for Review or Notice of Appeal. The responding party (the appellee) is not required to file an answer or other pleading, since the brief the party will be required to file will sufficiently answer the allegations raised by the appellant's brief.

The record on appeal (exhibits, transcripts of the prior proceedings, etc.) is retained by the board or court. A certified list of the record of a board decision or a certified copy of the docket entries for a Court of Federal Claims decision is transmitted to the Court of Appeals instead of the record.[48]

The key documents in appeals before the Court of Appeals for the Federal Circuit are the briefs that are filed by the parties. The appellant's brief must be filed within 60 days after the date on which the appeal is docketed or the record filed. The appellee's brief must be filed within 40 days after the appellant's has been filed, and the appellant may file a reply brief within 14 days thereafter.[49]

The form and content of the briefs are strictly controlled. The appellant's brief must include (1) a table of contents, (2) a statement of the issues presented for review, (3) a brief statement of the nature of the case and the relevant facts, (4) legal argument with citations to authorities, and (5) a short conclusion stating the precise relief sought.[50] The appellee's brief follows the same requirements, except that another statement of the issues is not included absent disagreement.[51] The court, at its discretion, may also allow oral argument to supplement the written statements made in the briefs.[52]

Although by no means commonplace, the Federal Circuit will, when it believes it necessary, impose sanctions on a party for making frivolous arguments on appeal. In one case, the court awarded the Government double the costs it incurred in defending an appeal where the contractor's arguments were illogical and based on misstatements and distortions.[53]

b. Decision. A decision by the Federal Circuit is usually rendered by a panel of three judges.[54] It may be designated by the court as "precedential" or "nonprecedential." The court's Rules provide that "nonprecedential" opinions "shall not be employed or cited as precedent."[55] All opinions—"precedential" and "nonprecedential"—issued by the Court of Appeals for the Federal Circuit in cases involving Government contracts can be found in Federal Publications' FEDERAL COURT PROCUREMENT DECISIONS.

As a practical matter, the Federal Circuit's decision marks the end of the litigation. Although review of a Court of Appeals decision can be obtained in the Supreme Court, successful appeals to the Supreme Court on Government contract matters are extremely rare.

The Federal Circuit's decision may order the case *remanded* to the board of contract appeals or to the Court of Federal Claims for further proceedings. Thus, for example, if the court finds that the record from the board is inadequate, it "may render an opinion and judgment and remand the case for further action by the agency board...as appropriate, with such direction as the court considers just and proper."[56] Similarly, the court may also remand a case from the Court of Federal

Claims to that court for "such further proceedings as may be just under the circumstances."[57]

c. Rehearing. A petition for rehearing of a panel decision must ordinarily be filed within 14 days after entry of judgment.[58] Unless a majority of the panel agrees to rehear the case, the Clerk will enter an order denying the petition after 10 days.[59] A petition for rehearing may be combined with a suggestion for rehearing "in banc." If the panel denies the petition, the suggestion for "in banc" review will be presented to the Federal Circuit's active judges. "In banc" review—that is, rehearing by all the active judges of the court—"is an extraordinary procedure" and "is not favored."[60] It will be ordered only when the case requires "answer to a precedent-setting question of exceptional importance or resolution of a conflict between the panel opinion and precedent of the Supreme Court of the United States or of this circuit."[61]

REFERENCES

1. P.L. 97-164, 96 Stat. 25.

2. See generally Anthony & White, "Contract Suits in the Court of Claims," Briefing Papers No. 73-6 (Dec. 1973), 3 BPC 81.

3. See generally White, "The New Government Contract Courts," Briefing Papers No. 83-11 (Nov. 1983), 6 BPC 257.

4. P.L. 102-572, 104 Stat. 4506 (Oct. 29, 1992).

5. 28 USC § 1295(a).

6. 41 USC § 609(a)(1).

7. 28 USC § 1491(a)(3).

8. 28 USC § 1491(a)(2). See Overall Roofing & Const. Inc. v. U.S., 929 F.2d 687 (Fed. Cir. 1991), 10 FPD ¶ 39, 33 GC ¶ 133.

9. 41 USC § 609(a)(3). See Structural Finishing, Inc. v. U.S., 14 Cl. Ct. 447 (1988), 7 FPD ¶ 28 (receipt of Contracting Officer decision by contractor's attorney started one-year filing period), 30 GC ¶ 197.

10. Fed. Cl. R. 3(a).

11. Ross v. U.S., 16 Cl. Ct. 378 (1989), 8 FPD ¶ 28, 31 GC ¶ 154.

12. Olsberg Excavating Co. v. U.S., 3 Cl. Ct. 249 (1983), 2 FPD ¶ 33, 25 GC ¶ 296.

13. National Neighbors, Inc. v. U.S., 839 F.2d 1539 (Fed. Cir. 1988), 7 FPD ¶ 13, 30 GC ¶ 86.

14. See Fed. Cl. R. 8.

15. Fed. Cl. R. 12(a).

16. Note 15, supra.

17. See Fed. Cl. R. 16, app. G, ¶¶ 11–15.

18. Fed. Cl. R. 16(e).

19. See note 17, supra ¶¶ 9–10.

20. Fed. Cl. R. 16(f).

21. Fed. Cl. R. 26–37, 1(b).

22. Fed. Cl. R. 37(b).

23. See Ingalls Shipbldg., Inc. v. U.S., 857 F.2d 1448 (Fed. Cir. 1988), 7 FPD ¶ 126, 30 GC ¶ 361.

24. See Fed. Cl. R. 45.

25. Fed. Cl. R. 34(d). See 28 USC § 2507(a).

26. See Fed. Cl. R. 7(b) and app. H.

27. Fed. Cl. R. 56, 12(c).

28. Fed. Cl. R. 39(a). See 28 USC § 173.

29. 28 USC § 2503. See In re United States, 877 F.2d 1568 (Fed. Cir. 1989), 8 FPD ¶ 82, 31 GC ¶ 228.

30. 28 USC § 2503(b); Fed. Cl. R. 43(a).

31. Fed. Cl. R. 83.1(a).

32. Fed. Cl. R. 83.1(b).

33. 28 USC § 174.

34. Fed. Cl. R. 52.

35. Fed. Cl. R. 58.

36. Fed. Cl. R. 59.

37. 41 USC § 607(g)(1); 28 USC § 1295(a)(3). See generally Shea & Schaengold, "A Guide to the Court of Appeals for the Federal Circuit," Briefing Papers No. 90-13 (Dec. 1990), 9 BPC 267.

38. Fed. Cir. R. 15.

39. See Fed. Cl. R. 72. See Cleek Aviation v. U.S., 20 Cl. Ct. 766 (1990), 9 FPD ¶ 102, 32 GC ¶ 245.

40. 41 USC § 607(g)(1)(B).

41. 41 USC § 609(b).

42. SMS Data Products Group, Inc. v. U.S., 900 F.2d 1553 (Fed. Cir. 1990), 9 FPD ¶ 55, 32 GC ¶ 187.

43. Koppers Co. v. U.S., 405 F.2d 554 (Ct. Cl. 1968), 11 GC ¶ 26.

44. Universal Camera Corp. v. National Labor Relations Board, 340 U.S. 474 (1951).

45. Fed. Cl. R. 52(a).

46. See, e.g., Fed. R. Civ. P. 52(a); Bellevue Gardens, Inc. v. Hill, 297 F.2d 185 (D.C. Cir. 1961).

47. See Tandon Corp v. U.S. Intl. Trade Commn., 831 F.2d 1017 (Fed. Cir. 1987).

48. Fed. Cir. R. 11, 17.

49. Fed. Cir. R. 31(a).

50. Fed. Cir. R. 28(a).

51. Fed. Cir. R. 28(b).

52. Fed. Cir. R. 34.

53. Romala Corp. v. U.S., 927 F.2d 1219 (Fed. Cir. 1991), 10 FPD ¶ 33, 33 GC ¶ 124. See Fed. R. App. P. 38. See also Dungaree Realty, Inc. v. U.S., 13 FPD ¶ 56 (Fed. Cir. 1994) (sanctioning both contractor and attorney for frivolously arguing appeal).

54. Fed. Cir. R. 47.2(a).

55. Fed. Cir. R. 47.8(b) (Rev. No. 1, 1991).

56. 41 USC § 609(c).

57. 28 USC § 2106.

58. Fed. R. App. P. 40.

59. Fed. Cir. R. 40, practice note.

60. Fed. Cir. R. 35(a); Fed. R. App. P. 35(a).

61. Fed. Cir. R. 35(a).

Part VI

SUBCONTRACTING

chapters

22 | Subcontract Basics
23 | Subcontract Terms And Conditions

SUBCONTRACT BASICS

22

A. Nature Of Subcontracts

B. Subcontractor Disputes & Remedies
   1. Privity Rule
   2. Subcontractors vs. The Government
   3. Subcontractors vs. Prime Contractors

C. Government Control
   1. Contractor Purchasing System Review
   2. Consent To Subcontracts
   3. Flow-Down Clauses
   4. Policies Favoring Special Groups
   5. Payment

The complexity of modern Government contracts makes it necessary for prime contractors regularly to seek assistance during the course of their performance. Although the contractual arrangements may vary, the most common manner for providing this assistance is through a *subcontract* between the prime and a subcontractor. Because subcontracting is an important part of Government contracting, it is treated in this part—Part VI—of the book, composed of this chapter and one other. This chapter discusses the basic matters involving subcontracts as they pertain to Government contracts. The chapter that follows examines subcontract terms and conditions.

A. NATURE OF SUBCONTRACTS

The term "subcontractor" refers generally to any firm that supplies materials or performs services for a prime contractor. Government subcontracts have a dual character. On the one hand, the Government *disclaims* any direct *responsibility* for the subcontract or to the subcontracting parties—because of the lack of "privity of contract" (a direct contractual relationship between the subcontractor and the Government); on the other hand, the Government seeks to retain a large measure of *control* over the parties by, for example, requiring that certain clauses be included in subcontracts and maintaining the right to approve most subcontracts.

Thus, subcontracts under Government prime contracts are, in a sense, *hybrid* contractual documents. They include many of the characteristics of contracts between purely commercial entities (the prime contractor and the subcontractor), while at the same time imposing on the subcontractor many of the Government-unique duties and controls imposed on the prime contractor.

B. SUBCONTRACTOR DISPUTES & REMEDIES

1. Privity Rule

It is axiomatic that in order to enforce contractual rights against a party, there must be a *direct* contractual relationship with that party (i.e., there must be "privity of contract"). Thus, there are situations where, although the ultimate responsibility for a contract problem (such as defective drawings) can be readily traced to the Government, a subcontractor is unable to seek a remedy *directly* from the Government—unless the subcontractor is otherwise in privity with the Government through a direct contractual tie.[1] Similarly, although the Government may ultimately provide all the contract funding, it is not liable to a subcontractor for problems caused by the prime contractor. As one United States Court of Appeals stated:[2]

> [T]he fact that the entire cost of the project came from the Government did not create a contractual obligation between the Government and the subcontractors under contracts to which the Government was not a party. The subcontractor perforce was required to look to the one who promised to pay him for his work and to him alone. There being no privity of contract between [the subcontractor] and the Government, [the subcontractor] could not maintain an action against the Government for money due him from [the prime contractor] alone.

The rationale of the privity rule has merit—at least theoretically—since the Government normally deals *only* with the prime. The manner in which the prime has obligated itself to produce is the prime's concern. Thus, if Government activities cause damage to a subcontractor in the course of performance, it is the prime's duty to seek compensation from the Government and, in turn, to pass the recovery on to the subcontractor. Similarly, the Government will hold the prime contractor responsible for the actions of its subcontractor under the contract.[3]

2. Subcontractors vs. The Government

The FAR states specifically—with respect to disputes procedures—that the Contracting Officer may not give his approval to any subcontract clause that purports to give a subcontractor the right to obtain a *direct* decision of the Contracting Officer on a claim against the Government or the right of direct appeal to a board of contract appeals.[4] Even if a Contracting Officer erroneously approved such a clause, the board would deny a direct appeal.[5] However, the identical result may be obtained indirectly because it is commonplace for a subcontractor's claim to be prosecuted by either (a) the prime contractor on behalf of the subcontractor, or (b) (more typically) the subcontractor using the prime contractor's name with the prime's permission.[6]

Thus, the requirement that the prime contractor constantly act as a buffer between the Government and the subcontractor has been significantly modified in actual practice.[7] Sponsorship of subcontractor appeals by prime contractors is mainly a matter of form, since the prime contractor need not be actively involved in prosecuting the subcontractor's claim.[8] The prime contractor, however, must certify the accuracy of subcontractor claims over $100,000 (see Chapter 19, Section B.5), although the prime need only believe that there is "good ground" to support the sub's claim.[9] The FAR permits such indirect appeals, but it also provides that subcontracts giving such rights of appeal to subcontractors may not attempt to obligate the Contracting Officer or a board to (1) decide questions that do not arise between the Government and the prime contractor or (2) deal directly with the subcontractor.[10] Thus, the Government must have a financial interest in the subcontractor's appeal for a board to retain jurisdiction.

Moreover, since the subcontractor must proceed in the name of the prime, it is important that the prime not take any actions that would jeopardize the subcontractor's position. For example, if the prime executes a release of the Government from further liability, the subcontractor's indirect appeal rights would be extinguished.[11] Similarly, if the prime contractor fails to give timely notice of appeal, the subcontractor would be barred from taking an indirect appeal, even though the prime was at fault in not giving the required notice.[12] However, a subcontractor that erroneously files an appeal in its own name may be allowed to substitute the name of the prime contractor if the prime contractor had agreed to sponsor the appeal.[13]

Extraordinary contractual relief under Public Law 85-804 is available to subcontractors as well as prime contractors (see Chapter 18, Section D.2). A petition for such relief may be filed by the prime contractor on behalf of the subcontractor. Ordinarily, the relief, if granted, is passed through the prime by amending the prime's contract with the Government.

3. Subcontractors vs. Prime Contractors

In many cases, the Government has no liability for the problem encountered by either the prime or the sub. If Government liability is not in question—as where defective specifications are prepared and furnished to the sub by the prime—the subcontracting parties are free to pursue the same remedies that would be available under any commercial contract. Depending on the location of the parties, where the contract was entered into, and where the work was performed, lawsuits may be filed in state or federal courts or (if international subcontracts are involved) in foreign tribunals.

An alternative to litigation that is sometimes used is arbitration. Arbitration procedures offer an inexpensive and decisive means of resolving sub-prime disputes. If the parties wish, they may include a clause in their subcontract providing for arbitration of disputes by the American Arbitration Association (or some similar organization). The results of any arbitration, judicial determination, or voluntary settlement of the dispute between the prime and the sub are not binding on the Government.[14] However, the Government generally recognizes such decisions unless there is a substantial reason for not doing so.

C. GOVERNMENT CONTROL

Although there is no direct contractual relationship between the Government and subcontractors, the Government nevertheless exercises considerable control over subcontracts and subcontractors. This control is manifested in several notable ways: (a) a requirement for Government review of a contractor's purchasing system, (b) the requirement that the Government consent to certain subcontracts, (c) the requirement that many contract clauses in the prime contract be passed on ("flowed down") by the prime contractor to the subcontractor, (d) the Government's policy decision to encourage subcontracting with favored groups, and (e) provisions protecting subcontractors from late payment from prime contractors.

1. Contractor Purchasing System Review

The purpose of a Contractor Purchasing System Review (CPSR) by the Government "is to evaluate the efficiency and effectiveness with which the contractor spends Government funds and complies with Government policy when subcontracting."[15] The FAR requires a CPSR for each contractor whose sales to the Government (under prime or subcontracts), using other than sealed bid procedures, are expected to exceed $10 million during the next 12 months.[16] The $10-million threshold can be raised or lowered by agency heads if this is considered to be in the Government's best interest.[17] The review provides the Contracting Officer "a basis for granting, withholding, or withdrawing approval of the contractor's purchasing system."[18]

The Government's review procedures are designed to evaluate the manner in which the prime contractor selects and administers its subcontracts. Specifically, the FAR requires that special attention be given to (1) the degree of price competition achieved, (2) pricing policies and techniques, (3) methods of evaluating subcontractor responsibility, (4) treatment accorded affiliates, (5) practices pertaining to small business concerns, (6) management of major subcontract programs, (7) compliance with the Cost Accounting Standards in awarding subcontracts, (8) appropriateness of the types of contracts used, and (9) management control systems and audit procedures to administer progress payments to subcontractors.[19]

Approval of a CPSR greatly facilitates the contractor's ability to place subsequent subcontracts. The Contracting Officer may approve a CPSR only when he is satisfied that the contractor's practices and policies adequately protect the Government's interests.[20] Approval will be withheld where the system has major weaknesses. Follow-up reviews are generally conducted every three years, or more frequently when information reveals a deficiency or major change in the contractor's purchasing system.[21]

2. Consent To Subcontracts

The Government also exercises control over subcontracts when it includes a clause in certain types of prime contracts requiring the consent of the Government to subcontracts.[22] Consent to subcontracts is generally required "when the subcontract work is complex, the dollar value is substantial, or the Government's interest is not adequately protected by competition and the type of prime contract or subcontract."[23] The FAR provides that consent to subcontracts is required, for example, under (a) certain fixed-price prime contracts where the contractor does not have an approved purchasing system, (b) cost-reimbursement and letter prime contracts where the contractor does not have an approved purchasing system and the subcontracts are cost-reimbursement, time-and-materials, or labor-hour subcontracts, and (c) time-and-materials prime contracts (except for the purchase of raw material or commercial stock items) and architect-engineer services prime contracts.[24]

The subcontract approval clauses[25] provide for dollar amounts, percentage of total procurement, and other threshold criteria before they become operative. When operative, they require notice by the prime contractor to the Contracting Officer in advance of entering into any subcontract. The notice must include, for example, (1) a description of the work to be performed by the subcontractor, (2) identification of the type of subcontract to be used and an explanation of why that particular subcontractor was selected, (3) the proposed subcontract price and the contractor's cost or price analysis, (4) the subcontractor's cost or pricing data and Cost Accounting Standards Disclosure Statement, if required by other provisions, and (5) the subcontract price negotiation memorandum.[26]

Thirteen separate criteria are listed in the FAR for determining whether the Contracting Officer should consent to a subcontract.[27] They include consideration of (a) the prime contractor's basis for selecting the subcontractor, (b) whether adequate price competition was obtained, (c) the appropriateness of the type of subcontract used, and (d) whether the prime contractor has adequately translated prime contract technical requirements into subcontract requirements. The Contracting Officer is instructed by the FAR to exercise particular diligence where:[28]

(1) The prime contractor's purchasing system or performance is inadequate.

(2) Close working relationships or ownership affiliations between the prime and subcontractor may preclude free competition or result in higher prices.

(3) Subcontracts are proposed for award on a noncompetitive basis, at prices that appear unreasonable, or at prices higher than those offered to the Government in comparable circumstances.

(4) Subcontracts are proposed on a cost-reimbursement, time-and-materials, or labor-hour basis.

Despite the control over subcontract selection that the contracting agency enjoys, the Contracting Officer's consent to a subcontract does not constitute approval of the terms and price of the subcontract.[29]

The prime contractor's failure to obtain the requisite consent for subcontracts could result in a partial termination of the prime contract for default.[30] (Termination for default is discussed in detail in Chapter 16.)

3. Flow-Down Clauses

Flow-down clauses are clauses from a prime contractor's contract that are incorporated into the prime's subcontracts.[31] They are designed to protect the Government's rights and interests and to otherwise promote its procurement and socioeconomic policies.

Some flow-down clauses are mandatory; that is, they are *required* to be included in a particular subcontract by statute, Executive Order, the procurement regulations, or the terms of the clause itself. For example, the "Examination of Records by Comptroller General" clause[32] applies to many negotiated prime contracts and gives the Comptroller General the right, for three years after final payment, to review directly pertinent prime contract records. Paragraph (c) of this clause states the following:

> The Contractor agrees to include in first-tier subcontracts under this contract a clause to the effect that the Comptroller General or a duly authorized representative from

the General Accounting Office shall, until 3 years after final payment under the subcontract...have access to and the right to examine any of the subcontractor's directly pertinent books, documents, papers, or other records involving transactions related to the subcontract.

Other clauses, although not mandatory, may be required by a Contracting Officer to be flowed-down if he determines it is necessary to do so to protect the Government's interests. The type of work to be performed, the dollar amount of the contract, and the contract type normally determine which clauses must be flowed-down. A more thorough review of subcontract terms and conditions is contained in the next chapter, Chapter 23, in Section B.

4. Policies Favoring Special Groups

Another way in which the Government exerts control over subcontracts is through requirements that encourage subcontracts with special groups. Several of these requirements were discussed in Chapter 6.

Notable among the various Government policies favoring special groups is the Small Business Act of 1958,[33] which was amended in 1978 to require the utilization of small and minority businesses in many Government contracts.[34] Under the law as amended, certain prime contracts must include clauses that encourage subcontracting with small business concerns and small business concerns owned by socially and economically disadvantaged individuals.

The requirement is implemented primarily through the use of two FAR contract clauses. The first, required in most Government contracts exceeding the small purchase threshold, is the "Utilization of Small Business Concerns and Small Disadvantaged Business Concerns" clause,[35] which obligates prime contractors to provide small and small disadvantaged firms with a "maximum practicable opportunity" to participate in contract performance. The second, required in contracts exceeding $500,000 ($1 million for construction contracts involving public facilities), is the "Small Business and Small Disadvantaged Business Subcontracting Plan" clause.[36] Under this clause, prime contractors must prepare plans showing specific percentage goals for subcontracting with small and small disadvantaged businesses. Also, Contracting Officers are required to enforce the subcontracting plan after the prime contract is awarded,[37] and a prospective contractor's compliance with small business subcontracting plans under prior contracts is a factor in determining the contractor's responsibility (see Chapter 3, Section E.2).[38]

5. Payment

The Government encourages prime contractors to pay their subcontractors without delay. The Prompt Payment Act, for example, provides that construction contractors must pay subcontractors within seven days of receiving payment from the Government, imposes an interest penalty for late payments, and requires prime contractors to submit a certification with each invoice to the Government that timely payments have been and will be made to subcontractors (see Chapter 15, Section A.3).[39] Other laws require agencies to release information to subcontractors when requested on whether demands for progress payments or other payments have been submitted by a prime contractor and whether final payment has been made to the prime contractor.[40] Implementing regulations permit a Contracting Officer to investigate credible assertions made by a subcontractor or supplier that it has not been paid in accordance with its subcontract agreement and to take appropriate remedial action, including reduction or suspension of progress payments due the prime contractor.[41]

REFERENCES

1. E.g., McMillin Bros. Constructors, Inc., EBCA 328-10-84, 86-3 BCA ¶ 19179.

2. Nickel v. Pollia, 179 F.2d 160 (10th Cir. 1950).

3. E.g., D&H Const. Co., ASBCA 37482, 89-3 BCA ¶ 22070, 31 GC ¶ 240.

4. FAR 44.203.

5. Kinetic Engrg., Inc., ASBCA 13649, 70-1 BCA ¶ 8104, 12 GC ¶ 104.

SUBCONTRACT BASICS 22-11

6. See, e.g., Boeing Co., ASBCA 10524, 67-2 BCA ¶ 6693, 10 GC ¶ 464.

7. See generally Taylor, "Subcontractor Remedies," Briefing Papers No. 86-8 (July 1986), 7 BPC 339.

8. TRW, Inc., ASBCA 11373, 66-2 BCA ¶ 5882, 10 GC ¶ 388.

9. U.S. v. Turner Const. Co., 827 F.2d 1554 (Fed. Cir. 1987), 6 FPD ¶ 66, 29 GC ¶ 190. See also McCloud v. Twin City Const. Co., No. A3-86-76 (D.N.D. Apr. 13, 1987) (subcontractor cannot force contractor to certify claim), 29 GC ¶ 142.

10. FAR 44.203(c).

11. Ashton-Mardian Co., ASBCA 7912, 1963 BCA ¶ 3836, 5 GC ¶ 523.

12. Baltimore Contractors, Inc., GSBCA 3489, 73-1 BCA ¶ 9928, 15 GC ¶ 135.

13. Cousins Const. Co., EBCA 433-11-89, 90-2 BCA ¶ 22761.

14. FAR 44.203(b)(4).

15. FAR 44.301. See also DFARS subpt. 44.3.

16. FAR 44.302(a).

17. Note 16, supra.

18. FAR 44.301.

19. FAR 44.303.

20. FAR 44.305-1(a)(1).

21. FAR 44.302(b).

22. FAR subpt. 44.2.

23. FAR 44.102(a).

24. FAR 44.201-1, 44.201-2, 44.201-3.

25. See FAR 44.204.

26. See, e.g., FAR 52.244-1 ("Subcontracts (Fixed-Price Contracts)" clause), para. (b).

27. FAR 44.202-2(a).

28. FAR 44.202-2(b).

29. FAR 44.203(a).

30. Blake Const. Co., GSBCA 4013 et al., 75-2 BCA ¶ 11487, 18 GC ¶ 198.

31. See generally Hoe, Oliver & Abbott, "Flow-Down Clauses in Subcontracts," Briefing Papers No. 85-5 (May 1985), 7 BPC 83.

32. FAR 52.215-1.

33. 15 USC § 631 et seq.

34. P.L. 95-507, 92 Stat. 1757. See Allen & Shafferman, "Subcontracting Under P.L. 95-507," Briefing Papers No. 81-6 (Dec. 1981), 5 BPC 243.

35. FAR 52.219-8. See also FAR 19.708(a) (exceptions for personal service contracts and for contracts performed entirely outside U.S.).

36. FAR 52.219-9. See also FAR 19.708(b).

37. FAR 19.705-6(g).

38. FAR 9.104-3, 19.705-6.

39. 31 USC § 3905. See JP, Inc., ASBCA 38426 et al., 90-1 BCA ¶ 22348, 32 GC ¶ 70, affd. on reconsideration, 90-1 BCA ¶ 22616; JP, Inc., ASBCA 40068, 91-1 BCA ¶ 23607, 33 GC ¶ 28.

40. National Defense Authorization Act for Fiscal Years 1992 and 1993, P.L. 102-190, § 806 (Dec. 5, 1991), amended by the Federal Acquisition Streamlining Act of 1994, P.L. 103-355, § 2091, 108 Stat. 3243 (Oct. 13, 1994).

41. See, e.g., DFARS 232.970. See generally Nash, "Timely Payment of Subcontractors: Is the Government Responsible?," 7 Nash & Cibinic Rep. ¶ 34 (June 1993).

SUBCONTRACT TERMS AND CONDITIONS

23

A. Background
 1. Uniform Commercial Code
 2. Standard Government Contract Clauses

B. Flow-Down Clauses

C. ABA Model Terms & Conditions

The general provisions of Government prime contracts (sometimes referred to as "boilerplate") have, over the years, assumed a more-or-less standard form. Thus, although there are some variations, most contracts—whether they are for supplies, services, construction, etc.—contain the same basic clauses. This concept of standard general provisions is a good one. The various clauses, their operation, and their interpretation become familiar to the parties. Also, to some extent at least, these standard provisions minimize unexpected occurrences and allocate risks equitably. Moreover, their use saves time and effort because it reduces the need to negotiate specific and new contract language for each procurement.

Much of this standardization has also become a part of Government subcontract terms and conditions. This chapter discusses subcontract terms and conditions in general and reviews some of the more significant *individual* subcontract clauses that are important in Government contracting.

A. BACKGROUND

As noted in the preceding chapter (see Chapter 22, Section A), subcontracts under Government prime contracts are essentially hybrid documents; they have many of the characteristics of purely commercial contracts between private parties and, at the same time, include additional Government contract terms and obligations. As such, Government subcontracts are affected by both the Uniform Commercial Code (UCC) and the standard clauses that are found in Government prime contracts.

1. Uniform Commercial Code

The UCC was originally drafted by the National Conference of Commissioners on Uniform State Laws and the American Law Institute to simply, clarify, and modernize the law governing commercial transactions throughout the United States. Because all of the states, except Louisiana, have adopted the UCC (with minor variations), the UCC is the nationwide uniform law of commercial practices.

The "sales" article—Article 2—of the UCC sets forth the basic rules for contracts for the sale of goods. It is intended to be the sole statement of sales law for the points it actually covers. Therefore, Government subcontracts—to the extent that a particular point is not preempted by the federal procurement regulations—will be interpreted and enforced in accordance with the UCC.[1] Agency boards of contract appeals have also been quite willing to apply UCC Article 2 concepts in appropriate circumstances, particularly in the areas of implied warranty and unconscionability. As a result, where subcontracts are in use on a Government prime contract, the parties must have an awareness of the FAR and of the Article 2 provisions of the UCC as well.

2. Standard Government Contract Clauses

Just as the Government has issued standard clauses for inclusion in its prime contracts, many of these prime contracts, in turn, require that standard clauses be "flowed down" by the prime contractor to its subcontractors. These flow-down terms and conditions will vary depending on the specific desires and interests of the prime contractor that issues them.

As the discussion in Section B below demonstrates, the prime contract clauses that are required to be "flowed down" to a subcontractor sometimes need not be passed down verbatim. Therefore, a prime contractor could propose modified mandatory flow-down clauses that secure more or varying rights for the prime (perhaps at the subcontractor's expense), as long as the minimum Government requirements remain in effect. The Contracting Officer is normally not concerned about the clauses that a prime contractor attempts to impose on its subcontractor provided (1) the essence of the flow-down provisions have, in fact, been passed down to the subcontractor, and (2) no prohibited language is included in the subcontract clauses by the prime (such as language giving the subcontractor the right of direct appeal to an agency board of contract appeals[2]). Thus, subcontractors on Government prime contracts cannot rely on the Government to intercede on their behalf; they must carefully review each of the prime's proposed terms and conditions prior to accepting them.

Consider, for example, the Government's right to terminate a prime contract for the Government's convenience. A number of clauses give the Government power to terminate prime contracts "in whole or, from time to time, in part if the Contracting Officer determines that a termination is in the Government's interest" (see Chapter 17).[3] The concept of a termination for convenience is not regularly found in commercial contracts, and the "Termination for Convenience of the Government" clause is not a mandatory flow-down to Government subcontracts, although the FAR does contain convenience termination clauses that the Government "suggests" for use in fixed-price and cost-reimbursement subcontracts.[4] Most prime contractors, however, realize that they must reserve the right to terminate their subcontracts for convenience in the event that their prime contracts are terminated by the Government in that manner. For this reason, a "Termination for Convenience" clause almost always appears in Government subcontracts to protect a legitimate prime contractor right. But many prime contractors do not limit their right to terminate their subcontracts to only when the prime contract is terminated but also frequently provide an additional right to terminate their subcontracts at their *own option* unrelated to the Government's actions. Subcontractors would be well advised to question this broader termination right and to limit the application of the clause to situations where the Government has terminated the prime contract.

B. FLOW-DOWN CLAUSES

There is almost no limit to the standard clauses or variations of standard clauses that Government prime contractors can include in their subcontracts.[5] Four different general categories of clauses can be listed:

(a) Prime contract clauses directing that they be incorporated in subcontracts exactly as written ("mandatory" flow-down clauses).

(b) Prime contract clauses providing that their "substance" be incorporated in subcontracts.

(c) Clauses that are "automatically" applicable to subcontracts due to the operation of law.

(d) Prime contract clauses that, although not mandatory flow-downs, impose obligations on prime contractors that cannot be effectively fulfilled unless similar provisions are incorporated into the primes' subcontracts.

Set forth below are examples of some typical FAR and Department of Defense FAR Supplement prime contract clauses that are often flowed down to subcontracts. Note that not all clauses found in the procurement regulations are discussed below; the list is meant to be illustrative rather than comprehensive. Note also that for a subcontract under a prime contract for the procurement of commercial items or a subcontract for the procurement of commercial items, the FAR will provide by October 1, 1995 (1) that a prime contractor shall not be required to flow-down any contract clause that is not required by law or is inconsistent with commercial practice and (2) a list of the statutes inapplicable to such contracts. The FAR will also include a list of statutes inapplicable to subcontracts in amounts not greater than the simplified acquisition threshold (formerly called the small purchase threshold).[6]

(1) Changes clauses—It is not mandatory to flow down the "Changes" clause[7] to subcontracts. However, since the prime contractor cannot effectively perform changed work unless it can require its subcontractors to perform changed work, most subcontracts contain a "Changes" clause. The "Notification of Changes" clause[8] also is not a mandatory flow-down. However, since it imposes strict reporting and notification requirements on prime contractors, its substance should be passed on to subcontractors when it is included in prime contracts. Similarly, the "Change Order Accounting" clause,[9] which permits the Contracting Officer to require change order accounting when a change or series of changes exceeds $100,000, is not a mandatory flow-down, but its substance should be included in subcontracts where it is likely that subcontractor cooperation will be required.

(2) Inspection clauses[10]—These clauses are not mandatory flow-downs. However, since they (a) provide the Government with the right to inspect all work (including subcontracted work) at the place where it is being performed, and (b) instruct the prime contractor to require subcontractors to cooperate with Government inspectors—a subcontract "Inspection" clause covering at least these points will be found in most subcontracts.

(3) "Assignment of Claims" clause[11]—This is not a mandatory flow-down clause. Many prime contractors, however, require that subcontractors obtain prior consent before assigning either the subcontract work or monies due (or to become due) from the prime contractor. Note that the UCC states that prohibitions against the assignment of monies due or to become due are ineffective.[12]

(4) Termination clauses[13]—Here again, although prime contract "Default" clauses and "Termination for Convenience" clauses are not mandatory flow-downs, the prime contractor will undoubtedly wish to provide for the right to terminate its subcontracts in the event that the prime contract is terminated for default or convenience (see Section A.2 above).

(5) "Disputes" clause[14]—The prime contract "Disputes" clause is not a mandatory flow-down, and (as discussed in Chapter 22, Section B) a clause purporting to give a subcontractor a right to directly appeal a claim will not be approved by the Contracting Officer. Subcontractors should consider the use of a clause giving them the right to pursue appeals indirectly, in the name of the prime contractor. As noted in Chapter 22, a prime contractor and subcontractor may also want to agree to submit disputes between them to arbitration.

(6) Labor standards clauses—The "Walsh-Healey Public Contracts Act" clause[15] providing for overtime compensation in supply contracts is not a mandatory flow-down, but prime contractors frequently pass down a similar clause to subcontractors. The "Service Contract Act" clause ensuring minimum wages and fringe benefits for contractor employees must be flowed-down to all subcontracts subject to the Act.[16] The "Equal Opportunity" clause, which implements the policy of equal employment opportunity in Government contracts, must be incorporated in all Government prime and subcontracts over $10,000.[17]

(7) Patents and data rights clauses—The "Authorization and Consent" clause[18] is not a mandatory flow-down, but its provisions automatically apply to subcontractors if the clause appears in a prime contract. The "Notice and Assistance Regarding Patent and Copyright Infringement" clause[19] is a mandatory flow-down to subcontractors if it is included in a prime contract. The "Patent Indemnity" clause[20] and "Waiver of Indemnity" clause[21] are not

mandatory flow-downs, but if they are contained in the prime contract, their substance should be passed on to subcontractors. The "Filing of Patent Applications–Classified Subject Matter" clause[22] is a mandatory flow-down in all subcontracts that cover—or are likely to cover—subject matter with a security classification of "secret" or higher. Prime contract "Rights in Data" clauses[23] place the burden on prime contractors to obtain the necessary data rights from their subcontractors through inclusion of appropriate similar clauses in their subcontracts.

(8) "Buy American Act–Construction Materials" clause[24]—This clause is not a mandatory flow-down, but since it must be included in most prime construction contracts and requires both the prime and its subcontractors to use only domestic construction material, the clause's substance will normally be passed on to subcontractors.

(9) "Insurance–Work on a Government Installation" clause[25]—This clause—which requires the prime contractor to maintain, for the period of performance, the minimum insurance coverage called for by the contract—is a mandatory flow-down where subcontractors must work on a Government installation.

(10) "Notice to the Government of Labor Disputes" clause[26]—If the clause appears in a prime contract, its substance must be included in each subcontract for which a labor dispute may delay timely performance of the prime contract.

(11) "Security Requirements" clause[27]—All classified prime contracts must contain this clause. Its substance must be included in all subcontracts that involve access to classified information.

(12) "Superintendence by the Contractor" clause[28]—Although not a mandatory flow-down, the substance of this clause is generally passed on to appropriate subcontractors.

(13) "Examination of Records by the Comptroller General" clause[29]—Under the current FAR, this clause is mandatory in virtually all negotiated prime contracts exceeding the small purchase threshold. Its substance must be flowed down to all subcontracts exceeding the small purchase threshold, with certain exceptions (e.g., some subcontracts for public utility services).

(14) "Preference for Privately Owned U.S.-Flag Commercial Vessels" clause[30]—This clause is required in many prime contracts that stipulate the transport of supplies, materials, or equipment on privately owned U.S. vessels. Where it appears in a prime contract, a similar clause should be included in subcontracts.

(15) "Subcontracts (Fixed-Price Contracts)" clause[31]—This clause is mandatory for many negotiated fixed-price prime contracts. When it appears, each subcontract should contain a prohibition against making payments on a cost-plus-percentage-of-cost basis.

(16) "Subcontracts (Cost-Reimbursement and Letter Contracts)" clause[32]—This clause is designed for use in cost-reimbursement prime contracts and is the equivalent of the "Subcontracts (Fixed-Price Contracts)" clause mentioned above. When used in subcontracts, there should be a prohibition against the use of cost-plus-percentage-of-cost payments. Also, when used, specific clauses (e.g., the "Limitation on Payments" clause) must appear in certain types of subcontracts.

(17) "Government Property Furnished 'As Is'" clause[33]—This is not a mandatory flow-down clause, but since it eliminates any warranties with regard to Government-furnished property, a similar clause is usually included in subcontracts where the prime contractor proposes to transfer any such property "as is" to subcontractors.

(18) "Special Tooling" clause[34]—This clause must be included in all negotiated prime contracts where the Government is to acquire full rights to special tooling in addition to the specific end products required under the contract. Any subcontracts that involve the use of special tooling, the full cost of which is charged to such subcontracts, must include appropriate provisions to obtain rights comparable to those granted to the Government by the prime contract clause. The only exception to this requirement occurs when the Government determines—on the prime contractor's request—that such rights are not of substantial interest to the Government.

(19) "Special Test Equipment" clause[35]—This clause must be included in negotiated prime contracts that provide that the contractor will acquire or fabricate special test equipment for

SUBCONTRACT TERMS AND CONDITIONS   23-9

the Government but do not specify the items to be acquired or fabricated. The prime contractor is required to include the clause's substance in all subcontracts where special test equipment may be acquired or fabricated for the Government.

(20) Cost or pricing data clauses—The prime contractor must flow down to its subcontracts the substance of the "Subcontractor Cost or Pricing Data" clause[36] requiring certified cost or pricing data from subcontractors when it is contemplated that cost or pricing data will be required from the prime under the Truth in Negotiations Act. If the prime is found liable to the Government for a price reduction for defective cost or pricing data submitted to the Government in connection with subcontracts, the prime contractor may be indemnified for the loss by the subcontractor if the prime included a "Price Reduction for Defective Cost or Pricing Data" clause[37] or similar provision in its subcontracts.

(21) "Duty Free Entry" clause[38]—If this clause appears in the prime contract, the prime contractor must include its substance in all first-tier subcontracts if they provide that foreign supplies in excess of $10,000 may be imported by the subcontractor into the United States.

(22) "Advance Payments" clause[39]—This clause must appear in prime contracts where advance payments are to be made. It is not a mandatory flow-down. However, the prime contractor's obligations cannot be fully discharged unless subcontracts providing for advance payments also provide for a Government lien paramount to all other liens, and impose on the subcontractor and the depository bank substantially the same duties, and give the Government the same rights provided by the prime contract clause.

(23) "Audit–Sealed Bidding" clause[40]—This clause must be included in all prime contracts that result from sealed bidding and are expected to exceed $500,000. All provisions of the clause must be included in all subcontracts exceeding $10,000.

(24) "Value Engineering" clause[41]—If this clause appears in a prime contract, an "appropriate" clause must be included in any subcontract of $100,000 or more. It also may be included in subcontracts of lesser value.

(25) "Limitation of Liability" clause[42]—This clause is required in most prime contracts exceeding the small purchase threshold. Its substance must be included in all subcontracts.

(26) "New Material" clause[43]—If this clause is included in a prime contract, its substance should be passed on to subcontractors, although it is not a mandatory flow-down.

(27) "Utilization of Women-Owned Small Businesses" clause[44]—This clause is mandatory for all prime contracts expected to exceed the small purchase limitation except (a) those which are to be performed entirely outside the United States or its possessions, and (b) contracts for personal services. The prime is required to use its best efforts to carry out, in the award of subcontracts, the policy favoring women-owned small businesses that is expressed in the clause.

(28) "Cleaning Up" clause[45]—This clause, which requires that fixed-price demolition contractors leave the job site in a neat and orderly condition, is not a mandatory flow-down. However, its substance should be extended to appropriate subcontracts.

(29) "Government Delay of Work" clause[46]—This clause is required in all prime fixed-price supply contracts, except contracts for commercial items or modified commercial items. It is not a mandatory flow-down, but its substance may be included in appropriate subcontracts.

(30) Cost Accounting Standards (CAS) clauses—The "Cost Accounting Standards" clause[47] must appear in all negotiated prime contracts unless the contract is exempt or is subject to modified CAS coverage. The substance of the clause is a mandatory flow-down to all nonexempt negotiated subcontracts at any tier in excess of $500,000. The "Disclosure and Consistency in Cost Accounting Practices"[48] clause must be included in all negotiated prime contracts when the contract amount is over $500,000 and less than $10 million. The clause provides for modified CAS coverage, and its substance must be included in subcontracts. The "Administration of Cost Accounting Standards" clause[49] must be included in negotiated prime contracts on the same basis as the "CAS" clause or "Disclosure and Consistency" clause, and its substance must also be included in negotiated subcontracts.

(31) "Engineering Change Proposals" clause[50]—This clause is not a mandatory flow-down. However, where it appears in a

SUBCONTRACT TERMS AND CONDITIONS 23-11

defense prime contract, its substance should be passed on to those subcontractors whose cooperation would be required to prepare engineering change proposals.

(32) "Privacy Act" clause[51]—This clause must be included in all prime contracts that require the design, development, or operation of a system of records on individuals to accomplish an agency function. It is a mandatory flow-down to all subcontracts containing the same requirement.

(33) "Stop-Work Order" clause[52]—This clause is authorized for use in all negotiated fixed-price prime contracts where work stoppage may be required for reasons such as advancement in the state of the art, production or engineering breakthroughs, or realignment of programs. It is not a mandatory flow-down, but its substance will generally be passed on to subcontractors.

(34) Warranty clauses[53]—These clauses are not mandatory flow-downs, but where they are included in prime contracts, it is typical for their substance to be included in subcontracts.

(35) "Limitation of Cost" clause[54]—This clause for fully-funded cost-reimbursement clauses is not a mandatory flow-down. However, where it is included in a cost-reimbursement prime contract, it will usually be included in appropriate subcontracts.

(36) "Allowable Cost and Payment" clause[55]—This clause for cost-reimbursement prime contracts is generally passed on in cost-reimbursement-type subcontracts, although it is not a mandatory flow-down.

(37) "Excusable Delays" clause[56]—This clause is included in virtually all cost-reimbursement prime contracts. Although it is not a mandatory flow-down, its substance generally is included in appropriate subcontracts.

C. ABA MODEL TERMS & CONDITIONS

Based on the FAR, the Public Contract Law Section of the American Bar Association (ABA) has published "model" terms and conditions for fixed-price supply subcontracts.[57] These model terms and conditions are reproduced in Figure 23-1, which follows.

23-12 GOVERNMENT CONTRACT GUIDEBOOK

Figure 23-1

ABA MODEL FIXED-PRICE SUPPLY SUBCONTRACT TERMS & CONDITIONS

SECTION OF PUBLIC CONTRACT LAW
MODEL
FIXED-PRICE SUPPLY
SUBCONTRACT TERMS AND CONDITIONS

SECTION A — DEFINITIONS

The following definitions apply unless otherwise specifically stated:

A-1 *"Buyer"* — the legal entity issuing this Order
A-2 *"Purchasing Representative"* — Buyer's authorized representative identified elsewhere in this order
A-3 *"Seller"* — the legal entity which contracts with the Buyer
A-4 *"This Order"* — this contractual instrument, including changes
A-5 *"Government"* — the Government of the United States
A-6 *"Prime Contract"* — the Government contract under which this Order is issued
A-7 *"FAR"* — the Federal Acquisition Regulation – 48 CFR Chapter 1
A-8 *"Contracting Officer"* — the government contracting officer(s) for the Prime Contract, or authorized representative.

SECTION B — APPLICABLE CLAUSES

B-1 *Acceptance* — Acceptance of this order is limited to the terms and conditions stated herein. Any additions, deletions or differences in the terms proposed by Seller are objected to and hereby rejected unless Buyer agrees otherwise in writing.

B-2 *Packing, Marking and Shipping* — Seller shall pack, mark and ship all goods and supplies in accordance with the requirements of this Order so as to be in compliance with transportation regulations and good commercial practice for protection and shipment, and shall secure the most advantageous transportation service and rates consistent therewith. No separate or additional charge is payable by Buyer for containers, crating, boxing, bundling, dunnage, drayage or storage unless specifically stated in this Order.

B-3 *Public Releases* — Except as required by law or regulation, no news release, public announcement or advertising material concerned with this Order shall be issued by Seller without prior written consent of Buyer, which consent shall not unreasonably be withheld.

B-4 *Disputes* — Either party may litigate any dispute arising under or relating to this Order before any court of competent jurisdiction. Pending resolution of any such dispute by settlement or by final judgment, the parties shall proceed diligently with performance. Seller's performance shall be in accordance with Buyer's written instructions. All references to disputes procedures in Government clauses incorporated by reference shall be deemed to be superseded by this clause.

B-5 *Assignment and Subcontracting*

(a) Neither this Order nor any interest herein may be assigned, in whole or in part, by either party without the prior written consent of the other party except that without securing such prior consent, either party shall have the right to assign this Order to any successor of such party by way of merger or consolidation or the acquisition of substantially all of the business and assets of the assigning party relating to the subject matter of this Order. This right shall be retained provided that such successor shall expressly assume all of the obligations and liabilities of the assigning party under this Order, and that the assigning party shall remain liable and responsible to the other party hereto for the performance and observance of all such obligations.

(b) Notwithstanding the foregoing, any amounts due or to become due hereunder may be assigned by the Seller, provided that such assignment shall not be binding upon the Buyer unless and until the assignment agreement is received by Buyer.

(c) Neither all or substantially all of this Order may be further subcontracted by Seller without the prior written consent of Buyer.

B-6 *Waiver* — The failure of either party to insist on performance of any provision of this Order shall not be construed as a waiver of that provision in any later instance.

©1988 American Bar Association
This form may be reproduced without cost provided the copyright notice is also reproduced.

B-7 *Choice of Law* — Irrespective of the place of performance, this Order will be construed and interpreted according to the federal common law of government contracts as enunciated and applied by federal judicial bodies, boards of contract appeals, and quasijudicial agencies of the federal government. To the extent that the federal common law of government contracts is not dispositive, the laws of the state from which the Buyer's Order is issued shall apply.

The text of clauses identified in Sections C and D by FAR clause number are subject to the following definitions and to the modifications indicated.

"Contractor" means Seller except in the term *"Prime Contractor."*
"Subcontractor" means Seller's Subcontractor(s).
"Contract" means this Order except in the term "Prime Contract."

The FAR clauses incorporated herein are those dated April 1984 unless otherwise indicated.

SECTION C — APPLICABLE CLAUSES

The clauses in this section are incorporated by this reference.

C-1 52.203-7 *ANTI-KICKBACK PROCEDURES (FEB 1987).* The following is added to paragraph (c)(2): "Seller shall notify Buyer when such action has been taken." In the first sentence of paragraph (c)(4) "the Contracting Officer may —" is replaced by "after the Contracting Officer has effected an offset at the prime contract level or has directed Buyer to withhold any sum from the Seller, Buyer shall —."

C-2 52.208-1 *REQUIRED SOURCE(S) FOR JEWEL BEARINGS AND RELATED ITEMS.* Communication required under this clause from Seller to Contracting Officer shall be through Buyer's Purchasing Representative.

C-3 52.219-8 *UTILIZATION OF SMALL BUSINESS CONCERNS AND SMALL DISADVANTAGED BUSINESS CONCERNS (JUN 1985).*

C-4 52.219-13 *UTILIZATION OF WOMEN-OWNED SMALL BUSINESSES (AUG 1986).*

C-5 52.220-3 *UTILIZATION OF LABOR SURPLUS AREA CONCERNS.*

C-6 52.220-4 *LABOR SURPLUS AREA SUBCONTRACTING PROGRAM,* if this Order exceeds $500,000. "Contracting Officer" means Buyer's Purchasing Representative.

C-7 52.222-1 *NOTICE TO THE GOVERNMENT OF LABOR DISPUTES.* "Contracting Officer" means Buyer's Purchasing Representative.

C-8 52.222-4 *CONTRACT WORK HOURS AND SAFETY STANDARDS ACT — OVERTIME COMPENSATION (MAR 1986).* Buyer may withhold or recover from Seller such sum as the Contracting Officer withholds or recovers from Buyer because of liabilities of Seller or its subcontractors under this clause.

C-9 52.222-20 *WALSH-HEALY PUBLIC CONTRACTS ACT,* if this Order exceeds $10,000.

C-10 52.222-26 *EQUAL OPPORTUNITY,* but only subparagraphs (b) (1) through (b) (11) of FAR 52.222-26.

C-11 52.222-35 *AFFIRMATIVE ACTION FOR SPECIAL DISABLED AND VIETNAM ERA VETERANS,* if this Order is for $10,000 or more.

C-12 52.222-36 *AFFIRMATIVE ACTION FOR HANDICAPPED WORKERS,* if this Order exceeds $2,500.

C-13 52.233-3 *PROTEST AFTER AWARD (JUNE 1985).* The first sentence is revised to read: "In the event the Contracting Officer has directed Buyer to stop performance of the work under the prime contract under which this Order is issued pursuant to FAR subpart 33.1, Buyer may, by written order to Seller direct Seller to stop performance of the work called for by this order." In the balance of the clause, "Contracting Officer" means Buyer; the reference to "the Termination for Convenience of the Government" clause means the "Termination" clause; "30 days" means 20 days in paragraph (b)(2) and "Government" means Buyer in paragraphs (c) and(e).

C-14 52.229-3 *FEDERAL, STATE AND LOCAL TAXES.* "Government" means Buyer and "Contracting Officer" means Buyer's Purchasing Representative.

continued

Fig. 23-1 / continued

C-15 52.232-1 *PAYMENTS.* "Government" means Buyer. This clause is subordinate to any other payment provisions herein.
C-16 52.243-1 *CHANGES — FIXED PRICE (AUG 1987).* "Contracting Officer" means Buyer's Purchasing Representative and "Government" means Buyer, and in paragraph (c) "30 days" is changed to "20 days."
C-17 52.245-2 *GOVERNMENT PROPERTY (FIXED-PRICE CONTRACTS).*
- "Contracting Officer" means Buyer's Purchasing Representative.
- "Government" means Buyer except:
  1) in the terms "Government-furnished property," "Government-property," and "Government-owned property," and
  2) the second time it appears in paragraph (b) (1)(ii), and 3) in paragraph (c)(1).
- "Government" means Government or Buyer:
  1) in paragraph (f) and in the following phrase "its" becomes "their" and
  2) in paragraph (j) and subparagraphs (j)(1).
- The fourth sentence of paragraph (h) is changed to read: "Neither the Government nor the Buyer shall be liable...

C-18 52.246-16 *INSPECTION OF SUPPLIES (FIXED-PRICE) (JUL 1985).* "Contracting Officer" means Buyer's Purchasing Representative or authorized designee, and "Government" means Buyer except that, the first time it appears in the first sentence of paragraph (b) and in the fourth sentence of paragraph (b) it means Government and Buyer (provided, however, that an inspection system accepted by the Government will be deemed acceptable to the Buyer, and the first time it appears in paragraph (k) it means Government or Buyer. The provisions in the clause for access, rights to inspect, safety protection and relief from liability apply equally to Buyer and the Government.

C-19 52.246-16 *RESPONSIBILITY FOR SUPPLIES.* "Government" means Buyer except in paragraph (d) where "Government" means Government or Buyer.

C-20 52.249-2 *TERMINATION FOR CONVENIENCE OF THE GOVERNMENT (FIXED-PRICE).* "Contracting Officer" means Buyer's Purchasing Representative, and "Government" means Buyer except in paragraph (m). Paragraph (c) is deleted. The term "1 year" in paragraph (d) is changed to "6 months." In paragraph (k) "90 days" is changed to "45 days." If the Government is unable or unwilling in a timely manner to conduct any audit of Seller's books and records, an audit may be conducted by a mutually acceptable independent certified public accounting firm.

C-21 52.249-8 *DEFAULT (FIXED-PRICE SUPPLY AND SERVICE).* "Contracting Officer" means Buyer's Purchasing Representative and "Government" means Buyer except in paragraph (c), where it means Government and in paragraph (e) where it means Government or Buyer. In the second sentence of paragraph (c) add "acts of Buyer" to the list of examples.

SECTION D — OPTIONAL CLAUSES

The clauses in this section do not apply unless specifically designated in the Order.

D-1 52.203-6 *RESTRICTIONS ON SUBCONTRACTOR SALES TO THE GOVERNMENT (JUL 1985).*
D-2 52.204-2 *SECURITY REQUIREMENTS.*
D-3 52.210-5 *NEW MATERIAL.* "Contracting Officer" means Buyer's Purchasing Representative and "Government" means Buyer in the last two sentences of the clause.
D-4 52.210-7 *USED OR RECONDITIONED MATERIAL, RESIDUAL INVENTORY AND FORMER GOVERNMENT SURPLUS PROPERTY.* "Contracting Officer" means Buyer's Purchasing Representative.
D-5 52.212-8 *DEFENSE PRIORITY AND ALLOCATION REQUIREMENTS (MAY 1986).*
D-6 52.212-13 *STOP WORK ORDER.* "Contracting Officer" means Buyer's Purchasing Representative, the title "Termination for Convenience of the Government" in paragraph (a)(2) means "Termination" and the words "for the convenience of the Government" in paragraph (c) are replaced by "in accordance with the Termination clauses." "90 days" and "30 days" are changed to "100 days" and "20 days" respectively.
D-7 52.212-15 *GOVERNMENT DELAY OF WORK.* "Contracting Officer" means Buyer's Purchasing Representative.
D-8 52.214-26 *AUDIT—SEALED BIDDING (APR 1985).* If the Government is unable or unwilling in a timely manner to conduct any audit of Seller's books and records, an audit may be conducted by a mutually acceptable independent certified public accounting firm.
D-9 52.214-27 *PRICE REDUCTION FOR DEFECTIVE COST OR PRICING DATA–MODIFICATIONS—SEALED BIDDING (APR 1985).* The obligations which FAR clause 52.214-26 in the Prime Contract requires of subcontractors

are required of Seller. In addition to any other remedies provided by law or under this Order, if Buyer is subjected to any liability as the result of Seller's or its lower-tier subcontractors' failure to comply with the requirements of clauses D-8, then Seller agrees to indemnify and hold Buyer harmless to the full extent of any loss, damage or expense (excluding profit) resulting from such failure.

D-10 52.214-28 *SUBCONTRACTOR COST OR PRICING DATA–MODIFICATIONS—SEALED BIDDING (APR 1985),* if Clause D-8 applies to this Order. The certificate required by paragraph (c) is that set forth in FAR 15.804-4, substituting Buyer's name for "Contracting Officer."

D-11 52.215-1 *EXAMINATION OF RECORDS BY COMPTROLLER GENERAL,* paragraph (c) of the clause is deleted. The term "of the prime contract" is added after "Disputes clause" in paragraph (d).

D-12 52.215-2 *AUDIT—NEGOTIATION.* If the Government is unable or unwilling in a timely manner to conduct any audit of Seller's books and records, an audit may be conducted by a mutually acceptable independent certified public accounting firm. The term "of the prime contract" is added after "Disputes clause" in paragraph (d)(2).

D-13 52.215-22 *PRICE REDUCTION FOR DEFECTIVE COST OR PRICING DATA.* The obligations which FAR clause 52.215-24 in the Prime Contract requires of subcontractors are required of Seller. In addition to any other remedies provided by law or under this Order, if Buyer is subjected to any liability as the result of Seller's or its lower-tier subcontractors' submission and certification of defective cost or pricing data as set forth in subparagraphs (a)(1) or (2) of this clause, or their furnishing of data of any description that is inaccurate as set forth in subparagraph (a)(3) of this clause, then Seller agrees to indemnify and hold Buyer harmless to the full extent of any loss, damage or expense (excluding profit) resulting from such failure.

D-14 52.215-23 *PRICE REDUCTION FOR DEFECTIVE COST OR PRICING DATA—MODIFICATIONS (APR 1985).* The obligations which FAR clause 52.215-25 in the Prime Contract requires of subcontractors are required of Seller. In addition to any other remedies provided by law or under this Order if Buyer is subjected to any liability as the result of Seller's or its lower-tier subcontractors' submission and certification of defective cost or pricing data as set forth in subparagraphs (a)(1) or (2) of this clause, or other furnishing of data of any description that is inaccurate as set forth in subparagraph (a)(3) of this clause, then Seller agrees to indemnify and hold Buyer harmless to the full extent of any loss, damage or expense (excluding profit) resulting from such failure.

D-15 52.215-24 *SUBCONTRACTOR COST OR PRICING DATA (APR 1985),* if Clause D-12 applies to this Order. The certificate required by paragraph (b) is that set forth in FAR 15.804-4 substituting Buyer's name for "Contracting Officer."

D-16 52.215-25 *SUBCONTRACTOR COST OR PRICING DATA–MODIFICATIONS (APR 1985),* if Clause D-13 applies to this Order. The certificate required by paragraph (c) is that set forth in FAR 15.804-4, substituting Buyer's name for "Contracting Officer."

D-17 52.215-26 *INTEGRITY OF UNIT PRICES (APR 1987).* Paragraph (c) is deleted.

D-18 52.219-9 *SMALL BUSINESS AND SMALL DISADVANTAGED BUSINESS SUBCONTRACTING PLAN.* "Contracting Officer" means Buyer's Purchasing Representative in the first sentence of paragraph (c).

D-19 52.219-9 (Alternate 1) *SMALL BUSINESS AND SMALL DISADVANTAGED BUSINESS SUBCONTRACTING PLAN.* "Contracting Officer" means Buyer's Purchasing Representative in the first sentence of paragraph (c).

D-20 52.223-2 *CLEAN AIR AND WATER.*

D-21 52.223-3 *HAZARDOUS MATERIAL IDENTIFICATION AND MATERIAL SAFETY DATA (AUG 1987).* "Government" means Government or Buyer except in the legend.

D-22 52.225-10 *DUTY-FREE ENTRY.* "Contracting Officer" means the Buyer's Purchasing Representative, except the first time it appears in paragraph (b)(2) and (b)(3) and paragraph (e). Change "20 days" to "30 days" in paragraph (b)(1). Change "10 days" to "20 days" in paragraph (b)(2). Change "The Government agrees" to "The Government has agreed" in paragraph (e). The terms "the Schedule" and "the contract Schedule" in paragraphs (a), (b) and (h) mean "the Order." In the last sentence of paragraph (h) "the contract" means the Prime Contract.

D-23 52.225-11 *CERTAIN COMMUNIST AREAS.*

D-24 52.227-1 *AUTHORIZATION AND CONSENT.* Except in subparagraph (a)(1) "this contract" means the Prime Contract and "through the Contracting Officer" in subparagraph (a)(2)(ii).

D-25 52.227-2 *NOTICE AND ASSISTANCE REGARDING PATENT AND COPYRIGHT INFRINGEMENT.* Except "Contracting Officer" means Buyer's Purchasing Representative and "Government" means Government or Buyer

continued

23-14 GOVERNMENT CONTRACT GUIDEBOOK

Fig. 23-1 / continued

D-26 52.227-8 *REPORTING OF ROYALTIES (FOREIGN).* Except "Contracting Officer" means Buyer's Purchasing Representative.

D-27 52.227-9 *REFUND OF ROYALTIES.* Except "Contracting Officer" means Buyer's Purchasing Representative in paragraphs (a) and (c) and the third time it appears in paragraph (d), and means Contracting Officer and Buyer's Purchasing Representative in paragraph (e). In paragraph (e) "this contract" means the Prime Contract.

D-28 52.227-10 *FILING OF PATENT APPLICATIONS — CLASSIFIED SUBJECT MATTER.*

D-29 52.227-11 *PATENT RIGHTS — RETENTION BY THE CONTRACTOR (SHORT FORM).*

D-30 52.227-12 *PATENT RIGHTS — RETENTION BY THE CONTRACTOR (LONG FORM).*

D-31 52.227-13 *PATENT RIGHTS* — ACQUISITION BY THE GOVERNMENT.

D-32 52.227-14 *RIGHTS IN DATA — GENERAL (JUN 1987).* In paragraphs (e)(1)(i) and (e)(1)(ii) the 30 day period is reduced to 25 days if the Contracting Officer's notice is given to the Buyer for delivery to the Seller. Paragraph (e)(4) is deleted. In paragraph (f)(1)(iv) "Government has" is changed to "Government and Buyer have." In paragraphs (g)(1) and (i) "Government" means Government or Buyer.

D-33 52.227-14 *RIGHTS IN DATA — GENERAL (ALTERNATE I) (JUN 1987).*

D-34 52.227-14 *RIGHTS IN DATA — GENERAL (ALTERNATE II) (JUN 1987).* "Government" means Government and Buyer and in the second sentence at paragraph (g)(2).

D-35 52.227-14 *RIGHTS IN DATA — GENERAL (ALTERNATE III) (JUN 1987).* "Government" means Government or Buyer in the second sentence at paragraph (a) of the first Restricted Rights Notice.

D-36 52.227-14 *RIGHTS IN DATA — GENERAL (ALTERNATE V) (JUN 1987).*

D-37 52.227-16 *ADDITIONAL DATA REQUIREMENTS (JUN 1987).* The term "this contract" is changed to "prime contract" in paragraph (a).

D-38 52.227-21 *TECHNICAL DATA CERTIFICATION, REVISION, AND WITHHOLDING OF PAYMENT — MAJOR SYSTEMS (JUN 1987).* In paragraph (d) "Contracting Officer" means Buyer's Purchasing Representative and "Government" means Buyer.

D-39 52.227-22 *MAJOR SYSTEMS—MINIMUM RIGHTS (JUN 1987).*

D-40 52.227-23 *RIGHTS TO PROPOSAL DATA (TECHNICAL) (JUN 1987).*

D-41 52.229-4 *FEDERAL, STATE AND LOCAL TAXES (NONCOMPETITIVE CONTRACT).* "Government" means Buyer except in the definition of "Excepted tax," and "Contracting Officer" means Buyer's Purchasing Representative. When this clause is included, clause C-11 is deleted.

D-42 52.230-3 *COST ACCOUNTING STANDARDS (AUG 1988).* Paragraph (b) of the clause is deleted. Seller shall communicate and otherwise deal directly with the Contracting Officer to the extent practicable and permissible as to all matters relating to Cost Accounting Standards. Seller shall provide Buyer with copies of all communications between Seller and the Contracting Officer respecting this clause, and clauses D-43, provided Seller shall not be required to disclose to Buyer such communications containing information which is privileged and confidential to the Seller. In addition to any other remedies provided by law or under this Order, Seller agrees to indemnify and hold Buyer harmless to the full extent of any loss, damage, or expense (excluding profit) if Buyer is subjected to any liability as the result of a failure of the Seller or its lower-tier subcontractors to comply with the requirements of this clause or clause D-43.

D-43 52.230-4 *ADMINISTRATION OF COST ACCOUNTING STANDARDS.* Seller shall communicate and otherwise deal directly with the Contracting Officer to the extent practicable and permissible as to all matters relating to Cost Accounting Standards.

D-44 52.230-5 *DISCLOSURE AND CONSISTENCY OF COST ACCOUNTING PRACTICES (AUG 1988).* Paragraph (b) of the clause is deleted. Seller shall communicate and otherwise deal directly with the Contracting Officer to the extent practicable and permissible as to all matters relating to Cost Accounting Standards. Seller shall provide Buyer with copies of all communications between Seller and the Contracting Officer respecting this clause, and clause D-43, provided Seller shall not be required to disclose to Buyer such communications containing information which is privileged and confidential to the Seller. In addition to any other remedies provided by law or under this Order, Seller agrees to indemnify and hold Buyer harmless to the full extent of any loss, damage, or expense (excluding profit) if Buyer is subjected to any liability as the result of a failure of the Seller or its lower-tier subcontractors to comply with the requirements of this clause or clause D-43.

D-45 52.232-9 *LIMITATION ON WITHHOLDING OF PAYMENTS.* Paragraph (d) of the clause is deleted.

D-46 52.243-7 *NOTIFICATION OF CHANGES.* "Contracting Officer" and "Administrative Contracting Officer" mean Buyer's Purchasing Representative and "Government" means Buyer. Insert "10 calendar days" in the space provided in paragraphs (b) and (d).

D-47 52.244-1 *SUBCONTRACTS (FIXED-PRICE CONTRACTS) (JAN 1986).* "Contracting Officer" means Buyer's Purchasing Representative.

D-48 52.244-5 *COMPETITION IN SUBCONTRACTING.*

D-49 52.245-2 *GOVERNMENT PROPERTY (FIXED-PRICE CONTRACTS) (Alternate I).* "Contracting Officer" means Buyer's Purchasing Representative and "Government" means Buyer except in the term "Government Property" and in paragraph (4)(i).

D-50 52.245-17 *SPECIAL TOOLING.* "Contracting Officer" means Buyer's Purchasing Representative, and "Government" means Buyer except in paragraphs (e)(1), (i)(1) and (i)(4) where it means Government or Buyer. The term "90 days" is changed to "120 days" in paragraph (i).

D-51 52.245-18 *SPECIAL TEST EQUIPMENT.* "Contracting Officer" means Buyer's Purchasing Representative. "Government" means Buyer except in paragraphs (b) and (d) and in the terms "Government owned" and Government Property." In paragraphs (b) and (c) "30 days" is changed to "45 days." Insert "Government-owned" before "special test equipment" in the first sentence of paragraph (c).

D-52 52.246-1 *CONTRACTOR INSPECTION REQUIREMENTS.* "Government" means Government or Buyer. When this clause is included, clause C-15 is deleted.

D-53 52.246-23 *LIMITATION OF LIABILITY.* "Acceptance of supplies delivered under this contract" means acceptance of such supplies by the Government under the prime contract.

D-54 52.246-24 *LIMITATION OF LIABILITY — HIGH VALUE ITEMS.* Insert the following preamble before paragraph (a) of the clause: "This clause shall apply only to those items identified in this Order as being subject to the clause." "Acceptance of supplies delivered under this contract" means acceptance of such supplies by the Government under the prime contract.

D-55 52.247-63 *PREFERENCE FOR U.S.-FLAG AIR CARRIERS.*

D-56 52.247-67 *PREFERENCE FOR PRIVATELY-OWNED U.S.-FLAG COMMERCIAL VESSELS.* In paragraph (c)(2) "20" and "30" are changed to "10" and "20" respectively.

D-57 52.248-1 *VALUE ENGINEERING.* "Contracting Officer" means Buyer's Purchasing Representative except in the third sentence of paragraph (j). "Government" means Buyer in paragraphs (e)(1), (e)(2), (g)(4), and (i)(4), and means Government and Buyer in the legend prescribed in paragraph (m). Replace the share percentage figures in paragraphs (f) and (j) with those the parties agree upon.

A complete subcontract, using the model, would be comprised of (a) the FAR-compatible terms and conditions completed to indicate which of the optional clauses apply, (b) the agency terms and conditions, similarly completed, and (c) a purchase order or other form containing the essential terms of the transaction such as quantity, price, delivery, special financing, and any other provisions specifically agreed to by the parties.

The model includes all mandatory flow-downs and the substance of all FAR clauses required in the subcontract by practical necessity. Several "standard" subcontract clauses are conspicuous by their absence. These include clauses on (1) warranty, (2) patent infringement indemnity, (3) special payment provisions (i.e., progress, advance, and milestone payments), (4) order of precedence, (5) integration and merger, (6) invoices, and (7) buyer-furnished property. The ABA concluded that these provisions did not lend themselves to standardization due to their transactionally unique risks and were, therefore, best left to the negotiation and drafting skills of the parties.

REFERENCES

1. See Power Systems & Controls, Inc. v. Keith's Electrical Const. Co., 765 P.2d 5 (Utah App. 1989) (subcontract under Government contract is governed by UCC), 31 GC ¶ 172 (Note). See generally Paul, "Subcontracting Under the Uniform Commercial Code," Briefing Papers No. 66-4 (Aug. 1966), 1 BPC 185.

2. See FAR 44.203(b)(3).

3. See, e.g., FAR 52.249-2 ("Termination for Convenience of the Government (Fixed-Price)" clause), para. (a).

4. See FAR 49.502(e) (fixed-price subcontracts), 49.503(c) (cost-reimbursement subcontracts).

5. See generally Hoe, Oliver & Abbott, "Flow-Down Clauses in Subcontracts," Briefing Papers No. 65-5 (May 1965), 7 BPC 83; Greenberg, "Construction Subcontract Terms," Briefing Papers No. 72-3 (June 1972), 2 BPC 173.

6. Federal Acquisition Streamlining Act of 1994, P.L. 103-355, §§ 8002, 8003, 4101, 4102, 108 Stat. 3243 (Oct. 13, 1994).

7. See, e.g., FAR 52.243-1.

8. FAR 52.243-7.
9. FAR 52.243-6.
10. See, e.g., FAR 52.246-2.
11. FAR 52.232-23.
12. See UCC § 9-318.
13. See, e.g., FAR 52.249-8, 52.249-2.
14. FAR 52.233-1.
15. FAR 52.222-20.
16. FAR 52.222-41.
17. FAR 52.222-26, 22.807.
18. FAR 52.227-1.
19. FAR 52.227-2.
20. FAR 52.227-3.
21. FAR 52.227-5.
22. FAR 52.227-10.
23. E.g., FAR 52.227-14; DFARS 252.227-7013.
24. FAR 52.225-5.
25. FAR 52.228-5.
26. FAR 52.222-1.
27. FAR 52.204-2.
28. FAR 52.236-6.
29. FAR 52.215-1.
30. FAR 52.247-64.
31. FAR 52.244-1.
32. FAR 52.244-2.
33. FAR 52.245-19.
34. FAR 52.245-17.
35. FAR 52.245-18.

SUBCONTRACT TERMS AND CONDITIONS   23-17

36. FAR 52.215-24. See generally Arnavas & Gildea, "Subcontractor Cost or Pricing Data/Edition II," Briefing Papers No. 93-8 (July 1993).
37. FAR 52.215-22.
38. FAR 52.225-10.
39. FAR 52.232-12.
40. FAR 52.214-26.
41. FAR 52.248-1.
42. FAR 52.246-23.
43. FAR 52.210-5.
44. FAR 52.219-13.
45. FAR 52.236-12.
46. FAR 52.212-15.
47. FAR 52.230-2.
48. FAR 52.230-3.
49. FAR 52.230-5.
50. DFARS 252.243-7000.
51. FAR 52.224-2.
52. FAR 52.212-13.
53. E.g., FAR 52.246-17, 52.246-18, 52.246-19.
54. FAR 52.232-20.
55. FAR 52.216-7.
56. FAR 52.249-14.
57. See ABA, Public Contract Law Section, "Model Fixed-Price Supply Subcontract Terms & Conditions" (1988) (based on the FAR, as amended up to Sept. 1987).

Part VII

CONSTRUCTION CONTRACTING

chapters

24 | Construction Contract Basics
25 | Differing Site Conditions
26 | Construction Delays And Liquidated Damages
27 | Construction Labor Standards

CONSTRUCTION CONTRACT BASICS

24

A. Overview
B. Construction Contracts vs. Supply Contracts
   1. Similarities
   2. Differences

The Federal Government is, undoubtedly, the largest "owner" of buildings and other real property in the world. Billions of dollars are spent every year in constructing and renovating the many different kinds of structures needed by the Government throughout the world. And many building contractors enjoy a prosperous existence doing business primarily—if not entirely—with the Government.

Thus far, this book has concentrated mainly on Government supply contracting. Although many of the differences between supply and construction contract clauses and procedures have been pointed out in the preceding chapters of the book, this last part of the book—Part VII—examines the peculiarities of construction contracting in greater depth, emphasizing the contract clauses and special problems that most frequently concern Government construction contractors. This chapter provides an overview of the basics of construction contracting and some of the similarities and differences between construction and supply contracts. The chapters that follow discuss the subjects of differing site conditions (Chapter 25), construction delays and liquidated damages (Chapter 26), and some special labor standards that apply to most federal construction projects (Chapter 27).

A. OVERVIEW

Any major Government construction project is usually preceded by a contract between the Government and an architect-engineering (A-E) firm to develop the design of the structures to be built and draft the drawings and specifications that will be followed by the construction contractor.[1] Sometimes, however, the Government elects to use so-called "turnkey" contracting by which a general construction contractor assumes *complete* responsibility for a project—from design to completion of construction ready for use. Another alternative is the simultaneous award of contracts to a number of prime contractors to perform separate portions of a construction project.[2]

Nevertheless, in most construction projects, design work is still entrusted to an A-E firm or to Government employees, and a single contract is awarded to a general contractor for the entire project. The general contractor is required by contract clause to provide a superintendent to oversee the performance of any subcontractors' work—as well as the work of the contractor's own forces.[3]

In addition to supervising the performance of subcontractors *after* award of the contract, the prime contractor should review *all* of the drawings and specifications *before* bidding and bring to the attention of potential subcontractors the requirements that affect their responsibilities. A clearly specified requirement is binding on the prime contractor even if it is set forth in a section of the specifications (or on a drawing) that is not likely to be consulted by the subcontractor. For example, in one case, requirements concerning backfill were binding on a prime contractor even though they were included in the "heat distribution" section of the specifications rather than in the "excavation, trenching and backfill" specifications.[4] Note, too, that the "Specifications and Drawings for Construction" clause included in most contracts provides that "[a]nything mentioned in the specifications and not shown on the drawings, or shown on the drawings and not mentioned in the specifications, shall be of like effect as if shown or mentioned in both."[5] A contractor or subcontractor is permitted to rely on the provision in the clause that "[i]n case of a difference between the specifications and drawings, the specifications shall govern."[6]

Sealed bidding procedures are usually employed in construction contracting, and the contract award most likely will be for a lump sum—that is, the contract will be for a fixed price. However, the various items of work may be broken down into individual items with separate unit prices in a bidding or pay schedule. Even though not included in any *specific* pay item, work that is clearly required by the contract must be performed without additional compensation.[7]

It should be noted that some contracts contain elements of both construction and supply. Therefore, contractors should carefully check which clauses of the contract apply to different aspects of their work. If there is any question, inquiry should be made to the Contracting Officer before bidding.

B. CONSTRUCTION CONTRACTS vs. SUPPLY CONTRACTS

1. Similarities

The basic principles of Government contracting are the same whether a contract is for supplies or construction (although supply contracts involve more varied procedures and contract types than construction contracts). Thus, the policy of obtaining the widest competition possible, small business and minority business preferences,[8] the rules limiting the authority of Government agents, the Government's duty of fairness and noninterference with contractors, policies regarding patents and data, and the other fundamental policies and procedures explored in earlier chapters in this book with regard to supply contracts apply with equal force to construction contracts.

For example, if a contract is awarded through sealed bidding, the rules governing that method of contracting (see Chapter 3) are generally the same whether the contract is for supplies or construction.[9] Similarly, the rules of fixed-price contracting are the same for supply and construction contracts. In addition, although there are differences between supply and construction contract clauses and circumstances, similar rights and obligations attach in connection with terminations for default (see Chapter 16) or terminations for convenience (see Chapter 17), furnishing of Government property (see Chapter 9), contract changes (see Chapter 11), equitable adjustments (see Chapter 13), payment (see Chapter 15), inspections and warranties (see Chapter 14), and disputes (see Chapters 18–21).

2. Differences

Not surprisingly, the differences between supply and construction contracts are primarily traceable to the different physical environments in which they are performed and to the differences in the nature of the contract work. Some of the most significant differences between supply and construction contracting are briefly reviewed below.

a. Government Control. Whereas supply contracts are typically performed in a production facility owned or leased by the contractor and generally under its control, a construction contract is performed at a location owned or controlled by the Government. The construction contractor—even when it is responsible for quality control (see Chapter 14)—is subject to a great deal more surveillance and control by Government inspectors and other Government representatives than the supply contractor.[10]

A burdensome feature of construction contracts is the number of reports the contractor is required to file with the Government. Daily reports of work accomplished are often required, as well as reports involving (a) quality control activities, (b) safety procedures, (c) labor disputes, (d) construction or completion schedules, and (e) descriptions—even samples—of materials the contractor proposes to use.

b. Work Site. The fact that the contract is performed on a Government-owned site or in a Government-controlled facility also poses problems of *access* to the work site by the contractor's workers, subcontractors, and material suppliers. Other difficulties faced by the construction contractor are *interference* from Government activities conducted while work is being performed and from the activities of other Government contractors, as well as the possible damage or loss of equipment and materials after work hours.[11] The contractor is also responsible for maintaining a safe and clean site.[12] Moreover, even though the work is done on federal property, the construction contractor is responsible for properly disposing of hazardous substances.[13]

c. Contract Clauses. Construction contractors also must comply with the standard clauses used only in construction contracts.[14] For example, the standard "Permits and Responsibilities" clause makes the contractor "responsible for all damages to persons or property that occur as a result of [its] fault or negligence."[15] That clause also makes the contractor responsible for all materials delivered and work performed "until completion and acceptance of the entire work, except for any completed unit of work which may have been accepted under the contract." Thus, under this clause, a contractor could be required to bear the cost of construction material stolen or otherwise removed from the contract site or damaged by the weather.[16] The "Permits and Responsibilities" clause also requires the contractor to obtain necessary permits and comply with federal, state, and local safety standards.

Another important standard clause in construction contracts is the "Material and Workmanship" clause.[17] This clause requires the work to be performed in "a skillful and workmanlike manner"[18] and also states that "[a]ll equipment, material, and articles incorporated into the work covered by [the] contract shall be new and of the most suitable grade for the purpose intended."[19]

When the contract is over $1 million (as is not unusual), the "Performance of Work by the Contractor" clause[20] requires that the general contractor perform a stipulated percentage of the work with its own forces. For purposes of this clause, "work" includes both labor and materials.[21]

Examples of other standard clauses typically found in Government construction contracts (besides the "Specifications and Drawings" clause mentioned above in Section A) include (1) the "Accident Prevention" clause,[22] (2) the "Differing Site Conditions" clause[23] (see Chapter 25), (3) the "Other Contracts" clause[24] requiring the contractor to cooperate with other contractors and Government employees working at or near the work site, (4) the "Use and Possession Prior to Completion" clause[25] permitting the Government to take possession of or use any completed or partially completed part of the project without legally "accepting" the contract work (see Chapter 14, Section D), and (5) the "Cleaning Up" clause.[26]

d. Bonds. Construction contractors must also comply with many pervasive statutory requirements. For example, the Miller Act[27] requires construction contractors in the United States to furnish payment and performance bonds.[28] Failure to furnish Miller Act bonds[29] or furnishing forged bonds[30] is a basis for termination of a contract for default.

e. Labor Standards. Construction contractors are subject to stringent statutory requirements regarding the treatment and payment of laborers. Construction contract labor standards laws are reviewed in Chapter 27.

f. Contract Changes. One of the most notable features of construction contracts is the number of contract modifications that may be necessary in performing the contract. Although modifications of supply contracts are not uncommon, it is rare when a construction contract is not changed during performance as to some aspect of the work. In fact, most construction projects usually undergo numerous modifications. These modifications take the form of ordered changes under the "Changes" clause or constructive changes, such as acceleration of the contract schedule or defective specifications (see Chapter 11). Such changes to the contract work invariably disrupt the project's schedule and increase its costs.

g. Default Termination. As mentioned in Chapter 16, Section B, terminations for default are much less frequent in construction than in supply contracts. In construction contracts, the imposition of liquidated damages for delayed completion of work is more common (see Chapter 26, Section C). A major advantage for construction contractors is that they are entitled to payment for the value of work they have performed at the time of a termination for default,[31] whereas supply contractors may get nothing for the work they have completed but not delivered.

Even when termination of a construction contract does occur, disputes concerning repurchase actions and excess costs of completion are relatively rare. This is because defaulted construction contracts are usually completed by the surety company that has guaranteed performance by issuing a performance bond.[32] However, if the surety company is unwilling or unable to complete performance, a performance bond has not been furnished (as is the case, for example, in most contracts performed outside the United States), or there is an urgent need to complete the work, the Government may finish the job with its own forces and charge the defaulted contractor its costs of completing performance[33] or may award a contract to another construction firm to finish the project and assess the defaulted contractor any excess costs.[34] (See Chapter 16, Section E.)

REFERENCES

1. See generally Ness & Medill-Jones, "A-E Government Contracts," Construction Briefings No. 88-11 (Oct. 1988), 4 CBC 215; Blasky, "Architect-Engineer Contracts," Briefing Papers No. 63-5 (Nov. 1963), 1 BPC 39; Baugh, "Architects' Contractual Responsibilities," Briefing Papers No. 69-6 (Dec. 1969), 1 BPC 427.

2. See generally Gaede & Bynum, "The Multi-Prime Job," Construction Briefings No. 79-3 (May 1979), 1 CBC 101.

3. See FAR 52.236-6 ("Superintendence by the Contractor" clause). See Davis Constructors, Inc., ASBCA 40630, 91-1 BCA ¶ 23394 (Government is entitled to reduce contract price if contractor fails to have an onsite superintendent who has no other duties), 33 GC ¶ 44.

4. Mason & Dulion Co., ASBCA 22530, 80-2 BCA ¶ 14499. See also Stallings & McCorvey, Inc., ASBCA 25125, 81-1 BCA ¶ 15094, 23 GC ¶ 305; Franchi Const. Co. v. U.S., 609 F.2d 984 (Ct. Cl. 1979), 21 GC ¶ 518.

5. FAR 52.236-21, para. (a).

6. E.g., Hensel Phelps Const. Co. v. U.S., 886 F.2d 1296 (Fed. Cir. 1989), 8 FPD ¶ 129 (even if a discrepancy between a specification and drawing is patent, the contractor or subcontractor ordinarily is not obliged to seek clarification before bidding), 31 GC ¶ 335; Nu-Way Builders of Va., Inc., ASBCA 31771, 89-1 BCA ¶ 21515.

7. Zisken Const. Co., ASBCA 7875, 1963 BCA ¶ 4001.

8. See generally Dauer, "Complying With MBE/WBE Programs," Construction Briefings No. 90-11 (Oct. 1990), 5 CBC 243; Tolle, "Small Business Contracting," Construction Briefings No. 89-12 (Nov. 1989), 4 CBC 503.

9. See FAR subpt. 36.3 ("Special Aspects of Sealed Bidding in Construction Contracting").

10. See generally Abernathy & Kelleher, "Inspection Under Fixed-Price Construction Contracts," Briefing Papers No. 76-6 (Dec. 1976), 4 BPC 89.

11. See generally Wickwire, Hurlbut & Shapiro, "Rights & Obligations in Scheduling," Construction Briefings No. 88-13 (Dec. 1988), 4 CBC 249.

12. E.g., FAR 52.236-12, 52.236-13.

13. See generally Person, "Risk Management in Environmental Contracting," Construction Briefings No. 93-7 (June 1993); Hatfield & Ferring, "Environmental Risks in Construction Contracting," Construction Briefings No. 91-8 (July 1991), 5 CBC 437; Lifschitz & O'Riordan, "Handling Environmental Incidents at the Jobsite," Construction Briefings No. 91-10 (Sept. 1991), 5 CBC 467; Hall & Davis, "Environmental Compliance at Federal Facilities," Briefing Papers No. 88-9 (Aug. 1988), 8 BPC 183.

14. See generally Wilson & Tieder, "Risk-Shifting Clauses in Construction Contracts," Construction Briefings No. 91-9 (Aug. 1991), 5 CBC 451.

15. FAR 52.236-7. See generally Nagle & Ferring, "'Permits and Responsibilities' Clause," Construction Briefings No. 92-8 (July 1992).

16. George Okano Electrical Contracting Corp., ASBCA 20978, 78-1 BCA ¶ 12914, 20 GC ¶ 87; DeRalco, Inc., ASBCA 41063, 91-1 BCA ¶ 23576; 32 GC ¶ 395. But see Wolff & Munier Inc., GSBCA 5634, 80-1 BCA ¶ 14417, 22 GC ¶ 198.

17. FAR 52.236-5. See generally Nagle & Ferring, "'Material and Workmanship' Clause," Construction Briefings No. 93-12 (Nov. 1993).

18. FAR 52.236-5, para. (c).

19. FAR 52.236-5, para. (a). See, e.g., Williams & Burrows Contractors, Inc., ASBCA 8415, 1963 BCA ¶ 3781 ("new" material does not mean "never used" material; contractor had to use recently-manufactured cable and not unused surplus cable that had been stored for five years), 6 GC ¶ 85.

20. FAR 52.236-1.

21. Blinderman Const. Co., ASBCA 35376, 88-3 BCA ¶ 21052, 30 GC ¶ 312.

22. FAR 52.236-13.

23. FAR 52.236-2.

24. FAR 52.236-8.

25. FAR 52.236-11.

26. FAR 52.236-12.

27. 40 USC § 270a. See generally, Watt, Tolle & Hill, "Surety Miller Act Rights," Construction Briefings No. 88-3 (Feb. 1988), 4 CBC 57.

28. See FAR 28.102. See also Office of Federal Procurement Policy, Policy Letter 91-4 (56 Fed. Reg. 58932, Nov. 22, 1991) (small business may use an irrevocable letter of credit in lieu of surety bond).

29. Aetna Casualty & Surety Co. v. U.S., 526 F.2d 1127 (Ct. Cl. 1975), 18 GC ¶ 11; United Baeton Intl., VACAB 1335 et al., 80-1 BCA ¶ 14211.

30. Dry Roof Corp., ASBCA 29061, 88-3 BCA ¶ 21096, 30 GC ¶ 329.

31. Brooklyn & Queens Screen Mfg. Co. v. U.S., 97 Ct. Cl. 532 (1942); Valda Const. Co., ASBCA 18550, 74-2 BCA ¶ 10705.

32. See generally Stephenson, Patin & Mitchell, "Surety's Role in Default Terminations," Construction Briefings No. 90-4 (Mar. 1990), 5 CBC 77.

24-10 GOVERNMENT CONTRACT GUIDEBOOK

33. Collins Electronics, Inc., ASBCA 16956, 72-2 BCA ¶ 9542, 14 GC ¶ 415; Superior Disposal, ASBCA 19350 et al., 75-2 BCA ¶ 11523, 18 GC ¶ 10.

34. Olson Plumbing & Heating Co., ASBCA 17965, 75-1 BCA ¶ 11203, 17 GC ¶ 427; Charleston Shipyards, Inc., ASBCA 27230, 83-1 BCA ¶ 16400.

DIFFERING SITE CONDITIONS

25

A. Standard "Differing Site Conditions" Clause
B. Notice To Government
C. Types Of Differing Site Conditions
   1. Type I Conditions
   2. Type II Conditions
   3. Conditions Occurring After Award
   4. Excluded Conditions
D. Contractor's Duty To Investigate Site
   1. Standard "Site Investigation" Clause
   2. Limitations
   3. Failure To Investigate Or Inquire
   4. Government's Duty To Disclose
E. Government Disclaimers

When a construction contractor encounters a subsurface or otherwise concealed site condition that differs from what was indicated in the contract or from what would normally be expected, the condition encountered is often referred to as a "differing site condition." In the absence of a contract clause allocating the risk of unknown subsurface conditions between the parties, a construction contractor generally assumes the risk of increased costs that may result from unforeseen site conditions. Therefore, a prudent contractor would protect itself by including a contingency factor in its bid price to cover the unexpected costs it might encounter. To discourage contractors from including contingency factors in their prices—and thus increasing the cost of Government construction—the Government has developed a contract clause—the "Differing Site Conditions" clause—that substantially shifts the risk of subsurface or unknown site conditions to the Government.[1]

A. STANDARD "DIFFERING SITE CONDITIONS" CLAUSE

The FAR's standard "Differing Site Conditions" clause[2] (formerly called the "Changed Conditions" clause) is reproduced in Figure 25-1. It requires the contractor to "promptly, and before such conditions are disturbed" provide written notice to the Contracting Officer of any (1) subsurface or latent physical conditions at the site that differ materially from those indicated in the contract, or (2) unknown physical conditions at the site of an unusual nature that differ materially from those ordinarily encountered (see Paragraph (a) of the clause in Figure 25-1). If such conditions increase or decrease the contractor's cost of—or time required for—performance, the clause requires that an equitable adjustment in the contract's price and schedule be made (see Paragraph (b) of the clause).

The Court of Claims stated that the clause assures contractors that they "will have no windfalls and no disasters."[3] Note that if the differing site condition makes performance *less* expensive, the clause permits the Government to reduce the contract price (see Paragraph (b)).[4] For example, the Government has been granted a price reduction where rock excavation re-

> **Figure 25-1**
>
> **"DIFFERING SITE CONDITIONS" CLAUSE**
> (FAR 52.236-2)
>
> (a) The Contractor shall promptly, and before the conditions are disturbed, give a written notice to the Contracting Officer of (1) subsurface or latent physical conditions at the site which differ materially from those indicated in this contract, or (2) unknown physical conditions at the site, of an unusual nature, which differ materially from those ordinarily encountered and generally recognized as inhering in work of the character provided for in the contract.
>
> (b) The Contracting Officer shall investigate the site conditions promptly after receiving the notice. If the conditions do materially so differ and cause an increase or decrease in the Contractor's cost of, or the time required for, performing any part of the work under this contract, whether or not changed as a result of the conditions, an equitable adjustment shall be made under this clause and the contract modified in writing accordingly.
>
> (c) No request by the Contractor for an equitable adjustment to the contract under this clause shall be allowed, unless the Contractor has given the written notice required; *provided,* that the time prescribed in (a) above for giving written notice may be extended by the Contracting Officer.
>
> (d) No request by the Contractor for an equitable adjustment to the contract for differing site conditions shall be allowed if made after final payment under this contract.

quired at a work site was substantially less than the amount of rock excavation that had been foreseeable.[5] Most frequently, however, the clause has been the basis for contractor claims for increased costs.

B. NOTICE TO GOVERNMENT

The "Differing Site Conditions" clause requires the contractor to give *prompt written notice* to the Contracting Officer after encountering a differing site condition but before the condition is disturbed (Paragraph (a) of the Figure 25-1 clause).[6] The notice need not be detailed, but it should fairly alert the Government to the nature of the condition.[7]

The notice requirement affords the owner (the Government) the opportunity to inspect the condition and modify the contract requirements if necessary or even abandon the contract work if it is no longer feasible. Usually, the Government modifies the contract. Failure to follow the notice requirements strictly may result in rejection of the contractor's otherwise valid differing site conditions claim.

It is well established that the notice provision of the "Differing Site Conditions" clause will not be enforced, however, if the Government, in fact, knew of the physical conditions that the contractor encountered.[8] In addition, if the Contracting Officer decides a claim for a differing site condition on its merits, the Government may be held to have waived the notice requirement.[9] Similarly, where the contractor's failure to give notice does not *prejudice* the Government's interest, the contractor's claim usually will not be barred.[10] However, if the contractor's failure to give notice deprives the Government of an opportunity to verify that a differing site condition was actually encountered, the contractor's claim will be denied.[11]

Just as the contractor is obliged to proceed with contract performance in the case of a contract change (see Chapter 11, Section C), the contractor is obliged to proceed with work if so directed after notifying the Government of a differing site condition. A contractor is not entitled to stop work while waiting for a Government decision on its equitable adjustment claim.[12]

C. TYPES OF DIFFERING SITE CONDITIONS

Differing site conditions are usually classified as "Type I" or "Type II" conditions. The major difference between the two types of conditions is that in "Type I" conditions, the contractor compares conditions actually encountered with the conditions *represented in the contract*, while in a "Type II" differing site condition, the contractor compares the conditions actually encountered with the conditions that would *usually be encountered*, given the nature and location of the work.

1. Type I Conditions

A Type I differing site condition is described in Paragraph (a) of the "Differing Site Conditions" clause (see Figure 25-1) as a "subsurface or latent physical condition" at the site that "differ[s] materially from those indicated in [the] contract." Thus, there must be a material difference between the conditions encountered and the conditions indicated by the contract documents. The condition need not be contrary to *express representations* in the contract; it is enough that there are "indications" in the documents that would lead a contractor reasonably to infer that it would not encounter the condition.[13] The Armed Services Board of Contract Appeals (ASBCA) summarized the rule very well when it observed:[14]

> The absence of an explicit indication does not preclude assertion of a Type I claim: Sometimes the "indications" are implicit:
>
>> [T]here must be reasonably plain or positive indications in the bid information or contract documents that such subsurface conditions would be otherwise than actually found in contract performance, or to view the other side of the coin, that there were such indications which induced reasonable reliance by the successful bidder that subsurface conditions would be more favorable than those encountered.

Since the clause refers to "subsurface or latent" in the disjunctive, the condition need not be *underground*.[15] Indeed, even the term "subsurface" has been held not limited to underground conditions.[16] Examples of Type I conditions include the following:

(1) Rock in an excavation or dredging area where the rock was not indicated by soil boring information made available by the Government to bidders and included in the contract.[17]

(2) Larger or more dense boulders than indicated by Government test borings.[18]

(3) A substantially greater quantity of rock in an excavation area than indicated in test borings.[19]

(4) Rock that was substantially harder to drill than indicated on plans and specifications.[20]

(5) Decomposed rock, when sound rock had been indicated by Government borings.[21]

(6) Soil conditions different than those indicated in Government soil reports.[22]

(7) Permafrost where Government borings gave no indication of the extent of the permafrost.[23]

(8) Unsuitable material in a borrow pit substantially in excess of that shown in the contract.[24]

(9) Insufficient stone in a stone quarry where Government representations indicated enough stone to complete the work.[25]

(10) A trench in a river bed.[26]

(11) Ground water at an unforeseeably high level.[27]

(12) A perforated pipe without a required identifying label.[28]

(13) Denial of access to the work site by an Indian tribe on whose reservation a portion of the trail was located where the contract represented the land was owned by the Government.[29]

2. Type II Conditions

The second type of differing site condition is an "unknown physical condition" of an "unusual nature" differing "materially from those ordinarily encountered and generally recognized as inhering in work of the character provided for in the contract" (see Paragraph (a) of the clause in Figure 25-1). The Type II differing site condition is less frequently alleged and more difficult to prove than the Type I condition. The ASBCA again aptly summed up the rule for recovery under Type II when it stated:[30]

In asserting a Type II Differing Site Condition Claim, [the contractor] is "confronted with a relatively heavy burden of proof."...When nothing is said in the contract documents about subsurface or latent conditions, [the contractor] "must demonstrate that he has encountered something materially different from the 'known' and the 'usual'."... One need not encounter a geological freak like permafrost in the tropics to recover. When we speak of an "unusual" condition...we mean one which might not reasonably be anticipated based on the contract work and the location at which it was to be performed. Of course part of the difficulty in establishing a Type II claim arises from the broad range of subsurface experiences which one may encounter...."A contractor is not entitled to expect the most favorable conditions but he need not anticipate the worst."

Type II claims have succeeded, for example, where the contractor encountered highly corrosive ground water,[31] the presence of cattle bones beneath an inlet structure,[32] concrete beams, automobile parts, and railroad ties in an excavation contract,[33] and the failure of rock to fracture in the manner anticipated.[34] However, Type II claims have been denied where, for instance, the condition was common to structures built during a particular era even though the contractor was not accustomed to the existence of the condition,[35] and the condition was subsurface water and the site was located near a large body of water.[36] If the contractor should have reasonably anticipated the condition, it will not be regarded as "unknown" or "unusual."[37]

3. Conditions Occurring After Award

To fall within the "Differing Site Conditions" clause, the condition need not necessarily exist at the time of award of the contract. It may be the result of a man-made change occurring after contract award. For example, a diversion of a river by another Government contractor working upstream from where the contractor was building a bridge—which caused flooding of the bridge site—was held in one decision to be a differing site condition, even though the flooding occurred after contract award.[38] In a similar case, recovery was allowed for the cost of removing sand washed down on the contractor's work site from the site of another contractor.[39] Recovery has also been allowed where a condition arising after award combines with a preexisting condition to cause the loss.[40]

The rationale of these decisions appears to be that the Government has a duty to protect contractors from differing site conditions created by its other contractors in the same area. However, the circumstances must be such that the Government could have corrected the condition but failed to do so.[41]

4. Excluded Conditions

Certain types of conditions—such as conditions resulting solely from unusually severe weather, acts of God, or acts of the Government taken in its sovereign capacity—are not considered to fall within the protection of the "Differing Site Conditions" clause. Examples of such conditions include the following:

(a) Hurricanes,[42] excessive rainfall,[43] excessive snowfall,[44] drought,[45] and flooding due to natural causes.[46] (However, relief under the clause may be available when the severe weather condition combines with another condition to cause a loss; for example, heavy rainfall combined with inadequate drainage conditions not indicated by the contract documents.[47])

(b) High water level in a lake where work was to be performed.[48]

(c) Changes in wage rates during contract performance.[49]

(d) Inability to obtain materials.[50]

(e) Imposition of strict fire laws by the local government subsequent to contract award.[51]

(f) Flooding of a contractor's site as a result of flood control measures taken by the Government in its sovereign capacity.[52]

(g) Assault by a mob on the contractor's work force.[53]

(h) Insect infestation.[54]

D. CONTRACTOR'S DUTY TO INVESTIGATE SITE

Closely connected with the "Differing Site Conditions" clause is the duty of a contractor to conduct a reasonable site investigation.[55] The Government often attempts to limit its liability for differing site conditions by including a "Site Investigation" clause in the contract. An adequate site investigation by the contractor is particularly important in contracts for the renovation of existing facilities.[56]

1. Standard "Site Investigation" Clause

When a bid solicitation calls on bidders to make a site investigation before submitting their bids, they have a duty to do so.[57] This duty is included in a contract clause, typically the FAR's "Site Investigation and Conditions Affecting the Work" clause[58] set forth in Figure 25-2 on the next page. If the contractor does not conduct a site investigation, or does so in a careless manner, it will not be compensated for differing site conditions that a reasonable investigation would have revealed.

2. Limitations

The site investigation requirement does not void the "Differing Site Conditions" clause. Rather, the site investigation requirement relates to the *foreseeability* of the differing site condition.[59] If the condition could have been discovered by a "reasonably prudent contractor" during a reasonable site inspection, a claim based on the condition will be denied.[60] A *reasonable* site investigation does not require the employment of geologists or other experts; the test is what a reasonably experienced and intelligent contractor-layman could discover.[61]

A contractor's duty to investigate the site also does *not* extend to the verification of Government representations in any of the contract documents.[62] For example, a bidder need not conduct its own investigation of subsurface conditions to determine the truth or falsity of the Government's statements regarding those conditions.[63] In one case, recovery was allowed where a contractor justifiably relied on inaccurate Government soil borings—

> **Figure 25-2**
>
> **"SITE INVESTIGATION AND CONDITIONS AFFECTING THE WORK" CLAUSE**
> (FAR 52.236-3)
>
> (a) The Contractor acknowledges that it has taken steps reasonably necessary to ascertain the nature and location of the work, and that it has investigated and satisfied itself as to the general and local conditions which can affect the work or its cost, including but not limited to (1) conditions bearing upon transportation, disposal, handling, and storage of materials; (2) the availability of labor, water, electric power, and roads; (3) uncertainties of weather, river stages, tides, or similar physical conditions at the site; (4) the conformation and conditions of the ground; and (5) the character of equipment and facilities needed preliminary to and during work performance. The Contractor also acknowledges that it has satisfied itself as to the character, quality, and quantity of surface and subsurface materials or obstacles to be encountered insofar as this information is reasonably ascertainable from an inspection of the site, including all exploratory work done by the Government, as well as from the drawings and specifications made a part of this contract. Any failure of the Contractor to take the actions described and acknowledged in this paragraph will not relieve the Contractor from responsibility for estimating properly the difficulty and cost of successfully performing the work, or for proceeding to successfully perform the work without additional expense to the Government.
>
> (b) The Government assumes no responsibility for any conclusions or interpretations made by the Contractor based on the information made available by the Government. Nor does the Government assume responsibility for any understanding reached or representation made concerning conditions which can affect the work by any of its officers or agents before the execution of this contract, unless that understanding or representation is expressly stated in this contract.

notwithstanding the Government's assertion that the borings were solely for informational purposes.[64] However, the contractor will be held responsible for discovering "patent indications, plainly, to a layman, contradicting the contract documents."[65]

3. Failure To Investigate Or Inquire

A contractor that does not conduct a necessary site inspection may be deemed to have *assumed the risk* for problems that an investigation would have disclosed. For example, a contractor has been held to have assumed the risk of a differing site condition when a snowstorm prevented a site investigation before bid opening, but the contractor nonetheless proceeded to bid.[66]

On the other hand, where Government activity at the site *prevented* a contractor from performing a site inspection, the contractor was allowed to recover when it later encountered an unusual condition that a site inspection would have revealed.[67] A contractor was also able to recover when the Government did not allow sufficient time for a complete site inspection and the contractor had to rely on the Government's estimates that later proved to be incorrect, as a full site inspection would have revealed.[68]

If the contract documents are silent as to what conditions may be encountered, the contractor may have an obligation to inquire whether the Government has borings or other pertinent data,[69] or to seek clarification of inconsistent drawings.[70] This would be particularly true where the specifications, as a whole, indicate that such information is available and would be of use in determining the overall contract conditions. Contractors are generally not required to inspect documents that are not a part of the contract, however.[71]

4. Government's Duty To Disclose

When the Government possesses important information regarding site conditions, which it knows or should know that the contractor does not possess, it is under a duty to disclose its "superior knowledge." For example, in one case a contractor was able to recover based on the Government's failure to disclose reports of unusual sea conditions that it should have known the contractor did not have.[72]

E. GOVERNMENT DISCLAIMERS

Efforts by the Government to disclaim liability[73]—in contract specifications or other contract documents (such as through inclusion in the contract of the "Site Investigation" clause discussed above in Section D)—for differing site conditions do not normally preclude the contractor's recovery, provided the contract contains the standard "Differing Site Conditions" clause and the contractor is otherwise able to prove it is entitled to recovery under the clause. For example, the boards of contract appeals and courts have ruled that the "Differing Site Conditions" clause overrides the following *general* disclaimer language: (1) that the information in boring logs furnished by the Government was not intended as representations or warranties but was furnished "for information only,"[74] and (2) that "sounding and probing data" appearing on the contract drawings represented "average existing conditions" intended to "serve only as a general guide."[75] However, *specific* and unambiguous language that gives clear warning to the contractor—such as a statement that fill materials in a borrow pit shown on the contract drawings "are estimated to be less than the amount required" to perform the entire contract[76]—may bar the contractor's claim.

REFERENCES

1. See generally Lane, "Differing Site Conditions," Construction Briefings No. 92-11 (Oct. 1992), and Currie, Ansley, Smith & Abernathy, "Differing Site [Changed] Conditions," Briefing Papers No. 71-5 (Oct. 1971), 2 BPC 133.

2. FAR 52.236-2.

3. Foster Const. Co. v. U.S., 435 F.2d 873 (Ct. Cl. 1970), 13 GC ¶ 23.

4. Hoffman v. U.S., 166 Ct. Cl. 39 (1964), 6 GC ¶¶ 228, 231.

5. AFGO Engrg. Corp., VACAB 1236, 79-2 BCA ¶ 13900.

6. Mingus Constructors, Inc., IBCA 2117, 88-2 BCA ¶ 20529, 30 GC ¶ 108 (Note).

7. Farnsworth & Chambers Co. v. U.S., 346 F.2d 577 (Ct. Cl. 1965), 9 GC ¶ 287. But see Saturn Const. Co., ASBCA 22653, 82-1 BCA ¶ 15704.

8. Roy I. Strate, ASBCA 19914, 78-1 BCA ¶ 13128; Jack Crawford Const. Corp., GSBCA 4089, 75-2 BCA ¶ 11387, 17 GC ¶ 404; Troup Bros., ENGBCA 3030, 70-2 BCA ¶ 9491.

DIFFERING SITE CONDITIONS 25-13

9. Dittmore-Freimuth Corp. v. U.S., 390 F.2d 664 (Ct. Cl. 1968), 10 GC ¶ 111; Fox Valley Engrg. Inc. v. U.S., 341 F.2d 639 (Ct. Cl. 1960), 2 GC ¶ 580. But see Schnip Bldg. Co., ASBCA 21637, 78-2 BCA ¶ 13310.

10. CSH Contractors, Inc., NASA 476-2, 77-2 BCA ¶ 12814; ETS-Hokin Corp., IBCA 842-6-70, 71-1 BCA ¶ 8733, 13 GC ¶ 244.

11. DeMauro Const. Corp., ASBCA 17029, 77-1 BCA ¶ 12511, 19 GC ¶ 388.

12. American Dredging Co. v. U.S., 207 Ct. Cl. 1010 (1975).

13. E.g., P.J Dick Inc. v. General Services Admin., GSBCA 12036 et al. (July 20, 1994); J.E. Robertson Co. v. U.S., 437 F.2d 1360 (Ct. Cl. 1971), 13 GC ¶ 89; Pacific Alaska Contractors, Inc. v. U.S., 436 F.2d 461 (Ct. Cl. 1971), 13 GC ¶ 76; United Telecommunications, Inc., NASA 771-13, 72-2 BCA ¶ 9754, 15 GC ¶ 75; Peabody N.E., Inc., ASBCA 26410, 85-1 BCA ¶ 17867.

14. Kinetic Builders, Inc., ASBCA 32627, 88-2 BCA ¶ 20657 (quoting Pacific Alaska Contractors v. U.S., 436 F.2d 461 (Ct. Cl. 1971), 13 GC ¶ 76), 30 GC ¶ 121.

15. Jefferson Const. Co. v. U.S., 348 F.2d 968 (Ct. Cl. 1965), 7 GC ¶ 362.

16. I. Alper Co., GSBCA 2233, 68-1 BCA ¶ 6774, 10 GC ¶ 122.

17. Cosmo Const. Co. v. U.S., 207 Ct. Cl. 966 (1975), 17 GC ¶ 381; Bernard McMenamy Contractor, Inc., ENGBCA 3413, 77-1 BCA ¶ 12335, 19 GC ¶ 149; Dunbar & Sullivan Dredging Co., ENGBCA 3165 et al., 73-2 BCA ¶ 10285, 15 GC ¶ 473; Electronic & Missile Facilities, Inc., GSBCA 2203, 69-1 BCA ¶ 7781.

18. E. Arthur Higgins, AGBCA 76-128, 79-2 BCA ¶ 14050, 21 GC ¶ 458; J&T Const. Co., DOTCAB 73-4, 75-2 BCA ¶ 11358; Harris Paving & Const. Co., IBCA 487-3-65, 67-2 BCA ¶ 6468.

19. General Gas Co. v. U.S., 130 Ct. Cl. 520 (1955); Pennsylvania Drilling Co., IBCA 1187-4-78, 78-2 BCA ¶ 13465, 20 GC ¶ 465; JB&C Co., IBCA 1020-2-74, 77-2 BCA ¶ 12782; American Structures, Inc., ENGBCA 3410, 76-1 BCA ¶ 11683; Tecon Corp., ENGBCA 2782, 75-1 BCA ¶ 11282, 17 GC ¶ 255.

20. Note 12, supra; Minnis & Wright, AGBCA 332, 74-2 BCA ¶ 10685; K&M Const., ENGBCA 3012, 69-2 BCA ¶ 8052. But see Southwest Engrg. Co. v. U.S., 206 Ct. Cl. 892 (1975).

21. Brown Engrs. Intl., ENGBCA 2313, 65-2 BCA ¶ 4981.

22. Pennsylvania Drilling Co., note 19, supra; Perini Corp., ENGBCA 3745, 78-1 BCA ¶ 13191, 20 GC ¶ 293; Continental Drilling Co., ENGBCA 3455, 75-2 BCA ¶ 11541; F.D. Rich Co., ASBCA 14023, 75-2 BCA ¶ 11537; R.L. Spencer Const. Co., ASBCA 18450, 75-2 BCA ¶ 11604.

25-14 GOVERNMENT CONTRACT GUIDEBOOK

23. Morrison-Knudson Co. v. U.S., 170 Ct. Cl. 712 (1965), 7 GC ¶ 229.

24. S.J. Groves & Sons v. U.S., 106 Ct. Cl. 93 (1946); Nielson, Inc., IBCA 525-11-65, 67-2 BCA ¶ 6667.

25. Stock & Grove, Inc. v. U.S., 493 F.2d 629 (Ct. Cl. 1974), 16 GC ¶ 168.

26. Farnsworth & Chambers Co. v. U.S., note 7, supra. But see Stevedore Dredging Corp. v. U.S., 207 Ct. Cl. 1044 (1975).

27. United Contractors v. U.S., 368 F.2d 585 (Ct. Cl. 1966), 8 GC ¶ 491; Bosen & Dybevik Const. Co., AGBCA 243, 69-1 BCA ¶ 7581, 11 GC ¶ 286.

28. Caesar Const., Inc., ASBCA 41059, 91-1 BCA ¶ 23639, 33 GC ¶ 69.

29. E.R. McKee Const. Co. v. U.S., 500 F.2d 525 (Ct. Cl. 1974), 16 GC ¶ 305. See also D&L Const. Co. & Assocs. v. U.S., 402 F.2d 990 (Ct. Cl. 1968), 10 GC ¶ 476.

30. Kinetic Builders, Inc., note 14, supra. See also Youngdale & Sons Const. Co. v. U.S., 27 Fed. Cl. 516 (1993), 12 FPD ¶ 3.

31. Blount Bros. Corp., ENGBCA 2803, 70-1 BCA ¶ 8256.

32. Panhandle Const. Co., DOTCAB 77-31, 79-2 BCA ¶ 13756.

33. Maverick Diversified, Inc., ASBCA 19838, 76-2 BCA ¶ 12104, 18 GC ¶ 462.

34. R.A. Heintz Const. Co., ENGBCA 3380, 74-1 BCA ¶ 10562.

35. Northwest Painting Service, Inc., ASBCA 27854, 84-2 BCA ¶ 17474.

36. E.g., Robert McMullan & Son, Inc., ASBCA 22168, 78-2 BCA ¶ 13228; Quality Services of N.C., Inc., ASBCA 34851, 89-2 BCA ¶ 21836.

37. Southwest Engrg. Co. v. U.S., note 20, supra; Stevedore Dredging Corp. v. U.S., note 26, supra; John E. Moyer, AGBCA 417, 75-1 BCA ¶ 11338.

38. Note 4, supra.

39. Frank W. Miller Const. Co., ASBCA 22347, 78-1 BCA ¶ 13039, 20 GC ¶ 149.

40. Premier Electrical Const. Co., FAACAP 66-10, 65-2 BCA ¶ 5080, 8 GC ¶ 530.

41. Arkansas Rock & Gravel Co., ENGBCA 2895, 69-2 BCA ¶ 8001, 12 GC ¶ 274; Security Natl. Bank of Kansas City v. U.S., 184 Ct. Cl. 741 (1968), 10 GC ¶ 257.

42. Norfolk Dredging Co. v. U.S., 360 F.2d 619 (Ct. Cl. 1966), 8 GC ¶ 260.

43. Reinhold Const., Inc., ASBCA 23770, 79-2 BCA ¶ 14123.

44. Warren Painting Co., ASBCA 18456, 74-2 BCA ¶ 10834, 17 GC ¶ 12. See also S.S. Mullen, Inc., ASBCA 8533, 65-1 BCA ¶ 4644.

45. Turnkey Enterprises, Inc. v. U.S., 597 F.2d 750 (Ct. Cl. 1979), 21 GC ¶ 219.

46. Lenry, Inc., ASBCA 4674, 58-2 BCA ¶ 1849.

47. D.H. Dave & Gerben Contracting Co., ASBCA 6257, 1962 BCA ¶ 3493, 5 GC ¶ 105.

48. Roen Salvage Co., ENGBCA 3670, 79-2 BCA ¶ 13882, 21 GC ¶ 382.

49. R.G. Brown, Jr. & Co., IBCA 241, 61-2 BCA ¶ 3230, 4 GC ¶ 39.

50. George A. Rutherford Co., NASA 12, 1962 BCA ¶ 3561, 4 GC ¶ 608.

51. George R. MacKay, AGBCA 454, 75-2 BCA ¶ 11395, 17 GC ¶ 403.

52. Amino Bros. Co. v. U.S., 372 F.2d 485 (Ct. Cl. 1967), 9 GC ¶ 86.

53. Cross Const. Co., ENGBCA 3676, 79-1 BCA ¶ 13707, 21 GC ¶ 136.

54. Acme Missiles & Const. Corp., ASBCA 10784, 66-1 BCA ¶ 5418; Central Fla. Const. Co., IBCA 246, 61-1 BCA ¶ 2903, 3 GC ¶ 40.

55. J.S. Alberici Const. Co., ASBCA 9897, 89-3 BCA ¶ 22224.

56. See Ambrose-Augusterfer Corp. v. U.S., 394 F.2d 536 (Ct. Cl. 1968), 10 GC ¶ 263.

57. Puget Sound Bridge & Dredging Co. v. U.S., 131 Ct. Cl. 490 (1955); Tri-Messine Const. Co., PSBCA 312, 78-1 BCA ¶ 13023; Mojave Enterprises, AGBCA 75-114, 77-1 BCA ¶ 12337; Martin Const. Co., ENGBCA 3192, 75-2 BCA ¶ 11384, 17 GC ¶ 331; Coliseum Const., Inc., ASBCA 35953 et al., 89-1 BCA ¶ 21484, 31 GC ¶ 120.

58. FAR 52.236-3.

59. See Farnsworth & Chambers Co. v. U.S., note 7, supra; Vann v. U.S., 420 F.2d 968 (Ct. Cl. 1970), 12 GC ¶ 88.

60. Nineteenth Seed Co., AGBCA 450, 78-2 BCA ¶ 13537; Parkland Design & Development Corp., IBCA 1442-3-81, 82-2 BCA ¶ 15975. See also Price/CIRI Const., J.V., ASBCA 36988, 89-3 BCA ¶ 22146.

61. Note 25, supra; Kaiser Industries Corp. v. U.S., 169 Ct. Cl. 310 (1965), 7 GC ¶¶ 79, 80; Empire Const. Inc., ASBCA 27540, 84-3 BCA ¶ 17531. See also Moon Const. Co. v. General Services Admin., GSBCA 11766, 93-3 BCA ¶ 26017.

25-16 GOVERNMENT CONTRACT GUIDEBOOK

62. Perini Corp., note 22, supra; JB&C Co., note 19, supra; Klefstad Engrg. Co., VACAB 787, 69-1 BCA ¶ 7485.

63. Note 23, supra. But see G&H Const. Inc., ASBCA 26856, 82-2 BCA ¶ 16111; Titan Atlantic Const. Co., ASBCA 23588, 82-2 BCA ¶ 5808, 24 GC ¶ 406.

64. Jack Crawford Const. Corp., note 8, supra. See also Davho Co., VACAB 1004, 73-1 BCA ¶ 9848, 15 GC ¶ 87; Ragonese v. U.S., 128 Ct. Cl. 156 (1954); Key, Inc., IBCA 690-12-67, 68-2 BCA ¶ 7385, 11 GC ¶ 317; Tri-Ad Constructors v. U.S., 8 FPD ¶ 98 (Fed. Cir. 1989) (unpublished), revg., 89-1 BCA ¶ 21250, 31 GC ¶ 274.

65. Note 25, supra.

66. Cal-Pacific Foresters, AGBCA 230, 70-1 BCA ¶ 8087, 12 GC ¶ 132.

67. Pavement Specialists, Inc., ASBCA 17410, 73-2 BCA ¶ 10082, 15 GC ¶ 289.

68. Raymond Intl. of Del., Inc., ASBCA 13121, 70-1 BCA ¶ 8341, 12 GC ¶ 360.

69. Daymar, Inc., DOTCAB 77-13, 78-1 BCA ¶ 12903; Flippin Materials Co. v. U.S., 160 Ct. Cl. 357 (1963), 5 GC ¶ 60.

70. Rockford Corp., ASBCA 37198, 89-2 BCA ¶ 21734.

71. E.g., Klefstad Engrg., VACAB 602, 68-1 BCA ¶ 6965; American Structures, Inc., ENGBCA 3408, 75-1 BCA ¶ 11283, 17 GC ¶ 463.

72. Hardeman-Monier-Hutcherson v. U.S., 458 F.2d 1364 (Ct. Cl. 1972), 14 GC ¶ 224. See also Morrison-Knudson Co., ENGBCA 3856, 79-1 BCA ¶ 13798. Compare Brooks & Rivellini, Inc. v. U.S., 3 FPD ¶ 141 (Fed. Cir. 1985) (unpublished).

73. See generally Pettit, "Government Disclaimers of Liability," Briefing Papers No. 77-5 (Oct. 1977), 4 BPC 159; Pratt & Davis, "Disclaimers of Subsurface Conditions," Construction Briefings No. 82-4 (July 1982), 2 CBC 73.

74. E.g., Fehlhaber Corp. v. U.S., 138 Ct. Cl. 571, cert. denied, 355 U.S. 877 (1957).

75. Minnis & Wright, note 20, supra. See also Jack Crawford Const. Corp., note 8, supra.

76. Jefferson Const. v. U.S., 364 F.2d 420 (Ct. Cl.), cert. denied, 386 U.S. 914 (1966).

CONSTRUCTION DELAYS AND LIQUIDATED DAMAGES

26

A. Government Suspensions Of Work
1. Ordered Suspensions
2. Constructive Suspensions
3. Recoverable Costs
4. Limitations On Recovery

B. Excusable Delays
1. Weather Delays
2. Labor Delays
3. Subcontractor Delays
4. Acts Of Another Contractor

C. Liquidated Damages
1. Standard Clause
2. Enforceability
3. Relief From Liquidated Damages

The subject of delays in performance of the contract work was discussed from the perspective of supply contracts in Chapter 12. It was also treated in the discussion of default termination in Chapter 16—again, primarily in terms of supply contracts. Although the subject is important for the supply contractor, it is especially so for the construction contractor. A construction contractor is particularly hard hit by delays that cause a contract to continue beyond the scheduled completion date. Usually, the contractor has nowhere to go and nothing else to do but stay on the project site until the job is completed. And, when a contractor remains on the site beyond the originally scheduled completion date, its overhead rises and its profits fall.

Innumerable conditions and circumstances can intervene during contract performance to prevent adherence to the original contract schedule. The Government may suspend the contractor's work[1] (see Section A below), the contractor may fail to meet the contract performance schedule (making it liable in many instances for liquidated damages, see Section C), or events beyond the control of either party may delay the project's completion (see Section B). Contract clauses have been specially designed by the Government to allocate the risks for these delays between the parties. These clauses, and the various legal decisions bearing on them, are the focus of this chapter.

A. GOVERNMENT SUSPENSIONS OF WORK

The "Suspension of Work" clause is designed to provide an expeditious and inexpensive method of compensating a contractor for Government interruption, delay, or suspension of work. The standard clause for all fixed-price construction and architect-engineer contracts[2] found in the FAR is set forth in Figure 26-1. The clause provides for both ordered and constructive suspensions.

1. Ordered Suspensions

Paragraph (a) of the clause set forth in Figure 26-1 states that the "Contracting Officer may order the Contractor, in writ-

> **Figure 26-1**
>
> **"SUSPENSION OF WORK" CLAUSE**
> (FAR 52.242-14)
>
> (a) The Contracting Officer may order the Contractor, in writing, to suspend, delay, or interrupt all or any part of the work of this contract for the period of time that the Contracting Officer determines appropriate for the convenience of the Government.
>
> (b) If the performance of all or any part of the work is, for an unreasonable period of time, suspended, delayed, or interrupted (1) by an act of the Contracting Officer in the administration of this contract, or (2) by the Contracting Officer's failure to act within the time specified in this contract (or within a reasonable time if not specified), an adjustment shall be made for any increase in the cost of performance of this contract (excluding profit) necessarily caused by the unreasonable suspension, delay, or interruption, and the contract modified in writing accordingly. However, no adjustment shall be made under this clause for any suspension, delay, or interruption to the extent that performance would have been so suspended, delayed, or interrupted by any other cause, including the fault or negligence of the Contractor, or for which an equitable adjustment is provided for or excluded under any other term or condition of this contract.
>
> (c) A claim under this clause shall not be allowed (1) for any costs incurred more than 20 days before the Contractor shall have notified the Contracting Officer in writing of the act or failure to act involved (but this requirement shall not apply as to a claim resulting from a suspension order), and (2) unless the claim, in an amount stated, is asserted in writing as soon as practicable after the termination of the suspension, delay, or interruption, but not later than the date of final payment under the contract.

ing, to suspend, delay, or interrupt all or any part of the work of [the] contract for the period of time that the Contracting Officer determines appropriate for the convenience of the Government." Such express suspensions are relatively rare. Generally, suspensions will be ordered only when (a) it is advisable to suspend work pending a decision by the Government, and (b) execution of a supplemental agreement providing for a suspension is not feasible.

In certain circumstances, the suspension order may arise from a combination of communications from Government officials.

For example, in one case, a memorandum from a Government inspector strongly suggesting that a contractor suspend work—coupled with a threat by the Contracting Officer to withhold progress payments—was held to be a stop-work order entitling the contractor to relief under the "Suspension of Work" clause.[3] Note that—except for the conjunction of the inspector's memorandum with the Contracting Officer's threat—an actionable suspension probably would not have been found, since inspectors generally do not have authority to order suspensions of work.[4]

2. Constructive Suspensions

The language in Paragraph (b) of the clause set forth in Figure 26-1 covers "constructive" suspensions of work. In essence, this means that a suspension of work will be deemed to have occurred if an act or failure to act on the part of the Contracting Officer interferes with the contractor's performance of contract work, but there was no express order from the Government to stop work. The primary purpose of the clause language is to establish machinery for a fair and speedy administrative settlement to compensate the contractor if its performance is suspended, delayed, or interrupted for an *unreasonable* period of time *and* relief is not available under any other contract provision, such as the "Changes" clause.

a. Government Fault. Proof of Government fault is a prerequisite to recovery in all constructive suspension cases. The contractor must show that the Government did something it should not have done—or failed to do something it should have done—and that the contractor's performance was adversely affected. The Government's action must be the sole proximate cause of the delay for the contractor to be compensated under the clause.[5]

The following types of Government-caused delays illustrate the factual situations that can be held to constitute constructive suspensions of work:

(1) *Delay in issuing notice to proceed*—Even though no time for issuing this notice to the contractor is provided for in a contract,

the Government's delay beyond a reasonable time after award of the contract may constitute a constructive suspension.[6]

(2) *Delay in making site available*—The Government will be liable to a contractor for its unreasonable delay in making the construction site available to start the work,[7] but where the delay is caused by another contractor—rather than the Government—the contractor will not be compensated unless the Government has expressly promised that the site will be available by a certain date.[8] For example, approval by the Government of another contractor's progress schedule with full knowledge that it would result in interference with the contractor's work has been held to be a compensable suspension.[9] Similarly, where the Government issued a notice to proceed knowing that the contractor would not be able to enter the work site because of a previous contractor's failure to clear the site, the contractor may be compensated under the clause.[10] However, the contractor must make more than a nominal effort to gain access to the site.[11]

(3) *Delay in issuing change orders*—Where there is an unreasonable delay in investigating a differing site condition (see Chapter 25) or in issuing a change order (see Chapter 11) under a construction contract, a contractor may recover under the "Suspension of Work" clause.[12]

(4) *Delay in responding to contractor requests*—Unreasonable Government delay in responding to a contractor's request for a contract deviation may constitute a constructive suspension of work if the contractor's procurement of a required item is delayed as a result.[13] Similarly, an unreasonable delay in responding to a contractor's request for the Contracting Officer's interpretation of a contract provision will entitle the contractor to recover under the "Suspension of Work" clause.[14]

(5) *Delay in approval of shop drawings, samples, or models.*[15]

(6) *Delay caused by defective Government specifications or drawings*—Any delay that results from defective drawings or specifications is unreasonable and thus compensable.[16]

b. Unreasonable Delay. Recovery of costs under the "Suspension of Work" clause is granted, as the language of Paragraph (b) of the clause (see Figure 26-1) indicates, only for delays of an "unreasonable" duration. Some delays, such as those caused by defective Government specifications (see the preceding section), are always unreasonable and thus fully compensable. In many situations, however, the amount of delay for which the Government is liable will depend on the reason for the Government's interference with the contractor's work. For example, if the delay is due to the Government's exercise of a contractual right (such as the issuance of a change order), the contractor is compensated only for the unreasonable portion of the delay, which is determined by the circumstances of the case.[17] In one case, an unusually long delay caused by a change in Government regulations for issuing security clearances was considered unreasonable, entitling the contractor to a time extension and recovery of costs.[18]

Although the contractor usually has the burden of proving the unreasonableness of the period of delay, if the Government has *exclusive* knowledge of the facts relating to the suspension, the Government is obligated to prove the reasonableness of the delay period. For example, the Government had the burden of proof in one case where it had ordered all contractor personnel off the site during the movement of highly classified weapons.[19]

3. Recoverable Costs

Paragraph (b) of the "Suspension of Work" clause provides for an adjustment in the contract price "for any increase in the cost of performance of this contract (excluding profit) necessarily caused by the unreasonable suspension, delay, or interruption." To recover its increased costs, therefore, the contractor must establish not only the amount of the costs, but that the costs would not have been incurred *but for* the suspension.[20]

Compensation for delays under the "Suspension of Work" clause may include both actual delay costs as well as the impact costs of the delay on the other parts of the contract work. Examples of recoverable costs are listed below:

(a) *Overhead*—The cost of both *office* overhead[21] and *work site* overhead[22] during extended performance are recoverable.

(b) *Idle time*—The cost of equipment lying idle because of a suspension is recoverable.[23]

(c) *Increased costs of labor and materials*—Where a suspension causes the contractor to perform a portion of the work in a later, more expensive time period—for example, after a wage increase has gone into effect—the amount of the cost increase is recoverable.[24] The same is true for increases in material costs.[25]

(d) *Insurance and bond premiums*—Additional bond and insurance premiums that must be paid in the extended performance period are recoverable.[26]

(e) *Increased costs of performing during adverse weather conditions*—If the Government delays the contract, and the contractor is foreseeably forced to perform under more difficult weather conditions, the increased cost of performance is recoverable. Such recovery may occur, for example, if performance is extended into seasons for rain,[27] cold weather,[28] or flooding.[29] However, if the weather conditions would have been encountered regardless of the suspension, no recovery is allowed.[30]

(f) *Loss of efficiency*—If work is necessarily performed less efficiently in the extended period because of the delay, recovery is allowed.[31]

(g) *Interest on borrowings*—Interest on borrowings necessary to finance the contractor's performance in the extended period caused by the delay may also be recovered.[32]

4. Limitations On Recovery

a. Notice & Claim Requirements. Paragraph (c) of the "Suspension of Work" clause (see Figure 26-1) provides that the contractor may not recover any costs incurred more than 20 days prior to the time the contractor notifies the Contracting Officer in writing of the existence of a constructive suspension (see Section A.2 above). The purpose of the notice requirement is to alert the Government to the conduct that the contractor believes constitutes a suspension of the work.[33] Note that the 20-day notice provision does not apply to an *ordered* suspension (see Section A.1 above).

Despite the seeming rigidity of this 20-day notice requirement, failure to give such notice will not bar a claim for suspension if the Government knows or should have known that it was called upon to act. This is in accord with the general rule that notice provisions should not be applied too strictly where the Government is aware of the operative facts.[34]

Paragraph (c) of the clause also contains a separate limitation on the period within which the contractor can file its claim for increased costs. It provides that a claim stated in a definite amount must be presented in writing as soon as practicable after the end of the suspension period—but not later than the date of final payment under the contract.

b. Concurrent Delays. Paragraph (b) of the "Suspension of Work" clause precludes recovery for delay if the delay is due to concurrent causes attributable to both the contractor and the Government. In this instance, neither party is generally allowed to benefit. This means that the Government cannot recover liquidated damages for the period of delay caused by the contractor (see Section C.3.b below), and the contractor cannot recover its delay costs under the "Suspension of Work" clause (or under the "Changes" clause (see Chapter 11)).[35]

Similarly, a contractor will not be allowed to recover where the Government-caused delay is concurrent and intertwined with delay for which the Government is *not* responsible—such as delay attributable to a third party.[36] However, if the Government was responsible for the third party's delay, the contractor may recover.[37] The contractor may also recover for Government-caused delay—despite the concurrent existence of contractor-caused delay—if it can show that its delay did *not* affect work that was on the "critical path," i.e., was not work that was crucial to the overall performance of the contract.[38]

Although neither party is usually allowed to recover when delay is attributable to both the Government and the contractor, courts and boards have on occasion taken a more liberal view. Thus, in one case where the overall delay in completing a contract was attributable not only to late delivery of Government-furnished equipment but also partly to contractor inexperience and inefficiency, the Court of Claims found that the contractor could recover to the extent the Government's delay in delivering the equipment was responsible for one-third of the extra expense incurred by the contractor because of the overall delay.[39]

B. EXCUSABLE DELAYS

Under the standard "Default (Fixed-Price Construction)" clause[40]—set forth in full in Figure 16-2 in Chapter 16—a contractor is excused from full compliance with the original contract schedule and the contract is not subject to termination for default when the delay in performance or failure to perform arises out of "unforeseeable causes beyond the control and without the fault or negligence of the Contractor" (Paragraph (b)(1) of the clause in Figure 16-2). As pointed out in Chapter 16, Section D.1, the examples of excusable delay set forth in Paragraph (b) of the construction contract "Default" clause are basically the same as set forth in the supply contract "Default" clause (see also Chapter 12, Section B). Note, however, that the list of enumerated excusable delays for construction contracts includes one cause of excusable delay in addition to those enumerated for supply contracts: "acts of another Contractor in the performance of a contract with the Government."[41] In addition, the construction contract "Default" clause requires that the contractor give the Government notice of any delays,[42] although the supply and service contract "Default" clause does not contain a notice requirement.

It must be remembered that the examples of excusable delay enumerated in the "Default" clause are not exclusive—the sole test is whether the delay is "beyond the control and without the fault or negligence" of the prime contractor, its subcontractors, and suppliers.[43] With this in mind, the following sections focus on the four major types of excusable delay that are most common in construction contracting—weather delays, labor delays, subcontractor delays, and delays due to the acts of another contractor.

1. Weather Delays

One of the enumerated examples of excusable delay in the "Default" clauses—"unusually severe weather"—is more frequently involved in construction delays than in supply contract delays.[44] "Unusually severe weather" has been defined as "adverse weather which at the time of year in which it occurred is unusual for the place in which it occurred."[45]

To substantiate a claim of unusually severe weather, a contractor must present weather records of the same period in prior years to show that the weather it encountered surpassed in severity the weather usually encountered or reasonably expected in the particular locality during the time of year involved.[46] For example, in one case where precipitation over a two-month period was 9.44 inches and 6.98 inches, while normal totals for those months were 4.15 inches and 4.90 inches as shown by weather records, a construction contractor was given a time extension for the resulting floods that delayed the work.[47] But a roofing contractor was not entitled to an extension of time for high winds in Kansas because "Kansas is a windy state" and the contractor failed to show the weather's "unusual severity."[48] On the other hand, a contractor was entitled to a time extension in a brick-laying contract where it showed that low temperatures between 11 degrees and 20 degrees Fahrenheit in December were not normal for Georgia.[49]

Even where a contractor could reasonably have expected a wet season, weather has been held to be unusually severe not only because more rain fell than normal, but also because the rain occurred at such intervals that the area did not dry out to permit proper compaction.[50] Other occurrences that have been held to be unusually severe weather excusing delays include (1) abnormally high humidity,[51] (2) an abnormal amount of fog,[52] and (3) an unusually heavy snowfall.[53]

Unusually severe weather occurring *before* award of the contract can be the cause of an excusable delay. Thus, an excusable delay was found in one case where excavation could not be started promptly because the ground had been saturated by heavy rains prior to award.[54]

Of course, the mere occurrence of unusually severe weather is not enough to justify a delay. The contractor must show that the bad weather actually prevented it from meeting the performance schedule.[55]

2. Labor Delays

a. Strikes. Another excusable delay listed in the "Default" clause is "strikes." In a construction contract, a strike generally must be *unforeseeable* to excuse delay.[56] In addition, the contractor must establish that the strike actually delayed the contractor's performance,[57] and the contractor must act reasonably to avoid the effects of the strike or to end the strike if possible.[58] For example, when a steel strike began several months before the contractor submitted its bid and was still in progress at the time of bidding, the contractor was not allowed to cite the strike as an excusable cause of its delay.[59] Similarly, if there is a shortage of material caused by a strike, the contractor is expected to make reasonable efforts to obtain the supplies from another source.[60] It should be noted that a delay caused by a labor action that is not technically a strike—such as a refusal by the contractor's employees to cross a picket line protesting another contractor at the site[61]—may also be considered excusable.

b. Labor Shortages. Hiring and retaining skilled workers to perform the contract is frequently difficult in construction contracts. Generally, the contractor is responsible for assuring an adequate labor force.[62] Particularly when a labor shortage was known to the contractor at the time the contract was executed, no extension of time will be granted based on a shortage of laborers during contract performance,[63] unless, for example, the labor shortage was caused by Government action.[64] However, in one unusual case, a board of contract appeals recognized an excusable delay where highly-skilled operators were hired away by the contractor's competitors and the contractor "left no stone unturned" in its efforts to overcome the difficulty.[65]

3. Subcontractor Delays

The standard "Default" clauses provide that to be excusable, a delay or failure by a subcontractor at any tier must be beyond the control of and without the fault or negligence of *both* the subcontractor and the contractor. This means to be excusable to the contractor, the delay must be excusable to the subcontractors at each tier—i.e, all intervening subcontractors between the contractor and the delayed sub (see Chapter 12, Section B.3.d). The construction contract "Default" clause adds the requirement that subcontractor delays must arise from *unforeseeable* causes to be excusable.[66]

4. Acts Of Another Contractor

The standard construction contract "Default" clause includes an enumerated cause of excusable delay not listed in the supply and service contract clause—"acts of another contractor in the performance of a contract with the Government."[67] This type of delay commonly arises in construction contracts where the Government enters into agreements with several contractors for concurrent or sequential performance. In this situation, the delay of one contractor may affect the ability of another contractor to perform on time, and thus entitle the affected contractor to additional time to perform.[68]

C. LIQUIDATED DAMAGES

The topic of liquidated damages is closely connected to the subject of delays in construction contracting. "Liquidated Damages" clauses are occasionally used in Government supply or service contracts (see Chapter 16, Section E.3), but they are common in construction contracts. Liquidated damages afford the Government an exceedingly valuable remedy in instances where a construction contractor's delay is caused by its own fault. This section reviews the "Liquidated Damages" clause and its enforceability in construction contracts, as well as the means by which contractors may seek relief when the Government asserts its rights under the clause.[69]

1. Standard Clause

The FAR sets forth the clause appearing in Figure 26-2 as the "Liquidated Damages" clause that a Contracting Officer *may* insert in any construction contract, except one that is on a cost-plus-fixed-fee basis.[70] According to the FAR, a "Liquidated Damages" clause "should be used only when both (1) the time of delivery or performance is such an important factor in the award of the contract that the Government may reasonably expect to suffer damage if the delivery or performance is delinquent, and (2) the extent or amount of such damage would be difficult or impossible to ascertain or prove."[71] Thus, liquidated damages are intended as a substitute for actual damages for late completion or delivery of the contract work.[72]

Figure 26-2

"LIQUIDATED DAMAGES—CONSTRUCTION" CLAUSE
(FAR 52.212-5)

(a) If the Contractor fails to complete the work within the time specified in the contract, or any extension, the Contractor shall pay to the Government as liquidated damages, the sum of . . . . [*Contracting Officer insert amount*] for each day of delay.

(b) If the Government terminates the Contractor's right to proceed, the resulting damage will consist of liquidated damages until such reasonable time as may be required for final completion of the work together with any increased costs occasioned the Government in completing the work.

(c) If the Government does not terminate the Contractor's right to proceed, the resulting damage will consist of liquidated damages until the work is completed or accepted.

---

a. Measuring The Damages Period. As the language of the "Liquidated Damages–Construction" clause indicates, it requires payment by the contractor of a specific amount to the Government for each day that the contractor does not meet the contract's performance schedule. Generally, liquidated damages are assessed starting at the completion date of the contract. The completion date is generally determined by adding the number of calendar days of the performance period to the date on which the contractor acknowledged receipt of the Government's "notice to proceed."[73]

The "Liquidated Damages" clause also spells out the duration period for the assessment of damages based on the Government's rights in connection with termination of the contract for default: (1) if the contractor's right to proceed *is terminated*, liquidated damages accrue "until such reasonable time as may be required for final completion of the work" (usually by another contractor that would be solicited by the Government after the default), and (2) if the contractor's right to proceed is *not terminated*, liquidated damages accrue "until the work is completed or accepted." Thus, the clause, in theory, seeks to put the Government in as good a position on completion of the work as it would have been in had the delay not occurred—that is, it allows the Government to obtain the completed work at the contract price, less the amount of damages for delay.

b. Per Diem Rate. The rate of liquidated damages will be prescribed in the contract as a specific sum for each day of delay. The FAR requires that the rate "should as a minimum cover the estimated cost of inspection and superintendence for each day of delay in completion."[74] It also advises that if the Government will suffer other specific losses due to the failure of the contractor to complete the work on time—such as the cost of substitute facilities, the rental of building or equipment, or the continued payment of quarters allowance—the per diem rate should include these amounts.[75] However, where the peculiar circumstances in which the contract was to be performed made it obvious that *no* daily inspection and superintendence by the Government would be required, liquidated damages based on additional inspection and superintendence expenses for late performance have been held to constitute an unenforceable penalty.[76] The FAR further provides that the contract may—but is not required to—include an overall *maximum* dollar amount or period of time, or both, during which liquidated damages may be assessed, "to ensure that the result is not an unreasonable assessment of liquidated damages."[77]

2. Enforceability

Liquidated damages provisions must meet two criteria to be valid and enforceable. First, the amount stipulated in the "Liquidated Damages" clause must be a *reasonable forecast* of the harm that the breach of the contract (the contractor's delay) would cause to the Government. Second, the harm that would result from the breach must be *difficult* or impossible to *estimate*. A "Liquidated Damages" clause that does not meet both of these criteria may be viewed as a penalty and therefore unenforceable. If a "Liquidated Damages" clause is held to be unenforceable, the Government may recover its actual damages for breach of contract.[78]

a. Reasonableness Of The Forecast. In Government contracts, the reasonableness of the forecast of liquidated damages is determined by looking at the situation at the time the parties executed the contract.[79] The stipulated amount must be reasonable in light of the harm the Government anticipates in the case of a breach.[80] In other words, the per diem damages rate must not be disproportionate to the actual damages expected in the event of breach based on the Government's knowledge at the time the contract was made. Liquidated damages may be assessed only when they bear some "reasonable relation to the probable actual damages which the Government would suffer from the contractor's breach."[81] For example, if the Government knew at the time it awarded the contract that it would not suffer any damages from late performance by the contractor, a "Liquidated Damages" clause is inappropriate.[82]

"Liquidated Damages" clauses have been enforced despite great discrepancies between the actual and liquidated damages. The fact that actual damages far exceed or fall far short of the liquidated amount will not necessarily invalidate an otherwise proper provision.[83] Similarly, even liquidated damages that exceed the contract price have been upheld where the rate fixed in the clause was reasonable as of the time the contract was awarded,[84] although if the assessment becomes too protracted, a court or board may regard it as a penalty.[85]

b. Difficulty In Estimating Loss. The second part of the test of enforceability of a "Liquidated Damages" clause is that the harm to the Government from a breach is difficult or impossible to determine accurately. As a practical matter, this hurdle is rarely a problem for the Government since testimony by Government personnel that the Government could not accurately estimate its damages in the event of a delay or default is difficult for the contractor to dispute.

3. Relief From Liquidated Damages

If the "Liquidated Damages" clause is enforceable and the Government assesses damages against the contractor, the contractor may nevertheless have ground to seek relief from the assessment.

a. Substantial Completion. Liquidated damages cannot properly be assessed after the contract is "substantially complete."[86] A contract is substantially complete when a large portion of the work is complete and the project is available for its intended use. There is no specific percentage of completion that triggers "substantial completion"; it depends on the facts of the case. A building may be fit for its intended use even if some items remain uncompleted.[87] On the other hand, even if the percentage of completion is high, a building may nevertheless be unfit for its intended purpose if an essential area or feature remains incomplete, and liquidated damages may be assessed.[88] Once a project is substantially complete, the Government may not properly assess liquidated damages against the contractor, regardless of whether the Government takes actual occupancy of the building or not.[89]

b. Excusable & Concurrent Delays. The most common defense to an assessment of liquidated damages is excusable delay. If proved, the delivery schedule will be extended by the number of days of excusable delay, and thereby reduce or eliminate the liquidated damages. For a detailed discussion of excusable delay, see Section B above and Chapter 16, Section D.1.

If a delay is caused by *both* the Government and the contractor, and the extent to which each party has contributed to the delay is difficult to ascertain, most courts and boards will find that the "Liquidated Damages" clause should be "annulled,"[90] especially where the Government's delays interfered with the contractor's progress on a "critical path" schedule.[91] If the Government can prove that the total project delay was caused by contractor fault despite the concurrent Government delays, however, the liquidated damages may be assessed.[92] See Section A.4.b above for a further discussion of concurrent delays.

c. Remission By Comptroller General. The Comptroller General is authorized by law to remit (i.e., forgive) the whole or any part of a liquidated damages assessment.[93] Thus, even though the assessment of liquidated damages by the Government was legal, the Comptroller General has the equitable power in certain circumstances to return to the contractor liquidated damages sums collected by the Government.

A request by the contractor for remission must first be transmitted to the head of the contracting agency involved,[94] and the contractor must exhaust its administrative remedies.[95] The Comptroller General will not exercise his remission power unless he receives a recommendation from the agency head.[96] The decision of the agency head to recommend remission, as well as the decision of the Comptroller General to grant remission, is wholly discretionary—remission is not a matter of legal right[97] and is granted only rarely.

The Comptroller General has required the "existence of strong and persuasive equities" before remitting liquidated damages.[98] Where remission has been granted, usually the Comptroller General has merely accepted the agency's favorable recommendation without describing the factual situation.[99]

REFERENCES

1. See generally McWhorter, "Suspension of Work," Briefing Papers No. 66-6 (Dec. 1966), 1 BPC 215; McWhorter, "Suspension of Work/Edition II," Briefing Papers No. 76-2 (Apr. 1976), 4 BPC 15.

2. FAR 52.212-12. See FAR 12.505(a).

3. Stamell Const. Co., DOTCAB 68-27J, 75-1 BCA ¶ 11334, 17 GC ¶ 449. See also Southland Const., ASBCA 32677, 87-1 BCA ¶ 19672 (shutdown of work site for three days for ceremony and congressional visit entitled contractor to time extension), 30 GC ¶ 115.

4. Frank K. Blas Plumbing & Heating Co., ASBCA 16563, 73-2 BCA ¶ 10279.

5. Triax-Pacific v. Stone, 11 FPD ¶ 33 (Fed. Cir. 1992), 34 GC ¶ 210.

6. E.g., Freeman Electric Const. Co., DOTCAB 74-23A, 77-1 BCA ¶ 12258, 19 GC ¶ 156; GMC Contractors, Inc., GSBCA 3730, 75-1 BCA ¶ 11083, 17 GC ¶ 99; Ross Engrg. Co. v. U.S., 92 Ct. Cl. 253 (1940); T.C. Bateson Const. Co., ASBCA 6028, 1963 BCA ¶¶ 3692, 3733, 5 GC ¶ 505. See also De Matteo Const. Co., PSBCA 187, 76-2 BCA ¶ 12172, 18 GC ¶ 487; Welch Const. Co., PSBCA 217, 77-1 BCA ¶ 12322, 19 GC ¶ 283.

7. Eickhof Const. Co., ASBCA 20049, 77-1 BCA ¶ 12398; John A. Johnson & Sons, Inc. v. U.S., 180 Ct. Cl. 969 (1967), 9 GC ¶ 313; Merritt-Chapman & Scott Corp. v. U.S., 429 F.2d 431 (Ct. Cl. 1970), 12 GC ¶ 432; Lea County Const. Co., ASBCA 10093, 67-1 BCA ¶ 6243.

8. Freuhauf Corp., PSBCA 479, 73-1 BCA ¶ 9897. See also Hoel-Steffen Const. Co. v. U.S., 456 F.2d 760 (Ct. Cl. 1972), 14 GC ¶ 116; Asheville Contracting Co., DOTCAB 74-6, 76-2 BCA ¶ 12027, 19 GC ¶ 87.

9. Warrior Constructors, Inc., ENGBCA 3134, 71-1 BCA ¶ 8915, 13 GC ¶ 357.

10. Head Const. Co., ENGBCA 3537, 77-1 BCA ¶ 12226. See also Hensel Phelps Const. Co., ENGBCA 3368, 74-2 BCA ¶ 10728, 16 GC ¶ 406; Pierce Assocs., Inc., GSBCA 4163, 77-2 BCA ¶ 12746, 19 GC ¶ 398.

11. Boro Developers, Inc., ASBCA 40146, 90-3 BCA ¶ 23192, 32 GC ¶ 273.

12. DeMauro Const. Corp., ASBCA 12514, 73-1 BCA ¶ 9830, 15 GC ¶ 105; William Passalacqua Builders, Inc., GSBCA 4205, 77-1 BCA ¶ 12406; Day & Zimmerman-Madway, ASBCA 13367, 71-1 BCA ¶ 8622; Marigold Electric Co., ASBCA 15984, 72-2 BCA ¶ 9646; Martin Const. Co., ENGBCA 3192, 75-2 BCA ¶ 11384, 17 GC ¶ 331. But see B.J. Larvin, General Contractor, Inc., ASBCA 20945, 77-2 BCA ¶ 12717.

13. Thomas W. Yoder Co., VACAB 1010, 74-2 BCA ¶ 10960, 17 GC ¶ 19.

14. Royal Painting Co., ASBCA 20034, 75-1 BCA ¶ 11311, 17 GC ¶ 283. See also Edgemont Const. Co., ASBCA 16759, 73-2 BCA ¶ 10234.

15. C.W. Schmid v. U.S., 351 F.2d 651 (Ct. Cl. 1965), 7 GC ¶ 472; S. Patti, Massman & MacDonald Const. Cos., ASBCA 8423, 1964 BCA ¶ 4225; Shiff Const. Co., ASBCA 9029, 1964 BCA ¶ 4478; L.B. Gallimore, Inc., GSBCA 3327, 72-1 BCA ¶ 9232; Sydney Const. Co., ASBCA 21377, 77-2 BCA ¶ 12719, 19 GC ¶ 388.

16. S. Patti, Massman & MacDonald Const. Cos., note 15, supra; Carl M. Halvorson, Inc. v. U.S., 461 F.2d 1337 (Ct. Cl. 1972), 14 GC ¶ 281; E.W. Sorrells, Inc., ASBCA 13348, 70-2 BCA ¶ 8515, 13 GC ¶ 72; Desonia Const. Co., ENGBCA 3231, 73-1 BCA ¶ 9797. See, e.g., Chaney & James Const. Co. v. U.S., 421 F.2d 728 (Ct. Cl. 1970), 12 GC ¶ 101.

17. See, e.g., Gregory & Reilly Assocs., Inc., FAACAP 65-30, 65-2 BCA ¶ 4918; Barnet Brezner, ASBCA 6207, 61-1 BCA ¶ 2895, 3 GC ¶ 153; George A. Fuller Co., ASBCA 8524, 1962 BCA ¶ 3619, 5 GC ¶ 379; Paccon, Inc., ASBCA 7890, 1963 BCA ¶ 3659, 5 GC ¶ 532; Lee Electric Co., FAACAP 67-26, 67-1 BCA ¶ 6263.

18. G&S Const., Inc., ASBCA 28677, 86-2 BCA ¶ 18791, 28 GC ¶ 93.

19. M.A. Santander Const., Inc., ASBCA 15882, 76-1 BCA ¶ 11798, 18 GC ¶ 348.

20. R.C. Hedreen Co., ASBCA 20599, 77-1 BCA ¶ 12328; Joseph Pickard's Sons Co., ASBCA 13585, 73-1 BCA ¶ 10026, 15 GC ¶ 342.

21. Eichleay Corp., ASBCA 5183, 60-2 BCA ¶ 2688, 61-1 BCA ¶ 2894, 2 GC ¶ 485, 3 GC ¶ 138(a); Chaney & James Const. Co., FAACAP 67-18, 66-2 BCA ¶ 6066; Continental Consolidated Corp., ASBCA 10662, 67-1 BCA ¶ 6127; Capital Electric Co. v. U.S., 729 F.2d 743 (Fed. Cir. 1984), 2 FPD ¶ 109, 26 GC ¶ 49.

22. Bruno Law, Trustee v. U.S., 195 Ct. Cl. 370 (1970), 13 GC ¶ 344; Paccon, Inc., note 17, supra.

23. Merritt-Chapman & Scott Corp. v. U.S., 528 F.2d 1392 (Ct. Cl. 1976), 18 GC ¶ 73; Cornell Wrecking Co. v. U.S., 184 Ct. Cl. 289 (1966), 10 GC ¶ 215; Fullerton Const. Co., ASBCA 11500, 67-2 BCA ¶ 6394, 9 GC ¶ 406.

24. Sydney Const. Co., note 15, supra; Norair Engrg. Corp., ASBCA 12054, 71-1 BCA ¶ 8835; Paccon, Inc., note 17, supra; Keco Industries, Inc., ASBCA 15184 et al., 76-2 BCA ¶ 9576, 15 GC ¶ 9.

25. Samuel N. Zarpas, Inc., ASBCA 4722, 59-1 BCA ¶ 2170, 1 GC ¶ 363; Paccon, Inc., note 17, supra.

26. Stapleton Const. Co. v. U.S., 92 Ct. Cl. 551 (1940); Barnet Brezner, ASBCA 6194, 1962 BCA ¶ 3381, 4 GC ¶ 449; E.V. Lane Corp., ASBCA 9741, 65-2 BCA ¶ 5076, 66-1 BCA ¶ 5472, 8 GC ¶ 204.

27. Merritt-Chapman & Scott Corp. v. U.S., note 23, supra.

28. Chris Berg, Inc. & Assocs., ASBCA 3466, 58-1 BCA ¶ 1792.

29. B.J. Lucarelli & Co., ASBCA 8422, 65-1 BCA ¶ 4523.

30. Paccon, Inc., note 17, supra; Merritt-Chapman & Scott Corp. v. U.S., note 23, supra.

31. Luria Bros. & Co. v. U.S., 369 F.2d 701 (Ct. Cl. 1966), 9 GC ¶ 11; Eisen-Magers Const. Co., ASBCA 4694, 59-1 BCA ¶ 2171, 1 GC ¶ 363; Allied Contractors, Inc., ASBCA 5326, 59-2 BCA ¶ 2441, 2 GC ¶ 42; Algernon Blair, Inc., GSBCA 4072, 76-2 BCA ¶ 12073.

32. Luzon Stevedoring Corp., ASBCA 11650, 68-2 BCA ¶ 7193, 69-1 BCA ¶ 7545, 10 GC ¶ 481, 11 GC ¶ 98; Industrial Research Assocs., Inc., DCAB WB-5, 67-1 BCA ¶ 6309, 71-1 BCA ¶ 8680, 9 GC ¶ 210, 13 GC ¶ 405.

33. Hoel-Steffen Const. Co. v. U.S., note 8, supra.

34. E.g., GMC Contractors, Inc., GSBCA 3730, 75-1 BCA ¶ 11083, 17 GC ¶ 99; Davis Decorating Service, ASBCA 17342, 73-2 BCA ¶ 10107, 15 GC ¶ 378.

35. Framlau Corp., ASBCA 14479, 71-2 BCA ¶ 9082, 13 GC ¶ 492; Hardeman-Monier-Hucherson, ASBCA 11869, 67-2 BCA ¶ 6522, 11 GC ¶ 197; William Passalacqua Builders, Inc., note 12, supra; Scona, Inc., IBCA 1094-1-76, 78-1 BCA ¶ 12934, 20 GC ¶ 254; O'Bryant Plumbing Co., ASBCA 20896, 76-2 BCA ¶ 12128, 19 GC ¶ 43.

36. Note 4, supra.

37. Paccon, Inc. v. U.S., 399 F.2d 162 (Ct. Cl. 1968), 10 GC ¶ 329; note 9, supra.

38. Fischbach & Moore Intl. Corp., ASBCA 18146, 77-1 BCA ¶ 12413, 19 GC ¶ 239.

39. Raymond Constructors of Africa, Ltd. v. U.S., 411 F.2d 1227 (Ct. Cl. 1969), 11 GC ¶ 309. See also Grumman Aerospace Corp. v. U.S., 549 F.2d 767 (Ct. Cl. 1977), 19 GC ¶ 109; Dynalectron Corp. v. U.S., 518 F.2d 594 (Ct. Cl. 1975), 17 GC ¶ 307; Circle Electrical Contractors, Inc., DOTCAB 76-27, 77-1 BCA ¶ 12339, 19 GC ¶ 133.

40. FAR 52.249-10.

41. FAR 52.240-10, para. (b)(1)(iii).

42. FAR 52.249-10, para. (b)(2).

43. U.S. v. Brooks-Callaway Co., 318 U.S. 120 (1943); Blinderman Const. Co., ASBCA 20725, 77-2 BCA ¶ 12723.

44. See Crowell & Dees, "The Weather," Briefing Papers No. 65-4 (Aug. 1965), 1 BPC 129.

45. Broome Const. Co. v. U.S., 492 F.2d 829 (Ct. Cl. 1974), 16 GC ¶ 123.

46. Allied Contractors, Inc., IBCA 265, 1962 BCA ¶ 3501, 4 GC ¶ 512; Alpha Roofing & Sheet Metal Corp., GSBCA 1115, 1964 BCA ¶ 4461; Bateson-Cheves Const. Co., IBCA 52210-65, 67-2 BCA ¶ 6466.

47. William F. Klingensmith, Inc., GSBCA 3329, 73-2 BCA ¶ 10198.

48. Federal Builders, Inc., ASBCA 30164, 86-3 BCA ¶ 19235.

49. Bracewell Const. Co., GSBCA 1353, 65-1 BCA ¶ 4556.

50. Electronic & Missile Facilities, Inc., ASBCA 9031, 1964 BCA ¶ 4338, 6 GC ¶ 488.

51. Wilmington Shipyard, Inc., ENGBCA 3378, 73-2 BCA ¶ 10040, 15 GC ¶ 251; R&R Const. Co., VACAB 1101, 74-2 BCA ¶ 10857, 16 GC ¶ 420.

52. Thomas J. Doyle, ASBCA 13786, 72-2 BCA ¶ 9480.

53. K-Mor Const. Co., ASBCA 23397, 81-2 BCA ¶ 15460.

54. F.D. Rich Co., ASBCA 13234, 70-2 BCA ¶ 8599.

55. Jonathan Woodner Co., ASBCA 4113, 59-1 BCA ¶ 2120, 1 GC ¶ 293; Dillon Const., Inc., ENGBCA PCC-12, 67-2 BCA ¶ 6495; Empire Const. Co., ASBCA 27540, 84-3 BCA ¶ 17531.

56. Charles J. Cunningham, IBCA 242, 60-2 BCA ¶ 2816, 2 GC ¶ 518.

57. E.g., Santa Fe Engrs., Inc., PSBCA 902 et al., 84-2 BCA ¶ 17377; International Electronics Corp. v. U.S., 646 F.2d 496 (Ct. Cl. 1981).

58. E.g., FAR 22.101-2(b); Diversacon Industries, Inc., ENGBCA 3284 et al., 76-1 BCA ¶ 11875, 18 GC ¶ 304.

59. Allied Contractors, Inc., note 46, supra.

60. Alabama Bridge & Iron Co., ASBCA 6124, 61-1 BCA ¶ 2970, 3 GC ¶ 298(f).

61. Montgomery Ross Fisher, Inc., ASBCA 16843 et al., 73-1 BCA ¶ 9799.

62. Old Dominion Corp., ASBCA 11553, 67-1 BCA ¶ 6347, 10 GC ¶ 34.

63. Forsberg & Gregory, ASBCA 17163 et al., 76-2 BCA 12037, 18 GC ¶ 391.

64. E.g., Space Systems Lab., Inc., ASBCA 12162, 68-1 BCA ¶ 6859, 10 GC ¶ 226.

65. Bannercraft Clothing Co., ASBCA 6247, 1963 BCA ¶ 3995, 6 GC ¶ 112.

66. FAR 52.249-10, para. (b)(1)(xi).

67. Note 41, supra.

68. See, e.g., Modern Home Mfg. Corp., ASBCA 6523, 66-1 BCA ¶ 5367, 8 GC ¶ 416.

69. See generally Barba, Kozek & Benson, "Liquidated Damages," Construction Briefings No. 84-4 (Apr. 1984), 2 CBC 373.

70. FAR 52.212-5, 12.204(b).

71. FAR 12.202(a).

72. See Priebe & Sons, Inc. v. U.S., 332 U.S. 407 (1947).

73. See Urban Industries Corp., GSBCA 3050, 72-2 BCA ¶ 9604, 14 GC ¶ 421.

74. FAR 12.203(b).

75. Note 74, supra.

76. Garden State Painting Co., ASBCA 22248, 78-2 BCA ¶ 13499, 20 GC ¶ 463.

77. FAR 12.203(c), 12.202(b).

78. Steffen v. U.S., 213 F.2d 266 (6th Cir. 1954).

79. E.g., Schouten Const. Co., FAACAP 65-20, 65-1 BCA ¶ 4803, 8 GC ¶ 257. See generally Cibinic, "Liquidated Damages or Penalty: A Rose by Any Other Name," 8 Nash & Cibinic Rep. ¶ 46 (Aug. 1994).

80. Note 72, supra. See also Southwest Engrg. Co. v. U.S., 341 F.2d 998 (8th Cir. 1965), 7 GC ¶ 41; Martin Const. Co., ENGBCA 3192, 75-2 BCA ¶ 11384, 17 GC ¶ 331.

81. Arctic Seafood Corp., ASBCA 20833, 77-1 BCA ¶ 12476. See also John Cunningham Co., ASBCA 28262, 84-3 BCA ¶ 17691; W.H. Smith Hardware Co., ASBCA 34532, 89-2 BCA ¶ 21606, 31 GC ¶ 153 (Note).

82. E.g., notes 79 and 76, supra.

83. Lane Co., ASBCA 21691, 79-1 BCA ¶ 13651; J.K. Prince & Sons, ASBCA 22721, 78-2 BCA ¶ 13380. But see Madsen Const. Co., ASBCA 22945, 79-1 BCA ¶ 13586; D.L. Muns Engrg. & Bldg. Contractors, ASBCA 30104, 87-2 BCA ¶ 19709, 29 GC ¶ 143.

84. E.g., Parker-Schram, IBCA 96, 59-1 BCA ¶ 2127, 1 GC ¶ 289; Merchants Storage Co. of Va., ASBCA 19115, 75-1 BCA ¶ 11094.

85. E.g, Fred A. Arnold, ASBCA 21661 et al., 86-1 BCA ¶ 18701; Tri-State Const. Co., ASBCA 22558, 79-1 BCA ¶ 13644.

86. Triad, Inc., VABCA 1774, 89-2 BCA ¶ 21661, 31 GC ¶ 153.

87. Lane Co., note 83, supra; Martin Const. Co., note 80, supra; Minmar Builders, Inc., GSBCA 3430, 72-2 BCA ¶ 9599, 14 GC ¶ 453.

88. Thermodyne Contractors, Inc. v. General Services Admin., GSBCA 12510 (July 8, 1994), 36 GC ¶ 443. See also Skipper & Co., PSBCA 445, 79-2 BCA ¶ 13984; Roberts Const. Co., ASBCA 35570, 89-2 BCA ¶ 21870; Southland Const. Co., VABCA 2579, 89-2 BCA ¶ 21704.

89. See Lindwall Const. Co., ASBCA 23148, 79-1 BCA ¶ 13822, 21 GC ¶ 198.

90. Acme Process Eqpt. Co. v. U.S., 347 F.2d 509 (Ct. Cl. 1965); Stramese Const. Corp., VACAB 1332, 79-2 BCA ¶ 13940; David M. Cox, Inc., IBCA 1092-12-75, 76-2 BCA ¶ 12003.

91. E.g., Consolidated Const., Inc., GSBCA 8871, 88-2 BCA ¶ 20811, 30 GC ¶ 253. See also O'Bryant Plumbing Co., note 35, supra (liquidated damages reduced where delay was caused by strained relations between the contractor and Government inspector for which both parties were responsible).

92. E.g., Blackhawk Heating & Plumbing Co., GSBCA 2432, 76-1 BCA ¶ 11649 (1975), 18 GC ¶ 123; Industrial Design Labs., Inc., ASBCA 21603, 80-1 BCA ¶ 14269, 22 GC ¶ 194.

93. 41 USC § 256a; 10 USC § 2312.

94. FAR 12.202(d).

95. E.g., Pine Belt Helicopters, Inc., Comp. Gen. Dec. B-181787, 74-2 CPD ¶ 115.

96. Turner-Pilkinton Const. Co., Comp. Gen. Dec. B-191646, 78-2 CPD ¶ 22.

97. Note 94, supra.

98. 32 Comp. Gen. 67 (1952).

99. See, e.g., Scanforms, Inc., Comp. Gen. Dec. B-186144, 76-2 CPD ¶ 184.

CONSTRUCTION LABOR STANDARDS

27

A. Davis-Bacon Act
  1. Coverage
  2. Determination Of "Prevailing" Wage Rate
  3. Contractor Obligations
  4. Administration & Enforcement

B. Work Hours Act
  1. Coverage
  2. Contractor Obligations
  3. Administration & Enforcement

C. Construction In Foreign Countries

As mentioned in the first chapter of this part of the book (see Chapter 24, Section B.2.e), a contractor engaged in Government construction work is tightly controlled by federal statutes governing the treatment of workers. Extensive uniform guidance regarding labor standards in Government construction contracts is contained in the FAR.[1] This chapter discusses the two key federal labor laws—the Davis-Bacon Act and the Contract Work Hours and Safety Standards Act (referred to as the Work Hours Act for short)—that pertain to construction contracts.[2] In addition, it touches briefly on the labor requirements that pertain to construction work performed for the United States in foreign countries.

A. DAVIS-BACON ACT

The most important requirement of the Davis-Bacon Act[3] is that contractors (and subcontractors) must pay mechanics and laborers employed directly on the work site no less than minimum wages, including basic hourly rates and fringe benefits payments, as determined by the Secretary of Labor.[4] Mechanics and laborers (including apprentices and trainees) are those who work primarily with the strength and skills of their hands and bodies.[5] Clerks, bookkeepers, superintendents, guards and watchmen, technical workers, and engineers are generally *not* considered mechanics and laborers.[6]

1. Coverage

The Act applies to contracts in excess of $2,000 for the construction, alteration, or repair (including painting and decorating) of public buildings or public works *within the United States*.[7] Thus, the Act applies to domestic *construction-type* work—as distinguished from (a) manufacturing or furnishing of supplies, materials, and equipment and (b) rendering of services. Generally, the Act applies only if the contract *as a whole* is for construction, alteration, or repair; it does not apply to contracts only incidentally involving construction work (even if such work exceeds $2,000).[8] However, the Act has been held to cover construction of a building to be leased to the Government.[9]

2. Determination Of "Prevailing" Wage Rate

The minimum wages to be paid various classes of laborers and mechanics are based on the wages the Secretary of Labor determines to be the "prevailing" wages being paid to corresponding classes of laborers and mechanics employed on similar projects in the political subdivision (city, town, village, county, etc.) where the work is performed. The Secretary of Labor determines the prevailing wage rates based on data voluntarily submitted, field surveys, or formal hearings.[10] Often, wage rates bargained for by building trade unions are accepted as "prevailing." Where little or no similar work has been performed in the immediate area, the nearest employment center from which workers might be drawn—even though outside the county in which the work is to be performed—can be used.[11] Determinations of prevailing wages by the Secretary of Labor generally are not reviewable.[12]

Wage determinations set forth minimum rates to be paid by craft (painter, laborer, carpenter, etc.). Apprentices registered in Government programs may be paid lower rates.[13] A Contracting Officer's order to pay a higher wage rate to correct an erroneous wage determination rate is a compensable contract change.[14] Note that wage determinations may not prescribe *how* the work will be performed (for example, by brush painting rather than by spray painting).[15] Such instructions are the province of the contract specifications.

The most critical problem in the administration and enforcement of these wage determinations is the *classification* of workers by craft. An employer may attempt to pay workers in a *low-wage* classification (e.g., as helpers) rather than pay the higher wages specified for craftsmen. The standard for classification of workers is the "area practice."[16] Any generally accepted practice in the construction area will usually be acceptable.[17]

3. Contractor Obligations

a. Wage Schedule. The Invitation for Bids must indicate which "wage schedule" is to apply to which work. For example, it may specify a "building" wage schedule for certain work and a "heavy and highway construction" wage schedule for other work.[18]

If the contractor desires to use a craft classification not included in the wage determination, it must propose a wage rate conforming to those in the wage determination and obtain the approval of the Contracting Officer, but the final authority for wage rates is the Secretary of Labor.[19]

The minimum wage schedule is not a representation that such wages will be sufficient to attract workers to the particular job.[20] However, where the Government *mistakenly* incorporates wage rate schedules that are *lower* than the actual minimums, it *may* be required to correct the schedules and grant the contractor an adjustment in the contract price.[21] Conversely, the Government cannot obtain credit on reduction of an erroneous wage determination.[22]

The contractor is required to post the scale of wages in a prominent and easily accessible place at the work site.[23]

b. Wage Payments. The Davis-Bacon Act also requires that wages must be paid not less often than *once a week*.[24] Rebates and kickbacks cannot be taken after wages are paid, and only certain listed deductions from wage payments are permitted.[25] Nor can payment of the prescribed wage rates be avoided by special arrangements with workers—such as "subcontracting" with a partnership made up of workers—or obtaining their agreement to lower wages.[26]

The contractor must submit to the Contracting Officer payrolls and a certificate affirming payment, and must maintain payroll records for three years.[27] False payrolls may result in civil and criminal penalties.[28]

c. Fringe Benefits. The minimum wage determination may include "fringe benefits," which are contributions made—or obligations incurred—for medical or hospital care, pensions, compensation for injuries or illness resulting from occupational activity, unemployment benefits, life insurance, disability and sickness insurance, accident insurance, vacation and holiday pay, apprenticeship, or any other fringe benefit specifically enumerated in the wage determination or expressly approved by the Secretary of Labor.[29] Fringe benefits may be conferred by (1) paying amounts in cash to the laborer or mechanic, (2) irrevocable contributions to a fund, (3) incurring obligations to provide benefits, or (4) any combination of these methods.[30]

4. Administration & Enforcement

Failure by the contractor to pay required wages can result in several *sanctions*, including termination of the contract for default and assessment of excess reprocurement costs[31] (see Chapter 16) and debarment of the contractor for three years from contracting with the Government[32] (see Chapter 7, Section C.3). The Government may also withhold payment due the contractor to the extent necessary to cover any wage underpayment, and may pay these funds directly to the contractor's work force.[33] However, the funds can only be taken from payments due under the contract on which the violations occurred; they cannot be withheld from sums owed to the contractor under another contract.[34] If the withheld funds are insufficient to cover the underpayments, the workers may sue the contractor and its surety for the difference.[35]

Administration and enforcement responsibilities under the Davis-Bacon Act are divided between three Government agencies:

(a) The procuring agency's *Contracting Officers*, who are responsible for administration (inserting wage determinations in contracts, reviewing payrolls for compliance, and conducting investigations to determine compliance with labor standards provisions) and enforcement (for example, withholding contract funds for wage underpayments and initiating debarments).[36]

(b) The *Secretary of Labor*, who makes wage determinations and is responsible for assuring coordination of administration by all federal agencies.[37]

(c) The *Comptroller General*, who pays laborers and mechanics accrued wages from amounts withheld from contract payments and lists firms debarred from Government business for violating the Act.[38]

B. WORK HOURS ACT

The Contract Work Hours and Safety Standards Act[39] supplements the Davis-Bacon Act by providing that Government contractors and subcontractors must calculate the wages of every laborer and mechanic employed on a public works contract on the basis of a standard workweek of 40 hours. Work in excess of this amount is permitted, but the contractor must pay *overtime* wages of not less than one-and-one-half times the basic rate of pay.[40] These requirements are similar to the overtime provisions imposed on supply contractors by the Walsh-Healey Act[41] (see Chapter 6, Section E.1). The Work Hours Act also forbids working conditions that are unsanitary, hazardous, or dangerous to employee health or safety.[42]

1. Coverage

By its terms, the Work Hours Act applies to (1) any contract involving the employment of laborers or mechanics on a *public work* of the United States, a territory, or the District of Columbia and (2) any *other* contracts involving employment of laborers and mechanics (a) to which the United States, the District of Columbia, or any territory is a party, (b) which are made on their behalf, or (c) which are financed by loans or grants from, or insured or guaranteed by, the United States and are subject to wage standards.[43] Mere Government insurance or guarantee of the *financing* of work does not bring a contract under the coverage of the Act.

The Act excludes from coverage (a) contracts for transportation or communications, (b) contracts for the purchase of materials available in the open market, (c) contracts subject to the Walsh-Healey Act, and (d) contracts below $100,000.[44] Also, under a provision of the Work Hours Act giving the Secretary of Labor the authority to provide exemptions to the Act,[45] exemptions have been made, for example, for construction contracts involving work in foreign countries.[46]

The "laborers and mechanics" covered by the Act include apprentices, trainees, watchmen, guards, firefighters, fireguards, and workmen who perform services in connection with dredging or rock excavation in rivers or harbors (excluding seamen).[47]

2. Contractor Obligations

a. Maximum Hours & Overtime Pay. Contractors must compute the wages of laborers and mechanics on the basis of a "standard" workweek of 40 hours.[48] Compensation for hours worked in *excess* of 40 in one week must be not less than one-and-one-half times the basic rate of pay.[49] Both contractors and their subcontractors must keep and preserve employment records for three years.[50]

b. Health & Safety Standards. Working conditions must not be unsanitary, hazardous, or dangerous to employee health or safety, as determined by construction health and safety standards issued by the Secretary of Labor.[51]

3. Administration & Enforcement

Administration and enforcement of the Act is handled by Contracting Officers, the Secretary of Labor, and the Comptroller General. There are several methods by which these parties enforce the Act.

a. Maximum Hours & Overtime Pay. Contractors that fail to comply with overtime pay differentials may be liable for the amount of the wage underpayment plus liquidated damages for each calendar day on which the employee was permitted or required to work in excess of the standard workweek without payment of the overtime wages.[52] However, whenever the violations are found to be nonwillful or inadvertent—and to have occurred despite due care by the contractor—the Government may waive or adjust the liquidated damages.[53]

The Government is authorized to withhold from contract payments otherwise due the contractor sums necessary to pay laborers and mechanics the full wages due. The Comptroller General may pay the withheld sums directly to the laborers and mechanics if the contractor does not make restitution.[54] In addition, the laborers and mechanics themselves may sue the contractor, any offending subcontractors, and the contractor's sureties for overtime compensation due.[55]

A contractor and its subcontractors may also be declared ineligible to receive contract awards (for up to three years) if they are guilty of aggravated or willful violations of the Act.[56] Moreover, criminal penalties may be imposed—fines up to $1,000 and imprisonment up to six months.[57]

b. Health & Safety Standards. The Secretary of Labor is authorized to inspect workplaces, adjudicate complaints, and issue orders necessary to enforce and ensure compliance with the Act's health and safety standards.[58] If a contractor violates the standards, the contracting agency may cancel the contract, enter into other contracts to complete the project, and charge the original contractor the excess completion costs.[59] A willful or grossly negligent violation of the Act is grounds for debarment[60] and, as with intentional violations of the maximum hours provisions, may also result in a criminal fine of $1,000 and six-months' imprisonment.[61]

C. CONSTRUCTION IN FOREIGN COUNTRIES

When Government construction in a foreign country is contemplated, a technical working agreement with the foreign government involved is usually negotiated. This agreement covers all elements necessary for the construction required by the laws, regulations, and customs of the United States and the foreign government—including the applicability of labor laws to citizens of the United States, citizens of the host country, and citizens of other countries.

Contractors generally are required to comply with the applicable labor laws of the host country. However, exemption from such laws—by treaty or other appropriate means—may be sought where compliance with the laws is impractical or serves no purpose.

CONSTRUCTION LABOR STANDARDS 27-9

REFERENCES

1. E.g., FAR subpts. 22.4, 22.3.

2. See generally Speck, "Labor Standards in Government Contracts," Briefing Papers No. 67-3 (1967), 1 BPC 241.

3. Act of March 3, 1931, 46 Stat. 1491, as amended (codified at 40 USC § 276a et seq.).

4. 40 USC § 276a(a).

5. 29 CFR § 5.2(m).

6. Note 5, supra.

7. Note 4, supra.

8. Comp. Gen. Dec. B-144901, 1961 CPD ¶ 20, 40 Comp. Gen. 565, 3 GC ¶ 212; Comp. Gen. Dec. B-150905 (May 24, 1963), 5 GC ¶ 441.

9. Building & Const. Trades Dept., AFL-CIO v. Turnage, 705 F. Supp. 5 (D.D.C. 1988), 31 GC ¶ 43.

10. 29 CFR § 1.3.

11. 29 CFR § 1.7.

12. U.S. v. Binghamton Const. Co., 347 U.S. 171 (1954); Rodman Dam & Spillway, WAB 67-11 (1968), 10 GC ¶ 322; Jack Picoult, GSBCA 2923, 69-2 BCA ¶ 7845; Davho Co., GSBCA 4398-R, 78-1 BCA ¶ 13037, 20 GC ¶ 366. But see Virginia v. Marshall, 599 F.2d 588 (4th Cir. 1979), 21 GC ¶ 253.

13. See 29 CFR § 5.5(a)(4).

14. Dahlstrom & Ferrell Const. Co., ASBCA 30741, 85-3 BCA ¶ 18371, 28 GC ¶ 119 (Note).

15. 36 Comp. Gen. 806 (1957).

16. Comp. Gen. Dec. B-153051, 1964 CPD ¶ 8, 43 Comp. Gen. 623, 7 GC ¶ 50; note 15, supra.

17. Comp. Gen. Dec. B-160778 (Feb. 27, 1967); Comp. Gen. Dec. B-153051, note 16, supra.

18. Comp. Gen. Dec. B-157732 (Mar. 1, 1966), 8 GC ¶ 159.

19. 29 CFR § 5.11. See also Acme Missile & Const. Corp., ASBCA 11150, 66-2 BCA ¶ 5826; Nello L. Teer Co. v. U.S., 348 F.2d 533 (Ct. Cl. 1965), 7 GC ¶ 367.

27-10 GOVERNMENT CONTRACT GUIDEBOOK

20. U.S. v. Binghamton Const. Co., note 12, supra; Wilkinson & Jenkins Const. Co., ENGBCA 2776, 67-1 BCA ¶ 6169, 9 GC ¶ 359.

21. Comp. Gen. Dec. B-154443 (June 29, 1964), 6 GC ¶ 323; Blake Const. Co., ASBCA 41110, 58-1 BCA ¶ 1639; C&B Const. Co., ENGBCA 2698, 70-1 BCA ¶ 8089. But see Morrison-Hardeman-Perini-Leavell v. U.S., 392 F.2d 988 (Ct. Cl. 1968), 10 GC ¶ 206.

22. Burnett Const. Co. v. U.S., 413 F.2d 563 (Ct. Cl. 1969), 11 GC ¶ 306.

23. Note 4, supra.

24. Note 4, supra. See also FAR 52.222-6 ("Davis-Bacon Act" clause), para. (a).

25. 29 CFR §§ 3.5, 3.6. See Op. Sol. Labor DB-35 (May 10, 1963), 5 GC ¶ 311.

26. See note 4, supra.

27. See 29 CFR § 5.5(a)(3).

28. See, e.g., 31 USC § 3729; 18 USC § 1001. See U.S. v. Greenberg, 237 F. Supp. 439 (S.D.N.Y. 1965), 7 GC ¶ 96; Mark B. Horner, HUDBCA 79-410-D43 (Mar. 11, 1980), 22 GC ¶ 195.

29. See 29 CFR § 5.2(p).

30. See Op. Sol. Labor DB-49 (Nov. 9, 1965); Op. Sol. Labor DB-47 (Oct. 15, 1965); Op. Sol. Labor DB-46 (June 11, 1965). See also Sol. Labor Memo No. 62 (Jan. 21, 1965).

31. 40 USC § 276a-1.

32. See Ruel W. Bodily, Comp. Gen. Dec. B-196703, 80-1 CPD ¶ 328, 22 GC ¶ 254; FAR 52.222-12 ("Contract Termination–Debarment" clause).

33. 40 USC § 276a-2(a). See See 21 Comp. Gen. 197 (1941); Gevyn Const. Corp. v. U.S., 225 Ct. Cl. 580 (1980).

34. Victor Welsh, Comp. Gen. Dec. B-187142, 76-2 CPD ¶ 539, 19 GC ¶ 52.

35. 40 USC § 276a-2(b). Cf. Universities Research Assn. v. Coutin, 450 U.S. 754 (1981) (employees cannot file Davis-Bacon Act suit where contract does not contain minimum wage stipulations), 23 GC ¶ 167.

36. See note 4, supra; 29 CFR § 5.6. See also FAR 52.222-7 ("Withholding of Funds" clause).

37. See note 4, supra; 29 CFR § 5.6. See also 41 Op. Atty. Gen. 488; Comp. Gen. Dec. B-147602 (Jan. 23, 1963), 5 GC ¶ 398.

38. See 40 USC § 276a-2.

CONSTRUCTION LABOR STANDARDS 27-11

39. P.L. 87-581, 76 Stat. 357, as amended (codified at 40 USC § 327 et seq.).
40. 40 USC § 328(a).
41. See 41 USC § 35.
42. 40 USC § 333(a).
43. 40 USC § 329(a).
44. 40 USC § 329(b), (c).
45. 40 USC § 331.
46. See 29 CFR § 5.15(b).
47. FAR 22.300.
48. See FAR 52.222-4 ("Contract Work Hours and Safety Standards Act–Overtime Compensation" clause).
49. See 29 CFR § 5.5.
50. Note 42, supra.
51. 40 USC § 328(b)(2).
52. 40 USC § 330(c).
53. Note 52, supra.
54. 40 USC § 330(a).
55. 40 USC § 330(b).
56. See 29 CFR § 5.12. See also Copper Plumbing & Heating Co. v. Campbell, 290 F.2d 368 (D.C. Cir. 1961), 3 GC ¶ 250; Janik Paving & Const., Inc. v. Brock, 828 F.2d 84 (2d Cir. 1987), 30 GC ¶ 55.
57. 40 USC § 332.
58. 40 USC § 333(b).
59. Note 58, supra.
60. 40 USC § 333(d).
61. Note 57, supra.

APPENDIX

APPENDIX

STRUCTURE OF THE FAR TO THE SUBPART LEVEL

SUBCHAPTER A: GENERAL

PART 1
FEDERAL ACQUISITION REGULATIONS SYSTEM

Subparts

1.1 Purpose, Authority, Issuance
1.2 Administration
1.3 Agency Acquisition Regulations
1.4 Deviations from the FAR
1.5 Agency and Public Participation
1.6 Contracting Authority and Responsibilities
1.7 Determinations and Findings

PART 2
DEFINITIONS OF WORDS AND TERMS

Subparts

2.1 Definitions
2.2 Definitions Clause

PART 3
IMPROPER BUSINESS PRACTICES AND PERSONAL CONFLICTS OF INTEREST

Subparts

3.1 Safeguards
3.2 Contractor Gratuities to Government Personnel
3.3 Reports of Suspected Antitrust Violations
3.4 Contingent Fees
3.5 Other Improper Business Practices
3.6 Contracts With Government Employees or Organizations Owned or Controlled by Them
3.7 Voiding and Rescinding Contracts
3.8 Limitation on the Payment of Funds to Influence Federal Transactions

GOVERNMENT CONTRACT GUIDEBOOK

Part 4
Administrative Matters

Subparts
4.1 Contract Execution
4.2 Contract Distribution
4.3 [Reserved]
4.4 Safeguarding Classified Information Within Industry
4.5 [Reserved]
4.6 Contract Reporting
4.7 Contractor Records Retention
4.8 Contract Files
4.9 Information Reporting to the Internal Revenue Service

SUBCHAPTER B: ACQUISITION PLANNING

Part 5
Publicizing Contract Actions

Subparts
5.1 Dissemination of Information
5.2 Synopses of Proposed Contract Actions
5.3 Synopses of Contract Awards
5.4 Release of Information
5.5 Paid Advertisements

Part 6
Competition Requirements

Subparts
6.1 Full and Open Competition
6.2 Full and Open Competition After Exclusion of Sources
6.3 Other Than Full and Open Competition
6.4 Sealed Bidding and Competitive Proposals
6.5 Competition Advocates

Part 7
Acquisition Planning

Subparts
7.1 Acquisition Plans
7.2 Planning for the Purchase of Supplies in Economic Quantities

APPENDIX

7.3 Contractor Versus Government Performance
7.4 Equipment Lease or Purchase

PART 8
REQUIRED SOURCES OF SUPPLIES AND SERVICES

Subparts
8.1 Excess Personal Property
8.2 Jewel Bearings and Related Items
8.3 Acquisition of Utility Services
8.4 Ordering from Federal Supply Schedules
8.5 [Reserved]
8.6 Acquisition from Federal Prison Industries, Inc.
8.7 Acquisition from the Blind and Other Severely Handicapped
8.8 Acquisition of Printing and Related Supplies
8.9 [Reserved]
8.10 [Reserved]
8.11 Leasing of Motor Vehicles

PART 9
CONTRACTOR QUALIFICATIONS

Subparts
9.1 Responsible Prospective Contractors
9.2 Qualification Requirements
9.3 First Article Testing and Approval
9.4 Debarment, Suspension, and Ineligibility
9.5 Organizational and Consultant Conflicts of Interest
9.6 Contractor Team Arrangements
9.7 Defense Production Pools and Research and Development Pools

PART 10
SPECIFICATIONS, STANDARDS, AND OTHER PURCHASE DESCRIPTIONS

PART 11
ACQUISITION AND DISTRIBUTION OF COMMERCIAL PRODUCTS

GOVERNMENT CONTRACT GUIDEBOOK

Part 12
Contract Delivery Or Performance

Subparts
12.1 Delivery or Performance Schedules
12.2 Liquidated Damages
12.3 Priorities and Allocations
12.4 Variation in Quantity
12.5 Suspension of Work, Stop-Work Orders, and Government Delay of Work

SUBCHAPTER C: CONTRACTING METHODS AND CONTRACT TYPES

Part 13
Small Purchase And Other Simplified Purchase Procedures

Subparts
13.1 General
13.2 Blanket Purchase Agreements
13.3 Fast Payment Procedure
13.4 Imprest Fund
13.5 Purchase Orders

Part 14
Sealed Bidding

Subparts
14.1 Use of Sealed Bidding
14.2 Solicitation of Bids
14.3 Submission of Bids
14.4 Opening of Bids and Award of Contract
14.5 Two-Step Sealed Bidding

Part 15
Contracting By Negotiation

Subparts
15.1 General Requirements for Negotiation
15.2 [Reserved]
15.3 [Reserved]
15.4 Solicitation and Receipt of Proposals and Quotations

APPENDIX

15.5 Unsolicited Proposals
15.6 Source Selection
15.7 Make-or-Buy Programs
15.8 Price Negotiation
15.9 Profit
15.10 Preaward, Award, and Postaward Notifications, Protests, and Mistakes

PART 16
TYPES OF CONTRACTS

Subparts
16.1 Selecting Contract Types
16.2 Fixed-Price Contracts
16.3 Cost-Reimbursement Contracts
16.4 Incentive Contracts
16.5 Indefinite-Delivery Contracts
16.6 Time-and-Materials, Labor-Hour, and Letter Contracts
16.7 Agreements

PART 17
SPECIAL CONTRACTING METHODS

Subparts
17.1 Multiyear Contracting
17.2 Options
17.3 [Reserved]
17.4 Leader Company Contracting
17.5 Interagency Acquisitions Under the Economy Act
17.6 Management and Operating Contracts

PART 18
[RESERVED]

SUBCHAPTER D: SOCIOECONOMIC PROGRAMS

PART 19
SMALL BUSINESS AND SMALL DISADVANTAGED BUSINESS CONCERNS

Subparts
19.1 Size Standards
19.2 Policies

19.3 Determination of Status as a Small Business Concern
19.4 Cooperation With the Small Business Administration
19.5 Set-Asides for Small Business
19.6 Certificates of Competency and Determinations of Eligibility
19.7 Subcontracting With Small Business and Small Disadvantaged Business Concerns
19.8 Contracting With the Small Business Administration (The 8(a) Program)
19.9 Contracting Opportunities for Women-Owned Small Businesses
19.10 Small Business Competitiveness Demonstration Program

Part 20
Labor Surplus Area Concerns

Subparts
20.1 General
20.2 Set-Asides
20.3 Labor Surplus Area Subcontracting Program

Part 21
[Reserved]

Part 22
Application Of Labor Laws To Government Acquisitions

Subparts
22.1 Basic Labor Policies
22.2 Convict Labor
22.3 Contract Work Hours and Safety Standards Act
22.4 Labor Standards for Contracts Involving Construction
22.5 Open Bidding on Federal Construction Contracts— [Reserved]
22.6 Walsh-Healey Public Contracts Act
22.7 [Reserved]
22.8 Equal Employment Opportunity
22.9 Nondiscrimination Because of Age

APPENDIX

22.10 Service Contract Act of 1965, as Amended
22.11 Professional Employee Compensation
22.12 [Reserved]
22.13 Special Disabled and Vietnam Era Veterans
22.14 Employment of the Handicapped

PART 23
ENVIRONMENT, CONSERVATION, OCCUPATIONAL SAFETY, AND DRUG-FREE WORKPLACE

Subparts
23.1 Pollution Control and Clean Air and Water
23.2 Energy Conservation
23.3 Hazardous Material Identification and Material Safety Data
23.4 Use of Recovered Materials
23.5 Drug-Free Workplace
23.6 Notice of Radioactive Material

PART 24
PROTECTION OF PRIVACY AND FREEDOM OF INFORMATION

Subparts
24.1 Protection of Individual Privacy
24.2 Freedom of Information Act

PART 25
FOREIGN ACQUISITION

Subparts
25.1 Buy American Act—Supplies
25.2 Buy American Act—Construction Materials
25.3 Balance of Payments Program
25.4 Trade Agreements
25.5 Payment in Local Foreign Currency
25.6 Customs and Duties
25.7 Restrictions on Certain Foreign Purchases
25.8 International Agreements and Coordination
25.9 Additional Foreign Acquisition Clauses
25.10 Implementation of Sanctions Against Countries That Discriminate Against United States Products or Services in Government Procurement

GOVERNMENT CONTRACT GUIDEBOOK

PART 26
OTHER SOCIOECONOMIC PROGRAMS

Subparts
26.1 Indian Incentive Program

SUBCHAPTER E: GENERAL CONTRACTING REQUIREMENTS

PART 27
PATENTS, DATA, AND COPYRIGHTS

Subparts
27.1 General
27.2 Patents
27.3 Patent Rights Under Government Contracts
27.4 Rights in Data and Copyrights
27.5 [Reserved]
27.6 Foreign License and Technical Assistance Agreements

PART 28
BONDS AND INSURANCE

Subparts
28.1 Bonds
28.2 Sureties
28.3 Insurance

PART 29
TAXES

Subparts
29.1 General
29.2 Federal Excise Taxes
29.3 State and Local Taxes
29.4 Contract Clauses

PART 30
COST ACCOUNTING STANDARDS

Subparts
30.1 General
30.2 CAS Program Requirements
30.3 CAS Rules and Regulations—[Reserved]

APPENDIX

30.4 Cost Accounting Standards—[Reserved]
30.5 [Reserved]
30.6 CAS Administration

PART 31
CONTRACT COST PRINCIPLES AND PROCEDURES

Subparts
31.1 Applicability
31.2 Contracts With Commercial Organizations
31.3 Contracts With Educational Institutions
31.4 [Reserved]
31.5 [Reserved]
31.6 Contracts With State, Local, and Federally Recognized Indian Tribal Governments
31.7 Contracts With Nonprofit Organizations

PART 32
CONTRACT FINANCING

Subparts
32.1 General
32.2 [Reserved]
32.3 Loan Guarantees for Defense Production
32.4 Advance Payments
32.5 Progress Payments Based on Costs
32.6 Contract Debts
32.7 Contract Funding
32.8 Assignment of Claims
32.9 Prompt Payment

PART 33
PROTESTS, DISPUTES, AND APPEALS

Subparts
33.1 Protests
33.2 Disputes and Appeals

SUBCHAPTER F: SPECIAL CATEGORIES OF CONTRACTING

PART 34
MAJOR SYSTEM ACQUISITION

GOVERNMENT CONTRACT GUIDEBOOK

PART 35
RESEARCH AND DEVELOPMENT CONTRACTING

PART 36
CONSTRUCTION AND ARCHITECT-ENGINEER CONTRACTS

Subparts
36.1 General
36.2 Special Aspects of Contracting for Construction
36.3 Special Aspects of Sealed Bidding in Construction Contracting
36.4 Special Procedures for Negotiation of Construction Contracts
36.5 Contract Clauses
36.6 Architect-Engineer Services
36.7 Standard and Optional Forms for Contracting for Construction, Architect-Engineer Services, and Dismantling, Demolition, or Removal of Improvements

PART 37
SERVICE CONTRACTING

Subparts
37.1 Service Contracts—General
37.2 Advisory and Assistance Services
37.3 Dismantling, Demolition, or Removal of Improvements
37.4 Nonpersonal Health Care Services

PART 38
FEDERAL SUPPLY SCHEDULE CONTRACTING

Subparts
38.1 Federal Supply Schedule Program
38.2 Establishing and Administering Federal Supply Schedules

PART 39
ACQUISITION OF INFORMATION RESOURCES

APPENDIX

PART 40
[RESERVED]

PART 41
[RESERVED]

SUBCHAPTER G: CONTRACT MANAGEMENT

PART 42
CONTRACT ADMINISTRATION

Subparts
42.1 Interagency Contract Administration and Audit Services
42.2 Assignment of Contract Administration
42.3 Contract Administration Office Functions
42.4 Correspondence and Visits
42.5 Postaward Orientation
42.6 Corporate Administrative Contracting Officer
42.7 Indirect Cost Rates
42.8 Disallowance of Costs
42.9 Bankruptcy
42.10 Negotiating Advance Agreements for Independent Research and Development/Bid and Proposal Costs
42.11 Production Surveillance and Reporting
42.12 Novation and Change-of-Name Agreements
42.13 [Reserved]
42.14 Traffic and Transportation Management

PART 43
CONTRACT MODIFICATIONS

Subparts
43.1 General
43.2 Change Orders
43.3 Forms

PART 44
SUBCONTRACTING POLICIES AND PROCEDURES

Subparts
44.1 General
44.2 Consent to Subcontracts
44.3 Contractors' Purchasing Systems Reviews

GOVERNMENT CONTRACT GUIDEBOOK

PART 45
GOVERNMENT PROPERTY

Subparts
45.1 General
45.2 Competitive Advantage
45.3 Providing Government Property to Contractors
45.4 Contractor Use and Rental of Government Property
45.5 Management of Government Property in the Possession of Contractors
45.6 Reporting, Redistribution, and Disposal of Contractor Inventory

PART 46
QUALITY ASSURANCE

Subparts
46.1 General
46.2 Contract Quality Requirements
46.3 Contract Clauses
46.4 Government Contract Quality Assurance
46.5 Acceptance
46.6 Material Inspection and Receiving Reports
46.7 Warranties
46.8 Contractor Liability for Loss of or Damage to Property of the Government

PART 47
TRANSPORTATION

Subparts
47.1 General
47.2 Contracts for Transportation or for Transportation-Related Services
47.3 Transportation in Supply Contracts
47.4 Air Transportation by U.S.-Flag Carriers
47.5 Ocean Transportation by U.S.-Flag Vessels

PART 48
VALUE ENGINEERING

Subparts
48.1 Policies and Procedures
48.2 Contract Clauses

APPENDIX

Part 49
Termination Of Contracts

Subparts
49.1 General Principles
49.2 Additional Principles for Fixed-Price Contracts Terminated for Convenience
49.3 Additional Principles for Cost-Reimbursement Contracts Terminated for Convenience
49.4 Termination for Default
49.5 Contract Termination Clauses
49.6 Contract Termination Forms and Formats

Part 50
Extraordinary Contractual Actions

Subparts
50.1 General
50.2 Delegation of and Limitations on Exercise of Authority
50.3 Contract Adjustments
50.4 Residual Powers

Part 51
Use Of Government Sources By Contractors

Subparts
51.1 Contractor Use of Government Supply Sources
51.2 Contractor Use of Interagency Fleet Management System (IFMS) Vehicles

SUBCHAPTER H: CLAUSES & FORMS

Part 52
Solicitation Provisions And Contract Clauses

Subparts
52.1 Instructions for Using Provisions And Clauses
52.2 Texts of Provisions And Clauses
52.3 Provision And Clause Matrix

GOVERNMENT CONTRACT GUIDEBOOK

PART 53
FORMS

Subparts
53.1 General
53.2 Prescription of Forms
53.3 Illustrations of Forms

GLOSSARY

GLOSSARY

This Glossary is designed to serve two purposes. First, it is an abbreviations key—a tool for translating the numerous specialized abbreviations and acronyms used throughout the text and in the References sections at the end of each chapter of the book. The list focuses on "specialized" abbreviations used in writing about and citing Government contract authorities; it excludes many of the common abbreviations used in citing standard legal authorities. (Such abbreviations may generally be found in A Uniform System of Citation *published by the Harvard Law Review Association.)*

Second, the Glossary defines many of the specialized terms used in the field of Government contracts. These definitions have been included to give the reader a working familiarity with relevant terminology. In connection with this second purpose, a number of definitions have been taken verbatim from the procurement regulations. A cautionary note—because this Glossary is necessarily brief, the definitions provided are general and should not be considered exhaustive.

A-E—Architect-engineer

abstract of bids—A list of the bidders for a particular sealed bid procurement showing the significant portions of their bids

ACAB—Army Contract Adjustment Board

accelerated procedure—Procedure under the Contract Disputes Act whereby an appellant before an agency board of contract appeals can elect, for certain small claims, to have a decision issued on a claim within six months after making the election

ACO—Administrative Contracting Officer (responsible for contract administration)

ADP—Automatic data processing

advance payment—Monetary advance made by the Government to a contractor prior to, but in anticipation of, contract performance

AECBCA—Atomic Energy Commission Board of Contract Appeals

GL-1

GOVERNMENT CONTRACT GUIDEBOOK

affirmative action plan—A plan submitted with a bid, under which the bidder agrees to use its best efforts to employ certain percentages of minority workers

AGBCA—Department of Agriculture Board of Contract Appeals

allocable cost—A cost that is assignable or chargeable to one or more cost objectives in accordance with the relative benefits received or other equitable relationship

allowable cost—Any cost that can be included in prices, cost reimbursements, or settlements under the contract to which it is allocable (to be allowable, a cost must be five basic requirements: (1) the cost is "reasonable," (2) the cost is allocable to the contract, (3) the treatment of the cost is in accordance with the Cost Accounting Standards, if applicable (or otherwise conforms to generally accepted accounting principles), (4) the cost is in accordance with the terms of the contract, and (5) the allowability of the cost is subject to any specific limitations or exclusions set forth in the cost principles

appeal notice—A notice to a board of contract appeals that a Contracting Officer's final decision is being appealed

arbitration—Procedure whereby a dispute is referred to one or more impartial persons (selected by the disputing parties) for a final and binding determination

Armed Services Procurement Act—General federal statute that governs contracting by the Department of Defense and its military services

Armed Services Procurement Regulation—Set of procurement regulations that once governed procurements by military agencies and later (in 1978) became known as the Defense Acquisition Regulation

ASBCA—Armed Services Board of Contract Appeals

ASPR—Armed Services Procurement Regulation (superseded by DAR in 1978)

audit—The systematic examination of records and documents and the securing of other evidence by confirmation, physical inspection, or otherwise, for one or more of the following purposes: determining the propriety or legality of transactions; ascertaining whether all transactions have been recorded and are reflected accurately in accounts; determining the existence of recorded assets and inclusiveness of recorded liabilities; determining the accuracy of financial or statistical statements or reports and the fairness of the facts they present; determining the degree of compliance with established policies and procedures relative to financial transactions and business management; and appraising an accounting system and making recommendations concerning it

BCA—*Board of Contract Appeals Decisions* (published by Commerce Clearing House, Inc.)

bid bond—A surety bond that indemnifies the Government against a winning bidder's failure to execute the contract documents and proceed with performance (also called a bid guarantee)

bid protest—A disappointed bidder's protest against the award of a Government contract

bidders mailing list—A Government list of contractors to whom invitations for bids for particular procurements should be sent

boards of contract appeals—Judicial-type administrative boards established by the various Government procuring agencies to hear and decide Government contract disputes

BPC—BRIEFING PAPERS COLLECTION (published by Federal Publications Inc.)

BPD—BOARD OF CONTRACT APPEALS BID PROTEST DECISIONS (published by Federal Publications Inc.)

"brand name or equal"—Type of purchase description that identifies one or more commercial products by brand name or other appropriate nomenclature and sets forth the physical, functional, or other characteristics of the named product that are essential to the Government's needs

GOVERNMENT CONTRACT GUIDEBOOK

Buy American Act—Federal law that carries out the Government's preference for the use of American-made materials and the purchase of domestically-manufactured goods by requiring that acquisitions for public use be for materials, supplies, or articles substantially composed of domestic products

buy-in—Attempt to win a contract by submitting a price so low that a loss will result, with the hope of recouping the loss through change orders or follow-on contracts

CAA Council—Civilian Agency Acquisition Council

CAB—Contract Adjustment Board

cardinal change—Contract change having the effect of making the work as performed not essentially the same work as the parties bargained for when the contract was awarded, and thus constituting a breach of contract by the Government

CAS—Cost Accounting Standard

CBC—CONSTRUCTION BRIEFINGS COLLECTION (published by Federal Publications Inc.)

CBD—*Commerce Business Daily*

CCF—*Contract Cases Federal* (published by Commerce Clearing House, Inc.)

CDA—Contract Disputes Act of 1978

Certificate of Competency—Certification by the Small Business Administration that a small business has the capacity and credit to perform a particular Government contract

Certificate of Current Cost or Pricing Data—Prescribed certificate required to be executed by contractors that must submit certified cost or pricing data under the Truth in Negotiations Act

certification of claim—The requirement under the Contract Disputes Act that contract claims over $100,000 be

GLOSSARY

accompanied by a statement asserting that the claim is made in good faith, that supporting data are accurate and complete, and that the amount requested reflects the contract adjustment believed due

CFR—Code of Federal Regulations (official codification of United States administrative regulations)

change order—A written order signed by the Contracting Officer directing the contractor to make changes that the "Changes" clause of the contract authorizes the Contracting Officer to make without the consent of the contractor

Civilian Agency Acquisition Council—A group composed of members from federal civilian agencies which has joint responsibility with the Defense Acquisition Regulations Council for revision of the Federal Acquisition Regulation

claim—Under the Contract Disputes Act, a written demand or written assertion by one of the contracting parties, seeking (as a matter of right) the payment of money in a sum certain, the adjustment or interpretation of contract terms, or other relief regarding a Government contract

COC—Certificate of Competency

Commerce Business Daily—A Department of Commerce publication which is issued every business day to provide information on Government contract opportunities and awards

commercial item—An item of a type customarily used by the general public or by nongovernmental entities for purposes other than governmental purposes and defined by the Office of Federal Procurement Policy Act; a statutory preference for the acquisition of commercial items by both civilian and defense agencies was established by the Federal Acquisition Streamlining Act of 1994

Comp. Gen.—The Comptroller General of the United States or the official reports of his decisions, *Decisions of the Comptroller General of the United States* (published by the Government Printing Office)

Comp. Gen. Dec.—A specific decision of the Comptroller General

Competition in Contracting Act—Federal law (effective in 1985) designed to promote full and open competition, which brought about several significant changes in procurement practices, such as the elimination of the past bias for formal advertising of procurements in favor of negotiation as a primary procurement method

competitive negotiation—One of the two basic procurement methods, this means of contracting is used when sealed bidding cannot be employed and (1) is initiated by a request for proposals which sets out the Government's requirements and the criteria for evaluation of offers, (2) contemplates the submission of timely proposals by the maximum number of possible offerors, (3) usually provides discussion with those offerors found to be within the competitive range, and (4) concludes with the award of a contract to the one offeror whose offer (price and other factors considered) is most advantageous to the Government

Comptroller General of the United States—Government official who controls and directs the General Accounting Office

constructive acceleration—A requirement (based on the reasonable interpretation of the words, acts, or inaction of authorized Government employees) that a contractor complete its work by a date earlier than one that would reflect the time extensions to which it is entitled because of excusable delays

constructive contract change—An alteration to a contract resulting from conduct by the Government (for example, defective specifications) or its authorized employees that has the effect of requiring the contractor to perform additional work

Contract Adjustment Board—Agency board to which authority has been delegated to decide extraordinary contractual relief petitions

GLOSSARY

contract auditor—Professional accountant representing the Government who is responsible for examining the books and records of contractors

contract change—An alteration to a contract made by the Government, within the general scope of the contract, which calls for an adjustment in the contract price and/or delivery schedule

Contract Disputes Act—Comprehensive federal statute, effective since 1979, which establishes procedures for the adjudication of all Government contract disputes

contract modification—Any unilateral or bilateral written alteration in the specifications, delivery point, rate of delivery, contract period, price, quantity, or other provision of an existing contract, accomplished in accordance with a contract clause

Contract Work Hours and Safety Standards Act—Federal law governing Government construction contracts which forbids allowing any laborer or mechanic to work more than 40 hours in any week unless overtime wages of at least 1½ times the basic pay rate are paid, and which also forbids working conditions that are unsanitary, hazardous, or dangerous to employee health or safety

Contracting Officer—Employee of a Government procuring agency with authority to legally bind the Government in matters under a particular contract

contractor purchasing system review—Review of a contractor's procurement system conducted on a periodic basis to allow the Government to monitor its contractors' activities and protect Government interests

Cost Accounting Standards—The set of 19 rules on cost accounting for Government contracts promulgated by the Cost Accounting Standards Board

Cost Accounting Standards Board—Agency established by Congress in 1970 which developed the Cost Accounting Standards and implementing regulations—the Board was dissolved in 1980 but reestablished in 1988 within the Office of Federal Procurement Policy

cost principles—The regulations that establish rules and policies relating to the general treatment of costs in Government contracts, particularly the allowability of costs

cost-reimbursement contract—Basic category of Government contract in which the pricing arrangement involves the Government's payment of "allowable" costs incurred by the contractor during performance

CO—Contracting Officer of a Government procuring agency

CP&A Rep.—COSTS, PRICING & ACCOUNTING REPORT (published by Federal Publications Inc.)

CPAF contract—Cost-plus-award-fee contract

CPD—COMPTROLLER GENERAL'S PROCUREMENT DECISIONS (published by Federal Publications Inc.)

CPFF—cost-plus-fixed-fee contract

CPIF contract—cost-plus-incentive-fee contract

CPSR—Contractor purchasing system review

DAC—Defense Acquisition Circular

DAR—Defense Acquisition Regulation (superseded by the FAR)

DAR Council—Defense Acquisition Regulations Council

Davis-Bacon Act—Federal law covering Government construction contracts which requires contractors to pay mechanics and laborers employed directly at the work site no less than the prevailing wage, including basic hourly rates and fringe benefits, determined by the Secretary of Labor

DCAA—Defense Contract Audit Agency

DCAB—Department of Commerce Appeals Board

DCMC—Defense Contract Management Command

GLOSSARY

deductive change—A change to a contract resulting in a reduction in contract price because of a net reduction in the contractor's work

defective cost or pricing data—Certified contractor cost or pricing data subsequently found to have been inaccurate, incomplete, or noncurrent as of the effective date of the certificate; it entitles the Government to an adjustment of the negotiated price, including profit or fee, to exclude any significant sum by which the price was increased because of the defective data, provided that the data were relied on by the Government

Defense Acquisition Circular—Circular that is issued to revise or supplement the Department of Defense Federal Acquisition Regulation Supplement

Defense Acquisition Regulation—One of the two major sets of procurement regulations—this set governed procurements by military agencies—which were replaced by the Federal Acquisition Regulation in 1984

Defense Acquisition Regulations Council—Group composed of representatives from the military departments, the Defense Logistics Agency, and the National Aeronautics and Space Administration which has joint responsibility with the Civilian Agency Acquisition Council for revision of the Federal Acquisition Regulation

Defense Contract Audit Agency—Separate and independent entity within the Defense Department which provides contract audit functions and accounting-financial advisory services for all Defense Department components as well as for other Government agencies

Defense Contract Management Command—Component of the Defense Logistics Agency which is the largest of all Government contract administration agencies (formerly the Defense Contract Administration Service)

Defense Logistics Agency—Component organization within the Department of Defense which provides consumable supply items and logistics services common to the military services

GOVERNMENT CONTRACT GUIDEBOOK

Department of Defense—Department within the Executive Branch of Government which is responsible for the military security of the United States and which is the largest purchaser of goods and services within the Government

Department of Defense Federal Acquisition Regulation Supplement—This set of regulations supplementing the Federal Acquisition Regulation is the most comprehensive of the various Government agency supplementing regulations and governs all of the military and Defense Department agencies

descriptive data—Literature, brochures, catalogs, or other documentation describing a bidder's product

design specification—Category of specification which sets out in detail the materials used for contract work and the mode and manner in which contract work is to be performed

DFARS—Department of Defense Federal Acquisition Regulation Supplement

Disclosure Statement—A statement (typically a Form CASB-DS-1) designed to meet Cost Accounting Standards requirements on which contractors describe their contract cost accounting practices

disputes procedure—The administrative procedure within a Government procuring agency, generally prescribed by the Contract Disputes Act, for processing disputes arising under or relating to contracts; it involves a decision on the dispute by the Contracting Officer which (if unfavorable to the contractor) may be appealed to a board of contract appeals or to the United States Court of Federal Claims

DLA—Defense Logistics Agency

DOD—Department of Defense

DOEBCA—Department of Energy Board of Contract Appeals (superseded by the EBCA)

DOTBCA—Department of Transportation Board of Contract Appeals

DOTCAB—Department of Transportation Contract Appeals Board (superseded by the DOTBCA)

EAJA—Equal Access to Justice Act

EBCA—Department of Energy Board of Contract Appeals

ECR—EXTRAORDINARY CONTRACTUAL RELIEF REPORTER (published by Federal Publications Inc.)

ENGBCA—Army Corps of Engineers Board of Contract Appeals

Equal Access to Justice Act—Federal law designed to aid small businesses and individuals to recover attorney fees if they prevail in certain actions against the Government

equitable adjustment—An adjustment in the contract price (and/or schedule) which certain contract clauses prescribe to accommodate increases or decreases in the contract work under defined conditions

excess reprocurement costs—Costs that the Government is entitled to charge a defaulted contractor to cover the difference between the price of the defaulted contract and the price the Government is required to pay to the reprocurement contractor for the defaulted quantity of supplies, services, or unfinished work

excusable delay—Type of delay in contract performance which, in the absence of contractor control, fault, or negligence, will excuse delay and prevent a termination of the contract for default

expedited procedure—Procedure under the Contract Disputes Act whereby an appellant before an agency board of contract appeals can elect, for certain small claims, to have a decision issued on a claim within four months after making the election

extraordinary contractual relief—Form of relief for contractors under federal law giving the President the power to

GOVERNMENT CONTRACT GUIDEBOOK

>authorize federal agencies to enter into contracts, or amendments or modifications of contracts, without regard to other provisions of law relating to the making, performance, amendment, or modification of contracts when he believes the action will facilitate the national defense

FAACAP—Federal Aviation Administration Contract Appeals Panel

FAC—Federal Acquisition Circular

FACNET—Federal Acquisition Computer Network, which under the Federal Acquisition Streamlining Act of 1994 must be established Government-wide to permit procurement through "electronic commerce"

FAR—Federal Acquisition Regulation

Fed. Reg.—Federal Register

Federal Acquisition Circular—Document issued by the Defense Acquisition Regulations Council and the Civilian Agency Acquisition Council to amend the Federal Acquisition Regulation

Federal Acquisition Regulation—Uniform set of procurement regulations which went into effect on April 1, 1984 as the primary set of regulations governing all Government contracting

Federal Acquisition Streamlining Act—Federal law enacted in 1994 to reform Government procurement practices, most notably by establishing a "simplified acquisition threshold" of $100,000 for small purchases, establishing a statutory preference for the acquisition of commercial items, and promoting the use of electronic commerce procedures

Federal Courts Administration Act—Federal law enacted in 1992 that, among other things, clarified the jurisdiction of the United States Claims Court and renamed it the United States Court of Federal Claims

GLOSSARY

Federal Courts Improvement Act—Federal law which, in 1982, replaced the United States Court of Claims as the primary federal court involved in Government contract litigation with two courts—the United States Claims Court (a trial court) and the United States Court of Appeals for the Federal Circuit

Federal Procurement Regulations—One of the two major sets of procurement regulations—this set governed procurements by civilian agencies—which were replaced by the Federal Acquisition Regulation in 1984

Federal Property and Administrative Services Act—General federal statute that governs contracting by the civilian agencies of the Government

Federal Rules of Appellate Procedure—The procedural rules governing appeals before the U.S. Courts of Appeals, including the Court of Appeals for the Federal Circuit

Federal Rules of Civil Procedure—The procedural rules of the U.S. District Courts which have heavily influenced the development of the rules of the Court of Federal Claims and the agency boards of contract appeals

Federal Rules of Evidence—The rules of evidence applicable to trials in the U.S. District Courts which are also applied by boards of contract appeals and the Court of Federal Claims

federal specification—Type of specification issued or controlled by the General Services Administration and listed in the "Index of Federal Specifications, Standards and Commercial Item Descriptions"

FFP contract—Firm-fixed-price contract

final decision—For purposes of the Contract Disputes Act, a Contracting Officer's unilateral adjudication of a contract claim that is a prerequisite to jurisdiction over the claim by a board of contract appeals or federal court

fixed-price contract—Basic category of Government contract in which the pricing arrangement involves a ceiling beyond which the Government bears no responsibility for payment

flow-downs—Clauses from a prime contractor's Government contract that are incorporated into the contractor's subcontracts

FPD—FEDERAL COURT PROCUREMENT DECISIONS (published by Federal Publications Inc.)

FPI contract—Fixed-price-incentive contract

FPR—Federal Procurement Regulations (superseded by the FAR)

G&A expenses—General and administrative expenses

GAO—General Accounting Office of the United States

GC—THE GOVERNMENT CONTRACTOR (published by Federal Publications Inc.)

General Accounting Office—Government agency, headed by the Comptroller General of the United States, which is charged by law to settle and adjust claims by and against the Government, and which, in the Government contract area, renders advance opinions for Government disbursement officers, audits their accounts, and decides the merits of protests regarding contract awards

GFP—Government-furnished property

Government property—All property that is owned by or leased to the Government or that is acquired by the Government under the terms of a contract

Government-furnished property—Property of the Government that is made available to the contractor

grant—An agreement by the Government to provide funds for a particular purpose

GSA—General Services Administration

GSBCA—General Services Administration Board of Contract Appeals

HUDBCA—Department of Housing and Urban Development Board of Contract Appeals

GLOSSARY

IBCA—Department of the Interior Board of Contract Appeals

IFB—Invitation for bids

IG—Inspector General

invitation for bids—Solicitation packet containing all of the information required by a bidder to submit a responsive bid when the sealed bidding method of procurement is used

LBCA—Department of Labor Board of Contract Appeals

liquidated damages—Damages provided under a contract in a sum certain to be awarded to the Government if a contractor fails to perform as agreed

LSA—Labor surplus area

micro-purchase—A purchase by an executive agency of $2,500 or less, which may be made without obtaining competitive quotations if the price is reasonable

military specification—Type of specification (often referred to as "milspecs") issued by the Department of Defense for use by its activities; since 1994, the Department has emphasized the use of performance and commercial standards instead

NASA—National Aeronautics and Space Administration

NASABCA—National Aeronautics and Space Administration Board of Contract Appeals (merged with the ASBCA effective July 12, 1993)

negotiated procurement—The statutory procedure for purchasing under which (a) contractors' proposals are not publicly disclosed, (b) there is bargaining between the Government and contractors (on both price and technical requirements) after submission of proposals, and (c) an award is made to the contractor whose final proposal is most advantageous to the Government

OFCCP—Office of Federal Contract Compliance Programs

Office of Federal Procurement Policy—Government agency established as a branch of the Office of Management

GOVERNMENT CONTRACT GUIDEBOOK

and Budget to provide overall direction to the procurement process and formulate procurement policy

OFPP—Office of Federal Procurement Policy

OMB—Office of Management and Budget

P.L.—United States Public Law

payment bond—A bond required of Government construction contractors which secures their obligation to pay their laborers and materialmen

PCO—Procuring Contracting Officer (responsible for supervising contract award)

performance bond—A bond required primarily of Government construction contractors which secures their obligation to properly complete their work

performance specification—Type of specification issued or controlled by the General Services Administration and listed in the "Index of Federal Specifications, Standards and Commercial Item Descriptions"

PODBCA—Post Office Department Board of Contract Appeals (superseded by the PSBCA)

PR—Purchase request or purchase requisition

PRBs—Postretirement benefits

progress payment—Monetary payment made as work progresses under a contract on the basis of percentage of completion accomplished, or for work performed at a particular stage of completion

Prompt Payment Act—A statute requiring payment of invoices by the Government within a designated time period and subjecting the Government to interest penalties for late payments

proposal—Any offer or other submission used as a basis for pricing a contract, contract modification, or termination settlement, or for securing payments thereunder

GLOSSARY

protest—A complaint that a certain procurement action violates the applicable rules

PSBCA—Postal Service Board of Contract Appeals

purchase description—A description of the essential physical characteristics and functions required to meet the Government's minimum needs

QAR—Quality Assurance Representative

QBL—Qualified bidders list

QML—Qualified manufacturers list

QPL—Qualified products list

qualified product—An item that has been examined and tested for compliance with specification requirements and qualified for inclusion in a qualified products list

qualified products list—A list of prequalified products which are the only ones eligible for award of a particular procurement

Quality Assurance Representative—Individual responsible for assuring that quality standards are met in Government procurements

R&D—Research and development

request for proposals—Packet of information used in the competitive negotiation method of procurement to communicate Government requirements and solicit proposals

request for quotations—Packet of information used in the competitive negotiation method of procurement to communicate Government requirements and solicit indications of prices that might be expected

responsibility—The ability of a bidder to properly perform contract work

responsiveness—A bid's conformity with, and commitment to meet, the material terms of an invitation for bids

RFP—Request for proposals

RFQ—Request for quotations

RFTP—Request for technical proposals

SBA—Small Business Administration

sealed bidding—One of the two basic methods of procurement, this method involves the solicitation of bids and the award of a contract to the responsible bidder submitting the lowest responsive bid

Service Contract Act—Federal law establishing labor standards for such matters as wages and working conditions, which applies to every Government contract over $2,500 when its principal purpose is to furnish services to the Government

SF—Standard Form

simplified acquisition—An acquisition of supplies, services, or construction in the amount of $100,000 or less using streamlined procurement procedures

Small Business Act—Federal law providing preferences for small and small disadvantaged businesses in Government contracting

Small Business Administration—Government agency which administers federal laws giving small businesses preferences in Government contracts

small purchase—An acquisition of supplies, services, or construction in the amount of $25,000 or less using simplified acquisition procedures; a new "simplified acquisition" threshold (increased to $100,000) was set by the Federal Acquisition Streamlining Act of 1994

specification—A description of the technical requirements for a material, product, or service that includes the criteria for determining whether these requirements are met

standard—A document that establishes engineering and technical limitations and applications of materials, processes, methods, designs, and engineering practices

GLOSSARY

Standard Form—A set of standard provisions or terms issued for use by all Government agencies in regard to procurement matters

substantial performance—Doctrine which prohibits termination of a contract for default if a contractor's performance deviates only in minor respects from the contract's requirements

TCO—Termination Contracting Officer (responsible for the settlement of terminated contracts)

termination for convenience—Right reserved to the Government, under standard "Termination for Convenience of the Government" contract clauses, to bring an end to contracts that are made obsolete by technological and other developments or that are otherwise no longer advantageous to the Government

termination for default—Termination of a contract by the Government under the standard contract "Default" clause for a contractor's unexcused failure to perform

TINA—Truth in Negotiations Act

Truth in Negotiations Act—Federal law enacted to provide the Government with sufficient information prior to award of certain negotiated contracts to ensure that it does not pay excessive prices for its procurements, which requires contractors to submit cost or pricing data and to certify that, to the contractor's best knowledge and belief, the data submitted are accurate, complete, and current

two-step sealed bidding—Hybrid procurement method whereby, under "step one," contractors submit technical proposals (without prices) in response to Government performance specifications, and then, under "step two," each contractor whose technical proposal was acceptable submits a sealed bid in accordance with normal bidding procedures

UCC—Uniform Commercial Code

unallowable cost—Any cost which, under the provisions of any pertinent law, regulation, or contract, cannot be

GL-19

included in prices, cost reimbursements, or settlements under a Government contract to which it is allocable

Uniform Commercial Code—Uniform law governing commercial transactions, which has been adopted by all states in the United States except Louisiana, and which is sometimes used to aid in the interpretation and enforcement of Government subcontracts

United States Claims Court—Federal court which, upon dissolution of the United States Court of Claims in 1982, assumed the role of the Court of Claims' trial division and which, in 1992, was renamed the United States Court of Federal Claims

United States Court of Appeals for the Federal Circuit—Federal court which, upon dissolution of the United States Court of Claims in 1982, assumed the role of the Court of Claims' appellate division

United States Court of Claims—Until its dissolution in 1982, the federal court that resolved most Government contract disputes brought in federal court

United States Court of Federal Claims—Federal court with jurisdiction to resolve most Government contract disputes

USC—United States Code (official codification of United States laws)

VABCA—Department of Veterans Affairs Board of Contract Appeals

VACAB—Veterans Administration Contract Appeals Board (superseded by the VABCA)

VECP—Value engineering change proposal

Walsh-Healey Act—Federal law establishing labor standards covering such things as work hours, the payment of overtime, and worker health and safety, which applies to contractors having a Government contract in excess of $10,000 to manufacture or furnish materials, supplies, or equipment

SUBJECT INDEX

SUBJECT INDEX

— A —

Abbreviated proceedings
Administrative appeals (see Board of contract appeals)

Ability to perform
Certificates of Competency in small business preferences 6-4, 6-5

Accelerated appeals
Board of contract appeals, small claims procedures before 20-10

Acceleration of work
Constructive changes theory, application of 11-21, 11-22

Acceptance of supplies (see Inspection of work by Government)

Accounting
Audit rights of Government .... 5-36 to 5-40
Cost Accounting Standards (see Cost Accounting Standards (CAS))

Acknowledgment
Amendments to sealed bid 3-20, 3-21

Act of God
Excusable delay, what constitutes 12-6, 12-7, 12-9
Weather conditions (see Weather)

"Actual" and "apparent" authority to issue changes
Distinguished .... 11-7 to 11-10

Actual cost data
Equitable adjustment claims, proving 13-11, 13-12

Added work
Equitable adjustment claims, basic rules of computation 13-3, 13-4

Administrative appeals (see Board of contract appeals)

Administrative Dispute Resolution Act 18-11

Advance payments (see Payment)

Affirmative action plans
Preferential procurement treatment 6-12

Age discrimination
Preferential procurement treatment 6-12, 6-13

Agencies
Acquisition regulations (see Federal Acquisition Regulation)
Agency employees:
  Procurement activities, generally .... 2-23 to 2-24
  Procurement authority, generally .... 2-24 to 2-26
Appeals (see Board of contract appeals)
Authority to grant extraordinary contractual relief 18-12, 18-13
Department of Defense organization for procurement .... 2-13 to 2-14
Civilian agencies organization for procurement 2-14

Allocation of costs
Generally 5-7, 5-8

Allowability of costs
Principles applied to 5-5

Alternative dispute resolution 18-11

Ambiguities
Sealed bidding 3-28

Amendments
Amendments without consideration 18-14
Competitive negotiation, amendments to RFP or RFQ 4-5
Sealed bid, acknowledgment of amendments to 3-20, 3-21

American Bar Association model terms and conditions
Subcontractors, application to .... 23-11 to 23-15

Answers
Board of contract appeals proceedings 20-4, 20-5
Court of Federal Claims proceedings 21-4

Anticipated profits
Recovery of 17-2

Anticipatory breach of contract
Default termination arising from 16-10, 16-11

GOVERNMENT CONTRACT GUIDEBOOK

Anti-Kickback Enforcement Act .... 7-12 to 7-14

"Apparent" and "actual" authority to issue changes
Distinguished .... 11-7 to 11-10

Appeals
Board of contract appeals (see Board of contract appeals)
Court system (see Courts)

Approval of work (see Inspection of work by Government)

Architectural firms (see Design work)

Armed Services Board of Contract Appeals (see Department of Defense (DOD))

Asserting a "claim" .... 19-3 to 19-7

Assumption of risk
Differing site conditions, assumption of risk in (see Differing site conditions)

Attorneys
Board of contract appeals (see Board of contract appeals)
Fees:
Protests 3-38, 3-42
Recovery by small business (see Equal Access to Justice Act (EAJA))

Audits and auditing
Audit rights of Government .... 5-36 to 5-40

Award of contract
Sealed bids (see Sealed bidding)

— B —

Background or history
Construction contracts 24-2, 24-3
Disputes process 18-2, 18-3
Federal court proceedings 21-2, 21-3
Subcontract terms and conditions .... 23-2 to 23-4

Bad faith (see Ethical considerations)

Basics of Government contracts (see Contract basics)

Basics of procurement process
Generally .... 2-15 to 2-26

Basics of subcontracting (see Subcontractors and subcontracting)

Best and final offers
Competitive negotiation ... 4-15, 4-16

Bids and bidding requirements
Basic procurement process .... 2-15 to 2-26
Competitive proposal procurements (see Competitive negotiation)
Sealed bidding (see Sealed bidding)

Bilateral change orders 11-16

Board of contract appeals
Abbreviated proceedings:
Small claims procedures (see Small claims procedures, this topic)
Submission without hearing ... 20-9
Answer 20-4, 20-5
Appeal to Court of Appeals for Federal Circuit .... 21-7 to 21-9
Armed Services Board of Contract Appeals (see Department of Defense (DOD))
Attorneys
Privileged communications, claim of 20-7
Representation by 20-3, 20-4
Briefs 20-14
Choice of forum to appeal Contracting Officer's decision 19-11, 19-12
Complaint 20-4
Contractor's choice of forum to appeal to 19-11, 19-12
Court of Appeals review of decisions of 2-8, 20-15, 20-16
Decisions:
Generally .... 20-14 to 20-16
Appeal to Court of Appeals for Federal Circuit ... 21-7 to 21-9
Discovery 20-6, 20-7
Docketing of appeal notice 20-3
Forum to appeal Contracting Officer's decision, choice of 19-11, 19-12
Framework of 2-6

SI-2

10/94

SUBJECT INDEX

General Services Administration Board of Contract Appeals, protests 3-42
Generally .... 18-8, 18-9, 20-1 to 20-19
Hearings:
   Abbreviated proceedings 20-9
   Conduct of 20-13
   Generally .... 20-11 to 20-14
   Location and date 20-12, 20-13
   Posthearing briefs 20-14
   Prehearing conference 20-11, 20-12
Initial steps in appeal .... 20-2 to 20-6
Judicial review of decision of 2-8, 20-15, 20-16
Location and date of hearings 20-12, 20-13
Motions 20-8
Notice of appeal 20-2, 20-3
Pleadings 20-4
Posthearing briefs 20-14
Prehearing conference 20-11, 20-12
Reconsideration of decision 20-15
Remand of case to 21-10, 21-11
Review of decision of 2-8, 20-15, 20-16
Rule 4 File 20-5, 20-6
Small claims procedures:
   Accelerated appeals 20-10
   Expedited appeals 20-10
   Generally .... 20-9 to 20-11
Subpoenas 20-8
Time:
   Abbreviated proceedings (see Abbreviated proceedings, this topic)
   Hearings, date of 20-12, 20-13
   Notice of appeal, timing of ... 19-11, 20-2, 20-3
U.S. Court of Appeals review of decisions of 2-8, 20-15, 20-16

Bonds
Construction contracts 24-6

Borrowing to finance contract (see Payment)

Brand name or equal
Purchase descriptions 8-7, 8-8

Breach of contract
Changes, effect of (see Constructive changes)
Termination of contracts (see Default termination)

Breach of warranty
Remedies for 14-16, 14-19, 14-20

Bribery
Anti-Kickback Enforcement Act .... 7-12 to 7-14
Bribery statute 7-14
Commercial bribery (see Kickbacks)
Illegal gratuities statute ... 7-14, 7-15

Briefs
Board of contract appeals, posthearing briefs 20-14
Court of Appeals for Federal Circuit proceedings 21-9, 21-10
Court of Federal Claims proceedings 21-6

Burden of proof
Civil False Claims Act 7-3, 7-4
Equitable adjustment claims (see Equitable adjustment claims)
Excusable delay, what constitutes 12-7

Buy American Act
Requirements .... 6-17 to 6-19

Buy-ins
Sealed bidding 3-30

Byrd Amendment .... 7-16 to 7-18

— C —

Cancellation
Of contract (see Termination)
Of solicitation 4-8

"Cardinal changes" outside scope of contract, authority to order 11-9, 11-10

Certificates and certification
Claims, certification of 19-6, 19-7
Conformance of supplies 14-7
Small business preferences, Certificates of Competency 6-4, 6-5
Truth in Negotiations Act, certification of cost or pricing data .... 5-34 to 5-36

Changes or modifications
Amendments to contracts (see Amendments)

SI-3

GOVERNMENT CONTRACT GUIDEBOOK

"Changes" clauses (see Contract requirements, changes to, this topic)
Construction contracts 24-7
Constructive changes (see Constructive changes)
Contract requirements, changes to:
   Authority to issue ...... 11-7 to 11-10
   Constructive changes (see Constructive changes)
   Contractor's duty to proceed .... 11-10 to 11-12
   Equitable adjustment claims (see Equitable adjustment claims)
   Formal change orders .... 11-14 to 11-16
   Generally .... 11-17 to 11-22
   Standard "Changes" clauses ... 11-2 to 11-7
   "Value Engineering" clauses .... 11-12 to 11-14
   Sealed bids (see Sealed bidding)
   Termination for convenience (see Termination for convenience)

Civil False Claims Act
   Generally 7-3, 7-4
   "Qui tam" provisions .... 7-4 to 7-7

Civilian Agency Acquisition Council
   Description and function 2-6, 2-7

Claims
   Asserting a "claim" .... 19-3 to 19-7
   Certification of claim 19-6, 19-7
   Construction contracts, notice of claim for suspension of work 26-7, 26-8
   Contractor claims vs. Government claims 19-2, 19-3
   Defined 19-4, 19-5
   Disputes giving rise to, generally (see Disputes and remedies)
   Equitable adjustments (see Equitable adjustment claims)
   Generally .... 19-2 to 19-7
   Preexisting dispute, necessity of 19-5
   "Sum certain" requirement 19-5, 19-6

Clerical errors
   Sealed bids 3-31, 3-32

Commercial bribery
   Anti-Kickback Enforcement Act affecting .... 7-12 to 7-14

"Commitment" of funds
   Defined or construed 2-15

Compensable delays (see Delays)

Competency
   Small business preferences, Certificates of Competency required in 6-4, 6-5

Competition in Contracting Act
   Competitive negotiation 4-3
   Effect of, generally 2-16, 2-17
   Procurement protests 3-34
   Sealed bidding 3-2

Competitive advantage
   Neutralizing of (see Government property)

Competitive negotiation
   Amendments to Request for Proposals (RFP) or Quotations (RFQ) 4-5
   Best and final offers 4-15, 4-16
   Best response 4-9
   Cancellation of RFP or RFQ 4-8
   Competitive range concept, discussions relating to .... 4-10 to 4-15
   Conditions permitting use 4-3
   Cost-reimbursement contracts, types of .... 4-18 to 4-21
   Debriefing and postaward notice 4-22
   Discussions with offerors in competitive range .... 4-10 to 4-15
   Evaluation factors .... 4-6 to 4-8
   Fixed-price contracts, types of .... 4-16 to 4-18
   Generally .... 2-16, 2-17, 4-1 to 4-29
   Government property, neutralizing competitive advantage 9-5
   Late proposals, handling of 4-10
   Postaward notice and debriefing 4-22
   Preparation of proposal 4-8, 4-9
   Protests 4-25
   RFPs or RFQs:
      Amendments 4-5

SUBJECT INDEX

Cancellation 4-8
Comparison of RFP and
   RFQ 4-3, 4-4
Evaluation factors .... 4-6 to 4-8
Generally .... 4-3 to 4-8
Proposal conferences 4-5, 4-6
Soliciting offers 4-4, 4-5
Standard forms 4-4
Soliciting offers 4-4, 4-5
Submission of proposal 4-9, 4-10
Timeliness of submission of
   proposal 4-9, 4-10
Types of contracts, generally ..... 4-16 to 4-22

Competitive range concept
Application to competitive negotiation procedures .... 4-10 to 4-15

Complaints
Board of contract appeals 20-4
Court of Federal Claims 21-3

Comptroller General
Construction contracts, remission of liquidated damages 26-17
Procurement protests .... 3-36 to 3-40, 4-25

Computers and electronic equipment
FAX machines (see FAX and FAX machines)
Information rights (see Data or information rights)
Protests of procurements of 3-42
Sealed bidding procedures via FACNET 3-25

Concurrent delays (see Construction contracts)

Congress
Framework of procurement process .... 2-2 to 2-4

Consent
Subcontracts, consent by Government to .... 22-6 to 22-8

Construction contracts
Another contractor's acts causing excusable delays 26-12
Bonds 24-6
Changes or modifications 24-7

Comptroller General, remission of liquidated damages by 26-17
Concurrent delays:
   Effect of 26-8, 26-9
   Relief from liquidated
     damages 26-16, 26-17
Constructive suspensions .... 26-4 to 26-6
Contract Work Hours and Safety Standards Act (see Work Hours Act, this topic)
Cost principles applied to (see Costs)
Davis-Bacon Act:
   Administration and enforcement 27-5
   Contractor obligations .... 27-3 to 27-5
   Coverage 27-2
   "Prevailing" wage rate, determination of 27-3
   Work Hours Act (see Work Hours Act, this topic)
"Default (Fixed-Price Construction)" clause (see Excusable delays, this topic)
Default termination 24-7
Delays:
   Concurrent delays (see Concurrent delays, this topic)
   Excusable delays (see Excusable delays, this topic)
   Liquidated damages (see Liquidated damages, this topic)
   Suspension of work by Government (see "Suspension of Work" clause, this topic)
Differing site conditions (see Differing site conditions)
Enforceability of liquidated damages provisions .... 26-14 to 26-16
Enforcement of Davis-Bacon Act 27-5
Enforcement of Work Hours Act 27-7, 27-8
Excusable delays:
   Acts of another contractor 26-12
   Generally .... 26-9 to 26-12
   Labor delays 26-11
   "Liquidated Damages" clause, relief from 26-16, 26-17

SI-5

10/94

Subcontractor delays 26-11, 26-12
Weather 26-9, 26-10
Foreign countries, construction in 27-8
Fringe benefits 27-4, 27-5
Generally .... 24-1 to 24-10
Government control 24-5
Hours of labor (see Work Hours Act)
Invitation for Bids, standard form 3-3, 3-9
Labor delays as excusable 26-11
Labor standards requirements:
  Davis-Bacon Act (see Davis-Bacon Act, this topic)
  Foreign countries, construction in 27-8
  Generally .... 24-6, 24-7, 27-1 to 27-11
  Work Hours Act (see Work Hours Act, this topic)
Limitations on recovery for suspension of work .... 26-7 to 26-9
Liquidated damages:
  Enforceability .... 26-14 to 26-16
  Generally .... 26-12 to 26-17
  Relief from 26-16, 26-17
  Standard clause .... 26-12 to 26-14
Notice:
  Differing site conditions, notice to Government of 25-3, 25-4
  Suspension of work, notice of claim for 26-7, 26-8
Ordered suspensions ...... 26-2 to 26-4
Overtime (see Work Hours Act, this topic)
Overview 24-2, 24-3
Place or location:
  Subsurface or unknown conditions (see Differing site conditions)
  Work site 24-4
"Prevailing" wage rate, determination of 27-3
Recoverable costs under "Suspension of Work" clause 26-6, 26-7
Relief from liquidated damages 26-16, 26-17
Safety standards under Work Hours Act 27-7, 27-8
Salaries and wages (see Labor standards requirements, this topic)

Standard contract clauses:
  "Differing Site Conditions" 25-2, 25-3
  Generally 24-5, 24-6
  "Liquidated Damages" .... 26-12 to 26-14
  "Suspension of Work" (see "Suspension of Work" clause, this topic)
Subcontractors (see Subcontractors and subcontracting)
Substantial performance doctrine 8-13, 8-14
Subsurface or unknown conditions (see Differing site conditions)
Supply contracts compared .... 24-4 to 24-7
"Suspension of Work" clause:
  Constructive suspensions .... 26-4 to 26-6
  Generally .... 26-2 to 26-9
  Limitations on recovery .... 26-7 to 26-9
  Ordered suspensions ... 26-2 to 26-4
  Recoverable costs 26-6, 26-7
Unknown conditions (see Differing site conditions)
Wages (see Labor standards requirements, this topic)
Weather as excusable delay 26-9, 26-10
Work Hours Act:
  Administration and enforcement 27-7, 27-8
  Contractor obligations 27-7
  Coverage 27-6, 27-7
  Generally .... 27-6 to 27-8
Work site 24-5

Construction or interpretation
Bribery statute 7-14
Constructive change, contract interpretation as 11-18, 11-19
Procurement Integrity Act 7-15
Termination for convenience, "changed circumstances" rule 17-8

Constructive changes
Compensable delays .... 12-2 to 12-6
Development of doctrine 11-17
Generally .... 11-17 to 11-22
Types of .... 11-18 to 11-22

SUBJECT INDEX

Constructive suspensions of work
Construction contracts ... 26-4 to 26-6

Constructive termination for convenience .... 17-11 to 17-13

Contract Adjustment Boards
Described 18-12, 18-13
Relief, power to grant (See Extraordinary contractual relief)

Contract adjustments
Extraordinary contractual relief 18-13, 18-14

Contract basics
Changes to contract (see Changes or modifications)
Competitive negotiation (see Competitive negotiation)
Construction contracts, generally (see Construction contracts)
Costs (see Costs)
Construction contracts vs. supply contracts .... 24-4 to 24-7
Ethical matters (see Ethical considerations)
Generally .... 2-15 to 2-21
Performance (see Performance)
Preferential procurement treatment (see Socioeconomic considerations)
Sealed bids (see Sealed bidding)
Standard clauses (see Standard contract clauses)
Subcontracting basics (see Subcontractors and subcontracting)
Supply contracts, generally (see Supply contracts)

Contract clauses (see Standard contract clauses)

Contract Disputes Act, generally (see Disputes and remedies)

Contract Work Hours and Safety Standards Act (see Construction contracts)

Contracting Officers
Appeal from decision (see Board of contract appeals)
Authority of, generally 2-22
Changes in contract requirements, authority to order .... 11-7 to 11-9

Claims, procedural matters (see Claims)
Decisions:
Appeal from (see Board of contract appeals)
Content .... 19-8 to 19-10
Duty to proceed 19-11
Generally .... 19-8 to 19-11
Timing 19-10
Default termination, discretion as to 16-12
Defined 2-22
Final decisions (see Decisions, this topic)
Generally .... 2-24 to 2-26, 18-8
Notice of claim to Contracting Officer 19-3, 19-4
Value engineering proposals, authority .... 11-13 to 11-14

Contractor Purchasing System Review
Subcontractors and subcontracting 22-6

Convenience, termination for (see Termination for convenience)

Cooperation with contractor
Government's failure in 11-19, 11-20

Copyright protection
Rights of contractors and Government 10-12, 10-13

Correction of rejected work by contractor 14-10, 14-11

Corruption
Anti-Kickback Enforcement Act .... 7-12 to 7-14
Bribery statute 7-14
Byrd Amendment .... 7-16 to 7-18
Debarment of contractors for 7-20, 7-21
Enforcement .... 7-18 to 7-21
Illegal gratuities statute ... 7-14, 7-15
Procurement Integrity Act 7-15, 7-16
Suspension of contractors for 7-19, 7-20

Cost Accounting Standards (CAS)
CAS Board 5-20

SI-7

10/94

Cost Accounting Standards:
　Applicability 5-21, 5-22
　Contractor obligations 5-22, 5-23
　Disclosure statements 5-23, 5-24
　Generally .... 5-21 to 5-28
　Individual CAS .... 5-25 to 5-27
Cost Accounting Standards Board
　Cost Accounting Standards of (see Cost Accounting Standards (CAS))
　Description and history 5-20
Cost-plus-award-fee contracts 4-20, 4-21
Cost-plus-fixed-fee contracts
　Cost principles applied to, generally (see Costs)
　Described 2-20, 4-21
Cost-plus-incentive-fee contracts 4-19, 4-20
Cost-reimbursement contracts
　"Changes—Cost-Reimbursement" clause .... 11-4 to 11-7
　Competitive negotiation, types of contracts in .... 4-18 to 4-21
　Cost principles applied to (see Costs)
　Generally 2-20, 2-21
　Termination for convenience, general limitations 17-16
Costs
　Allocability 5-7, 5-8
　Allowability 5-5
　Audit rights of Government .... 5-36 to 5-40
　Cost Accounting Standards (see Cost Accounting Standards (CAS))
　Cost or pricing data (see Truth in Negotiations Act)
　Cost principles, generally .... 5-2 to 5-19
　Default terminations, excess costs of reprocurement .... 16-18 to 16-21
　Defense Contract Audit Agency, audit conducted by 2-13, 5-37
　Equitable adjustment claims, preparation costs ..... 13-14 to 13-16
　General Accounting Office, audit duties of 5-39
　Generally .... 5-1 to 5-49
　Government property (see Government property)

Inspection of work, costs of 14-8
Inspectors General, audit and investigative rights of 5-40
Reasonableness .... 5-5 to 5-7
Selected costs, treatment in regulations .... 5-8 to 5-19
Termination for convenience, contractor's recovery of, generally .... 17-13 to 17-23
Truth in Negotiations Act (see Truth in Negotiations Act)
Court of Appeals for Federal Circuit
　Appeal from decision of 21-10
　Board of contract appeals decisions, review of .... 21-7 to 21-9
　Court of Federal Claims decisions, review of 21-9
　Decision of 21-10, 21-11
　Generally .... 2-8, 21-7 to 21-11
　Procedures:
　　Decision of 21-10, 21-11
　　Filings and record 21-9, 21-10
　　Rehearing 21-11
　Questions of law and fact:
　　Review of board decisions 21-7, 21-8
　　Review of Court of Federal Claims decisions 21-9
　Rehearing, petition for 21-11
Court of Federal Claims
　Answer 21-4
　Appeal to Court of Appeals for Federal Circuit 21-9
　Complaint 21-3
　Contractor's choice of forum ... 19-11, 19-12
　Decisions:
　　Appeal to Court of Appeals for Federal Circuit 21-9
　　Generally 2-7, 21-6, 21-7
　Discovery 21-5
　Equitable adjustment claims (see Equitable adjustment claims)
　Generally .... 2-7, 18-9, 21-3 to 21-7
　Motions 21-5
　Post-trial briefs 21-6
　Pretrial orders and conferences 21-4, 21-5
　Procurement protests 3-38, 3-42

SUBJECT INDEX

Remand of case to 21-10, 21-11
Trial 21-6

Courts
Claims Court (see Court of Federal Claims)
Court of Appeals for Federal Circuit (see Court of Appeals for Federal Circuit)
Court of Claims (see Court of Federal Claims)
History of federal court proceedings .... 21-2 to 21-3
U.S. Court of Appeals, role of 2-8, 18-9
U.S. District Courts, role of 2-8, 3-41
U.S. Supreme Court (see Supreme Court of U.S.)

Criminal False Claims Act .... 7-7 to 7-9

Criminal matters
Corruption (see Corruption)
Fraud (see Fraud)

— D —

Damages
Breach of contract:
  Changes, effect of (see Constructive changes)
  Termination of contracts (see Default termination)
Government property, contractor's duty to mitigate damages 9-14, 9-15
Liquidated damages (see Liquidated damages)

Data or information rights
Actual cost data, proving equitable adjustment claims 13-11, 13-12
Cost or pricing data (see Truth in Negotiations Act)
Government data, suitability .... 9-12 to 9-14
Procurement policies, obtaining information on 2-14, 2-15
Technical data:
  DOD policy and procedures, generally ...... 10-8, 10-10 to 10-12
  Enforcement of data rights ... 10-12
  Generally .... 10-8 to 10-12
  Government policy 10-9, 10-10
  Regulations, generally ... 10-8, 10-9
  Types of Government rights ... 10-9

Davis-Bacon Act (see Construction contracts)

Debarment of contractors from Government contracting 7-20, 7-21

Debt Collection Act
Offset, Government debt collection through 15-19, 15-20

Decisions
Board of contract appeals (see Board of contract appeals)
Contracting Officer's decisions (see Contracting Officers)
Court of Appeals for Federal Circuit (see Court of Appeals for Federal Circuit)
Court of Federal Claims (see Court of Federal Claims)

Deductive change vs. partial termination 17-23, 17-24

"Default (Fixed-Price Construction)" clause (see Construction contracts)

"Default (Fixed-Price Supply and Service)" clause (see Delays)

Default termination
Anticipatory breach of contract 16-10, 16-11
Breach of contract:
  Anticipatory breach 16-10, 16-11
  Generally 16-21, 16-22
Changes to contract, refusal to proceed following 11-11, 11-12
Completion of contract, Government's discretion in ... 16-21
Construction contracts 24-7
Contesting 16-23, 16-24
Conversion to termination for convenience 17-11
Costs of reprocurement, excessiveness of .... 16-18 to 16-21
Damages for breach of contract (see Breach of contract, this topic)
Decision to terminate .... 16-11 to 16-14

SI-9

10/94

GOVERNMENT CONTRACT GUIDEBOOK

Defenses available to contractor ...... 16-14 to 16-17
Delivery, failure to make .... 16-6 to 16-8
Discretion of Contracting Officers as to 16-12
Excusable delay 16-14, 16-15
Generally .... 16-1 to 16-32
Grounds for .... 16-6 to 16-13
Improper motive or grounds for 16-12, 16-13
Liquidated damages .... 16-21 to 16-23
Mitigation of costs of reprocurement, duty as to 16-20, 16-21
Motive or grounds for, propriety of 16-12, 16-13
Notice requirements 16-13, 16-14
Performance, failure in ... 16-6 to 16-8
Progress, failure to make .... 16-8 to 16-10
Remedies available to contractor 16-24
Remedies available to Government .... 16-17 to 16-23
Reprocurement, excess costs of .... 16-18 to 16-21
Similarity of repurchase 16-19, 16-20
Standard "Default" clauses .... 16-2 to 16-6
Substantial performance doctrine precluding (see Specifications)
Waiver of due date as defense to .... 16-15 to 16-17

Defective pricing (see Truth in Negotiations Act)

Defects or deficiencies
Acceptance of work with latent defects by Government 14-13, 14-14
Constructive change theory, defective specifications giving rise to 11-20
Errors (see Mistakes or errors)
Sealed bids, defects in (see Sealed bidding)
Specifications (see Specifications)
Truth in Negotiations Act, liability for defective data 5-36

Defense Acquisition Circulars
Described 2-12

Defense Acquisition Regulations Council
Description and function 2-6, 2-7

Defense Contract Audit Agency 2-13, 5-37

Defense FAR Supplement (see Department of Defense (DOD))

Defense Logistics Agency 2-13

Delays
Compensable delays:
  Constructive suspensions, recovery for 12-4
  Standard contract clauses .... 12-2 to 12-4
  "Suspension of Work" clause (see Construction contracts)
  Types of .... 12-4 to 12-6
Construction contracts (see Construction contracts)
"Default (Fixed-price Supply and Service)" clause (see Excusable delays, this topic)
Excusable delays:
  Burden of proof 12-7
  Causes of .... 12-6 to 12-10
  Construction contracts (see Construction contracts)
  Default terminations 16-14, 16-15
  Elements of 12-7
  Standard clause 12-6, 12-7
Generally .... 12-1 to 12-12
"Government Delay of Work" clause .... 12-2 to 12-4
"Suspension of Work" clause:
  Construction contracts (see Construction contracts)
  Supply contracts (see Compensable delays, this topic)

Deleted work
Equitable adjustment claims, computation of 13-4, 13-5
Termination for convenience compared .... 17-23 to 17-24

Delivery of supplies
Default termination for failure to make .... 16-6 to 16-8

SI-10

10/94

SUBJECT INDEX

Department of Defense (DOD)
Armed Services Board of Contract Appeals:
  Framework 2-6
  Procedures of, generally (see Board of contract appeals)
Defense Acquisition Regulations Council 2-6, 2-7
Defense Contract Audit Agency 2-13, 5-37
Defense FAR Supplement:
  Deviations 2-12
  Generally 2-11, 2-12
  Revision of 2-12
  Technical data, DOD policy and procedures .... 10-8, 10-10 to 10-12
Defense Logistics Agency 2-13
Extraordinary contractual relief, authority to grant 18-12, 18-13
Purchasing offices 2-13
Specifications 8-5, 8-6
Technical data, DOD policy and procedures .... 10-8, 10-10 to 10-12

Department of Justice
Fraud and corruption statutes, enforcement of 7-19

Design work
Role of architectural firms in 24-2, 24-3
Specifications, generally 8-2, 8-3

Deviations from regulations
Allowance of 2-12
Specifications 8-8

Differing site conditions
Disclaimers by Government ... 25-11, 25-12
Disclosure, duty of Government 25-11
Duty to investigate site .... 25-9 to 25-11
Excluded conditions 25-8
Generally .... 25-1 to 25-16
Notice to Government 25-3, 25-4
Standard contract clause:
  Generally 25-2, 25-3
  "Site Investigation" clause 25-9
  Types of .... 25-4 to 25-8

Disabled persons
Prohibition against discrimination 6-12, 6-13

Disclaimers by Government
Differing site conditions 25-11, 25-12
Specifications 8-11, 8-12

Disclosure
Constructive changes doctrine, nondisclosure of vital information 11-20, 11-21
Cost Accounting Standards requirements 5-23, 5-24
Differing site conditions, Government's superior knowledge 25-11
Discovery (see Discovery)

Discovery
Board of contract appeals proceedings 20-6, 20-7
Court of Federal Claims proceedings 21-5

Discretion of Contracting Officers, generally (see Contracting Officers)

Discrimination, prohibition against (see Socioeconomic considerations)

Disputes and remedies
Alternative dispute resolution 18-11
Appeals:
  Board of contract appeals (see Board of contract appeals)
  Court system (see Courts)
Board of contract appeals, appeal to (see Board of contract appeals)
Breach of warranty, remedies for 14-16, 14-19, 14-20
Changes to contract, duty to proceed .... 11-10 to 11-12
Claim arising from dispute, procedural matters (see Claims)
Contracting Officer's role in, generally (see Contracting Officers)
Courts, review by, generally (see Courts)
Default terminations:
  Contractor, remedies available to 16-24

SI-11

10/94

Government, remedies available
to .... 16-17 to 16-23
Duty to proceed pending resolution of dispute .... 11-10 to 11-12, 19-11
Equitable adjustments (see Equitable adjustment claims)
Exclusions from disputes
process ....,.................. 18-4, 18-5
Extraordinary remedies (see Extraordinary contractual relief)
Generally .... 18-1 to 21-14
History 18-2, 18-3
Procedure, generally .... 18-1 to 18-18
Route of disputes process .... 18-7 to 18-10
Standard "Disputes" clause ...... 18-2, 18-5 to 18-7
Subcontractors and subcontracting .... 22-2 to 22-5

District Courts
Role of 2-8

Docketing
Appeal to board of contract appeals, docketing of notice of 20-3

Drugs and narcotics
Drug-free workplace requirements .... 6-19 to 6-21

— E —

Electronic equipment (see Computers and electronic equipment)

Embargoes
Excusable delay, what constitutes 12-6

Employment (see Labor headings)

Environmental protection
Requirements 6-19

Epidemics
Excusable delays, what constitutes 12-6

Equal Access to Justice Act
Small business, award of attorney fees .... 6-7 to 6-9

Equal employment opportunity
Preferential procurement treatment 6-11, 6-12

Equitable adjustment claims
Added work 13-3, 13-4
Borrowings, interest on 13-17
Burden of proof:
 Actual cost data 13-11, 13-12
 Generally .... 13-6 to 13-14
 "Jury verdict" method 13-13, 13-14
 "Total cost" method 13-12, 13-13
Claims, interest on 13-16, 13-17
Computation, basic rules of .... 13-2 to 13-6
Deleted work 13-4, 13-5
Generally .... 13-1 to 13-20
Interest, payment of...... 13-16, 13-17
Notice of claims 13-17
Overhead 13-5
Preparation costs .... 13-14 to 13-16
Profit 13-5, 13-6
Proving (see Burden of proof, this topic)

Errors (see Mistakes or errors)

Ethical considerations
Corruption (see Corruption)
Fraud (see Fraud)
Generally .... 7-2 to 7-27
Responsibility determinations ... 3-29 to 3-30

Evidence
Burden of proof (see Burden of proof)
Discovery (see Discovery)
Questions of law and fact (see Court of Appeals for Federal Circuit)

Excusable delays
Construction contracts (see Construction contracts)
Supply contracts (see Delays)

Executive Branch (see also specific departments and agencies)
Byrd Amendment's effect on lobbying of 7-16
Framework of procurement process .... 2-5 to 2-7

Executive Orders
Defined 2-5

SUBJECT INDEX

Executive privilege
Board of contract appeals
proceedings 20-7

Expedited appeals
Board of contract appeals, small
claims procedures 20-10

Expenses (see Costs)

Express warranties 14-15
to 14-20

Extraordinary contractual relief
Generally .... 18-11 to 18-15
Procedures 18-15
Subcontractors, availability
of remedy to 22-4
Types of relief available,
generally .... 18-13 to 18-15

— F —

FACNET (Federal Acquisition Computer Network)
Sealed bidding procedures 3-25

Facsimiles (see FAX and FAX machines)

"Fair compensation"
Termination for convenience
cases 17-14, 17-15

False Claims Act
Civil suits (see Civil False Claims Act)
Criminal suits .... 7-7 to 7-9

False representations (see Fraud)

False Statements Act ... 7-9 to 7-10

FAR (see Federal Acquisition Regulation (FAR))

FAX and FAX machines
Competitive negotiation, submission
of offers 4-10
Sealed bids 3-25

Federal Acquisition Circular
Revision of FAR by 2-9

Federal Acquisition Regulation (FAR)
Changes in contract requirements
(see Changes or modifications)

Competitive negotiation (see
Competitive negotiation)
Contract payments (see Payment)
Cost principles (see Costs)
Default termination (see Default termination)
Defense FAR Supplement (see
Department of Defense (DOD))
Deviations 2-12
Disputes (see Disputes and remedies)
Equitable adjustment claims (see
Equitable adjustment claims)
Function and composition of 2-7
Generally 2-8, 2-9
Government property (see Government property)
Implementation of policies,
generally .... 2-9 to 2-12
Inspection of work (see Inspection of
work by Government)
Patents as within coverage
of 10-4, 10-5
Payment, matters of (see Payment)
Preferential procurement treatment
(see Socioeconomic considerations)
Revision of FAR by Federal
Acquisition Circulars 2-9
Sealed bids (see Sealed bidding)
Specifications (see Specifications)
Subcontractors, generally (see
Subcontractors and subcontracting)
Technical data, rights to (see Data or
information rights)
Termination of contract:
Convenience, termination for (see
Termination for convenience)
Default termination (see Default termination)
Warranties (see Inspection of work
by Government)

Federal Acquisition Streamlining Act of 1994 .... 1-6, 6-2, 18-3, 18-5

Federal Circuit (see Court of Appeals for Federal Circuit)

Federal courts (see Courts)

Federal Courts Administration Act of 1992 18-3

SI-13

10/94

Federal Courts Improvement Act of 1982 18-3

Final decisions
By Contracting Officer on claim (see Contracting Officers)

Financing of contract (see Payment)

Fires
Excusable delays, what constitutes 12-6

Firm-fixed-price contract (see Fixed-price or firm-fixed-price contracts)

Fixed-price-incentive contracts
Cost principles applied to (see Costs)
Described 4-18

Fixed-price or firm-fixed-price contracts
"Changes—Fixed-Price" clause .... 11-2 to 11-4
Competitive negotiation, types of contracts in .... 4-16 to 4-18
Cost principles applied to (see Costs)
Default termination (see Default termination)
Delays:
  Compensable delays (see Delays)
  Excusable delays (see Delays)
  Generally .... 2-19 to 2-21
Government property, risks in contracts involving 9-17, 9-18
Inspection of work (see Inspection of work by Government)
Payments under (see Payments)
Termination of contract:
  Convenience, termination for (see Termination for convenience)
  Default, termination for (see Default Termination)

Floods
Excusable delays, what constitutes 12-6

Flow-down clauses (see Subcontractors and subcontracting)

Foreign countries
Construction in 27-8
Purchase descriptions 8-8

Forfeitures (see Penalties and forfeitures)

"Forgiveness"
Comptroller General 26-17

Formal change orders .... 11-14 to 11-16

Forum to appeal Contracting Officer's decision, choice of 19-11, 19-12

Fraud
Acceptance of work or supplies, postacceptance rights of Government 14-14
Civil False Claims Act (see Civil False Claims Act)
Criminal False Claims Act .... 7-7 to 7-9
Debarment of contractors for 7-20, 7-21
Enforcement of statutes .... 7-18 to 7-21
False Claims Act:
  Civil suits (see Civil False Claims Act)
  Criminal False Claims Act .... 7-7 to 7-9
False Statements Act .... 7-9 to 7-10
Generally .... 7-2 to 7-12
Mail and wire fraud 7-10
Major Fraud Act of 1988 .... 7-11, 7-12
Program Fraud Civil Remedies Act 7-10, 7-11
"Qui tam" provisions of civil False Claims Act .... 7-4 to 7-7
Suspension of contractors for fraud or corruption 7-19, 7-20
Wire and mail fraud 7-10

Fringe benefits
Construction contracts 27-4, 27-5

Furnishing property or materials
Constructive delay caused by failure in 12-5
Government-furnished property, generally (see Government property)

SI-14

10/94

SUBJECT INDEX

— G —

General Accounting Office
Audit rights of Government 5-39
Framework of procurement process .... 2-2 to 2-5

General Services Administration Board of Contract Appeals
Procurement protests 3-42

Gifts
Illegal gratuities statute prohibiting 7-14, 7-15

Good faith
Default termination, decision by Contracting Officer (see Default termination)
Termination for convenience (see Termination for convenience)

Government control
Construction contracts 24-5
Subcontracting (see Subcontractors and subcontracting)

"Government Delay of Work" clause
Compensable delays (see Delays)

Government-furnished property (see Government property)

Government property
Construction of (see Construction contracts)
Contractor's obligations .... 9-14 to 9-16
Costs, contractor's recovery of 9-16, 9-17
Data or information, suitability .... 9-12 to 9-14
Definitions 9-2, 9-3
Extension of time 9-17
Furnishing property, Government's duties as to 9-11
Generally .... 9-1 to 9-23
Government obligations .... 9-11 to 9-14
Information or data, suitability .... 9-12 to 9-14
Maintenance and repair of, contractor's duties as to .... 9-14 to 9-16
Mitigation of damages 9-14, 9-15

Neutralizing competitive advantage:
Generally .... 9-3 to 9-6
Negotiated procurements 9-5
Other costs and savings 9-5
Sealed bid procurements 9-4
Notice requirements, contractor's duties as to 9-15, 9-16
Obligations of contractor .... 9-14 to 9-16
Obligations of Government .... 9-11 to 9-14
Remedies available to contractor 9-16, 9-17
Renovation of (see Construction contracts)
Repair of, contractor's duties as to .... 9-14 to 9-16
Risk of loss .... 9-17 to 9-19
Standard contract clauses 9-5, 9-6
Suitability of .... 9-12 to 9-14
Time:
Extension of 9-17
Timely delivery, Government's duties to effect 9-11, 9-12
Title to .... 9-6 to 9-10

Government Purpose License Rights
Technical data 10-9, 10-10

Guide to use of this text .... 1-3 to 1-6

— H —

Handicapped persons
Prohibition against discrimination 6-12, 6-13

Hearings
Board of contract appeals (see Board of contract appeals)
Court of Appeals for Federal Circuit, petition for rehearing 21-11

History (see Background or history)

Hours of work (see Labor standards requirements)

SI-15

10/94

GOVERNMENT CONTRACT GUIDEBOOK

— I —

Implied warranties
Contractor's warranty of quality
of work 14-20
Specifications 8-10, 8-11

Impossibility of performance
Defective specifications 8-16, 8-17

Incentive contracts
Cost principles applied to (see Costs)
Cost-plus-incentive-fee
contracts 4-19, 4-20
Fixed-price-incentive contracts ... 4-18

Indemnification of Government
Patents 10-7

Industry specifications
Defined 8-6

"Influence peddling"
Commercial lobbyists, Byrd Amendment affecting .... 7-16 to 7-18

Information rights (see Data or information rights)

Infringement
Copyright 10-13
Patents .... 10-5 to 10-7

Inspection of site by contractor
Differing site conditions .... 25-9 to 25-11

Inspection of work by Government
Acceptance of contractor supplies:
Generally .... 14-11 to 14-15
Method of 14-12, 14-13
Postacceptance rights .... 14-13 to 14-15
Breach of warranty, remedies
for 14-16, 14-19, 14-20
Contractor inspection 14-6, 14-7
Correction by contractor 14-10, 14-11
Costs of 14-8
Delay caused by 12-5, 12-6
Express warranties .... 14-15 to 14-20
Generally .... 14-1 to 14-24
Implied warranties 14-20
Manner of 14-9
Place of 14-8
Postacceptance rights .... 14-13 to 14-15

Procedures .... 14-6 to 14-9
Rejection .... 14-9 to 14-11
Remedies for breach of warranty 14-16, 14-19, 14-20
Right of Government to
inspect .... 14-2 to 14-6
Time:
Inspection, time of 14-7, 14-8
Rejection notice, timing
of 14-9, 14-10
Warranties:
Express warranties .... 14-15 to 14-20
Implied warranties 14-20

Inspectors General
Audit and investigative
rights of 5-40
Fraud or corruption statutes ..... 7-18 to 7-21

Instructions
Sealed bid, preparation
of 3-17, 3-18

Intellectual property rights
Copyright 10-12, 10-13
Generally .... 10-1 to 10-16
Patents (see Patents)
Technical data (see Data or information rights)

Intent
Bribery and illegal gratuities
statutes, distinguished ... 7-14, 7-15
Criminal False Claims Act 7-7

Interest on money
Equitable adjustment
claims 13-16, 13-17
Late payment 15-7

Interference in progress of work
Constructive change 11-19, 11-20

Interpretation (see Construction or interpretation)

Inventory costs
Termination inventory costs,
recovery of 17-17, 17-18

Investigation of site by contractor
Differing site conditions .... 25-9 to 25-11

SI-16

10/94

SUBJECT INDEX

Invitation for Bids (see Sealed bidding)

Irregularities (see Defects or deficiencies)

— J —

Judicial Branch
Framework of procurement process 2-7, 2-8
Review by (see Courts)

"Jury verdict" method
Equitable adjustment claims, proving 13-13, 13-14

— K —

Kickbacks
Anti-Kickback Enforcement Act .... 7-12 to 7-14

Knowledge
Criminal False Claims Act 7-7
Disclosure (see Disclosure)
Notices (see Notice)
Unknown site conditions (see Differing site conditions)

— L —

Labor standards requirements
Compliance with, generally .... 6-14 to 6-16
Construction contracts (see Construction contracts)
Hours of work:
Walsh-Healey Act, compliance with .... 6-14 to 6-16
Work Hours Act, application of (see Construction contracts)

Labor strikes as excusable delay
Construction contracts 26-11
Supply contracts 12-6

Labor surplus area preferences 6-10, 6-11

Lateness or tardiness (see Time)

Latent defects
Acceptance of work with latent defects, rights of Government 14-13, 14-14

Lawyers (see Attorneys)

Legislative Branch
Framework of procurement process .... 2-2 to 2-5
General Accounting Office (see General Accounting Office)
Lobbying or "influence peddling," Byrd Amendment affecting .... 7-1 to 7-18

Licenses and licensing
Government Purpose License Rights 10-9, 10-11
Patents under research and development contracts (see Patents)

Limited Rights
Technical data 10-9, 10-11

Liquidated damages
Construction contracts (see Construction contracts)
Default termination .... 16-21 to 16-23

Loan guarantees 15-18

Lobbying or "influence peddling"
Byrd Amendment prohibiting use of federal funds for .... 7-16 to 7-18

Location (see Place or location)

Lump-sum contracts (see Fixed-price or firm-fixed-price contracts)

— M —

Mail and wire fraud 7-10

Major Fraud Act of 1988 .... 7-11, 7-12

Methods of procurement
Generally .... 2-16 to 2-19

"Micro-purchases"
Competition, exceptions to requirement of .... 2-17 to 2-19

"Minimum needs" of Government, specifications .... 8-3 to 8-5

Misrepresentations (see Fraud)

SI-17

10/94

GOVERNMENT CONTRACT GUIDEBOOK

Mistakes or errors
Bidding .... 3-31 to 3-34
Correction of rejected work by contractor 14-10, 14-11

Modifications (see Changes or modifications)

Motions
Board of contract appeals proceedings 20-8
Court of Federal Claims proceedings 21-5

— N —

Negotiation of contracts (see Competitive negotiation)

No-cost settlement
Termination for convenience cases 17-14

Noncompetitive contracts
Generally .... 2-17 to 2-19

Nondisclosure (see Disclosure)

Nondiscrimination requirements (see Socioeconomic considerations)

Notice
Asserting claim, early notice to Contracting Officer 19-3, 19-4
Board of contract appeals, notice of appeal 19-11, 20-2, 20-3
Competitive negotiation, postaward notice 4-22
Construction contracts (see Construction contracts)
Contracting Officer's decision, appeal of 19-11, 20-2, 20-3
Court of Appeals for Federal Circuit, filing notice of appeal to 21-9
Defective specifications 8-17, 8-18
Equitable adjustment claims ... 13-17
Government property, contractor's duties 9-15, 9-16
Patents, notice and assistance clause 10-7
Termination for convenience 17-9
Termination for default 16-13, 16-14

— O —

"Obligation"
Defined or construed 2-15

"Offerors," generally (see Competitive negotiation)

Office of Federal Procurement Policy
Description and function 2-6, 2-7

Offset
Contract payments, offsetting contract debts against 15-19, 15-20

Older persons
Prohibition against discrimination 6-12, 6-13

Opening of bids
Sealed bids (see Sealed bidding)

Ordered suspensions of work
Construction contracts .... 26-2 to 26-4

Overhead
Equitable adjustment claims, computation of 13-5

Overtime
Work Hours Act, application of (see Construction contracts)

Ownership (see Title)

— P —

Partial payment .... 15-3 to 15-6

Partial termination (see Termination for convenience)

Parties
Disputes, generally (see Disputes and remedies)
"Qui tam" suit, relators as parties to 7-5

Patents
Current policy of Government .. 10-3, 10-4
FAR coverage 10-4, 10-5
Generally .... 10-2 to 10-7
Indemnification of Government 10-7
Infringement .... 10-5 to 10-7

SUBJECT INDEX

License vs. title, generally 10-2, 10-3
Notice and assistance by contractor 10-7
Title vs. license, generally 10-2, 10-3

Payment
Advance payments:
  Contract financing 15-17, 15-18
  Extraordinary contractual relief 18-13
Borrowing (see Contract financing, this topic)
Contract financing:
  Advance payments 15-17, 15-18
  Change, recovery of interest on borrowings 13-17
  Generally .... 15-8 to 15-19
  Loan guarantees 15-18
  Private financing 15-18, 15-19
  Progress payments .... 15-8 to 15-17
Contract payment:
  Generally .... 15-2 to 15-8
  Partial payments .... 15-3 to 15-6
  Prompt payment .... 15-6 to 15-8
  Standard contract clauses 15-2, 15-3
Financing of contracts (see Contract financing, this topic)
Generally .... 15-1 to 15-23
Loan guarantees 15-18
Offsetting contract debts against contract payments 15-19, 15-20
Partial payments .... 15-3 to 15-6
Private financing 15-18, 15-19
Progress payments .... 15-8 to 15-17
Prompt Payment Act requirements .... 15-6 to 15-8
Setoff of contract debts against contract payments 15-19, 15-20
Standard contract clauses 15-2, 15-3
Subcontractor, Government control over payment of 22-10
Withholding payments 15-19

Penalties and forfeitures
Anti-Kickback Enforcement Act 7-14
Byrd Amendment 7-17, 7-18
Civil False Claims Act 7-4
Criminal False Claims Act 7-7

Default, termination for (see Default termination)
Interest penalties on late payments (see Payment)
Procurement Integrity Act 7-15, 7-16
Termination of contract for default (see Default termination)

Performance
Changes to contract affecting (see Changes or modifications)
Default termination for failure in .... 16-6 to 16-8
Delays (see Delays)
Equitable adjustment claims (see Equitable adjustment claims)
Excusable delays:
  Construction contracts (see Construction contracts)
  Supply contracts (see Delays)
Government property (see Government property)
Inspection by Government (see Inspection of work by Government)
Intellectual property (see Intellectual property rights)
Payment (see Payment)
Specifications (see Specifications)

Permission
Subcontracts, consent by Government to .... 22-6 to 22-8

Place or location
Board of contract appeals, location of hearings 20-12, 20-13
Construction contracts:
  Subsurface or unknown conditions (see Differing site conditions)
  Work site 24-4
Inspection of work by Government 14-8

Pleadings
Board of contract appeals proceedings 20-4
Court of Federal Claims proceedings 21-3, 21-4

Postacceptance rights of Government .... 14-13 to 14-15

Post-trial briefs (see Briefs)

SI-19

10/94

GOVERNMENT CONTRACT GUIDEBOOK

Preaward survey
Sealed bidding 3-31

Preferential procurement treatment (see Socioeconomic considerations)

Preparation costs
Equitable adjustment claims ... 13-14 to 13-16

Preparation of bid
Sealed bidding, procedures (see Sealed bidding)

President
Framework of procurement process 2-5

Presolicitation phase
Role of Government representatives in 2-23

Pretrial/prehearing orders and conferences
Board of contract appeals .... 20-11 to 20-12
Court of Federal Claims 21-4, 21-5

Price
Best and final offers .... 4-15 to 4-16
Competitive negotiation, as evaluation factor .... 4-6 to 4-8
Sealed bids (see Sealed bidding)
Truth in Negotiations Act data disclosure requirements .... 5-28 to 5-36

Private financing 15-18, 15-19

Privileged matters
Board of contract appeals, rules of discovery 20-6, 20-7

"Privity of contract" rule
Government and subcontractor, relationship between 22-2, 22-3

Probability of claim
Early notice to Contracting Officer 19-3, 19-4

Procedures
Board of contract appeals, generally (see Board of contract appeals)
Claims, procedural matters, generally (see Claims)
Court of Appeals for Federal Circuit (see Court of Appeals for Federal Circuit)
Default termination, contesting 16-23, 16-24
Disputes and remedies, generally .... 18-1 to 18-18
Extraordinary contractual relief 18-15
Formal change orders 11-16
Notices (see Notice)
"Qui tam" suits 7-6
Technical data, DOD policy and procedures regarding ...... 10-8, 10-10 to 10-12
Termination for convenience ..... 17-8 to 17-11
Termination for default .... 16-12 to 16-14

Procurement, methods of, generally .... 2-16 to 2-19

Procurement Integrity Act 7-15, 7-16

Profit
Anticipated profits, recovery of after termination 17-2, 17-22
Equitable adjustment claims, computation of 13-5, 13-6
Termination for convenience, recovery following 17-22

Program Fraud Civil Remedies Act 7-10, 7-11

Progress
Contract financing, progress payments to facilitate .... 15-8 to 15-17
Default termination for failure to make .... 16-8 to 16-10

Prompt Payment Act .... 15-6 to 15-8

Proof (see Evidence)

Proposals
Bidding requirements, generally (see Bids and bidding requirements)
Competitive proposal procurements (see Competitive negotiation)
Request for proposals (see Competitive negotiation)

SI-20

10/94

SUBJECT INDEX

Protests
Competitive negotiation 4-25
Sealed bids (see Sealed bidding)

Public corruption (see Corruption)

Public Law 85-804 (see Extraordinary contractual relief)

Purchase descriptions
Specifications 8-7, 8-8

Purchase requisition or request
Defined or construed 2-16

Purchasing offices
Generally .... 2-12 to 2-15

— Q —

Qualification as small business (see Socioeconomic considerations)

Qualified products
Specifications 8-9, 8-10

Quality assurance
Contractor's warranty of quality of work (see Inspection of work by Government)
Inspection of work (see Inspection of work by Government)
Quality Assurance Representative, authority of 2-22

Quality Assurance Representative
Authority of 2-22

Quarantine restrictions
Excusable delay, what constitutes 12-6

Questions of law and fact
Judicial review (see Court of Appeals for Federal Circuit)

"Qui tam" provisions of civil False Claims Act .... 7-4 to 7-7

Quotations
Request for Quotations (see Competitive negotiation)
Sealed bidding, formulation of price quotations 3-19, 3-20

— R —

Ratification
Acts of unauthorized Government employees 2-25, 2-26

Reasonable costs
What constitutes .... 5-5 to 5-7

Reconsideration of decision
Board of contract appeals, decision of 20-15

Regulations
Deviations from FAR 2-12
Executive Branch, rulemaking organizations of 2-6, 2-7
Federal Acquisition Regulation (see Federal Acquisition Regulation (FAR))
Generally .... 2-8 to 2-12
Revision of (see Revision of rules)
Technical data, generally 10-8, 10-9

Rehabilitation Act
Implementation of 6-12, 6-13

Rejection of work
Failure to meet specifications .... 14-9 to 14-11

Remand of case
Court of Appeals for Federal Circuit, remand ordered by 21-10, 21-11

Remedies (see Disputes and remedies)

Remission of liquidated damages
Comptroller General 26-17

Repairs
Government property, contractor's duty to repair .... 9-14 to 9-16

Reprocurement, excess costs of
Default termination ... 16-18 to 16-21

Request for Proposals or Quotations (see Competitive negotiation)

Request for Technical Proposals
Two-step sealed bidding 3-45, 3-46

"Requirement"
Defined or construed 2-15

SI-21

GOVERNMENT CONTRACT GUIDEBOOK

Research and development
Department of Defense, purchasing offices 2-13
Intellectual property, protection of (see Intellectual property rights)

Residual powers
Agencies' powers to grant relief 18-15

Responsiveness-responsibility relationship
Competitive negotiation 4-13
Sealed bidding .... 3-29 to 3-31

Revision of rules
Agencies charged with, generally 2-7
Defense FAR Supplement 2-12
Federal Acquisition Circulars, revision of FAR by 2-9

Risk
Differing site conditions, assumption of risk in (see Differing site conditions)
Government-furnished property, contract involving .... 9-17 to 9-19

Route of disputes process (see Disputes and remedies)

Rules (see Regulations)

— S —

Safety standards
Work Hours Act 27-7, 27-8

Salary
Compliance with labor standards, generally .... 6-14 to 6-16
Construction contracts (see Construction contracts)

"Schemes to defraud" 7-10

"Scope" of contract
Authority to order "cardinal changes" outside of 11-9, 11-10

Sealed bidding
Acknowledgment of amendments 3-20, 3-21
Ambiguities 3-28
Award of contract:
Generally 3-42, 3-43
Preaward survey 3-31

Buy-ins 3-30
Completeness of bid:
Preparation of bid 3-17
Responsiveness 3-28
Comptroller General, protests ... 3-36 to 3-40
Construction contracts 24-3
Defects or deficiencies:
Ambiguities 3-28
Invitation for Bids (IFB), correction of 3-11, 3-12
Minor informalities 3-26, 3-27
Mistakes in bids .... 3-31 to 3-34
Eligibility for award .... 3-25 to 3-31
FACNET bids and modifications 3-25
FAX and FAX machine bids or modifications 3-25
Federal courts, protests 3-38, 3-41
General Services Administration Board of Contract Appeals, protests 3-42
Generally .... 3-1 to 3-52
Government property, neutralizing competitive advantage 9-4
IFBs:
Generally .... 3-2 to 3-12
Two-step sealed bidding 3-46
Late opening or receipt of (see Time, this topic)
Mistakes in bids .... 3-31 to 3-34
Modification of bid:
Acknowledgment of amendments 3-20, 3-21
FACNET bids and modifications 3-25
FAX and FAX machine, use of 3-25
Telegraphic bids 3-24
Opening of bids:
Early or late openings 3-22, 3-23
Generally .... 3-21 to 3-25
Initial handling 3-21, 3-22
Late bids 3-23, 3-24
Procedures 3-22
Telegraphic bids and modifications 3-24
Preaward survey 3-31
Preparation of bid:
Acknowledgment of amendments 3-20, 3-21

SUBJECT INDEX

Completeness 3-17
Generally .... 3-16 to 3-21
Instructions 3-17, 3-18
Price quotations, formulation
   of 3-19, 3-20
Price:
  Definiteness 3-28
  Mistakes in .... 3-31 to 3-34
  Quotations, formulation
   of 3-19, 3-20
Protests:
  Comptroller General 3-36
   to 3-38
  Contracting agency 3-35, 3-36
  Federal courts 3-38, 3-41
  General Services Administration
   Board of Contract Appeals ... 3-42
  Generally .... 3-35 to 3-42
Rejection of all bids 3-44, 3-45
Responsibility of bidders 3-29
  to 3-31
Responsiveness of bids .... 3-26 to 3-28
Soliciting bids .... 3-13 to 3-16
Special requirements 3-30, 3-31
Telegraphic bids and modifica-
  tions 3-24
Time:
  Early or late bid openings 3-22,
   3-23
  Late bids 3-23, 3-24
Two-step sealed bidding ... 3-45, 3-46
Verification of bid, duty to
  pursue .... 3-32 to 3-34

Selected costs
Treatment under FAR ..... 5-8 to 5-19

Service Contract Act 6-16

Service contracts (see Supply contracts)

Services as Government-furnished property 9-11

Set-asides (see Socioeconomic considerations)

Setoff
Contract payments, setoff of
  contract debts against 15-19,
  15-20

Settlement
Contracting Officers, authority
  regarding disputes 18-8

Termination for convenience,
  settlement proposals 17-13
  to 17-16

Shortage of labor as excusable delay
Construction contract provi-
  sions 26-11

Site (see Place or location)

Small business preferences
Certificate of Competency 6-4, 6-5
Contract set-asides 6-3
Equal Access to Justice Act 6-7
  to 6-9
Generally .... 6-2 to 6-9
Qualification 6-3
Subcontracting .... 6-5 to 6-7
Women-owned small business
  preferences 6-9, 6-10

Small claims procedures (see Board of contract appeals)

Small purchases
Competitive bidding, exceptions
  to requirement of .... 2-17 to 2-19

Socioeconomic considerations
Affirmative action plans 6-12
Buy American Act require-
  ments .... 6-17 to 6-19
Drug-free workplace require-
  ments .... 6-19 to 6-21
Environmental protection
  requirements 6-19
Equal employment opportu-
  nity 6-11, 6-12
Generally .... 6-1 to 6-28
Labor standards requirements ... 6-14
  to 6-16
Labor surplus area prefer-
  ences 6-10, 6-11
Nondiscrimination requirements:
  Administration and enforce-
   ment 6-13, 6-14
  Equal employment opportu-
   nity 6-11, 6-12
  Miscellaneous requirements ... 6-12
   to 6-13
Qualification for preferential
  treatment:
  Labor surplus area prefer-
   ences 6-10

GOVERNMENT CONTRACT GUIDEBOOK

Small business preference 6-3
Service Contract Act, compliance
  with 6-16
Set-asides:
  Labor surplus area prefer-
    ences 6-10, 6-11
  Small business preferences 6-3, 6-4
  Small business preferences (see
    Small business preferences)
Subcontracting:
  Generally 22-9, 22-10
  Labor surplus area prefer-
    ences 6-11
  Small business preferences .... 6-5 to 6-7
Walsh-Healey Act, compliance
  with .... 6-14 to 6-16
Women-owned small business
  preferences 6-9, 6-10

Solicitation
Advertising requirements,
  generally 2-21
Competitive negotiation,
  soliciting offers 4-4, 4-5
Role of Government represen-
  tatives in 2-23
Sealed bids .... 3-13 to 3-16

Sources
Solicitation of 2-21

Sovereign act of Government
Excusable delay, what consti-
  tutes 12-8

Specifications
Brand name or equal, purchase
  descriptions 8-7, 8-8
Combination of design and per-
  formance specifications 8-2
Compliance with specifica-
  tions 8-12, 8-13
Construction contracts, application
  of substantial performance
  doctrine 8-13, 8-14
Contractor compliance with
  specifications 8-12, 8-13
Default termination for failure
  to comply with 16-8
Defective specifications:
  Constructive changes theory,
    application of 11-20

Constructive delay caused
  by 12-5
Generally .... 8-15 to 8-18
Impossibility of perfor-
  mance 8-16, 8-17
Notice of 8-17, 8-18
Right to stop work 8-18
Defined 8-5, 8-6
Design specifications 8-2, 8-3
Deviations 8-8
Disclaimers 8-11, 8-12
Federal specifications,
  defined 8-5
Foreign purchase descriptions 8-8
Generally .... 8-1 to 8-23
Government implied warranty
  of 8-10, 8-11
Impossibility of performance 8-16, 8-17
Industry specifications, defined ... 8-6
Inspection of work (see Inspection of
  work by Government)
Invitation for Bids (see Sealed
  bidding)
Military specifications, defined 8-5, 8-6
Minimum compliance with 8-12, 8-13
"Minimum needs" of Govern-
  ment .... 8-3 to 8-5
Notice of defective specifica-
  tions 8-17, 8-18
Performance specifications 8-2, 8-3
Purchase descriptions 8-7, 8-8
Qualified products 8-9, 8-10
Right to stop work for defective
  specifications 8-18
Service contracts, application
  of substantial performance
  doctrine to 8-14, 8-15
Standards, defined 8-6, 8-7
Strict compliance with 8-12
Substantial performance
  doctrine:
  Construction contracts 8-13, 8-14
  Service contracts 8-14, 8-15
  Supply contracts 8-14
Supply contracts, application
  of substantial performance
  doctrine to 8-14

SI-24

SUBJECT INDEX

Waiver 8-8
Warranty of .... 8-10 to 8-12

Standard contract clauses
Changes .... 11-2 to 11-7
Compensable delays .... 12-2 to 12-4
Construction contracts:
    Differing site conditions 25-2, 25-3, 25-9
    Generally 24-5, 24-6
    Liquidated damages .... 26-12 to 26-14
Contract payments 15-2, 15-3
Default termination clauses ...... 16-2 to 16-6
Differing site conditions (see Differing site conditions)
"Disputes" .... 18-2, 18-5 to 18-7
Excusable delays 12-6, 12-7
Express warranties .... 14-16 to 14-19
Government property 9-5, 9-6
Inspection rights .... 14-2 to 14-6
Progress payments .... 15-9 to 15-15
Subcontractors and subcontracting:
    Flow-down clauses .... 23-4 to 23-11
    Generally 23-3, 23-4
Termination for convenience ..... 17-2 to 17-7
Termination for default .... 16-2 to 16-6

Statutes (see specific statutes by name)

Strikes (see Labor strikes)

Subcontractors and subcontracting
Background .... 23-2 to 23-4
Basics of subcontracting:
    Disputes and remedies .... 22-2 to 22-5
    Generally .... 22-1 to 22-12
    Nature of 22-2
Conditions (see Terms and conditions, this topic)
Consent by Government to subcontracts .... 22-6 to 22-8
Construction contracts:
    Excusable delays caused by subcontractor 26-11, 26-12
    Role in, generally 24-3
Contractor Purchasing System Review 22-6

Davis-Bacon Act (see Construction contracts)
Definitions 22-2
Excusable delays caused by subcontractor 12-9
Flow-down clauses:
    Defined 22-5
    Standard clauses and variations .... 23-4 to 23-11
Generally .... 22-1 to 22-12
Government, subcontractor vs. 22-3, 22-4
Government control:
    Consent to subcontracts .... 22-6 to 22-8
    Contractor Purchasing System Review 22-6
    Flow-down clauses (see Flow-down clauses, this topic)
    Generally .... 22-6 to 22-10
    Payment 22-10
    Preferential procurement treatment (see Socioeconomic considerations)
History .... 23-2 to 23-4
Labor standards (see Construction contracts)
Model contract terms and conditions .... 23-11 to 23-15
Nature of 22-2
Payment 22-10
Preferential procurement treatment (see Socioeconomic considerations)
Prime contractor, subcontractor vs. 22-5
"Privity of contract" rule ... 22-2, 22-3
Special groups, policies favoring (see Socioeconomic considerations)
Standard Government contract clauses:
    Flow-down clauses .... 23-4 to 23-11
    Generally 23-3, 23-4
Termination for convenience, recovery of subcontractor's costs 17-21, 17-22
Terms and conditions:
    American Bar Association model subcontract terms and conditions .... 23-11 to 23-15
    Background .... 23-2 to 23-4

GOVERNMENT CONTRACT GUIDEBOOK

Flow-down clauses (see Flow-down clauses, this topic)
Generally .... 23-1 to 23-15
Uniform Commercial Code, effect of 23-2, 32-3

Subpoenas
Board of contract appeals 20-8
Inspector General authority 5-40, 7-19

Substandard working conditions
Walsh-Healey Act, compliance with .... 6-14 to 6-16

Substantial evidence test
Court of Appeals for Federal Circuit, application of 21-8, 21-9

Substantial performance doctrine
Termination by Government, defense to (see Specifications)

Subsurface or unknown conditions (see Differing site conditions)

"Sum certain" requirement
Claims 19-5, 19-6

Supply contracts
Basics of (see Contract basics)
Construction contracts compared .... 24-4 to 24-7
Delays (see Delays)
Disputes (see Disputes and remedies)
Performance (see Performance)
Substantial performance doctrine 8-14
Termination for convenience (see Termination for convenience)
Termination for default (see Default Termination)

Supreme Court of U.S.
Court of Appeals for Federal Circuit, appeal from 21-10
Role of 2-8, 18-9

Surveys
Sealed bidding, preaward survey 3-31

Suspension
Fraud or corruption, suspension of contractor for 7-19, 7-20

Progress payments, suspension or reduction of 15-16, 15-17

Suspension of work
Construction contracts (see Construction contracts)
Supply contracts (see Delays)

— T —

Tardiness (see Time)

"Target fee"
Defined 4-19, 4-20

"Team" of procurement officers
What constitutes .... 2-21 to 2-23

Technical data (see Data or information rights)

"Technical leveling" or "technical transfusion"
Prohibition against 4-14, 4-15

Telecommunications
Procurement of equipment (see Computers and electronic equipment)
Sealed bids and modifications ... 3-24

Termination
Convenience termination for (see Termination for convenience)
Default termination (see Default termination)
Substantial performance doctrine, effect of (see Specifications)
Termination Contracting Officer, defined 2-22

Termination for convenience
Abuse by Government 17-7, 17-8
Anticipated profits, recovery of 17-2
Bad faith in Government's exercise of 17-7, 17-8
Cancellation of contract, award, or work, effect of ...... 17-11 to 17-13
"Changed circumstances" rule ... 17-8
Constructive termination .... 17-11 to 17-13
Contractor recovery:
Generally .... 17-13 to 17-23
Partial termination 17-24, 17-25
Contractor's obligations 17-10, 17-11

SI-26

10/94

SUBJECT INDEX

Conversion of improper default termination 17-11
Deductive change vs. partial termination 17-23, 17-24
"Fair compensation" rule 17-14, 17-15
Generally .... 17-1 to 17-31
Government's obligations 17-9, 17-10
Initial costs, recovery of 17-17
Loss adjustments 17-22, 17-23
No-cost settlement 17-14
Notice requirement 17-9
Partial termination:
   Contractor recovery 17-24, 17-25
   Deductive change compared 17-23, 17-24
   Generally .... 17-23 to 17-25
Post-termination costs, recovery of 17-18, 17-19
Post-termination duties 17-9, 17-10
Precontract costs, recovery of .. 17-17
Procedures .... 17-8 to 17-11
Profit, recovery of 17-22
Recovery by contractor, generally .... 17-13 to 17-23
Right of Government to effect .... 17-2 to 17-8
Scope of right 17-7, 17-8
Settlement expenses, recovery of .... 17-19 to 17-21
Settlement principles and limitations .... 17-14 to 17-16
Settlement proposals 17-13, 17-14
Special costs .... 17-16 to 17-19
Standard contract clause .... 17-3 to 17-7
Subcontractor costs, recovery of 17-21, 17-22
Termination inventory costs, recovery of 17-17, 17-18

Termination for default (see Default Termination)

Time
Audit rights of Government 5-36
Board of contract appeals proceedings (see Board of contract appeals)
Change orders 11-16
Claim, early notice of claim to Contracting Officer 19-3, 19-4
Competitive negotiation, timeliness of submission of proposal 4-9, 4-10
Contracting Officer's decision, appeal from (see Board of contract appeals)
Default termination (see Default termination)
Delays (see Delays)
Government-furnished property (see Government property)
Hours of work (see Labor standards requirements)
Inspection of work (see Inspection of work by Government)
Notices, time for filing, generally (see Notice)
Overtime, application of Work Hours Act (see Construction contracts)
Payment, effect of Prompt Payment Act .... 15-6 to 15-8
Sealed bids, early or late opening or receipt of (see Sealed bidding)
Work Hours Act (see Construction contracts)

Title
Government property, title to .... 9-6 to 9-10
Patent developed under research and development contract (see Patents)
"Progress Payments" clause provisions 15-16

"Total cost" method
Equitable adjustment claims, proving 13-12, 13-13

Trial
Court of Federal Claims 21-6

Truth in Negotiations Act
Applicability 5-28, 5-29
Certification of data .... 5-34 to 5-36
"Cost or pricing data," defined 5-31, 5-32
Defective data, liability for 5-36
Exemptions and waiver 5-29, 5-30
Generally .... 5-28 to 5-36
Submission of data .... 5-32 to 5-34

GOVERNMENT CONTRACT GUIDEBOOK

Two-step sealed bidding 3-45, 3-46

Types of contracts .... 2-19 to 2-21

— U —

Underemployment
Implementation of labor surplus area preferences 6-10, 6-11

Underground or subsurface conditions (see Differing site conditions)

Unemployment
Implementation of labor surplus area preferences 6-10, 6-11

Uniform Commercial Code
Application to subcontracts 23-2, 23-3

Unilateral change orders 11-16

Unknown conditions (see Differing site conditions)

Unlimited Rights
Technical data 10-9, 10-11

U.S. courts (see Courts)

— V —

Value engineering
Contracting Officer authority ... 11-13 to 11-14
Types of savings .... 11-12 to 11-13
Value engineering change proposals .... 11-12 to 11-13

— W —

Wages
Compliance with labor standards, generally .... 6-14 to 6-16
Construction contracts (see Construction contracts)

Waiver
Competition, exceptions to requirements for .... 2-17 to 2-19
Cost Accounting Standards 5-21
Default terminations, waiver of due date as defense to .... 16-15 to 16-17
Specifications 8-8
Truth in Negotiations Act 5-29, 5-30

Walsh-Healey Act
Compliance with .... 6-14 to 6-16

Warranties
Contractor's warranty of quality of work (see Inspection of work by Government)
Implied warranties (see Implied warranties)
Specifications, Government warranty of .... 8-10 to 8-12

Weather as excusable delay
Construction contracts 26-9, 26-10
Supply contracts 12-9

"Weighted guidelines method"
Defined 4-16, 4-17

"Whistleblower" protection 7-11

Wire and mail fraud 7-10

Withholding payments 15-19

Women-owned small business preferences 6-9, 6-10

Work Hours Act (see Construction contracts)

Writing requirements
Generally 2-25
Notice requirements (see Notice)

1999 Supplement

GOVERNMENT CONTRACT GUIDEBOOK

Limited Softcover Version

Editor:
Herman D. Levy, Esquire

Federal Publications—A West Group Company
Copyright © 1999

★

...about the 1999 Supplement

This *1999 Supplement* (blue pages) updates the GOVERNMENT CONTRACT GUIDEBOOK (white pages) with discussions of new decisions, new laws, new regulations, and other developments that have occurred since the GUIDEBOOK's initial publication...up through the end of June 1999. The *Supplement* assumes that the user is familiar with the basic contents of the GUIDEBOOK.

Materials in the *Supplement* are keyed to the GUIDEBOOK's organizational scheme, arranged chapter-by-chapter. In the *Supplement*, new material for each chapter appears under pertinent chapter heads and subheads (including ones labeled *"New Section"* that were added to the GUIDEBOOK's structure). The new material under a chapter head or subhead can consist of (a) text in large type, (b) ANNOTATIONS—numbered items in small type presented under any of three categories [■ *Legislation & Regulations*, ■ *Cases & Decisions*, ■ *Miscellaneous*], or (c) both text and ANNOTATIONS.

Particularly helpful in using the *Supplement* are the complete listings of chapter heads and subheads given at the beginning of each *Supplement* chapter. Starred entries in these listings indicate heads and subheads for which there are *Supplement* materials, and page numbers after the starred entries show the *Supplement* page on which those materials begin. Use these listings of chapter contents to quickly find where new developments have occurred.

★

ABOUT THIS BOOK

1

1999 Supplement

> There are no materials in the *1999 Supplement* for Chapter 1 of the GOVERNMENT CONTRACT GUIDEBOOK since this chapter contains only introductory material. The chapter serves the basic purpose of explaining how the GUIDEBOOK is organized and how the material in it has been presented.

THE SETTING

2

1999 Supplement

Chapter Introduction

A. Institutional Framework
   1. Legislative Branch
      a. Congress
      b. General Accounting Office
   2. Executive Branch
      a. President
      b. Executive Departments & Agencies
      c. Rulemaking Organizations
   3. Judicial Branch
B. Regulations
   ★ 1. Federal Acquisition Regulation / 2-2
   2. Agency Acquisition Regulations
   3. Deviations
C. Purchasing Offices
   1. Department Of Defense
   2. Civilian Agencies
   3. Obtaining Information

■ GOVERNMENT CONTRACT GUIDEBOOK

    D. Basic Procurement Process
        1. Government "Requirement"
        2. Procurement Methods
    ★   a. Competitive Contracts / **2-5**
           b. Noncompetitive Contracts
    ★   c. Special Procedures For Small Purchases / **2-5**
        3. Contract Types
        4. Soliciting Sources
        5. Government Procurement Team
        6. Activities Of Government Representatives
★ 7. Dealing With Government Representatives / **2-6**

* * *

B. REGULATIONS

* * *

1. Federal Acquisition Regulation

The structure of the FAR has been revised since publication of this GUIDEBOOK. The arrangement of the FAR by subchapter as of January 1, 1999, is presented in Figure 2-1.

Figure 2-1 [*Revised*]

FEDERAL ACQUISITION REGULATION STRUCTURE

Subchapter A: General

Part 1—Federal Acquisition Regulations System
Part 2—Definitions of Words and Terms
Part 3—Improper Business Practices and Personal Conflicts of Interest
Part 4—Administrative Matters

continued

Fig. 2-1 / continued

Subchapter B: Competition and Acquisition Planning

Part 5—Publicizing Contract Actions
Part 6—Competition Requirements
Part 7—Acquisition Planning
Part 8—Required Sources of Supplies and Services
Part 9—Contractor Qualifications
Part 10—Specifications, Standards, and Other Purchase Descriptions
Part 11—Describing Agency Needs
Part 12—Acquisition of Commerical Items

Subchapter C: Contracting Methods and Contract Types

Part 13—Simplified Acquisition Procedures
Part 14—Sealed Bidding
Part 15—Contracting by Negotiation
Part 16—Types of Contracts
Part 17—Special Contracting Methods
Part 18—[Reserved]

Subchapter D: Socioeconomic Programs

Part 19—Small Business Programs
Part 20—[Reserved]
Part 21—[Reserved]
Part 22—Application of Labor Laws to Government Acquisitions
Part 23—Environment, Conservation, Occupational Safety, and Drug-Free Workplace
Part 24—Protection of Privacy and Freedom of Information
Part 25—Foreign Acquisition
Part 26—Other Socioeconomic Programs

Subchapter E: General Contracting Requirements

Part 27—Patents, Data, and Copyrights
Part 28—Bonds and Insurance
Part 29—Taxes
Part 30—Cost Accounting Standards
Part 31—Contract Cost Principles and Procedures
Part 32—Contract Financing
Part 33—Protests, Disputes, and Appeals

Subchapter F: Special Categories of Contracting

Part 34—Major System Acquisition
Part 35—Research and Development Contracting

continued

GOVERNMENT CONTRACT GUIDEBOOK

Fig. 2-1 / continued

Part 36—Construction and Architect-Engineer Contracts
Part 37—Service Contracting
Part 38—Federal Supply Schedule Contracting
Part 39—Acquisition of Information Technology
Part 40—[Reserved]
Part 41—Acquisition of Utility Services

Subchapter G: Contract Management

Part 42—Contract Administration and Audit Services
Part 43—Contract Modifications
Part 44—Subcontracting Policies and Procedures
Part 45—Government Property
Part 46—Quality Assurance
Part 47—Transportation
Part 48—Value Engineering
Part 49—Termination of Contracts
Part 50—Extraordinary Contractual Actions
Part 51—Use of Government Sources by Contractors

Subchapter H: Clauses and Forms

Part 52—Solicitation Provisions and Contract Clauses
Part 53—Forms

───────ANNOTATIONS───────

■ *Legislation & Regulations*

[1] **FAR Amendment**—A final rule announced that the FAR, as well as Federal Acquisition Circulars and other informational items, are available on the Internet at *http://www.arnet.gov/far*. 63 Fed. Reg. 34058 (June 22, 1998, effective Aug. 21, 1998). See 40 GC ¶ 322.

* * *

D. BASIC PROCUREMENT PROCESS

* * *

2. Procurement Methods

* * *

THE SETTING

a. Competitive Contracts

―――――ANNOTATIONS―――――

■ *Legislation & Regulations*

[1] **National Defense Authorization Act For Fiscal Year 1996**—P.L. 104-106 (Feb. 10, 1996), § 4101, retained the "full and open competition" requirement for federal procurement, but directs that the FAR be amended to ensure that the requirement to obtain full and open competition "is implemented in a manner that is consistent with the need to efficiently fulfill the Government's requirements." See 38 GC ¶ 69; FAR pt. 6.

* * *

c. Special Procedures For Small Purchases

―――――ANNOTATIONS―――――

■ *Legislation & Regulations*

[1] **DFARS Amendment**—Effective January 15, 1999, DOD amended the DFARS to bring it into line with the FAR reorganization of simplified acquisition procedures, including provisions governing the ordering of commercial items. 64 Fed. Reg. 2595 (Jan. 15, 1999). See 41 GC ¶ 33.

[2] **FAR Amendment**—Pursuant to § 4202 of P.L. 104-106, the FAR was amended to give Contracting Officers the discretion to use simplified procedures, "to the maximum extent practicable," for acquisitions of commercial items falling between the simplified acquisition threshold ($100,000) and $5 million. Contracting Officers may use any simplified acquisition procedure, but only when the Contracting Officer reasonably expects, on the basis of the items' nature and on market research, that offers will include only commercial items. This authority expires on January 1, 2000. 62 Fed. Reg. 224 (Jan. 2, 1997, effective Jan. 1, 1997). See 39 GC ¶ 7.

[3] **National Defense Authorization Act For Fiscal Year 1996**—For three years after the enactment of P.L. 104-106 (Feb. 10, 1996), agencies will be allowed to use the simplified acquisition procedures currently available for procurements under the $100,000 simplified acquisition threshold to purchase *commercial items* worth up to $5 million. This provision (§ 4202) is effective until January 1, 2000. See 38 GC ¶ 69.

[4] **FAR Amendment**—A final rule was issued to implement the "micro-purchase" requirements of the Federal Acquisition Streamlining Act of 1994, P.L. 103-355, for purchases under $2,500 ($2,000 for construction). Such purchases may be awarded without soliciting competitive quotations if the Contracting Officer considers the price reasonable. Contract clauses are not required. The rule (see FAR subpt. 13.2) also encourages agencies to use the "Governmentwide commercial purchase card" (as defined in FAR 13.001) for micro-purchases. 61 Fed. Reg. 39192 (July 26, 1996, effective Aug. 26, 1996). See 38 GC ¶ 365.

[5] FAR Amendment—A final rule was issued to implement the simplified acquisition procedures mandated by FASA for purchases under the simplified acquisition threshold of $100,000. The final rule amends primarily FAR Part 13 and sets forth procurement notice requirements, the degree of required competition, the requirements regarding purchasing via FACNET (the Federal Acquisition Computer Network), and award procedures. 61 Fed. Reg. 39192 (July 26, 1996, effective Aug. 26, 1996). See 38 GC ¶ 365.

■ *Miscellaneous*

[1] Nash & Cibinic Report Articles—The simplified acquisition procedures that were set forth in the FAR in July 1995 on an interim basis to implement the Federal Acquisition Streamlining Act of 1994 are critiqued in "Simplified Acquisitions: Keep It Simple," 10 NASH & CIBINIC REP. ¶ 4 (Jan. 1996); "Simplified Acquisition: Specifying the Basis for Award," 11 NASH & CIBINIC REP. ¶ 52 (Oct. 1997); and "Simplified Acquisition: Late Quotations," 11 NASH & CIBINIC REP. ¶ 19 (Apr. 1997).

★ ★ ★

7. Dealing With Government Representatives

─────────ANNOTATIONS─────────

■ *Cases & Decisions*

[1] COFC Improperly Failed To Consider Whether Government Ratified Proposed Contract—To investigate suspected corruption, the Federal Bureau of Investigation (FBI) asked a vending business owner to turn his business into an FBI-operated facade and verbally promised to indemnify the owner. He submitted a proposed contract under which the Government agreed to pay him according to a formula. Shortly before the FBI submitted a counteroffer, the FBI indirectly exposed the owner as an informant and told him that they would protect him and his family only if he continued to cooperate. Ultimately, the FBI made several arrests and seized $650,000. The owner sued for compensation in the Court of Federal Claims (COFC), which granted summary judgment to the Government on the ground the Government agents lacked contracting authority. On appeal, the U.S. Court of Appeals for the Federal Circuit reversed the COFC, holding (among other things) that the COFC erred in dismissing the claim without considering whether the FBI had ratified the owner's proposed contract by continuing the sting operation and receiving the resulting benefits. **Janowsky v. U.S., 133 F.3d 888 (Fed. Cir. 1998), 17 FPD ¶ 5, 40 GC ¶ 73.**

★ **Note**—See also *Salles v. U.S.*, 156 F.3d 1383 (Fed. Cir. 1998), 17 FPD ¶ 116 (oral promise by Government officials to pay informant for confidential information was not authorized contract; dissent filed), 40 GC ¶ 532; *Henke v. U.S.*, 43 Fed. Cl. 15 (1999), 18 FPD ¶ 15 (court stated in dicta that official's silence while knowing that party was performing with contractual expectation of payment might establish ratification), 41 GC ¶ 175.

SEALED BIDDING

3

1999 Supplement

Chapter Introduction

A. Invitation For Bids
★ 1. Standard Forms / **3-3**
    2. Specifications
    3. Correction Of IFB Deficiencies
B. Soliciting Bids
C. Preparing The Bid
    1. Complete Bid Package
    2. Instructions To Bidders
    3. Other Aids
    4. Formulation Of Price Quotations
    5. Acknowledgment Of Amendments
D. Bid Opening
    1. Initial Handling
    2. Procedures
★ 3. Early Or Late Openings / **3-3**

GOVERNMENT CONTRACT GUIDEBOOK

★ 4. Late Bids / 3-4
    5. Telegraphic Bids & Modifications
★ 6. Facsimile Bids & Modifications / 3-7
★ 7. FACNET Bids & Modifications / 3-8
E. Eligibility For Award
    1. Responsiveness Of Bids
    ★ a. Minor Informalities / 3-9
       b. Bid Acceptance Period
    ★ c. Binding Legal Obligation / 3-10
       d. Firm Price
    ★ e. Completeness / 3-11
       f. Ambiguities
★ 2. Responsibility Of Bidders / 3-11
    ★ a. Responsibility Determinations / 3-11
       b. Buy-Ins
       c. Special Requirements
       d. Preaward Survey
F. Mistakes In Bids
    1. Preaward Mistakes
       a. Apparent Clerical Errors
       b. Other Preaward Mistakes
       c. Bid Verification
    ★ 2. Postaward Mistakes / 3-12
★ G. Protests / 3-13
    ★ 1. Contracting Agency / 3-14
       a. Procedures
       b. Remedies
    ★ 2. Comptroller General / 3-15
       ★ a. Procedures / 3-18
       ★ b. Remedies / 3-18
    ★ 3. Federal Courts / 3-19
    ★ 4. GSBCA / 3-21

SEALED BIDDING

H. Contract Award
  1. Award Procedures
  2. Rejection Of All Bids
I. Two-Step Sealed Bidding
  1. Step One: Request For Technical Proposals
  2. Step Two: Invitation For Bids

---

* * *

A. INVITATION FOR BIDS

* * *

1. Standard Forms

─────────ANNOTATIONS─────────

■ *Legislation & Regulations*

[1] **FAR Amendment**—Pursuant to the Federal Acquisition Streamlining Act of 1994 (FASA), P.L. 103-355, the FAR was amended to adopt contract terms and conditions in accordance with standard commercial practice, including a new Standard Form 1449 ("Solicitation/Contract/Order for Commercial Items"). 60 Fed. Reg. 48231 (Sept. 18, 1995). See 37 GC ¶ 489.

* * *

D. BID OPENING

* * *

3. Early Or Late Openings

─────────ANNOTATIONS─────────

■ *Cases & Decisions*

[1] **Delivery Of Bid During Exact Minute Specified For Submission Did Not Prevent Its Rejection As Late**—The IFB required that bids be delivered to Room 204 of a certain building by 3 P.M. on September 19. When the time/date stamp clock changed to 3 P.M., the bid-opening officer announced that the bid opening time had arrived and that no more bids

GOVERNMENT CONTRACT GUIDEBOOK

would be accepted. After the announcement but while the clock still showed 3 P.M., Nueva delivered its bid to Room 204 where a secretary stamped the bid in at that time. When the bid was declared late and unacceptable, Nueva protested, contending that the instructions to submit the bid by 3 P.M. meant that bids might be submitted at any time prior to 3:01 P.M. Denying the protest, the Comptroller General held that the controlling factor was not the clock but the agency's reasonable declaration of the start of bid-opening time. Because the bid was not submitted until after that declaration, it was properly rejected as late. **Nueva Const. Co., Comp. Gen. Dec. B-270009, 96-1 CPD ¶ 84, 38 GC ¶ 224.**

4. Late Bids

———————ANNOTATIONS———————

■ *Legislation & Regulations*

[1] **FAR Amendment**—Effective March 3, 1997, the FAR has been amended to broaden the conditions under which the Government may accept late offers. A late offer may be accepted if Government mishandling after receipt at an installation was the *primary cause* of delay, rather than the sole cause as in the prior FAR provision. The rule also recognizes the use of hand-carried offers (including delivery by commercial carrier) as a common business practice, and provides flexibility in determining when an offer was received at a Government activity per standards used by the Comptroller General. The rule expands the definition of acceptable evidence to support acceptance of a late offer and adds an exception at paragraph (a)(5) of the FAR 52.215-10 contract clause to allow consideration of a proposal that is misdirected or misdelivered, not necessarily by mishandling, to an office other than that designated in the solicitation. The changes do not apply to commercial item solicitations, however. 61 Fed. Reg. 69286 (Dec. 31, 1996). See 39 GC ¶ 6.

■ *Cases & Decisions*

[1] **Agency Stamp Did Not Conclusively Establish Time Bid Was Received**—The Navy solicitation provided that hand-carried bids would be received at the depository ("bid box") until 10 A.M. on January 8. Six days after bid opening, CM informed the Navy that it was surprised to note another firm (PT) listed as the low bidder at a price higher than that of CM. The Navy opened the bid box, found a bid envelope from CM bearing an agency time/date stamp of 8:38 A.M. on January 8, and decided to consider the CM bid. PT protested the decision to the Comptroller General. A CM employee stated that he time/date-stamped the bid envelope and placed it in the bid box. The Comptroller General found that the stamp device was in a lobby area relatively open to the public and was not continuously monitored by the agency. Most significantly, bidders might operate the device; they did not have to place a stamped envelope in the bid box immediately. The language of FAR 14.304-1(c) clearly contemplates that to be acceptable evidence of time of receipt, the time/date stamp device must be securely under the agency's control, which was not the

SEALED BIDDING

case here. The Comptroller General recommended that CM's bid be rejected as late and sustained PT's protest. **Pacific Tank Cleaning Services, Inc., Comp. Gen. Dec. B-279111.2, 98-2 CPD ¶ 2, 40 GC ¶ 452.**

★ Note—In a later decision regarding the same procurement, *California Marine Cleaning, Inc. v. U.S.*, 42 Fed. Cl. 281 (1998), 17 FPD ¶ 119, 41 GC ¶ 9, the Court of Federal Claims found that the Comptroller General's decision in 98-2 CPD ¶ 2 was "irrational"; the preponderance of the evidence supported CM's assertion that its bid was timely. Therefore, the Navy could not rely on the earlier decision and cancel the solicitation.

[2] **Closing Mail Room During Lunch Hour Was Not Government Mishandling Of Mailed Bid**—The IFB provided that bids were due at 2 P.M. on October 15, 1997. Denny's bid package arrived by U.S. Postal Service Express Mail at 6:25 P.M. on October 14. The postal carrier attempted to deliver the package to the installation mail room at 11:30 A.M. on October 15 but found it locked for the regularly scheduled lunch hour. The carrier alleged that he did not go to the installation's main entrance because he knew that the security guards there would not sign for express mail or permit access to the installation. The package was delivered the next day and was rejected as late. Denny's protested, contending that closing the mail room only hours before bid opening constituted Government "mishandling." The Comptroller General denied the protest, finding that the installation was accessible by the main entrance when the carrier arrived and the agency specifically notified the security personnel of the bid opening location and time. Thus, Denny's own actions and those of his carrier were the paramount cause for late receipt. **Denny's Rock & Driveway, Comp. Gen. Dec. B-278597, 98-1 CPD ¶ 30, 40 GC ¶ 122.**

★ Note—Because the protester had sent the bid by Express Mail less than two days before bid opening, it could not take advantage of the standard "Late Submission of Bids" clause set forth in FAR 52.214-7 and included in the solicitation.

[3] **Late Bid Rejected Where Installation's Security Exercise Did Not Prevent Its Timely Delivery To Contracting Office**—The solicitation required that bids be sent to a specified address on an Air Force base, to be opened at 2 P.M. on March 15. The bid, delivered by commercial carrier, did not arrive at the specified location until March 18. The Contracting Officer rejected it as late. A base security exercise was in effect on March 15 and the carrier driver, on his own initiative, delivered the bid package to the base freight terminal instead of to the specified address. Although he later stated that such delivery was customary during security exercises, other commercial carriers were able to deliver packages to the specified location on March 15. The bidder argued that the terminal's failure to timely deliver the bid package to the specified location constituted "Government mishandling." The Comptroller General held that improper Government action was not the paramount cause of delay, and denied the protest. **Great Plains Asbestos Control, Inc., Comp. Gen. Dec. B-271841, 96-2 CPD ¶ 19, 38 GC ¶ 420.**

[4] **Bid Received In Agency Mail Room By Specified Time Is Timely Unless Solicitation Provides Otherwise**—The Naval Facilities Engineering Command invited sealed bids on a contract for an air system. The solicitation provided that bids would be opened at 2:30 P.M. on a certain date. In lieu of specifying an office (e.g., by name or room number) respon-

sible for ultimately receiving the bids (see FAR 14.302(a)), the solicitation stated the agency's generic address. Ely's bid (the low one) arrived in the agency's mailroom at 2:28 P.M.; at about 2:31 P.M. a clerk handed it to the bid-opening official, who accepted it and opened it and the bids from the bid box. A competitor protested, contending that the bid was late. The Comptroller General held the bid timely, stating that where the solicitation gives only a generic address, a bid received at the agency's point of receipt by bid opening time is timely. **C.R. Hipp Const. Co., Comp. Gen. Dec. B-274328, 96-2 CPD ¶ 195, 39 GC ¶ 36.**

[5] Government Mishandling Caused Lateness Of Hand-Carried Bid Not Placed In Bid Box—The solicitation stated that bids would be opened at 2 P.M. on February 7 and directed bidders to deposit bids in the bid box at the Plans office. When PBM attempted to enter the office shortly before noon on February 7, it found the door locked; a sign directed persons with emergencies to go to the Contracts office, where a purchasing agent directed PBM to the contract specialist in charge of bid opening. The specialist time-stamped the bid envelope at 12:05 P.M. but forgot to take the bid with her to bid opening. The Contracting Officer determined that the bid could be considered because the Government's actions were the paramount cause of the bid's lateness, and the Comptroller General upheld the Contracting Officer's determination, further noting that since the bid was in the agency's sole custody after receipt and before opening, PBM could not have changed the bid or gained any competitive advantage. **Ed Kocharian & Co., Comp. Gen. Dec. B-271186, 96-1 CPD ¶ 170, 38 GC ¶ 275.**

[6] Bidder Was Obligated To Determine Which Of Two Inconsistent Bid Opening Times Was Correct—The Department of Agriculture issued a solicitation inviting sealed bids on a contract for emergency watershed protection work. The cover sheet stated that bids must arrive at the time shown in Block 13a, which was 1 P.M. Elsewhere on the cover sheet and in Block 10 of the solicitation the bid opening time was stated as 1:45 P.M. The contractor delivered its bid between 1:15 and 1:30 P.M. and the Contracting Officer refused to open or consider it. In denying the contractor's protest, the Comptroller General conceded that the Contracting Officer had been careless and should have clarified the matter prior to bid opening. Nonetheless, in the event of an obvious discrepancy, a bidder is obligated to request clarification and may not simply act on assumption. **Delta Const. Co., Comp. Gen. Dec. B-258518, 94-2 CPD ¶ 235, 37 GC ¶ 59.**

★ **Note**—Although bidders are usually charged with asking the contracting agency to clarify solicitation inconsistencies, in *Department of Agriculture*, Comp. Gen. Dec. B-259262, 96-1 BCA ¶ 163, 38 GC ¶ 331, the Comptroller General held that a bid that was late because the bidder used the agency-furnished preprinted misaddressed envelope could nevertheless be considered. The Comptroller found that it would be unreasonable to expect bidders to examine agency-furnished envelopes to ensure that the address in the solicitation and the address on the preprinted envelope were the same.

[7] Bid's Lateness Was Not Excused By Agency's Erroneous Advice That It Had Been Timely Received—Six hours before bid opening, the contractor telephoned the contracting agency to ask if its bid had arrived. Evidently as a result of confusion between bidders of somewhat similar names, the agency erroneously advised the contractor that the bid had been received. The bid, sent by commercial courier, arrived a day late.

SEALED BIDDING

The contractor argued that if the agency had advised that the bid had not been received, it could have hand-delivered another copy on time. Denying the protest, the Comptroller General held that the rule allowing acceptance of a late bid where improper Government action was the cause for the delay is to be narrowly interpreted. The Government is not obligated to advise bidders whether their bids have arrived; in any event, the primary responsibility for the delay lay with the courier, the bidder's agent. **Selrico Services, Inc., Comp. Gen. Dec. B-259709.2, 95-1 CPD ¶ 224, 37 GC ¶ 351.**

* * *

6. Facsimile Bids & Modifications

———————ANNOTATIONS———————

■ *Cases & Decisions*

[1] **Bid's Signature Page Could Be Replaced By Fax Even Though That Method Could Not Be Used To Submit Original Bid**—The IFB advised bidders that bids (1) could not be submitted by telegraphic or telefacsimile (fax) methods but (2) could be modified or withdrawn by those methods. The low bidder noted "revised by FAX" in the price box of its properly-signed and timely-submitted bid. Prior to the time set for bid opening, the low bidder sent a fax modification to the bid instructing the contracting agency to replace the bid's first two pages; the replacement pages included a price and an authorized signature. The Comptroller General denied the protest of the second low bidder against the agency's decision to award to the low bidder. **American Eagle Industries, Inc., Comp. Gen. Dec. B-256907, 94-2 CPD ¶ 156, 36 GC ¶ 620.**

★ **Note**—The solicitation specifically authorized fax modifications but failed to contain the clause at FAR 52.214-31 authorizing the submission of original bids by fax. In a footnote, the Comptroller General seems to hint that this constituted a solicitation defect because FAR 14.303 only envisions permitting fax modifications where original fax bids are also authorized.

[2] **Delay In Delivering Fax Bid Modification Constituted Government Mishandling**—A Corps of Engineers solicitation authorized bid modifications to be sent by facsimile to a designated telephone number at the facility's mail room. Bid opening time was 2 P.M. About 1:30 P.M., a bidder unsuccessfully tried to send his bid by fax and telephoned the mail room. The mail room clerk told the bidder that the agency machine had jammed and advised him to resend the transmission. The bidder did so, and the mail room received the transmission about 1:53 P.M. The mail room clerk gave the transmission to another clerk instructing him to deliver it "to the bid opening room right away." The other clerk did not do so, and the modification failed to reach the bid opening room on time. As modified, the bid was low. The Comptroller General held that the Corps' failure to follow its internal procedures constituted mishandling, recommended that the bidder receive award at the modified price, and ruled that the bidder was entitled to protest costs. **Butt Const. Co., Comp. Gen. Dec. B-258507, 95-1 CPD ¶ 45, 37 GC ¶ 122.**

GOVERNMENT CONTRACT GUIDEBOOK

★ **Note**—See also *Brazos Roofing, Inc.,* Comp. Gen. Dec. B-275113, 97-1 CPD ¶ 43, 40 GC ¶ 452, where the solicitation advised bidders choosing to submit a bid by fax machine that the Government was not responsible for any failure of receipt attributable to the "availability or condition" of the receiving fax machine. When the protester was unable to complete transmission to the solicitation-designated fax machine, which had run out of ink, he made four unsuccessful attempts to telephone the agency's official point of contact for advice, and another agency official gave the bidder an alternative fax number. The agency did not discover the transmitted modification until after bid opening, however. Although the Government argued that the solicitation language relieved it of responsibility for the late bid, the Comptroller General held that it was received on time because the bid's lateness was the result of a "chain of events" for which the agency was solely responsible.

7. FACNET Bids & Modifications

———————ANNOTATIONS———————

■ *Legislation & Regulations*

[1] **Interim FAR Amendment**—The National Defense Authorization Act for Fiscal Year 1998, P.L. 105-85 (Nov. 18, 1997), repealed language mandating use of FACNET for electronic commerce but required agencies to consider use of existing electronic commerce systems (such as FACNET) before developing new systems. The FAR was revised to eliminate language requiring the use of FACNET for electronic commerce. 63 Fed. Reg. 58586 (Oct. 30, 1998).

[2] **National Defense Authorization Act For Fiscal Year 1996**—P.L. 104-106 (Feb. 10, 1996), § 4302, amended 41 USC § 413 to allow agencies to experiment with alternative procurement systems even without implementing FACNET, and deleted the requirement imposed in 1994 by FASA that agencies achieve "interim" FACNET capability before using simplified acquisition procedures. Full FACNET capability of agencies is still required by the year 2000, however, or the ceiling for simplified acquisitions for that agency will drop from $100,000 to $50,000. This provision is effective on the date specified in the final implementing regulations but not later than January 1, 1997. See 38 GC ¶ 69.

[3] **FAR Amendment**—A final rule amending primarily FAR Parts 4, 5, and 13 was issued to implement requirements of FASA regarding the use of FACNET to make purchases. The FAR provides that FACNET shall be used to acquire supplies and services for contract actions exceeding the micro-purchase threshold ($2,500) but not exceeding the simplified acquisition threshold ($100,000) when practicable and cost effective. FACNET is described in FAR Subpart 4.5. Synopses in the *Commerce Business Daily* are not required for simplified acquisitions made through FACNET. FAR 5.202(a)(13). To promote the use of FACNET, FASA had tied an agency's ability to fully use simplified acquisition procedures to the implementation of FACNET capability, but this requirement was deleted in 1996 (see item [2], above). Nevertheless, the final FAR rule provides that for agencies

SEALED BIDDING

without full FACNET capability by January 1, 2000, the simplified acquisition threshold will revert to $50,000. 61 Fed. Reg. 39192 (July 26, 1996, effective Aug. 26, 1996). See 38 GC ¶ 365.

■ *Cases & Decisions*

[1] **Digital Electronic Signatures Can Be Used To Create Valid Government Contracts**—The Comptroller General found that Electronic Data Interchange systems using message authentication codes following the National Institute of Standards and Technology's (NIST's) Computer Data Authentication Standard, or digital signatures following NIST's Digital Signature Standard, can produce a form of evidence of intent to be bound on a par with a written signature. **National Institute of Standards & Technology, Comp. Gen. Dec. B-245714, 96-2 CPD ¶ 225, 39 GC ¶ 100.**

★ **Note**—For a general discussion of FACNET and recent Comptroller General decisions, see Yukins, "Feature Comment: FACNET—New Risks and New Potential," 38 GC ¶ 511.

■ *Miscellaneous*

[1] **Briefing Paper**—For (1) a discussion of the evolution of electronic commerce in Government procurement and (2) a summary of current initiatives and future plans of DOD and other federal agencies for transition from a paper-based to a more fully automated electronic procurement system, see Swennen & McCarthy, "Electronic Commerce in Federal Procurement," BRIEFING PAPERS No. 98-8 (July 1998).

E. ELIGIBILITY FOR AWARD

* * *

1. Responsiveness Of Bids

* * *

a. Minor Informalities

———————ANNOTATIONS———————

■ *Cases & Decisions*

[1] **Bid Could Not Be Rejected For Minor Violation Of Provision Intended To Prevent Front-Loading**—An IFB for construction of employee housing required submission of separate prices on site and utility work, the housing unit, and stabilization rock, and further required that the price for the site and utility work was not to exceed 20% of the total base bid. Because the low bidder's price for the site and utility work exceeded 20% of its total base bid by $13,300, the Government deemed the bid nonresponsive and awarded the contract to a bidder whose total price was $27,000 higher than the low bid. The Comptroller General held that the low bid's discrep-

■ GOVERNMENT CONTRACT GUIDEBOOK

ancy would neither prejudice other bidders nor fail to satisfy the Government's actual needs. The discrepancy was therefore a minor informality pursuant to FAR 14.405 and rejection of the low bid was improper. **Legare Const. Co., Comp. Gen. Dec. B-257735, 94-2 CPD ¶ 173, 37 GC ¶ 42.**

[2] **Bid's Failure To Comply With Requirement To Submit Equipment History Did Not Affect Its Responsiveness**—An IFB to install air conditioning equipment in a building required bidders to provide with their bids a five-year history of the equipment they proposed to furnish, including a listing of its applications and successful installations. The solicitation did not indicate what would constitute an acceptable history, and the agency admitted that it had inserted the requirement to provide the history by mistake. The bidder took no exception to the solicitation requirements but failed to submit the equipment history. Nonetheless, it received award, and a competitor protested. The Comptroller General, denying the protest, held the omission to be a minor informality under FAR 14.405. **W.M. Schlosser Co., Comp. Gen. Dec. B-258284, 94-2 CPD ¶ 234, 37 GC ¶ 57.**

★ ★ ★

c. Binding Legal Obligation

———————ANNOTATIONS———————

■ *Cases & Decisions*

[1] **Bid Did Not Have To Be Signed By Every Participant In Joint Venture**—Two corporations established a joint venture (JV) to submit a sealed bid on an IFB for a contract to modernize a building. The JV's bid, bid bond, and Certificate of Procurement Integrity were signed by one company's president as the JV's "partner" or "managing partner." The JV's bid was low. Because FAR 4.102(d) states that a "contract with joint venturers...shall be signed by each participant in the joint venture," the Contracting Officer rejected the JV's bid. The JV filed a preaward protest at the Court of Federal Claims seeking an injunction against award to any other bidder. The court observed that the IFB did not explicitly require that a JV's bid be signed by each partner, and held that the agency could not consider factors not stated in the IFB. In addition, the regulation applies only to contracts and not to bids. The court held that absent an explicit agreement to the contrary, each member of a JV has authority to act for and bind the enterprise, and it enjoined the agency from treating the bid as nonresponsive. **PCI/RCI v. U.S., 36 Fed. Cl. 761 (1996), 15 FPD ¶ 109, 39 GC ¶ 129.**

[2] **Agency Properly Rejected Bid Of Joint Venture That Was Not Created To Perform Contract**—A purported JV was apparent low bidder on a contract for road construction. The JV agreement stated that its purpose was to prepare proposals, and that should the parties be awarded a contract, contract performance would be governed by a JV agreement to "be negotiated at that time." In that acceptance of the bid would have meant award to a nonbidding entity, the Comptroller General upheld the Contracting Officer's rejection of the bid and denied the protest. **Calvin Corp./CRIT Constructors, Comp. Gen. Dec. B-258756, 95-1 CPD ¶ 71, 37 GC ¶ 181.**

SEALED BIDDING

* * *

e. Completeness

————————ANNOTATIONS————————

■ *Cases & Decisions*

[1] **Using Dash Did Not Violate Requirement To Bid On All Items Using Only Figures Or Words**—The solicitation required that bids be "submitted on all line items" and that "amounts and prices shall be indicated in either words or figures." Failure to submit a bid on all line items would render the bid nonresponsive. The low bidder entered a handwritten dash for one of 28 line items. The agency awarded the contract to the low bidder; the second low bidder protested to the Comptroller General, contending that the dash rendered the bid nonresponsive. The Comptroller General, citing prior decisions, held that the dash was synonymous with "zero dollars" or "no cost," which obligated the low bidder to perform the work of the line item at no cost to the Government. Accordingly the Comptroller General held the bid to be responsive and denied the protest. **Sverdrup Civil, Inc., Comp. Gen. Dec. B-278627, 98-1 CPD ¶ 31, 40 GC ¶ 198.**
★ **Note**—Other Comptroller General decisions have held that a dash has no particular meaning apart from the context in which it is used or constitutes an ambiguity as to whether the bidder intended to perform the work at no cost to the Government.

* * *

2. Responsibility Of Bidders

————————ANNOTATIONS————————

■ *Miscellaneous*

[1] **Briefing Paper**—For an examination of the definition and elements of bidder responsibility, the relationship of responsibility to responsiveness and to technical acceptability, and a review of agency responsibility determinations, see Bodenheimer, "Responsibility of Prospective Contractors," BRIEFING PAPERS No. 97-9 (Aug. 1997).

a. Responsibility Determinations

————————ANNOTATIONS————————

■ *Legislation & Regulations*

[1] **FAR Amendment**—FAR 52.209-1 has been revised to provide that a Contracting Officer may not reject a bid solely because the bidder did

■ GOVERNMENT CONTRACT GUIDEBOOK

not provide evidence of qualification at the time of bid opening. This corrects inconsistencies in the FAR. 59 Fed. Reg. 67055 (Dec. 28, 1994, effective Feb. 27, 1995). See 37 GC ¶ 7.

* * *

F. MISTAKES IN BIDS

* * *

2. Postaward Mistakes

─────────ANNOTATIONS─────────

■ *Cases & Decisions*

[1] **Contract Reformation Allowed Where Contractor Relied On CO's Misrepresentation Regarding Government's Exemption From State Tax**—The contractor's best and final proposal on a fixed-price contract to construct a ranger station in New Mexico included an amount for the New Mexico gross receipts tax, which contractor believed was applicable. The Contracting Officer insisted that the tax was inapplicable. The parties agreed that the contract price would exclude the tax but that the agency would either obtain a state tax-exemption certificate for the contractor or reimburse the contractor for the tax amount paid. Despite the agreement, the contract incorporated the standard "Permits and Responsibilities" clause (FAR 52.229-3), which made the contractor responsible for all existing state and local taxes. When the state forced the contractor to pay the tax, the Government refused to reimburse the contractor. The Department of Interior Board of Contract Appeals held that, at very least, both parties were mistaken as to whether the Government could obtain a tax-exemption certificate from the state. Even innocent Government misrepresentation does not prevent equitable reformation of a contract where the misrepresentation misled the contractor and caused the contractor to suffer a substantial detriment. The Board reformed the contract to allow the contractor to recover the tax. **Jim Sena Const. Co., IBCA 3761 et al., 98-2 BCA ¶ 29891, 40 GC ¶ 500.**

[2] **CO's Bid Verification Request Was Adequate Despite Failure To Expressly State Suspicion Of Mistake**—The contractor's $145,000 bid was the lowest and was $28,000 lower than the second lowest bid and about half of the Government's cost estimate. Noticing the disparity before award, the Contracting Officer suspected a mistake and sent the contractor a bid verification request, which enclosed the Abstract of Offers and asked the contractor to "review your bid worksheets for possible errors or omissions." After reviewing its bid, the contractor confirmed its accuracy and was awarded the contract. After losing money on performing the contract, the contractor discovered that in error it had failed to transfer an amount to its recapitulation sheet, leaving its bid $16,530 lower than intended. The Armed Services Board of Contract Appeals refused to reform the contract to increase the price, and

the Court of Appeals for the Federal Circuit affirmed the board, holding that even though the Contracting Officer's verification request did not expressly state suspicion of a mistake, it was sufficient to place the contractor on notice of the possibility of error. **McClure Electrical Constructors, Inc. v. Dalton, 132 F.3d 709 (Fed. Cir. 1997), 16 FPD ¶ 152, 40 GC ¶ 120.**

[3] **Government Not Liable For Unauthorized Employee's Misinformation Regarding State Tax Liability**—A Corps of Engineers IFB for construction of a sewage treatment facility at Fort Knox stated that the contract price would include all applicable federal, state, and local taxes. Before submitting its bid, the contractor telephoned the Corps to ask whether the project was exempt from Kentucky taxes. A Corps employee erroneously advised that the project was exempt. The contractor thereupon submitted its bid excluding Kentucky sales taxes, and received award. Ultimately, Kentucky required the contractor to pay almost $291,000 in sales taxes. The contractor brought suit in the U.S. Court of Federal Claims for reformation of the contract on the ground of mutual mistake. Denying the claim, the court held that the contractor failed to prove that the Corps' employee had authority to bind the Corps in what would have been tantamount to a pre-bid modification of the solicitation; and, in any event, the solicitation clearly required that any contract questions be in writing and that oral interpretations would not bind the Corps. **Foley Co. v. U.S., 36 Fed. Cl. 788 (1996), 15 FPD ¶ 111, 39 GC ¶ 66.**

G. PROTESTS

To respond to changes in the law made by FASA, new regulations were issued in 1995 by the FAR Council, the GAO, and the GSBCA to make significant revisions in the procedures for the adjudication of protests. Many of the FASA-required changes applied to both the GAO and the GSBCA, such as the change in the computation of statutory deadlines from "working days" to "calendar days," the cap on the payment of expert witness, consultant, and attorney fees to prevailing parties (except small businesses), and the alteration of certain time periods in the protest process. In 1996, GAO made further changes to implement reforms in the National Defense Authorization Act for Fiscal Year 1996. (See Annotations in Sections G.1, G.2, and G.4 below.)

In 1996, Congress repealed the jurisdiction of the GSBCA to hear bid protests regarding computer-related acquisitions, effective August 8, 1996 (see Section G.4, *Legislation & Regulations*, item [1], below).

In 1996, Congress also amended the Tucker Act to grant fully concurrent jurisdiction over bid protests to the Court of

■ GOVERNMENT CONTRACT GUIDEBOOK

Federal Claims and the U.S. District Courts (see Section G.3, *Legislation & Regulations*, item [1], below).

The revised GAO Protest Time Chart presented in Figure 3-6 summarizes the more significant time limitations in a typical GAO bid protest.

─────────ANNOTATIONS─────────

■ *Miscellaneous*

[1] **Briefing Paper**—For an examination of the FAR, GAO, and GSBCA protest rules revised in 1995, see Humphrey & Corrao, "Changes in the Notice of Award, Debriefing, and Protest Rules After FASA," BRIEFING PAPERS No. 95-10 (Sept. 1995).

1. Contracting Agency

─────────ANNOTATIONS─────────

■ *Legislation & Regulations*

[1] **FAR Amendment**—A final rule (new FAR 15.507) encourages the use of agency protest procedures that incorporate alternative dispute resolution provisions for pre- and post-award protests. 62 Fed. Reg. 51224 (Sept. 30, 1997, effective Oct. 10, 1997). See 39 GC ¶ 466.

[2] **FAR Amendment**—Following up on and clarifying the interim rule (see item [4] below) implementing Executive Order 12979, the final rule requires that agency procedures and solicitations notify potential bidders and offerors that independent review of a protest is available as an alternative to consideration by the Contracting Officer. Pursuant to FAR 33.103(d)(4), agencies shall designate the official(s) to conduct the independent review. Such official(s) need not be in the Contracting Officer's chain, but when practicable should have had no personal involvement in the procurement. Nevertheless, FAR 33.103(d)(4) makes it clear that agency appellate review of the Contracting Officer's decision will not extend the time for filing a protest with the Comptroller General. In addition, FAR 33.103(f)(4) explains that pursuing an agency protest does not extend the time for obtaining a GAO stay; an agency may include in its protest process a voluntary suspension period in the event that the agency denies the protest and the protester subsequently files at GAO. 62 Fed. Reg. 224 (Jan. 2, 1997). See 39 GC ¶ 7.

★ **Note**—See generally Kessler, "Feature Comment: Tips for Agencies in Establishing Protest Procedures, and Factors Potential Protesters Should Consider in Selecting a Forum," 39 GC ¶ 81.

[3] **FAR Amendments**—The FAR Part 33 protest regulations were revised to implement the requirements of FASA. 60 Fed. Reg. 48224 (Sept. 18, 1995, effective Oct. 1, 1995). See 37 GC ¶ 478. Changes include (a) an expanded

SEALED BIDDING

definition of "protest," (b) a new method for computing the time period in which to obtain a suspension of contract performance, (c) creation of a ceiling on the payment of expert witness, consultant, and attorney fees to a successful protester (other than a small business), (d) authority for agencies to pay costs and fees in settlement of protests on a finding by the agency that its actions were inconsistent with law or regulation, (e) authority for agencies to obtain from the initial awardee reimbursement for any protest costs paid to a successful protester if the protest is sustained based on a negligent or intentional mirepresentation by the awardee, and (f) a requirement, for GAO protests, that the procuring agency prepare a "protest file" to be available to actual or prospective offerors.

[4] **Interim FAR Amendment**—Effective July 26, 1996, agency procurement protest procedures were revised to provide for the informal, procedurally simple, and inexpensive resolution of protests. FAR 33.103 implements Executive Order 12979 (60 Fed. Reg. 55171, Oct. 27, 1995; see 37 GC ¶ 554), which called for agencies to establish procedures for the resolution of bid protests at the agency level as an alternative to resolving protests in outside forums. The rule requires parties to use their "best efforts" to resolve protests, and agencies to use such techniques as alternative dispute resolution and third-party neutrals. Interested parties may request review at a level above the Contracting Officer, and the rule requires a stay of contract performance or award pending disposition of a protest. 61 Fed. Reg. 39219. See 38 GC ¶ 365.

* * *

2. Comptroller General

───────ANNOTATIONS───────

■ *Legislation & Regulations*

[1] **National Defense Authorization Act For Fiscal Year 1996**—P.L. 104-106 (Feb. 10, 1996), § 5501, shortened the time for an agency to make a report on a protested procurement from 35 to 30 days, and shortened the time for GAO to issue a final decision from 125 to 100 days of a protest's submission. The effective date is 180 days after the date of enactment (i.e., Aug. 8, 1996), but proceedings underway on the effective date are allowed to continue under the old law. See 38 GC ¶ 69.

[2] **GAO Bid Protest Rules Revised**—GAO issued revised bid protest regulations on August 10, 1995 (60 Fed. Reg. 40737, applying to all protests filed on or after Oct. 1, 1995). See 37 GC ¶ 424. GAO further revised its protest rules on July 26, 1996 (61 Fed. Reg. 39039, effective for protests filed on or after Aug. 8, 1996). See 38 GC ¶ 362. The revised rules are codified at 4 CFR pt. 21. The 1995 revised rules include most of the same changes discussed in Section G.1, *Legislation & Regulations*, item [3], above, that were required by FASA and implemented in the FAR. In addition, the revised GAO rules, among other things, set forth explicit practices regarding protective orders and include a number of clarifying provisions not required by FASA. The revisions made in 1996 shortened

GOVERNMENT CONTRACT GUIDEBOOK

Figure 3-6 [*Revised*]
GAO PROTEST TIME CHART

	Action		Deadline
			[*Must be received by Comptroller General within the deadline]
1.	Filing protest (a) For automatic suspension (b) For consideration of the merits (may be filed at Comptroller General or contracting agency)	*	Before award or the later of 10 days after award or 10 days after debriefing (or within 5 days after debriefing for automatic stay)
	(1) Deficiency in the IFB	*	Before bid opening
	(2) Other matters	*	Within 10 days after basis of protest was or should have been known
2.	Appeal of adverse contracting agency decision to Comptroller General	*	10 days after initial adverse agency action (protest to agency must have been filed on time)
3.	Copy of protest to Contracting Officer		Within 1 day after filing of protest
4.	Comptroller General notification of protest to contracting agency		Within 1 day after Comptroller General's receipt of protest
5.	Request for express option	*	Within 5 days after protest is filed
6.	Comptroller General decision on whether to grant express option		"Promptly" after request is received
7.	Agency report due under express option	*	Within 20 days after notice that express option invoked
8.	Comments on agency report under express option	*	Within 5 days after receipt of report
9.	Decision issued on express option case		Within 65 days after filing of protest

Items 5–9: EXPRESS OPTION ONLY

continued

1999 SUPPLEMENT

SEALED BIDDING

Fig. 3-6 / continued

10.	Contracting agency report due	*	30 days after notice of protest
11.	Request for protective order	*	May be filed with original protest
12.	Requests for exclusion of documents from protective order	*	2 days after receipt of protective order request
13.	Request for documents	*	Concurrent with protest at Comptroller General
14.	Request for supplemental documents	*	2 days after existence or relevance of documents is known or should have been known
15.	Agency response to request for supplemental documents		2 days after receipt of request
16.	Request for hearing (optional)		As early as practicable (not later than promptly after receipt of agency report)
17.	Comments on agency report due		10 days after receipt of report
18.	Hearing (at discretion of Comptroller General)		As soon as practicable after parties receive agency report and relevant documents
19.	Posthearing comments	*	Within 5 days of hearing unless Comptroller General sets a different time
20.	Comptroller General decision		Within 100 days after filing of protest
21.	Request for reconsideration	*	Within 10 days after basis is known or should have been known
22.	Claim for protest costs and bid or proposal preparation costs	*	Within 60 days after receipt of Comptroller General's recommendation that agency pay costs

1999 SUPPLEMENT

■ **GOVERNMENT CONTRACT GUIDEBOOK**

many of the time limits for protest procedures to facilitiate the 100-day statutory deadline for issuing bid protest decisions imposed by the 1996 National Defense Authorization Act, as well as streamlined other procedures.

★ **Note**—The FAR was amended to conform to the revised GAO Bid Protest Rules. 62 Fed. Reg. 64912 (Dec. 9, 1997, effective Feb. 9, 1998). See 39 GC ¶ 593.

■ *Miscellaneous*

[1] **Briefing Papers**—For an analysis of the important deadlines imposed on protesters by the GAO regulations, see McGovern & Palmer, "GAO Protest Timelines Rules," BRIEFING PAPERS No. 99-3 (Feb. 1999). For a discussion of the 1996 revisions to GAO's bid protest rules, see Shnitzer, "The 1996 GAO Bid Protest Rules," BRIEFING PAPERS No. 96-13 (Dec. 1996). See also Shnitzer, "GAO Bid Protests: Similarities & Differences in the Treatment of the Government & Private Parties," BRIEFING PAPERS No. 98-6 (May 1998).

a. Procedures

————————ANNOTATIONS————————

■ *Cases & Decisions*

[1] **Fax Notice Denying Unsuccessful Offeror's Agency-Level Protest Starts GAO Protest Filing Period**—The protester received a facsimile message on December 2 denying its agency-level protest, but failed to file a protest with the Comptroller General within the prescribed time (10 working days from that date). The protester argued that the protest was not late because the filing time begins to run when the agency mails an "official hard copy" of the denial. The Comptroller General disagreed, holding that the rule requiring filing within 10 days of "actual or constructive knowledge of initial adverse agency action" does not require that notice of adverse agency action be in the form of an "official" written document. **American Mediquip, Comp. Gen. Dec. B-259474.3, 96-1 CPD ¶ 173, 38 GC ¶ 274.**

b. Remedies

————————ANNOTATIONS————————

■ *Cases & Decisions*

[1] **CICA Required That GAO's Corrective Action Recommendation Ignore Cost And Disruption Impact On Agency**—The Comptroller General sustained a protest, ruling that the Navy had improperly excluded the protester's proposal from the competitive range. The decision recommended that the Navy reinstate the protester's proposal and recompete the procurement and, should the protester be selected for award, allow the awardee to complete a portion of the work and award the remainder of the procure-

ment to the protester. The Navy requested the Comptroller General to modify the recommendation, asserting that terminating the awardee's contract and rewarding might make the total cost unaffordable and cause delay. The Navy continued contract performance notwithstanding the protest based on a written finding of the Government's "best interests." Under the Competition in Contracting Act, if the agency has invoked that provision, the Act requires that the Comptroller General's recommendation be made "without regard to any cost or disruption from terminating, recompeting, or rewarding the contract." Therefore, the Comptroller General held that neither of the Navy's concerns justified modifying the recommendation. **Department of the Navy, Comp. Gen. Dec. B-274944.4, 97-2 CPD ¶ 16, 40 GC ¶ 61.**

★ **Note**—CICA alternatively permits an agency to continue performance based on a determination that "urgent and compelling circumstances that significantly affect interests of the U.S. will not permit waiting for the...decision" (see 31 USC § 3553(d)(3)(C)(i)). If an agency elects that basis to continue, the Comptroller General has held that CICA permits it to consider all circumstances, including cost and disruption, in fashioning a remedy under a sustained protest. *Arthur Young & Co.*, Comp. Gen. Dec. B-216643, 85-1 CPD ¶ 598, 27 GC ¶ 201.

3. Federal Courts

———————ANNOTATIONS———————

■ *Legislation & Regulations*

[1] **Administrative Dispute Resolution Act Of 1996**—P.L. 104-320, 110 Stat. 380 (Oct. 19, 1996) amended 28 USC § 1491(b)(1) to grant fully concurrent jurisdiction to the U.S. District Courts and to the Court of Federal Claims over bid protests, effective December 31, 1996. The jurisdiction extends to both preaward and postaward protests. The Act states that, in exercising their jurisdiction, the courts shall review the agency's decision under the standards set forth in the Administrative Procedure Act (APA, 5 USC § 706), setting aside agency action, findings, and conclusions found to be "arbitrary, capricious, an abuse of discretion, or otherwise not in accordance with law." Discovery may be limited because, under the APA, review is restricted (with several exceptions) to "the agency record." The new Act grants authority to both courts to award declaratory and injunctive relief, but limits monetary relief to bid preparation and proposal costs. The Act also imposes a four-year "sunset" provision on the District Courts' jurisdiction over bid protests based on *Scanwell Labs. v. Shaffer*, 424 F.2d 859 (D.C. Cir. 1970), 12 GC ¶ 64, unless Congress acts to preserve it before January 1, 2000. GAO is directed to begin a study no earlier than January 1999 to determine, among other things, whether "concurrent jurisdiction is necessary." See 38 GC ¶ 465.

★ **Note**—See generally Churchill, Papson & Closser, "Feature Comment: Congress Enacts Major Changes in Federal Judicial Authority To Hear Protests," 38 GC ¶ 475; Petrillo, Powell & Conner, "Feature Comment: Where To File the Protest? Implications of the Expanded Bid Protest Jurisdiction of the Court of Federal Claims," 38 GC ¶ 536. For a discussion

GOVERNMENT CONTRACT GUIDEBOOK

of Court of Federal Claims bid protest decisions during the first and second years of expanded jurisdiction pursuant to the Administrative Dispute Resolution Act of 1996, see Kennedy & Yukins, "Feature Comment: A Year of Progress—The New Federal Court Bid Protest Jurisdiction," 40 GC ¶ 40, and McCullough, Pollack & Pafford, "Feature Comment: The COFC's New Bid Protest Jurisdiction and Procedures—The Second Year," 41 GC ¶ 122.

■ Cases & Decisions

[1] COFC Has No Jurisdiction To Bar Agency From Overriding Stay Of Award Pending Issuance Of GAO Bid Protest Decision—Ramcor filed a preaward protest with GAO, and the agency chose to override the stay (see 31 USC § 3553) and award the contract to another offeror. Ramcor then requested the Court of Federal Claims (COFC) to issue an injunction barring the agency from proceeding with award until GAO issued its decision. The COFC granted a preliminary injunction on the ground that the agency had been unable to justify overriding the stay. The Government requested the COFC to reconsider its action and dismiss the suit for lack of jurisdiction to review an agency decision to override the stay. Before the COFC could respond, GAO issued its decision on Ramcor's protest, and the COFC lifted its injunction. Subsequently, Ramcor, under the Equal Access to Justice Act, requested the COFC to allow it to recover the legal fees and expenses it incurred to obtain the injunction and respond to the Government's reconsideration request. The COFC, however, noted that it had jurisdiction to grant an EAJA award only if it had jurisdiction over the dispute that led to the underlying decision and therefore had to decide the issue raised in the Government's reconsideration request. The COFC opined that although the Administrative Dispute Resolution Act (ADRA) expanded the COFC's jurisdiction to entertain postaward as well as preaward bid protests, its legislative history indicates that it did not confer general "federal question" jurisdiction on the COFC. If Ramcor had wanted to challenge the propriety of the agency's award of the contract, it could have done so by simply amending its complaint to conform to a typical postaward protest. In such a protest, Ramcor could have raised the stay issue. By its choice Ramcor sought a remedy from the COFC that was beyond its jurisdiction; review of agency overrides of a GAO stay lay exclusively in the District Courts. **Ramcor Services Group, Inc. v. U.S., 41 Fed. Cl. 264 (1998), 17 FPD ¶ 75, 40 GC ¶ 402.**

★ **Note**—*Ramcor* is significant in that it appears to be the first judicial decision on this aspect of ADRA. If correct, it demonstrates one way in which District Court bid protest jurisdiction remains broader than that of the COFC. For one example of a situation in which COFC bid protest jurisdiction may be broader than that of the District Courts, see *Hewlett-Packard Co. v. U.S.*, 41 Fed. Cl. 99 (1998), 17 FPD ¶ 67, 40 GC ¶ 300.

[2] Federal Circuit Limits Court Of Federal Claims' Ability To Enjoin Contract Awards—A company (CAM) was excluded from the competitive range in a procurement and sought declaratory and injunctive relief in an action that was eventually transferred to the Court of Federal Claims. After a hearing, the court found that the Government had properly excluded CAM from the competitive range, and also determined that the successful offeror (F-W) had violated the Procurement Integrity Act due to a conflict of interest. The court found, however, that the procurement

SEALED BIDDING

integrity violation did not prevent CAM's proposal from receiving fair and honest consideration. Although the court acknowledged that under its jurisdictional statute only statutory or regulatory violations that breach the contracting agency's implied-in-fact contractual obligation to treat a proposal in a full, fair, and honest manner are grounds for injunctive relief, it nevertheless enjoined the agency from awarding the contract to F-W, finding that conflicts of interest merit exercise of broader injunctive powers. On appeal, the U.S. Court of Appeals for the Federal Circuit held that the lower court had exceeded its equitable powers. It stated: "we see no authority for [the court] to exercise its injunctive powers absent a finding that the government has breached its implied contract to consider bids honestly and fairly." **Central Arkansas Maintenance, Inc. v. U.S., 68 F.3d 1338 (Fed. Cir. 1995), 14 FPD ¶ 91, 37 GC ¶ 553.**

■ *Miscellaneous*

[1] **Nash & Cibinic Report Article**—The 1996 legislation expanding the jurisdiction of the federal courts to hear bid protests is examined in "Bid Protests: Additional Authority for the Courts," 11 NASH & CIBINIC REP. ¶ 14 (Mar. 1997).

4. GSBCA

————————ANNOTATIONS————————

■ *Legislation & Regulations*

[1] **National Defense Authorization Act For Fiscal Year 1996**—P.L. 104-106 (Feb. 10, 1996), § 5101, repealed 40 USC § 759, eliminating GSA's central authority over computer purchases and the GSBCA's jurisdiction over protests regarding information technology procurements. Such protests will have to be brought to the agency, GAO, the Court of Federal Claims, or to the U.S. District Courts within existing jurisidictional limitations. These provisions are effective 180 days after date of enactment (i.e., Aug. 8, 1996), but proceedings underway on the effective date are allowed to continue under the old law. See 38 GC ¶¶ 69, 70.

[2] **GSBCA Bid Protest Rules Revised**—The GSBCA issued revised protest rules on April 4, 1995. 60 Fed. Reg. 17023 (applying to all protests filed on or after May 5, 1995; codified at 48 CFR pt. 6101). See 37 GC ¶ 205.

★ ★ ★

COMPETITIVE NEGOTIATION

4

1999 Supplement

Chapter Introduction

A. Conditions Permitting Use
B. Requests For Proposals Or Quotations
   1. RFP vs. RFQ
   2. Standard Forms
   3. Soliciting Offers
   4. Amendments
   ★ 5. Preproposal Conferences / **4-2**
   ★ 6. Evaluation Factors / **4-3**
   ★ 7. Cancellation / **4-9**
C. Proposal Preparation & Submission
   1. Proposal Preparation
   2. Best Response
   3. Timeliness
D. Discussions
   ★ 1. Award Without Discussions / **4-10**
   2. Competitive Range Concept
      ★ a. Determining The Range / **4-11**
      ★ b. Responsiveness-Responsibility Relationship / **4-12**

GOVERNMENT CONTRACT GUIDEBOOK

    ★ 3. Scope Of Discussions / **4-13**
  ★ E. Best & Final Offers / **4-14**
    F. Contract Types
      1. Fixed-Price Contracts
        a. Firm-Fixed-Price
        b. Fixed-Price With Economic Price Adjustment
        c. Fixed-Price Incentive
        d. Fixed-Price Redeterminable
      2. Cost-Reimbursement Contracts
        a. Cost
        b. Cost-Sharing
        c. Cost-Plus-Incentive-Fee
    ★   d. Cost-Plus-Award-Fee / **4-16**
        e. Cost-Plus-Fixed-Fee
      3. Other Contract Types
  ★ G. Postaward Notice & Debriefing / **4-16**
    H. Protests

* * *

B. REQUESTS FOR PROPOSALS OR QUOTATIONS

* * *

5. Preproposal Conferences

———————ANNOTATIONS———————

■ *Legislation & Regulations*

[1] **FAR Amendment**—A final rule (FAR 15.201) encourages agencies to exchange information with industry before receipt of proposals, and these exchanges may include, among other things, public hearings, market research, and presolicitation and preproposal conferences, including one-on-one meetings with potential offerors. 62 Fed. Reg. 51224 (Sept. 30, 1997, effective Oct. 10, 1997). See 39 GC ¶ 466.

COMPETITIVE NEGOTIATION

■ *Miscellaneous*

[1] **Briefing Paper**—For an analysis of the presolicitation exchanges between the Government and potential contractors advocated and authorized by FAR Part 15, see Thrasher, "Government Exchanges With Industry Before Receipt of Proposals," BRIEFING PAPERS No. 99-4 (Mar. 1999).

6. Evaluation Factors

———————ANNOTATIONS———————

■ *Legislation & Regulations*

[1] **FAR Amendments**—FAR Part 15, "Contracting by Negotiation," was completely revised in September 1997. Among the many changes are a new FAR 2.201 defining "best value" as "the expected outcome of an acquisition that, in the Government's estimation, provides the greatest overall benefit in response to the requirement." Agencies can obtain best value by using one or more source selection approaches. The revised rules also describe a "best value continuum" recognizing that in different types of acquisitions, the importance of cost or price relative to technical or past performance considerations may vary. FAR 15.101. In addition, what were once known as best value source selections are now called "tradeoff processes" that require documentation of perceived benefits to the Government in awarding a contract to a higher-priced proposal. FAR 15.101-1 and -2. The rule permits "lowest price technically acceptable source selection" when best value is expected to result from selection of the technically acceptable proposal with the lowest evaluated cost; in that event, tradeoffs are not allowed. FAR 15.101-2. Contractor past performance must also be evaluated in all competitively negotiated procurements expected to exceed $1 million ($100,000 for solicitations issued on or after January 1, 1999) unless the Contracting Officer documents why past performance is not an appropriate evaluation factor. FAR 15.304(c)(3). 62 Fed. Reg. 51224 (Sept. 30, 1997, effective Oct. 10, 1997). See 39 GC ¶ 466.

★ **Note**—For an in-depth discussion and analysis of the FAR Part 15 final rule and several remaining problems it failed to address, see Pachter, Shaffer & Pirrello, "The FAR Part 15 Rewrite," BRIEFING PAPERS No. 98-5 (Apr. 1998).

[2] **FAR Amendment**—The FAR was amended to require solicitations for competitive proposals to list all significant evaluation factors and subfactors and to state whether they are more important, of equal importance to, or less important than cost or price. The rating method need not be disclosed, however. FAR 15.304. 62 Fed. Reg. 51224 (Sept. 30, 1997, effective Oct. 10, 1997).

■ *Cases & Decisions*

[1] **Agency Could Give "Satisfactory" Rating To Offeror For Which It Did Not Have Enough Data To Evaluate Past Performance Fully**—The Navy's Request for Proposals for a fixed-price negotiated contract to repair a vessel stated that the offeror whose proposal was most advanta-

geous to the Government on the bases of past performance and price would receive award. Although the solicitation stated that the agency had readily available past performance information, it permitted offerors to submit any information they considered relevant. The offeror the agency ultimately chose for award did not submit a list of prior contracts, and the agency lacked past performance information on that offeror's completed contracts. It had, however, a favorable oral report on the offeror's work on an ongoing ship repair contract. The Navy assigned a "satisfactory/neutral" rating to the offeror for past performance. A competitor protested, arguing that the Navy should have assigned the awardee less than a satisfactory rating. The Comptroller General noted that FAR 15.608(a)(2)(iii) provides that firms "lacking relevant past performance history shall receive a neutral evaluation for past performance." An offeror's failure to list any previous contracts in itself does not justify a neutral rating if the agency is aware of such contracts. In this case, though, the awardee would have been entitled to a rating higher than "neutral" if the agency had based its evaluation on the oral information it had. The Comptroller General also rejected the protester's contention that the Navy should not have equated "neutral" with "satisfactory." **Braswell Services Group, Inc., Comp. Gen. Dec. B-278921.2, 98-2 CPD ¶ 10, 40 GC ¶ 414.**

[2] Offeror Experienced In Producing Same Item Can Receive Higher Score Even If RFP Listed Experience On "Similar" Item As Acceptable—The agency requested proposals on a negotiated contract for aircraft fuel nozzle test stands. One of the listed evaluation factors was the contractor's "past performance"; the solicitation instructed offerors to describe their "experience with producing the same or similar items within the last three years." Because Bauer had manufactured stands of the same type as those specified, agency evaluators assigned Bauer the maximum score on past performance. Although Chant had designed and installed many types of test stands, its proposal provided no evidence that it had designed the item required by the RFP, and it received the minimum acceptable past performance score. In its protest to the Comptroller General, Chant argued that absent a solicitation-stated preference for a firm that had previously manufactured the same (as opposed to a "similar") type of stand, the agency should have given it a past performance score equal to that of Bauer. The Comptroller General denied the protest, holding that agencies may properly consider specific experience so long as it is "logically encompassed by or related to" the solicitation's requirements and stated basis for evaluation. **Chant Engrg. Co., Comp. Gen. Dec. B-280250, 98-2 CPD ¶ 38, 40 GC ¶ 423.**

[3] Allowing One Offeror To Substantially Exceed Solicitation's Page Limitation Created Unequal Competition—The Navy's solicitation for a contract to upgrade ship equipment stated that technical proposals could not exceed 150 pages in three binders. Litton's initial proposal included (1) one 149-page binder labeled "Technical Proposal" and (2) two additional binders of "attachments" consisting of about 1,700 pages, to which the first binder made frequent references. The Navy informed Litton that the proposal exceeded the page limitation and asked for advice on which 150 pages it should consider for evaluation. Litton responded that the agency should evaluate the binder labeled "Technical Proposal" and disregard the others. Eventually, the Navy included all of the proposals in the competitive range and opened discussions, advising all offerors that

COMPETITIVE NEGOTIATION

they could present any information they wished. The agency permitted Litton to include all of the proposal pages it previously submitted that exceeded the page limitation. Based on the degree to which this improved Litton's technical proposal, the Navy awarded the contract to Litton. Electronic Design protested on the ground that its proposal consisted of only 136 pages, including all attachments. The Comptroller General found that the Navy created an unequal competition; in effect, the Navy had considered the entire 1,900-page submission that Litton had submitted as its initial proposal while all the other offerors adhered to the specified page limitation. The Comptroller General sustained the protest, stating that that the appropriate way to place all offerors on an equal footing would be to allow all to prepare and submit proposals with no page limitation and to benefit equally from discussions on those proposals. **Electronic Design, Inc., Comp. Gen. Dec. B-279662.2, 98-2 CPD ¶ 69, 40 GC ¶ 513.**

[4] **Pure Mathematical Analysis Could Not Be Used To Justify Source Selection**—The solicitation for a contract to provide janitorial services stated that the agency would make a "best value" award by "comparing differences in the value of technical features with differences in the offerors' prices" but did not specify the relative importance of price and technical factors. Teltara's proposal offered the lowest price ($3.71 million as compared with TMI's $4.58 million); TMI's proposal had the highest technical score (93 compared to Teltara's 78). Concluding that Teltara's 16.65% price advantage did not offset TMI's 16.11% technical advantage, the Contracting Officer decided that TMI's proposal represented the best value to the Government and awarded TMI the contract. Teltara protested to the Comptroller General. The Comptroller General noted that where the solicitation fails to indicate the relative importance of price and technical factors, they are considered to be equal in weight. Nevertheless, the Contracting Officer had discretion to determine whether the technical advantage associated with TMI's proposal was worth its higher price. Here, the record does not support the source selection decision. There is no indication either that the evaluators discussed the proposals' strengths and weaknesses or otherwise looked beyond the individual point scores or that the Contracting Officer based his award decision on anything beyond his percentage comparisons. Such agency reliance on a purely mathematical cost/technical tradeoff is improper unless consistent with the solicitation evaluation scheme, which was not the case here. The Comptroller General sustained the protest and recommended that the agency make a proper and documented source selection decision. **Teltara Inc., Comp. Gen. Dec. B-280922, 98-2 CPD ¶ 124, 41 GC ¶ 85.**

[5] **Solicitation Making Past Performance More Important Than Price Does Not Bar Award To Lower-Priced Offeror With No Performance History**—The Navy requested proposals on items for its sensor system improvement program. The solicitation provided for color-coded evaluation of offerors' past performance to assist determination of "best value" to the Government. Although price would be a significant factor, past quality performance would be "essentially more important." Nevertheless, proposals classified as "insufficient data" (no past performance on the items) would be evaluated "solely on the basis of price" and "past quality performance shall not be a consideration in their evaluation." The Navy assigned low risk ratings both to ESI (the incumbent) and to Condor; the

latter had never produced the items it offered. Condor's price was 1% lower than that of ESI. The Navy awarded to Condor and ECI protested, arguing that the Navy should have assigned Condor an "insufficient data" rating and, in view of ESI's rating and the minimal price difference, should have awarded to ESI. Denying the protest, the Comptroller General upheld the Government's position that even if Condor had been given an "insufficient data" rating the Navy still could have awarded to Condor. **Excalibur Systems, Inc., Comp. Gen. Dec. B-272017, 96-2 CPD ¶ 13, 38 GC ¶ 424.**

★ **Note**—See generally Pachter & Shaffer, "Feature Comment: Past Performance as an Evaluation Factor—Opening Pandora's Box," 38 GC ¶ 280.

[6] Agency Evaluator's Failure To Use Personal Knowledge Of Offeror's Experience Was Improper—The Internal Revenue Service (IRS) requested proposals on a negotiated contract to provide janitorial and related services at one of its automatic data processing (ADP) centers, listing "project experience" as a technical evaluation subfactor assigned 25% of the available score. The solicitation advised offerors to list at least three projects they had performed of similar size and complexity to the one being procured, and to emphasize their experience in custodial operations in ADP centers. Safeguard's proposal listed 28 custodial projects but did not specify any involving an ADP center. The Chairman of the IRS Technical Evaluation Panel specifically noted that the listed projects included the IRS headquarters complex, a building he knew contained significant ADP space, but failed to consider this personal knowledge in evaluating the proposal because he believed that he was prohibited from doing so. The IRS excluded Safeguard's proposal from the competitive range, and Safeguard protested. The Comptroller General held that an agency may not ignore information personally known about an offeror's prior experience and recommended that the IRS reevaluate the proposals and establish a new competitive range. **Safeguard Maintenance Corp., Comp. Gen. Dec. B-260983.3, 96-2 CPD ¶ 116, 38 GC ¶ 505.**

[7] Federal Circuit Finds GSBCA's Reversal Of Agency's "Best Value" Determination Was Improper—The Air Force (AF) selected TRW's proposal on the "ULANA II" procurement as representing the "best value" to the Government after an extensive evaluation process. In performing the evaluation, the Source Selection Authority (SSA) was not bound by quantitative factors but was allowed to weigh various qualitative ones, which the SSA discussed and explained in her report. Nevertheless, the GSBCA sustained a protest from a competitor (Unisys), directing the AF to make another selection based on a new "best value" analysis. On appeal, the Court of Appeals for the Federal Circuit reversed the GSBCA, invoking the reasoning in *B3H Corp.* (see item [8], below) that the board may overturn the agency's best value procurement determination only if it is "not grounded in reason" (i.e., "arbitrary or capricious"). Otherwise, the board must defer to the agency's decision, even if it might have chosen another proposal. **TRW, Inc. v. Unisys Corp., 98 F.3d 1325 (Fed. Cir. 1996), 15 FPD ¶ 104, 38 GC ¶ 544.**

★ **Note**—*TRW* is noteworthy in that it seems to equate the Competition in Contracting Act's "not grounded in reason" standard of administrative review with the Administrative Procedure Act's "arbitrary and capricious" standard.

COMPETITIVE NEGOTIATION

[8] Federal Circuit Upholds "Grounded In Reason" Standard For Reviewing Best Value Determinations—The Air Force solicited offers for technical support for the AF Materiel Command. Award was to be made on a "best value to the Government" basis. After evaluating several offers, the AF determined that although the estimated cost of the LOGTEC offer was higher than that of B3H and Aries, LOGTEC and Aries were rated higher in the technical area than B3H, and LOGTEC was rated higher in the management area than the other two. After conducting a price/technical tradeoff analysis, the AF determined that award to B3H would result in unnecessary cost overruns and a cost higher than an estimated value adjusted cost, and awarded contracts to LOGTEC and to Aries. B3H protested to the GSBCA, contending, among other things, that the AF failed to select the "best value" offer. The GSBCA granted the protest on the best value issue. See 36 GC ¶ 619. On appeal, the Federal Circuit held that the GSBCA must limit its review to determining whether the awarding agency's procurement decision was "grounded in reason" and not substitute its own judgment for that of the agency. Applying this test, the court reversed the GSBCA's decision. **Secretary of the Air Force v. B3H Corp., 75 F.3d 1577 (Fed. Cir. 1996), 15 FPD ¶ 9, 38 GC ¶ 120, on remand, GSBCA 12813-P-REM, 1996 BPD ¶ 62, 38 GC ¶ 254.**

★ **Note**—Although the Federal Circuit's decision in *B3H* is an authoritative reaffirmation of the broad discretion that agencies enjoy to select a higher-priced offeror for award in a best value procurement, the potential impact of the decision is somewhat diminished by the repeal of the GSBCA's bid protest jurisdiction effective August 9, 1996 (see *Supplement* Chapter 3, Section G.4, *Legislation & Regulations*, item [1]; see 38 GC ¶ 70). The decision is consistent, however, with the approach that other protest forums have been taking in resolving bid protests. See "Postscript VI: Best Value Procurements," 10 NASH & CIBINIC REP. ¶ 15 (Apr. 1996). See also *Grumman Data Systems Corp. v. Dalton*, 88 F.3d 990 (Fed. Cir. 1996), 15 FPD ¶ 65, 38 GC ¶ 384.

[9] Solicitation Provided Adequate Information On How Past Performance Would Be Evaluated Without Point Scoring—A solicitation on an ammunition contract listed in Section M.3 the critical technical evaluation factors (e.g., the contractor's capability and performance of its product) in descending order of importance. Nevertheless, Section M.4. provided that the Government also would evaluate the quality of the offeror's past performance, a factor not listed as a critical evaluation factor. The solicitation stated that although past performance would not be scored independently, it would be "highly influential" in the selection process. Rejecting a protest, the Comptroller General held that the solicitation included sufficient detail to enable offerors to compete intelligently and on a relatively equal basis. **Talon Mfg. Co., Comp. Gen. Dec. B-257536, 94-2 CPD ¶ 140, 36 GC ¶ 598.**

[10] Agency Could Assess Offeror's Past Performance On Dissimilar Projects And For Period Prior To Required References—A solicitation on a negotiated construction contract provided that offerors' past performance was the most important of three factors to be evaluated regarding technical merit, and instructed offerors to furnish at least three references for projects they had completed in the past five years that were similar in size and scope to the one in the solicitation. Young and White received identical scores for the technical factors other than past performance; the agency awarded to White after scoring White higher in past performance. Part of Young's lower score was unfavorable comments on its performance on a contract completed more than five years prior to issuance of the solicitation. Rejecting Young's protest, the Comptroller General ruled that although the solicitation requested references only on projects completed in the past five years, it did not imply that evaluation would be based solely on those references. **Young Enterprises, Inc., Comp. Gen. Dec. B-256851.2, 94-2 CPD ¶ 159, 36 GC ¶ 649.**

[11] **GSBCA Finds Flaws In Agency's Conduct Of "Best Value" Procurement**—The Air Force solicited proposals on a contract to replace outdated telephone switching systems with the latest available digital systems; award was to be made on the basis of "best value." The Source Selection Evaluation Team (SSET) concluded that although the proposals of Nortel and AT&T were "strong," AT&T's was better. Nevertheless, because Nortel's evaluated price was lower, Nortel received award on the basis of SSET's recommendation that AT&T's technical superiority was not worth the additional cost. AT&T protested. The Board found that (a) the SSET failed to give appropriate consideration to the offerors' differing pricing strategies, (b) the Performance Risk Assessment Group raised AT&T's performance risk rating on the basis of the slowness of AT&T's proposal writers but refused to listen to knowledgeable input that on the prior contract Nortel had had difficulties in meeting software requirements, and (c) contrary to the solicitation requirements, the SSET gave little consideration to the proposed equipment's commercial availability. The Board directed the Air Force to weigh the criteria according to the solicitation and to make another decision. A dissenting opinion held that the Board should confine its review to violations of statutes, regulations, and solicitations. **AT&T Corp. v. Department of the Air Force, GSBCA 13107-P, 95-1 BCA ¶ 27551, 1995 BPD ¶ 54, 37 GC ¶ 195.**

[12] **Agency Improperly Used Unpublished Factor To Break Tie Between Offerors On A-E Contract**—Pursuant to the Brooks Architect-Engineering Act, the Navy solicited offers for A-E services. Under the Act, A-E contractors must be selected on the basis of established and published criteria. Prior to submitting an offer, ABB asked the Navy if a firm's previous volume of work would be an evaluation factor and was told it would not. After finding the top three firms equally qualified to perform the contract, the Navy decided to break the tie on the basis of "equal distribution of the work"—a factor not among those published in the *Commerce Business Daily*—and awarded to B&R. DFARS 236.602-1(6) authorizes the Navy to use equitable distribution as a factor in selection. ABB protested the award. The Comptroller General held that the Navy should not have applied a factor not published, even though DFARS listed it as a permissible one. Nevertheless, the Comptroller denied the protest on the ground that ABB was not prejudiced by application of the unpublished factor; the Comptroller General did not believe that ABB would have declined to offer had it known that the Navy would apply the factor solely to break a tie. **ABB Environmental Services, Inc., Comp. Gen. Dec. B-258258.2, 95-1 CPD ¶ 126, 37 GC ¶ 207.**

[13] **Resolution Of Past Performance Problems Did Not Justify Reversing Agency's Evaluation**—A solicitation requested proposals on a con-

COMPETITIVE NEGOTIATION

tract to remove, transport, and dispose of hazardous waste and required that offerors provide detailed information about their performance over the prior two years of Government and commercial contracts for similar services. The solicitation stated that although past performance was significant, it was "a somewhat lesser factor of importance" than price. Although FESI's $3.3-million proposed price was almost $1 million lower than that of Tri-State, the agency awarded the contract to Tri-State on the basis that Tri-State's higher past performance rating justified paying the higher price. FESI protested the award, contending that most if not all of its performance problems had been satisfactorily resolved and that Tri-State's performance record did not justify the significantly higher rating the Government assigned to it. The Comptroller General denied the protest, stating that significant problems reasonably can lead to an overall negative evaluation even if there were far more positive than negative reports, especially where even a small number of improper actions could endanger health and safety. **Federal Environmental Services, Inc., Comp. Gen. Dec. B-260289, 95-1 CPD ¶ 261, 37 GC ¶ 459.**

[14] **Agency Improperly Based Award Decision On Proposal's Offer Of Extended Warranty**—A solicitation for proposals on a contract to furnish various items of computer hardware and software required a one-year warranty on the hardware. Although the agency had requested comments on an earlier draft version of the solicitation indicating it would seek an option to extend the warranty for a second year and give "special emphasis to" the length of the warranty offered, in answers to questions it received, the agency stated that there was no longer a need for a two-year warranty and that no "subjective evaluation points" would be given for providing a warranty of over one year. The final solicitation did not include any provision for a warranty of over one year. Nevertheless, EDS offered a two-year warranty, and the agency found the warranty to be the "only quantified discriminator" which provided "a significant additional value to the Government" and awarded the contract to EDS. In sustaining the protest, the GSBCA held that the agency had violated the statutory requirement that agencies evaluate proposals solely on the basis of factors stated in the solicitation. **Zenith Data Systems Corp. v. Department of the Treasury, GSBCA 13306-P et al., 95-2 BCA ¶ 27863, 1995 BPD ¶ 160, 37 GC ¶ 499.**

7. Cancellation

───────────ANNOTATIONS───────────

■ *Cases & Decisions*

[1] **Cancellation Of Solicitation Was Improper Absent Finding That Procurement Irregularities Benefited Or Prejudiced Anyone**—The agency received 10 proposals in response to a solicitation on a negotiated painting contract. Subsequently, two of the offerors allegedly received information from agency officials disclosing prices and stating that one of the offerors was low, and the offerors also discussed their proposed prices regarding possible subcontracting arrangements should either receive the award. The second low bidder (Flammann) advised the agency of two clerical mistakes

GOVERNMENT CONTRACT GUIDEBOOK

in its offer, and the Contracting Officer allowed Flammann to correct the errors, thus making Flammann the low offeror. After an agency-level protest against the correction, expressing concern about the conduct of contracting officials, the Contracting Officer decided to cancel the solicitation and to resolicit the procurement. Flammann then protested that action to the Comptroller General. The Comptroller General noted that the Contracting Officer was justified in being concerned that the procurement's integrity might have been compromised and that the matter required prompt investigation. Nevertheless, the decision to cancel the solicitation without first determining that the "irregularities" actually compromised an award was unreasonable. The Contracting Officer had no information that anyone benefited from or was prejudiced by the price disclosures by the agency officials. In any event, there was no evidence that Flammann was involved in any of the irregularities. The Comptroller General recommended that the contract be awarded to Flammann based on its low offer. **R.&W. Flammann GmbH, Comp. Gen. Dec. B-278486, 98-1 CPD ¶ 40, 40 GC ¶ 366.**

* * *

D. DISCUSSIONS

1. Award Without Discussions

————————ANNOTATIONS————————

■ *Legislation & Regulations*

[1] **FAR Amendment**—A final rule (FAR 15.306(a)(1)) provides that "clarifications"—defined as "limited exchanges, between the Government and offerors"—may occur if the agency intends to award a contract without discussions. In these exchanges, offerors may be given the opportunity to clarify certain aspects of proposals, for example, past performance information or minor or clerical errors. 62 Fed. Reg. 51224 (Sept. 30, 1997, effective Oct. 10, 1997). See 39 GC ¶ 466.

■ *Cases & Decisions*

[1] **Conversations With Government Personnel During Site Visit To Offeror's Customer Did Not Constitute "Discussions"**—The solicitation provided for the agency to evaluate offerors' past performance, including how well the offeror had satisfied its customers. Agency evaluators conducted a site visit at offeror Meridian's designated building, then awarded the contract to Meridian without discussions. A competitor protested, contending that the site visit itself constituted discussions, requiring discussions with other offerors and a request for best and final offers. The Comptroller General noted that "discussions" occur when (1) information requested and provided by an offeror is essential for determining the proposal's acceptability and (2) the offeror is given an opportunity to revise or modify its proposal. None of the information Meridian provided modified or revised the proposal; the information only confirmed the evaluators' scores. The Comptroller General held that the conversations did not

COMPETITIVE NEGOTIATION

constitute discussions and denied the protest. **UNICCO Govt. Services, Inc., Comp. Gen. Dec. B-277658, 97-2 CPD ¶ 134, 40 GC ¶ 48.**

[2] **Agency Award Of Contract Without Discussions Was Improper—** The Air Force solicited offers on a contract for 354 pentium laptop computers and spare parts, with an option to purchase up to an additional 500 laptops. The solicitation provided for award to the lowest-priced, technically acceptable proposal, and that award might be made without discussions. CLW, lowest of the 52 responding offerors and one of five found to be technically acceptable, offered an unusually low price. The AF requested verification, and CLW indicated that its price was based on a misinterpretation of the somewhat ambiguous solicitation. The AF rejected CLW's proposal without advising CLW of its misinterpretation. Without giving CLW or any of the six lowest offerors an opportunity to correct proposal defects, the AF awarded to the seventh lowest offeror without discussions, and the rejected offerors protested. The GSBCA held that although FAR 15.610 permits award without discussions where the solicitation so advises, the Contracting Officer's discretion was not unlimited. In this case the AF was in a position to save money by holding limited discussions and conducting BAFOs. Moreover, expiring funds were not an excuse for failing to do so. **Computer Literacy World, Inc. v. Department of the Air Force, GSBCA 13438-P, 1995 BPD ¶ 231, 38 GC ¶ 127.**

[3] **Agency Held Improper Discussions—**The Navy issued a solicitation to provide design, development, fabrication, and testing for the Seasparrow missile system. The competition was limited to two offerors. During negotiations, in response to Navy communications regarding the technical data rights it would be conveying to the Government, Hughes changed its proposal in a meaningful way. The Comptroller General held that the exchange of communications with Hughes constituted discussions and not mere clarifications, and that the Navy must conduct discussions with both offerors. **Raytheon Co., Comp. Gen. Dec. B-261959.3, 96-1 CPD ¶ 37, 38 GC ¶ 161.**

2. Competitive Range Concept

* * *

a. Determining The Range

————————ANNOTATIONS————————

■ *Legislation & Regulations*

[1] **FAR Amendments—**The FAR was amended to permit the Contracting Officer to include in the *competitive range* "all of the most highly rated proposals, unless the range is further reduced for purposes of efficiency." The rule emphasizes that proposals are to be evaluated in accordance with the solicitation criteria. Only after all proposals are so evaluated may the Contracting Officer limit the number in the competitive range "to the greatest number that will permit an efficient competition among the most highly rated proposals." FAR 15.306(c). The FAR also provides for *"commu-*

■ GOVERNMENT CONTRACT GUIDEBOOK

nications" before establishment of the competitive range with offerors whose inclusion in (or exclusion from) the competitive range is uncertain and requires precompetitive-range exchanges with offerors whose past performance is the determining factor preventing them from being placed within the competitive range. FAR 15.306(b). The FAR permits offerors excluded from the competitive range to request a *preaward debriefing* from the Contracting Officer. The Contracting Officer "shall make every effort to debrief the unsuccessful offeror as soon as practicable" but may refuse or delay the debriefing where it is in the best interests of the Government. FAR 15.505. 62 Fed. Reg. 51224 (Sept. 30, 1997, effective Oct. 10, 1997). See 39 GC ¶ 466.

[2] **National Defense Authorization Act For Fiscal Year 1996**—P.L 104-106 (Feb. 10, 1996), § 4103, gives Contracting Officers new power to limit the competitive range to the greatest number of proposals "that will permit an efficient competition among the offerors rated most highly" in accordance with the solicitation criteria. So long as a Contracting Officer remains true to the solicitation's criteria, the Contracting Officer may discard offers—even those arguably with a reasonable chance for award and therefore within the competitive range under prior law—in the interest of a more "efficient" procurement. An excluded offeror has a right to a preaward debriefing "as soon as practicable," although the Contracting Officer may refuse the debriefing request "if it is not in the best interests of the Government to conduct a debriefing at that time." The provisions are effective for solicitations issued and contracts awarded on or after January 1, 1997, unless an earlier date is set forth in implementing regulations. See 38 GC ¶ 69.

■ *Cases & Decisions*

[1] **Comptroller General Refuses To Consider Protest Against Agency's Use Of Statute's "Best Interests" Exception To Reject Preaward Debriefing Request**—An offeror the Corps of Engineers had excluded from the competitive range requested a preaward debriefing pursuant to P.L. 104-106 (see *Legislation & Regulations*, item [2] above). The Corps denied the request, invoking the "best interests" exception, stating that a preaward debriefing would require redirecting the agency's resources, "which would not best serve our customers' needs or be a wise expenditure of U.S. tax dollars." The Comptroller General declined to review the Corps' "best interests" determination, noting Congress' express determination that agencies need to retain discretion to delay debriefings until after award. **Global Engrg. & Const. Joint Venture, Comp. Gen. Dec. B-275999.3, 97-1 CPD ¶ 77, 39 GC ¶ 270.**

b. Responsiveness-Responsibility Relationship

——————ANNOTATIONS——————

■ *Legislation & Regulations*

[1] **FAR Amendment**—A final rule provides that contractors' past performance shall be evaluated in all competitively negotiated procurements expected to exceed $1 million ($100,000 for solicitations issued on or after

COMPETITIVE NEGOTIATION

January 1, 1999). FAR 15.304. The Contracting Officer should consider "the currency and relevance of the information, source of the information, context of the data, and general trends in contractor's performance." Offerors must be given opportunity to provide information to the Government on problems encountered in identified contracts and corrective action taken. Offerors without a record of performance may not be rated favorably or unfavorably on past performance. This assessment of past performance information is separate from the responsibility determination under FAR Subpart 9.1. FAR 15.305. 62 Fed. Reg. 51224 (Sept. 30, 1997, effective Oct. 10, 1997). See 39 GC ¶ 466.

★ **Note**—For a discussion of the use of contractor past performance as an evaluation factor, including changes incorporated in the 1997 FAR Part 15 rewrite, see Pachter & Shaffer, "Feature Comment: Past Performance as an Evaluation Factor—Getting It Right," 41 GC ¶ 1.

■ Cases & Decisions

[1] **Evaluators May Use Their Personal Knowledge Of Offeror's Past Performance To Downgrade Proposal**—A solicitation for travel management services listed "customer service/satisfaction/past performance" as the most important evaluation factor for technical proposals. The incumbent contractor protested that its proposal was downgraded on the basis of undocumented personal knowledge of the evaluators. The Comptroller General noted that the mere fact that the extrinsic evidence on which the evaluators relied was not physically included in or attached to the evaluation score sheets did not invalidate reference to that evidence in deciding the protest. That evidence included internal agency documents and traveler surveys, and all three evaluators stated awareness of undocumented complaints regarding the incumbent's performance. The Comptroller General found that the evaluation of past performance was reasonable and denied the protest. **Omega World Travel, Inc., Comp. Gen. Dec. B-271262.2, 96-2 CPD ¶ 44, 38 GC ¶ 459.**

■ Miscellaneous

[1] **Nash & Cibinic Report Articles**—For discussions of the proper use by the Government of contractor past performance in making award decisions—and a critique of ways the Government evaluates past performance—see "Postscript II: Past Performance," 9 NASH & CIBINIC REP. ¶ 47 (Aug. 1995), "Customer Relations: Valid Procurement Tool, Means for Extortion, or Open Door to Cronyism?," 10 NASH & CIBINIC REP. ¶ 37 (July 1996), and "Past Performance Evaluations: Are They Fair?," 11 NASH & CIBINIC REP. ¶ 21 (May 1997).

3. Scope Of Discussions

———————ANNOTATIONS———————

■ Legislation & Regulations

[1] **FAR Amendments**—The revised FAR authorizes the Contracting Officer to discuss with each offeror being considered for award "significant weak-

nesses, deficiencies, and other aspects of its proposal (such as cost, price, technical approach, past performance, and terms and conditions) that could...be altered or explained to enhance materially the proposal's potential for award." In addition, the Contracting Officer may engage in "negotiations," which are "exchanges...between the Government and offerors, that are undertaken with the intent of allowing the offeror to revise its proposal." Negotiations may include "bargaining." FAR 15.306(d). 62 Fed. Reg. 51224 (Sept. 30, 1997, effective Oct. 10, 1997). See 39 GC ¶ 466.

■ *Cases & Decisions*

[1] **FAR Part 15 Rewrite Did Not Alter Rule That CO Need Not "Spoon-Feed" Offeror During Discussions**—An agency solicitation for real estate assessment and analysis services required offerors (1) to provide evidence of qualifications of key staff performing related work and (2) to submit job descriptions and other documentation on key personnel to perform the contract tasks. After determining that D&A's initial proposal was within the competitive range, the agency conducted discussions with the firm. It requested D&A to provide assurance that it (a) had the capacity and financial ability to perform the contract and (b) would dedicate adequate resources to the contract. After receiving D&A's revised proposal, the Contracting Officer made a new competitive range determination that excluded D&A. In a debriefing, the agency informed D&A that evaluation disclosed significant weaknesses in its proposal, including lack of specific information as to the experience of its proposed key personnel and how it would manage its subcontractors. D&A protested to the Comptroller General, contending that in the discussions the agency improperly failed to inform it about the agency's concern on these matters. Noting that this solicitation was subject to the revised FAR Part 15, the Comptroller General noted that new FAR 15.306(d)(3) specifically directs Contracting Officers to indicate "significant weaknesses, deficiencies, and other aspects of its proposal...that could...be altered or explained to enhance materially the proposal's potential for award." Nevertheless it left "the scope and extent of discussions" to the Contracting Officer's judgment. The rule therefore remains that an agency is not required to "spoon-feed" an offeror as to each and every item that it could revise to improve its proposal. The Comptroller General therefore denied the protest. **Du & Assocs., Inc., Comp. Gen. Dec. B-280283.3, 98-2 CPD ¶ 156, 41 GC ¶ 97.**

E. BEST & FINAL OFFERS

——————ANNOTATIONS——————

■ *Legislation & Regulations*

[1] **FAR Amendments**—The revised FAR requires the Contracting Officer, after conducting discussions, to give all remaining competitive range offerors the opportunity to submit a "final proposal revision" and to set a cut-off date for receipt of the proposal revisions. FAR 15.307. This step replaces the "best and final offer" procedure under the previous FAR Part 15. 62 Fed. Reg. 51224 (Sept. 30, 1997, effective Oct. 10, 1997). See 39 GC ¶ 466.

■ Cases & Decisions

[1] Failure To Amend Solicitation Required Agency To Permit Revised Technical As Well As Cost Proposals—The solicitation included the agency's estimate of the number of hours required to perform the contract. After receiving proposals, the agency substantially changed its estimate of labor hours but failed to amend the solicitation to reflect the change. Although there was no change in the labor skill mix or labor categories, among other things the total number of estimated hours declined by about 22%, estimated requirements for the project manager decreased by over 33%, and requirements for two classes of engineers increased by 257% and 175%. The agency then allowed offerors within the competitive range to submit new cost BAFOs but refused to allow submission of new technical BAFOs. The GSBCA held that by so refusing the agency had violated the statutory requirement for full and open competition and directed the agency to cancel the award and to request technical and cost BAFOs based on the amended requirement. **Materials, Communication & Computers, Inc. v. Defense Logistics Agency, GSBCA 12930-P et al., 1994 BPD ¶ 269, 95-1 BCA ¶ 27312, 37 GC ¶ 16.**

[2] Federal Circuit Rules BAFO Notice Need Not Expressly State It Is A Request For BAFOs—The agency issued an RFP on a contract for computer support services. After discussions and receipt of BAFOs, the agency discovered that some offerors had misunderstood discussions regarding wage rates. It then sent to all offerors within the competitive range a notice stating that the Government "has determined a need to conduct a second round of discussions" and gave the offerors an opportunity to submit any amendments to their proposals within five days. The agency's notice did not include the words "best," "final," or "offer." The U.S. Court of Appeals for the Federal Circuit held that the FAR does not require that the notice expressly state that it is a request for BAFOs, and that the notice given satisfied FAR requirements. **Cleveland Telecommunications Corp. v. Goldin, 43 F.3d 655 (Fed. Cir. 1994), 13 FPD ¶ 105, 37 GC ¶ 58.**

■ Miscellaneous

[1] Nash & Cibinic Report Article—For an examination of current BAFO procedures, see "BAFOs and Common Cut-Off Dates: Costly and Unnecessary Relics," 9 NASH & CIBINIC REP. ¶ 25 (Apr. 1995).

F. CONTRACT TYPES

* * *

2. Cost-Reimbursement Contracts

* * *

■ GOVERNMENT CONTRACT GUIDEBOOK

d. Cost-Plus-Award-Fee

————————ANNOTATIONS————————

■ *Cases & Decisions*

[1] Government Cannot Contractually Prevent Contractors From Obtaining Board Review Of Award Fee Determination—In affirming a decision by the Armed Services Board of Contract Appeals, the Federal Circuit reiterated that the board's review of the Contracting Officer's determination of the award fee amount is limited to whether the Contracting Officer's action was arbitrary or capricious. In this case, the fee-determining official determined the fee by a formula not directly corresponding to the contractor's numerical score in performance evaluation, and the Contracting Officer approved the determination. The contract contained no formula for converting performance scores into fee ranges, as had prior contracts, and the contractor based its proposal on the expectation that it would receive an award fee proportional to its performance evaluation score. **Burnside-Ott Aviation Training Center v. Dalton, 107 F.3d 854 (Fed. Cir. 1997), 16 FPD ¶ 27, 39 GC ¶ 153.**

* * *

G. POSTAWARD NOTICE & DEBRIEFING

————————ANNOTATIONS————————

■ *Legislation & Regulations*

[1] FAR Amendment—The FAR was amended to allow both successful and unsuccessful offerors on negotiated procurements to request a debriefing within three days of notice of contract award. Agencies must, to the maximum extent practicable, conduct debriefings within five days. At a minimum, debriefings must include (1) the Government's evaluation of the significant weaknesses or deficiencies in the offeror's proposal, (2) the overall evaluated cost and technical rating of the successful and debriefed offerors, (3) the overall ranking of each offer (where applicable), (4) a summary of the rationale for award, (5) where the proposal includes a commercial item that is an end item under the contract, the make and model of the item being provided by the awardee, and (6) responses to relevant questions as to whether source selection procedures in the solicitation and in applicable regulations were followed. The debriefings may be done orally, in writing, or by any other method acceptable to the Contracting Officer. FAR 15.506. 62 Fed. Reg. 51224 (Sept. 30, 1997, effective Oct. 10, 1997). See 39 GC ¶ 466.

■ *Miscellaneous*

[1] Briefing Paper—For an examination of the implemention of notice of award and debriefing rules originally established by the Federal Acquisition Stream-

COMPETITIVE NEGOTIATION

lining Act of 1994, see Humphrey & Corrao, "Changes in the Notice of Award, Debriefing, and Protest Rules After FASA," BRIEFING PAPERS No. 95-10 (Sept. 1995).

* * *

COSTS

5

1999 Supplement

Chapter Introduction

A. Cost Principles
  ★ 1. Applicability / **5-3**
  2. Allowability
  3. Reasonableness
  4. Allocability
  ★ 5. Selected Costs / **5-3**
★ B. Cost Accounting Standards / **5-9**
  1. Applicability
    ★ a. Exemptions & Waiver / **5-9**
    b. Types Of Coverage
  2. Contractor Obligations
  3. Disclosure Statements
    a. Requirements
    b. Time Of Submission

GOVERNMENT CONTRACT GUIDEBOOK

★ c. Form Of Submission / **5-11**
★ 4. Individual Standards / **5-11**
★ C. Truth In Negotiations Act / **5-12**
  ★ 1. Applicability / **5-12**
  ★ 2. Exemptions & Waiver / **5-12**
    ★ a. Adequate Price Competition / **5-13**
    ★ b. Established Catalog Or Market Price / **5-13**
    c. Price Set By Law Or Regulation
    ★ d. Commercial Item Procurements / **5-13**
    e. Waiver
  3. "Cost Or Pricing Data" Defined
  4. Submission Of Data
    ★ a. Form / **5-14**
    ★ b. When Submitted / **5-15**
    ★ c. Subcontractor Data / **5-15**
    d. Failure To Submit Data
  ★ 5. Certification Of Data / **5-16**
  ★ 6. Liability For Defective Data / **5-16**
  D. Government Audit Rights
  ★ 1. Procuring Agencies / **5-18**
    ★ a. Price Proposal Audits / **5-18**
    b. Contract Settlement Audits
    ★ c. Cost Or Pricing Data Audits / **5-19**
  2. General Accounting Office
  3. Inspectors General

★ ★ ★

A. COST PRINCIPLES

★ ★ ★

1999 SUPPLEMENT
5-2

COSTS

1. Applicability

———————ANNOTATIONS———————

■ *Legislation & Regulations*

[1] **OMB Circulars A-21, A-87, A-102, A-110, and A-122**—Reflecting the Single Audit Act Amendments of 1996, the Office of Management and Budget (OMB) issued final revisions to the following OMB Circulars: A-21 ("Cost Principles for Educational Institutions"), A-87 ("Cost Principles for State and Local Governments"), A-102 ("Grants and Cooperative Agreements with State and Local Governments"), A-110 ("Uniform Administrative Requirements for Grants and Agreements with Institutions of Higher Education, Hospitals, and Other Non-Profit Organizations"), and A-122 ("Cost Principles for Non-Profit Organizations"). These revisions are effective September 29, 1997. OMB also has issued interim final amendments to Circular A-110 reflecting the rescission and consolidation of other OMB Circulars. 62 Fed. Reg. 45934 (Aug. 29, 1997). See 39 GC ¶ 439.

[2] **OMB Circular A-87**—In 1995, OMB issued final revisions to OMB Circular A-87, "Cost Principles for State and Local Governments" (60 Fed. Reg. 36484, May 17, 1995). Applicable to all federal agencies, it covers cost-reimbursement-type contracts, grants, and cooperative agreements except those with educational institutions subject to OMB Circular A-21 and hospitals and other medical care providers subject to sponsoring agency regulations. See 37 GC ¶ 289.

■ *Miscellaneous*

[1] **Briefing Paper**—For a discussion of the framework for the Federal Government's administration of contracts and grants awarded to educational and nonprofit institutions, including cost principles, CAS, and audits, see Zumwalt & Lawrence, "Special Rules for Educational & Nonprofit Institutions/Edition II," BRIEFING PAPERS No. 97-8 (July 1997).

★ ★ ★

5. Selected Costs

———————ANNOTATIONS———————

■ *Legislation & Regulations*

[1] **National Defense Authorization Act For Fiscal Year 1998**—P.L. 105-85 (Nov. 18, 1997), § 808, limits the reimbursable executive compensation under defense and civilian contracts. The amount of compensation paid to a contractor's chief executive officer and the next four most highly compensated employees is limited to "the benchmark compensation amount determined applicable for the fiscal year" determined by the Office of Federal Procurement Policy (OFPP). The "benchmark compensation amount" is defined as "the median amount of the compensation" provided to all senior

GOVERNMENT CONTRACT GUIDEBOOK

executives of "benchmark corporations" (publicly-owned U.S. corporations with annual sales over $50 million). "Compensation" is defined as the total amount of wages, salary, bonuses, and deferred compensation for the year concerned. The cap applies to compensation costs incurred after January 1, 1998, under "covered contracts entered into before, on, or after" November 18, 1997. The effective date is February 16, 1998, by which date OFPP must prescribe implementing regulations. See 40 GC ¶ 1; 39 GC ¶ 516.

★ **Note**—The National Defense Authorization Act for FY 1999, P.L. 105-261, § 804 (Oct. 17, 1998), broadened the applicability of the compensation cap to cover the five most highly compensated contractor employees at "each home office or segment."

[2] **National Defense Authorization Act For Fiscal Year 1997**—P.L 104-201 (Sept. 23, 1996), §§ 809, 810, imposed a one-year $250,000 cap on allowable annual compensation paid to any one "officer" of a contractor under civilian agency and defense contracts over $500,000 funded with FY 1997 appropriations, except fixed-price contracts without cost incentives and firm, fixed price contracts for commercial items. The Act defines "officer" as "a person who is determined to be in a senior management position as established by regulation." The Act defines the term "compensation" broadly to include both wages and elective deferrals as defined in the Internal Revenue Code and implementing regulations to cover, among others, salaries, fees, bonuses, commissions on sales or insurance premiums, pensions, retired pay, and employer contributions to 401(k) plans. The Act also directed OFPP to develop a legislative proposal establishing a Government-wide policy on allowable executive compensation costs, due to Congress by March 1, 1997. See 38 GC ¶ 439.

★ **Note**—See generally Perry, "Feature Comment: Untangling the FY 1997 Limitations on Allowable Individual Compensation Costs," 38 GC ¶ 498.

[3] **Defense Appropriations Act For Fiscal Year 1997**—P.L. 104-208 (Sept. 30, 1996), § 8071, caps at $250,000 the amount of individual compensation costs that may be charged to the Government on new contracts funded under the Act. See 38 GC ¶¶ 464, 498.

[4] **Defense Appropriations Act For Fiscal Year 1996**—P.L. 104-61 (Nov. 30, 1995), § 8086, addressed the issue of perceived excessive compensation for high-level contractor employees by providing that FY 1996 funds may not be obligated for payment on new contracts where allowable costs charged to the Government include payments for individual compensation at a rate in excess of $200,000 per year, unless OFPP establishes guidance in the FAR governing the allowability of individual compensation. This limitation was effective July 1, 1996 and expired September 30, 1996. Section 8122 of the Act further prohibited DOD from using FY 1996 funds to reimburse a contractor for bonuses or other payments in excess of the normal salary paid to an employee when such payments are part of restructuring costs associated with a business combination. See 37 GC ¶ 612.

★ **Note**—On June 10, 1996, OFPP announced that it would not remove or alter by regulation the dollar limit on allowable individual compensation costs under defense contracts imposed by P.L. 104-61. See 38 GC ¶ 281.

[5] **FAR Amendment**—Effective March 4, 1999, an interim rule modifies the limits on the amount of allowable compensation contractors pay to their "senior executives" (FAR 31.205-6(p)). The rule extends allowable cost lim-

COSTS

its to "the five most highly compensated employees in management positions at each home office and each segment of the contractor" whether or not the home office or segment reports directly to the contractor's headquarters. Section 804 of the FY 1999 National Defense Authorization Act (P.L. 105-261) mandated the change, which applies to executive compensation costs incurred under Government contracts after January 1, 1999, regardless of the date of contract award (see item [1], above). 64 Fed. Reg. 10529 (Mar. 4, 1999). See 41 GC ¶ 116.

[6] **FAR Amendment**—Effective December 29, 1998, a final rule amended FAR 31.205-47 to generally disallow costs contractors incur in defending qui tam actions. Nevertheless, amended FAR 31.205-47(c)(2) permits a contractor to recover "reasonable costs" incurred in connection with such proceedings, provided that (a) the costs are not otherwise unallowable and (b) the Contracting Officer "determines that there was very little likelihood that the third party would have been successful on the merits." In the event that the contractor meets those requirements, FAR 31.205-47(e)(3) limits recovery to 80% of otherwise allowable legal costs incurred; the Contracting Officer may at his or her discretion set a lower percentage. 63 Fed. Reg. 58586 (Oct. 30, 1998). See 40 GC ¶ 508.

[7] **FAR Amendment**—Effective December 29, 1998, a final rule deleted the "Civil defense" cost principle, FAR 31.205-5, as no longer necessary (see 40 GC ¶ 149(g)). The general allocability, allowability, and reasonableness criteria set forth in FAR Part 31 will govern acceptability of former FAR 31.205-5 costs. 63 Fed. Reg. 58586 (Oct. 30, 1998). See 40 GC ¶ 508.

[8] **FAR Amendment**—Effective May 3, 1999, a final rule streamlines the "Recruitment Costs" cost principle (FAR 31.205-34) and replaces the current allowability criteria for help-wanted advertising with more general criteria. The final rule disallows the costs of advertising that does not describe specific positions or that includes irrelevant material (e.g., extensive illustrations or descriptions of the company's products or capabilities). The final rule also incorporates the allowability criteria for recruitment costs by reference in the "Public relations and advertising costs" cost principle, FAR 31.205-1. 64 Fed. Reg. 10529 (Mar. 4, 1999). See 41 GC ¶ 116.

[9] **FAR Amendment**—An interim FAR rule implementing § 808 of the FY 1998 National Defense Authorization Act (P.L. 105-85) (see item [1], above) to disallow senior executive compensation in excess of the OFPP benchmark (see 40 GC ¶ 78) was finalized. The amendment incorporates the $340,650 benchmark by reference and applies to costs incurred after January 1, 1998, regardless of whether the affected contracts were previously subject to a statutory cap on such costs. The amendment defines "senior executives" as the chief executive officer (or any individual acting in a similar capacity at the contractor's headquarters) and the four other most highly compensated employees in management positions. If the contractor has intermediate home offices or segments reporting directly to corporate headquarters, the definition also applies to the five most highly compensated employees in each such office or segment. The limit defines "compensation" as the total amount of wages, salary, bonuses, deferred compensation, and employer contributions to defined pension plans for the fiscal year. 63 Fed. Reg. 70264 (Dec. 18, 1998). See 41 GC ¶ 6.

★ **Note**—Effective March 26, 1998, a final rule amended the DOD FAR Supplement to remove differing limitations on allowability of executive

GOVERNMENT CONTRACT GUIDEBOOK

compensation costs. The FAR contains the sole statutory limitation on allowable senior executive compensation costs incurred after January 1, 1998 under new or previously existing contracts. 63 Fed. Reg. 14640 (Mar. 26, 1998). See 40 GC ¶ 159(g).

[10] **FAR Amendment**—A new paragraph (p) has been added to FAR 31.205-6, "Compensation for Personal Services," to implement § 809 of the FY 1997 National Defense Authorization Act (see item [2] above). The new language places a Government-wide ceiling of $250,000 per year on allowable compensation costs for contractor management personnel in senior management positions under contracts awarded during FY 1997. It defines "officer in a senior management position" as (1) the contractor's Chief Executive Officer or individual acting in a similar capacity, (2) the contractor's four other most highly compensated officers in senior management positions, and (3) in the case of contractors divided into intermediate home offices/segments, the five most highly compensated individuals in senior management positions at each such intermediate home office. 62 Fed. Reg. 64912 (Dec. 9, 1997, effective for contracts awarded on or after Jan. 2, 1997). See 39 GC ¶¶ 593, 7.

[11] **FAR Amendment**—Effective December 20, 1996, FAR 31.205-22 has been amended to make allowable the costs of lobbying activities to influence local legislation when the activities (1) directly reduce contract costs or (2) avoid material impairment of the contractor's authority to perform the contract. The rule treats the lobbying of local legislation in a manner consistent with the treatment of state legislation lobbying. 62 Fed. Reg. 44802 (Aug. 22, 1997). See 39 GC ¶ 424.

[12] **FAR Amendment**—A final rule effective December 31, 1996, amends FAR 31.205-6(e)(1) to state explicitly that contractors may properly consider increased federal income taxes in the allowable foreign differential pay provided to overseas employees. 62 Fed. Reg. 44802 (Aug. 22, 1997). See 39 GC ¶ 424.

[13] **FAR Amendment**—Effective October 7, 1996, FAR 31.205-47 was amended to disallow the costs of protesting Government solicitations or contract awards, except those incurred to defend against a protest pursuant to a written request of the Contracting Officer. 61 Fed. Reg. 41466 (Aug. 8, 1996). See 38 GC ¶ 389.

[14] **FAR Amendment**—A final rule, effective September 24, 1996, amends FAR 31.205-6(b), "Compensation for Personal Services," to provide guidance on evaluating the reasonableness of contractor compensation systems (61 Fed. Reg. 39217, July 26, 1996). Among other things, the rule clarifies the standard for reasonableness of labor-management compensation agreements and clearly allows offsets of allowable compensation elements against allegedly unallowable elements among jobs of the same pay grade or level. See 38 GC ¶ 365.

[15] **FAR Amendment**—Revised FAR 31.205-6, "Compensation for Personal Services," regarding the treatment of costs for postretirement benefits other than pensions that are attributable to employees' past service, provides guidance for any transfer of pension funds to another employee benefit fund. FAR 31.205-6(o)(2) was also amended to allow all contractors, whether or not covered by CAS, to use the "terminal funding method" for

prefunding retiree insurance programs. 59 Fed. Reg. 67010 (Dec. 28, 1994). See 37 GC ¶ 7.

[16] **FAR Amendment**—The cost principle on "Executive Lobbying Costs" (FAR 31.205-50) has been removed and its reimbursement prohibition transferred to the list of expressly unallowable lobbying costs at FAR 31.205-22(a). 61 Fed. Reg. 31656 (June 20, 1996, effective Aug. 19, 1996). See 38 GC ¶ 309.

[17] **FAR Amendment**—FAR 31.205-6 has been amended to disallow costs of severance payments to foreign nationals employed under a service contract or subcontract performed outside the U.S. to the extent that such payments exceed amounts typically paid to employees providing similar services in the same industry in the U.S. 60 Fed. Reg. 42648 (Aug. 16, 1995). See 37 GC ¶ 442.

[18] **FAR Amendment**—A final rule (60 Fed. Reg. 42662, Aug. 16, 1995) makes expressly unallowable the costs of gifts, recreation, and entertainment for contractor employees. The rule does, however, allow the costs of company-sponsored employee sports teams and employee organizations designed to improve company loyalty, team work, or physical fitness. The rule, which amends FAR 31.205-13 and FAR 31.205-14, also permits reimbursement for otherwise reasonable costs of employee performance and recognition awards and of "wellness/ fitness centers." See 37 GC ¶ 441.

[19] **FAR Amendment**—FAR 31.205-22 has been amended to disallow the costs of lobbying the legislative body of a state political subdivision. 60 Fed. Reg. 42648 (Aug. 16, 1995). See 37 GC ¶ 442.

[20] **FAR Amendment**—FAR 31.205-43 has been amended to add "convention" to the list of activity costs that are allowable under certain conditions. 60 Fed. Reg. 42648 (Aug. 16, 1995). See 37 GC ¶ 442.

■ *Cases & Decisions*

[1] **Federal Circuit Reverses ASBCA Decision Regarding FAR Prohibition Against Reimbursement Of Penalties**—The Longshore and Harbor Workers' Compensation Act (LHWCA) (33 USC § 901 et seq.) requires employers to pay workers' compensation to employees for job-related injuries. Section 914(e) imposes on employers a 10% surcharge (called "additional compensation") on installment payments not paid to employees on time. The contractor made about $191,000 in payments to current and former employees under § 914(e), and contended that it was entitled to recover these costs as employee compensation under its Government cost-reimbursement contracts. The Armed Services Board of Contract Appeals (ASBCA), however, held the § 914(e) payments were a penalty for the contractor's violation of a federal statute and, as such, were unallowable under FAR 31.205-15, which generally bars reimbursement for "fines and penalties." The U.S. Court of Appeals for the Federal Circuit reversed the board, noting that unlike nine other sections of the LHWCA that expressly provide for "fines" and "penalties," § 914(e) provides for "additional compensation." Moreover, the LHWCA provides that amounts collected as "fines and penalties" be paid into an administrative fund, while § 914(e) payments are made to individual claimants and are meant to compensate employees for inconvenience and delay in receiving payments. For these and other reasons, the court concluded that the § 914(e) payments are not

"fines and penalties." **Ingalls Shipbldg., Inc. v. Dalton, 119 F.3d 972 (Fed. Cir. 1997), 16 FPD ¶ 90, 39 GC ¶ 450.**

[2] **Federal Circuit Reverses ASBCA And Finds Interest On Back Taxes Allowable**—The Federal Circuit held interest paid by a contractor on *inadvertent* underpayment of state taxes did not represent "interest on borrowings" that otherwise would have been unallowable under the cost principles. The Federal Circuit reasoned that borrowing required an element of intent that was absent in this case; the record did not indicate that the contractor used tax underpayments as a means of deliberately raising capital. **Lockheed Corp. v. Widnall, 113 F.3d 1225 (Fed. Cir. 1997), 16 FPD ¶ 59, 39 GC ¶ 250.**

★ **Note**—This case is noteworthy as one of the few decisions allowing payment of interest-related costs. For another case on this subject, see *Superstaff, Inc.*, ASBCA 48062 et al., 97-1 BCA ¶ 28845, which disallowed interest on borrowings associated with changed work.

[3] **Federal Circuit Reverses ASBCA Decision Disallowing Costs Of Contractor's Claims Consultant**—Reversing a split decision of the ASBCA, the Federal Circuit ruled that whether "claim preparation costs" are recoverable as part of an equitable adjustment depends on "why the contractor incurred the cost." That is, if the contractor incurred the cost with the genuine purpose of materially furthering negotiation, the cost normally should be allowable, even though negotiation eventually fails and the contractor later submits a Contract Disputes Act (CDA) claim. Conversely, if the contractor's underlying purpose is to promote prosecution of a CDA claim, the cost is unallowable under FAR 31.205-47(f)(1), "Costs Related to Legal and Other Proceedings." The court remanded the case for determinations of reasonableness and allocability of the costs involved. **Bill Strong Enterprises, Inc. v. Shannon, 49 F.3d 1541 (Fed. Cir. 1995), 14 FPD ¶ 18, 37 GC ¶ 141.**

★ **Note**—Compare *Plano Builders Corp. v. U.S.*, 40 Fed. Cl. 635 (1998), 17 FPD ¶ 36, 40 GC ¶ 208, where a contractor made several written submissions to the Government requesting additional compensation for additional work, and then hired a consultant to assist it in clarifying the claims for the Government. The contractor ultimately sought to recover the consultant fees as allowable costs under its Government contracts. The U.S. Court of Federal Claims ruled that because the contractor's written submissions to the Government constituted CDA "claims," the consultant costs were incurred in connection with "the prosecution of claims" and were unallowable.

■ *Miscellaneous*

[1] **Costs, Pricing & Accounting Report Articles**—The case law developed by various agency boards of contract appeals following the Federal Circuit's decision in *Bill Strong* (see *Cases & Decisions*, item [3] above) is examined in Stafford & Pompeo, "Life After *Bill Strong*," 96-12 CP&A REP. 3 (Dec. 1996). Issues raised by the limits on allowable personal compensation for contractor employees imposed by the Fiscal Year 1995 DOD Appropriations Act are examined in Chierichella & Weitzel, "Complying With the New Limits on Personal Compensation Under FY 1995 DOD Contracts," 95-1 CP&A REP. 3 (Jan. 1995). The Administration's legislative proposal for a statutory allowability standard for executive compensation costs is discussed in Worthington, Roberts & Manos, "Executive Compensation: A Critical

Examination of the Proposed 'Contract Costs Act of 1997,'" 97-3 CP&A REP. 3 (Mar. 1997). The laws and rules enacted from 1995-1997 governing limits on allowable executive compensation are reviewed and analyzed in Dempsey, "Statutes & Regulations Governing Allowable Executive Compensation," 98-2 CP&A REP. 3 (Feb. 1998). The amended cost principles, FAR 31.205-13 and FAR 31.205-14, on employee morale and entertainment costs are discussed in Nibley & Thompson, "The Allowability of Employee Morale & Entertainment Costs After FASA: Questions Remain," 95-11 CP&A REP. 3 (Nov. 1995).

[2] **Briefing Paper**—For a detailed analysis of the statutory caps on allowable executive compensation enacted in each fiscal year since 1995 as well as the regulatory limitations applicable to specific elements of compensation typically included in compensation packages for contractors' senior management, see Manos, "Allowability of Executive Compensation Costs," BRIEFING PAPERS No. 97-13 (Dec. 1997).

B. COST ACCOUNTING STANDARDS

——————————ANNOTATIONS——————————

■ *Legislation & Regulations*

[1] **FAR Amendments**—The FAR was amended to reflect the 1993 recodification of the CAS in 48 CFR Chapter 99. 59 Fed. Reg. 67041 (Dec. 28, 1994). The rule removes the CAS rules and regulations from FAR Subpart 30.3 and the Standards from Subpart 30.4. Also, FAR Part 30 and related provisions in Part 52 were amended to conform to CAS Board changes regarding the criteria, thresholds, and procedures for applying the CAS to negotiated Government contracts. 59 Fed. Reg. 67041, 67042 (Dec. 28, 1994). See 37 GC ¶ 7.

■ *Miscellaneous*

[1] **Briefing Paper**—For a survey of the Cost Accounting Standards, see Boyd & Villet, "Cost Accounting Standards Fundamentals," BRIEFING PAPERS No. 96-12 (Nov. 1996).

1. Applicability

* * *

a. Exemptions & Waiver

——————————ANNOTATIONS——————————

■ *Legislation & Regulations*

[1] **FAR Amendment**—A final rule revised FAR Part 12 to conform to a CAS rule (see item [3], below) exempting commercial item contracts and firm

■ GOVERNMENT CONTRACT GUIDEBOOK

fixed-price or fixed-price with economic price adjustment subcontracts (provided that the price adjustment is not based on actual costs incurred) from the CAS requirements. The rule also made corresponding changes to applicable contract clauses. The CAS rule implemented § 4205 of P.L. 104-106, which removed "contracts or subcontracts for the acquisition of commercial items" from mandatory CAS coverage. 63 Fed. Reg. 9048 (Feb. 23, 1998, effective Apr. 24, 1998). See 40 GC ¶ 106.

[2] **National Defense Authorization Act For Fiscal Year 1996**—P.L. 104-106 (Feb. 10, 1996), § 4205, includes a mandatory exemption from CAS coverage for "[c]ontracts and subcontracts for the acquisition of commercial items." The exemption will take effect on January 1, 1997, unless implementing regulations set forth an earlier date. See 38 GC ¶ 69.

[3] **Cost Accounting Standards Board**—Implementing § 8301 of the Federal Acquisition Streamlining Act of 1994 (P.L. 103-355) and § 4205 of the National Defense Authorization Act (P.L. 104-106), the CAS Board has revised the CAS applicability criteria to exempt individual firm, fixed-price contracts and subcontracts and fixed-price contracts with economic price adjustment provisions for the acquisition of "commercial items" from CAS requirements. The exemption, which is set forth in a final rule, applies without regard to the submission of cost data. 62 Fed. Reg. 31294 (June 6, 1997), 39 GC ¶ 294.

[4] **Cost Accounting Standards Board**—The CAS Board has deleted the exemption (48 CFR § 9903.201-1(b)(10)) from CAS requirements for negotiated contracts and subcontracts awarded to educational institutions other than Federally Funded Research and Development Centers. 59 Fed. Reg. 55746 (Nov. 8, 1994). The Board created a new 48 CFR Part 9905, effective January 9, 1995, containing separate CAS for educational institutions that essentially parallel the "modified" CAS coverage that applies to qualifying commercial contractors. The requirements for CAS compliance are two-fold: (1) an educational institution must disclose its actual cost accounting practices on a new Disclosure Statement (CASB-DS-2), and (2) the educational institution must consistently follow its disclosed cost accounting practices. The CAS Board has established a phased-in transition period for filing new DS-2s, depending on an institution's rank in receipt of federal funds as listed in Appendix A of OMB Circular A-21. See 36 GC ¶ 594.

■ *Miscellaneous*

[1] **Costs, Pricing & Accounting Report Article**—For an analysis of the new CAS for educational institutions, see Lemmer & Pompeo, "Cost Accounting Standards for Government Contracts With Educational Institutions," 94-12 CP&A REP. 3 (Dec. 1994).

* * *

3. Disclosure Statements

* * *

c. Form Of Submission

———————ANNOTATIONS———————

■ *Legislation & Regulations*

[1] **Cost Accounting Standards Board**—The CAS Board finalized the first full-scale revision of the CAS Disclosure Statement for commercial organizations (CASB-DS-1). The revision is effective February 28, 1996 (61 Fed. Reg. 7616); however, contractors will have a phase-in period within which to begin using the new form. The new form retains the eight-part format of the original DS-1, but alters its substance to address, among other things, certain cost measurement topics, such as cost of money, postretirement benefits, and employee stock option plans. In furtherance of its goal of balancing the need for disclosure against administrative burdens on contractors, the revised DS-1 reduces some detailed reporting requirements and clarifies the requirements for annual updating of the form. The greatest number of changes are in Part VII, "Deferred Compensation and Insurance Costs." See 38 GC ¶ 111.

■ *Miscellaneous*

[1] **Costs, Pricing & Accounting Report Article**—The new CASB-DS-1 Disclosure Statement is analyzed and its key terms compared to those in the original form in Barsalona & Kaplan, "The New CASB DS-1—Potential Pitfalls & Opportunities," 96-3 CP&A REP. 3 (Mar. 1996).

4. Individual Standards

———————ANNOTATIONS———————

■ *Legislation & Regulations*

[1] **Cost Accounting Standards Board**—on March 30, 1995, the CAS Board issued revisions to CAS 412 and CAS 413, which govern the measurement, adjustment, and allocation of pension costs. 60 Fed. Reg. 16533. The new rules address specific situations that the CAS Board viewed as problems, including pension cost determination, nonqualified pension plans, and termination accounting. See 37 GC ¶ 189.

■ *Miscellaneous*

[1] **Costs, Pricing & Accounting Report Articles**—For an analysis of the new CAS 412 and CAS 413, see McQuade & Buss, "The New CAS 412 & 413: Significant Pension Accounting Changes," 95-4 CP&A REP. 3 (Apr. 1995). The special allocations prescribed by CAS 403, 410, 418, and 420 are discussed in Manos & Giskin, "Special Allocations Under the Cost Accounting Standards," 96-10 CP&A REP. 3 (Oct. 1996).

■ GOVERNMENT CONTRACT GUIDEBOOK

[2] **Briefing Paper**—For discussion and practical suggestions about the CAS 412 and CAS 413 cost recovery rules applicable to pension and postretirement benefit costs, see Lemmer, Dwyer & Meagher, "Pension & Postretirement Benefit Costs: Current Rules & Future Issues," BRIEFING PAPERS No. 98-9 (Aug. 1998).

C. TRUTH IN NEGOTIATIONS ACT

───────────ANNOTATIONS───────────

■ *Miscellaneous*

[1] **Costs, Pricing & Accounting Report Article**—The regulatory implementation of the Federal Acquisition Streamlining Act of 1994 (FASA) amendments to TINA are discussed in Ryland, "The TINA Regulations Under FASA," 95-9 CP&A REP. 3 (Sept. 1995).

[2] **Briefing Papers**—For an examination of the 1994 amendments to TINA, see Simchak & Gildea, "Impact of FASA on the Truth in Negotiations Act," BRIEFING PAPERS No. 95-8 (July 1995). The new rules regarding selling commercial items to the Government, including the exemptions from TINA requirements for such procurements, are discussed in Wall & Sherry, "Pricing Commercial Items," BRIEFING PAPERS No. 95-13 (Dec. 1995).

[3] **Nash & Cibinic Report Article**—See "Truth in Negotiations: The FAR Implementation of FASA," 9 NASH & CIBINIC REP. ¶ 57 (Nov. 1995), for an explanation and critique of the revised rules implementing the 1994 TINA amendments.

1. Applicability

───────────ANNOTATIONS───────────

■ *Legislation & Regulations*

[1] **FAR Amendment**—Pursuant to FASA §§ 1201 and 1251, the FAR was revised to reflect the new uniform data submission threshold for civilian and military agency contracts—$500,000—subject to adjustment for inflation beginning October 1, 1995, and every five years thereafter (60 Fed. Reg. 48208, Sept. 18, 1995). However, the FAR Council found that an adjustment of the threshold for inflation was not required in 1995 (60 Fed. Reg. 49707, Sept. 26, 1995). The next adjustment will be made in 2000. See 36 GC ¶ 613; 37 GC ¶¶ 476, 507.

2. Exemptions & Waiver

───────────ANNOTATIONS───────────

■ *Legislation & Regulations*

[1] **National Defense Authorization Act For Fiscal Year 1996**—P.L. 104-106 (Feb. 10, 1996), § 4201 provides a clear statutory exemption from the

COSTS

requirement to submit cost or pricing data for contractors and subcontractors that are supplying a "commercial item" to the Government. Although FASA and its implementing regulations created a "commercial item" exemption from TINA's cost or pricing data submission requirements, P.L. 104-106 eliminates the existing "catalog or market price" exemption to TINA and substitutes an unqualified exemption for commercial items (as defined in FASA). The exemption is effective for solicitations issued or contracts awarded on or after January 1, 1997, unless implementing regulations set forth an earlier date. See 38 GC ¶ 69.

a. Adequate Price Competition

──────────ANNOTATIONS──────────

■ *Legislation & Regulations*

[1] **FAR Amendment**—The "adequate price competition" exception has been broadened to apply if only one offer is received from a responsible, responsive offeror provided "there was a reasonable expectation, based on market research or other assessment, that two or more responsible offerors, competing independently, would submit priced offers in response to the solicitation's expressed requirement." FAR 15.403-1(c). 60 Fed. Reg. 48208 (Sept. 18, 1995); 62 Fed. Reg. 51224 (Sept. 30, 1997, effective Oct. 10, 1997). See 39 GC ¶ 466. The FAR previously required that at least two responsive offers be received for the exception to apply.

b. Established Catalog Or Market Price

──────────ANNOTATIONS──────────

■ *Legislation & Regulations*

[1] **FAR Amendment**—Pursuant to § 4201 of P.L. 104-106, the FAR was amended to delete the "catalog or market price" exemption and substitute a straight exemption for commercial items as defined in FAR 2.101. 62 Fed. Reg. 224 (Jan. 2, 1997, effective Jan. 1, 1997). 39 GC ¶ 7.

[2] **FAR Amendment**—Pursuant to FASA, the FAR was amended to make the "established catalog or market price" exception more flexible. For example, the rule eliminated limitations on counting sales by affiliates and competitors. FAR 15.804-(b)(2). 60 Fed. Reg. 48208 (Sept. 18, 1995); see 37 GC ¶¶ 338, 476.

★ ★ ★

d. Commercial Item Procurements

──────────ANNOTATIONS──────────

■ *Legislation & Regulations*

[1] **FAR Amendment**—Pursuant to § 4201 of P.L. 104-106, the FAR was amended to eliminate the subordination (previously required by FASA) of

GOVERNMENT CONTRACT GUIDEBOOK

the "commercial item" exception to the traditional exceptions for adequate price competition, catalog- or market-priced commercial items, or prices set by law or regulation. The revision also deleted (1) the criteria established for the commercial item exception by FASA (i.e., that an exception could not be granted unless price reasonableness could be determined based on specific information requirements) and (2) the authority to obtain cost or pricing data for commercial item acquisitions when those criteria are not met. 62 Fed. Reg. 224 (Jan. 2, 1997, effective Jan. 1, 1997). See 39 GC ¶ 7.

[2] **FAR Amendment**—Pursuant to FASA §§ 1204(d)(2) and 1251(d)(2), the FAR was amended to provide a special "commercial item" exception to TINA requirements that may be granted if the Contracting Officer "does not have sufficient information to support an exception under" the three original exceptions and the Contracting Officer obtains sufficient pricing information to determine that the price is reasonable. 60 Fed. Reg. 48208 (Sept. 18, 1995); see 37 GC ¶ 476.

■ *Miscellaneous*

[1] **Costs, Pricing & Accounting Report Article**—The impact of the changes to the pricing of commercial items made by FASA, P.L. 104-106, the 1997 rewrite of FAR Part 15, and the revisions to the General Services Administration's multiple award schedule contracting procedures are analyzed in Ebert, "'Commercial Item' Acquisitions: A Primer on the New Pricing & Accounting Rules," 97-12 CP&A REP. 3 (Dec. 1997).

* * *

4. Submission Of Data

a. Form

The Standard Form 1411 presented in Figure 5-1 of the chapter text, which was used when submission of cost or pricing data was required, has been eliminated. The FAR still requires submission of essentially the same information but permits the information to be submitted in the contractor's own formats (see *Legislation & Regulations*, item [1], below).

———————ANNOTATIONS———————

■ *Legislation & Regulations*

[1] **FAR Amendment**—Standard Form 1411 (used for submitting cost or pricing data) and SF 1448 (used for submitting information other than cost or pricing data) have been eliminated. The FAR still requires essentially the same information to be submitted but permits the information to be submitted in prime contractors' and subcontractors' own formats or in an

alternate format specified in the solicitation. See FAR 15.403-5(b)(2), 15.404-3(c)(3). 62 Fed. Reg. 51224 (Sept. 30, 1997, effective Oct. 10, 1997). See 39 GC ¶ 467.

b. When Submitted

——————ANNOTATIONS——————

■ *Legislation & Regulations*

[1] **FAR Amendment**—Pursuant to FASA, the FAR was amended to specifically provide that data be submitted or identified in writing by the time of agreement on price or another time agreed upon by the parties. 60 Fed. Reg. 48208 (Sept. 18, 1995). See FAR 15.406-2; 37 GC ¶¶ 338, 476.

c. Subcontractor Data

——————ANNOTATIONS——————

■ *Legislation & Regulations*

[1] **FAR Amendment**—A final rule (FAR 15.404-3(c)(1)) raised the threshold to $10 million (from $1 million) for requiring a prospective subcontractor to submit cost or pricing data. 62 Fed. Reg. 51224 (Sept. 30, 1997, effective Oct. 10, 1997). See 39 GC ¶ 467.

■ *Cases & Decisions*

[1] **Prime Contractor Liable For Subcontractor's Failure To Disclose Unallowable Facilities Capital Charge In G&A Rate**—The Air Force (AF) sought to recover from the prime contractor under the "Price Reduction for Defective Cost or Pricing Data" clause the difference between the subcontractor's proposed 45% general and administrative rate and the 23.9% rate actually experienced. The difference was the unallowable facilities capital cost. The AF did not learn of the subcontractor's inclusion of the unallowable costs until two years after (1) the AF and the prime contractor had agreed on the prime contract price, and (2) the prime contractor and subcontractor had agreed on the subcontract price and the subcontractor had certified its cost or pricing data. The nature of the facilities capital charge was not evident from the subcontractor's CAS Disclosure Statement or the monthly accounting worksheets it furnished the Defense Contract Audit Agency. The Armed Services Board of Contract Appeals denied the prime contractor's appeal from the AF's action, concluding that the cost or pricing data the subcontractor actually furnished did not adequately disclose the unallowable facilities capital charge and that the AF detrimentally relied on the subcontractor's defective data. **Martin Marietta Corp., ASBCA 48223, 98-1 BCA ¶ 29592, reconsideration denied, 98-2 BCA ¶ 29741, 40 GC ¶ 326.**

[2] **Prime Contractor Was Required To Furnish Prospective Subcontractor Pricing Data It Did Not Possess Or Know About**—The contractor negotiated with a prospective first-tier subcontractor (Ford) to sup-

■ GOVERNMENT CONTRACT GUIDEBOOK

ply a component for an aircraft. A prospective second-tier sub (Ferranti) sent the first-tier sub a quotation to provide one of the component's subsystems. Based on this quotation, Ford submitted its proposal to the contractor in December 1987. In February 1988, Ferranti furnished Ford with a revised proposal, and in April Ford drafted a "memorandum" analyzing the revised proposal. In March 1988, the contractor disclosed the December 1987 proposal to the Government and subsequently executed a "Certificate of Current Cost or Pricing Data" as of June 1988. In January 1989, the contractor and Ford executed a fixed-price subcontract for the component, and Ford executed its own "Certificate." The Government alleged defective pricing against the contractor based on the contractor's failure to disclose Ford's April 1988 cost "memorandum." The board held that a contractor's duty to obtain and update pricing data from actual and prospective subs cannot be reduced by the contractor's subjective lack of knowledge or nonpossession of such data. **McDonnell Aircraft Co., ASBCA 44504, 97-1 BCA ¶ 28977, 39 GC ¶ 369.**

* * *

5. Certification Of Data

The language of the "Certificate of Current Cost or Pricing Data" set forth in Figure 5-2 of the text has been modified to permit the Contracting Officer and contractor to establish a cut-off date for the submission of cost or pricing data.

6. Liability For Defective Data

————————ANNOTATIONS————————

■ *Legislation & Regulations*

[1] FAR Amendment—A final rule (FAR 15.407-1(b)(7)(i)) expressly permits the Government to recover for defective pricing, in addition to the price adjustment amount, "any overpayment plus interest on the overpayments." 62 Fed. Reg. 51224 (Sept. 30, 1997, effective Oct. 10, 1997). See 39 GC ¶ 467.

■ *Cases & Decisions*

[1] "Christian Doctrine" Used To Incorporate "Price Reduction" Clause—The university's contract with the Government did not include the "Price Reduction for Defective Cost or Pricing Data" clause mandated by FAR 15.804-8(a). After negotiating an extension of a 1990 contract that increased the monthly rate over that paid during 1990 by 27%, the Contracting Officer issued a final decision reducing the price on the ground that the contractor had failed to supply certified cost or pricing data to support the 27% increase. In its appeal, the contractor argued that the Government's right to a reduction must be based on the "Price Reduction" clause, which was absent from the contract. The Department of Veterans Affairs Board

COSTS

Figure 5-2 [*Revised*]

**CERTIFICATE OF CURRENT COST
OR PRICING DATA**

This is to certify that, to the best of my knowledge and belief, the cost or pricing data (as defined in section 15.401 of the Federal Acquisition Regulation (FAR) and required under FAR subsection 15.403-4) submitted, either actually or by specific identification in writing, to the Contracting Officer or to the Contracting Officer's representative in support of ____* are accurate, complete, and current as of ____**. This certification includes the cost or pricing data supporting any advance agreements and forward pricing rate agreements between the offeror and the Government that are part of the proposal.

Firm _____

Signature _____

Name _____

Title _____

Date of execution*** _____

* Identify the proposal, request for price adjustment, or other submission involved, giving the appropriate identifying number (e.g., RFP No.).

**Insert the day, month, and year when price negotiations were concluded and price agreement was reached or, if applicable, an earlier date agreed upon between the parties that is as close as practicable to the date of agreement on price.

***Insert the day, month, and year of signing, which should be as close as practicable to the date when the price negotiations were concluded and the contract price was agreed to.

---

of Contract Appeals held that the "Price Reduction" clause is a mandatory clause that expresses a "significant or deeply ingrained strand of public procurement policy." As such, under the "Christian doctrine," when the clause has been omitted from a contract, it will be incorporated by operation of law. **University of Cal., San Francisco, VABCA 4661, 97-1 BCA ¶ 28642, 39 GC ¶ 39.**

[2] **Failure To Prepare Learning Curve Analysis Was Not TINA Violation**—The Government brought a defective pricing claim against a contractor alleging that the contractor failed to disclose a downward trend in labor hours. The downward trend was revealed by a learning curve analysis performed after award on the contractor's cost or pricing data by Government auditors. The Government argued that TINA required the contractor to present labor hour data in the form that the Government's

■ GOVERNMENT CONTRACT GUIDEBOOK

auditors later used. On appeal, the board granted summary judgment for the contractor finding that the Government had failed to prove that learning curves would have been used in contract negotiations. **Rosemount, Inc., ASBCA 37520, 95-2 BCA ¶ 27770, 37 GC ¶ 540.**

D. GOVERNMENT AUDIT RIGHTS

* * *

1. Procuring Agencies

————————ANNOTATIONS————————

■ *Legislation & Regulations*

[1] **FAR Amendment**—FAR Part 42 relating to policies and procedures for assigning and performing contract audit services was revised to designate the agency with the largest dollar amount of negotiated contracts as the "cognizant Federal agency" for purposes of establishing final indirect and forward pricing rates and administering the CAS under all contracts for a contractor business unit. The rule also clarifies the policy for delegating responsibility for establishing forward pricing and billing rates and final indirect cost rates and directs agencies to avoid duplicate audits, reviews, inspections, and examinations of contractors or subcontractors through the use of interagency agreements. 63 Fed. Reg. 9048 (Feb. 23, 1998, effective Apr. 24, 1998). See 40 GC ¶ 106.

■ *Miscellaneous*

[1] **Costs, Pricing & Accounting Report Article**—For a review of DCAA's history and roles in claims litigation, as well as suggestions for litigants facing DCAA audits, see Barnes, "Understanding DCAA's Roles in Contract Claims Litigation," 97-11 CP&A REP. 3 (Nov. 1997).

a. Price Proposal Audits

————————ANNOTATIONS————————

■ *Legislation & Regulations*

[1] **FAR Amendment**—A final rule (FAR 15.404-2) provides that audit assistance should be obtained only when the Contracting Officer needs additional information to determine a fair and reasonable price. Requests for field pricing assistance should be limited to selected areas, with full technical and audit reviews as the exceptions. 62 Fed. Reg. 51224 (Sept. 30, 1997, effective Oct. 10, 1997). See 39 GC ¶ 467.

* * *

1999 SUPPLEMENT

COSTS

c. Cost Or Pricing Data Audits

──────────ANNOTATIONS──────────

■ *Legislation & Regulations*

[1] **Federal Acquisition Streamlining Act**—FASA merged the audit provisions of TINA and of 10 USC § 2313 into a single section at 10 USC § 2313. FASA also consolidated audit rights for civilian agencies making them consistent Government-wide. P.L. 103-355, § 2201, 108 Stat. 3243 (Oct. 13, 1994).

[2] **FAR Amendments**—Pursuant to FASA, FAR 52.215-2(g) subjects to audit all cost-reimbursement, incentive, time-and-materials, labor-hour, or price-redeterminable subcontracts and requires the flow-down of the "Audit and Records–Negotiation" clause to all subcontracts of these types when certified cost or pricing data or cost performance records are required. All subcontracts below the simplified acquisition threshold are exempt from the flow-down requirement. Also pursuant to FASA, the FAR has been amended to (1) permit contractors to store records in electronic form, (2) restrict Contracting Officers from requesting preaward audits of indirect costs if the results of a recent audit are available, (3) delete the clause at FAR 52.215-1, "Examination of Records by Comptroller General," and revise the clauses at FAR 52.214-26, "Audit and Records–Sealed Bidding," and 52.215-2, "Audit and Records–Negotiation," to provide for examination of records by the Comptroller General, and (4) delete the requirement for TINA-related postaward audits. 60 Fed. Reg. 42648 (Aug. 16, 1995); 60 Fed. Reg. 48208 (Sept. 18, 1995); 60 Fed. Reg. 54045 (Oct. 19, 1995). See 37 GC ¶¶ 442, 476, 546.

★   ★   ★

SOCIOECONOMIC CONSIDERATIONS

6

1999 Supplement

Chapter Introduction / 6-2

A. Small Business Preferences
   ★ 1. Qualification / 6-3
   ★ 2. Contract Set-Asides / 6-4
       a. Total Set-Asides
       b. Partial Set-Asides
   ★ 3. Certificates Of Competency / 6-4
   ★ 4. Subcontracting / 6-4
       ★ a. By Private Firms / 6-6
       ★ b. By The SBA / 6-6
      5. Equal Access To Justice Act
         a. History
       ★ b. Eligibility / 6-7
         c. "Prevailing Party"
         d. Government Position Not "Substantially Justified"
       ★ e. Amount Of Recovery / 6-7
★ B. Women-Owned Small Business Preferences / 6-10
★ C. Labor Surplus Area Preferences / 6-10

■ GOVERNMENT CONTRACT GUIDEBOOK

   1. Qualification
   2. Contract Set-Asides
   3. Subcontracting
  D. Nondiscrimination Requirements
   1. Equal Employment Opportunity
    a. "Equal Opportunity" Clause
    b. Affirmative Action Plans
   2. Miscellaneous Requirements
   3. Administration & Enforcement
  E. Labor Standards Requirements
   1. Walsh-Healey Act
★   a. Coverage / **6-10**
    b. Administration & Enforcement
   2. Service Contract Act
    a. Coverage
    b. Administration & Enforcement
★ F. Buy American Act Requirements / **6-11**
  G. Environmental Protection Requirements
★ H. Drug-Free Workplace Requirements / **6-12**
★ I. Hiring Restrictions [*New Section*] / **6-12**
★ J. Distressed Communities [*New Section*] / **6-13**

CHAPTER INTRODUCTION

——————ANNOTATIONS——————

■ *Legislation & Regulations*

[1] **National Defense Authorization Act For Fiscal Year 1996**—P.L. 104-106 (Feb. 10, 1996), § 4203, establishes "commercial off-the-shelf" (COTS) items as a subset of "commercial items" and defines COTS items to include only commercial items that are "offered to the Government, without modification, in the same form in which [they are] sold in the commercial marketplace." Section 4203 exempts procurements of COTS items from even more procurement laws than "commercial items" and requires that the Office of Federal Procurement Policy publish a list of federal laws

1999 SUPPLEMENT

SOCIOECONOMIC CONSIDERATIONS

inapplicable to COTS items. The list will include any law imposing "Government-unique policies, procedures, requirements, or restrictions for the procurement of property or services," except those relating to certain unique protections to the Government (e.g., penalties for civil or criminal fraud). The provisions are effective January 1, 1997, unless an earlier date is set forth in implementing regulations. See 38 GC ¶ 69.

[2] **FAR Amendment**—Pursuant to the Federal Acquisition Streamlining Act of 1994 (FASA), P.L. 103-355, §§ 8105, 8301, FAR Subpart 12.5 lists provisions of laws that are not applicable (wholly or partially) to contracts for the acquisition of commercial items. The socioeconomic requirements that are inapplicable to commercial item buys include the following: (a) Drug Free Workplace Act, (b) Fly American requirements, (c) Contract Work Hours and Safety Standards Act certification, (d) Walsh-Healey Act, (e) Federal Water Pollution Control Act certification, (f) Clean Air Act certification, and (g) Service Contract Act (for subcontracts). 60 Fed. Reg. 48231 (Sept. 18, 1995). See 37 GC ¶ 489.

A. SMALL BUSINESS PREFERENCES

* * *

1. Qualification

———————ANNOTATIONS———————

■ *Legislation & Regulations*

[1] **FAR Amendment & SBA Final Rules**—Guidelines issued by the Clinton Administration on June 24, 1998, revised the process for determining the eligibility of small disadvantaged businesses (SDBs) to win federal contracts. According to the guidelines, only SDBs "in industries that show the ongoing effects of discrimination" as determined by the Commerce Department will be able to receive up to a 10% "price evaluation adjustment" in bidding for Government contracts at the prime contract level. The new program is intended to restore limited affirmative action preferences in federal procurement. The FAR has been amended to implement the Administration's guidelines (see FAR subpt. 19.11). 63 Fed. Reg. 35719 (June 30, 1998, effective Oct. 1, 1998); 64 Fed. Reg. 36221 (July 2, 1999). In addition, the SBA has issued final rules that, among other things, establish the procedures for certifying firms as SDBs and revise program eligibility procedures. 63 Fed. Reg. 35767 (June 30, 1998, effective Aug. 24, 1998). See 40 GC ¶ 318, 41 GC ¶ 304.

■ *Miscellaneous*

[1] **Briefing Paper**—For a survey of SBA regulations and case law reflecting major revisions to SBA rules on the eligibility of small businesses for participation in federal programs that provide preferences in Government contracting to small businesses, see Hordell & Hoffman, "Small Business Size Appeals/Edition III," BRIEFING PAPERS No. 96-9 (Aug. 1996).

GOVERNMENT CONTRACT GUIDEBOOK

2. Contract Set-Asides

────────────ANNOTATIONS────────────

■ *Legislation & Regulations*

[1] **FAR Amendment**—FAR Part 19 (and related clauses at FAR Part 52) have been amended to implement a provision of the Federal Acquisition Streamlining Act of 1994, P.L. 103-355, reserving each contract for the purchase of goods or services that has an anticipated value greater than $2,500 but not greater than $100,000 for exclusive small business participation (unless the Contracting Officer determines there is no reasonable expectation of obtaining competitive offers from two or more small businesses). 61 Fed. Reg. 39207 (July 26, 1996). See 38 GC ¶ 365.

* * *

3. Certificates Of Competency

────────────ANNOTATIONS────────────

■ *Cases & Decisions*

[1] **SBA Can Refuse To Issue COC On Basis Not Questioned By Contracting Officer**—The Contracting Officer (CO) determined that the low bidder on a dredging contract lacked capacity in that its dredge did not meet contract requirements and referred the matter to the SBA under COC procedures. The SBA found the bidder had adequate capacity; nevertheless, the SBA denied the COC request on financial grounds. The bidder sought an injunction in the Court of Federal Claims citing FAR 19.602-2(a)(2), which only requires the SBA to conduct a field investigation for those responsibility elements that the CO's referral stated that the bidder did not meet. The court dismissed the suit finding FAR 19.602-2(a)(2) inconsistent with both FAR 19.601(a) (which appears to authorize the SBA to evaluate all factors underlying a responsiblity determination) and SBA regulations (which do not limit the SBA's site investigation to the elements in the CO's decision). Once the CO refers a responsibility matter to the SBA, SBA procedures generally govern. *C&G Excavating, Inc. v. U.S.*, 32 Fed. Cl. 231 (1994), 13 FPD ¶ 91, 36 GC ¶ 599.

4. Subcontracting

────────────ANNOTATIONS────────────

■ *Legislation & Regulations*

[1] **FAR Amendments**—After the Supreme Court's 1995 *Adarand* decision (see *Cases & Decisions,* item [1], below) the Department of Justice proposed a structure to reform affirmative action in federal procurement (see 38 GC ¶ 255). Two interim FAR rules implemented that structure. See

SOCIOECONOMIC CONSIDERATIONS

FAC 97-06, 63 Fed. Reg. 35719 (June 30, 1998, effective for solicitations issued on or after Oct. 1, 1998), and FAC 97-07, 63 Fed. Reg. 36120 (July 1, 1998, effective for solicitations issued on or after Jan. 1, 1999); 40 GC ¶¶ 318, 458. The FAR has now been amended to finalize the interim policies providing for (a) a price evaluation adjustment of up to 10% to SDBs in certain Standard Industrial Classification groups where there has been a history of "persistent and significant underutilization of minority firms...attributable to past or present discrimination" either regionally or nationwide, (b) a source selection factor or subfactor in favor of a prime contractor that plans to use an SDB as a subcontractor, and (c) monetary incentives to prime contractors to encourage subcontracts with SDBs. 64 Fed. Reg. 36221 (July 2, 1999). See 41 GC ¶ 304.

[2] **FAR Amendment**—A final rule updated the definition of "small disadvantaged business concern" to reflect new categories of individuals considered to be socially and economically disadvantaged. Another final rule clarified eligibility and procedural requirements for § 8(a) procurements, making several changes to the interim rule issued in December 1996 (see 39 GC ¶ 5). 62 Fed. Reg. 44802 (Aug. 22, 1997). See 39 GC ¶ 424.

■ Cases & Decisions

[1] **Supreme Court Finds Constitutionality Of Federal Race-Based Affirmative Action Programs Subject To "Strict Scrutiny"**—A federal highway construction contract awarded by the Department of Transportation contained a Subcontracting Compensation Clause (SCC) program which authorized an additional payment to the prime contractor as an incentive to award subcontracts to small disadvantaged businesses (SDBs)—up to 1.5% for using one SDB subcontractor or up to 2% for hiring two or more SDBs. The SCC program implemented a requirement under the Surface Transportation and Uniform Relocation Assistance Act that not less than 10% of the appropriations be spent with SDBs. Although a nonminority subcontractor submitted the lowest bid on a guardrail subcontract, the prime contractor awarded the subcontract to an SDB. The nonminority subcontractor sued, contending that the SCC program was unconstitutional as a denial of equal protection. The Supreme Court, in a divided opinion, ruled that all race-based classifications must withstand "strict scrutiny" under the U.S. Constitution. In other words, the program must serve a compelling Government interest and must be "narrowly tailored" to further that interest. The Court remanded the case for further consideration. The opinion overruled earlier decisions holding federal race-based programs subject to a lower standard of scrutiny. **Adarand Constructors, Inc., v. Peña, 115 S. Ct. 2097 (1995), 37 GC ¶ 332.**

★ **Note**—Because affirmative action programs have been widely used in federal contracting—often through subcontracting quotas, requirements, and preferences—the *Adarand* decision will have a significant impact on the future of many such programs. Contractors have begun to challenge minority preference programs in court (see generally 37 GC ¶ 598), although many of the challenges have failed (see generally 38 GC ¶ 321). In addition, pursuant to a Memorandum issued by President Clinton in July 1995, all federal affirmative action and other sheltered competition programs are undergoing review in light of the principles set forth in *Adarand*. See 37 GC ¶ 385. As part of the Government's review of affirmative action

■ GOVERNMENT CONTRACT GUIDEBOOK

programs after the *Adarand* decision, in 1996 the Department of Defense suspended DFARS sections that prescribe acquisition set-asides for small disadvantaged businesses. 61 Fed. Reg. 7739 (Feb. 29, 1996), 18195 (Apr. 24, 1996). See 38 GC ¶¶ 112, 209. In addition, on the remand of the *Adarand* case, the District Court rejected the constitutionality of the affirmative action programs, *Adarand Constructors, Inc. v. Peña*, 965 F. Supp. 1556 (D. Colo. 1997), 39 GC ¶ 287, *vacated*, 169 F.3d 1292 (10th Cir. 1999), 41 GC ¶ 132.

a. By Private Firms

─────────ANNOTATIONS─────────

■ *Legislation & Regulations*

[1] **FAR Amendment**—FAR 52.219-9 has been amended to clarify that prime contractors may rely on the information contained in the SBA's Procurement Automated Source System (PASS) as an accurate representation of a concern's size and ownership characteristics for the purpose of maintaining a small business source list. 59 Fed. Reg. 67056 (Dec. 28, 1994). See 37 GC ¶ 7.

b. By The SBA

─────────ANNOTATIONS─────────

■ *Cases & Decisions*

[1] **Agency Cannot Manipulate Contract's Minimum Value To Avoid Competing Procurement**—The Public Health Service (PHS) issued a solicitation for workstations and related equipment and services, intending to procure the items as an 8(a) Program set aside. The PHS divided the $24.5-million requirement among equipment, software, and services so as to avoid the $5-million contract price threshold for requiring competition under the 8(a) Program. In a protest from an unsolicited firm, the board held that the PHS's breakdown of the procurement was not based on any established budgetary limitations or any true analysis of the agency's requirements and violated the sole-source threshold of the 8(a) Program. **Dynamic Decisions, Inc. v. Department of Health & Human Services, GSBCA 13170-P et al., 95-2 BCA ¶ 27732, 1995 BPD ¶ 102, 37 GC ¶ 409.**

■ *Miscellaneous*

[1] **Delegation Of Authority**—On May 6, 1998, the SBA signed agreements with 25 federal agencies that will allow the agencies to contract directly with firms participating the the SBA's 8(a) Program. These "delegations of authority" remove the SBA from its traditional contract "middleman" or oversight role in the 8(a) Program. The agencies signing delegation agreements account for 95% of all federal procurement activity. The delegations of authority do not affect the SBA's authority to accept or reject firms from participating in the 8(a) Program. See 40 GC ¶ 228.

SOCIOECONOMIC CONSIDERATIONS

5. Equal Access To Justice Act

* * *

b. Eligibility

―――――――――ANNOTATIONS―――――――――

■ *Cases & Decisions*

[1] **Small Subcontractor Cannot Obtain EAJA Relief Unless Sponsoring Prime Contractor Meets Statute's Size Standards**—Affirming the District Court's decision and following rulings of the Armed Services Board of Contract Appeals, the U.S. Court of Appeals for the Ninth Circuit held that a prime contractor sponsoring a subcontractor's Contract Disputes Act claim may prevail under the EAJA only if the prime meets the EAJA's size and net worth standard. In this case, the subcontractor met the EAJA's size and net worth standards but the prime did not. **Southwest Marine, Inc. v. U.S., 43 F.3d 420 (9th Cir. 1994), 37 GC ¶ 150.**

* * *

e. Amount Of Recovery

―――――――――ANNOTATIONS―――――――――

■ *Cases & Decisions*

[1] **EAJA Recovery Rate For Expert Witness Costs Can Exceed DFARS Maximum**—The contractor sought to recover from the Government the fees it paid to its expert witnesses. The EAJA (5 USC § 504(b)(1)(A)) states that "no expert witness shall be compensated at a rate in excess of the highest rate of compensation for expert witnesses paid by the agency involved." Defense FAR Supplement 237.104(f)(1) provided that "[p]ayment to each expert or consultant for personal services...shall not exceed the highest rate fixed...for grade GS-15," which at that time was $41.49 per hour. Although the Government argued that the DFARS-specified rate was the maximum that the contractor could recover under the EAJA, the Armed Services Board of Contract Appeals (ASBCA) noted that the Government paid its own expert witness at an hourly rate of $210 and presumed that this rate was proper and appropriate. Because the Government did not rebut that presumption, the Board held the rate did not exceed "the highest rate of compensation for expert witnesses paid by the agency involved." **Techplan Corp., ASBCA 41470 et al., 98-2 BCA ¶ 29954, 40 GC ¶ 474.**

[2] **Federal Circuit Determines Meaning Of Word "Agent" In EAJA—Contractor Appearing "Pro Se" Cannot Recover Fees**—After prevailing before the Department of Veterans Affairs Board of Contract Appeals (VABCA) in various disputes under a services contract, the contractor filed an EAJA request to recover its litigation expenses. Included were (1) wages for several employees (including one who had testified as an expert witness)

GOVERNMENT CONTRACT GUIDEBOOK

paid for all hours worked on the claims, and (2) the salary (plus overhead and profit) of a partner, Molnar, who represented the partnership in the Board appeal. The VABCA held that the EAJA (a) only permits recovery of fees paid to *outside* consultants or independent expert witnesses and (b) does not permit recovery for the salaries of an *applicant's officers or employees*. VABCA 3856E, 97-2 BCA ¶ 29008. In its appeal to the U.S. Court of Appeals for the Federal Circuit, the contractor noted that the EAJA expressly allows recovery of "reasonable attorney or agent fees" and urged that the word "agent" includes all "non-attorney representatives of a prevailing party," including Molnar. The court first noted that the EAJA requires that fees awarded be based on the prevailing market rates for the "kind and quality of the services furnished." The court reasoned that the "fees" must be those of a person who normally furnishes the services needed to prosecute a claim. The prevailing party's employees generally do not regularly furnish that type of service and are not usually people "qualified...for the proceedings involved." The statutory language therefore indicates that "agents" are *specialized representatives* of litigants; they include nonattorney practitioners authorized to represent clients with the special permission of a tribunal. Molnar was not a specialized nonattorney practitioner retained to prosecute the claim; the VABCA's rules do not expressly authorize contractors to hire such outside agents. Furthermore, the EAJA's legislative history shows that Congress deleted proposed language that would have allowed compensation at an hourly rate for a litigating party's personal absence from a business. Based on the above reasoning, the Federal Circuit affirmed the VABCA's decision. **Fanning Phillips & Molnar v. West, 160 F.3d 717 (Fed. Cir. 1998), 17 FPD ¶ 121, 40 GC ¶ 555.**

★ **Note**—Procuring agency boards of contract appeals apparently have split on the question of whether a contractor representing itself in an appeal through a nonattorney principal may obtain EAJA recovery; *Fanning* appears to clarify the issue to some extent. See, e.g., *Simpson Contracting Corp.*, EBCA E-9602-190, 96-2 BCA ¶ 28471, 38 GC ¶ 599, and cases cited therein, and *Joseph R. DeClerk & Assocs., Inc.*, ASBCA 49595, 97-2 BCA ¶ 29268. The boards also have split on the question of whether a contractor represented by a principal or employee who is an attorney may obtain EAJA recovery. Compare *Giancola & Assocs. v. GSA*, GSBCA 12305-C, 93-3 BCA ¶ 26146, 35 GC ¶ 182, with *Dalton v. Gaffny Corp.*, item [4], below. Because contractor's representative in *Fanning* was not an attorney, the court did not have to decide the in-house attorney issue. For additional discussion of these issues, see Nash, "Postscript II: Equal Access to Justice Act," 8 NASH & CIBINIC REP. ¶ 51 (Sept. 1994).

[3] Boards Continue To Differ On How To Compute EAJA Recovery For Paralegal Services—A qualifying applicant for EAJA fees claimed for 14.5 hours of paralegal services at the $45 per hour billed by its attorneys. The Government argued that the contractor can recover only the amount the paralegals actually cost the attorneys, not the amount the attorneys billed. The VABCA noted a split among agency boards on the issue, citing as an example the ASBCA holding in *Walsky Const. Co.*, ASBCA 41541, 95-2 BCA ¶ 27889, 37 GC ¶ 526 (see item [6], below), which limited recovery for paralegal services to the law firm's cost. The VABCA, however, noted that the EAJA expressly states that the tribunal "shall award" the prevailing party the "fees and expenses incurred by that party," and that preventing an applicant from fully recovering the amount it was charged would dis-

SOCIOECONOMIC CONSIDERATIONS

courage use of paralegals and serve as an undesirable disincentive to cost-efficient litigation. The board allowed the applicant to recover for paralegal services at the rate billed, subject to "the statutory cap on attorney fees" and VABCA's determination of the rates' reasonableness. **Adams Const. Co., VABCA 4669E et al., 98-1 BCA ¶ 29479, 40 GC ¶ 123.**

★ Note—The same board has held that recovery under the EAJA is not available to an accounting firm seeking fees for "representation" of a contractor before the board. *Landscaping by Femia Assocs., Inc.*, VABCA 5099E, 99-1 BCA ¶ 30276 (noting, however, that fees paid for *accounting services* "under certain circumstances" might be recoverable under the EAJA), 41 GC ¶ 209.

[4] **Federal Circuit Finds No Substantial Evidence Supporting ASBCA Finding That Contractor Was Represented By Attorney**—In a 1988 appeal before the ASBCA, the contractor was represented by Michael Gaffny, who became a corporate officer in 1977 and "worked as in-house counsel" from 1990 (on becoming an attorney) until leaving the company to enter private practice in July 1991. After his admission to the bar, Gaffny's correspondence generally used the title "Vice President" or "Attorney Pro Se." He did not notify ASBCA of his new capacity, but did sign a March 1991 submission as "Michael Gaffny, Esq." and an April 1991 paper as "Michael Gaffny, Esq., Attorney Pro Se." At the board hearing in June 1991, Gaffny served as the contractor's principal witness. The ASBCA awarded the contractor EAJA legal fees for Gaffny's services. See 38 GC ¶ 139. The Federal Circuit reversed the ASBCA, holding that there was no substantial evidence for the board's finding that Gaffny's 1991 correspondence gave the board or the agency reason to believe that he was a licensed attorney after his having represented the company as a corporate officer or "attorney pro se" for over two years. Also, Gaffny's service as a witness raised further presumption that he was acting as a corporate officer. **Dalton v. Gaffny Corp., 16 FPD ¶ 19 (Fed. Cir. 1997) (nonprecedential), 39 GC ¶ 127.**

★ Note—The Federal Circuit avoided answering the question of whether the board could properly award EAJA legal fees for a corporate in-house attorney.

[5] **EAJA Allows Contractor To Recover Cost Of Experts It Did Not Introduce As Witnesses**—The EAJA permits a qualifying prevailing contractor to recover "expert witness fees." The ASBCA held that this includes fees paid to experts that failed to appear as witnesses in the appeal. **Applied Cos., ASBCA 43210, 95-1 BCA ¶ 27371, 37 GC ¶ 33.**

[6] **Contractor Recovers Certain Fax/Courier Expenses But Not Others**—In view of the distances between the locations of the contractor's attorney, the Government's attorney, and the board, the contractor's attorney's limited use of telefacsimile and courier services to exchange appeal information among the principals was reasonable. However, the costs of similar communications between the attorney and either the contractor or third parties must be excluded. Similarly, the contractor may not recover travel-related costs in having an Anchorage-based court reporter provide stenographic services for depositions in Fairbanks; absent "exigent circumstances" not present in this case, attorneys should use a local reporter. Finally, the EAJA provision for recovery of expenses of expert witnesses bars recovery of expenses for lay witnesses. **Walsky Const. Co., ASBCA 41541, 95-2 BCA ¶ 27889, 37 GC ¶ 526.**

GOVERNMENT CONTRACT GUIDEBOOK

★ **Note**—Compare *Freedom, NY, Inc.*, ASBCA 35671, 98-1 BCA ¶ 29711 (EAJA permits recovery for attorney's fax/courier communications to client), 40 GC ¶ 314.

B. WOMEN-OWNED SMALL BUSINESS PREFERENCES

————————ANNOTATIONS————————

■ *Legislation & Regulations*

[1] **FAR Amendment**—The FAR was amended to delete separate coverage relating to women-owned businesses and revise the coverage to place women-owned businesses on the same footing as small disadvantaged businesses. 60 Fed. Reg. 48258 (Sept. 18, 1995, effective Oct. 1, 1995). See 37 GC ¶ 477.

C. LABOR SURPLUS AREA PREFERENCES

————————ANNOTATIONS————————

■ *Legislation & Regulations*

[1] **Federal Acquisition Streamlining Act**—FASA § 7101(a) deleted the statutory priority for award of set asides to and the statutory basis for a procurement preference for concerns located in LSAs. P.L. 103-355, 108 Stat. 3243 (Oct. 13, 1994) (deleting 15 USC § 644(e), (f)).

[2] **FAR Amendment**—Pursuant to FASA, the LSA set-aside and subcontracting programs were removed from the FAR. 60 Fed. Reg. 48258 (Sept. 18, 1995, effective Oct. 1, 1995). See 37 GC ¶ 477.

* * *

E. LABOR STANDARDS REQUIREMENTS

* * *

1. Walsh-Healey Act

a. Coverage

————————ANNOTATIONS————————

■ *Legislation & Regulations*

[1] **FAR Amendment**—A final rule adopted without change the interim rule published in December 1996 (see 39 GC ¶ 5) eliminating the requirement

SOCIOECONOMIC CONSIDERATIONS

that contractors subject to the Walsh-Healey Act be either manufacturers or regular dealers. The amendment is pursuant to § 7201 of FASA and conforms to Department of Labor regulations. 62 Fed. Reg. 44802 (Aug. 22, 1997). See 39 GC ¶ 424.

* * *

F. BUY AMERICAN ACT REQUIREMENTS

————————ANNOTATIONS————————

■ *Legislation & Regulations*

[1] **FAR Amendment**—A final rule implements revised thresholds for application of the Trade Agreements Act and the North American Free Trade Agreement. 63 Fed. Reg. 34058 (June 22, 1998, effective Aug. 21, 1998). See 40 GC ¶ 322.

[2] **FAR Amendment**—The FAR has been amended to implement the renegotiated GATT Agreement on Government Procurement (Uruguay Round) that became effective January 1, 1996. Although the interim rule does not impose any new requirements on contractors, it changes the list of designated foreign countries and extends applicability of the Trade Agreements Act to all agencies for supply and service contracts over certain dollar thresholds. 60 Fed. Reg. 67514 (Dec. 29, 1995); 61 Fed. Reg. 31612 (June 20, 1996). See 38 GC ¶¶ 9, 309.

[3] **DFARS Amendment**—DFARS 225.402 and the accompanying clause at DFARS 252.225-7007 have been amended to implement the DOD-unique requirements of the renegotiated 1996 GATT Agreement on Government Procurement (Uruguay Round) so as to permit the purchase of non-designated country end products if sufficient U.S.-made, qualifying country, or eligible products are not available. 61 Fed. Reg. 130 (Jan. 3, 1996). See 38 GC ¶ 9.

[4] **DFARS Amendment**—DFARS 225.402 has been amended to provide that the value of an acquisition for purposes of determining the applicability of both the NAFTA Act and the Trade Agreements Act is the total value of all end products subject to the Acts. 61 Fed. Reg. 7739 (Feb. 29, 1996), 18195 (Apr. 24, 1996). See 38 GC ¶¶ 112, 209.

[5] **National Defense Authorization Act For Fiscal Year 1995**—P.L. 103-337, § 812, 108 Stat. 2815 (1994), amended 10 USC § 2533 specifying the factors to be considered by DOD in determining whether to grant a public interest exception to the Buy American Act (e.g., the need to ensure access to state-of-the-art commercial technology, to maintain the same source of supply for spare parts, or to protect national security). An interim rule implements the change by amending DFARS 225.102. 60 Fed. Reg. 34470 (July 3, 1995). See 37 GC ¶ 367.

[6] **Customs Service Final Rule**—The U.S. Customs Service issued a final rule implementing the provisions of NAFTA governing the determination of country of origin. The final rule establishes the standard for determining when the

■ GOVERNMENT CONTRACT GUIDEBOOK

country of origin of a good is one of the parties to NAFTA (the U.S., Mexico, and Canada). 60 Fed. Reg. 46334 (Sept. 6, 1995). See 37 GC ¶ 465.

* * *

H. DRUG-FREE WORKPLACE REQUIREMENTS

————————ANNOTATIONS————————

■ *Legislation & Regulations*

[1] **FAR Amendment**—Implementing § 4301(a) of P.L. 104-106 (Feb. 10, 1996), the FAR has been amended to delete the requirement that an offeror provide a drug-free workplace certification. 61 Fed. Reg. 69286 (Dec. 31, 1996). See 39 GC ¶ 6.

I. HIRING RESTRICTIONS [*NEW SECTION*]

On March 8, 1995, President Clinton signed an Executive Order authorizing the Secretary of Labor to terminate contracts (worth over $100,000) between the Federal Government and contractors that hire permanent replacement workers for strikers during a lawful strike and to debar such contractors from receiving future contracts. The Order was later set aside by a federal court. (See *Legislation & Regulations*, item [1], and *Cases & Decisions*, item [1], below.) President Clinton also issued an Executive Order on February 13, 1996, subjecting contractors that knowingly hire illegal immigrants to debarment from federal contracting (see *Legislation & Regulations*, item [2], below.)

————————ANNOTATIONS————————

■ *Legislation & Regulations*

[1] **Executive Order 12954**—President Clinton issued an Executive Order barring the Government from doing business with companies that hire permanent replacement workers during lawful strikes (60 Fed. Reg. 13023, Mar. 10, 1995). The Order, which applies to contracts over the simplified acquisition threshold ($100,000), charges the Secretary of Labor with administering and enforcing the policy. If the Secretary determines that a federal contractor has permanently replaced lawfully striking workers (*after* the effective date of the Order, March 8, 1995), the Secretary may direct the agency involved to terminate the contract for convenience. The Secretary may also debar from future contracts any contractor that has hired permanent striker replacements even if before the March 8 effective date of the Order. The Secretary issued final regulations implementing the Executive Order on May 25, 1995 (60 Fed. Reg. 27856). See 37 GC ¶ 142.

SOCIOECONOMIC CONSIDERATIONS

[2] **Executive Order 12989**—Under an Executive Order issued by President Clinton, federal contractors who knowingly hire illegal immigrants will face debarment from federal contracting (61 Fed. Reg. 6091, Feb. 15, 1996). The Order vests the Attorney General (AG) with responsibility to both administer and enforce the Order. The AG may investigate to determine whether a contractor has hired illegal immigrants and hold hearings. If the AG finds that the contractor is not in compliance with the Immigration and Nationality Act employment provisions, the AG must transmit that determination to the contracting agency, and the agency head then "shall consider the contractor or an organizational unit thereof for debarment" or other appropriate action. See 38 GC ¶ 87.

■ *Cases & Decisions*

[1] **Court Sets Aside Striker Replacement Executive Order**—The U.S. Court of Appeals for the District of Columbia Circuit has set aside Executive Order 12954 (see *Legislation & Regulations*, item [1], above), which permitted debarment of federal contractors that hire permanent replacements for lawful strikers. The court held that the Order was judicially reviewable and that it conflicted with the National Labor Relations Act, which guarantees the right to hire permanent replacements. **Chamber of Commerce v. Reich, 74 F.3d 1322 (D.C. Cir.), 38 GC ¶ 78, rehearing denied, 83 F.3d 442 (D.C. Cir. 1996), 38 GC ¶ 254.**

★ **Note**—On September 9, 1996, the Clinton Administration decided not to appeal this decision. See 38 GC ¶ 449.

J. DISTRESSED COMMUNITIES [*NEW SECTION*]

On May 21, 1996, President Clinton issued an Executive Order granting incentives to encourage business activity in areas of general economic distress (see *Legislation & Regulations*, item [1], below). The incentives include a price or an evaluation credit in assessing offers for Government contracts in unrestricted competitions.

———————ANNOTATIONS———————

■ *Legislation & Regulations*

[1] **Executive Order 13005**—President Clinton issued an Executive Order (61 Fed. Reg. 26069, May 24, 1996) granting incentives, such as a price or an evaluation credit in assessing offers for Government contracts in unrestricted competitions, to encourage business activity in areas of general economic distress. The Order defines an area of general economic distress as any census tract having a poverty rate of at least 20% or any designated Federal Empowerment Zone, Supplemental Empowerment Zone, Enhanced Enterprise Community, or Enterprise Community. The Secretary of Commerce, who is charged with implementing the Order, may designate additional rural or Indian reservation areas as areas of general economic distress based on the unemployment rate, degree of poverty, extent of

GOVERNMENT CONTRACT GUIDEBOOK

outmigration, and rates of business formation and business growth. In developing policies and procedures, the Order directs the Commerce Secretary to consider also the size of the businesses qualified under the Order; qualified large or small businesses must employ a significant number of residents from an area of general economic distress and have either a significant physical presence in such an area or a direct impact on generating significant economic activity therein. The Commerce Secretary must draft all rules, regulations, and guidelines necessary to implement the Order within 90 days of May 21, and must issue a report to the President on the status and effectiveness of the program by December 1, 1996. See 38 GC ¶ 261.

FRAUD AND ETHICAL CONSIDERATIONS

7

1999 Supplement

★ *Chapter Introduction* / **7-3**

A. Fraud
    1. Civil False Claims Act
        a. Key Definitions
        b. Burden Of Proof
        c. Penalties
★   2. "Qui Tam" Provisions / **7-3**
    ★ a. Relators / **7-4**
    ★ b. Limitations / **7-4**
    ★ c. Procedures / **7-6**
    ★ d. Recovery / **7-7**
    3. Criminal False Claims Act
        a. "Claim"
        b. Knowledge & Intent

GOVERNMENT CONTRACT GUIDEBOOK

      c. Presentation Against Government

      d. Penalties

   4. False Statements Act

      a. Included Offenses

★   b. Elements / 7-7

      c. Penalties

   5. Mail & Wire Fraud

   6. Program Fraud Civil Remedies Act

★7. Major Fraud Act / 7-8

B. Corruption

   1. Anti-Kickback Enforcement Act Of 1986

      a. Prohibited Conduct

      b. Penalties

   2. Bribery & Illegal Gratuities Statutes

      a. Bribery Statute

      b. Illegal Gratuities Statute

★ 3. Procurement Integrity Act / 7-8

  ★ a. Prohibitions / 7-10

  ★ b. Penalties / 7-11

   4. Byrd Amendment

  ★ a. Prohibitions / 7-11

      b. Penalties

★ 5. Lobbying Activities [*New Section*] / 7-12

C. Enforcement

★ 1. Inspectors General / 7-13

   2. Department Of Justice

★ 3. Suspension & Debarment / 7-13

      a. Suspension

  ★ b. Debarment / 7-14

FRAUD AND ETHICAL CONSIDERATIONS

CHAPTER INTRODUCTION

──────────ANNOTATIONS──────────

■ *Miscellaneous*

[1] **Book**—THE GOVERNMENT CONTRACT COMPLIANCE HANDBOOK (Federal Publications, 3d ed. 1999), by attorneys at the law firm of Seyfarth, Shaw, Fairweather & Geraldson, provides in-depth substantive information as well as practical tips to help Government contractors avoid civil and criminal liability to the Government for fraud and other offenses.

A. FRAUD

★ ★ ★

2. "Qui Tam" Provisions

──────────ANNOTATIONS──────────

■ *Cases & Decisions*

[1] **Federal Court Finds "Qui Tam" Provisions Unconstitutional**—A U.S. District Court in Texas held that the "qui tam" provisions of the False Claims Act are unconstitutional because they violate the "irreducible constitutional minimum" standing requirement of Article III, § 2, of the U.S. Constitution. The court also intimated in dicta that the provisions may violate the Constitution's Appointments Clause (Article II, § 2), which vests the power to appoint officers of the U.S. exclusively in the Executive Branch and "would raise serious concerns under the separation of powers principles [Article II, § 3] as well." **U.S. ex rel. Riley v. St. Luke's Episcopal Hosp.**, No. H-94-3996 (S.D. Tex., Oct. 24, 1997), 39 GC ¶ 549.

★ **Note**—The ruling conflicts with decisions of the U.S. Courts of Appeals for the Ninth and Second Circuits.

■ *Miscellaneous*

[1] **Department Of Justice Statistics**—Since the adoption of the 1986 qui tam amendments to the False Claims Act, the Government has recovered $2.2 billion in civil fraud penalties in whistleblower-initiated cases, while whistleblowers have received about $300 million. Half of that recovery has occurred in the last three years. The number of whistleblower suits filed since the 1986 amendments has steadily increased from 33 cases in Fiscal Year 1987 to 534 cases in FY 1997. Although the whistleblower suits have involved fraud against a wide range of Government agencies, the majority of them have involved health care fraud. For example, since 1997 two suits against health care companies have resulted in recoveries of over $450 million. 40 GC ¶ 507.

GOVERNMENT CONTRACT GUIDEBOOK

a. Relators

————————ANNOTATIONS————————

■ *Cases & Decisions*

[1] **In-House Attorney May Bring "Qui Tam" Suit Against Former Employer**—A former in-house attorney of a Government contractor filed a "qui tam" suit against the company alleging that the contractor had committed fraud against the Government. The U.S. District Court for the Eastern District of Virginia held that nothing in the False Claims Act prevents in-house counsel from being a relator in a "qui tam" suit. However, state law duties independent of the False Claims Act may have the practical effect of precluding such actions. In this case, Virginia law prevented the attorney from disclosing his client's confidential information on which the "qui tam" claims were based. Therefore, the court dismissed the "qui tam" suit. **U.S. ex rel. Doe v. X Corp., 862 F. Supp. 1502 (E.D. Va. 1994), 36 GC ¶ 596.**

b. Limitations

————————ANNOTATIONS————————

■ *Cases & Decisions*

[1] **Supreme Court Rejects Retroactive Application Of 1986 FCA Amendment**—Before 1986, the False Claims Act (FCA) barred any qui tam action that was based on evidence or information the Government had when the action was brought. In 1986, however, the FCA was amended to remove that bar and permit suits based on information in the Government's possession, provided that if the allegations in the complaint are based on public information, then the relator must be the "original source" of the information. In this case, the defendant had disclosed to the Government, in the early 1980s, the alleged violation that was the subject of a qui tam suit filed in 1989. The U.S. Court of Appeals for the Ninth Circuit had ruled that the 1986 FCA amendment should be applied retroactively in this case to permit the suit to go forward. The U.S. Supreme Court reversed, finding that the 1986 FCA amendment does not apply to actions that took place before its enactment, and therefore the defendant's disclosure of information about the alleged illegalities to the Government constituted a full defense to the qui tam action. **Hughes Aircraft Co. v. U.S. ex rel. Schumer, 117 S. Ct. 1871 (1997), 16 FPD ¶ 77, 39 GC ¶ 301.**

[2] **Former Agency Employee Barred From Filing Qui Tam Suit**—Reversing an earlier panel decision (see 39 F.3d 957 (9th Cir. 1994), 36 GC ¶ 650), the U.S. Court of Appeals for the Ninth Circuit en banc held that the False Claims Act bars an employee from a Government agency's Inspector General office from bringing a qui tam suit under the FCA. The auditor could not meet the FCA "original source" test in that the nature of

FRAUD AND ETHICAL CONSIDERATIONS

his duties and accompanying salary precluded his disclosures from meeting the further test of having been "voluntarily provided." **U.S. ex rel. Fine v. University of Cal., 72 F.3d 740 (9th Cir. 1995), 38 GC ¶ 104, cert. denied, No. 95-1445 (U.S. June 3, 1996).**

★ **Note**—See a companion en banc decision by the Ninth Circuit rejecting agency IG employees as qui tam relators, *U.S. ex rel. Fine v. Chevron*, 72 F.3d 740 (9th Cir. 1995), 38 GC ¶ 104 (Note). See also *U.S. ex rel. Burns v. A.D. Roe Co.*, 919 F. Supp. (W.D. Ky. 1996) (Government construction representative does not qualify as "original source" because such employees are required to investigate and report fraud as part of their job responsibilities), 38 GC ¶ 357; *U.S. ex rel. Biddle v. Board of Trustees of Leland Stanford, Jr. Univ.*, 147 F.3d 821 (9th Cir.) (Contracting Officer can not be "original source" for qui tam purposes), 40 GC ¶ 401, *amended to add dissent*, 161 F.3d 533 (9th Cir. 1998) (arguing majority opinion is inconsistent with *Hagood v. Sonoma County Water Agency*, 81 F.3d 1465 (9th Cir. 1996), 38 GC ¶ 357 (Note), which found Government attorney was "original source" despite his fiduciary duty to disclose to his superiors what he thought the law required), 41 GC ¶ 25; *U.S. ex rel. Foust v. Group Hospitalization & Medical Services, Inc.*, 26 F. Supp. 2d 60 (D.D.C. 1998) (auditors who were Government employees or contractors could not be considered "original sources" for purpose of filing qui tam suit), 40 GC ¶ 472.

[3] Citizen Whose Qui Tam Suit Was Dismissed Cannot File Suit Seeking Share Of Government's Settlement—Stinson (a law firm) brought a qui tam suit in U.S. District Court against a Medicare contractor. The court dismissed the suit on the ground Stinson did not satisfy the FCA's "original source" rule, having apparently learned of the contractor's allegedly improper practices while representing an accident victim in his dealings with the contractor. Stinson appealed the dismissal, and while the appeal was pending Stinson and the contractor settled their dispute. The Government, declining to intervene in Stinson's qui tam suit, sued the contractor separately and settled for about $27 million. Stinson then filed a Tucker Act suit against the Government in the Court of Federal Claims (COFC), claiming that as the source of much of the Government's information regarding the contractor's wrongdoing it was entitled to its FCA-allotted share of the Government's recovery. The COFC dismissed the suit for lack of jurisdiction, and the U.S. Court of Appeals for the Federal Circuit affirmed the dismissal, finding, among other things, that since Stinson already had been adjudicated not to be a qui tam relator under the FCA, it had no right to file a Tucker Act suit based on an alleged obligation of the Government under the FCA. **Stinson, Lyons & Bustamante, P.A. v. U.S., 79 F.3d 136 (Fed. Cir. 1996), 15 FPD ¶ 27, 38 GC ¶ 227.**

[4] "Qui Tam" Suit Barred Because Union Representative Did Not Have Direct Knowledge Of Contractor's Violations—The U.S. Court of Appeals for the Eighth Circuit held that a union representative was not an original source of false claims allegations because he had not seen the misconduct "with his own eyes." The union representative discovered the alleged false claims while gathering information on the union's behalf regarding whether the defendant contractor was paying wages at a level required by federal law. Because he did not have direct knowledge of the manner in which the contractor classified its employees but had obtained

■ GOVERNMENT CONTRACT GUIDEBOOK

the knowledge through intermediary sources, the court considered him a recipient rather than a direct source of the information on which the "qui tam" action was based. **U.S. ex rel. Barth v. Ridgedale Electric, Inc., 44 F.3d 699 (8th Cir. 1995), 37 GC ¶ 197.**

c. Procedures

──────────ANNOTATIONS──────────

■ *Cases & Decisions*

[1] **Government Has Unlimited Right To Veto Settlement Of Qui Tam Suit Despite Failure To Intervene**—The Government had decided not to intervene in a "qui tam" suit that ultimately proceeded to a settlement with the contractor under which the District Court would enter a $1 million judgment against the contractor and the contractor would be released from all claims asserted or that "could have been asserted" in the action. Although the Government argued that it was entitled to veto the settlement even absent intervention, the court approved the settlement over the Government's objection. The U.S. Court of Appeals for the Fifth Circuit reversed the court's order and held that the Government retains the right to veto voluntary settlements reached by a "qui tam" relator by withholding its consent to dismissal under 31 USC § 3730(b)(1), even though the Government has declined to assume control of the case. **Searcy v. Philips Electronics N. Amer. Corp., 117 F.3d 154 (5th Cir. 1997), 39 GC ¶ 389.**

★ **Note**—This decision is contrary to a 1994 Ninth Circuit decision (see 36 GC ¶ 220). In reaching its decision in *Searcy*, the Fifth Circuit cited the danger that relators can manipulate settlements to unfairly enrich themselves to the Government's detriment.

[2] **Government's Settlement Of False Claim Against Contractor Was Equivalent To Taking Over "Qui Tam" Suit And Entitled Relator To Share Of Recovery**—After failing to intervene in a "qui tam" suit alleging bid-rigging on the part of a contractor, the Government entered into a settlement of the matter with the contractor. The Government then contended that the relator was not entitled to recover a percentage of the settlement's proceeds because the Government was not a party to the "qui tam" suit and therefore its action did not settle that suit and trigger the "qui tam" recovery provision. The U.S. Court of Appeals for the 11th Circuit held that the Government's settlement with the contractor constituted an "election to intervene" in and prosecute the "qui tam" suit, and therefore the relator was entitled to a 15% share of the Government's settlement recovery. **U.S. ex rel. Neher v. NEC Corp., No. 92-2854 (11th Cir. Apr. 28, 1995) (unpublished), 37 GC ¶ 340.**

[3] **Relator Can Add Claims After Government Declines To Take Over Suit**—When the Government declined to take over the "qui tam" suit, the relator filed an amended complaint two months later that included a claim relating to defective parts. The contractor, contending that the defective parts allegations constituted a "new claim" that the Government had not reviewed, urged that that claim be dismissed. The District

FRAUD AND ETHICAL CONSIDERATIONS

Court disagreed, noting that the Government had taken eight months to decide not to intervene and had received a copy of the amended complaint, which appeared to be "a mere expansion" of earlier claims. In addition, the False Claims Act permits later intervention for "good cause." **U.S. ex rel. Walle v. Martin Marietta Corp., 39 CCF ¶ 76720 (E.D. La. 1994), 37 GC ¶ 92.**

d. Recovery

————————ANNOTATIONS————————

■ *Cases & Decisions*

[1] Legal Fees Should Be Paid Directly To Lawyer Rather Than To "Qui Tam" Relator—A "qui tam" relator reached a settlement with the defendant and apparently requested the U.S. District Court to award expenses and legal fees pursuant to 31 USC § 3730(d)(1). Ruling that it did not have jurisdiction to decide how fees should be allocated under the parties' agreement, the court held that it would have the fees paid to the relator. The U.S. Court of Appeals for the Ninth Circuit reversed, holding that the legal fee must be paid directly to the attorney. **U.S. ex rel. Virani v. Lewis Truck Parts & Eqpt. Inc., 89 F.3d 574 (9th Cir. 1996), 39 GC ¶ 88.**

★ ★ ★

4. False Statements Act

★ ★ ★

b. Elements

————————ANNOTATIONS————————

■ *Cases & Decisions*

[1] A Promise Made Without Intent To Perform May Violate False Statements Act—The defendant certified in a bid that it would not share its bid prices with other bidders. However, the evidence showed that at the time of making the certification, the defendant was in the process of trying to convince another bidder to exchange price information so that they could rig the bids for the contract. The U.S. Court of Appeals for the Fifth Circuit found that while breaking a promise cannot retroactively render the promise false when stated, "the making of a promise will necessarily imply an intent to perform, the absence of which may itself make a promise false when stated." **U.S. v. Shah, 44 F.3d 285 (5th Cir. 1995).**

★ **Note**—See also *U.S. v. Gatewood*, 173 F.3d 983 (6th Cir. 1999) (a statement is only actionable under the False Statements Act if it is literally false), 41 GC ¶ 283.

★ ★ ★

GOVERNMENT CONTRACT GUIDEBOOK

7. Major Fraud Act

———————ANNOTATIONS———————

■ *Cases & Decisions*

[1] Major Fraud Act Did Not Justify Separate Indictment Count For Every Individual Act Furthering Single Scheme—A contractor was indicted under the Major Fraud Act for 12 counts involving 12 invoices in one scheme of false estimates of labor and vendor costs. The Government relied on the "multiple counts" provision of the Act, under which there is a limit of a $10-million fine. Holding that neither the Major Fraud Act's language nor its legislative history is clear as to whether each act furthering a scheme to defraud is a separate indictable offense, and contrasting that Act with the mail and wire fraud statutes, the U.S. District Court for the Northern District of New York concluded that the 12 counts should be consolidated into a single count. **U.S. v. Wiehl, 904 F. Supp. 81 (N.D.N.Y. 1995), 38 GC ¶ 140.**

★ **Note**—Two prior U.S. District Court decisions arguably reached a contrary result. See *U.S. v. Frequency Electronics*, 862 F. Supp. 834 (E.D.N.Y. 1994), 38 GC ¶ 140 (Note), and *U.S. v. Broderson*, No. CR 93-1177 (E.D.N.Y. Apr. 1, 1994), *remanded on other grounds*, 67 F.3d 452 (2d Cir. 1995), 38 GC ¶ 140 (Note). See also *U.S. v. Sain*, 141 F.3d 463 (3d Cir. 1998) (defendants could be separately punished under Major Fraud Act for each of 46 false contract modification claims submitted to the Government), 40 GC ¶ 265.

[2] Small Subcontract Is Subject To Major Fraud Act If Prime Contract Exceeds $1 Million—On two prime contracts, one worth over $9 million and another over $5 million, a subcontractor was awarded a $52,000 subcontract and a $1,500 subcontract. The subcontractor was later convicted of having violated the Major Fraud Act (MFA). In appealing the conviction, the subcontractor argued that it was not subject to the MFA because the subcontracts involved were for less than the statute's $1-million threshold. In rejecting this argument, the U.S. Court of Appeals for the Fourth Circuit found that the MFA imposes liability on any subcontractor involved with a Government prime contract valued at $1 million or more, regardless of the value of the subcontract. **U.S. v. Brooks, 111 F.3d 365 (4th Cir. 1997), 39 GC ¶ 391.**

★ **Note**—The Fourth Circuit acknowledged that its ruling in *Brooks* conflicts with the Second Circuit's ruling in *U.S. v. Nadi*, 996 F.2d 548 (2d Cir. 1993), 35 GC ¶ 635, which held that under the MFA "the value of the contract is determined by looking to the specific contract upon which the fraud is based."

B. CORRUPTION

* * *

3. Procurement Integrity Act

Congress completely revised the Procurement Integrity Act in 1996 to streamline its complex requirements and proce-

FRAUD AND ETHICAL CONSIDERATIONS

dures and delete some of the more burdensome provisions to make compliance by contractors easier and procurement integrity requirements more uniform. For example, all requirements for certifications by contractors have been eliminated. Also eliminated is the gratuities portion of the Act which prohibited gifts to "procurement officials" in certain circumstances. The Act simplifies permissible contacts between contractors and Government officials regarding future employment, and simplifies the limits on private-sector employment for former Government employees. The Act also repeals several provisions pertaining to separate Government agencies and lower-level procurement officials. (See Annotations, below.)

—————ANNOTATIONS—————

■ *Legislation & Regulations*

[1] **FAR Amendment**—The FAR was amended, effective January 1, 1997, to implement § 4304 of P.L. 104-106 (Feb. 10, 1996). The amendment removed the procurement integrity certifications at FAR 52.203-8 and 52.203-9 and reorganized and revised the sections on procurement integrity at FAR 3.104. 62 Fed. Reg. 224 (Jan. 2, 1997). See 39 GC ¶ 7.

[2] **National Defense Authorization Act For Fiscal Year 1996**—P.L. 104-106 (Feb. 10, 1996), § 4304, completely revised § 27 of the Office of Federal Procurement Policy Act (41 USC § 423), which governs procurement integrity. To create a uniform procurement integrity system, it repeals several overlapping statutory restrictions on the conduct of current, former, and retired Government officials, such as 10 USC § 2397 et seq. (procurement integrity requirements at the Department of Defense), 42 USC § 5918 (contractor conflict-of-interest reporting requirements applicable to the Department of Energy), 41 USC § 428 (exempting lower-level procurement officials), and 18 USC § 281 (employment constraints on former military officers). To the extent P.L. 104-106 sets forth new law, its provisions take effect on the date of enactment, whereas provisions that amend existing law will be effective on the date specified in implementing regulations but not later than January 1, 1997. See 38 GC ¶ 69.

■ *Miscellaneous*

[1] **Briefing Papers**—The "revolving door" restrictions contained in the 1996 amendments to the Procurement Integrity Act, as well as in other statutes and rules, are discussed in Levy, Pankowski & Flyer, "A Contractor's Guide to Hiring Government Employees," BRIEFING PAPERS No. 96-8 (July 1996). For an analysis of the substantial revisions to the Procurement Integrity Act made by P.L. 104-106 and implemented in revisions to the FAR effective January 1, 1997, see Arnavas, "The Procurement Integrity

GOVERNMENT CONTRACT GUIDEBOOK

Act/Edition II," BRIEFING PAPERS No. 97-12 (Nov. 1997). The PAPER also compares many of the changes to the provisions of the old Act.

[2] **Nash & Cibinic Report Article**—The revised procurement integrity rules set forth in P.L. 104-106 (Feb. 10, 1996) and the amendment to the FAR issued in January 1997 are examined in "The New Procurement Integrity Rules," 11 NASH & CIBINIC REP. ¶ 12 (Mar. 1997).

a. Prohibitions

──────────ANNOTATIONS──────────

■ *Legislation & Regulations*

[1] **National Defense Authorization Act For Fiscal Year 1996**—P.L. 104-106 (Feb. 10, 1996), § 4304, bans disclosure or receipt of contractor bid, proposal, or source selection information before contract award. It sets a uniform requirement for recusal and eliminates the rules that both Government and contractor officials certify that they have not improperly disclosed or obtained procurement sensitive information. If a federal official working on a procurement worth more than the simplified acquisition threshold has had contact with a bidder regarding potential employment, the official must report the contact to his superiors and to the designated agency official. The procurement official must then either reject the employment or recuse himself from the procurement; failure of the official to do so and knowledge of the bidder of the failure to do so are subject to penalty. The new law also simplifies the restrictions on employment of former Government officials. The restrictions apply only to those involved in source selection or program management of a contract of over $10 million or those personally making decisions on contract rates, payments, or claims in excess of $10 million. Such officials are barred for one year from working for the contractor holding the affected contract, except that this does not bar the official from working for an unrelated division or affiliate of the contractor. The statute removes the prohibition on all gifts to procurement officials having a value in excess of $10. The statute provides that implementing regulations must include procedures for officials or former officials to obtain ethics counseling. To the extent P.L. 104-106 sets forth new law, its provisions take effect on the date of enactment, while provisions that amend existing law will be effective on the date specified in implementing regulations but not later than January 1, 1997. See 38 GC ¶ 69.

★ **Note**—Section 4304 was implemented in amendments to the FAR, effective January 1, 1997. The implementing regulations, among other things, define the terms "compensation," "contract," "decision to award a subcontract or modification of a subcontract," "contractor bid or proposal information," and "contact." 62 Fed. Reg. 224 (Jan. 2, 1997). See 39 GC ¶ 7. See generally Pushkar & Levy, "Feature Comment: Guidelines and Observations on the Procurement Integrity Rules Affecting the Hiring of Government Employees," 39 GC ¶ 15, and Rector, "Feature Comment: Disclosure and Receipt of Procurement Information Under the Revised Procurement Integrity Act," 39 GC ¶ 68.

FRAUD AND ETHICAL CONSIDERATIONS

b. Penalties

──────────ANNOTATIONS──────────

■ *Legislation & Regulations*

[1] **National Defense Authorization Act For Fiscal Year 1996**—P.L. 104-106 (Feb. 10, 1996), § 4304, amends prior law to set forth the following penalties for procurement integrity violations. Criminal penalties include fines and up to five years' imprisonment; civil penalties may be up to $50,000 per violation plus twice the unlawful compensation the individual received or offered and, for organizations, up to $500,000 plus twice the prohibited compensation. Administrative penalties include cancellation of a procurement, rescission of a contract, recovery of all amounts paid, and suspension and debarment from contracting with the Government. To the extent P.L. 104-106 sets forth new law, its provisions take effect on the date of enactment, while provisions that amend existing law will be effective on the date specified in implementing regulations but not later than January 1, 1997. See 38 GC ¶ 69.

★ **Note**—Section 4304 was implemented in amendments to the FAR, effective January 1, 1997. FAR 3.104-10 provides that an agency may take appropriate administrative action when the agency official's contact with a bidder or offeror regarding postfederal employment interferes with the official's ability to perform assigned duties. The rule also specifically refers to criminal and civil penalties that may result from violation of applicable law. 62 Fed. Reg. 224 (Jan. 2, 1997). See 39 GC ¶¶ 7, 15, 68.

4. Byrd Amendment

★ ★ ★

a. Prohibitions

──────────ANNOTATIONS──────────

■ *Legislation & Regulations*

[1] **Lobbying Disclosure Act Of 1995**—Section 10 of P.L. 104-65 (Dec. 19, 1995, effective Jan. 1, 1996), 109 Stat. 691, substantially reduced the disclosure requirements of the Byrd Amendment. Contractors and awardees now must file a declaration in connection with an individual award containing only (1) the name of the registrant under the Lobbying Disclosure Act who has made lobbying contacts on behalf of the contractor or other awardee with respect to the relevant federal contract, grant, loan, or cooperative agreement, and (2) a certification that the person making the declaration has not made and will not make any prohibited payment.

★ ★ ★

5. Lobbying Activities [*New Section*]

The Lobbying Disclosure Act of 1995 repealed and replaced many prior statutes governing the registration and disclosure of lobbying activities by individuals and companies, effective January 1, 1996. (See *Legislation & Regulations*, item [1], below.) Although the Act was not primarily targeted at federal contractors, it is sufficiently broad to cover many contractor marketing and business development contacts with Federal Government officials, as well as routine communications relating to contract administration. It covers lobbying firms as well as organizations that employ in-house lobbyists. The 1995 Act imposes requirements for registration, semiannual reporting, disclosure in connection with individual awards, and identification of interests.

The Act requires (with a few exceptions) individuals spending at least 20% of their time on lobbying activities and any organization employing at least one "lobbyist" to register with the Clerk of the House and the Secretary of the Senate within 45 days after first making a lobbying contact or being employed or retained to make a lobbying contact. A "lobbying contact" is defined as any oral or written communication to a covered Legislative or Executive Branch official (including staff) on behalf of a client with regard to the administration or execution of a federal program or policy, including the negotiation, award, or administration of a federal contract, grant, loan, permit, or license. A "lobbyist" is defined as one who (1) is employed to provide services to his or her employer that include more than one "lobbying contact" in a semiannual reporting period and (2) spends at least 20% of his or her time in "lobbying activities." Each registrant under the Act must file semiannual reports with the House Clerk and Senate Secretary that disclose the specific issues being lobbied and estimates of lobbying income and expenses.

The Act requires many federal contractors to register for the first time as lobbying organizations and to file semiannual reports on their lobbying activities. Penalties for violations of the Act include a civil fine of up to $50,000 for knowing failure to (a) remedy a defective filing within 60 days of notification of the defect or (b) comply with any other provision of the Act. The amount of the civil fine depends on "the extent and gravity of the violation."

FRAUD AND ETHICAL CONSIDERATIONS

---------------ANNOTATIONS---------------

■ *Legislation & Regulations*

[1] **Lobbying Disclosure Act Of 1995**—P.L. 104-65 (Dec. 19, 1995, effective Jan. 1, 1996), 109 Stat. 691 (to be codified at 2 USC § 1601 et seq.) repealed and replaced most prior lobbying statutes, including the Federal Regulation of Lobbying Act (2 USC § 261 et seq.), and amended the Foreign Agents Registration Act (2 USC § 1602(8)(A)(iii)) and Byrd Amendment (see *Supplement* Section B.4 above). See 38 GC ¶ 33.

■ *Miscellaneous*

[1] **Briefing Paper**—For a detailed discussion of the Lobbying Disclosure Act of 1995, see Kenney & Schroer, "The Lobbying Disclosure Act of 1995," BRIEFING PAPERS No. 96-5 (Apr. 1996).

C. ENFORCEMENT

* * *

1. Inspectors General

---------------ANNOTATIONS---------------

■ *Cases & Decisions*

[1] **Federal IG Subpoena Statute Preempts State Banking Confidentiality Law**—The Agency for International Development's IG issued subpoenas to a Maryland bank for records pertaining to corporate customers. The bank contended that it need not comply with the subpoenas because the IG had not provided certain certifications required under Maryland law. The District Court, citing the Supremacy Clause of the U.S. Constitution, noted that properly enacted federal laws nullify state or local laws that obstruct accomplishment of Congress' objectives. If the IG had to comply with different state statutes governing bank records, this would substantially frustrate the IG in its work. Therefore, the court held that the IG was not required to comply with the Maryland statute. **U.S. v. First Natl. Bank of Md.**, 866 F. Supp. 884 (D. Md. 1994), 36 GC ¶ 597.

* * *

3. Suspension & Debarment

---------------ANNOTATIONS---------------

■ *Legislation & Regulations*

[1] **Final Rules Give Government-Wide Effect To Procurement And Nonprocurement Debarments/Suspensions**—Implementing § 2455 of

GOVERNMENT CONTRACT GUIDEBOOK

the Federal Acquisition Streamlining Act of 1994, P.L. 103-355, and Executive Order 12689, amendments to FAR Part 9 (60 Fed. Reg. 33064, June 26, 1995) and to the nonprocurement Common Rule (60 Fed. Reg. 33037, June 26, 1995) require that all agencies honor an agency's action to exclude a person or entity placed on the "List of Parties Excluded from Federal Procurement and Nonprocurement Programs." This reciprocity requirement is effective for any exclusion action initiated on or after August 25, 1995. Nevertheless, the reciprocity requirement neither dictates identical procedures nor affects the flow-down of the two debarment/suspension systems. For example, under FAR Subpart 9.4, a proposed debarment excludes a party from receiving a contract, but under the Common Rule a proposed debarment has no effect on a person's eligibility to participate in a nonprocurement program. See 37 GC ¶ 364.

* * *

b. Debarment

―――――――ANNOTATIONS―――――――

■ *Legislation & Regulations*

[1] **FAR Amendment**—An amendment to FAR 9.405 provides that an agency may renew or extend the duration of existing contracts with contractors that are debarred, suspended, or proposed for debarment, provided that the agency head or designee states in writing the compelling reasons for renewal or extension. 59 Fed. Reg. 67032 (Dec. 28, 1994). See 37 GC ¶ 7.

■ *Cases & Decisions*

[1] **Agency's Disparate Treatment Of Contractors Is One Factor Leading Board To Reject Debarment Proposal**—In 1987, a competitor (UAI) approached the contractor to "cooperate" rather than compete for certain roofing contracts. The contractor resisted the advances until UAI threatened economic harm. For approximately the next three years, the contractor, UAI, and other roofing contractors had an oral agreement to submit collusive bids for public and private contracts in two states. In late 1992, the contractor pleaded guilty to one count of conspiracy under the Sherman Act, paid a fine, and fully cooperated in DOJ's prosecution of its co-conspirators. The Department of Housing and Urban Development (HUD) suspended the contractor and proposed a five-year debarment; the contractor protested to the HUD Board of Contract Appeals. The board noted that even during the conspiracy the contractor had refrained from charging its customers higher prices, and that the prosecutor had described it as the least culpable of the co-conspirators. Further, in the nearly six years since the conviction, the contractor had been acting responsibly and had instituted programs designed to prevent recurrence of the conspiratorial actions. Lastly, HUD did not debar three of the co-conspirators, and the could find no justification for the disparity. The board directed that the suspension be ended and that no debarment be imposed. **S.D. Carruthers Sons, Inc., HUDBCA 95-A-124-D17 (June 28, 1996), 38 GC ¶ 407.**

FRAUD AND ETHICAL CONSIDERATIONS

[2] **Criminal Prosecution Following Debarment Did Not Violate U.S. Constitution's "Double Jeopardy" Clause**—The Army debarred the contractor for 26 months for fraud. Subsequently, the Government filed a criminal indictment in U.S. District Court based on the same alleged conduct. The contractor requested the court to dismiss the indictment, arguing, among other things, that proceeding with the prosecution would result in a second punishment violating the "Double Jeopardy" clause of the Fifth Amendment of the U.S. Constitution. The court denied dismissal, and the contractor appealed to the U.S. Court of Appeals for the Fourth Circuit. Affirming the District Court, the Fourth Circuit noted that debarment is a civil proceeding imposed not for punishment but to protect the Government, and that the 26-month debarment was not unreasonable or excessive in view of the Government's estimated contractor-caused direct losses of between $40,000 and $60,000. **U.S. v. Hatfield, 108 F.3d 67 (4th Cir. 1997), 39 GC ¶ 233.**

★ **Note**—Although the debarment in *Hatfield* preceded the indictment, the Fourth Circuit indicated that the result would have been the same if the order of the proceedings had been reversed. Because a debarment often is based on a prior criminal conviction, the Fourth Circuit would have substantially undermined the Government's use of debarment had it held debarment to be a punishment implicating the "Double Jeopardy" clause. See also *Hudson v. U.S.*, 118 S. Ct. 488 (1997) (criminal prosecution following civil sanctions does not violate "Double Jeopardy" clause), 40 GC ¶ 162.

SPECIFICATIONS

8

1999 Supplement

Chapter Introduction

A. Design vs. Performance Specifications
   1. Design Specifications
   2. Performance Specifications
★ B. Government's "Minimum Needs" / 8-2
★ C. Specifications, Standards & Purchase Descriptions / 8-3
   1. Specifications
      a. Federal Specifications
   ★ b. Military Specifications / 8-4
      c. Industry Specifications
   2. Standards
   3. Purchase Descriptions
      a. Definition
      b. Brand Name Or Equal
      c. Foreign Purchase Descriptions
   4. Deviations & Waivers
D. Qualified Products

■ GOVERNMENT CONTRACT GUIDEBOOK

    E. Government Warranty Of Specifications
    ★ 1. The "Implied Warranty" / **8-4**
    ★ 2. Government Disclaimers / **8-5**
    F. Contractor Compliance With Specifications
      1. Strict Compliance
      2. Minimum Compliance
    G. Substantial Performance
      1. Construction Contracts
      2. Supply Contracts
      3. Service Contracts
    H. Defective Specifications
      1. Impossibility Of Performance
        a. Types Of Impossibility
        b. Allocation Of Risk
      2. Notice
    ★ 3. Right To Stop Work / **8-5**

* * *

B. GOVERNMENT'S "MINIMUM NEEDS"

———————ANNOTATIONS———————

■ *Cases & Decisions*

[1] Agency Fails To Establish That Safety Requirement Is Necessary To Satisfy Its "Minimum Needs"— The agency requested proposals for supplying shotguns, requiring that the guns have a crossbolt safety mechanism located at the rear of the trigger guard and that the receiver be of "parkerized" steel. The protester offered shotguns with a safety switch on top of the receiver and anodized aluminum receivers. The protester argued that the solicitation's requirements unduly restricted competition, and that the protester's safety mechanism was superior to the crossbolt type. The agency asserted that it specified the crossbolt in the interest of standardization and safety. The record, however, contained no evidence supporting the agency's safety rationale. The Comptroller General sustained the protest, finding that the record did not adequately establish that the challenged requirements were necessary to meet the agency's "minimum needs." **Mossberg Corp., Comp. Gen. Dec. B-274059, 96-2 CPD ¶ 189, 39 GC ¶ 50.**

SPECIFICATIONS

★ **Note**—*Mossberg* is significant because it is relatively rare for the Comptroller General to sustain a protest against a requirement that the agency maintains it needs to protect human safety.

■ *Miscellaneous*

[1] **Nash & Cibinic Report Article**—Problems created by the use of the term "minimum needs" in federal procurement and some arguments for changing the term are discussed in "'Minimum Needs': A Contentious Term?," 11 NASH & CIBINIC REP. ¶ 10 (Feb. 1997).

C. SPECIFICATIONS, STANDARDS & PURCHASE DESCRIPTIONS

—————————ANNOTATIONS—————————

■ *Legislation & Regulations*

[1] **FAR Amendment**—FAR Parts 10, 11, and 12 were completely revised to implement provisions of the Federal Acquisition Streamlining Act of 1994, P.L. 103-355, establishing a clear preference for the acquisition of commercial items by the Government. The FAR now requires in Part 10 that before developing new requirements documents for acquisitions, all agencies, unless otherwise authorized by law, conduct market research to determine if commercial items or nondevelopmental items are capable of meeting the Government's need. Where market research establishes that a commercial item or nondevelopmental item will meet the Government's need or can be modified to meet the Government's need, then the agency should solicit that item using the streamlined procedures, terms, and conditions of new FAR Part 12, "Acquisition of Commercial Items." In addition, FAR Part 11 has been completely revised to address the process of describing agency needs. Although it contains some of the language on specifications and standards previously found in Part 10, it adopts a more streamlined approach. It establishes a new policy that, to the maximum extent practicable, agencies should ensure that acquisition officials state requirements with respect to an acquisition of supplies or services in terms of (a) functions to be performed, (b) performance required, or (c) essential physical characteristics, and define requirements in terms that enable and encourage offerors to supply commercial items. FAR 11.002. With respect to developing requirements documents, agencies may select from existing requirements documents (such as the GSA's "Index of Federal Specifications, Standards and Commercial Item Descriptions" and DOD's "Index of Specifications and Standards"), modify or combine existing requirements documents, or create new requirements to meet agency needs consistent with the following order of precedence: (1) documents mandated for use by law, (2) performance-oriented documents, (3) detailed design-oriented documents, and (4) standards and specifications issued by the Government outside the defense or federal series for the nonrepetitive acquisition of items. FAR 11.101. 60 Fed. Reg. 48231 (Sept. 18, 1995, effective Oct. 1, 1995). See 37 GC ¶ 489.

GOVERNMENT CONTRACT GUIDEBOOK

■ *Miscellaneous*

[1] **Briefing Paper**—For a discussion of recent reforms mandating preferences for the procurement of commercial items by the Federal Government and an explanation of the current rules governing commercial item acquisitions, see O'Sullivan & Perry, "Commercial Item Acquisitions," BRIEFING PAPERS No. 97-5 (Apr. 1997).

1. Specifications

* * *

b. Military Specifications

————————ANNOTATIONS————————

■ *Legislation & Regulations*

[1] **Department Of Defense Memorandum**—In a memorandum issued on December 8, 1995, DOD announced its intention to implement "block changes" to existing contracts to replace military-unique processes, specifications, and standards with more general performance standards. The memorandum directs that "block changes to the management and manufacturing requirements of existing contracts be made on a facility-wide basis" to permit contractors to use "common, facility-wide systems" for federal and commercial production "wherever such changes are technically acceptable to the government." See 37 GC ¶ 626.

* * *

E. GOVERNMENT WARRANTY OF SPECIFICATIONS

* * *

1. The "Implied Warranty"

————————ANNOTATIONS————————

■ *Cases & Decisions*

[1] **Agency Was Not Required To Design For Worst Possible Circumstances That Might Occur During Construction**—A U.S. Postal Service (USPS) contract to develop and install a mechanized mail handling system at a facility made the contractor responsible for the equipment until acceptance. After the contractor had installed the equipment but before the USPS had tested and accepted it, an earthquake (of about .6g lateral movement) severely damaged the equipment. The contractor sought to recover (among other things) the cost of repairs. The contract included a provision that the system meet applicable state and local requirements

SPECIFICATIONS

for seismic zone 4 (.4g lateral movement); otherwise it left the equipment's design to the contractor. The contractor contended that the zone 4 provision constituted a defective design requirement in view of the USPS's knowledge that during the project's life an earthquake of a magnitude exceeding .4g might occur. The board held that the USPS was not required to design the project for the worst possible scenario; the system met local code requirements for zone 4, and the purpose of the zone 4 requirement was safety of building occupants in exiting, not protecting the building and its systems from harm. **HK Systems, Inc., PSBCA 3712, 97-2 BCA ¶ 29079, 39 GC ¶ 476.**

2. Government Disclaimers

————————ANNOTATIONS————————

■ *Miscellaneous*

[1] **Briefing Paper**—For a review of the extent to which exculpatory contract clauses effectively shield the Government from liability for defective specifications, property, drawings, and other documentation that it furnishes to its contractors, see Arnavas, "Exculpatory Clauses," BRIEFING PAPERS No. 98-10 (Sept. 1998).

* * *

H. DEFECTIVE SPECIFICATIONS

* * *

3. Right To Stop Work

————————ANNOTATIONS————————

■ *Cases & Decisions*

[1] **Contractor Was Justified In Stopping Work Despite Ignorance That Performance Was Impossible**—The contract required the contractor to produce 7,787 cartridges for the Navy using the technical data package (TDP) provided by the Navy. The contract required delivery in 11 production lots, and provided that a lot would be accepted only if there were "zero defects" in the 31 cartridges randomly-selected for testing in each lot. After attempting for 39 months to produce the cartridges, the contractor had only produced two lots, both of which had failed to meet the stringent testing criteria. Alleging that the specifications were defective, contractor sought additional compensation and then stopped work, and the Navy terminated the contract. Based on the Navy's own records, the board found that the contract was impossible to perform because (1) the flaws in the TDP could only be corrected by uncontracted-for research engineering work, (2) the "zero defect" performance criterion was totally unrealistic for

GOVERNMENT CONTRACT GUIDEBOOK

the TDP, and (3) other manufacturers had been able to produce the cartridges only after obtaining deviations from the TDP. **Defense Systems Corp., ASBCA 42939 et al., 95-2 BCA ¶ 27721, 37 GC ¶ 469.**

GOVERNMENT PROPERTY

9

1999 Supplement

Chapter Introduction

★ A. Overview / 9-2
 1. Definitions
   a. Government Property
   b. Government-Furnished Property
 2. Neutralizing The Competitive Advantage
   a. Sealed Bid Procurements
   b. Negotiated Procurements
   c. Other Costs & Savings
 3. Standard Contract Clauses
 4. Title
B. Government Obligations
 1. Furnishing Property
 2. Timely Delivery
 3. Suitability Of Property
 4. Suitability Of Data & Information

■ GOVERNMENT CONTRACT GUIDEBOOK

    C. Contractor Obligations
        1. Mitigation Of Damages
        2. Notice To Government
        3. Maintenance & Repair
    D. Contractor Remedies
        1. Recovery Of Extra Costs
        2. Performance Time Extension
    E. Risk Of Loss
        1. Competitive, Fixed-Price Contracts
        2. Other Contracts

* * *

A. OVERVIEW

———————ANNOTATIONS———————

■ *Legislation & Regulations*

[1] **Rewrite Of FAR Part 45**—The Director of Defense Procurement announced sponsorship of an initiative to rewrite FAR Part 45, "Government Property," and the related FAR Part 52 contract clauses. 59 Fed. Reg. 47583 (Sept. 16, 1994). See 36 GC ¶ 479. The goal of the rewrite is to streamline and improve current policies and procedures, eliminate unnecessary burdens on contractors and Contracting Officers, and make the rules easier to read and understand. Issues to be addressed include property storage, accountability and reporting, allowability of profits, contractor access to the Department of Defense Supply System, and property rollover from contract to contract. A proposed new FAR Part 45 was issued for comment in June 1997. 62 Fed. Reg. 30186 (June 2, 1997). See 39 GC ¶ 286.

* * *

INTELLECTUAL PROPERTY RIGHTS

10

1999 Supplement

Chapter Introduction

A. Patents
    1. Title vs. License
    2. Current Government Policy
    3. FAR Coverage
        a. Contractor Title
        b. Government License
    4. Patent Infringement
    5. Contractor Indemnification Of Government
    6. Contractor Notice & Assistance

B. Technical Data
    ★ 1. The Regulations / 10-2
    2. Types Of Government Rights
    3. Government Policy

GOVERNMENT CONTRACT GUIDEBOOK

    ★ 4. DOD Policy & Procedures / **10-2**
       a. Policy
       b. Procedures
    5. Enforcing Data Rights
  C. Copyright

* * *

B. TECHNICAL DATA

* * *

1. The Regulations

————ANNOTATIONS————

■ *Legislation & Regulations*

[1] **FAR Amendment**—Pursuant to the Federal Acquisition Streamlining Act of 1994, P.L. 103-355, FAR 12.211 was revised to state the general principle that in regard to acquisitions of commercial items, the Government will acquire only the technical data customarily provided to the public, except as provided by agency-specific statutes. The rule also adds FAR 12.212, "Computer Software," to require that commercial computer software and documentation be acquired under licenses customarily provided to the public to the extent that the licenses are consistent with federal procurement law. 60 Fed. Reg. 48231 (Sept. 18, 1995). See 37 GC ¶ 489.

* * *

4. DOD Policy & Procedures

————ANNOTATIONS————

■ *Legislation & Regulations*

[1] **DFARS Amendment**—DOD issued its long-awaited final regulations on rights in technical data and computer software and software documentation. This comprehensive revision applies to solicitations issued on or after September 29, 1995, and replaces the "interim rule" that had been in effect since 1988. The significant substantive changes made by the final rule include the following: (1) deletion of the provision that the Government obtains unlimited rights in technical data relating to items, components, or processes developed at private expense if development was "required for

INTELLECTUAL PROPERTY RIGHTS

the performance of a Government contract or subcontract"; (2) clarification that all development accomplished with costs charged to indirect cost pools is considered development at private expense; (3) the Government automatically receives a standard license granting "Government purpose rights" where development of an item, component, process, or computer software or software documentation is accomplished with mixed funding; (4) a requirement that DOD, with some exceptions, acquire "only the technical data customarily provided to the public with a commercial item or process"; and (5) separate treatment and separate contract clauses for (a) technical data and (b) computer software and computer software documentation. The new DFARS Subpart 227.71, dealing with technical data, is subdivided into provisions addressing commercial and noncommercial items, components, or processes. The new DFARS Subpart 227.72, dealing with computer software and software documentation, is similarly structured. 60 Fed. Reg. 33464 (June 28, 1995) (codified at DFARS pts. 211, 227, and 252). See 37 GC ¶ 356.

■ Miscellaneous

[1] **Briefing Paper**—An examination of the 1995 revision of the DFARS provisions on technical data and computer software rights—and how the DFARS rules applicable to defense contracts and the FAR rules applicable to civilian agency contracts differ—is contained in Burgett, Sweeney & Kunzi, "Government Rights in Data and Software/Edition II," BRIEFING PAPERS No. 95-11 (Oct. 1995).

[2] **Nash & Cibinic Report Article**—For an explanation and critique of the new DOD policies on rights in computer software, see "The New DOD 'Rights in Software' Policy: Half a Loaf," 10 NASH & CIBINIC REP. ¶ 12 (Mar. 1996).

★ ★ ★

CHANGES

11

1999 Supplement

Chapter Introduction

A. Standard "Changes" Clauses
   1. Fixed-Price Contracts
   2. Cost-Reimbursement Contracts
B. Changes Authority
   1. Non-Contracting Officers
   2. Changes Outside Contract's "Scope"
C. Contractor's Duty To Proceed
   1. Scope Of Duty
   2. Effect Of Failure To Proceed
★ D. Value Engineering / 11-2
   1. Value Engineering Change Proposals
   ★ 2. Administration / 11-3
E. Formal Change Orders
   1. Origination
      a. Contractor-Proposed Changes
      b. Government-Originated Changes

GOVERNMENT CONTRACT GUIDEBOOK

    2. Procedures
        a. Bilateral Change Orders
        b. Unilateral Change Orders
        c. Timing
 F. Constructive Changes
    1. Development Of The Doctrine
    2. Types Of Constructive Changes
        a. Contract Interpretation
        b. Interference & Failure To Cooperate
        c. Defective Specifications
        d. Nondisclosure Of Vital Information
        e. Acceleration

---

* * *

D. VALUE ENGINEERING

————————ANNOTATIONS————————

■ *Cases & Decisions*

[1] **CO Could Not Defeat Value Engineering Claim By Asserting That Contract Required Contractor To Use Cheapest Method**—During the initial stages of performance of a construction contract, lead contamination producing hazardous wastes was discovered on the site. The Contracting Officer (CO) directed the contractor to excavate the contaminated material and transport it to a landfill. However, the contractor discovered a process was available to treat the lead contaminate on-site to render it not hazardous, thus simplifying loading, trucking, and dumping the material, saving time and money. The contractor filed a VECP seeking a share of the savings that would be achieved by using the process. The CO rejected the claim, arguing that the contractor already was required to use the best and most cost-effective method of performance. On appeal, the board held that accepting the CO's reasoning would render the "Value Engineering" clause entirely meaningless, and that the CO should have granted the proposal. **Morse Diesel Intl., Inc. v. General Services Admin., GSBCA 13419, 97-1 BCA ¶ 28634, 39 GC ¶ 12.**

* * *

CHANGES

2. Administration

———————ANNOTATIONS———————

■ *Cases & Decisions*

[1] CO's Value Engineering Action Is Subject To CDA—Contrary Regulation Is Invalid—On a Corps of Engineers contract that contained most of the standard "Value Engineering" clause (FAR 52.248-1), the contractor submitted a VECP to the Contracting Officer (CO) providing savings in electricity and labor. The CO responded that the proposed reduction in electricity costs did not constitute "acquisition savings" under the clause. Although he conceded the savings could be "collateral" savings, the contract did not include the provision in FAR 52.248-1, paragraph (j), that would have allowed the contractor to share in collateral savings arising from an accepted VECP. The contractor sued in the Court of Federal Claims contending that it was entitled to share in the savings. The Government argued the court lacked jurisdiction because the contractor never submitted its claim to the CO for a decision under the CDA. The contractor then argued that the "Value Engineering" clause (FAR 52.248-1, paragraph (e)(3)), specifically exempts such disputes from the CDA. The court held that under the CDA, all disputes arising from a contract are subject to the CDA's administrative dispute resolution mechanisms. Therefore, because paragraph (e)(3) purports to insulate VECP disputes from board or court review, it conflicts with the CDA and is invalid. **Rig Masters, Inc. v. U.S., 42 Fed. Cl. 369 (1998), 17 FPD ¶ 133, 41 GC ¶ 11.**

★ **Note**—The court cited *Burnside-Ott Aviation Training Center v. Dalton*, 107 F.3d 854 (Fed. Cir. 1997), 16 FPD ¶ 27, 39 GC ¶ 153, in which the Federal Circuit held that a regulation purporting to insulate an award fee dispute from board or court review directly conflicted with the CDA and therefore was unenforceable.

[2] VECP Can Be "Constructively" Accepted Even After Contractor Has Furnished All Contract Items—Bianchi's Government contract to supply certain garments contained a "Value Engineering" clause which provided that, for any VECP accepted by the Government, the contractor would receive a share of savings realized on its own contract and on future contracts for essentially the same items. During contract performance, Bianchi submitted a VECP on packing and packaging, but the agency rejected the proposal. After rejection, Bianchi completed all contract deliveries, but did not invoice the Government for final payment. Shortly thereafter, the agency contracted with another contractor for essentially the same items, and that contractor submitted a similar VECP regarding the packing of the items. The agency accepted this proposal in modified form. Bianchi submitted a claim for royalties for its previously rejected VECP, asserting the agency had "constructively accepted" Bianchi's VECP on the second contract. The Government admitted that the agency had constructively accepted Bianchi's VECP, but the board denied Bianchi's claim on the ground that a contractor cannot recover where a VECP is accepted after completion of the contractor's contract. On appeal, the Court of Appeals for the Federal Circuit agreed and remanded the case to the board to permit Bianchi to present evidence to prove the VECP had been ac-

GOVERNMENT CONTRACT GUIDEBOOK

cepted before contract termination. *M. Bianchi of Cal. v. Perry*, 31 F.3d 1163 (Fed. Cir. 1994), 13 FPD ¶ 65, 36 GC ¶ 481. On remand, the board determined that because Bianchi had neither billed for nor received final payment at the time the Government accepted the other firm's VECP, the contract had not ended and Bianchi was entitled to recover for savings calculated according to its own VECP. **M. Bianchi of Cal., ASBCA 37029 et al, 96-2 BCA ¶ 28410, 38 GC ¶ 434, vacated & remanded on other grounds, 1998 WL 838337 (Fed. Cir. 1998) (nonprecedential), 17 FPD ¶ 135, 41 GC ¶ 108.**

■ *Miscellaneous*

[1] **Nash & Cibinic Report Articles**—A critique of the *Bianchi* case and other value engineering decisions can be found in "Value Engineering: Another Illusory Promise?," 9 NASH & CIBINIC REP. ¶ 20 (Mar. 1995), and "Postscript: Value Engineering," 10 NASH & CIBINIC REP. ¶ 51 (Oct. 1996).

* * *

DELAYS

12

1999 Supplement

> As of the June 30, 1999, cutoff date for preparation of this *Supplement*, there was no significant legislative, regulatory, court, or administrative activity to be reported on the topics covered in Chapter 12. Therefore, the latest developments can be found in the text chapter.

12

DELAYS

1999 Supplement

As of the June 30, 1999, cutoff date for preparation of this Supplement, there was no significant legislative, regulatory, court, or administrative activity to be reported on the topics covered in Chapter 12. Therefore, the latest developments can be found in the text chapter.

EQUITABLE ADJUSTMENT CLAIMS

13

1999 Supplement

Chapter Introduction

A. Basic Rules Of Computation
   1. Added Work
 ★ 2. Deleted Work / 13-2
   3. Overhead & Profit
      a. Overhead
  ★ b. Profit / 13-2
B. Proving The Equitable Adjustment Amount
   1. Actual Cost Data
   2. "Total Cost" Method
 ★ 3. "Jury Verdict" Method / 13-3
★ C. Claim Preparation Costs / 13-3
D. Interest
   1. Interest On Claims
   2. Interest On Borrowings
E. Notice Of Claims

GOVERNMENT CONTRACT GUIDEBOOK

* * *

A. BASIC RULES OF COMPUTATION

* * *

2. Deleted Work

——————ANNOTATIONS——————

■ *Cases & Decisions*

[1] **Deductive Change Measured By Price That Was Separately Specified In Proposal But Not In Contract**—The Government awarded a contract for environmental remediation work pursuant to a Request for Proposals. An attachment to the contractor's proposal showed the figure of $52,226 for "encapsulation." This price apparently remained the same in the contractor's offer, which included certified cost or pricing data. The sub-item was not separately priced in the contract, however. After award, the contractor awarded a subcontract for the encapsulation at $1,638. The Government issued a change order deleting the encapsulation, contending that it was entitled to a $46,609 deduction. The contractor argued that the Government could reduce the price by only the $1,638 subcontract amount. The board held that even though the contract did not state that price separately, the parties in effect agreed on the $52,226 price for the encapsulation. Therefore, the Government was entitled to a credit based on contractor's proposal. **Bral Environmental Services, Inc., DOTBCA 2980 et al., 97-1 BCA ¶ 28762, 39 GC ¶ 178.**

★ **Note**—See "Equitable Adjustments for Deleted Work: The Severability Exception to the 'Would Have Cost' Rule," 11 NASH & CIBINIC REP. ¶ 39 (Aug. 1997), and "Postscript: Equitable Adjustments for Deleted Work," 12 NASH & CIBINIC REP. ¶ 15 (Mar. 1998), for analyses of the *Bral* decision.

3. Overhead & Profit

* * *

b. Profit

——————ANNOTATIONS——————

■ *Cases & Decisions*

[1] **Equitable Adjustment Under "Changes" Clause Of Loss Contract Includes Profit—ASBCA Overrules Prior Inconsistent Case**—The contractor bid on an Army contract expecting to lose over $1 million. The Contracting Officer issued unilateral change orders; the Government argued that it was not entitled to add any profit to the contractor's equitable adjustment to cover the contractor's costs of complying with the change

orders. The Armed Services Board of Contract Appeals (ASBCA) cited the general rule that an equitable adjustment should make a contractor "whole" and should not increase or decrease a contractor's loss at the Government's expense. Nevertheless, awarding a reasonable profit on changed work only applies to it and does not reprice the unchanged work, and therefore does not violate the general rule. The board cited two inconsistent ASBCA decisions on this issue and, unable to reconcile the two, chose to follow the decision allowing the contractor to recover profit on the changed work as being "consistent with sound procurement policy." **Stewart & Stevenson Services, Inc., ASBCA 43631, 97-2 BCA ¶ 29252, 39 GC ¶ 566.**

B. PROVING THE EQUITABLE ADJUSTMENT AMOUNT

* * *

3. "Jury Verdict" Method

———————ANNOTATIONS———————

■ *Cases & Decisions*

[1] **COFC Should Have Made "Jury Verdict" Award For Government's Constructive Change**—The contractor under an erosion control works contract experienced unusually severe rainfall. After advising the Contracting Officer on June 16 and July 15 that overtime work would be needed to complete a portion of the work before it was flooded, the Contracting Officer informed the contractor on July 27 that he would determine responsibility for the delay after the work was completed. On September 30 the Contracting Officer modified the contract to extend the completion date. The Court of Federal Claims (COFC) ruled that the Contracting Officer's delay in issuing a time extension constituted an implied order to accelerate the contract schedule, but denied recovery because the contractor had improperly failed to segregate its resulting increased costs. The U.S. Court of Appeals for the Federal Circuit found that the COFC erred in not using the jury verdict method to award damages. The Federal Circuit noted that determining severe weather damages with precision is difficult if not impossible, and the contractor's engineering expert testified that his estimates were as accurate as the contractor's accounting system could provide. Therefore, the Federal Circuit found that the COFC had enough information to award damages. **Azure v. U.S., 16 FPD ¶ 128 (Fed. Cir. 1997) (nonprecedential), 39 GC ¶ 574.**

C. CLAIM PREPARATION COSTS

———————ANNOTATIONS———————

■ *Cases & Decisions*

[1] **COFC Finds Consultant Costs Are Unallowable Claim Prosecution Costs**—The Court of Federal Claims (COFC) found that a contractor's claim

GOVERNMENT CONTRACT GUIDEBOOK

for consulting fees associated with the quantification of excess asbestos removal and other work on a contract with the Army Corps of Engineers was not an allowable cost because the consulting services were associated with the contractor's claim for additional compensation. The contractor argued that the fees should be allowed because this case was similar to the situation in the *Bill Strong* decision [see item [2], below] where the contractor hired a consultant to address inadequacies the Contracting Officer had identified in the contractor's "claim" documents, and the U.S. Court of Appeals for the Federal Circuit had viewed the costs of the consultant as contract administration costs rather than costs incurred "in connection with the prosecution" of a claim. The COFC found, however, that *Bill Strong* is no longer good law because it was effectively overruled by *Reflectone, Inc. v. Dalton*, 60 F.3d 1572 (Fed. Cir. 1995), 14 FPD ¶ 63, 37 GC ¶¶ 411, 516. Under the *Reflectone* definition of "claim," the consultant's work product in this case was presented to the Contracting Officer contemporaneously with the contractor's "claim" and therefore the consultant's fees are unrecoverable claim prosecution costs. **Plano Builders Corp. v. U.S., 40 Fed. Cl. 635 (1998), 17 FPD ¶ 36, 40 GC ¶ 208.**

[2] **Federal Circuit Reverses ASBCA Decision Disallowing Costs Of Contractor's Claims Consultant**—Reversing a split decision of the Armed Services Board of Contract Appeals, the U.S. Court of Appeals for the Federal Circuit ruled that the meaning of the word "claim" is the same in both the "Costs Related to Legal and Other Proceedings" cost principle (FAR 31.205-47(f)(1)) and in the Contract Disputes Act (CDA). According to the court, whether "claim preparation costs" are recoverable as part of an equitable adjustment depends on "why the contractor incurred the cost." That is, if the contractor incurred the cost with the genuine purpose of materially furthering negotiation, the cost normally should be allowable, even though negotiation eventually fails and the contractor later submits a CDA claim. Conversely, if the contractor's underlying purpose is to promote prosecution of a CDA claim, the cost is unallowable. The court remanded the case for determinations of reasonableness and allocability of the costs involved. **Bill Strong Enterprises, Inc. v. Shannon, 49 F.3d 1541 (Fed. Cir. 1995), 14 FPD ¶ 18, 37 GC ¶ 141.**

■ *Miscellaneous*

[1] **Costs, Pricing & Accounting Report Article**—For a discussion of the relationship of the allowability of professional fees under the FAR cost principles, as set forth by the Federal Circuit in *Bill Strong*, to the definition of a CDA "claim," see Zupa, "*Reflectone & Bill Strong*: A Concordance," 95-12 CP&A REP. 3 (Dec. 1995).

[2] **Nash & Cibinic Report Articles**—The Federal Circuit's *Bill Strong* decision and its implications are discussed in "Allowable Contract Administration Costs vs. Unallowable Claim Costs: *Bill Strong* Reversed," 9 NASH & CIBINIC REP. ¶ 27 (Apr. 1995). Subsequent decisions are examined in "Unallowable Claims Costs vs. Allowable Contract Administration Costs: The *Bill Strong* Legacy," 12 NASH & CIBINIC REP. ¶ 35 (June 1998).

* * *

INSPECTION AND WARRANTY

14

1999 Supplement

Chapter Introduction

A. Government Inspection Rights
  ★ 1. Regulations / 14-2
   2. Standard Contract Clauses
B. Inspection Procedures
   1. Contractor Inspection
   2. Time Of Inspection
   3. Place Of Inspection
   4. Costs Of Inspection
   5. Manner Of Inspection
C. Rejection & Correction
   1. Rejection Notice
      a. Timing
      b. Form
   2. Contractor Correction
D. Acceptance
   1. Effect
   2. Method Of Acceptance

■ GOVERNMENT CONTRACT GUIDEBOOK

      3. Government's Postacceptance Rights

    ★ a. Latent Defects / **14-3**

    ★ b. Fraud & Gross Mistakes / **14-3**

      c. Other Contract Terms

  E. Warranties

    1. Express Warranties

      a. Regulations

      b. Standard Contract Clauses

      c. Government's Remedies

★ 2. Implied Warranties / **14-4**

* * *

A. GOVERNMENT INSPECTION RIGHTS

1. Regulations

————————ANNOTATIONS————————

■ *Legislation & Regulations*

[1] **FAR Amendment**—A final rule amended the FAR to replace preferences for Government specifications with preferences for commercial quality standards as examples of higher-level contract quality requirements. 63 Fed. Reg. 70264 (Dec. 19, 1998; effective Feb. 16, 1999). See 41 GC ¶ 6.

[2] **FAR Amendment**—Pursuant to the Federal Acquisition Streamlining Act of 1994 (FASA), P.L. 103-355, the FAR was amended to require that contracts for commercial items rely on contractors' existing quality assurance systems in lieu of Government inspection and testing, unless customary market practices for the item being acquired include in-process inspection by the buyer. FAR 12.208, 46.102, 46.202-1. Also, FAR 12.208 was revised to clarify that any in-process inspection by the Government will be done in a manner consistent with commercial practice. Agencies are also permitted to take advantage of vendors' standard commercial warranties. These changes will bring contracting with the Federal Government more in line with standard commercial practices. 60 Fed. Reg. 48231 (Sept. 18, 1995). See 37 GC ¶ 489.

* * *

INSPECTION AND WARRANTY

D. ACCEPTANCE

* * *

3. Government's Postacceptance Rights

* * *

a. Latent Defects

————————ANNOTATIONS————————

■ *Cases & Decisions*

[1] **Contractor Was Presumed To Have Been Prejudiced By Agency's Nine-Year Delay In Asserting Latent Defect Claim**—A contract for installation of floating slabs and isolation pads contained an "Inspection" clause stating that acceptance would be final and conclusive except for, among others, latent defects. The agency accepted the work in September 1975. In 1982, the agency received an engineering report stating that the slabs were failing "both structurally and elastically." Nevertheless, the agency did not give notice of the defect to the contractor until 1991, claiming that its acceptance of the pads was not final. The board found the notice delay unreasonable as a matter of law, holding that to the extent that a showing of prejudice was required to enforce a notice requirement, a delay of nine years is presumed prejudicial. **Ball Healy (JV), ENGBCA 5892, 96-2 BCA ¶ 28429, 39 GC ¶ 114.**
★ **Note**—See also *Traylor Bros., Inc.,* ENGBCA 5884, 99-1 BCA ¶ 30136, 41 GC ¶ 83, where the same board later held that a three-year delay in asserting a latent defect claim was unreasonable and that the contractor need not show resulting prejudice.

b. Fraud & Gross Mistakes

————————ANNOTATIONS————————

■ *Cases & Decisions*

[1] **Preponderance Of The Evidence Can Establish Fraud Under "Inspection" Clause**—The Government attempted to revoke its acceptance of military equipment based on contractor fraud when it found the equipment was defective and had to be replaced. The Government alleged that the contractor had committed fraud in failing to perform contract-required inspections and to disclose that fact to the Government. The contractor argued that fraud must be proved by clear and convincing evidence. The Court of Federal Claims ruled that, for "general" Government claims of contractor fraud, such as in the context of this case where a finding of fraud would merely result in revocation of acceptance, the Government must prove fraud only by a "preponderance of the evidence." The Court

GOVERNMENT CONTRACT GUIDEBOOK

then held that although there was no "direct evidence" of the contractor's intent to deceive the Government (which is an element of fraud), the Government had presented sufficient *circumstantial* evidence to meet its burden of proof on this issue. **BMY–Combat Systems v. U.S., 16 FPD ¶ 63 (Fed. Cl. 1997), 39 GC ¶ 388.**

* * *

E. WARRANTIES

* * *

2. Implied Warranties

————————ANNOTATIONS————————

■ *Legislation & Regulations*

[1] **FAR Amendment**—Pursuant to FASA, new FAR 12.404 establishes the implied warranties of merchantability and fitness for a particular purpose as the Government's minimum warranties in contracts for commercial items. 60 Fed. Reg. 48231 (Sept. 18, 1995). See 37 GC ¶ 489.

PAYMENT

15

1999 Supplement

Chapter Introduction

  A. Contract Payments
    1. Standard Contract Clauses
    2. Partial Payments
    3. Prompt Payment Act Requirements
      a. Interest Penalties
      b. "Proper" Invoices
      c. Applicability Of The Act
★ B. Contract Financing / 15-2
    1. Progress Payments
      a. Standard Contract Clause
      b. Amount
      c. Title To Property
    ★ d. Suspension Or Reduction Of Payments / 15-2
    2. Advance Payments
    3. Other Financing Methods
      a. Loan Guarantees
      b. Private Financing

GOVERNMENT CONTRACT GUIDEBOOK

    C. Government Withholding
★ D. Government Debt Collection Through Offset / **15-3**
      1. Applicability Of Debt Collection Act
      2. Regulations

---

* * *

B. CONTRACT FINANCING

————————ANNOTATIONS————————

■ *Legislation & Regulations*

[1] **FAR Amendment**—The FAR was amended to implement the contract financing provisions of the Federal Acquisition Streamlining Act of 1994 (FASA), P.L. 103-355, providing authority for the financing of commercial item purchases and revising the authority for Government financing of purchases of noncommercial items. The regulations now make a fundamental distinction between financing of purchases of commercial items (FAR Subpart 32.2) and noncommercial items (FAR Subpart 32.1). Also, the FAR now provides, in Subpart 32.10, a new financing technique for contracts for noncommercial items that bases payment on contractor performance. 60 Fed. Reg. 49707 (Sept. 26, 1995). See 37 GC ¶ 504.

■ *Miscellaneous*

[1] **Costs, Pricing & Accounting Report Article**—FASA's contract financing reforms and the final regulatory implementation of those reforms are examined in Wall & Gustin, "FASA Contract Financing Reforms (An Offer You Can't Refuse?)," 95-10 CP&A REP. 3 (Oct. 1995).

1. Progress Payments

* * *

d. Suspension Or Reduction Of Payments

————————ANNOTATIONS————————

■ *Legislation & Regulations*

[1] **FAR Amendment**—Pursuant to FASA, FAR 32.006 through 32.006-5 extend to civilian agencies the right to suspend payments to a contractor when the agency head determines that there is substantial evidence that a

contractor's request for advance, partial, or progress payments is based on fraud. 60 Fed. Reg. 49728 (Sept. 26, 1995). See 37 GC ¶ 507.

* * *

D. GOVERNMENT DEBT COLLECTION THROUGH OFFSET

——————ANNOTATIONS——————

■ *Miscellaneous*

[1] **Costs, Pricing & Accounting Report Article**—For a discussion of the roles and responsibilities of Government and contractor representatives during the debt determination and collection process under FAR Subpart 32.6, see Stafford & Farley, "Contract Debts—Navigating the Determination & Collection Process," 96-4 CP&A REP. 3 (Apr. 1996).

* * *

TERMINATION FOR DEFAULT

16

1999 Supplement

★ Chapter Introduction / **16-2**

★ A. Standard "Default" Clauses / **16-2**
B. Bases For Termination
 1. Failure To Deliver Or Perform
  a. Timely Delivery
  b. Compliance With Specifications
 2. Failure To Make Progress
 3. Failure To Perform Other Contract Provisions
 ★ 4. Anticipatory Breach Of Contract / **16-3**
C. The Termination Decision
 ★ 1. Contracting Officer Discretion / **16-4**
 ★ 2. Improper Motive Or Grounds / **16-5**
 3. Notices
D. Contractor Defenses
 1. Excusable Delay
 ★ 2. Waiver Of Due Date / **16-6**
  a. Forbearance vs. Waiver
  b. Termination After Waiver

■ GOVERNMENT CONTRACT GUIDEBOOK

    E. Government Remedies
      1. Excess Costs Of Reprocurement
      ★ a. Measure Of Excess Costs / **16-8**
      ★ b. Similarity Of Repurchase / **16-8**
      ★ c. Government Duty To Mitigate / **16-9**
      d. Government Completion Of Work
      2. Other Remedies
      3. Liquidated Damages
    F. Contesting Default Terminations
      1. Procedures
      2. Contractor Remedies

CHAPTER INTRODUCTION

───────ANNOTATIONS───────

■ *Miscellaneous*

[1] **Book**—Pettit, Vacketta & Anthony, GOVERNMENT CONTRACT DEFAULT TERMINATION (Federal Publications 1991), mentioned in the text as a more thorough treatment of the subject of default termination, has been updated with a 1999 *Supplement*.

A. STANDARD "DEFAULT" CLAUSES

───────ANNOTATIONS───────

■ *Miscellaneous*

[1] **Briefing Paper**—For an examination of the new FAR provisions and contract terms addressing contractor default and related issues in procurements of "commercial items" and a comparison of those terms with the standard Government supply contract "Default" clause, see Vacketta & Moynihan, "'Commercial Item' Contracts: Default & Related Topics," BRIEFING PAPERS No. 96-3 (Feb. 1996).

[2] **Briefing Paper**—For a review of the grounds for default termination and the possible contractor defenses to default termination, plus practical advice on how to avoid termination, respond to Government "cure" and "show cause" notices, and challenge a default termination if it occurs, see

TERMINATION FOR DEFAULT

Seidman & Banfield, "How To Avoid & Overturn Terminations for Default," BRIEFING PAPERS No. 98-12 (Nov. 1998).

B. BASES FOR TERMINATION

* * *

4. Anticipatory Breach Of Contract

————————ANNOTATIONS————————

■ *Cases & Decisions*

[1] **Contractor's Demand For Termination Costs Was Inconsistent With Intent To Complete Performance**—After the contractor delivered the microscope inspection system to the agency, a dispute arose as to whether the system was performing properly. After unsuccessfully attempting to repair the system to meet a certain requirement, the contractor asked the agency to relax the requirement. The contractor neither delivered the documentation needed to make the system fully useful nor made any effort to correct any of the other defects the agency noted. The contractor removed its system, and the Contracting Officer stated that she would terminate the contract for default. The parties discussed a termination for convenience; the contractor stated that it had another buyer for the system willing to pay a higher price than the agency would have paid. The agency default terminated the contract, and the contractor appealed. Denying the appeal, the board found that the contractor's removal of its system constituted abandonment of contract performance and the contractor's conduct showed inconsistency with intent to complete performance. **Micro-Metric v. Department of Commerce, GSBCA 12766-COM, 97-1 BCA ¶ 28645, 39 GC ¶ 164.**

[2] **Default Termination Was Not Justified By Contractor's Threat To Stop Performing**—Under a four-year contract with the Postal Service (PS) to deliver mail, the contractor twice threatened to cease performance unless the PS renegotiated its payment rate. The PS did not take any action in reliance on these statements, and the contractor continued performing the contract. After one instance by the contractor of failure to complete its route, the PS default terminated the contract. The board found that (1) there was no evidence the single failure by the contractor was in any way connected to its earlier threats to cease performance, and (2) the one day of incomplete performance after months of otherwise satisfactory performance was insufficient in itself to justify default termination of the contract. **Talano Transportation, PSBCA 3812, 97-1 BCA ¶ 28898, 39 GC ¶ 299.**

C. THE TERMINATION DECISION

* * *

■ GOVERNMENT CONTRACT GUIDEBOOK

1. Contracting Officer Discretion

──────────ANNOTATIONS──────────

■ *Cases & Decisions*

[1] **Default Termination Decision Should Have Considered Contractor's Attempt To Satisfy Agency's Nonrequired Preference**—During the solicitation process for a contract to produce 20,000 etched-image lapel pins for the Bureau of Land Management (BLM), the BLM expressed a desire to conduct a press sheet inspection. Although the low offeror normally manufactured the pins in Asia, it decided to have them manufactured in Florida to facilitate the inspection. BLM later rejected the contractor's preproduction samples for noncompliance with the specifications and sent the contractor a "cure notice," giving it three days to cure the discrepancies. The contractor replied the same day, stating that (1) the required etching process no longer was available in the U.S., (2) it had tried to produce the pins in the U.S. to placate the BLM, and that (3) it was prepared to complete the job within five weeks at the contract price through production in Asia. The Contracting Officer (CO) terminated the contract for default and subsequently awarded a reprocurement contract. The contractor appealed both the termination and the assessment of excess costs. The board found that, among other factors, Government delay in notifying the contractor of the unacceptable preproduction samples entitled the contractor to an extension of the delivery date to February 8, which was only a week before the date the contractor had told BLM that it could complete delivery of Asian pins. There was no evidence that the CO considered this in determining that default termination and reprocurement were appropriate, as regulations required. Nor was there any evidence that the later delivery agreed to by the Government in the reprocurement contract was more advantageous to the Government. The board therefore sustained the appeal, holding that the CO failed to act in the Government's best interest and abused his discretion in terminating the contract. **Vatex America, GPOBCA 08-96, 1998 WL 750866 (Oct. 14, 1998), 41 GC ¶ 21.**

★ **Note**—See also *McDonnell Douglas Corp. v. U.S.*, 35 Fed. Cl. 358 (1996), 15 FPD ¶ 37 (although the CO is not absolutely required to consider every FAR factor before default terminating a contract, he "must assess all of the relevant circumstances of the contract"), 38 GC ¶ 165.

[2] **Default Termination Decision Can Be That Of CO Even If Action Was Ordered By Superiors**—The contractor argued that the decision to terminate its grain storage contract was improper because it was made by a committee of Government officials other than the CO. By following the committee's instructions, the CO failed to exercise independent judgment in making the termination decision. The Court of Appeals for the Federal Circuit found that although the committee did instruct the CO to terminate the contract, the CO reviewed, agreed with, and revised the termination order before it was executed. These actions were sufficient to make the CO the final decisionmaker. **PLB Grain Storage Corp. v. Glickman, 16 FPD ¶ 55 (Fed. Cir. 1997) (nonprecedential), 39 GC ¶ 340.**

[3] **CO Abuses Discretion By Default Terminating Contract Based On Materially Erroneous Information**—A contracting official recommended

TERMINATION FOR DEFAULT

termination of a contract to replace an underground hot water heating pipeline system at an Air Force Base, but due to the size of the contract, termination could be ordered only by the Termination Contracting Officer (TCO) at the agency headquarters. The TCO terminated the contract on the basis of a written recommendation replete with material misinformation. The TCO terminated the contract on alternative grounds: (a) failure to complete the work on time and (b) failure to prosecute the work with diligence required for timely completion. The Armed Services Board of Contract Appeals (ASBCA) held that termination on the basis of materially erroneous information was not a reasonable exercise of discretion under the "Default" clause, and converted the default termination into one for convenience. **L&H Const. Co., ASBCA 43833, 97-1 BCA ¶ 28766, 39 GC ¶ 195.**

★ Note—In the factual findings, the board noted lack of evidence that the TCO had considered any of the factors in FAR 49.402-3(f) in deciding to terminate or prepared a memorandum to the file per FAR 49.402-5. Although the majority opinion does not emphasize this, it implies that even if the TCO had considered the factors and prepared the memorandum, the termination would have been improper for lack of accurate, complete, and true information as a basis.

[4] **Default Termination Can Be Affirmed Even If CO Failed To Consider Factors Set Forth In FAR**—The ASBCA denied the contractor's appeal from termination of a contract for failure to timely submit a first article test report. Contending among other matters that the Contracting Officer had not considered the factors set forth in FAR 49.402-3(f) when making his termination decision, the contractor appealed to the Federal Circuit. The Federal Circuit affirmed the ASBCA decision, holding that the CO's contemporaneous memorandum and hearing testimony demonstrated that he did consider the pertinent factors and found that they did not "counsel against" termination. In any event, although a determination of whether the CO complied with the FAR factors may help a tribunal decide whether he abused his discretion, the regulation does not confer any rights on a defaulting contractor. **DCX, Inc. v. Perry, 79 F.3d 132 (Fed. Cir. 1996), 15 FPD ¶ 24, 38 GC ¶ 174.**

[5] **Contracting Agency Not Obligated To Investigate Numerous Complaints Against Contractor Before Terminating For Default**—Where the postmaster received numerous complaints from customers regarding contractor's performance of a delivery services contract, the Postal Service Board of Contract Appeals concluded that he was not obligated to follow up each telephoned complaint in writing or investigate each complaint received. Although there might be such a duty if the termination relied on only one or two major irregularities, the significant number of complaints about similar problems justified the termination. **Dinah Wolverton Perkins, PSBCA 3691, 95-2 BCA ¶ 27670, 37 GC ¶ 515.**

2. Improper Motive Or Grounds

———————ANNOTATIONS———————

■ *Cases & Decisions*

[1] **COFC Finds Government's Grounds For Termination Were Pretext—Federal Circuit Reverses**—In 1994, the Court of Federal Claims

GOVERNMENT CONTRACT GUIDEBOOK

(COFC) ruled that the Navy improperly terminated for default the A-12 aircraft contract because the contract had been terminated not because of the contractors' default but because the Secretary of Defense withdrew support and funding from the A-12 program. **McDonnell Douglas Corp. & General Dynamics Corp. v. U.S.**, 13 FPD ¶ 100 (Fed. Cl. 1994), 36 GC ¶ 625. The court later converted the termination for default to a termination for convenience and awarded the contractors in excess of $1.2 billion. 40 Fed. Cl. 529 (1998), 17 FPD ¶ 41, 38 GC ¶ 604. The U.S. Court of Appeals for the Federal Circuit reversed the COFC's ruling, holding that the COFC must first determine if the contractors were actually in default before it can convert a default termination into a termination for convenience, and stating that if the Government can show that the contractors were in default, the termination would be valid. **McDonnell Douglas Corp. & General Dynamics Corp. v. U.S., 1999 WL 450934 (Fed. Cir., July 1, 1999), 18 FPD ¶ 88, 41 GC ¶ 297.**

* * *

D. CONTRACTOR DEFENSES

* * *

2. Waiver Of Due Date

————————ANNOTATIONS————————

■ *Cases & Decisions*

[1] Contractor's Continued Performance Did Not Constitute Detrimental Reliance On Government's Delay In Default Terminating Contract— An Air Force (AF) contract to manufacture and supply 16 jet engine compressor case assemblies required incremental delivery of the units, with delivery of the first three due on June 30, 1996. On that date, the parts were 83% complete. On August 7, 1996, the AF sent the contractor a "show cause" letter stating that it was considering termination of the contract for default and that "it is not the intention of the Government to condone any delinquency or to waive any rights the Government has under the contract." On receiving the letter, the contractor stopped production of the undelivered parts, which by then were 90% complete. On August 27, the AF terminated the contract for default, and the contractor appealed to the ASBCA. The board noted that it may find Government waiver of a default if (1) the Government fails to terminate within a reasonable time after the default under circumstances indicating forbearance, and (2) the contractor relies on the failure by continuing to perform with the Government's knowledge and implied or express consent. In this case, however, the board found that the contractor did not continue to perform because the Government induced continuation but rather because of the contractor's own business practice and policy. Moreover, the contractor made only 7% progress on the undelivered parts between June 30 and August 7. Absent clear proof that the Government knew of the contractor's

TERMINATION FOR DEFAULT

continuing performance, 7% progress was "not sufficiently material" to establish detrimental reliance. For these reasons (among others), the board denied the appeal. **Electro-Methods, Inc., ASBCA 50215, 99-1 BCA ¶ 30230, 41 GC ¶ 176.**

[2] Contractor's Default Was Not Waived By Government's Routine Monitoring Or Lack Of Need For Contract Items—In an earlier decision, the ASBCA affirmed the CO's default termination of a contract for life raft door assemblies, holding (among other things) that the Government's Quality Assurance Representative's routine visits to the contractor's plant and telephone calls to the contractor after the delivery date did not (absent "some affirmative act") constitute waiver of the delivery date. The U.S. Court of Appeals for the Federal Circuit affirmed the board, finding that the contract does not require and "reason does not demand" that the Government cease routine monitoring actions after default and before termination; such a requirement would unduly burden contract administration. The Federal Circuit also rejected the contractor's argument that the agency improperly used its lack of need for the assemblies as a reason to terminate for default. There was no evidence that the agency would have terminated for convenience but for the default, and an agency is not required to terminate for convenience merely because it no longer has a critical need for the item. **Precision Standard, Inc. v. Widnall, 1997 WL 794107 (Fed. Cir. 1997), 16 FPD ¶ 159 (nonprecedential), 40 GC ¶ 34.**

[3] Government Waives Delivery Delay By Failing To Default Terminate Within Reasonable Time—Under Navy contracts to refurbish submarine pumps and motors, in 1989 the contractor failed to deliver the units on time. The Contracting Officer left the contractor "in a delinquent status," and the contractor delivered about 14 delinquent units between August and December 1989. On December 13, 1989, the CO notified the contractor that all delinquent units would have to be shipped by January 31, 1990. There was no evidence that in setting that date, the CO consulted the contractor, Navy technical advisors, or available documentation as to the contractor's capability. The date set meant that the contractor would have to ship in about 40 days more units than it had shipped in the prior 4-½ months. January 31 passed without all units having been made ready to ship. The CO, although aware that the contractor was spending time and money continuing to perform in reliance on the Navy's inaction, did not terminate the contract until April 1990. The board sustained the contractor's appeal, holding that the date set for delivery in the December 13 notice was unreasonable under the most favorable conditions, and that even if the date had been reasonable, the Navy waived it by failure to terminate promptly. **Precision Dynamics, Inc., ASBCA 41360 et al., 97-1 BCA ¶ 28722, 39 GC ¶ 165.**

* * *

E. GOVERNMENT REMEDIES

* * *

GOVERNMENT CONTRACT GUIDEBOOK

1. Excess Costs Of Reprocurement

* * *

a. Measure Of Excess Costs

——————ANNOTATIONS——————

■ *Cases & Decisions*

[1] **Default Termination Allowed Government To Recover Cost Of Remedying Defects That Contractor Was Not Permitted To Correct—Dissent Filed**—The "Inspection" clause in a contract to construct a refrigeration system provided that if the contractor failed to correct rejected work, the Government could contract to have the defective work corrected and charge the contractor with the cost of that work or terminate the contract for default. The Government rejected some of the contractor's work for defects, but never gave the contractor an opportunity to correct them. The Government terminated the contract for default and the termination was affirmed (on a basis unrelated to the defects). The Government had another firm correct the defective work and charged the terminated contractor with the cost of correction. Denying the contractor's appeal, the Armed Services Board held that the "Inspection" clause did not limit the Government's "Default" clause right to reprocure the defective work and charge the contractor. A dissenting judge would have held, however, that the "Inspection" clause permitted the Government to charge the contractor for the correction costs only where the contractor failed to correct the work promptly within the contract performance period. **Kirk Bros. Mechanical Contractors, Inc., ASBCA 47801 et al., 96-2 BCA ¶ 28291, 38 GC ¶ 305.**

b. Similarity Of Repurchase

——————ANNOTATIONS——————

■ *Cases & Decisions*

[1] **Reprocurement Contract Changes Did Not Invalidate Excess Cost Assessment—Defaulted Contractor Gets Benefit Of Prompt Payment Discount**—The Government awarded a $12,845 fixed-price contract to print 2,002 course catalogs by September 4, 1996 (26-day performance period). The Contracting Officer rejected the catalogs. When the contractor refused to reprint them, the CO terminated the contract for default on September 18. On September 30, the CO awarded a reprocurement contract for $21,961, with a 14-day performance period and then assessed the defaulted contractor the $9,116 difference. The contractor challenged the assessment, claiming major differences between the defaulted and reprocurement contract specifications, including the shortened performance period and the CO's failure to take into account the reprocurement contract's prompt payment discount. On appeal, the board held the shorter delivery

period to be reasonable in that it arose from the terminated contractor's delinquency and refusal to return Government-furnished material in its possession, and from the customer agency's "must have" date of October 15. Nevertheless, because the Government had taken advantage of the reprocurement contract's prompt payment discount, the board reduced the excess cost assessment by the amount of the discount ($439), a figure the board determined to be "more than a trifling amount." **VP Printing, Inc., GPOBCA 30-96 (Jan. 26, 1999), 41 GC ¶ 187.**

c. Government Duty To Mitigate

————————ANNOTATIONS————————

■ *Cases & Decisions*

[1] **Comptroller General Refuses To Review Exclusion Of Defaulted Contractor From Reprocurement Competition**—Following a default termination, the Navy solicited three firms, but not the defaulted contractor, for a reprocurement contract. The defaulted contractor protested to the Comptroller General, contending that the exclusion violated the requirement for maximum practicable competition. The Comptroller General held, however, that the current regulation at FAR 49.402-6(b) requires agencies to "obtain competition to the maximum extent practicable for the repurchase" but does not require full and open competition. It also authorizes use of "any terms and acquisition method deemed appropriate." The Comptroller General held that this language gives agencies sufficient latitude to exclude defaulted contractors from reprocurement. **Montage, Inc., Comp. Gen. Dec. B-277923.2, 97-2 CPD ¶ 176, 40 GC ¶ 98.**

★ **Note**—See also *Walsh Const. of Ill.*, ENGBCA 6325, 98-1 BCA ¶ 29683 (Contracting Officer must act reasonably in deciding whether to allow defaulted contractor to compete for reprocurement), 40 GC ¶ 291.

★ ★ ★

TERMINATION FOR CONVENIENCE

17

1999 Supplement

Chapter Introduction

A. Government's Convenience Termination Right
   1. Standard "Termination For Convenience" Clause
   ★ 2. Scope Of Right / 17-2
B. Termination Procedures
   1. Government's Obligations
      a. Written Notice
      b. Post-Termination Duties
   2. Contractor's Obligations
C. Constructive Termination
   1. Conversion Of Improper Default Termination
   ★ 2. Cancellation Of Contract, Award, Or Work / 17-4
★ D. Contractor Recovery / 17-5
   1. Settlement Proposals
      a. Form & Content
      b. Settlement Basis
      c. No-Cost Settlement

■ GOVERNMENT CONTRACT GUIDEBOOK

    2. Settlement Principles & Limitations
       ★ a. "Fair Compensation" / **17-5**
       b. General Limitations
    3. Special Termination Costs
       ★ a. Precontract Costs / **17-6**
       b. Initial Costs
       ★ c. Termination Inventory Costs / **17-6**
       d. Post-Termination Costs
    4. Settlement Expenses
    5. Subcontractor Claims
    6. Profit
    7. Loss Adjustments
  E. Partial Terminations
    1. Partial Termination vs. Deductive Change
    2. Contractor Recovery

* * *

A. GOVERNMENT'S CONVENIENCE TERMINATION RIGHT

* * *

2. Scope Of Right

———————ANNOTATIONS———————

■ *Cases & Decisions*

[1] **Inducing Contractor To Base Proposal On Quantities Agency Should Have Known Were Overstated Constituted Bad Faith**—The Government entered into an indefinite quantity/indefinite delivery contract with Travel Centre (TC) to establish and operate a travel management center for Government agencies in several states for a one-year period. The awardee was to be the "preferred" rather than mandatory source for such services. The solicitation had included estimates of the number of airline tickets the agencies would purchase during the period of performance, and offerors were required to base their offers on the Government estimates. However, the Government was negligent in developing the estimates and

TERMINATION FOR CONVENIENCE

grossly overstated the number of tickets that would be purchased. TC lost so much money that it went out of business, and the Government terminated the contract for default but later converted it to a termination for convenience. TC appealed to the General Services Administration Board of Contract Appeals contending that the Government's conduct constituted a breach of contract (presumably entitling TC to recover greater compensation than under a convenience termination). The board agreed, finding that the Government's knowing failure to provide crucial information it had in its possession to offerors indicated that it had "no intention of fulfilling its promises" and constituted bad faith and breach of contract, entitling TC to breach damages. **Travel Centre v. General Services Admin., GSBCA 14057, 98-1 BCA ¶ 29536, 40 GC ¶ 136, reconsideration denied, 98-2 BCA ¶ 29849, 40 GC ¶ 358.**

★ **Note**—Arguably, the board based its decision on the Government's bad faith in the *estimate* rather than on the Government's bad faith in the *termination*. For an analysis of *Travel*, see "Postscript: The Limits of Convenience Terminations," 12 NASH & CIBINIC REP. ¶ 29 (May 1998). Also, compare *T&M Distributors, Inc. v. U.S.*, 17 FPD ¶ 31 (Fed. Cl. 1998) (Government's gross understatement of contract quantities did not constitute bad faith and justified convenience termination), 40 GC ¶ 276.

[2] **Cardinal Change Allowed Government To Terminate Contract For Its Convenience**—A $415,000 contract for demolition of an abandoned air base called for removal and disposal of asbestos during site restoration. The agency had estimated asbestos removal to cost about 10% of the total contract price. A few days after receiving the notice to proceed, the contractor informed the agency that asbestos had been found in locations not referred to in the contract (e.g., vinyl tile flooring). The agency then estimated that an additional 36,000 square feet of asbestos would have to be removed, adding $320,000 to the contract's cost. The Contracting Officer (CO) decided that a price increase of this magnitude constituted a "cardinal change," terminated the contract for convenience, and reprocured the work pursuant to the Competition in Contracting Act. The agency awarded the reprocurement to the low offeror at $443,000; the original contractor was sixth lowest. The Court of Federal Claims held that the termination constituted a breach of contract. Reversing the court, the Court of Appeals for the Federal Circuit ruled that the principles enunciated in *Torncello v. U.S.* (cited in the text chapter) were inapplicable in this case because *Torncello* involved a termination for convenience done in bad faith; in this case, there was no evidence of that. The Federal Circuit held that the CO was amply justified in terminating and recompeting the contract. **Krygoski Const. Co. v. U.S., 94 F.3d 1537 (Fed. Cir. 1996), 15 FPD ¶ 88, 38 GC ¶ 522, cert. denied, 117 S. Ct. 1691 (1997), 39 GC ¶ 248.**

★ **Note**—For an extensive critical analysis of *Krygoski*, see "Convenience Terminations: What Are the Limits?," 10 NASH & CIBINIC REP. ¶ 52 (Oct. 1996). See also O'Donnell & Ackerman, "Feature Comment—Bucking the Trend: Limiting the Grounds for Terminations for Convenience," 38 GC ¶ 547.

[3] **Postaward Discovery Of Solicitation Defect Entitles Contracting Officer to Terminate Contract For Government's Convenience**—The Federal Circuit emphasized that Government bad faith is a prerequisite

for a claim under *Torncello v. U.S.* (cited in the text chapter) for wrongful termination for convenience. In this case, the agency concluded after contract award that ambiguous specifications had caused the contractor to fail to include costs for certain equipment in its bid. The contractor argued that the Contracting Officer had known before award that the bid did not include the costs but had nevertheless found no reason to suspect error in the bid. Concluding that adding the equipment would increase the contract price by as much as $300,000 and would constitute a material alteration of the contract prejudicial to other bidders, the CO terminated the contract for convenience. The contractor contended that there was no postaward change in circumstances that would justify the convenience termination. The court held that the Government is barred from using convenience terminations only when the Government has a preaward intent to terminate, not where the Government contracts in good faith but has knowledge of facts placing it on notice that future termination for convenience may be appropriate. **Caldwell & Santmyer, Inc. v. Glickman, 55 F.3d 1578 (Fed. Cir. 1995), 14 FPD ¶ 46, 37 GC ¶ 423.**

* * *

C. CONSTRUCTIVE TERMINATION

* * *

2. Cancellation Of Contract, Award, Or Work

———————ANNOTATIONS———————

■ *Cases & Decisions*

[1] **Agency Cannot Use "Termination" Clause Retroactively To Avoid Consequences Of Breaching Requirements Contract**—The agency awarded a requirements contract to fill the Government's vehicle parts and accessories requirements at an Air Force base for a period extending through January 1996. The contract required the Government to order from the contractor all of the schedule-specified supplies "that are required to be purchased by the Government activity." In December 1995, the contractor discovered that the Government had been purchasing some of its requirements from outside sources. The contractor sought to recover the profits it lost as a result of the Government's failure to purchase those items from it. In this appeal by contractor to the Armed Services Board of Contract Appeals, the Government contends that the purchases from outside sources constituted constructive partial terminations of the requirements contract for convenience, and the "Termination for Convenience" clause bars recovery of profit on terminated work. The Government also cited the contractor's failure to allege Government bad faith, abuse of discretion, or arbitrary or capricious conduct. The board held that the Government cannot attempt retroactively to avoid a breach of contract situation in order to change its obligations under a completed contract. Further, the contractor had no duty to allege Government bad faith, abuse

TERMINATION FOR CONVENIENCE

of discretion, or arbitrary or capricious conduct. In addition, the contract's "Termination" clause does not conclusively foreclose the recovery of lost profit because the CO in this case actually already determined that the contractor was entitled to an "equitable adjustment" for lost profit in one of the contract years. **Carroll Automotive, ASBCA 50993, 98-2 BCA ¶ 29864, 40 GC ¶ 482.**

D. CONTRACTOR RECOVERY

———————ANNOTATIONS———————

■ *Miscellaneous*

[1] **Briefing Papers**—For practical advice for contractors (including a set of guidelines) on preparing settlement proposals for convenience termination of fixed-price contracts, see Seidman & Banfield, "Preparing Termination for Convenience Settlement Proposals for Fixed-Price Contracts," BRIEFING PAPERS No. 97-11 (Oct. 1997). This PAPER is a companion to an earlier PAPER by the same authors, "Maximizing Termination for Convenience Settlements," BRIEFING PAPER No. 95-5 (Apr. 1995).

[2] **Costs, Pricing & Accounting Report Article**—See generally Hildebrant, "Recent Developments in the Law of Terminations for Convenience," 98-4 CP&A REP. 3 (Apr. 1998), for a discussion of recent U.S. Court of Federal Claims and Federal Circuit decisions affecting many areas of termination for convenience claims and recovery.

* * *

2. Settlement Principles & Limitations

a. "Fair Compensation"

———————ANNOTATIONS———————

■ *Legislation & Regulations*

[1] **FAR Amendment**—The FAR has been clarified (FAR 12.403) to provide that the negotiation of termination charges in a termination of a commercial item contract for the Government's convenience does not require Government-unique recordkeeping or compliance with the Cost Accounting Standards or the FAR Part 31 cost principles. 60 Fed. Reg. 48231 (Sept. 18, 1995). See 37 GC ¶ 489.

* * *

3. Special Termination Costs

* * *

■ GOVERNMENT CONTRACT GUIDEBOOK

a. Precontract Costs

————————ANNOTATIONS————————

■ *Cases & Decisions*

[1] **Convenience Termination Recovery May Not Include Precontract Costs Not Needed to Meet Delivery Schedule**—The Air Force terminated a roof repair contract for convenience. Among the costs the contractor sought to recover in its settlement proposal were those it had paid to an architect for review, revision, and approval of drawings for the contractor's bid on the project. The board denied recovery, stating the general rule against recovery of precontract costs and holding that this case did not come within the exception for costs incurred to meet the delivery schedule. **Aislamientos y Construcciones Apache S.A., ASBCA 45437, 97-1 BCA ¶ 28632, 38 GC ¶ 610.**

* * *

c. Termination Inventory Costs

————————ANNOTATIONS————————

■ *Cases & Decisions*

[1] **Costs Of Producing Defective Items Are Allowable Convenience Termination Costs**—Although the Court of Federal Claims held that the contractor was entitled to recover under the standard "Termination for Convenience" clause contained in the contract, the Government denied liability, contending that the items produced by the contractor under the contract did not meet certain inspection requirements All evidence, however, demonstrated that the contractor's inspection procedures complied with the inspection standard. The court held that neither the "Termination" clause nor the applicable regulations require the contractor to prove that the terminated work conforms strictly to specifications, and ruled that the contractor generally was entitled to recover its claimed costs. **Best Foam Fabricators, Inc. v. U.S., 38 Fed. Cl. 627 (1997), 16 FPD ¶ 89, 39 GC ¶ 485.**

* * *

THE DISPUTES PROCESS

18

1999 Supplement

★ *Chapter Introduction* / **18-2**

A. Contract Disputes Act Overview
  1. History
  2. Coverage
    ★ a. Excluded Contracts / **18-2**
    ★ b. Excluded Claims / **18-4**
B. Standard "Disputes" Clause
C. The Disputes Path
  1. Contracting Officer
  ★ 2. Board Of Contract Appeals / **18-5**
  3. Court Of Federal Claims
  4. Appellate Review
D. Other Remedies
  ★ 1. Alternative Dispute Resolution / **18-5**
  2. Extraordinary Contractual Relief
    a. Agency Implementation
    b. Types Of Relief
    c. Procedures

■ GOVERNMENT CONTRACT GUIDEBOOK

CHAPTER INTRODUCTION

————————ANNOTATIONS————————

■ *Miscellaneous*

[1] **Book**—For an in-depth examination of the Contract Disputes Act of 1978 and how its statutory provisions have been interpreted in case law and implemented through regulations, see Peacock & Ting, CONTRACT DISPUTES ACT ANNOTATED (Federal Publications 1997).

* * *

2. Coverage

* * *

a. Excluded Contracts

————————ANNOTATIONS————————

■ *Cases & Decisions*

[1] **AGBCA Has No CDA Jurisdiction Over United Soybean Board Contract Appeal**—The United Soybean Board (USB) of the U.S. Department of Agriculture (USDA) awarded a contract to provide producer communication services. When the contractor submitted contract claims involving disputes between itself and the USB, the USDA refused to consider them on the ground that the contract was not subject to the CDA, and the contractor appealed to the Department of Agriculture Board of Contract Appeals. The board noted that the USB is a nonappropriated fund activity, and the CDA expressly limits its coverage of such activities' contracts to those described in 28 USC §§ 1346 and 1491, e.g., various military exchanges. That USDA had fiscal and contractual oversight responsibilities regarding USB was not sufficient to create CDA coverage. No law or rule required the USDA to be a party to a USB contract, and only the USB signed the contract. Accordingly, the board dismissed the appeal for lack of jurisdiction. **Trent-Jones, Inc., AGBCA 98-104-1, 99-1 BCA ¶ 30196, 41 GC ¶ 74.**

[2] **AGBCA Shifts Position On Its Authority To Consider Settlement Agreement Breach Claims**—To resolve a contract dispute, the agency and the contractor entered into a settlement agreement (SA). The Contracting Officer later decided that the contractor had breached the SA, declared the SA null and void, and refused to make the specified payment. The contractor requested the Department of Agriculture Board of Contract Appeals (AGBCA) to enforce the agreement, but the agency contended that the matter was beyond the board's CDA jurisdiction in that the SA was not a contract for (a) procurement of property, services, or construction or (b) disposition of personal property. Notwithstanding an earlier contrary AGBCA

THE DISPUTES PROCESS

position, but consistent with decisions of two other boards, the AGBCA held that because the settlement involved a CDA contract, the board had jurisdiction to resolve the dispute regarding the SA. Nevertheless, the board held that before it could consider the appeal, the contractor must submit a CDA claim to the Contracting Officer with respect to the SA and demand a final decision. **Barnes, Inc., AGBCA 97-111-1 et al., 97-2 BCA ¶ 29237, 39 GC ¶ 501.**

[3] **CHAMPUS Medical Facility Sharing Arrangements Are Contracts Subject To CDA**—TMM entered into several Memoranda of Understanding (MOUs) with an Army hospital providing that all in-patient services could be billed at specified percentages of the current Civilian Health and Medical Program of the Uniformed Services (CHAMPUS) prevailing rate. Although none of the MOUs referred to the use of the Medicare Economic Index (MEI) to limit payments, the Army only reimbursed TMM at that rate. TMM brought suit under the CDA in the Court of Federal Claims for the difference between the MEI rate and the MOU rate, and the court issued a summary judgment in favor of TMM. On appeal to the Court of Appeals for the Federal Circuit, the Government contended, among other things, that the MOUs were not subject to the CDA because they were not procurement contracts for the benefit of the Government but were solely for the benefit of the military dependents who receive the medical care. The court ruled the CDA applicable, noting that (1) the MOUs were valid contracts, (2) Congress' failure to label the MOUs as contracts was not controlling, and (3) the MOUs were of benefit to the Government, which has obligations to military dependents to obtain medical care. **Total Medical Mgmt., Inc. v. U.S., 104 F.3d 1314 (Fed. Cir. 1997), 16 FPD ¶ 4, 39 GC ¶ 67.**

[4] **Board Had CDA Jurisdiction Over Appeal Involving Concession Contract**—A National Park Service (NPS) concession contract required the contractor to make significant facilities improvements in accordance with Government-furnished specifications. The contract contained language acknowledging that the contractor would be performing services for the benefit of the Government and the public and did not require the contractor to pay a franchise fee to the Government. The contractor appealed to the Department of the Interior Board of Contract Appeals in a claim for additional costs allegedly incurred because of defective Government specifications. The Government argued the board lacked CDA jurisdiction over concession contract cases. The board ruled that in view of the contract language, the NPS was procuring services within the meaning of the CDA. Nevertheless, the board denied the claim on the merits for lack of proof. **National Park Concessions, Inc., IBCA 2995, 94-3 BCA ¶ 27104, 36 GC ¶ 563.**

[5] **CDA Did Not Apply To Transportation Services Contract**—The Government awarded a contract to transport Government freight on a Government bill of lading. When a dispute arose regarding overages, the Court of Federal Claims held that the CDA does not apply to transportation services contracts. The Transportation Act of 1940, 31 USC § 3726, specifically applies to claims against the Government "relating to freight and passenger transportation services" and provides a claim review mechanism notably different from that of the CDA. The court held 31 USC § 3726 preempts the CDA. **Northeastern Pa. Shippers Cooperative Assn. v. U.S., 32 Fed. Cl. 72 (1994), 13 FPD ¶ 81, 36 GC ¶ 586.**

■ GOVERNMENT CONTRACT GUIDEBOOK

★ **Note**—The Armed Services Board of Contract Appeals has apparently reached the contrary conclusion regarding 31 USC § 3726, ruling that the board's CDA authority exists independently of the disputes resolution process provided under other statutes. *Merchants Moving & Storage, Inc.,* ASBCA 47370, 95-1 BCA ¶ 27298, 36 GC ¶ 652 (Note).

[6] CDA Did Not Cover Spot Movement Transportation Contract—The Federal Circuit held that the CDA does not cover Government bill of lading (GBL) transactions. The Navy had entered into a GBL transaction with Sherwood to transport household goods, and it set off funds to satisfy claims for damaged goods. Sherwood appealed under the CDA. The Federal Circuit noted the disputes procedure for transportation contracts in 31 USC § 3726, which predates the CDA and differs from it. Moreover, the informal procedure of 31 USC § 3726 is better suited to GBL matters than is the more formal CDA procedure. **Dalton v. Sherwood Van Lines, Inc., 50 F.3d 1014 (Fed. Cir. 1995), 14 FPD ¶ 22, 37 GC ¶ 234.**

b. Excluded Claims

───────ANNOTATIONS───────

■ *Cases & Decisions*

[1] Assertion Of Contractor Fraud In Contracting Officer's Final Decision Did Not Deprive Court Of CDA Jurisdiction—The Contracting Officer default terminated the contract based on the contractor's defective performance and alleged falsification of records. The contractor brought suit under the CDA in the Court of Federal Claims (COFC) challenging the default termination. The Government argued, among other things, that the contractor's claim was tainted by fraud and therefore barred under the Forfeiture Statute (28 USC § 2514); it also asserted counterclaims for return of progress payments and for damages under the False Claims Act. The COFC denied the merits of the contractor's claim and granted the Government some affirmative recovery under its counterclaims. On appeal to the Federal Circuit, the contractor argued that the COFC lacked jurisdiction over either the contractor's claim or the Government's counterclaims in that there was no valid Contracting Officer's decision because Contracting Officers lack authority under the CDA to decide fraud claims. The Federal Circuit held that the COFC had jurisdiction over (1) the default termination decision because fraud was only one of two grounds for the termination and (2) the Government's counterclaims because a Contracting Officer's decision is not a jurisdictional prerequisite to the Government's right to assert a counterclaim. **Daff, Trustee v. U.S., 78 F.3d 1566 (Fed. Cir. 1996), 15 FPD ¶ 19, 38 GC ¶ 176.**

★ **Note**—See also *TRW, Inc.*, ASBCA 5112 et al., 1999 WL 381089 (June 1, 1999) (board took jurisdiction of contract interpretation claim despite pending fraud litigation), 41 GC ¶ 309.

* * *

C. THE DISPUTES PATH

* * *

THE DISPUTES PROCESS

2. Board Of Contract Appeals

——————————ANNOTATIONS——————————

■ *Cases & Decisions*

[1] **CDA Does Not Authorize Boards To Grant Relief Based On U.S. Constitution**—While the Court of Federal Claims may consider constitutional issues pursuant to its Tucker Act jurisdiction, the CDA does not authorize procuring agency contract appeals boards to grant relief based on the U.S. Constitution. **United Technologies Corp., ASBCA 46880 et al., 95-1 BCA ¶ 27456, 37 GC ¶ 446 (Note).**

★ ★ ★

D. OTHER REMEDIES

★ ★ ★

1. Alternative Dispute Resolution

——————————ANNOTATIONS——————————

■ *Legislation & Regulations*

[1] **Administrative Dispute Resolution Act Of 1996**—In 1996, Congress enacted P.L. 104-320 (Oct. 19, 1996), which permanently reauthorized the Administrative Dispute Resolution of 1990. The 1996 Act reaffirmed the goal of the 1990 Act of encouraging agencies to resolve disputes through means other than litigation, and eliminated several undesirable features of the 1990 Act, such as (a) the requirement that contractors, when choosing ADR to resolve their CDA claims, certify contract claims below $100,000, and (b) the ability of federal agencies to "opt out" of arbitration decisions with which they disagree.
★ **Note**—See generally Gomez, "Feature Comment—ADR in Government Contracting: Trend or Revolution?," 39 GC ¶ 210.

■ *Miscellaneous*

[1] **Nash & Cibinic Report Article**—For an examination of the proper time to schedule ADR during the disputes process, see "Alternative Dispute Resolution: When Should It Be Done?," 10 николай & Cibinic Rep. ¶ 26 (June 1996).

[2] **Briefing Paper**—For an analysis of various ADR methods for resolving contract disputes and protests and a review of the recent legislative and regulatory initiatives and reforms in the use of ADR, such as the Administrative Dispute Resolution Act of 1996, see Arnavas & Hornyak, "Alternative Dispute Resolution/Edition II," Briefing Papers No. 96-11 (Oct. 1996).

★ ★ ★

THE CLAIM AND CONTRACTING OFFICER DECISION

19

1999 Supplement

Chapter Introduction

A. Contractor Claims vs. Government Claims

B. Asserting A "Claim"

    1. Early Notice To Contracting Officer

    2. Definition Of "Claim"

★ 3. Need For Preexisting Dispute / **19-2**

★ 4. Sum Certain / **19-3**

★ 5. Claim Certification / **19-4**

       a. Who Signs The Certification

       b. Content Of Certification

C. Contracting Officer's Decision

★ 1. Content / **19-4**

★ 2. Timing / **19-5**

    3. Contractor's Duty To Proceed

■ GOVERNMENT CONTRACT GUIDEBOOK

D. Contractor's Decision To Appeal Or Bring Suit
1. Practical Considerations
★ 2. Binding Election Of Forum / **19-6**

---

* * *

B. ASSERTING A "CLAIM"

* * *

3. **Need For Preexisting Dispute**

————————ANNOTATIONS————————

■ *Cases & Decisions*

[1] **Federal Circuit Addresses Status Of Convenience Termination Settlement Proposals As CDA "Claims"**—After its contract was terminated for convenience, Ellett submitted a termination for convenience settlement proposal. The settlement proposal sought recovery of basically the same costs Ellett had sought earlier from the Contracting Officer (CO) through submission of a CDA changes claim. The CO concluded that Ellett was entitled to significantly less than it requested. Ellett filed suit in the Court of Federal Claims, and the court dismissed the suit for lack of a "preexisting dispute." The Court of Appeals for the Federal Circuit reversed, citing *Reflectone* (see item [2] below). The court first noted that a termination settlement proposal, when initially submitted, is not a "claim" because "it is for the purpose of negotiation, not for a contracting officer's decision." However, the proposal ripens into a CDA "claim" if (1) negotiations reach an impasse, (2) the CO issues a final decision, or (3) the contractor's submissions indicate the contractor "desires" a final decision. Since the CO had basically denied Ellett's proposal, the Court of Federal Claims had jurisdiction to hear it under the CDA as a "claim." **James M. Ellett Const. Co. v. U.S., 93 F.3d 1537 (Fed. Cir. 1996), 15 FPD ¶ 90, 38 GC ¶ 426.**

★ **Note**—Subsequent Armed Services Board of Contract Appeals (ASBCA) decisions shed additional light on when termination for convenience settlement proposals constitute CDA "claims." See *Mid-America Engrg. & Mfg.*, ASBCA 48831, 96-2 BCA ¶ 28558 (settlement proposal constituted "claim" because it was a nonroutine request for payment, it provided sufficient information regarding the claim, it was certified, and contractor had requested final decision), 38 GC ¶ 477; *National Interior Contractors, Inc.*, ASBCA 46012, 96-2 BCA ¶ 28560 (settlement proposal ripened into "claim" when parties reached "an impasse"), 38 GC ¶ 477; and *Rex Systems, Inc.*, ASBCA 49502, 99-1 BCA ¶ 30179 (failure to request CO decision or reach impasse prevents termination settlement proposal from becoming CDA

1999 SUPPLEMENT

THE CLAIM AND CONTRACTING OFFICER DECISION

claim), 41 GC ¶ 72. See also West & Handwerker, "Feature Comment: The 'In Dispute' Requirement After *Ellett*: A Resuscitation of the *Dawco* Standards?," 38 GC ¶ 574.

[2] Federal Circuit Rejects "Pre-Existing Dispute" Requirement For CDA Claims—Overruling an earlier panel decision in this case and its 1991 decision in *Dawco Const. Co. v. U.S.* (cited in the text chapter), the Federal Circuit held en banc that, to satisfy the CDA definition of "claim," a nonroutine, written demand for payment need not be in dispute as to either amount or liability when submitted to the Contracting Officer. The court noted that the FAR 33.201 definition of "claim" only explicitly excludes those "routine request[s] for payment that are not in dispute when submitted to the contracting officer." Therefore, by implication, "all other written demands seeking payment as a matter of right are 'claims,' whether in dispute or not." **Reflectone, Inc. v. Dalton, 60 F.3d 1572 (Fed. Cir. 1995), 14 FPD ¶ 63, 37 GC ¶ 411, rehearing denied (Sept. 27, 1995), 37 GC ¶ 516.**

■ *Miscellaneous*

[1] Nash & Cibinic Report Articles—The *Reflectone* decision, its history, and its significance are discussed in "Reflections on *Reflectone*: Narrowing the 'In Dispute' Requirement," 9 NASH & CIBINIC REP. ¶ 55 (Oct. 1995), and "Postscript: Further Reflections on *Reflectone*," 9 NASH & CIBINIC REP. ¶ 59 (Nov. 1995). See also "Postscript II: More Reflections on *Reflectone*," 10 NASH & CIBINIC REP. ¶ 35 (July 1996), for an examination of board cases decided after *Reflectone* that provide some insight on the decision's effects. The status of termination for convenience settlement proposals as CDA "claims" is discussed in "The *Ellett* Case: What's All the Fuss About?," 11 NASH & CIBINIC REP. ¶ 8 (Feb. 1997), and "Postscript: The *Ellett* Case," 13 NASH & CIBINIC REP. ¶ 5 (Jan. 1999).

4. Sum Certain

———————ANNOTATIONS———————

■ *Cases & Decisions*

[1] Contractor Could File CDA Claim For Costs It Had Not Yet Incurred—An Air Force (AF) contract included a clause that stated that in the event of a break in production, the parties would negotiate an equitable adjustment for the break's impact, and that any disagreement as to the adjustment's validity would be treated as a "dispute." The clause indicated that if there was no fiscal year 1983 buy, the contractor's "phase-out" costs would be considered part of the adjustment. When there was no fiscal year 1983 buy, the contractor submitted a certified claim for "phase-out" costs. The AF denied the claim, stating that "many of the costs have not been incurred…may never be incurred…and are speculative in amount." On appeal, the AF argued the contractor's claim should be dismissed because the claim was not for a "sum certain" and therefore was not cognizable under the CDA. The board disagreed, citing a decision by the Federal Circuit (*Servidone v. U.S.*, 10 FPD ¶ 48 (Fed. Cir. 1991), 33 GC ¶ 149) which had held that interest runs from the date a claim is received "without regard to whether the contractor incurred the costs." Because the Federal Circuit had allowed interest on such a claim, it must necessarily have considered the claim to have been properly filed. Thus, under *Servidone*, the contractor had stated a proper CDA claim in this case. **Fairchild Industries, Inc., ASBCA 46197, 95-1 BCA ¶ 27594, 37 GC ¶ 308.**

5. Claim Certification

──────────ANNOTATIONS──────────

■ *Cases & Decisions*

[1] **Claim Amount May Be Different From Amount Specified In CDA Certification**—The contractor submitted a claim, which the Contracting Officer received in May 1993. The contractor's original certification (in October 1994) was defective for not mentioning a claim amount; on March 10, 1995, the contractor submitted a corrected certification claiming entitlement to $81,137, an amount different from that in the 1993 submission. The Government contended that the contractor could recover CDA interest only as of the date of the corrected submission, and that the "claim" was not submitted in 1993 because the amount in that claim differed from that in the 1995 submission. The General Services Administration Board of Contract Appeals observed that any CDA interest due on a claim with a defective certification is paid from the date the Contracting Officer initially received the claim. Furthermore, the GSBCA found no absolute requirement that a claim certification must itself specify the sum sought, and did not see how inserting a sum into an otherwise valid certification renders the certification invalid. **Herman B. Taylor Const. Co. v. General Services Admin., GSBCA 12915-R, 97-2 BCA ¶ 29127, 39 GC ¶ 488.**

* * *

C. CONTRACTING OFFICER'S DECISION

* * *

1. Content

──────────ANNOTATIONS──────────

■ *Cases & Decisions*

[1] **CO Was Entitled To Rely On His Subordinates In Reaching Final Decision**—The Contracting Officer reviewed the materials sent to him by the Resident Officer in Charge of Construction (ROICC), which included the contractor's claims and the ROICC's written position on the claims, together with attachments. The CO did not attempt to independently verify

THE CLAIM AND CONTRACTING OFFICER DECISION

any of the facts that the ROICC and other subordinates provided him primarily because the ROICC had first-hand knowledge of the facts concerning the contract's performance. The CO arrived at his final decision by reviewing the memoranda provided him and putting those positions into his own words. The ASBCA ruled that a CO is not required to independently investigate the facts of a claim but need only exercise independent discretion in deciding the claim. One member of the board dissented, stating that a contractor is entitled to a final decision that (a) results from the CO's personal and independent consideration of the issues and (b) reflects his own independent judgment. **Prism Const. Co., ASBCA 44682 et al., 97-1 BCA ¶ 28909, 39 GC ¶ 315.**

[2] **Contractor Must Prove That It Relied On Agency's Incorrect Advice Regarding Its Appeal Rights**—The Contracting Officer's decision terminating a contract for default contained a technical error in its statement of the contractor's appeal rights, stating that the contractor could appeal either to a board of contract appeals within 90 days or to the Court of Federal Claims (COFC) within 12 months. The CO's decision was a so-called "pure" default termination that did not mention monetary issues, and at the time the decision was issued, the COFC did not have jurisdiction to consider the challenges to "pure" default terminations. When the contractor appealed to the board almost two years after the decision was issued, the Government claimed the appeal was untimely. The board disagreed, finding that the error in the statement of appeal rights did not start the appeal-filing period running. The Federal Circuit reversed the board, holding that a contractor seeking to bring an appeal outside of the 90-day statutory period based on a defective termination notice must show detrimental reliance on the error. Here, the contractor received correct advice regarding its right to appeal to the board within 90 days. **Decker & Co. v. West, 76 F.3d 1573 (Fed. Cir. 1996), 15 FPD ¶ 12, 38 GC ¶ 173.**
★ **Note**—"Notice of Appeal Rights: Prejudice Required," 10 NASH & CIBINIC REP. ¶ 36 (July 1996), examines the law before and after the *Decker* case.

2. Timing

————————ANNOTATIONS————————

■ *Cases & Decisions*

[1] **Precertification Period Considered In Deciding If CO Has Unreasonably Delayed Issuing Decision**—On January 3, 1995, the contractor submitted to the Contracting Officer a $5.9-million "request for equitable adjustment" (REA). On April 11, the CO requested the Defense Contract Audit Agency (DCAA) to audit the REA. The DCAA suspended its work between August 9 and October 1 because the contracting agency lacked sufficient funds. On August 21, the contractor submitted a CDA certification and asked the CO when a final decision would be issued. The CO advised that he would issue a final decision by February 29, 1996. On October 31, the contractor requested the board, as permitted by the CDA (41 USC § 605(c)(4)), to direct the CO to issue a decision within a specified time period. The board found that although the claim was certified on

1999 SUPPLEMENT
19-5

GOVERNMENT CONTRACT GUIDEBOOK

August 21, the CO had had almost one year to consider contractor's request for additional compensation. Stating that it could not completely disregard the precertification time in deciding what is a "reasonable time" for issuing a CO decision, the board ordered the CO to issue a final decision not later than January 5, 1996 (one year after submission of the REA). In addition, the board found that lack of funds does not excuse the Government from expeditious consideration of claims. **VECO, Inc., DOT-BCA 2961, 96-1 BCA ¶ 28108, 38 GC ¶ 102.**

★ **Note**—See also *Dillingham/ABB-SUSA*, ASBCA 51195 et al., 98-2 BCA ¶ 29778 (CO's establishment of 16-month decisionmaking period was unreasonable where claim had already been extensively analyzed and audited), 40 GC ¶ 341.

[2] **CDA Does Not Require That CO Wait Reasonable Time Before Issuing Final Decision**—On December 1, 1993, contractor submitted a claim to the Contracting Officer. On January 5, 1994, the CO sent the contractor a letter requesting documentation justifying the claim and stating that on receipt of the documentation the claim would be evaluated. The contractor failed to furnish the documentation promptly, and on February 8, 1994, the CO issued a letter purporting to be a final decision denying the December 1 claim. On March 20, 1995, more than 12 months after the contractor's receipt of the February 8, 1994, letter, the contractor filed suit in the Court of Federal Claims appealing the denial. The contractor argued (among other things) that the CDA (41 USC § 605(c)(3)) requiring the CO to issue the decision "within a reasonable time...taking into account such factors as...the adequacy of the information in support of the claim provided by the contractor," requires the CO to wait a reasonable time before issuing a decision to allow the contractor to submit supporting information, and that therefore the February 8 letter was not a final decision. The court held that the CDA established a maximum rather than a minimum time within which a CO must act, that the February 8 letter was a final decision, and that the contractor's appeal was untimely. **L&D Services, Inc. v. U.S., 34 Fed. Cl. 673 (1996), 15 FPD ¶ 5, 38 GC ¶ 291.**

* * *

D. CONTRACTOR'S DECISION TO APPEAL OR BRING SUIT

* * *

2. Binding Election Of Forum

————ANNOTATIONS————

■ *Cases & Decisions*

[1] **Board Had CDA Jurisdiction Over Dual-Purpose Contract**—After the contractor had conveyed title on a contract to alter, repair, and sell a building to the Government, the Contracting Officer issued a final decision

THE CLAIM AND CONTRACTING OFFICER DECISION

demanding that the contractor pay $5.2 million to correct structural defects and improve the heating, ventilating, and air conditioning (HVAC) system. Damages assessed for the alleged structural defects were based on the "Warranty" clause; damages for the HVAC system were based on the repair and alteration provisions. The contractor initially appealed to the General Services Administration Board of Contract Appeals (GSBCA) but withdrew its appeal; GSBCA dismissed it without prejudice. The contractor then filed suit in the Court of Federal Claims. The court dismissed the suit on the ground that the claim fell under the CDA and by having first appealed to GSBCA, the contractor was bound by its initial election to resort to the board rather than to the court. 12 FPD ¶ 116 (Fed. Cl. 1993), 36 GC ¶ 58. On appeal, the Federal Circuit noted that § 602(a) of the CDA denies the board jurisdiction over contracts to procure real property but gives the board jurisdiction over contracts to repair and alter real property. In this case, the contract was for a dual purpose—for both the procurement of property and the repair of property. Because the parties' dispute and the CO's decision pertained to the contractor's failure to repair and alter the building and not to the procurement of the building, the GSBCA had jurisdiction pursuant to § 602(a)(3) of the CDA, and the Federal Circuit affirmed the dismissal by the Court of Federal Claims. **Bonneville Assocs. v. U.S., 49 F.3d 649 (Fed. Cir. 1994), 13 FPD ¶ 103, 37 GC ¶ 60.**

★ **Note**—The GSBCA later ruled that the contractor could not reinstate its appeal, even though the appeal had been dismissed without prejudice, because the date of the refiling of the appeal was after expiration of the CDA's 90-day filing period. *Bonneville Assocs.*, GSBCA 13134 (11595)-REIN, 96-1 BCA ¶ 28122, 38 GC ¶ 65.